THE PRISONERS' HAND

THE PRISONERS' HANDBOOK 1995

EDITED BY
MARK LEECH

Oxford University Press · 1995

Oxford University Press, Walton Street, Oxford OX2 6DP
Oxford New York
Athens Auckland Bangkok Bombay
Calcutta Cape Town Dar es Salaam Delhi
Florence Hong Kong Istanbul Karachi
Kuala Lumpur Madras Madrid Melbourne
Mexico City Nairobi Paris Singapore
Taipei Tokyo Toronto
and associated companies in
Berlin Ibadan

Oxford is a trade mark of Oxford University Press

Published in the United States
by Oxford University Press Inc., New York

British Library Cataloguing in Publication Data
Data available

Library of Congress Cataloging in Publication Data
Data available

ISBN 0–19–825960–3
ISBN 0–19–825939–5 (Pbk)

Set by Hope Services (Abingdon) Ltd.
Printed in Great Britain
on acid-free paper by
Biddles Ltd
Guildford & King's Lynn

THIS HANDBOOK IS DEDICATED TO

THOMAS NOLAN

A PRISONER NO LONGER

ACKNOWLEDGEMENTS

Editing the first edition of *The Prisoners' Handbook* has incurred a debt of gratitude to so many people, I could not possibly hope to name them all here. Below are those to whom I am especially grateful, they each gave me their time without complaint and without whose help, inspiration, patience, faith, encouragement or advice this Handbook could not have been written.

I owe an immense debt of gratitude to my Commissioning Editor at Oxford University Press, **Richard Hart**, for his courage and foresight in taking this project on and his belief in my abilities to complete the task from inside a prison cell. OUP Assistant Editors, **Sandra Sinden** and **Margaret Shade**, have both been a much valued source of encouragement for whom no request was too difficult.

A huge 'thank you' to my partner **Thomas Nolan**. Without complaint he processed all the questionnaires, took endless phone messages, wrote a plethora of notes—and achieved it all despite having his arm in plaster.

To **Vicky King** and **Simon Creighton** (Prisoners' Advice Service) I owe a particular debt of gratitude: they wrote the chapter on *Prisoners & The Law* almost at the last minute, and produced a section of such clarity and detail it deserves particular recognition. I also owe a big 'thank you' to **Peter Quinn**, Governor grade at Prison Service Headquarters, who wrote and revised the powerful article on disciplinary adjudications in Section Four and to **Basil Blackwell Ltd**, his publishers, for their kind permission to publish without fee. I am very grateful to the **Prison Reform Trust** for their permission to use the Prisoners' Information Pack and Foreign Prisoners Advice Pack, and to **HM.Prison Service**, for their permission to quote the policy documents shown in Annexe A. I also owe thanks to **HHJ Stephen Tumim** (HM.Chief Inspector of Prisons) for his authority to use his inspection reports, and also for the help given to me by his Staff Officer **Simon Boddis** and the Information Dept at **NACRO**, who helped me to obtain copies of them. Thanks are also due to **HMSO** for their permission to reproduce the Prison Act 1952/Prison Rules 1964 Young Offender Institution Rules 1988, and to the Rt.Hon **Betty Boothroyd MP**, Speaker of the House of Commons, who kindly provided the list of Members with prisons in their constituencies.

Special 'thanks' to **Jean Anderson** at HM Prison Service Secretariat, she worked absolute wonders in providing information and routing my many questions to the correct Cleland House desk. **Ian Chisholm**, **Tony Hall**, **Len Curran** and **J.J. O'Sullivan** at Prison Service HQ were models of openness. **Nigel Owens** (Home Office Publications Unit), **Roger Kendrick TD** (Mancare Ltd), **Stephen Twinn** and **Nick Metcalfe** (Group 4), **Pat Wilson** (Bristol), **Hilary Platt** (Manchester), **Stephen Shaw** (Prison Reform Trust), **Adam Sampson** (Assistant Prison Ombudsman), **Mervyn Barrett** (NACRO), **Eric McGraw** and **John Bowers** (The New Bridge), **Eric Allison** and **Tony Kavanagh** (Manchester), **Walter Cairns** (Scottish Arts Council), **Professor Rod Morgan** (Dean of Law, Bristol University), **Dougie Matthewson** (HMP Edinburgh), **John Durno** (Governor 1, HMP Edinburgh), and prison officer **Eric Lowe** (HMP Glenochil), have all in their own way helped to bring the Handbook to reality: I owe and record my sincere thanks to them all.

My chief thanks, however, must go to all those prisoners and Governors who provided detailed information from prisons around the country. Also into this category fall the handful of progressive Boards of Visitors who kindly supplied copies of their annual reports. For the help of these people I remain particularly indebted.

In addition to those above who have helped, I must also say 'thank you' to those few individuals who sought to obstruct me: your attempts at hindrance were a source of limitless motivation!

To each of you, I extend my deepest thanks and gratitude.

MARK LEECH
HMP Edinburgh
October 1994

CONTENTS

INTRODUCTION What's it all about?

HOW IT ALL STARTED

As anyone unfortunate enough to have been there will tell you, the reception at Wandsworth prison can take forever to get through. It was as I was sitting in a caged reception cubicle at Wandsworth, sandwiched between the concerned inquiries of those coming in, and the old-hand replies of those others lucky enough to be leaving, that the idea for the book you now hold in your hands was conceived.

QUESTIONS, QUESTIONS, QUESTIONS

What's it like here? What are the visits like? Is it difficult for visitors to get to? Is there any work available, and what are the wages like? What are the cells like? What about the food? Is it true they have a Radio and Television Course here? What is the doctor like? Can I see a dentist while I'm here, and is there a waiting list? Are there telephones for prisoners? How many phone cards can be bought? Is the canteen reasonable? Are the Board of Visitors any good? Who are the Board of Visitors? Is there a church service for Muslims? When is it? Is there a gymnasium? When can we use it? Who is the Governor? What about disciplinary adjudications, are they fair? How long will I be locked up weekdays? What about weekends? When is exercise time and how long do we get? Can we wear any civilian clothes in here? Do they allow sound systems, and what about pre-recorded cassettes . . . ?

NOT JUST FOR PRISONERS

As the questions flowed back and forth I suddenly realised that these were the same questions I had asked on my arrival—and would shortly be doing so again, in the prison to which I was then bound. In prison receptions across the country these questions are the only way the prisoner can discover what is in store for him at his new establishment; and his relatives and friends are in an even worse position. Unless they know someone who has been inside that particular prison, it is unlikely they will know anything about the place to which their loved one has been sent. Lawyers, CABx, advice workers, probation officers, penal reform groups, students, social workers and many others, are in precisely the same ignorant position and for the same unnecessary reason; the current dearth of information. Remedying this for the 50,000 prisoners in England and Wales—and the half a million others who make up our families, friends, advisers and campaigners, is what *The Prisoners' Handbook* is all about.

FROM RECEPTION TO RELEASE

The Prisoners' Handbook is the first comprehensive guide to every prison and YOI in England and Wales. Among other things the *Handbook* details the key-officials in each establishment, in addition to its regime, visiting conditions, educational & medical facilities, disciplinary adjudications, sports and games, chaplaincy team, workshops and wages—and often including the views of prisoners in that individual establishment. The *Handbook* contains a comprehensive advice section on everything from welfare services open to you in prison, to social security benefits and discharge grants available to you on your release. In the Advice Section you will find chapters giving advice on the prison disciplinary system, visits, letters, phone calls, race relations, health, hygiene, requests and complaints. Additionally, there are separate chapters for women prisoners, young offenders, unconvicted, civil, and foreign prisoners: all groups who are often marginalised and forgotten in our penal system. Much of the information given in these sections will be of equal interest to family and friends, and in relation to subjects such as visiting and obtaining financial assistance for those in receipt of DSS benefits, there are special sections of information.

USEFUL ORGANISATIONS, LEGAL ADVICE, ADJUDICATIONS

The Handbook contains a 'Useful Organisations' section, giving details of more than thirty organisations which exist to help, advise and support prisoners and their families and friends.

In addition the *Handbook* gives an authoritative tour of the legal rights which prisoners in England and Wales possess, written by Vicky King & (Solicitor) Simon Creighton of the Prisoners Advice Service: experts in this complex area. This is complemented by (Governor) Peter Quinn's powerful and cogently reasoned paper on reform of internal disciplinary hearings.

HMCIP REPORTS AND MORE

Section five of the Handbook details the Reports published in the last year by Judge Stephen Tumim, HM Chief Inspector of Prisons, who has earnt the respect of both sides of the prison divide with his hard-hitting, no nonsense, Inspection Reports. Section Six carries Annexes with full copies of the Prison Act 1952, the Prison Rules 1964, and official statements such as the Vision,

Values & Goals policy of HM Prison Service. The names of those who operate Headquarters are given, along with details of their respective areas of responsibility. Penal facts & figures are detailed, the standard list of items allowed in possession is shown, in addition to Parliamentary Questions on prisons during the last 12 months, and details of self-inflicted Deaths in Custody during the same period. All in all, *The Prisoners' Handbook* offers a comprehensive sweep of a complex system, providing detailed information that has not previously been drawn together: I hope you find it interesting, informative and of practical use during your day, whichever side of the prison wall you may be on.

THE PRISONERS' HANDBOOK 1996: An Invitation to Inmates

If you will be an inmate of a prison in England and Wales throughout 1995, and would like to register with Oxford University Press as a Compiler for **The Prisoners' Handbook 1996**, then please write to the address below with details about yourself: name, number, sentence, EDR, etc. Replies from all inmates are invited, juveniles, young offenders and female prisoners are particularly welcome, as are those who do not experience the normal prison regime: inmates in VPUs, Mother & Baby Units, SSUs, Segregation Units and prison hospital inpatients for example. A questionnaire will be sent to you for completion about your establishment in May 1995 and MUST arrive back with us no later than **30th June 1995**. You can apply to register as a Handbook Compiler by writing to the address below—mark your envelope '**Inmate Compiler**'. There is no need for a stamp.

GENERAL FEEDBACK

If there are general comments readers would like to make about content, whether you are a prisoner, a relative or friend of someone inside, a student, doctor, chaplain, teacher, lawyer, social worker, probation officer, voluntary associate, prison visitor, Samaritan, housewife, judge, member of the Board of Visitors or anyone else who has an interest in our £1.6bn per annum penal system—then please write to me at the address below. While I cannot promise that your suggestion will be taken up, I can assure you that all letters will be read and considered in a positive way. Please mark your envelope '**Feedback**'. I look forward to hearing from you.

Mark Leech
Editor
October 1994

All correspondence should be addressed to:

The Editor, The Prisoners' Handbook, c/o Richard Hart, Oxford University Press, Freepost 1777, Oxford. OX2 6YZ.

PREFACE The View From Here — MARK LEECH

NAMING NAMES

Three years ago the Prisons Board, made up of those senior Prison Service staff who have the last word in operational penal affairs, decreed as a mark of penal *Glasnost* that henceforth: '*all prison staff who come into contact with prisoners, or the public, should normally wear name badges.*'

With a flood of publicity, and acting under the banner of the **Citizen's Charter**, the Prison Service firmly pinned its colours to the 'More Open Government' mast and published its name badge commitment in glossy leaflets printed by the thousand at HMP Leyhill. This welcome 'nod' from the top-floor of Cleland House, indicating that the names of prison officials were no longer to be regarded (normally at least) as a national secret, appeared to signal an end to the Prison Service's practice of excessive secrecy once and for all: today, the colours are in danger of falling from the mast.

The Head of Custody at HMP Featherstone, to cite just one example, wrote to say that 'concern has been expressed' about my request for the names of Featherstone's 'key officials', and he refused to disclose the name of either the Education, Medical or Probation Officers, and nor would he identify the Governor, Area Manager, Chaplain or Chairman of the Board of Visitors without their express prior approval!

The Head of the BoV Liaison Section at Headquarters would not disclose the name of a single Chairman of any Board of Visitors: 'Some Chairmen do not want their names revealed' I was told. When I then asked for the names of those Chairmen who did not object, I was told that was not possible either, and for reasons which still remain unclear.

The Director of Prison Health Care, who is also a member of the Prisons Board, would not reveal the name of a single Medical Officer for any establishment in England and Wales, despite the fact that Medical Officers (like all members of the BoV) occupy an office created by statute, and it is accepted that the public have a right to know the names of individuals appointed to such posts. Writing in the *Prison Service Journal* in September 1994 the Director of Prison Health Care, Dr Rosemary Wool, said that since taking up the post of Director in 1990 she has sought to put into effect some of her 'personal ambitions' for prison medicine, 'not least to raise the standard in every aspect' and deliver a level of service equal to that provided by the National Health Service: perhaps Dr Wool would follow the example of the NHS, and reveal the names of her doctors?

When the Director General of HM Prison Service (who is also the Chairman of the Prisons Board) was contacted in a final attempt to make the practice fit the theory, it did not resolve the problem: the Director General did not reply to the letter. There has to be something completely illogical about a system that, on one hand, is quite happy to name the Head of MI5 but, on the other, seeks to conceal at all costs those of its prison Medical Officers and the Chairmen of its Board of Visitors: all of whom should normally be wearing name badges in any event.

Neatly it demonstrates how reform requires a practical change of attitude: glossy publications are not enough. The response from Headquarters may also explain why discipline staff have themselves been able to avoid wearing name badges for so long: for example, don't strain your eyes looking for one in places like Wandsworth. The Governor of that infamous establishment, when asked why he did not simply demand that his staff comply with the name badge policy, replied that it was 'never so simple as demanding'. Perfectly true, as the BoV at Wandsworth will confirm: they've been campaigning for discipline staff at Wandsworth to comply with the name badge policy for the last two years, and without any success at all. Opponents of the name badge claim it represents an unacceptable risk to the safety of staff: inmates could trace where officers live, and thereby pose a risk to them and their families. I recognise the concern is genuine and sincere, but equally it is quite irrational.

Prison Officers who print their name on a charge sheet every time they place a prisoner on report, do not use aliases. I doubt they are making up names as they go along each time they sign a VO, shout to a colleague, countersign a property card, answer a telephone or write their name on any one of a hundred different forms required by 'the system' each day. Opponents of the name badge have been unable to point to a single verified example in the last three years where the wearing of a name badge has resulted in the fears its opponents so passionately express. In any event, the solution to the problem is surely for opponents to argue for reversal of the Prisons Board name badge policy, rather than turning a blind eye to it just because they can't have their own way. Sooner or later it *has* to be as simple as 'demanding' if real progress is to be made, and the credibility of the Prisons Board maintained.

A MATTER OF INTEREST

Why is it that our penal system, which is capable of closing entire establishments overnight, arranging hundreds of transfers to all four corners of the country by the following morning, is unable to get a prisoner's **private cash** from one prison to another in less than six weeks? More to the point, if these funds are held in each prison's bank account, just what happens to the interest that is presumably accumulating while the private cash of thousands of prisoners is sitting dormant during this period?

While recently transferred prisoners around the country are left to stew without access to their private cash, the much needed money is presumably sitting in the prison's bank account earning interest the inmate never sees, and stemming from an unofficial loan that he never authorised: and the fact that there is absolutely no operational necessity for this obnoxious practice (as shown by the Scottish way of doing things) adds insult to what is an already grievous injury. All inmates on transfer in Scotland are credited, immediately on arrival at their receiving establishment, with the full balance of their private cash which accompanies them on transfer in the form of a cheque. Immediately, they are able to contact loved ones, reassure them, arrange visits and begin to settle down much faster than is currently the case in England and Wales. The Prison Service cannot expect to be taken seriously about promoting family contacts if, on transfer, it continues to severely restrict the ability of inmates to contact loved ones in this way. The penal system south of Hadrian's ruined Wall urgently needs to give the prisoner credit where it is already long overdue.

BOARDS OF VISITORS

All prisons have a BoV who are required by Rule 97 to submit an **Annual Report** to the Secretary of State on the state of the prison and the treatment of inmates within it. A small number of Boards publish their reports as a matter of course, but many others categorically refuse to do so and often without reason. The Chairman of the BoV at Woodhill prison, for example, tossed our request for a copy of their report back over the prison wall with the terse statement: '*We have decided not to forward to you a copy of the Board's Annual Report.*'

Why is that some Boards insist on unnecessary secrecy like this while others—such as Wandsworth, Pentonville and Wormwood Scrubs for example—not only publish their impressive reports, but issue press releases and place copies in the prison library for inmates and staff to read? Moreover, Judge Stephen Tumim, HM Chief Inspector of Prisons (who also reports to the Home Secretary), publishes ALL of his inspection reports and has won wide acclaim for his impartiality and openness as a result. HMCIP is *seen* to be professional, his criticisms of the prison authorities are seen to be balanced with an ability to dismiss complaints when they are without foundation. Many BoVs, and particularly those who shroud themselves in darkness, are often seen as little more than an extension of the prison governor: a chameleon device conveniently used for rubber-stamping his decisions and legitimising his actions.

The current BoV system, which even in its modern form is over 30 years old, is in need not so much of an overhaul but to be traded in completely for a newer and less secretive model. Incredibly, given the unfairness with which so many BoVs discharged their disciplinary functions before they were stripped of them by Parliament in April 1992, a number of Boards are now using their annual reports to campaign for a return of their disciplinary powers: could this be one reason why they do not want us to see them? All Boards should be required to publish their annual reports, so that we can all see what it is these people have to say about our prisons—or they should be required to explain, precisely, why they will not do so.

There are Boards with members who have served on the BoV for more than 20 years: while that may assist continuity, it can also act as a very great fetter on progress. Membership should be limited in duration so that fresher faces, and more enlightened minds, can be appointed to replace those who are well meaning but equally past their best.

In August 1994 The Prison Reform Trust published a report on the role of the BoV (***Have You Got a Minute: The Changing Role of Prison Boards of Visitors***), in which they warned the BoV system was under threat unless Boards improved their effectiveness and credibility. The creation of a Prisons Ombudsman may signal the thin end of the BoV wedge. The Prison Service has turned the post-Woolf corner, there can be no going back: the BoV system will have to reform itself and rapidly, or fade even further into disrepute.

STOP ME & BUY ONE

Official publications, such as the Prison Act, Prison Rules and certain Standing Orders, can be purchased by inmates—yet obtaining a copy often proves difficult, and an up to date edition is nigh on impossible. Why are establishments not required to stock these items (and display them) for purchase in each canteen? That would bring them to the attention of inmates, ensure that current editions are available and create an inmate population more informed about what they can and cannot do: isn't that why they are published?

Money-off coupons are still refused by prison

canteen staff, not because they are not applicable to prisons, but simply because it is administratively inconvenient for staff to deal with them: inconvenient it may be, but that is no longer a good enough reason for denying something that is correct in principle.

Far too many prisons are still shirking their legal responsibilities in respect of **defective phone cards**, sold through the prison canteen, insisting that inmates must raise the issue of defective cards with British Telecom and in the meantime suffer the loss in silence: that approach conflicts with the provisions of the UK-wide Sale of Goods Act 1979. This Act almost certainly extends to prison canteens in England and Wales, in the same way as the Scottish Secretary of State conceded it applied to canteens in Scottish prisons: **Leech v Secretary of State for Scotland** (March 1994). Where goods are defective the Governor is required to either refund the money or replace the item—*as the inmate-customer desires*—but far too many refuse to do this on the basis that they have no way of checking whether the card is actually faulty. I understand the difficulties that can arise in an environment where ingenious attempts at fraud are common, but that is not a sufficient basis for depriving prisoners of consumer rights that have been conferred upon us by statute. What's more, given the short period of telephone-time prisoners' receive for their units from British Telecom (who insist prison phones are classed as public pay phones, despite the fact that not a single member of the public can use them), it is time the Prison Service made serious enquiries with Mercury or cable operators to negotiate a better deal.

Shaw's Retail Guide, which gives the accepted everyday retail price of articles commonly sold in the shops, should be the yardstick for all prices in the prison canteen which, according to HM Prison Service, should make a profit of between 10 and 12.5%. Despite that, HMCIP has discovered establishments making twice that amount of profit, with prices being set quite arbitrarily by canteen staff. If these odious practices continue, then prison canteens must be prime candidates for market testing and privatisation.

PRIVATISATION

I have written elsewhere (The *Observer*, 9 August 1992) of my support for the process of prison privatisation and the reasons why I believe it represents a way forward for our penal system. Therefore it was with considerable regret that I found, when putting the *Handbook* together, that two of the three private companies who currently have prison contracts (**U.K.D.S.** at Blakenhurst, and **Premier Prisons** at Doncaster) were more secretive than many of their public sector counterparts—and far less forthcoming than **Group 4** (at The Wolds), who not only completed the questionnaires but provided an abundance of information and answered follow-up questions swiftly and without complaint. **U.K.D.S.** refused to complete the questionnaires we sent them, on the basis that Blakenhurst was a 'new establishment' where 'its culture and style is still developing': I suspect that was not an excuse they gave to Judge Tumim when he knocked on their gates to inspect the establishment a month before our request.

Premier Prisons, who had two inmate-suicides at Doncaster in its first three months, did not reply to any of our letters nor return our phone calls, despite promising a number of times to do so. While these actions of **U.K.D.S.** and **Premier Prisons** should not be allowed to damage the principle of privatisation, opponents of private sector involvement have already made much of the secrecy which they say surrounds such establishments—and this type of behaviour will do little except give credence to their claims.

READING BETWEEN THE LINES

In 1992 HM Prison Service announced the **abolition of censorship** of mail for the vast majority of prisoners: the evolution of the card phone had made its practice largely superfluous. All mail, in all penal establishments, is still opened. All of it is scanned for illicit enclosures and then, runs the theory, the envelope is passed to the inmate with its contents *unread* unless the addressee is in Category A, on the Escape List, or is the subject of a specific instruction from the Governor that his/her mail be censored. The still much resented practice, in far too many establishments according to returned inmate questionnaires, is that mail is opened out of sight of the prisoner concerned, often in a completely separate building behind closed and, sometimes, locked doors.

Asking prisoners to accept, or worse expecting us to believe, that only authorised mail is ever read in these circumstances is to demonstrate a negligent disregard of reality. Many hands make for light work in these days of ever more prisoners to the pound: why therefore is mail not distributed to the living units, and opened by Personal Officers in front of the inmate to whom it is addressed? In a stroke the task is completed in a fraction of the time, security is maintained, Personal Officer/inmate relationships are developed and the staff who would otherwise spend an entire morning opening inmates' mail are free for other duties far sooner so expanding the regime. Moreover, it removes any suspicion that the rules, which lay down the theory, may occasionally slip their handcuffs from the practice they ought to be shackled to, and it stops in its tracks any dispute as to what was (or wasn't) in the envelope when it arrived. In fact, there are so many reasons why it *should* happen this way, it does make you wonder why it doesn't.

SECTION ONE

PENAL ESTABLISHMENTS
(ENGLAND & WALES 1995)

Foreword

i GLOSSARY

ARD Automatic Release Date

Average Roll The number of prisoners in an establishment is called the 'Roll'. The figure shown in each entry is the average prisoner population for that particular prison, as published in the latest Annual Report of HM Prison Service or more recent official source. It should be treated only as an indication of how the establishment generally operates, viewed against the backdrop of its **CNA.**

BoV Board of Visitors. The body of people selected for each prison by the Home Secretary to act as watch-dogs.

BTEC Business Training Education Council.

C&R Control and Restraint. A series of physical locks and holds used by prison officers to move a resisting prisoner in a controlled manner from one location to another.

Category As all adult male inmates are placed into one of four security categories, ABCD, so the level of security of an establishment is similarly graded. There are no top security Category A prisons as such, all **Category A** inmates are 'dispersed' among one of six maximum security **Dispersal** prisons. **Category B** prisons cater for those inmates for whom escape must be made very difficult. **Category C** establishments hold those who have neither the intention nor resources to escape, while **Category D** prisons house those who can be trusted in open conditions.

CCE Church of England.

CES Clothing Exchange Store.

CIT Construction Industry Training.

CNA Certified Normal Accommodation. Section 14(2) Prison Act 1952 requires that all accommodation in which a prisoner can be located must be 'certified' by an inspector as being suitable for the purpose. There are two types of certified accommodation: **'Baseline'** and **'In-use'.** *Baseline* CNA is the maximum capacity of the prison, as certified by the inspector in terms of s.14(2). *In-use* CNA is the maximum capacity of a prison at any particular time; lower or equal to the Baseline CNA figure, it takes account of accommodation temporarily out of use for any reason. Unless otherwise stated, all CNA figures in the Handbook are

	Baseline CNA, and are from the latest Annual Report of HM Prison Service.
Con	Conservative.
CPC	Certificate of Professional Competence.
CRD	Conditional Release Date.
CSV	Community Service Volunteer.
CSLA	Community Sports Leader Award.
E.List	Escape List.
EMC	Effective Minimum Complement.
EN	Enrolled Nurse.
ESL	English as a Second Language.
FTE	Full Time Education.
FT	Full Time.
G5	Governor (Grade) 5. All governors fall into one of five categories: G1=highest, G5=lowest.
GUC	Genito-Urinary Clinic.
HCC	Health Care Centre.
HCO	Health Care Officer.
HCPO	Health Care Principal Officer.
HCSO	Health Care Senior Officer.
HLED	Home Leave Eligibility Date.
HMCIP	HM Chief Inspector of Prisons.
IO	Instruction Officer: prison officer qualified to instruct courses, workshops or works etc.
IP	In Possession.
JR	Judge's Remand. Inmates who have been convicted and remanded in custody by the judge for completion of pre-sentencing reports.
Lab	Labour.
LLO	Lifer Liaison Officer.
Local Purchase	Goods not stocked in the prison canteen which can be ordered and bought locally.
Long-Term	Over 3yrs (female), Over 4yrs (male).
M–F	Monday to Friday.
Medium-Term	Over 18mths & inc 3yrs (female), Over 18mths & inc 4yrs (male).
M&BU	Mother & Baby Unit.
NPD	Non-Parole Date.
NS	Nursing Sister.
OCA	Observation, Classification & Allocation Unit.
PED	Parole Eligibility Date.
PEO	Physical Education Officer.
PEPO	Physical Education Principal Officer.
PESO	Physical Education Senior Officer.
PNS	Principal Nursing Sister.
PO	Principal Officer.
PRES	Pre-Release Employment Scheme.
PSIF	Prison Service Industries & Farms.
PT	Part Time.
PTE	Part Time Education.
PV	Prison Visitor. Local people who visit prisoners, normally arranged by the Chaplain.
PVO	Privilege Visiting Order. Extra VO's which can ONLY be used on a weekday.;
RC	Roman Catholic.
Remand Centre	An establishment which holds untried and unsentenced inmates under the age of 21.
SAE	Stamped Addressed Envelope.
SED	Sentence Expiry Date. Formerly the Latest Date of Release (LDR).
Short-Term	Sentences up to & including 18 months.
SGO	Sports & Games Officer.
SNS	Senior Nursing Sister.
SO	Senior Officer.
Special Visits	All visits to inmates other than domestic visits.
SWIP	Shared Working in Prison.
Unified Grades	The eight ranks between G1 Governor and G8 Prison Officer.
VO	Visiting Officer. **Convicted** prisoners must send their visitor a VO before the date of the visit. VO's are valid for twenty-eight days from the date of issue and can be used on any day when convicted visits are allowed—see the respective establishment entry. VO's have to be presented to the officer in the prison gatelodge in order to gain access. Visitors to **Remand** prisoners are not normally required to have a VO on arrival, but will fill one in at the gate.
VTC	Vocational Training Course.
VPU	Vulnerable Prisoners Unit.
W/E	Weekends.
W/D	Weekdays.
Works	Prison maintenance.
YOI	Young Offenders Institution. The title given to establishments which hold prisoners under the age of 21.

ii PRISONER LOCATION SERVICE

Finding a recently imprisoned inmate
If your relative or friend has just been imprisoned, you could contact the Clerk of the Court in which he or she appeared and find out which prison they are in.

Finding an inmate imprisoned for some time
If your relative or friend has been in prison for some time and you do not know where they are, you can contact them via the **Prisoner Location Service**. You need to write to the Service giving as much information as possible, including the prisoner's:

name, age and date of birth;
their offence if convicted, or charge if untried;
your relationship to them, and
the reason for wanting to contact them.

How long does it take?
The process can take two or three weeks as the Service has to contact the prisoner to find out if they are happy for you to know where they are—a prisoner's whereabouts **cannot** be given over the telephone.

PRISONER LOCATION SERVICE
PO BOX 2152
BIRMINGHAM B15 1SD

iii IMPORTANT NOTES FOR VISITORS

The right day
Arrangements for visits vary considerably from one prison to another. The Establishment Section lists all prisons in England and Wales with details as to when visits take place, how to get there and what facilities are available. Further details, such as travel by road, can be obtained from the prison. No prison allows visits on Christmas Day, Boxing Day or Good Friday, and some do not allow visits on Sundays.

The right time
Multi-functional establishments (those that contain a mix of, say, Remand and Convicted prisoners, or young offenders and adults) often allow visits to the different groups on different days and at different times. For example, it would be pointless to visit a **Convicted** prisoner if the visiting session you attended catered for **Remand** prisoners only.

The right place
In some establishments, such as local prisons, prisoners can be transferred at very short notice and it therefore makes sense to phone the prison before making the journey, to check you are attending the right session and that the prisoner you wish to see is still there.

Financial assistance
You may be entitled to financial assistance to help you with the costs of visiting a close relative or spouse. Also if you travel to a prison only to find that the person who you were to visit has been transferred, you may be able to obtain the costs of visiting back from the prison—and the costs of any overnight stay that may have proved necessary in the circumstances. Detailed information for visitors is given in the **Visits, Letters and Phone Calls** chapter of the Advice Section.

iv DRUG TRAFFICKING: The Facts

In a growing number of prisons, particularly maximum security dispersal and local establishments, you may find that you are required to undergo a search before the visit is allowed. Your luggage may be examined or you may be required to leave it at the gate. Because of the growing number of visitors who are being caught and prosecuted after attempting to smuggle drugs into prisons, some establishments now secretly record visits on videotape and any evidence it reveals may be used against you. If you are caught trafficking then serious consequences will fall upon both you and the prisoner you are visiting: and the families of other prisoners will suffer also. Here are the facts.

If an illicit substance is suspected or detected you will be arrested and handed over to the local police. The least you can expect is a stressful day in police custody—longer if it happens on a weekend. You will be strip-searched, photographed, fingerprinted and your bodily orifices may be probed by medical hands. You will be interviewed and charged. Bail is by no means in your favour: the authorities take a very grave view of smuggling drugs into our prisons and you could quite easily spend much of the next six months in prison yourself awaiting trial. Thereafter a custodial sentence is almost inevitable and this will not only have a damaging effect on you and your family, but your future employment prospects will have been seriously damaged if not destroyed completely.

The person you are visiting will also suffer. All visits to that prisoner for the foreseeable future will take place behind a sheet of glass, and the Governor may ban you personally from entering the prison to visit at all—he has the legal powers to do that. Disciplinary or criminal charges could be brought against the prisoner you are visiting, and their prospects of obtaining Home Leave, Parole or a reduction in Security Category will be bleak to say the least.

Additionally your actions will be cited by the prison authorities to justify the imposition of even more stringent security measures in the future—it is other prisoners and their families who will suffer for your conduct long after you have gone. With modern technology and an increased awareness among prison staff of the need for vigilance during visits, the chances of success are very small and certainly short-term. Please think very carefully before you agree to become involved in such dangerous activities: once that cell door slams shut behind you, it's too late to say you didn't know the facts.

FINALLY

Remember . . . from 0100 hours on 16th April 1995, an additional '1' must be inserted in all telephone STD Area Codes after the '0'—for example 061 (Manchester) will become 0161.

HM Prison Acklington

Morpeth, Northumberland NE65 9XF
Tel: 0670-760411 **Fax:** 0670-761362
Opened: 1987 **CNA:** 676 **Average Roll:** 574 **Category:** C. Male

i **BACKGROUND** HM.Prison Acklington, the most northerly establishment in the Prison Service, is a Category C training prison situated adjacent to HM.YOI Castington at Morpeth in Northumberland. It is an establishment with a history of unrest and inter-prisoner violence. The prison holds short-medium term prisoners, up to 50 lifers progressing towards release, and operates the Core Sex Offender Treatment Programme. Neither the Governor nor the BoV replied to our requests for information about Acklington. HMCIP published their latest report in December 1992.

OFFICIALS
AREA MGR: Al Papps
CHAIR BOV:
GOVERNOR: F. Masserick
MEDICAL:
CHAPLAIN: Rev Truman
PROBATION: P. Fox
EDUCATION:
LOCAL MP: Alan Beith. Lib.Dem
STAFFING: 326 staff in unified grades.

REGIME *week days*: 0745 unlock, breakfast. 0800 treatments. 0845 work. 0900 sick parade. 1140 cease labour. 1145 lunch. 1215 yard association. 1305 work. 1645 tea. 1715 yard association. 1730–1930 evening classes. 2050 lock up.

week ends: 0800 unlock, breakfast. 0800 treatments. 0830 yard association. 0900 sick parade, CE Service(Sun). 1145 lunch. 1215 lock up. 1330 association. 1600 lock up. 1700 tea. 1715–1930 yard association. 2000 lock up.

Out of cell: 10.5/24hrs weekdays and 9.5/24hrs at weekends.

ACCOMMODATION & FACILITIES Seven main living units (A,B,C,D,E,F,G) with good size cellular accommodation, unrestricted access to showers and toilets or integral sanitation. Accommodation reported as filthy by HMCIP, who also castigated the establishment for the wanton destruction of fixtures and fittings. Personal officer scheme in operation, drug counselling and SWIP. Routine censorship abolished June 1992 but mail not opened in the presence of the inmate. Card phones on all living units with access throughout the day.

VISITS *How to get there*: Train to Newcastle upon Tyne. Metro to Haymarket. X18 bus takes an hour. Special Transport: West Yorks, Cumbria, Cleveland, Manchester, Merseyside and S.Yorks Probations Services, contact prison probation for details. HALOW (London) bus service: 071-793-7484. VISITING TIMES: Week Days: 1400–1600 Mon–Fri, no entry after 1530. Saturday: 1400–1600 no entry after 1530. Sunday: 1400–1600 no entry after 1530.

NOTES No staffed Visitors Centre but shelter for early arrivals. Buses come to prison gate. Canteen: Mon Wed Thurs Sat & Sun. Childrens Play Area with toys and games. For overnight stays, contact Boston Tourist Information on 0665-712313.

EDUCATION A total of seventy places per day on education. Comprehensive curriculum with classes in basic education, computing, maths, literacy, open learning.

WORKSHOPS VTC/CIT Courses: electrical wiring (12 places); furniture craft (12); engineering (12); welding (12); plastering (12); skilled ops (12); painting & decorating (12); carpentry (12). PSIF: heavy textiles (72); tailoring (120); laundry (16). gardens (38); kitchen (26). Usual domestic workers and orderlies.

DISCIPLINE A total of 1,072 adjudications in the 12 months prior to the inspection, mainly for work-related offences and awards on the lenient side. Places in the Segregation unit at a premium due to the large number of Rule 43(OR) inmates who found themselves in debt said HMCIP: 'We saw several black eyes and cut heads, and noted a large number of unexplained injuries in the Accident Investigation File'.

FOOD Staffing: 1×PO, 1×SO and 4×Officer (caterers), and there is a work party of 16. Food, which had been the root of many disturbances, had improved since the arrival of the new PO(Caterer) who had introduced meals that were popular with the inmates. Pre-select menu system now in operation.

ESTABLISHMENT REPORTS In a report (published 1st December 1992) of an inspection in

May 1992, Judge Stephen Tumim, HMCIP, said that Acklington was an expanding establishment with an open regime but with staff stretched to retain control. Vandalism was widespread and cleaning standards unsatisfactory. Positive throughcare arrangements were in their infancy. Many improvements proposed in the last major inspection had been adopted but HMCIP made a number of key recommendations: A visitors centre should be constructed, serving both Acklington and Castington; 1988 recommendations to improve the education block and chapel should be implemented without delay.

PRISONERS' COMMENTS New governor responds to requests and complaints far sooner than his predecessor or other established grades at Acklington. All cells have integral sanitation. Power points were tried on one unit but abandoned because it was a poor system. High prices in the canteen and no local purchase facility. Visits have to be pre-booked 48 hours in advance, No Smoking on visits. Basic education with lots of certificates that mean very little. Average wage £6.60, UB40 £2.50. Inmates not at worked banged up all day, for a Cat C establishment there is far too much lock up. New Health Care Centre with lovely grounds but limited facilities. Punishments are generally fair and even-handed, block is seldom full, but the Head of Custody seems very resistant to change or progression. Very good PE facilities. No limits on correspondence, opened on arrival but not in front of you, they say its not read but who knows? Handed out 1100 Mon–Sat. Management impose many unnecessary restrictions on movement and trust is not a word frequently used at Acklington.

HM Prison Albany

Newport, Isle of Wight PO30 5RS
Tel: 0983-524055 **Fax:** 0983-825827
Opened: 1967 **CNA:** 313 **Average Roll:** 254 **Category:** B. Male

i **BACKGROUND** Albany prison occupies the site of a former military barracks on the outskirts of Newport, Isle of Wight. The establishment was designed and built as a category C training prison in the early 1960's but soon after it opened in 1967, a decision was taken that security should be upgraded and in 1970 Albany became part of the dispersal system. Albany has never been popular with inmates, partly because of its location on 'The Island' and it suffered major disturbances in 1983 which closed most of the jail for over a year. A major review of the dispersal system concluded that Albany should no longer be a dispersal prison and, in September 1992, it was redesignated as a B.category closed training prison. Albany also operates as an Assessment Centre for the Core Sex Offender Treatment Programme. Albany suffered a disturbance in the summer of 1994. Neither the Governor nor BoV at Albany replied to our requests for information, and HMCIP published their latest inspection report in May 1991.

OFFICIALS

AREA MGR: Peter Kitteridge
CHAIR BOV:
GOVERNOR: Vacant
MEDICAL:
CHAPLAIN: Rev Roberts
PROBATION: Bernard Wiseman
EDUCATION:
LOCAL MP: Barry Field. Con
STAFFING: 11 Governor grades, 17 Principal Officers, 26 Senior Officers and 230 Officers, including specialist staff.

REGIME *week days*: 0745 unlock/breakfast. 0900 work. 1215 lunch. 1330 work. 1615 cease labour. 1700 tea. 1730–2000 association.

week ends: 0745 unlock/breakfast. 0900 association. 1215 lunch. 1400 association. 1700 tea. 1730–2000 association.

Out of cell: 8.5/24hrs weekdays and 8.5/24hrs at weekends.

ACCOMMODATION & FACILITIES Five four-storey cell blocks: A,B,C wings form the main prison, D,E Wings form the VPU. All wings identical and hold a maximum of 96 inmates all in single cells with access to electronic night sanitation. Three small spurs on each landing, with communal recesses housing showers, toilets and wash basins. Power points have been fitted but not wired for use at present. Five TV rooms, cooking facilities and card phones on each wing. Sentence planning, personal officer scheme undeveloped. Mail at Albany is opened in the presence of inmate and handed out at dinner time. Cat A phone calls have to be booked in advance.

VULNERABLE PRISONERS UNIT
Located in D and E wings the VPU has its own regime, staff and employment—VPU inmates operate the woodworking shop, contract services shops, cleaners, garden party or on education. Good inmate/staff relationships have resulted in an informal personal officer scheme being developed. Offence focused work in the pipeline. Out of cell hours as main prison.

CANTEEN Central canteen located on central corridor, staffed by two officers, and open two mornings, one afternoon and five evenings each week. Carries 180 lines of stock, local purchase facility, 10% profit within Prison Service guidelines and HMCIP was told that all prices are geared to Shaw's Retail Price Guide: though many inmates from Albany complained of high canteen prices.

VISITS *How to get there*: Train to Portsmouth or Southampton, then ferry to either Ryde or Cowes respectively. Hovercraft from Southsea to Ryde takes 10 min. Bus to prison gate. Special Transport: Every Sunday ABBA Coaches leaves Goldsmiths College, New Cross, at 0900. Adults £17, children £9—inclusive of ferry fares. Booking in advance crucial: 081 859 1808/8708 Mr O'Toole.
VISITING TIMES: Week Days: 1400–1600 M–F. Saturday: 1400–1600. Sunday : 1400–1600.

NOTES Childrens Play Area and canteen available each day, though no staffed Visitors Centre. Short and Long stay accommodation, contact prison probation officer. Disabled access is very difficult as Visiting Room is upstairs and there are narrow doorways. ALL visitors are searched and pass through a metal detection system, and ALL inmates are strip searched after visits.

EDUCATION Six f/t teaching staff and 39 p/t teachers, linked to the Isle of Wight College of arts and technology. Daytime classes in both the VPU and main prison during a 50 week year with evening classes three nights per week. Full range of studies, basic education to OU. Business Studies Course. Art & Craft Centre employs some 18 inmates produces art and craft for displays and charities in the community.

WORKSHOPS VTC/CIT Courses: Painting & Decorating. Micro Engineering. Five workshops: Tailors 1 & 2 (denims), Woodwork 1 and 2 (cupboards and lockers etc). Contract Services assembly work. Poor reports of working conditions in the shops, no tea, no talking and poor wages.

DISCIPLINE Segregation Unit with 26 ordinary cells, two strip cells and two dirty cells. Examination of adjudication records revealed minor errors, but correct procedures were being followed and hearings were fair: a view that contrasts markedly with the responses of inmates from Albany who complain of heavy–handed awards and reports for petty offences such as talking at work.

MEDICAL Part time Medical Officer, 1×HCSO, 4×HCO. All inpatient facilities at Parkhurst. Report sick morning unlock and see MO during morning. Dentist visits three times per week. Good reports of medical services and short waiting lists. Urine tests offered on admission—HMCIP comments that HMP Parkhurst next door has 'equipment which could detect cannabis, opiates, cocaine and amphetamines in urine'.

GYMNASIUM & SPORTS 1×PEPO, 1×3PESO and 2×PEO. Large gymnasium, sports field, red-gra and tarmac area. Gym has three badminton courts, and weights area on stage. Sports field in poor condition. Inmates report excellent PE facilities, but access restricted to four days and five evenings per week—due to the two separate halves of the establishment.

CHAPLAINCY Full time CE chaplain, RC priest and p/t Methodist minister. Two chapels at one end of central corridor (M1). Ethnic minorities catered for by visiting ministers, though poor facilities with no multi-faith room. Main church services Sunday, CE and RC at 0815. VPU inmates attend but are kept separate. Small attendances to both services. No Prison Visitor Scheme.

FOOD Staffing: 1×PO, 1×SO, 4×Officer (caterers) and an inmate work party of 18. Kitchen adequate for its purpose, pre-select menu system in operation, though complaints of too little variation, poor quality and small portions dominate the Albany responses. Three choices at dinner, two at tea.

ESTABLISHMENT REPORTS In their Report (published 4th August 1993) of a short inspection of Albany in October 1992, prison inspectors noted that the prison had been taken out of the dispersal system and was being asked to develop regimes for vulnerable prisoners and a smaller number of category B prisoners. Senior managers faced the challenge of bringing about change and encouraging staff to have different expectations of prisoners. The attitude and enthusiasm of many staff was impressive, though throughcare arrangements and the management of life sentence prisoners were among the poorest the inspectors had seen.

PRISONERS' COMMENTS Requests and complaints are usually dealt with within two weeks, though there are delays in getting the form. Wired for in-cell power but not connected yet. Fairly good accommodation, though no choice as to location and cell changes difficult to obtain. Canteen prices are high though good local purchase facility with wide choice. VPU inmates complain that there are no separate visiting facilities and often feel intimidated. All inmates are strip searched after visits. Poor education provision for long termers and there is a lack of training courses at work. Wages average £7.50, though the shops tend to be run like a Detention Centre with inmates being placed on report for talking when they should be working! Letters are opened in front of inmate. Punishments always on the heavy side, inmate/staff relationships in main prison said to be poor, though good in the VPU. Food is often cold, frequently undercooked and the portions are small with food being thrown away rather than given out. Good gym facilities, available every night apart from Wednesday and Friday.

HM Prison Aldington

Ashford Kent. TN25 7BQ
Tel: 0233-720436 **Fax:** 0233-720886
Opened: 1947 **CNA:** 127 **Roll:** 121 **Category:** C & D Male

i **BACKGROUND** Aldington is situated on the edge of Romney Marsh, some five miles inland. In 1940 it was requisitioned by the Ministry of Defence, having been a farm, and was used subsequently for a Heavy Anti-Aircraft Battery by the Royal Artillery. In 1944 Aldington House became a Prisoner-of-War camp and, late in 1947, it was acquired by the Prison Commissioners; serving as an 'open' satellite to Maidstone Prison. In 1961 Aldington became a Senior Detention Centre, changing in 1986 to a Category C prison. Neither the Governor nor BoV replied to requests for up-to-date information. HMCIP published their latest report on Aldington in August 1993.

OFFICIALS
AREA MGR: John Hunter
CHAIR BOV:
GOVERNOR: D. Bratton
MEDICAL:
CHAPLAIN: Rev Williams
PROBATION: M. Coldbeck
EDUCATION:
LOCAL MP: Keith Speed. Con
STAFFING: Three Governor grades, 2 Principal Officers, 4 Senior Officers and 28 Officers, including specialist staff.

REGIME *week days*: 0730 unlock 0815 breakfast/treatments. 0845 work. 1045 sick parade. 1220 cease labour. 1230 dinner/treatments. 1330 work. 1630 cease labour/treatments. 1645 tea. 1715 lock up. 1800–2100 association.

week ends: 0745 unlock. 0815 breakfast. 0900 association/cleaning. 1200 lunch. 1230 lock up. 1330 association/visits. 1600 cease visits. 1645 tea. 1700 lock up. 1800 association [1800–1830 applications]. 2100 lock up.

Out of cell: 12.75/24hrs weekdays and 11.25/24hrs at weekends.

ACCOMMODATION & FACILITIES Mix of dormitories and cubicles, the latter mainly for single occupancy though there are a few two or three-bedded rooms. Poor facilities and 'a tatty appearance'. One toilet per wing and no cooking facilities reported by HMCIP. Large association area provides table tennis, darts and TV. Central bath house with 32 sinks, 10 showers, 2 WCs and a urinal. Showers available outside working hours. One discipline officer 'largely at his own initiative' runs a drug counselling unit. Routine censorship abolished. Aldington was criticised by HMCIP for not posting out-going mail on a Friday.

CANTEEN Two storemen supervise the shop at Aldington, located centrally within the main accommodation building. Open Tuesdays and Wednesdays, and HMCIP found that 'apart from complaints about the price of items and low wages, they were genuinely satisfied with the service they received. Good range of stock held and local purchase facility allows orders on Monday for Wednesday delivery.

REQUESTS/COMPLAINTS An average of a dozen R/C forms issued each month, majority of subjects being temporary release, home leaves and transfers. 'Virtually all those requiring a local response were receiving an answer within seven days'. HMCIP, however, had difficulty examining the quality of the responses given 'as there was no central file of completed requests/complaints'.

VISITS *How to get there*: Train to Ashford, then bus (525,526) to Aldington from Park Street. Taxi roughly £6 each way from Ashford BR Station. Bus from Vicarage Lane (opposite old bus station) 1220 weekdays, 1300 Saturday—returning from Aldington 1621. No Special Transport.
VISITING TIMES: Week Days: 1400–1600 Wednesday only. Week Ends: 1400–1600 Sat & Sun. Duration: from arrival.

NOTES Canteen in Visiting Room, Childrens' Play Area, supervised only at weekends. No staffed Visitors Centre but small waiting room opposite side of drive to prison. Small clean visiting room. Two visits per month and HMCIP recommended this should be increased. Ample parking space at prison.

EDUCATION Spacious education department with well equipped classrooms. Forty places on FTE. Computer, woodwork, art/craft, cookery and interview rooms. Evening classes only twice a week. Day classes: maths, science, art & design, soft toys, cooking and open learning. Plans to introduce NVQs in catering and horticulture, and possibilities for a business studies course. VTC motor mechanics. Library with stock of 2000 books and magazines. Prison magazine.

WORKSHOPS VTC Motor Mechanics. Contract services workshop providing rubber pads for British Rail and paper folders for commercial company. Working week 32 hours and min of 3 weeks in workshop before change of labour. Labour Board meets every Thursday. Wages average of £7.

DISCIPLINE No Segregation Unit, inmates who require secure conditions are transferred usually to Canterbury. Two or three adjudications carried out each week 'for fairly minor transgressions'.

MEDICAL P/t Medical Officer, 2×HCO working alternate days. No night cover though HCC staff can be called in. Six-bedded ward. Well equipped dental room with sessions once per week, opticians and chiropodists visit as necessary. Morning surgery with average of 16 inmates per day. No psychologist services available to Aldington.

GYMNASIUM & SPORTS 1×PESO, 1×PEO. A small but 'very adequate' gymnasium with adjoining weights room. Toilet and shower areas 'dowdy'. Large sports field allows soccer, rugby, and a four hole golf course. Concrete foundation allows for cricket and a tarmac area for tennis: 'in short the facilities were very good'. Day classes football, carpet bowls, running, tennis, weights, softball. Evening classes Mon–Thur.

CHAPLAINCY Three p/t chaplains minister to Christians, meeting on Tuesdays. Visiting ministers of ethnic faiths available but rarely called for. Two services per week and Chaplains Hour each Friday evening. Average attendance at service between 20 and 30.

FOOD Staffing: 1×SO, 2×Officer (caterers), and a work party of 10. 'The kitchen has many defects' according to HMCIP: 'The wash pan area had recently been condemned by the Local Environmental Health Officer and the plate wash . . . [was] also deemed unsatisfactory'. HMCIP found the food to be 'of good quality and we received few complaints from inmates, indeed compliments were paid to the Catering staff'.

ESTABLISHMENT REPORTS In a report (published 5th August 1993) of an inspection in August 1992, Judge Stephen Tumim, HMCIP, said that Aldington had endured an unsettled past and now enjoyed a friendly atmosphere. The prison was well accepted by the local community, basic amenities were adequate, apart from the dormitories which should be partitioned to provide privacy. The work for inmates was boring and mundane, though interesting possibilities existed. 'The most that can be said of the regime is that prisoners are being contained reasonably cheaply in an undemanding environment'. Aldington needs to develop programmes that address attitudes, offending behaviour and self control. Derek Lewis, Chief Executive HM.Prison service, said in response to the report that improvements had now been made to the kitchen, a personal officer scheme had been introduced but a firm decision had still to be made on the prison's future.

HM Prison Ashwell

Oakham, Leicestershire. LE15 7LF
Tel: 0572-756075 **Fax:** 0572-724460
Opened: 1955 **CNA:** 404 **Average Roll:** 385 **Category:** C Male

i **BACKGROUND** Ashwell prison is situated some 1.5 miles from Oakham in Leicestershire. It first opened in 1955 as an open prison for short and medium term adult prisoners. In October 1987; after erection of a fence, it was converted to a category C prison. The site, which had previously been an Army camp, extends to about 10 hectares together with a few remaining houses on the nearby estate of officers quarters. The Governor did not reply to our request for information about the prison and Ron Haworth, Chairman of the prison's BoV, refused our request for a copy of their annual report. HMCIP published their latest full inspection report on Ashwell in March 1993.

OFFICIALS

AREA MGR: Jim Blakey
CHAIR BOV: Ron Haworth
GOVERNOR: H. Reid
MEDICAL:
CHAPLAIN: Rev Ridley
PROBATION: G. Peeters
EDUCATION:
LOCAL MP: Alan Duncan. Con
STAFFING: Six Governor grades, 7 Principal Officers, 13 Senior Officers and 52 Officers, including specialist staff.

REGIME *week days*: 0730 unlock. 0745 breakfast. 0825–1125 work. 1145–1215 lunch. 1300 work. 1625 cease labour. 1645–1705 tea. 1730–2030 association.

week ends: 0730 unlock. 0800 breakfast. 0830 wing cleaning. 0945 inspection (Sat). 1000 RC Mass (Sat). 1030 CE Service (Sun). 1140–1200 lunch. 1315 visits, association. 1630–1650 tea. 1700–1800 lock up. 1800–2030 association.

Out of cell: 10/24hrs weekdays and 10/24hrs at weekends.

ACCOMMODATION & FACILITIES

Four living units (A[CNA:102], B[102], C[102], D[98]) all three-storey buildings of similar design. D.wing was built in 1971, whereas A,B,C wings were completed in 1985. Apart from two dormitories in D.wing the rest of the prison has single rooms with privacy locks. No integral sanitation but access to toilet and showers available at all times. Many petty rules—inmates have internal light switches, but they are required to switch them off at 2300. Card phones on each unit, but maximum of FOUR cards per month can be purchased. Mail opened in the presence of the inmate. SAE's allowed from family and friends. Sentence planning, personal officer scheme, drug counselling. SWIP well established. Ashwell holds approximately 60 lifers spread evenly around the wings.

CANTEEN Housed in purpose-built accommodation close to the living units, it is staffed by two f/t auxiliaries assisted by a canteen orderly. Local purchase facility from Oakham once per week. All inmates have access to the canteen twice a week, earnings spent on Mon/Tues, private cash on Fridays. Reasonable 170 lines of stock, clearly displayed prices and including fresh fruit, cereals and milk. Profit margin of 10%.

REQUESTS & COMPLAINTS Average of 15–20 formal R/C forms issued each month. Almost 80% of forms requiring a local response received one within the seven day time target and the remainder within fourteen days. Replies were reasonably full, clear and understandable according to HMCIP.

VISITS *How to get there*: Train to Oakham (Birmingham/Peterborough line) then taxi or walk. Barton's bus No.2 from Nottingham. Special Transport available from Birmingham, Coventry, Leicester, Chesterfield & Northampton probation.
VISITING TIMES: Week Days: 1415–1550 Mon, Wed, Fri only. Saturday: 1315–1530. Sunday : 1315–1530.

NOTES Canteen sells light refreshments, Childrens Play Area, but no staffed Visitors Centre—PortaKabin in car park used as visitors waiting room. Some B&B in Oakham. Wheelchair ramp into Visiting area and shelter provided for early arrivals. All visitors' luggage is searched.

EDUCATION Located outside the inner security fence it makes access to inmate difficult. Good information technology room and a 'drop in centre' for performing arts well supported. Places for 65 on FTE and nine evening classes per week. Open learning and OU catered for with main curriculum based around three foundation courses: F1 basic education, F2 for improvers and F3 for those generally studying at O level standard. Business studies course (16 weeks) to BTEC standards. NVQ due to be introduced shortly. Library with a stock of 4,500 books.

WORKSHOPS Two industrial workshops (footwear and textiles), one VTC course in electrical installation. Kitchen, works, domestic cleaners, orderlies, and gardens. Labour Board meets each Thursday to consider change of labour applications. All inmates must generally spend three months on a party before being allowed a change of labour.

DISCIPLINE Segregation Unit with six cells adjacent to D.wing and unsuitable for anything but temporary location. Few formal adjudications as most offenders are shipped out to Leicester.

MEDICAL Part time Medical Officer contracted for 9.5 hours per week. 1×HCSO, 2×HCO. HCC situated in wooden hut, clean and well looked after. Six-bed ward and well-equipped dental surgery used twice per week 0915–1115: very short dental waiting list. Optician visits as required. One HCO trained as HIV/AIDS counsellor.

GYMNASIUM & SPORTS 1×PESO and 3×PEO. PE at four locations. Modern sports hall (1988), suitable for most types of indoor physical activities—no showers though. Old gymnasium across the road used as a carpet bowls and weights area. Large sports field providing for soccer, cricket and rugby. The old pavilion, several hundred yards from the gymnasium holds the only showers.

CHAPLAINCY Full time CE chaplain, p/t RC and Methodist ministers. Attractive chapel with space for 50, clean and well presented. Other faiths catered for by visiting Imam, Sikh minister, along with representatives of the Quaker, and Buddhist religions. Chaplaincy services or activities take place every day of the week.

FOOD Staffing: 1×SO, 5×Officers (Caterers), and an inmate work party of 26. Four choices of dinner and two for tea. all meals are eaten in large dining room next to kitchen. Three week menu cycle operated. Food complaints led to a serious disturbance at Ashwell in August 1991 though the arrival of a new catering manager has improved things since then.

ESTABLISHMENT REPORTS In a report (published March 1993) of an inspection in May 1992, HMCIP, said that the most refreshing part of Ashwell was that it retained many aspects of an open prison. Living accommodation for inmates was pleasant and relatively civilised. Management systems and administrative procedures were well constructed, though communication further down the line was not as effective and several staff felt themselves to be inadequately consulted and informed about developments inside the prison. As a Category C prison Ashwell has done well to hold onto its training ethos. This reflects credit on the Prison Service and Ashwell's managers and staff. Although it is good, it has the potential to provide a better training regime. Education needs to be at the forefront of what is offered to inmates, with much greater sophistication in using employment training, physical activity and offence-focused work to address the needs of inmates and thereby reduce the likelihood of reoffending.

PRISONERS' COMMENTS Poor request/complaint system, some answers still awaited after almost three months. Health care was not of the same standard as in the community, inmates had to report sick by 0800, even one minute late and you will not be seen. Fire doors on the end of wings were kept locked and fire barrier doors were often propped open. Lights have to be switched off at 2300 treating inmates like children. Little or no use was made of the sports field in the evenings or at weekends, and an allowance of four phone cards per month was insufficient. There was a reluctance by management to recategorise to D Category because of the financial implications of having to fund home leaves. Attendance of PE staff was designed to suit them, rather than the needs of the establishment. No civilian clothing other than trainers allowed. A number of mountain bikes had been bought, but these were only being used by staff. Inmates complained that they were being asked to denote their ethnic background when reporting sick. Poor work facilities, long delays in parole answers and a personal officer scheme which did not operate properly are just some of the other comments made to HMCIP by inmates at Ashwell, despite which many inmates made the point that it was a good prison, but hampered by far too many petty rules which have no purpose other than historical.

HM Prison Askham Grange

Askham Richard, York. YO2 3PT
Tel: 0904-704236 **Fax:** 0904-702931
Opened: 1947 **CNA:** 122 **Roll:** 105 **Category:** Female Open

i **BACKGROUND** Askham Grange is an open prison for women situated about seven miles west of York in the village of Askham Richard. The manor house was built in 1886, leased to the then Prison Commissioners in 1946 and sold to them in 1960. The prison, which contains a Mother & Baby Unit, occupies about five hectares of land which includes the Grange and a Pre-Release Hostel. The Governor supplied up-to-date information about the establishment, though the Askham Grange BoV did not reply to our request for a copy of their annual report. HMCIP published their latest report on Askham Grange in July 1993.

OFFICIALS
AREA MGR: M. Codd
CHAIR BOV: M.Dodd
GOVERNOR: H.E.Crew
MEDICAL: Dr Verity (Retires 11/94)
CHAPLAIN: Rev D. Watts
PROBATION: Mrs P. Flude
EDUCATION: Mrs C. Burke
LOCAL MP: Michael Alison. Con
STAFFING: Three Governor grades, 2 Principal Officers, 4 Senior Officers and 26 Officers. Total of 41 staff in post including specialist grades.

REGIME *week days*: Breakfast 0800, Activity 0830–11.45, Lunch 1200, Activity 13.30–16.45, Dinner 1700 hrs. No lock up.

week ends: Breakfast 0800, Activity 0830–11.45, Lunch 1200, Activity 13.30–16.45, Dinner 1700 hrs. No lock up. Temporary release and 'open' (ie off–site) visits as eligible, House cleaning, PE, Recreation and on-site visits.

Out of cell: 24/24hrs weekdays and 24/24hrs at weekends.

ACCOMMODATION & FACILITIES
Manor house built in 1886, takes 91 in dormitories, Mother & Baby Unit takes 15 & 17—being extended. Hostel takes 16 in single rooms. Internal switches & sockets in dorms but no pets. Askham Grange has: sentence planning, drug counselling, personal officer scheme, night sanitation, sexual abuse counselling and a pre-release hostel. SWIP and personal officer schemes. Routine censorship abolished June 1992. Mail opened in front of prisoner, usually handed out at lunchtime. No limit on letters or phone cards that can be bought, though chronic shortage of telephones reported by prisoners. HMCIP recommended that a further phone be installed.

CANTEEN Four Prison Auxiliaries share the duties of running the shop. Conditions are cramped, though HMCIP found a good service was provided. Over 200 items of stock, and local purchase facility for such things as fresh fruit and cards etc. Open only once a week, Monday or Thursday evening, dependent on work location. Private cash spends dealt with once per month.

REQUESTS/COMPLAINTS Four or five formal R/C submitted each month, parole and requests for restoration of lost remission make up the bulk of requests: 'A substantial majority of the requests/complaints received a reply within the stipulated target time, and most replies were full, well constructed and comprehensible'. HMCIP however thought it was 'insensitive' to cite a passage from official manuals to illustrate a point: 'every reference was to the male gender'.

VISITS *How to get there*: Train to York then taxi—£5.50 each way or (i) Tadcaster bus (843) from Leeds every hour from outside station then one mile walk from Buckles Inn or (ii) bus (87) from outside York Station 1220 to Askham Richard village (NOT Sundays). No Special Transport.
VISITING TIMES: Week Days: 1345–1515 (30 mins only, must be booked). Saturday: 1345–1515. Sunday : 1345–1515.

NOTES Canteen and Childrens Play Area available only at weekends. Plenty of B&B in York. Wheelchair ramp available, but as yet no disabled toilet facilities. No staffed Visitors Centre. Visiting described as 'excellent' by majority of prisoners, 'open visits' within 50 miles radius of prison being particularly appreciated by those eligible: 'they are well worth keeping clear of trouble'.

EDUCATION Education department opened 50 weeks of the year. Two full-time teachers, one part-time and 16 p/t lecturers. Evening classes available four nights of the week. The 'former unimaginative curriculum' had been replaced with one that now has VTC Home Economics, Catering, a hairdressing course and one that concentrates on business studies in the morning and dress-making in the afternoon. Between 40–50 women are normally engaged on day time education, with a small number following courses at external colleges.

WORKSHOPS No workshops as such, nearly half the inmates engaged on education, cleaning and orderlies accounted for a further 20 and of the remainder 15 could be employed on gardens, 8 in the kitchen and 5 on the works. Labour Board meets every Thursday at which inmates can attend and state their preferences: 'from what we observed, every effort was made to meet their wishes'. Average wage £7.

DISCIPLINE Average of one adjudication per day. Though many were for failure to return from home leave or temporary release HMCIP felt 'there were too many examples of petty offending which could have been dealt with informally'. Some rules at Askham Grange 'seemed excessively prescriptive'. Segregation unit normally used to hold inmates awaiting adjudication or transfer to closed conditions.

MEDICAL P/t Medical Officer visits twice per week for a two-hour session and HMCIP found the time given to medical interviews was sufficient and examinations were carried out sensitively. Other HCC staff visit as required. Four bed ward, though plans to move the HCC to a bungalow in the grounds. Dentist attends weekly and a non-urgent waiting list of about five weeks exists. Optician attends as required. Health screening did not include blood pressure or urine tests, though staff were to introduce a Well Woman clinic. No Listeners' scheme or befriending service. **Mother & Baby Unit**, located next to HCC, has a capacity for 17 women and up to 19 babies. Each mother and baby have separate rooms with either a bed or cot for the baby. HMCIP was concerned at the policy which separated mother and baby when the child reached 18 months: 'we reiterate our long held view that pregnant women and mothers with small babies should, except in exceptional circumstances, receive disposals from courts which avoid custody'.

PRE-RELEASE HOSTEL

Accommodation for 16 women. Bedrooms, though compact, are neatly furnished and a well appointed kitchen recently refurbished. Officer on duty 0700–2100. Night shift cover provided by Night Patrol officer. Lifers normally spend last six months, determinate sentence normally spend three months, on the hostel. Mixture of employment, with wages either paid directly to inmate or into a building society account opened for them by the prison. £8 per week compulsory savings, £8 per week emergency funds, £1.25 per week TV rental and all admissions to the hostel were credited with £100 to be repaid over subsequent weeks.

GYMNASIUM & SPORTS Good facilities for PE. Small swimming pool, separate weights and multigym area. Large flat tarmac area provides room for volleyball and netball as well as tennis. Adjacent lake allows fishing and canoeing. PE programme offers fitness sessions, walks, cycle rides, aerobics, swimming, badminton, remedial exercises and post-natal classes. Mothers encouraged to bring their babies to the pool to acclimatise them to the water. Despite these facilities HMCIP found the PE dept to be an 'unsatisfactory state of affairs' short of staff and where the six officers trained in Sports and Games had 'inexplicably' not been used at all.

CHAPLAINCY P/t CE, RC and Methodist chaplains, non-Christian faiths catered for as required. Ecumenical team of religious sisters, Salvation Army Officers and lay people. Inmates wishing to attend services usually do so in the local community. HMCIP report that: 'On the Sunday before our inspection two women had attended a Quaker meeting, one went to a Methodist service, five to an Anglican parish, two to a Roman Catholic Church and 12 to a Pentecostal service'.

FOOD Staffing: 2×Officer (caterers) and work party of 6. Choice of three meals for both dinner and tea on weekdays and two choices at weekends. 'Inmates complained that the menu was repetitive and that food was presented unimaginatively and in many cases cooked some hours before being served, from what we observed there was some substance to their complaints'. Pre-select menu system recently introduced and though the dining room had been recently refurbished, 'it would help if such items as table cloths, condiments, plants, water jugs and tumblers were provided'.

ESTABLISHMENT REPORTS In a report (published 14th July 1993) of an inspection in November 1992, Judge Stephen Tumim, HMCIP, said that all the facilities at Askham Grange were more than adequate, and both inmates and staff were to be congratulated on standards of hygiene and cleanliness. Increased opportunities were being provided for temporary release, chaplaincy services were of a high order though physical education was very disappointing, the PE staff had failed to achieve a consistent momentum for the programme. Control had been established by way of a large number of rules rather than encouraging responsibility and addressing offending behaviour, and the management at Askham Grange would learn much by looking to the regimes at such places as Blantyre House. There were no offence focused groups, pre-release training had come to a standstill and there was very little activity to assist drug abusers. Making progress at Askham Grange is the challenge for managers and staff, and the prison's continued existence in its current role may depend on the success of their efforts.

GOVERNOR'S COMMENTS The Governor of Askham Grange, Mr Crew, identified three objectives for the year ahead:

1. Develop towards quality service for prisoners.
2. Develop staff skill training, and
3. Develop buildings and grounds potential.

PRISONERS' COMMENTS Reasonably efficient with request and complaints, single room accommodation with internal light switch and power point. Queuing for the canteen is unpopular: 'a lot of bickering goes on in the line'. Visits are excellent as is education, and working conditions vary from average to very good. Medical services are very poor: 'I try never to be ill'. Quality of food varies between poor and average. Good gym facilities though could be open more at weekends. Excellent religious services, good mail procedures, handed out at lunchtime. Phone cards can be bought without limit but there is a 'desperate' need for more phones.

HM YOI Aylesbury

Bierton Road, Aylesbury, Bucks. HP20 1EH
Tel: 0296-24435 **Fax:** 0296-434139
Opened: 1847 **CNA:** 241 **Roll:** 239 **Category:** Closed YOI (Long-Term)

i **BACKGROUND** Aylesbury has had a gaol for many centuries. The present YOI, constructed well outside the town in 1847, was used to hold debtors, felons and women inmates. Its former inhabitants would have little difficulty in recognising many of the buildings today. A centre for inebriate women was added on land adjoining the prison in 1902; this functioned independently until 1930 then it was incorporated with the prison and used as a female borstal until 1959. Since 1960 Aylesbury has housed only male inmates including Cat.A's, though this was abolished in 1992 when HMCIP reported the security was inadequate. With Castington and Swinfen Hall, Aylesbury is designated to hold young offenders serving the longest sentences. Initially Aylesbury declined to provide up-to-date information, but a change of Governor in July 1994 brought a different response—though not alas from the BoV who declined to provide a copy of their annual report. HMCIP Report published their last inspection report on Aylesbury in June 1992.

OFFICIALS

AREA MGR: A. de Frisching
CHAIR BOV: G. Perrett
GOVERNOR: Mike Sheldrick
MEDICAL: Dr Haq
CHAPLAIN: Rev Alan Marley
PROBATION: T. Symmons
EDUCATION: Liz Vallis
LOCAL MP: D. Liddington. Con
STAFFING: Seven Governor grades, 11 Principal Officers, 20 Senior Officers and 140 Officers including specialist grades.

REGIME *week days*: 0805 unlock/breakfast. 0850–1135 work. 1150 dinner. 1200–1605 work. 1705 tea. 1730–2015 association.

week ends: 0805 unlock. 0825 breakfast. 0840–1120 association. 1120 dinner, lock up. 1320 unlock, association, visits. 1545 tea. 1605 lock up. 1700 slop out. No weekend evening association.

Out of cell: 8/24hrs weekdays and 3.5/24hrs at weekends.

ACCOMMODATION & FACILITIES Accommodation contained in two separate buildings: A,B,C Wings radiate from the traditional centre, F&G Wings constitute the former female centre. A&C have 67 cells, B has 62 and F&G Wings each have 45 cells spread over three landings. Single cells, no integral sanitation. Facilities generally poor in all wings. Space for association in A,B,C is limited to the bottom floor of each wing, F&G have separate TV room. System of 'split association' in which half the establishment get association one night and the remainder the next, was criticised by HMCIP who said inmates average just 32 hours a week out of their cells. Sentence planning, drug-counselling, card phones, personal officer scheme, anger management course, cognitive skills groups. Routine censoring was abolished at Aylesbury on 23 June 1991. There are no restrictions on the length of incoming or outgoing letters nor on the frequency they can be sent or received: letters however are not opened in front of the prisoner. Card phones have now been fitted and are available during association times.

CANTEEN The shop is located in a group of buildings at the end of F&G wings, it is spacious but poorly decorated and unimaginatively laid out. No price or stock list existed and inmates could only visit once per week. The range of goods was 'on the low side' at 120 items said HMCIP who recommended complete refurbishment.

REQUESTS/COMPLAINTS HMCIP said there had been 85 R/C forms issued in the six months prior to their inspection, of which 61 had been returned completed. The Head of Custody co-ordinated the process and the majority of issues that could be dealt with locally were replied to within seven days. Most R/C forms related to transfers, treatment and property queries.

VISITS *How to get there*: Train to Aylesbury then taxi or walk from town centre. No Special Transport.
VISITING TIMES: Week Days: 1315–15.30 Wed only. Last entry 1445. Saturday: 1315–15.30 Last entry 1445. Sunday : 1315–15.30 Last entry 1445.

NOTES Canteen in visiting room and creche available on Saturdays. B&B plentiful in Aylesbury. Disabled access is difficult, but arrangements can be made with advance notice. No staffed Visitors Centre. Property can only be handed in with a prison voucher.

EDUCATION Housed in a modern, purpose-built two-storey block with ten classrooms. Facilities are satisfactory though ventilation creates a problem in the summer because of small windows. Five f/t teachers and 25 p/t staff. Lack of admin support is a 'major difficulty' according to HMCIP. Links with Aylesbury College are good. The largest employer in Aylesbury with 45 on f/t education. Open 45 weeks of the year with evening class three nights a week for 36 weeks of the year. Classes: English, maths, social skills, handicrafts, cookery, business & finance course, French, German, music, art, pottery, soft-toy making, biology, creative writing, OU and yoga. See 'workshops' for details of VTC/CIT courses.

WORKSHOPS Five VTC courses: Braille, Catering, Electronic wiring, Electronic servicing and Engineering Drawing Office Skills (EDOS)—which won the Phil Guise Memorial Award in 1990 for the best VT course. Total number engaged on courses is around 40 (70%) and HMCIP said this figure should be increased. CIT course in Painting & Decorating. Average wage £7, top end £12.

DISCIPLINE HMCIP reported a reduction in the number of adjudications at Aylesbury at the time of his inspection, though a reduction in population actually means the rate of offending has remained unchanged 'at the high level of 4.8' per inmate. An internal review had revealed a growing tendency among staff to use Governor's Reports instead of the Minor Report procedure. HMCIP examined adjudication records and found 'a wide variation in punishment awards and considered some on the high side for the offences committed'.

MEDICAL The prison hospital at Aylesbury, said HMCIP, 'is a poor facility' which should have a properly equipped Health Care Centre, a full-time Medical Officer (who was subsequently appointed) and night cover. Staffing: 1×HCSO, and 3×HCO's, one of whom is a qualified nurse. HCC little used, 12 admissions in six months, contrasted with 120 visits to the outside hospital. Dentist visits four hours a week, on average deals with six inmates and HMCIP discovered a two month waiting list. Six psychiatric sessions provided per week, and four 'Self-Harm' forms had been completed in the previous 18 months: 'the reason for this very low total is that instances of self-harm are classified as "gestures" only and therefore not recorded'. A better genito-urinary service was needed. Psychiatric hospital due to be built in 1995.

GYMNASIUM & SPORTS Small purpose-built gym—dating from the early 1960's—good-sized weights room, large sports field and small unheated open-air swimming pool. Daily classes from 0900–1530, and 1730–2015 Mon–Fri. Two hours voluntary PE per inmate per week. Swimming pool required improvements to enable year-round use and CSLA and GCSE O level classes. Full programme: volleyball, basketball, weights, rugby, and cricket, softball. Olympic Lifting, canoeing, rugby union, hiking and VP programme.

CHAPLAINCY F/t CE chaplain, p/t RC, Methodist and minority faiths. HMCIP said a multi-faith room should be provided. CE service every Sunday at 0930 and RC at 1045. Muslims meet for prayers on Friday and Sikhs on Monday. Two discussion groups were in operation. The HMCIP concluded 'religious activities were in a satisfactory state'.

FOOD Staffing: 1×SO(Caterer), 4×Officer Caterers and 14 inmates. All staff had completed health and hygiene training, along with nine inmates. Though the kitchen was well laid out and equipped HMCIP found the food to be of a poor standard: 'the potatoes were bad and inedible on arrival . . . we were not impressed by the sweet, the scone was dry and hard'. No menu system in operation and meal times, particularly dinner and tea, were at least an hour too early.

ESTABLISHMENT REPORTS HMCIP last inspected Aylesbury in July 1991 and their report, published in June 1992, was critical of the poor regime, lack of work, poor food, the 'shabby' visiting room and poor medical facilities. It was a 'problematic' establishment that was however well-managed and well supported by its staff. The Home Secretary, responding to the Report, said food had now been improved, construction of a new gatelodge to open in 1994/5 would incorporate a new visiting room, and a visitors centre will be included towards the end of the building programme. New work for inmates had been obtained, a new sports hall was promised, and a central library had been created.

HM Prison Bedford

St. Loyes Street, Bedford. MK40 1HG
Tel: 0234-358671 **Fax:** 0234-273568
Opened: 1801 **CNA:** 206 **Roll:** 264 **Category:** Male Local

i **BACKGROUND** There has been a prison at Bedford for hundreds of years. Until 1801 the prison was situated in the city centre and was where John Bunyan was imprisoned for 14 years. Land purchased outside the town in 1796 allowed the building of a new prison, which was completed and opened in 1801. The prison was considerably enlarged in 1846 by extending the perimeter wall and building a large cellular block with ancillary accommodation. Since that date there have been many minor additions and amendments and all available space inside the prison has been taken up with small buildings. The site was further extended in 1992 with a new gatehouse, house block and medical centre. The Governor did not respond to our request for upto date information, though the Bedford BoV kindly supplied a copy of their latest annual report. HMCIP published their latest inspection report on Bedford in March 1992.

OFFICIALS
AREA MGR: Amy Edwards
CHAIR BOV: Major Tatham
GOVERNOR: E. Willets
MEDICAL:
CHAPLAIN: Rev Willcox
PROBATION: J. Williams
EDUCATION:
LOCAL MP: Trevor Skeet. Con
STAFFING: Five Governor grades, 7 Principal Officers, 24 Senior Officers and 161 Officers. A total of 201 unified grades including specialist staff.

☞ **REGIME** *week days*: 0730 unlock/breakfast. 0830 work/community centre. 1115 dinner. 1200 lock up. 1330 work/community centre. 1630 tea. 1645 lock up. 1830–2030 association.

week ends: 0745 unlock/breakfast. 0830 community centre. 1145 dinner. 1200 lock up. 1330 visits, community centre. 1630 tea. 1645 lock up. No evening association.

Out of cell: 8/24hrs weekdays and 8/24hrs at weekends. Twenty-four Purposeful Activity Hours per prisoner/wk.

ACCOMMODATION & FACILITIES Four main accommodation wings (A,B,C,D) with 86, 29, 46 and 50 cells respectively, many two per cell and all with integral sanitation. Bail Information scheme office (on B4), Personal Officer scheme in operation. Basement of B.wing used as Segregation Unit with six ordinary cells, two strip cells and a recess with shower. Limited facilities on all main wings with insufficient space for association or other out-of-cell activities. Workshop converted to Community Centre—see below. Exercise takes place in the afternoon for those who use the Community Centre in the morning, and *vice versa*. No evening association in community centre reported by HMCIP. VPU operates in F.Wing, with recreation room and small charity workshop. Routine censorship abolished and two censor officers redeployed to Bail Unit and SWIP. Mail opened out of sight of inmate except for recorded or registered packages. Incoming letters handed out by midday and outgoing mail collected am/pm and posted 1630. Card phones in all wings.

COMMUNITY CENTRE Workshop complex redesigned as a Community Centre. Ground floor large association area with pool, table tennis and PE facilities. First floor comprises education dept and library. Open 0845–1115 and 1400–1600. No use of centre in evenings which HMCIP said was 'disappointing. Use is split, morning and afternoon, between convicted and unconvicted inmates Mon–Thurs: HMCIP could not 'praise the facility too highly and we commend it to other local prisons'.

CANTEEN Located on the Centre and run by Prison Auxiliaries, the canteen is very small, ill-shaped and poorly decorated said HMCIP. Only about 120 lines were carried in stock and no fresh fruit was stocked at all. Remand prisoners can spend up to £20 private cash three times each week.

REQUESTS/COMPLAINTS There are an average of a dozen formal R/C forms issued each month, mainly dealing with transfer, allocation, food and diet, clothing, earnings and medical treatment. Three-quarters receive replies within 14 days. HMCIP concluded the system was operating properly, though they criticised the rule preventing R/C being taken on a Saturday and urged removal of this fetter.

VISITS *How to get there*: Train or bus to Bedford then walk. No Special Transport.
VISITING TIMES: Week Days: 1330–1530 Mon–Fri. Saturday: 0930–1030 (Rem) 1330–1530 (Rem/Con). Sunday : No Visits.

NOTES Canteen may be restricted on busy days. No staffed Visitors Centre or Childrens Play Area. Overnight stays contact prison probation officer. No disabled access but quite easy access. Clothing exchanges for unconvicted prisoners not allowed Saturday morning or afternoon.

EDUCATION Three f/t and 26 p/t teachers in conjunction with Amersham & Wycombe College. Dept open 50 weeks of the year. Housed in a newly converted PSIF workshop, providing five classrooms and two tutorial rooms, though HMCIP recommended that the poor ventilation and acoustics should be improved. Classes from 0845-1130 and 1345–1600: computers, sugar craft, pottery, art, basic skills, history, models, German, English, maths, general study, art therapy, woodwork, cookery. Evening classes, 1745–1945: English literature, French, jewellery, guitar, art, drama, current affairs, handicrafts, technical drawing and hygiene. No VTC or CIT courses though modular Caterbase in kitchen. First class library recently won a Charter Mark for the quality of its service. Prison magazine.

WORKSHOPS No workshops as such, most work domestic in nature: 23 cleaners, 11 kitchen workers, 76 education. Average wage £6.50.

DISCIPLINE A total of 489 adjudications in the 12 months prior to the inspection by HMCIP. Most 'appeared to be the result of confrontational behaviour or abusive language'. Hearings were fair and consistent with the rules. HMCIP concluded the 'formal disciplinary procedures were sound'.

MEDICAL P/t Medical Officer contracted for 22 hours per week. 13HCPO, 23HCSO and 10 HCO—only two of whom had nursing qualifications. New Health Care Centre recently opened. Dentist recently appointed and optician visits as necessary. No prisoner in Bedford was recorded as HIV+, but HMCIP felt this was 'not . . . an accurate reflection of the real position but was more likely the result of men being afraid to accept HIV counselling which was not totally confidential'. The two strip cells had been used 62 times in a single month and HMCIP 'considered the protective room was probably being used more often than was recorded'. A subsequent inquiry by the Area Manager rejected this criticism, though a thorough review of Bedford's medical services by Mr T. Ross, Health Care Manager at HMP Leeds, lead to a number of improvements.

GYMNASIUM & SPORTS Staffing: 1×PESO and 4×PEO. Classes daily from 0800–1930 weekdays, and 1600 weekends. Remedials. badminton, NVQ,s weights, fitness, carpet bowls, volleyball, tennis, hockey, and inter-wing fixtures.

CHAPLAINCY P/t CE (22hrs/wk), RC and Methodist (6hrs/wk) chaplains. All minority faiths catered for. Main CE service 0900 Sunday, with RC at 1000. Average attendance CE/45, RC/10. Separate communion service for VPU. Bible study classes Tuesdays and general discussion group Fridays.

FOOD Staffing: 1×SO, 5×Officer (caterers) and there is a work party of 14. All staff completed hygiene course and all inmates do a three week evening class course. Caterbase modular course. Meals served by kitchen workers and staff which HMCIP applauded and there were relatively few complaints about the standard of the food. No dine out facility though HMCIP recommended this be implemented.

ESTABLISHMENT REPORTS In a report (published 31st March 1992) of an inspection in June 1991, Judge Stephen Tumim, HMCIP, said that Bedford was a 'decidedly cheering' establishment. Overcrowding had been reduced and the Governor had made imaginative efforts to improve regime delivery and provide positive and purposeful activities for all prisoners. The BoV in their Annual Report (1993/4) stated there had been 'a dramatic improvement in the standard of accommodation at Bedford and the facilities offered by it'. The kitchen still requires replacing and workshops should be provided. The high ratio of staff/inmates (201/250) was justified by the large court commitment, the official Purposeful Activity Hours figures were 'distorted' with kitchen staff working 11 hours a day. It is 'unsatisfactory' that dinner was served at 1130 and the tea meal at 1630, 'the Board does not detect a mood to change'. The continued presence in Bedford of 'mentally disturbed inmates . . . is a reflection of a national problem': the appointment of a second Psychiatric Nurse would ease the problem.

BOARD OF VISITORS Major Tentham; Mr Brown; Mr Champion; Mrs Crarer; Mrs Evans; Dr Joseph; Mrs Kiddle; Mrs Muir; Mr Powell; Mrs Wells; Mr Charles.

HM Prison Belmarsh

Western Way, Thamesmead, London SE28 OEB
Tel: 081 317 2436 **Fax:** 081 317 2421
Opened: 1991 **CNA:** 841 **Roll:** 648 **Category:** Male Local

i **BACKGROUND** Work began on the design of HMP Belmarsh in 1982. The prison received its first prisoners in April 1991 and all accommodation at the prison was in use by February 1992. The prison was built on land that was previously a part of the Royal Arsenal estate, and occupies a 31 hectare site on a large flat area by the Thames known as Plumstead Marsh. Belmarsh is connected to Woolwich Crown Court by underground tunnel. Design faults have caused problems and HMCIP have reported that when designing the establishment 'The basic rule that detailed planning for use should precede the designing of buildings was largely ignored'. The Governor did not provide up-to-date information about Belmarsh, and the BoV did not reply to a request for a copy of their annual report. The majority of the information in this entry is therefore drawn from the HMCIP Report published in June 1993.

OFFICIALS
AREA MGR: Peter Kitteridge
CHAIR BOV:
GOVERNOR: H.D. Jones
MEDICAL: Dr
CHAPLAIN: Rev Herrett
PROBATION: J. Slaven
EDUCATION:
LOCAL MP: J.Austin-Walker. Lab
Nine Governor grades, 16 Principal Officers, 54 Senior Officers and 368 Officers including specialist grades.

☞ **REGIME** *week days*: 0730 unlock/breakfast. 0830 lock up, trays out. 0900 work. 1000–1100 exercise. 1115 return to wings. 1130 dinner. 1145 lock up. 1245 work, visits. 1745 tea. 1830 association. 2030 lock up.

week ends: 0730 unlock/breakfast. 0830 lock up, trays out. 0845 association. 1000–1100 exercise. 1130 dinner. 1215 lock up. 1345 association, visits. 1645 tea. 1745 lock up. 1830–2030 association.

Out of cell: Split shift system, allowing half to work while other half has association, gives weekly activity hours of only 15hrs/prisoner—the local prison model regime recommends 24 hrs.

ACCOMMODATION & FACILITIES Inmates on normal location housed in four identical living units (1,2,3,4). All have three spurs holding a total of 60 on three landings. Mix of double and single cells all with integral sanitation. Units 2&4 hold convicted while Units 1&3 are for remands. Showers, toilets and wash basins on each landing, launderette on each spur, television, pool, darts, and card phones available. No power points. All prisoners allowed to wear own clothing. HMCIP received complaints 'supported by residential staff' that there was a delay in in-coming mail being given out, and outgoing letters being posted.

Cat.A Unit, with CNA of 48, consists of four 12-cell spurs with common facilities. No workshop and temporary visiting facilities. Inmates describe the Unit as boring, phone calls have to be booked a day in advance, restricted cell hobbies, visitor approval took too long, there were too many strip searches and visits often started long after they should have done. **VPU**, one spur on Unit 1 has 60 places. Screening gives privacy and additional lock gives extra security. Inmate/staff relationships good, four education sessions a week provided, PE available Mon–Thurs and association (as on other spurs in Belmarsh) is offered three evenings one week and two the next.

CANTEEN Original plan for central canteen abandoned due to large numbers needing escorts and now small room on each wing has been converted. Canteens small, limited stock, and fraud is prevalent to the extent that identity cards are being introduced. Open 9–5 Tues–Fri, remand prisoners have access three times a week. Special orders catered for and goods delivered to those in the VPU or Cat.A Unit.

REQUESTS/COMPLAINTS An average of 60 written R/C forms submitted each month. Compensation for damage or missing property heads the list but complaints about food also played a large part. HMCIP discovered less than a third were receiving replies in the seven day period—'and only a further small number within 14 days'. This delay was attributed to 'departments passing requests/complaints between them, thus avoiding responsibility for preparing the reply'.

VISITS *How to get there*: Train to Woolwich, bus to prison. or train to Plumstead then 10 min walk to prison. No Special Transport. VISITING TIMES: Week Days: 0900–1100 & 1300–1700 M–F. Saturday: 0900–1100 & 1300–1700. Sunday : 0900–1100 & 1300–1700.

NOTES Canteen, staffed Visitors Centre and supervised Childrens Play Area though no overnight stays in the area. Disabled access and toilet facilities. Busy remand visits, but longer time for convicted. Funding for a Cat.A visiting room 'unlikely' before 1997.

EDUCATION Six f/t teachers, supplemented by 6,500 hours per year from sessional teachers. Ten purpose-built classrooms for art, pottery, woodwork, IT and home economics, and accommodation for three VT courses in motor mechanics, information technology and industrial cleaning. Induction programme does not include academic testing. Classes in English, maths, Afro-Caribbean history, open learning, craft work. The library was poorly attended and HMCIP discovered the official publications set out in Circular Instruction 20/92 'were not all available and there was nothing in the library drawing inmates' attention to these publications'.

WORKSHOPS Work opportunities better than other locals. Allocation part of induction process, pay scales allow bonus payments to those with good attendance records—those who refuse to work receive no wages. Workshop complex includes space for VT & CIT courses, 2 contracted services shops—one being manned by VP's. Farm and Gardens party of 30 looks after the grounds and polythene tunnels.

DISCIPLINE HMCIP reported there were 1,397 adjudications at Belmarsh in the 12 months prior to his inspection. There were few major incidents and management suggested the reason for the 'high number' was the regime allowing 9.5 hours/day out of cell. Adjudication procedures were being correctly followed said HMCIP. Staff thought awards were 'too lenient' though HMCIP who reviewed them said they were 'fair and appropriate'.

MEDICAL Health Care Centre a 3-storey building providing inpatient, out-patient and primary care facilities with about 900 admissions annually. Staffing: 1×SMO, 2×MO, 3×SR(Psych), 1×G4, 2×G5, 2×HCPO, 8×HCSO, 24 HCO and 32 nurses—2×F, 2×G, 28×D grades. Design faults in the HCC, including 31 rooms without integral sanitation and all with exposed bars, was 'substandard' and needed urgent attention. Patients had one hour association in the morning and two hours in the afternoon. The regime for Cat.A patients was 'particularly barren and unsatisfactory'. GUC clinic and Optician every fortnight, Dentist 4 sess/wk. X-ray and dark room. Approximately 16 per cent (103) inmates were likely to report sick each day.

GYMNASIUM & SPORTS Very large sports hall (29×17m), complemented by substantial weights room. Cat.A unit has own weights room. Tarmac areas for badminton and volleyball and Astroturf for football—together measuring half a mile in circumference. Three induction classes per week and a well balanced programme with four day classes per week. Main prison has use of gym each night 1830–2030, VPU 1630–1730 Mon–Thurs and Sunday morning.

CHAPLAINCY F/t CE & RC chaplains, assisted by p/t ministers of other faiths. Bible study classes, Christian Fellowship meetings. Staff service Tues/Thurs lunchtime. Main Christian service Sunday morning, average attendance of 20.

FOOD Contracted service, no inmates involved in preparation or delivery of food. General manager and 16 chefs operate the kitchen. HMCIP found a poor menu selection disliked by the inmates and a 3-week menu cycle which should be increased to 6-weeks. Inconsistency in food quality was a main grievance, though it was not helped said HMCIP by the contractor being forced to buy 'poor quality' veg from prison service farms.

ESTABLISHMENT REPORTS HMCIP conducted a full inspection of Belmarsh between 7–16 February 1993, the first since the prison opened, and published their report in June 1993. Though the prison had cost £110 million, there were many design faults: those in the Health Care Centre, Cat.A Unit and kitchen were of particular concern. The Governor was however 'to be congratulated' on opening the prison efficiently and it was 'encouraging to find the regime settling down with a distinctive culture'. Supervision of the catering contract by local management had been inadequate and the inconsistency of the food was a major complaint. Sentence planning was developing well, a personal officer scheme was in operation. The Chief Inspector concluded: 'Belmarsh appeared to be succeeding in introducing improvements widely acknowledged to be necessary throughout the prison system, the out-of-cell culture and importance placed on sentence planning and personal officer work, served as a model for other local prisons'.

HM Prison Birmingham

Winson Green Road, Birmingham. B18 4AS
Tel: 021 554 3838 **Fax:** 021 554 7990
Opened: 1848 **CNA:** 562 **Roll:** 738 **Category:** Male Local

i **BACKGROUND** Birmingham prison is situated about three miles from the city centre in an inner-city location. Winson Green, as the prison is known, has operated as a Local establishment since opening in 1848, and it currently serves four Crown Courts and 31 Magistrates Courts in the West Midlands. Since 1985 a new Pre-release Hostel, Staff Mess, Visitors Centre, Gate, Visits Room, Administration Department and Reception have been built. In 1991 new generators were installed and a new wing came into operation in 1993. The Head of Inmate Activities at Birmingham, David Seary, provided a comprehensive package of information about the establishment, though the Birmingham BoV did not reply to our request for a copy of their annual report. HMCIP published their latest inspection report on Birmingham in July 1992.

OFFICIALS
AREA MGR: J. Blakey
CHAIR BOV: Mrs Cox
GOVERNOR: C.B. Scott
MEDICAL: Dr J. Hall
CHAPLAIN: Rev B. Gracie
PROBATION: Mr P. Russell
EDUCATION: Mrs R. Royle
LOCAL MP: Clare Short. Lab
STAFFING: 431 in unified grades.

REGIME *week days*: 0730 unlock/breakfast. 0815 work. 1220 lunch. 1315 work. 1650 lock up. 1720 tea. 1815–2030 association. 2045 lock up.

week ends: 0730 unlock/breakfast. 0815 activities (0830 Sunday). 1130 lunch. 1215 lock up. 1315 activities 1630 activities cease. 1650 lock up. 1720 tea. 1815 activities. 2030 activities cease. 2045 lock up.

Out of cell: 7.62/24hrs weekdays and 7.62/24hrs at weekends.

ACCOMMODATION & FACILITIES Six cell blocks plus Health Care Centre: A=85; B=140; C=91; D(VPU)=49, all with in-cell sink, h/c water, light switch and night sanitation. G=closed for refurbishment, due to reopen May/June 1995 as a medium/long term regime for West Midlands' inmates. No power points at present. Beverage point (boiler) being installed on all landings, no access to toasters. Card phones on each landing. VPU, Bail Information Scheme, Drug Counselling, No Personal Officer Scheme but SWIP in operation. Sanitation completed in 95% of accommodation, remainder by early 1995. Impressive i/p list for Local prison, including combined sound system, typewriter, and battery shaver. Routine censorship abolished, mail opened centrally and delivered to wings for distribution. Phones installed in all wings, and phone cards available from private cash.

CANTEEN Currently located centrally, but funds have been made available to management at Birmingham for this financial year to upgrade and deliver a much enhanced Inmate Shop.

VISITS *How to get there*: Train to Birmingham then bus (82,87 & 88) to Summerfield Park, Dudley Road—then 5 min walk to prison: or 76 bus from Bull Street, city centre. No Special Transport.
VISITING TIMES: Week Days: 0830–1145 & 1315–1630 & 1810–2020. Last entry Convicted 1030 & 1515. Last entry Remand 1100 & 1545. Evening session 1810–1910 & 1920–2020. Saturday: 0830–1145 & 1315–1630. Sunday : 1315–1630. Cat A : 0900–1100 Mon–Sat only.

NOTES Staffed Visitors Centre (not w/e), Childrens Play Area (not Rem). Canteen in visiting room (Con only, Mon–Sat) none for remands. B&B available locally. All visitors must book in at the Visitors Centre (opp. prison) 1130–1500 Mon–Fri. At weekends go direct to gate. Wheelchair access, nappy changing facilities, creche and information centre. No smoking on visits.

EDUCATION Department open 50 weeks of the year, five f/t teachers employed by Dudley College, and evening classes five nights of the week. Day classes from 0845–1145 & 1330–1630 with range of f/t & p/t classes: Computing;

Art/Ceramics; Wordpower; ESOL; Maths; English; History; Music; Drama; GCSE. Evening classes, 1830–2030 M–F: Arabic; Business Studies; Woodwork; Bible Study; AA; Computing; Cultural Studies; Pottery; French; Spanish; Punjabi; Maths; Soft Toys; Food Hygiene; Yoga; Guitar. NACRO visit each month with advice on employment. NOTE: Don't apply for Computing if you only want to play games, and Art/Ceramic also requires study of maths and communication. CIT Painting & Decorating.

WORKSHOPS Kitchen (average £10.75p/w); Laundry (£8); Reception (£7.90); Works (£7.35); Officers Mess (£7.35); Stores (£7.35); Textile (shops 6&7, £7) Orderlies (£7); Pre-Release (£5.70); Social Skills (£5.70); Red Bands (£6.80); Cleaners (£5.40); CIT (£6.40); Education (f/t £6.30, p/t 50p per session); Servery (£5); UB40 (£2.50). Labour Board still in infancy and requires development.

MEDICAL Four f/t Medical Officers, supported by three locums. 36 Health Care staff including nurses. Ward for 19 and 21 cells. Very good liaison reported with Reaside Hospital. Daily receptions seen by nurse from Reaside to identify appropriate diversions to Health Service system. Report sick to landing/activity officers, no set times and no obstacles are put in the way of the system operating. Home Secretary reports that work on a new Health Care Centre 'unlikely' before 1996.

GYMNASIUM & SPORTS Six PE staff. Classes from 0815–1215 & 1315–1700, with evening programme 1800–2045 M–F. No evening use of gym at weekends. Generally unconvicted in morning, convicted in afternoon and evening. Swimming Tuesday evening.

CHAPLAINCY Full time CE and RC chaplains, p/t Methodist and visiting ministers. Chaplaincy Team: Rev Bryan Gracie and Assistant Chaplain Les Haughty (CE), Fr Walter Bance (RC) and Rev Terence Higgins (Methodist). Services: Sunday, 0830 RC Mass, 0850 CE Service. Monday 1330 bible class. Tuesday 1015 Sikh meeting, 1330 bible class. Wednesday 1330 bible class, 1800 RC class. Thursday, 0930 Holy Communion, 1330 bible class, 1400 Muslim prayers.

FOOD HMCIP reported that the food was good and they received few complaints during their inspection. The kitchen however was found to be 'obsolescent' and fell below acceptable modern hygiene standards. A new kitchen is planned—see Governors Comments. No pre-select menu system in operation though three choices usually given for dinner.

ESTABLISHMENT REPORTS In a report (published 23rd July 1992) of an inspection in January 1992, Judge Stephen Tumim, HMCIP, said that though Birmingham was gravely overcrowded, he commended the staff 'for their tactful management of prisoners' in difficult circumstances. With the opening of new establishments in the West Midlands (notably Blakenhurst) pressure on Birmingham should be reduced. Mentally disordered offenders have been a perennial problem at Birmingham and HMCIP was critical of their conditions. Arrangements have been made with Gartree and Stafford to absorb some of the load and a nearby hospital has agreed to accept others—the Home Office states that £4 million has been secured 'to encourage development of court diversion schemes on a national basis'. A new Health Care Centre cannot be built until the perimeter wall has been extended and is unlikely before 1996.

GOVERNOR'S COMMENTS
Birmingham prison in the year ahead: G.wing is being refurbished, expected to reopen mid-1995 as a long-term training wing for West Midlands' prisoners. CNA will rise to 724 with maximum occupational capacity rising to 995. Up to 45% of total establishment inmate population expected to remain unconvicted. The serious shortfall in the level of activity places per number of inmates will continue, though since 1992 the regime out of cell hours has significantly increased (August 1992=18 hrs/wk, January 1993=35 hrs/wk, November 1993=36 hrs/wk, June 1994=49 hrs/wk), and are expected to increase further to an average of 55 hours per week per inmate during the next year—this even after taking into account the very large unconvicted element. A new kitchen will be constructed which will speed up the service of meals and enable daytime activities to be halted later than at present. Two new Activity Areas to be created by 'filling-in' landing levels on two wings, and it is hoped that funding will be available to construct a mezzanine floor to the Chapel creating a third large activity area. Since November 1993, visits operate morning, afternoon and evenings weekdays. Normally visits last as long as the inmate and family-friends request, the only cut off being the end of one of the three sessions. It is expected that in 1995 visits to convicted inmates will be increased from two to three per month. The number of NVQ projects will increase from 2 to 6. There will be development of inmates working outside the prison.

HM Prison Blakenhurst

Hewell Lane, Reddith, Worcestershire. B97 6QS
Tel: 0527-543348 **Fax:** 0527-546382
Opened: 1993 **CNA:** 649 **Average Roll:** 546 **Category:** Male Local

i **BACKGROUND** HM Prison Blakenhurst is the second prison in the UK to be contracted out to private sector management, and it is the first such prison to house convicted inmates. On 4th December 1992 it was announced in the House of Commons that UK Detention Services (40 Bernard Street, London WC1N 1LG), a consortium of Corrective Corporation of America, John Mowlem & Co and Sir Robert McAlpine & Sons Ltd, formed in 1987, had been awarded the contract to manage Blakenhurst initially for five years but with renewable options for a maximum of fourteen years. Mowlem and McAlpine also won the contract to design and build The Wolds Remand Centre. Blakenhurst was handed over to UKDS in February 1993 with the first inmates arriving on 26th May 1993. The Director at Blakenhurst, Bernard Higgins, declined to complete the questionnaire about the prison, though the BoV provided a copy of their annual report. HMCIP are due to publish their first report on Blakenhurst as we go to press. Full details next edition.

OFFICIALS
CONTROLLER: Pat Hanglin
CHAIR BOV: Pru Earle
DIRECTOR: Bernard Higgins
MEDICAL: Dr Neil
CHAPLAIN: Rev Palmer
PROBATION: Jim Fairbrother
EDUCATION: Mrs Berrell
LOCAL MP: Eric Forth. Con

REGIME *week days*: 0700 unlock, breakfast. 0900 work. 1215 dinner. 1330 work. 1615 cease labour. 1700 tea. 1730–2100 association.

week ends: 0700 unlock/breakfast. 0900 association. 1215 dinner. 1400 association. 1700 tea. 1730–2100 association.

Out of cell: 14/24hrs weekdays and 14/24hrs at weekends.

ACCOMMODATION & FACILITIES Four House Blocks each of which hold 155 inmates in three units on three levels. Two Houses designated convicted and two for remands, each House has 71 single cells and 42 double cells. Communal medical treatment room, dining facilities, association rooms and a canteen within each House. All cells have integral sanitation and privacy locks on the doors. No in-cell power points—and much illegal wiring-up as a result. Card phones in each House, mail opened outwith the presence of the inmate and given out in the morning. VPU. BoV applications dealt with at weekly surgery on Mondays.

CANTEEN Canteen available in each House Block, well stocked, clearly displayed prices and special arrangements made for VPU inmates and those in segregation unit. Local purchase facility.

VISITS *How to get there*: Hewell Park bus 143 from Birmingham bus station. Redditch or Bromesgrove Hewell Park bus 318. No Special Transport.,
VISITING TIMES: Weekdays: 1300–2000 Last admission 1915. Saturday: 1300–2000. Sunday: 1300–2000.

NOTES Remand inmates receive a 1hr visit per day (or one 3hr visit per week), convicted inmates receive one 3hr visit per week. In peak periods—normally weekends—duration of visits may be reduced. Spacious well appointed visits room, decent furniture, and staffed Visitors Centre outside the prison is shared with HMPs Hewell Grange and Brockhill.

EDUCATION Sub-Contract awarded by UKDS to Mowlem Training. Excellent range of facilities and broad range of subjects from remedial education to GCSE and beyond. Trade and office skills training are available in addition to general studies. VTC/CIT Painting & Decorating, Plastering, Tiling, Food Studies and Multi-skills Engineering all leading to NVQ awards. Drop-In Centre operated for Remand inmates.

WORKSHOPS Five contract services workshops with tasks such as box folding, badge making and a local nappy hire service have been contracted to provide 'work' for the laundry! VPU inmates provided with cell work, though time is set aside in one workshop for VPU inmates. Other employment includes renovation of earth moving equipment and glass engraving.

DISCIPLINE All adjudications carried out by Home Office Controller, Pat Hanglin—though the BoV are campaigning for the Director (Governor) of Blakenhurst to deal with them. Segregation Unit has accommodation for 26 inmates in single cells and two strip cells. The unit is consistently full of those on punishment, Rule 43(GOAD) or Rule 43(OP). BoV comment: 'With the restricted level of punishment available to the Controller, we suspect that Rule 43(GOAD) is used as further punishment for the more troublesome inmates'. Special Wing with restricted regime now in operation, used as a halfway house from GOAD to normal location.

MEDICAL Contracted out medical service to Worcester Royal Infirmary. One f/t SMO (ex-HMP Barlinnie) and 2×f/t MO's. HCC on two floors with full facilities for medical care, including X-ray and dental clinics. Room for 29 inpatients in 23 single rooms and one 6-man dormitory. Strip cell. Serious problem with mentally disturbed inmates and lack of secure hospital places.

GYMNASIUM & SPORTS 1×PESO and 2×PEO. Excellent gymnasium facilities. Each inmate offered six hours per week, activities include football, volleyball, basketball, racquet games, circuit training, indoor cricket, weights, trampolining as well as table tennis and pool.

CHAPLAINCY Full time CE chaplain, p/t RC and Methodist ministers. Weekly programme of discussion groups and religious meetings. Main church services Sunday morning. Other faiths catered for by visiting ministers.

FOOD Staffing: 1×Catering Manager, 2×Chefs and an inmate work party of 11. Initial complaints about the menu were accepted and changed, the food is now said to be of a good standard and the necessary diets are catered for. Sealing gun used to seal containers so food cannot be contaminated. Varied menus with meals popular to the inmate population has lead to a decrease in complaints about the food.

ESTABLISHMENT REPORTS **BoV Annual Report 1993/94:** The initial plan for phased introduction of inmates was shattered in September 1993 when more than 200 prisoners arrived. There has been substantial vandalism, extensive illegal use of main power (wiring-up) to achieve in-cell power, frequent abuse of alarm bells, phones are put out of action and TV sets damaged all of which are costly to rectify. Rubbish thrown from cell windows litters the yards and is considerably worse outside the remand blocks. There is a lack of adequate provision for VPU inmates who have a poor regime. There are inadequate facilities for mentally disturbed prisoners, the Requests/Complaints system is in a mess with the system for applications to the BoV causing many problems. Far too much aggravation is caused by the delay in transferring private cash, and recording wages and private cash on the prison's computer system has also created problems. The Controller should transfer his responsibility for disciplinary adjudications to the prison's Director (Governor); inmates are committed to the care of the Director said the BoV, 'and it would seem to be his natural responsibility to deal with those who seek to undermine his authority'. [Members of the Blakenhurst BoV are invited to read the powerful paper by Governor Peter Quinn, in Section 4. Ed.]

HM Prison Blantyre House

Goudhurst, Cranbrook, Kent. TN17 2NA
Tel: 0580 211367 **Fax:** 0580-211060
Opened: 1911 **CNA:** 95 **Roll:** 95 **Category:** C. Male, Long Term Only

i **BACKGROUND** Blantyre House is situated three miles from the village of Goudhurst in Kent. It was built between 1911 and 1914 and served as a farm training school preparing boys from deprived backgrounds for service in the colonies. The house and some six hectares of grounds were taken over by the Prison Department in 1954, it was first used as a Detention Centre. In 1984 the Control Review Committee on the long-term prison system recommended that prisoners serving long sentences should be given the chance of serving a substantial part of their sentence in a prison which offers a relatively open regime. In light of this recommendation Blantyre House closed in June 1987 as a Detention Centre and reopened, in December 1987, as a Category C prison. The Governor provided detailed up-to-date information, though the Blantyre House BoV did not reply to a request for a copy of their annual report. HMCIP published their latest inspection report on Blantyre House in June 1993.

OFFICIALS

AREA MGR: John Hunter
CHAIR BOV: Derek Mason
GOVERNOR: Jim Semple
MEDICAL: Dr M. Davies
CHAPLAIN: Vacant

PROBATION: Ms C. Kelsey
EDUCATION: Mary Wheeler
LOCAL MP: Patrick Mayhew. Con
STAFFING: Six Governor grades, two Principal Officers, four Senior Officers, 26 Officers, three Prison Auxiliaries and three Night Patrols.

REGIME While there is a 'core day' at Blantyre House, both for weekdays and weekends, the establishment is almost unique in that it allows individuals to structure their day by pursuing a 'Personal Career Plan'. This consists of components which are negotiated between the individual and management. At weekends individuals can pursue activities in keeping with the 'personal priorities' stated in their Personal Career Plan. Inmates may exercise 'at will'. Breakfast 0815, dinner 12 noon and tea 1700.

Out of cell: 13/24hrs weekdays, and 13/24hrs at weekends.

ACCOMMODATION One 'Country House' residential building with personal services in keeping with a residential community. Single rooms, doubles and some trebles, internal light switch, no sockets at present but plans in the pipeline. Sentence planning, card phones, personal officer scheme and night-sanitation. Some inmates report the rooms to be very cold at times. Full range of own clothing allowed, personal furnishing in rooms: 'civilised agenda to go with wider personal obligations'. No seg unit or VPU. Little censorship of mail reported, limited number of phone cards but access to facility said to be good.

CANTEEN Central canteen operated by storeman and one inmate with 140 stock lines., prices reported as 'reasonable'. Local purchase facility at which inmates can 'order almost anything' and it is usually available within two days. Canteen officially open on Wednesdays, but the storeman opens at other times when possible.

REQUESTS/COMPLAINTS Not a great deal of recourse to formal Requests/Complaints procedures, most matters are dealt with by staff and individuals seeking to remedy potential problems and requests. Those who have resorted to use of the formal procedures report delays in obtaining replies. On average, less than two-dozen formal R/C forms submitted each year. The system was 'efficiently run with clear, neat records'. Replies were reasoned and within the time limits.

VISITS *How to get there*: Train to Marsden, then four mile journey from station. Special Transport: Minibus meets train before 1400 most days, phone prison for information.
VISITING TIMES: Week Days: 1400–1600 Tue, Wed, Thurs only. Saturday: 1400–1600. Sunday: 1400–1600.

NOTES Visiting room with space for 23 visits is a single storey building located in the centre of the prison. Canteen. Childrens Play Area with toys and television, no staffed Visitors Centre. B&B available locally but expensive, contact prison probation. Disabled access not a problem. Prisoners report relaxed atmosphere at visits, 'sweets and snacks but no hot food'. Weekly visits allowed. Eligibility for Town Visits after 12 months at Blantyre House.

EDUCATION Education department opened 50 weeks of the year—but available seven days a week. Three full-time teachers. Day/evening classes in woodwork, Spanish, English, art, tailoring, maths, music, computing, pottery, BTEC, CPC, Catering NVQ, decorative painting (fortnightly), literacy (by arrangement) and 'a wide range of Business Studies programmes, plus range of outside college courses'.

WORKSHOPS No production workshops, quality work available in catering, horticulture, and building maintenance. Paid work outside the prison which is in line with the positive philosophy of Blantyre House in fitting its inmates for return to the community on release. All receptions spend first month in kitchen.

MEDICAL Visiting GP, two Health Care Officers, visiting dentist, optician and physiotherapist. Report sick by attending GP's surgery or, at other times, when ill. Poor reports from prisoners, particularly complaining about the need for a full-time doctor at Blantyre House rather than visiting GP system.

GYMNASIUM & SPORTS Two PE Officers. Classes from 0845 to 1930 weekdays and 1600 weekends. Weights, squash, open golf, running, mini-gym, football, bowls, badminton, circuit training, yoga and external activities such as rambling.

CHAPLAINCY Part-time Chaplain, multi-faith approach with visiting ministers of world faiths. Blantyre has its own small Mosque.

FOOD Chef recently won award for his culinary skills and the food is reported as being 'first rate'. HMCIP said the kitchen was too small and the fabric needed repair, there was no staff toilet/shower, no changing area and inadequate cold store provision. SO Caterer and Catering Officer assisted by work party of six. Varied menu with special day menus, e.g. Greek Day, Chinese Day etc.

ESTABLISHMENT REPORTS HMCIP conducted a full inspection of Blantyre House in July 1992 and published their report in June 1993. The prison represents 'an unusual example' of the training concept matching the total regime of a prison. It was noticeable said HMCIP that inmates behaved 'in a civilised way with sensitivity towards each other and towards staff'. Security systems took a low profile and were not abused. 'We cannot believe that only a hundred out of the tens of thousands of prisoners held in England can profit by this remarkable regime'.

GOVERNOR'S COMMENTS Blantyre House provides a challenging, creative milieu, wherever prisoners and staff are invited to engage in an experience of growth and change. The regime of Blantyre House recognises the special dimensions of long-term imprisonment. We fulfil the strategy of progressive transfer of long-term prisoners from secure conditions to a more open lifestyle. We work to enhance the self esteem of the individual, in the spirit of a community styled prison. We involve staff and prisoners in an experience designed to improve personal and social relations, and the career competence and cultural awareness of our prisoners . . . The means to these ends are 1) a high degree of informal communication and participation in the life and development of the community both inside and outside the prison. 2) a substantial degree of self-determination on the parts of inmates—each person negotiating his regime/career package. 3) investment in good relationships between staff and men underpinned by a career planning role for officers, and 4) genuine shared responsibility for the well-being of the prison community, the individual, and for our environment.

PRISONERS' COMMENTS I came to Blantyre House after spending six years in the dispersal system and another four in a Cat B prison in Suffolk. Coming here was like a breath of fresh air, the atmosphere is relaxed, though the regime itself is probably the most challenging I have seen. The food is excellent, and the staff genuinely want to help. The management team is strong and knows where its going. Opportunities for outside work and visits are good and there have been improvements in the number of phones provided. For the first time in a decade I am no longer afraid of facing that day when the gates close behind me for the last time.

HM Prison Blundeston

Lowestoft, Suffolk. NR32 5BG
Tel: 0502-730591 **Fax:** 0502-730138
Opened: 1962 **CNA:** 408 **Roll:** 381 **Category:** B. Male

i **BACKGROUND** Blundeston prison is situated about four miles north-west of Lowestoft in Suffolk. It was purpose-built and opened in 1963 with four main cell blocks (A,B,C,D) holding 288 inmates. In 1975 two further wings (F,G) were added, each holding 60 inmates which brought the CNA to 408. The Governor of Blundeston, Mr Robinson, provided up-to-date information about the prison, though the BoV did not reply to our request for a copy of their latest annual report. HMCIP published their latest inspection report on Blundeston in June 1994.

OFFICIALS
AREA MGR: Mr Murtagh
CHAIR BOV: Mr Devereux
GOVERNOR: Mr Robinson
MEDICAL: Dr Khan
CHAPLAIN: Rev Cook
PROBATION: Mr Fullelove
EDUCATION: George Hutchings
LOCAL MP: David Porter. Con

STAFFING: Six Governor grades, 12 Principal Officers, 22 Senior Officers and 121 Officers, including specialist staff.

REGIME *week days*: 0755 unlock/breakfast. 0845 work. 1115 cease work 1130-1200 exercise. 1145–1215 dinner. 1345 work. 1645 cease work. 1655–1725 tea. 1740 association. (1800–1915 outdoor exercise, Summer only). 1955 lock up.

week ends: 0755 unlock 0845–0915 breakfast. 0945 exercise. 1135–1210 dinner. 1215 lock up. 1345 unlock, association, visits. 1615–1645 tea. 1700 lock up. 1800 association. 1955 lock up.

Our of cell: 12/24hrs weekdays and 9.5/24hrs at weekends.

ACCOMMODATION & FACILITIES Four wings (A,B,C,D) holding 72 in single cell accommodation with night san access. Two further wings (F,G, opened 1983) each hold 60 in multiple rooms with integral sanitation. Segregation Unit (E.wing). Large and comprehensive i/p list.

Sentence planning, drug counselling, Personal Officer scheme in operation. Low voltage power points some wings. Caged birds allowed. Mainly long-term population from London area. Routine censorship abolished. Card phones on all living units. Mail handed out lunchtime, not opened in presence of addressee other than in case of recorded/registered delivery for which inmates have to go to reception at lunchtime.

CANTEEN Central canteen, located opposite gymnasium entrance, restricted space and small stock. Local purchase facility once per week and £20 transfer private cash to earnings once per month.

REQUESTS/COMPLAINTS Between 30–40 formal R/C submitted each month, of these a third submitted to the area manager. HMCIP examined a selection of RC forms and found that time targets were being invariably achieved. Most issues were transfer or loss of property.

VISITS *How to get there*: Train to Lowestoft then taxi (5 miles) to prison. No public transport to prison. Prison minibus collects visitors from Lowestoft station on Wed, Sat & Sun (£1). Coach from London on Sundays, calls also at Chelmsford and Colchester—bookings: 071 237 8076/8039.
VISITING TIMES: Week Days: 1345–1525 M–F. Saturday: 1345–1525. Sunday : 1345–1525 very busy.

NOTES Canteen and Childrens Play area with video cartoons. No staffed Visitors Centre. No wheelchair ramps but easy access to visiting room. Contact prison probation for details of local guest houses.

EDUCATION Open 50 weeks of the year with three f/t teachers and evening classes four nights of the week. From September 1994 the vast majority of education at Blundeston will be on a part-time basis, with inmates being released from work to attend education. BTEC, ESL remain full time. Classes: English, Geography, Computers, Science, Afro-Carribean Studies, Maths, Woodwork, English Literature, Maritime Studies, German, Open Learning, Graphic art, Drama and Book-keeping. New education department to be built on site of present kitchen when that moves to its new site beside the hospital in 1995.

WORKSHOPS The whole concept of work at Blundeston is in the process of major change. This will take the form of work coupled with a form of day release to attend education, one of the Inmate Development courses or the gym. Should be in operation early 1995. Current work as follows: Tailoring (track suits & overalls, NVQ level 2, average, £7.30); Printers (all kinds of stationery, NVQ level 2, average £7.30); Laundry (all aspects of laundering, NVQ level 2, £7.30–8.51); Farm (inside gardens, pig farm, greenhouses, tunnels, average £6.40, outside work for those suitable on security grounds, NVQ introduced 1995); Handicraft tailoring (VTC NVQ level 3, average £5.40); Computers (VTC, NVQ level 2, average £5.40); Works, Kitchen, Cleaners etc (Kitchen with NVQ highly sought after, Blundeston is consistently praised for its food).

DISCIPLINE Segregation unit closed temporarily while integral sanitation is fitted. Located immediately beside B.wing the Seg Unit (E.wing) has seven ordinary cells and one strip cell. HMCIP was surprised to discover a high level of adjudications—681 in the six months to October 1993, and 1,236 in the previous twelve months. Records were correctly kept said HMCIP and awards were sensible for proven offences.

MEDICAL F/t Medical Officer, supported by 1×HCSO, 1×HCO and 2×Nurses. Report sick at unlock and then appointment provided. Dentist once per week, optician monthly.

GYMNASIUM & SPORTS Staff: 1×PESO, 3×PEO. 'Facilities for physical education were among the worst we have seen in a training prison'. Small gymnasium is totally inadequate, no drinking water, urinals or wash basins. No separate weights room. Outside Red-gra in very poor condition, and was soon to be lost to the PE Dept as the site for new kitchen. PE programme undergoing major change as we go to press.

CHAPLAINCY F/t CE chaplain and nine visiting ministers of other faiths. Muslim service Friday, other on Sunday. Good services with time to meet afterwards in relaxed surroundings with refreshments. Main church service Sunday morning.

FOOD HMCIP received no complaints about the food, which inmates feel to be very good in terms of both quality and quantity. HMCIP castigated the kitchen which was in a deplorable condition—work on a new kitchen started in March 1994. Blundeston won a Heartbeat Award from the Environmental Health Dept of the local council in May 1994, for its healthy eating options, there is no menu system in place yet but plans to introduce one when new kitchen comes on stream in 1995.

ESTABLISHMENT REPORTS In a report (published 29th June 1994) of an inspection in October 1993, Judge Stephen Tumim, HMCIP, said that despite the isolated location of Blundeston, the majority of inmates appeared to settle quickly and were content with their surroundings. There was however a shortage of training opportunities for long term inmates and HMCIP expressed concern at inmates being locked in their cells because of a lack of work for the Print Shop. Since the previous full inspection in 1987, Blundeston has been revitalised and the morale of staff has improved—though there is still room for improvement.

PRISONERS' COMMENTS
Request/complaints are normally dealt with the next day. Accommodation is very good, 90% single cells with night san, low voltage power points in some wings. Canteen is good, prices fair and local purchase facility. Visits are very relaxed but often noisy particularly at weekends. Education highly thought of with excellent facilities. Workshops are busy, conditions and wages are good. Medical facilities are average and adjudications are reported to be fair with even-handed punishments. The food, in both quality and quantity is 'excellent', but no menu system at present. The gymnasium also scores top marks at Blundeston for day and evening programmes, but not enough access at weekends. Good religious services. Mail is not opened in front of the inmate, and handed out at 1000 and 1500. Plenty of access to card phones.

HMRC & YOI Brinsford

New Road, Featherstone, Wolverhampton. WV10 7PY
Tel: 0902-791118 **Fax:** 0902-790889
Opened: 1993 **CNA:** 336 **Average Roll:** 325 **Category:** Closed YOI, Remand Centre & Juvenile Unit

i **BACKGROUND** Brinsford comprises a Remand Centre, holding unconvicted and unsentenced inmates under 21, a separate closed Young Offender Institution and a Juvenile Unit. The establishment, which has a total of 336 single cells, was first inspected by HMCIP in June 1994, though as we went to press no date for publication of the inspection report had been fixed. Neither the Governor of Brinsford, the Chairman of the Board of Visitors nor the Area Manager replied to our requests for information. Full details in the next edition.

OFFICIALS
AREA MGR: Jim Blakey
CHAIR BOV:
GOVERNOR: B. Payling
MEDICAL:
CHAPLAIN: Rev Robson
PROBATION: Nigel Byford
EDUCATION:
LOCAL MP: Patrick Cormack. Con

VISITS *How to get there*: Bus from Wolverhampton (Stand 'H' Nos: 870/872) Mon–Sat 1200; 1300; 1400; 1500. Return from outside prison 1331; 1431; 1531; 1631. Sunday 1055; 1255; 1455—returning 1430; 1603; 1800. Fare approx £1.50.
VISITING TIMES: Week Days: 1330–1600. Saturday: 1315–1615. Sunday : 1315–1615. Legal: 0930–1130 Mon–Fri.

NOTES No smoking policy in force. Staffed Visitors Centre(VC) opposite prison, open 30 mins before visits. All non-legal visitors must book in at the VC and are taken across in order of arrival. Last entry to VC 1515. Childrens Play Area in VC. Small tea bar in visiting room. Facilities for disabled and nappy-changing available.

HM PRISON Bristol

19, Cambridge Road, Horfield, Bristol. BS7 8PS
Tel: 0272-426661 **Fax:** 0272-244228 (Admin) 0272-244853 (Hosp) 0272-421192 (Works)
Opened: 1882 **CNA:** 374 **Roll:** 397 **Category:** Male Local

i **BACKGROUND** Originally opened in 1882 to serve the Bristol locality, the prison comprised a brick perimeter wall and Gatehouse, enclosing two four-storey brick cell blocks with associated ancillary buildings. The prison has remained in use ever since. Over the years considerable rebuilding and in-filling has taken place, to the point where all available space inside the perimeter wall has now been used. The prison suffered a serious disturbance in April 1990, into which Lord Justice Woolf subsequently inquired and HMCIP remarked that it is to the credit of the Governor and staff that positive dialogue has been re-established with inmates. Bristol is a multi-functional establishment, holding remands, convicted, VPU and long term inmates. Neither the Governor nor BoV at Bristol replied to our requests for information. HMCIP published their latest inspection report on Bristol in April 1993.

OFFICIALS
AREA MGR: John Wilkinson
CHAIR BOV:
GOVERNOR: R.D. Dixon
MEDICAL:
CHAPLAIN: Rev Peters
PROBATION: Sue James
EDUCATION:
LOCAL MP: Michael Stern. Con
STAFFING: 285 staff in unified grades including specialist.

REGIME *week days*: 0800–0900 unlock, breakfast in cell. 0900–0930 work, education, sick parade. 0930–1130 legal/probation visits, cell cleaning, Rule 43 education (Tuesday only). 1130–1215 cease labour, mail issued, dinner served by landing rota, treatments issued, duty governor takes applications, lock up. 1315–1345 trays out, work, main exercise, domestic visits, Rule 43 exercise (daily, or association Tues–Thurs). 1445–1630 library (Wed), kit changes (Tues), canteen (Fri). 1630–1715 cease labour/education, tea by landing rota, lock up. 1800–2030 unlock for association (all B.wing, others one landing per evening).

week ends: 0800–0900 unlock/breakfast. 0900–1015 kit changes, Rule 43 exercise. 1015–1115 main exercise. 1115–1215 dinner served by landing rota., lock up. 1315–1330 trays out, Rule 43 to exercise (return 1430). 1330–1530 wing association per landing rota, visits. 1530–1615 tea per landing rota, lock up. 1745–2030 trays out, association per landing rota.

Out of cell: Varies according to location.

ACCOMMODATION & FACILITIES Seven cells blocks (A,B,C,D,E,F,G). A/G closed for refurbishment & integral sanitation. B.wing (built 1967) for 102 long termers, single cells with night san. C.wing (built 1976) holding 192 convicted in mixture of double rooms and dormitories all with integral sanitation. C2 landing used as VPU (32 inmates). D.wing holding 100 remands with integral sanitation. E.wing seg unit. F.wing 11-man VPU. Routine censorship abolished other than on the instructions of the Governor or Medical Officer. Incoming mail collected from gate 0800, sorted and examined centrally and then handed out at midday. Outgoing mail delivered to gate by 1530 and posted same day. Card phones in all wings.

CANTEEN SO and 3×Officers man canteen situated between D.wing and exercise yard. Limited space, storage inadequate and stock of 170 items, over 50 of which are foodstuffs. HMCIP recommended involvement of inmates in stock selection. Profit margin between 10–12.5%.

REQUESTS/COMPLAINTS Average of 50 formal R/C per month. Though HMCIP did not research individual cases they were satisfied that the system was operating properly, time targets were generally being met and the system was properly administered. However, 'some replies, particularly those answering complaints about work opportunities and the regime for vulnerable inmates, were unsatisfactory to the extent that they did not offer any solution to the problem raised'.

VISITS *How to get there*: Train to Bristol Temple Meads, then bus (No: 8 or 9) from station to Debenhams. Then 74,77 or 78 to Bishop Road. No Special Transport. Taxi from station 5 miles.
VISITING TIMES: Week Days: 1320–1530 M–F. Saturday: 1320–1530. Sunday : 1320–1530. Long-term Wing visits only.

NOTES Staffed Visitors Centre. Canteen in visiting room. Childrens Play Area (weekdays only). Overnight stays possible, book through Warden 0272-425994. No smoking on visits and no wheelchair access.

EDUCATION Four f/t teachers and 15 p/t, open for 46 weeks of the year and all classes are full-time: HMCIP recommends introduction of p/t classes. Situated between B&C wings, comprising four general classrooms, woodwork room, cookery room art/craft rooms. Day & evening programme: adult education, woodwork, computer studies, English/maths, art, music, lifer group, guitar, cookery, typewriting, writers workshop, health & nutrition, media studies, ESOL. Shortage of staff causes many closures: '14 teaching sessions had been lost in the week before our inspection because no officers could be found to supervise inmates and we were told this was not unusual'.

WORKSHOPS All inmates interviewed after reception and allocated to work. Two main workshops (1,2) textiles and tailors respectively. HMCIP recommended that the textile shop should be given over to Rule 43's. Charity (PATCH) workshop praised by HMCIP. Average wage £6.10. CIT painting & decorating, well regarded by HMCIP, and with a waiting list for places of about a dozen.

DISCIPLINE Segregation unit of seven cells, 1 strip cell and 2 Cat A locations. Staffed by one SO and two officers, with poor regime and no work available. There had been 576 adjudications in the 12 months prior to the inspection: 'in keeping with that in similar establishments' said HMCIP.

MEDICAL Senior Medical Officer, 2×f/t MO's, 2×Visiting GP's, 1×G5, 1×HCPO, 4×HCSO, 13×HCO and 1×Nurse. Health Care Centre 'a claustrophobic and complicated building' said HMCIP. Ward with room for 18 patients with no integral sanitation. The rooms used for mentally disturbed inmates were not subject to appropriate supervision. Poor association facilities for patients with the association room being used for no more than four hours per day. Psych 2×sess/wk, Chiropodist 1 sess/2wks, standard of dental care 'diminishing rapidly' with waiting list of 60 and only one session/wk, Optician 1 sess/2wks.

GYMNASIUM & SPORTS PEPO, PESO and 2×PEO's. Facilities cramped and limited. Small unheated gymnasium and evening classes curtailed because of staff shortages. Small weights room, no changing area and just four showers. HMCIP felt that the staff were doing all they could to improve the situation, but 'it is difficult to see how more could be achieved without additional staff and better facilities'.

CHAPLAINCY Full time CE chaplain and p/t other faiths. Sunday 0815 RC Mass, 0915 worship, 1015 worship (R.43's and HCC). Monday 0930 R.43 class in chapel, 1800 Chaplain's class. Wednesday 0900 Holy Communion, 1800 Muslim class.

FOOD Staffing: 1×P0, 2×SO and 4×Officer (caterers) work party of 15. Kitchen five years old though design faults are many. Five week menu cycle in operation. 'The menu we sampled offered a choice of braised liver and onion, Lancashire hotpot or sliced gammon served with potatoes, cabbage, carrots and with apple-turnover and custard as a sweet . . . these meals were good'—HMCIP.

SPECIAL FEATURES Lifers and other long termers held in B.wing with relaxed regime and good support facilities. Work 0915-1130, 1330–1630, association available every weekday evening and weekend afternoons—not evenings though.

ESTABLISHMENT REPORTS In a report (published 14th April 1993) of an inspection in June 1992, Judge Stephen Tumim, HMCIP, said that Bristol was an example of 'piecemeal planning' and it is important that the pressure to accommodate more prisoners 'does not override the need to provide proper facilities'.

HM PRISON Brixton

Jebb Avenue, Brixton, London SW2 5XF
Tel: 081–647-9811 **Fax:** 081-647-6128
Opened: 1821 **CNA:** 636 **Average Roll:** 650 **Category:** Male Local & Remand Centre

i **BACKGROUND** In 1818 the Surrey Justices of the Peace purchased the present site to build what was then known as a House of Correction. The Surrey House of Correction opened in 1821 with accommodation for 175 men, though in practice up to 400 inmates were regularly housed there. The opening of Wandsworth in 1851 earmarked the Surrey House of Correction for demolition, but it was purchased by the Surveyor General of Prisons for £13,000 and opened in 1852 as a prison for 750 females. It remained a female prison until 1982 when it was briefly a military prison before becoming, in 1984, the local prison that it has remained ever since. Trenchant criticism from HMCIP, high profile escapes, a spate of suicides among both prisoners and staff, and appalling conditions in the F.Wing Acute Psychiatric Unit have all brought media attention to the prison over the last few years. Today, after a change of Governor, Brixton has made progress. Dr Andrew Coyle, Governor, supplied limited information about the prison, though the BoV did not reply to our request for a copy of their latest annual report. HMCIP published their latest inspection report on Brixton in August 1993.

OFFICIALS

AREA MGR: Peter Kitteridge
CHAIR BOV: S. Turquet
GOVERNOR: Andrew Coyle
MEDICAL: Dr Somasundaram
CHAPLAIN: Rev B. Dodsworth
PROBATION: S. Churchyard
EDUCATION: S. Gardner
LOCAL MP: Keith Hill. Lab
STAFFING: Seventeen Governor grades, 39 Principal Officers, 79 Senior Officers and 520 Officers, including specialist staff.

REGIME *week days*: Normal regime for local prison. No workshops, but all inmates have the opportunity for education and limited association each weekday. Limited regime at weekends.

Out of cell: 6–12/24hrs weekdays and 4–12/24hrs at weekends dependent on status, location or employment.

ACCOMMODATION & FACILITIES Two main remand wings, two convicted wings and separate unit for Vulnerable Prisoners and Cat A's. Brixton remains overcrowded, integral sanitation is partially installed and there are card phones in each wing. Bail Information Scheme, sentence planning, drug counselling. Normal restrictions apply to items allowed in-possession.

CANTEEN Five canteens located in various wings throughout the prison. About 120 lines of stock carried, no local purchase facility and only one visit per week for both private cash and earnings. Inmates report high prices, though HMCIP states a profit margin of 10% is operated and prices linked to Shaw's Retail Prices Guide.

VISITS *How to get there*: Underground to Brixton, then bus (50,95,109,133,159) to Jebb Avenue. No Special Transport.
VISITING TIMES: Week Days: 0915–1115, 1300–1545 Rem. 1330–1500 Con. Saturday: 0900–1115 Rem. 0900–1100 & 1300–1445 Con. Sunday : 1300–1415 Workforce only.

NOTES Sunday visiting only for 'workforce' in Brixton. Staffed Visitors Centre. No canteen or Childrens Play Area. No facilities for the disabled, access very difficult and max of 2 adults and babe-in-arms. Only one visit per day.

EDUCATION Open 48 weeks of the year, five full time staff and evening classes four nights per week. Special arrangements made for Cat A and VPU inmates. Excellent facilities though not a lot of space. No VTC or CIT courses.

MEDICAL Senior Medical Officer. Health Care Centre with 60 places in open wards, reasonable regime for inpatients with TV rooms and exercise daily. Inmates report sick to landing officer at morning unlock and are seen by doctor during the day. Full range of visiting specialists, dental and optical sessions each week.

GYMNASIUM & SPORTS Though the prison has a main gymnasium, each wing has a small gym of its own. Good facilities though access is too limited according to some inmates. Limited external facilities, tarmac yards, but good weights room and classes seven days per week.

CHAPLAINCY Full time CE chaplain, RC and Methodist ministers. Imam visits each Friday for Muslims and other faiths catered for as required. Separate chapels for RC and CE, but both suffer from limited space. CE Chaplain Brian Dodsworth well known in the system for providing an excellent religious programme of weekly groups and discussions.

FOOD Staffing: 1×PO, 2×SO and 6×Officer (caterers), and there is a work party of 25. Food much improved in recent years, three choices for dinner and three week menu cycle in operation. Inmates report little imagination is used in presentation of meals, portions are reasonable, though bread is sometimes stale.

ESTABLISHMENT REPORTS HMCIP last conducted a full inspection of Brixton in 1990, and found Brixton underfunded and underdeveloped. The defects were the product of a century's neglect, medical facilities in F Wing were an affront to humanity. Shortages of kit were at a serious level, education was available but under-resourced and the library was too small for the purpose. Accommodation required urgent and extensive refurbishment. Slopping out, perverse meal times, unhygienic accommodation made for a poor life. However in a report (published 5th August 1993) of an inspection in December 1992 that picture had changed dramatically. The new Governor, Dr Andrew Coyle, had introduced a comprehensive strategy that will take several years to complete but the transformation that had already taken place was described by HMCIP as 'remarkable'. The contrast between the squalid, overcrowded and desperate conditions in F wing in 1990 and the warm, light, open and positive atmosphere that prevailed at the latest inspection, was a credit to all concerned. Some of these improvements could be attributed to the reduced population and the quality of the Brixton staff, although conditions for prisoners in many respects remain unsatisfactory. Visiting arrangements, the reception area and facilities for association, education and PE as well as the working conditions of staff are unacceptable. Refurbishment and rebuilding are underway but, in spite of the improvements documented in the report, the quality of life for prisoners will remain unsatisfactory until the development is complete.

PRISONERS' COMMENTS Average request/complaints system. No power points in cells. Prices in the canteen are higher than outside. Visits are not too bad depending on location. Education also suffers from a lack of space but is doing well with the little there is. Average work opportunities for a local prison, and very good medical facilities. Adjudications are always very heavy handed, even for minor offences—definitely the worst part of Brixton. Food is not too bad. One phone per landing.

HM Prison Brockhill

Redditch, Worcestershire. B97 6RD
Tel: 0527-550314 **Fax:** 0527-550169
Opened: 1965 **CNA:** 160 **Roll:** 155 **Category:** C Male

i **BACKGROUND** Brockhill and its neighbouring establishments, HM Prisons Hewell Grange and Blakenhurst, occupy the former Hewell Grange estate—about four miles from Redditch in the open farming countryside of the West Midlands. Brockhill was one of five purpose-built Remand Centres built in the mid 1960's. Originally built to accommodate 115 males and 23 females it was opened in 1965 as a satellite of Birmingham prison some 16 miles away. Managerial independence came along in 1967 and a year later the female complement was moved out. Brockhill was earmarked for closure in 1991 when it was planned that Blakenhurst would take over the remand function. However the need for more convicted accommodation had led to its retention and conversion into a Category C training prison for male adults. Neither the Governor nor the BoV at Brockhill replied to our requests for information. HMCIP published their latest inspection report on Brockhill in March 1994.

OFFICIALS
AREA MGR: Dai Curtis
CHAIR BOV: Charles Gordon
GOVERNOR: Keith Naisbitt
MEDICAL: Dr Spoulding
CHAPLAIN: Rev Roy Loudge
PROBATION: Karen Mcleod
EDUCATION: Margaret Silkin
LOCAL MP: Roy Thomason. Con
STAFFING: Three Governor grades, 4 Principal Officers, 16 Senior Officers and 60 Officers, including specialist staff.

REGIME *week days*: 0800 unlock. 0810 breakfast. 0830 work. 1200 lunch. 1210 lock up. 1330 work. 1700 tea. 1730–2000 association.

week ends: 0800 unlock. 0810 breakfast. 0830 unit/cell cleaning. 0900 association. 1200 lunch. 1210 lock up. 1330 association/visits. 1700 tea. 2000 cease association.

Out of cell: 12/24hrs weekdays and 12/24hrs at weekends.

ACCOMMODATION & FACILITIES Five main living units (A,B,C,D,F,). A,B,C are identical in design and offer a total of 33 single cells, F wing (originally a hospital with large cells) operates as an induction unit holding a maximum of 15 inmates—some two per cell. Good recreational facilities available in main association rooms. D wing, which operates as a VPU with a CNA of 47, was once the female part of the establishment. Personal Officer scheme in operation, card phones in all living units and drug counselling available. Routine censorship abolished.

CANTEEN Staffed by a Prison Auxiliary Mon–Fri, the canteen is conveniently located to one side of the main passageway but is small and poorly ventilated. Adequate range of stock, carrying about 130 lines and, in 1993, the canteen made a profit of some £7,000 representing about 15% of turnover. Inmates visit canteen once per week and there is a restricted local purchase facility in operation.

REQUESTS/COMPLAINTS The custom at Brockhill appears to have developed whereby the majority of R/C forms are submitted to the Area Manager by way of Confidential Access. In early 1993, 90% of all R/C were submitted in this manner though there has been a reduction since. Issues dealt with locally received replies within seven days and HMCIP recommended that more explanation of the system be given to inmates who often waited extra weeks for an answer that would have been precisely the same had they used local procedures first.

VISITS *How to get there*: Hewell Park bus 143 from Birmingham bus station. Redditch or Bromesgrove Hewell Park bus 318. No Special Transport.
VISITING TIMES: Week Days: 1345–1545 Mon, Wed, Fri only. Saturday: 1345–1545. Sunday : 1345–1545.

NOTES Visitors Centre outside the prison is shared with HMPs Hewell Grange and Blakenhurst. Canteen and Childrens Play Area in visiting room. No overnight stays and maximum of three adults and children under ten.

EDUCATION Contracted service from Dudley College—which has won the contract to provide education to ten prisons in the West Midlands area. HMCIP reported that 'the single most important concern' he had about Brockhill 'was the paucity of educational provision'. Dept open just 47 weeks of the year and most hours consumed by just three daytime classes. There were 32 prisoners on FTE, 16 in the VPU—which has no evening classes at all. Evening classes in main prison just two nights per week, Tues & Thurs.

WORKSHOPS All inmates at Brockhill are employed. Labour board held weekly. Job vacancies advertised on wing notice boards. Kitchen (£8.00), Orderlies (£6.70), Cleaners (£5.50, Charity Workshop (£6.20), Gardens (£6.50), Tailors (VPU)(£5.70), Works (£6.20), FTE (£5.40), Induction (£4.00), UB40 (£2.50).

DISCIPLINE Formal disciplinary procedures were not being overused said HMCIP, average of 3.5 adjudications per week. Most charges were laid for possession of unlawful items or failure to comply with licence conditions. No recorded use of C&R techniques. Ten transfers out for disciplinary reasons.

MEDICAL P/t Medical Officer, cover provided by practice of five local GP's, 1×SHCO and 1×HCO(EN). Average of 8 inmates report sick each day and are seen by doctor between 0800–0830. Dentist visits one session per week.

GYMNASIUM & SPORTS Staffed by 1×PESO, 3×PEO assisted by 5×SGO. PE facilities were not good, though the PE programme was described by HMCIP as 'a remarkable achievement'. Modular course for NVQ in place (part of which is undertaken at Redditch swimming pool (for lifesaving), regular hiking trips for those who qualify and full range of normal sports and games.

CHAPLAINCY Full time CE chaplain shares work with Hewell Grange. P/t RC and Methodist ministers. Poor chaplaincy facilities. CE Service (Main prison) Sun 0930. CE Service (VPU) Sun 1030. RC Mass Mon 0930. Prayer Study (VPU) Tues 1800. Induction Group Wed 0900. Thurs 1800 Forum.

FOOD Staffing: 1×SO, 2×Officer (caterers), and there is a work party of 12. Meals for VPU collected early. All meals eaten in cell, dining area in VPU but is not used. Menu cycle only three weeks in length. Inmate representation on regimes committee, recent innovations had included the introduction of individual tea bags. Caterers had also introduced a substantial roll with a salad filling and either meat, egg or cheese as an alternative to the cooked midday meal—these had proved very popular. Metal trays replaced by earthenware plates on D wing. HMCIP, who tasted the food, found it to be 'piping hot, tasty and filling'.

ESTABLISHMENT REPORTS In a report (published 22nd March 1994) of an inspection in September 1993, Judge Stephen Tumim, HMCIP, said that Brockhill had recovered from the hiatus caused by the decision to close the establishment, followed by the decision to leave it open but change its role: 'Brockhill has made remarkable progress in a relatively short time'. There was much to commend at Brockhill, including physical education, the assessment and support groups for sex offenders, induction and pre-release courses, the regime development committee which included inmates, and the NVQ courses. Education was extremely poor: 'In an establishment which can offer little else to occupy prisoners' minds education becomes very important'.

HM Prison Bullingdon

PO Box 50, Bicester, Oxon. OX6 0PZ
Tel: 0869-322111 **Fax:** 0869-243383
Opened: 1992 **CNA:** 635 **Average Roll:** 421 **Category:** Male Local

i **BACKGROUND** Bullingdon is a multi-functional establishment located in Bicester, Oxfordshire, which became operational on 16th March 1992. The establishment holds primarily adult male prisoners. It provides a remand facility for courts in Oxfordshire and Berkshire, and a training facility for inmates serving 18 months or more, excluding lifers. Oxford resettlement prison operates as a satellite of Bullingdon. The Governor provided information about the establishment, the BoV did not provide a copy of their latest annual report, and the prison will undergo its first HMCIP inspection in February 1995.

OFFICIALS
AREA MGR: Arthur de Frishching
CHAIR BOV: Mrs Goff
GOVERNOR: S. Fielder
Medical : Dr R. Lyons
CHAPLAIN: Rev D. Wakefield
PROBATION: Maxine Myattl
EDUCATION: Rod Turner
LOCAL MP: Tony Baldry. Con

REGIME *week days*: 0800 unlock/breakfast. 0900 work. 1130-1345 dinner. 1345 work. 1630 tea. 1700 lock-up. 1800–2030 association. exercise 60 mins in morning.

week ends: 0800 unlock. 0815 breakfast, association/activities church etc. 1145 dinner, lock-up. 1345 association, exercise. 1700 tea, lock-up. 1800–2030 association. exercise 60 mins in afternoon.

Out of cell: 10.5/24hrs weekdays and 10.5/24hrs at weekends.

ACCOMMODATION & FACILITIES A.block with 100 remand places and (B.Block) 55 places for those on Rule 43. Two 'training prison' blocks (C&D) with 310 places for convicted prisoner, in single and double cells, all with integral sanitation. Card phones on landings. VPU, Bail Information Scheme, sentence planning, drug–counselling, card phones and personal officer scheme. Extensive in-possession list includes radio/cassette/CD, books, watch, though no pets, and is dependent on location.

CANTEEN Many prisoners report high prices and poor choice. Inadequate stock for minorities and a lack of hair and health products. Only one visit per week.

VISITS *How to get there*: Bus from Bicester every hour. Some link direct to Oxford (Thames Transit) 0865–727000. HALOW (London) bus service: 0171-793-7484.
VISITING TIMES: Week Days: 1400–1600 (Con: Wed, Fri) (Rem: Mon, Tue, Thur). Saturday: 0900–1100 (Rem). 1400–1600 (Rem). Sunday : 1400–1600 (Con).

NOTES Canteen and staffed Visitors Centre. Contact prison probation for more information. No smoking. Convicted 2×2hr visits per month.

EDUCATION North Oxfordshire College Further Education Corporation won the contract to deliver all educational services at Bullingdon from 1.9.93 to 31.7.98. An excellent 35 page booklet locally produced explains educational policies and practice to all receptions. Inmates give first class reports.

WORKSHOPS There are currently no workshops at Bullingdon, all activity is education-based. There are plans, however, to build and operate workshops during 1995.

MEDICAL Part time Medical Officer. Report sick via wing staff or calling at the Medical Centre. Long dental waiting list reported.

GYMNASIUM & SPORTS Staffing: 1 PEPO, 1 PESO and 6 PEO's. Excellent PE programme. Classes start at 0845 each morning, with remedial, over 35's and inductions. Thereafter, three classes go on simultaneously with the major components being football, basket ball, volleyball, circuit training, weights, badminton, gymnastics, trampoline, running, padder tennis, aerobics, and table-tennis. Evening classes 1800-2015, four evenings for prisoners and one for staff/families. Inmate PE Course, full time and leading to Community Sports Leaders Award, with half practical in the gym and half theory in education dept. Very good reports from Bullingdon prisoners.

CHAPLAINCY Full-time CE Chaplain assisted by part-time RC and Methodist ministers. Visiting ministers of other faiths.

FOOD Staffing: 2×Civilian Caterers, and an inmate work party of 11. Reported by prisoners as appalling. Almost all complained about the poor standard of the food at Bullingdon: indeed, not one inmate had a good word to say about it.

ESTABLISHMENT REPORTS HMCIP will conduct the first full inspection of Bullingdon in February 1995.

PRISONERS' COMMENTS Very slow Request/Complaint system, accommodation is clean, no power in cells. High prices in canteen, limited range of stock and doesn't cater for minorities. Comfortable visits, 2×2hr visits per month. Excellent education facilities, excellent business studies course, though low wages. New medical facilities though long waiting list to see dentist. Too few outside activities for PE, though excellent weights room. No privacy for making phonecalls, and no outgoing calls are allowed at all on a Saturday.

HM Prison & YOI Bullwood Hall

High Road, Hockley, Essex. SS5 4TE
Tel: 0702-202515 **Fax:** 0702-207464
Opened: 1962 **CNA:** 125 **Average Roll:** 104 **Category:** Closed Female (YOI <21> Adult)

i **BACKGROUND** Bullwood Hall functions as a closed Prison and Young Offender Institution in the East Anglia area of the Prison Service. Located at Hockley some six miles NW of Southend on Sea in Essex (A127, B1013), Bullwood Hall itself is a manor house built in 1900 which stands just outside the perimeter fence. It was a private residence until 1955 when it was purchased by the then Prison Commissioners. Bullwood Hall first opened as a penal establishment in 1962, when its role was that of a closed Borstal for females. In 1983 it changed to a Prison and Youth Custody Centre and, in 1988, the YCC became a YOI. The Governor did not reply to our request for information about Bullwood Hall, though the Chairman of the BoV kindly sent us a copy of their latest annual report. HMCIP published their latest inspection report on Bullwood Hall in August 1994.

OFFICIALS
AREA MGR : Tom Murtagh
CHAIR BOV: Mrs B.Crampin
GOVERNOR: Eva Butler
MEDICAL:
CHAPLAIN: Rev Kemp
PROBATION: D. Heining
EDUCATION:
LOCAL MP: Michael Clark. Con
STAFFING: 135 staff in post, 80 in unified grades. 1×PO, 6×SO and 8×Officers are male.

REGIME *week days*: 0730 unlock. 0800 breakfast. 0900 work. 1230 lunch. 1330 work. 1615 cease labour. 1700 tea. 1730–2030 association.

week ends: 0730 unlock. 0800 breakfast. 0900 association. 1215 lunch. 1400 association. 1700 tea. 1730–2030 association.

Out of cell: 11.25/24hrs weekdays and 9.3/24hrs at weekends.

ACCOMMODATION & FACILITIES Seven discrete living units. Condor, Kestrel, and Falcon hold a mix of inmates. Swan, holds lifers and long termers only, Osprey, operates as the Segregation Unit, Jay, is used to house inductions, and Eagle, is empty currently though here are plans for Eagle Unit to be used as new induction unit with Jay being used as a pre-release unit. Units are largely self-contained with their own serveries, toilet and shower areas, and with limited association facilities—TV, pool and board games and no inter-wing movement). The units are small, the largest having 32 cells, which promotes good inmate/staff relationships. Sentence planning, drug counselling, card phones, electronic night sanitation, and personal officer scheme.

VISITS *How to get there*: Train to Rayleigh from Liverpool St. Bus (7 or 8) to Bullwood Lane or taxi from station. Special Transport: HALOW (London) bus service: 0171-793-7484.
VISITING TIMES: Week Days: 1330–1530 Mon, Wed, Fri only. Saturday: 1330–1530. Sunday : 1330–1530.

NOTES Staffed Visitors Centre, canteen at weekends. Overnight stays not generally available, but contact prison probation officer. Childrens' visits (Mon pm) in relaxed surroundings are popular.

EDUCATION Provided by Essex County Council. Education department created out of a former workshop complex. Classrooms of reasonable size and adequate equipment levels. Hairdressing course popular. 30 FTE places. F/t secretarial skills course incorporating business English. Other day-time subjects include basic English, maths, cookery, arts and crafts. Evening classes Mon–Fri, mainly leisure based.

WORKSHOPS FTE (30 places), VTC Hairdressing (10), VTC fashion (10), PE Courses (10), Works (5), PSIF Workshop: Assembly (closed), Laundry (5). Farm (4), Gardens (6), Kitchen (8), Wing Cleaners (8), Prison Cleaners (3), Induction (6). Average pay £6.

DISCIPLINE High number of disciplinary hearings, with 426 between February 1993 and March 1994, mainly for minor acts of disobedience: a high proportion committed by a small number of inmates. Segregation Unit (Osprey) suffers from a lack of heating which HMCIP said should be remedied or the unit closed.

MEDICAL Part time Medical Officer, Senior Charge Nurse and HCO. Dentist, veneriologist and psychiatrist attend once per week, and optician as required. Part time psychologist. High number of self-harm incidents—113 in the 12 months prior to HMCIP's latest inspection. BoV report this has eased since, as a result of compacts and individual counselling by staff.

GYMNASIUM & SPORTS 1×PESO and 2×PEO. NVQs in Sports & leisure Activities. Indoor facilities good, excellent though small gymnasium, with multi-gym, clean showers and toilets. Outdoor facilities poor, hard standing area marked out for team games—netball, basketball, volleyball etc—and a redundant swimming pool which for a small cost, could be made operational.

CHAPLAINCY Part time CE chaplain, RC and Methodist ministers. Chapel moved to Activities Centre (old workshop) and the present situation is not ideal say the prison's BoV. Regular services are held by the Anglican, RC and Methodist ministers and visits from the Salvation Army and other bodies as necessary.

FOOD Staffing: 1×SO, 1×Officer (caterer) 1×Civilian and an inmate work party of 8. Very small kitchen with no showers for inmates or staff. HMCIP said he was impressed with the quantity, flavour and presentation of the food which was of a good quality. Three week menu cycle in operation with choices at dinner. Plan to build new kitchen with dining room 1995/6.

ESTABLISHMENT REPORTS In a report (published 4th August 1994) of an inspection in March 1994, HMCIP, said that Bullwood Hall had changed noticeably in the two years since the full inspection. The vast majority of the recommendations resulting from that inspection had been acted upon. Living and working conditions for both inmates and staff were satisfactory, though some toilets were in need of refurbishment. A new visitors centre and visiting room give good facilities, meals are served at reasonable times and inmate/staff relationships were very good. It was disappointing, however, to find so little enthusiasm among inmates for some existing activities in the evening, such as education and PE. The atmosphere within the establishment was generally calm and quiet; although frequent use was made of formal disciplinary reports, serious offences were relatively few and the overall figures were distorted by the number of offences committed by a disruptive minority. HMCIP was impressed by the attention given to recording incidents of self harm and by the way adjudications were conducted. The latter demonstrated a good balance between care and control, a balance which was evident in the attitude of staff which, said HMCIP, 'bodes well for the future development of the establishment'.

BOV Annual Report 1993/4: Changes in the conditions and regime at Bullwood Hall during 1993 have meant a more normal lifestyle for the women. The new shift patterns enable prisoners to be out of cell for 11.25 hours on weekdays and 9.3 hours weekends. The working day was extended by an extra half-hour in November. The library times extended during the day and on rota the evenings, lunch at 1230 and tea at 1700 and a choice of menu for the main meal have all helped tremendously. The extra hours out of cell required a considerable period of readjustment, but the women are now settled and established into a regular routine. There was a period of unrest in the middle part of the year; staff sickness and NEPO training led to split association in November, but by the end of the year, the commitment and dedication of the staff and management teams has resulted in a calmer, settled atmosphere at Bullwood Hall.

GOVERNOR'S COMMENTS I am delighted with the Inspectorate's Report and am very glad that they have recognised the positive work that goes on at Bullwood Hall. I would like to emphasise that it would have been impossible to introduce changes to the extent that has been done without the total co-operation of all staff, including the local branch of the POA. We will continue to develop new inmate programmes dealing with the special needs of female offenders.

PRISONERS' COMMENTS Health care is poor, doctors issue medication too readily, and the waiting time for dental treatment is too long. There is no inter-wing association, nor access to cooking facilities on the wings. The regime lacks opportunities for exercise and association in the open air. Cleaning materials are hard to obtain, disinfectant is never provided, toilets are dirty and the sanitary towel disposal bins are not emptied promptly. Some of the showers are in poor condition and there is often no hot water. Only six sets of clothes allowed (except leggings) and exchanges for clean clothing only allowed once every eight weeks.

HM Prison Camp Hill

Clissold Road, Newport, Isle of Wight. PO30 5PB
Tel: 0983-527661 **Fax:** 0983-520505
Opened: 1912 **CNA:** 469 **Roll:** 460 **Category:** C. Male

i **BACKGROUND** The then Home Secretary, Winston Churchill, opened Camp Hill in 1912 as a preventive detention establishment. Built with the help of inmate labour on a five hectare site adjoining Parkhurst prison, the establishment is situated one and a half miles north of Newport on the Isle of Wight. In 1932 Camp Hill became a Borstal. For the duration of the Second World War it reverted to prison use and, in 1946, Camp Hill again became a Borstal institution. In 1951 the establishment became a corrective training prison, ceasing that role in 1957 when the Criminal Justice Act that year abolished corrective training. Camp Hill now functions as a Category C training prison. The Head of Regimes at Camp Hill, Mr Gravett, kindly provided information about the establishment, though the BoV declined our request for a copy of their latest annual report. HMCIP published their latest inspection report on Camp Hill in June 1992.

OFFICIALS
AREA MGR: Peter Kitteridge
CHAIR BOV: J. Bolwell
GOVERNOR: W.A. Wood
MEDICAL: Dr E.Griffiths
CHAPLAIN: Rev R. Higginbottom
PROBATION: A. Bush
EDUCATION: Ms F. Newman
LOCAL MP: Barry Field. Con
STAFFING: 10 Governor grades, 10 Principal Officers, 20 Senior Officers, 104 Officers, 17 Night Patrol Officers and 4 Prison Auxiliaries.

REGIME *week days*: 0735 unlock, breakfast. 0830 work. 0900 sick parade. 1000 adjudications. 1210 cease work. 1220 dinner. 1335 work. 1650 cease work. 1710 lock up. 1750 unlock. 1800 association and evening classes. 2000 association ends. 2005 lock up.

week ends: 0735 unlock. 0745 treatments. 0815 breakfast. 0845 activities. 0900(Sun) C/E service. 1000(Sat) adjudications. 1040(Sun) RC service. 1140 return to cells. 1200 serve dinner. 1215 lock up. 1335 unlock. 1345 activities. 1645 tea. 1705 lock up. Evening association from 1750 to 2000 dependent on location.

Out of cell: 12/24hrs weekdays and 9.5/24hrs at weekends.

ACCOMMODATION & FACILITIES Inmates housed in eight accommodation units (St.Andrew's[CNA=25], St.David's [47] St.Edward's [51], St.George's [81], St.James' [86], St.Michael's, St.Patrick's [47] and St.Thomas' [86]) three of which (Edward's, David's and Andrew's) have specialist roles in the field of drugs, anger management and segregation/remand. Other units have their own identities: special needs, induction/receptions and Category Ds. Sentence planning and personal officer schemes, drug counselling and card phones. Night-san or integral sanitation dependent on location. Facilities include large in-possession list. Routine censorship abolished and card phones installed on all living units.

CANTEEN Central canteen located in purpose-built accommodation next to St.Michael's wing and staffed by four prison officers. Canteen available once per week, though for the handful of remand prisoners held at Camp Hill more frequent visits allowed. Local purchase facility and good range of stock. Prices said to be on the high side by some inmates.

VISITS *How to get there*: Train to Portsmouth or Southampton, then ferry to either Ryde or Cowes respectively. Hovercraft from Southsea to Ryde takes 10 mins. From Ryde, bus 1 or 1A from Ryde Esplanade. From Cowes, bus 1, 1A from Carvel Lane to St.Mary's Hsp. Special Transport: Every Sunday ABBA Coaches leaves Goldsmiths College, New Cross, at 0900. Adults £17, children £9—inclusive of ferry fares. Booking in advance crucial: 081 859 1808/8708 Mr O'Toole.
VISITING TIMES: Week Days: 1345–1545. Saturday: 1345–1545. Sunday: 1345–1545.

NOTES Staffed Visitors Centre, drinks machine in visits room (coins), creche available Wed & Fri. Overnight stay centre at Crocker St, Newport (0983-527970). No disabled facilities, but help can be obtained. Baby changing facilities. Town visits as appropriate.

EDUCATION Open 52 weeks of the year with five full-time teachers and evening classes Mon–Fri. Broad and comprehensive curriculum. Daytime classes (0830–1210/1345–1640hrs): business admin; basic education; essential food hygiene; health and safety; current affairs; int/adv maths; woodwork; cooking; information technology; science; and sociology. Evening classes (1800–1930hrs): Motor cycle club; hairdressing; drama; cookery; practical woodwork; computer games; motor cycle theory and maintenance—learn to ride on Sat & Sun 1400–1600. Excellent bonus payment scheme makes payments to inmates according to a scale based largely on the length of the course undertaken and the qualification obtained—e.g. first aid certificate £2 through to f/t NVQ/VTC/CIT qualification £10.

WORKSHOPS Full time education (£5). VTC: welding, domestic cleaning, information tech (£5). NVQ: painting & decorating, bricklaying, building ops (£5). PSIF Workshops: fabrication & spray assembly, light textiles, engineering, main and mfg stores (£7.90). Farm: stock, estate and maintenance parties—with weekend work dining outside (9.02). Kitchen (£10.08), Parkhurst Kitchen (£11). Orderlies (£5.50–9.50).

DISCIPLINE Segregation unit incorporated into St.Andrew's Wing, which also contains a group of 12 cells for remand prisoners attending Isle of Wight courts. HMCIP said that adjudications were averaging about 20 per month and was impressed with the procedures which complied with standing orders and natural justice'. HMCIP was however concerned at the number of times the body belt had been applied and he called for much greater control of its use by the Governor and Medical Officer.

MEDICAL F/t Medical Officer. Health Care Centre staffed by 1×HCPO, 1×HCSO and 6×HCO. HCC consists of seven single cells, and a six-bed ward. Conditions in 1992 were such that HMCIP stated the HCC should be 'condemned for in-patient use'—today in-patient facilities and the majority of clinics for Camp Hill are provided by Parkhurst.

GYMNASIUM & SPORTS Staffing, PO, SO and six officers. Classes from 0830–1930 each day. PE programme dependent on labour allocation with some areas, kitchen, works and FTE for example, being given priority.

CHAPLAINCY Full-time C/E chaplain and part-time ministers from other faiths. Holy Communion Thursday 0830–0900, main service Sunday 0900–1000. RC service Sunday 1040–1140. Chapel class Mon, Tues, Wed 1800–1930. Thursday prayer meeting 1800–1930. Muslim prayers Friday 1345–1445.

FOOD Staffing: 1×PO, 1×SO and 2×Officer (caterers), and there is a work party of 10. Kitchen compact and well laid out. Meals transported in heated trolleys to hotplates in each unit. Good choice of meals according to HMCIP, 'meals were tasty, well presented and reasonably varied, inmates on special diets were properly catered for'.

ESTABLISHMENT REPORTS In a report (published 2nd June 1992) of an inspection in June 1991, Judge Stephen Tumim, HMCIP, said that Camp Hill had many favourable aspects, new working arangements had been successfully implemented, though there was a need for the prison to shed its 'punishment prison' reputation. HMCIP found the medical facilities to be 'unsatisfactory in so many respects' that he arranged for a special investigation to be carried out at Camp Hill by Dr Faulk of the Knowle Hospital, Fareham, with the result that all in-patient services were transferred to Parkhurst.

GOVERNOR'S COMMENTS A progressive, developing institution. Good staff relationships with inmates, proactive and meets national operating standards in almost all areas of service, quality of care delivery. Our IoW location creates dificulties for visitors as Camp Hill has allocations from London and the south coast. We counter by offering opportunities for prisoners to progress if they respond. We offer a positive regime and provide home leave frequently. Town visits, employment interviews etc.

PRISONERS' COMMENTS Average request complaints procedure, single cells on some wings but no power points. canteen poor with poor selection. Visits are cold and depressing most of the time. Education is fair to good in some areas. Pay is poor and conditions and opportunities for work are fair. Average medical facilities. Punishments range from one end of the spectrum to the other and often with little relavance to the offence proved. Menu selection for food which has varied quality. Good gym facilities which are available on a daily basis. Religious needs are well catered for at Camp Hill, though there is a shortage of card phones with only one per wing.

HM Prison Canterbury

46 Longport, Canterbury, Kent. CT1 1PJ
Tel: 0227-762244 **Fax:** 0227-450203
Opened: 1808 **CNA:** 275 **Average Roll:** 175 **Category:** Male Local

i **BACKGROUND** Canterbury prison sits close to the city centre, housing remand and convicted adult males from courts in East Kent. The prison dates from 1808 when a County Gaol was built just outside the city limits, the front of the prison still bears the carved inscription 'House of Correction' though after recent refurbishment its description is now only of historic interest according to the prison's Board of Visitors. During the First World War the prison was used as a Home Office archive, later becoming a prison and a naval detention centre. In 1947 Canterbury once again became a local prison, the role that it continues to discharge today. The Governor did not reply to our request for information about the prison, though the BoV kindly supplied a copy of their latest annual report. HMCIP published their latest inspection report on Canterbury in January 1992.

OFFICIALS

AREA MGR: John Hunter
CHAIR BOV: B. Durban
GOVERNOR: J.L. Harrison
MEDICAL:
CHAPLAIN: Rev Crowie
PROBATION: Mr Swallow
EDUCATION:
LOCAL MP: Julian Brazier. Con
STAFFING: Five Governor grades and 158 other staff in unified grades including specialist staff.

REGIME *week days*: 0730 unlock, slop out, applications, breakfast. 0815 sick parade. 0820 trays out. 0830 slop out. 0845 gym. 0900 exercise A.wing, workshop (Mon, Wed, Fri), kit change (Thurs). 0930 reception board. 1000 adjudications. 1100 exercise convicted. 1130 dinner. 1330 work. 1340 VPU exercise. 1600 tea. 1730–2015 association by rota.

week ends: 0730 unlock, breakfast. 0820 trays out. 0830 slop out. 0845 VPU exercise. 0915 A.wing video, association (Sat), CE Service (Sun). 0950 B/C wings to exercise. 1100–1130 dinner. 1300 trays out, slop out. 1315 A.wing exercise, B.wing video, association. 1600 tea. No weekend evening association.

Out of cell: 4/24hrs weekdays and 7/24hrs at weekends.

ACCOMMODATION & FACILITIES

Three cell blocks, A,B,C, all of which are quite different in size. A&B wings have recently been refurbished throughout, most have single cells, some are two'd up but no threes. C.wing operates as a resettlement unit containing about a dozen inmates. All cells have integral sanitation, old recesses converted to showers and toilets for use during association. Laundry facilities available on the wings and card phones located in association areas. Each wing has its own servery. Original A.wing divided into A.East and A.West. Offence focused groups on C.wing, personal officer scheme undermined by lack of continuity. Mail opened centrally and handed out at midday—not opened in front of the prisoner.

BAIL INFORMATION SCHEME

Operated by Probation Department (SPO Mr Swallow) it provides a comprehensive information service, with considerable efforts being made to publicise legal rights.

FOREIGN NATIONALS Because of its location, Canterbury receives a large number of foreign nationals (FN) each year, comprising illegal immigrants, asylum seekers, deportees and drug couriers: the prison dealt with 26 different nationalities in 1993. Language Line is available but the governor has restricted its use because of high costs. If you have difficulty obtaining translation or interpretation, contact your Embassy or Consulate. Special advice for FN inmates is contained in Chapter 13 of the Section 2.

VISITS *How to get there*: Trains from London to either Canterbury East or Canterbury West. No Special Transport. Walk to prison in city centre.

VISITING TIMES: Week Days: 1330–1530. Saturday: 1330–1530 No PVOs. Sunday: 1330–1530 No PVOs.

NOTES No staffed Visitors Centre. Canteen in visiting room and Childrens Play Area. Creche available but sporadic supervision. No overnight stays but plenty of B&B in Canterbury. Privilege Visiting Orders cannot be used on Saturday. Disabled access to visits room possible.

EDUCATION Two f/t and one p/t teaching staff. Contracted out service retained by existing supplier, Canterbury College. Classes from 0845–1115 & 1345–1545 Monday to Friday, averaging 44 inmates per session. Inmates only allowed a morning or afternoon session, other session can be in the textile workshop or locked up. No evening classes due to a claimed lack of demand(!). Core subjects of English, English as a Foreign Language (heavily subscribed) and maths, other subjects include computing, pottery, French, cookery, music and art. All classes are mixed remand and convicted, Community Woodwork Shop proved popular—until an inmate cut off his index finger with a jigsaw—and there are open learning courses for those who want cell study. Good library with many books in other languages, all official publications available.

WORKSHOPS Charity workshop closed. Textile workshop main industrial employer. No VTC/CIT courses available. Kitchen, cleaners and usual orderlies. Shortage of work opportunities at Canterbury.

DISCIPLINE Refurbished segregation unit, partial integral sanitation but conditions are not suitable for long term prisoners transferred (ghosted) under CI 28/93. Inadequate exercise facilities with hospital garden having to be used. Seg inmates do have access to the gym however. Adjudications average about five per week, mainly for damage to cells or possession of small quantities of cannabis—all drug cases result in immediate closed visits.

MEDICAL Full and part time Medical Officers. HCC recently refurbished and now with partial integral sanitation. Small association area for inpatients, with TV, billiards and small library. Complaints that drug detoxification courses being undertaken in the community are not continued after admission to Canterbury, though the prison will notch up a first in placing homeopathic medicines on the wing drug trolleys. Report sick to landing officer at morning unlock, seen by HCO and doctor if required.

GYMNASIUM & SPORTS 1×PESO (Dave France) and 2×PEO. Good use made of old equipment by enthusiastic staff. High demand for gym by inmates, daily classes, evening classes four nights a week. CSLA. Good weights area and outside swimming for those who qualify. Local handicapped use gym once a week assisted by eight inmates.

CHAPLAINCY Full time CE chaplain, Hermon Crowie, p/t RC and Methodist ministers. Regular weekly programme of services, groups and discussions. No multi-faith area despite high proportion of ethnic minorities.

FOOD Staffing: 1×SO, 2×Officer (caterers), and an inmate work party of 11. New kitchen opened March 1993. Inmates complain bitterly about the quality of the food at Canterbury, overcooked, left to lie on hot plates too long before serving and no pre-select menu system.

ESTABLISHMENT REPORTS BoV Annual Report 1993/94: The prison has undertaken and almost completed an extensive refurbishment programme and this, combined with the educational and practical skills readily available, must serve to improve the life of a prisoner whilst in Canterbury and give him, on release, a sound basis to improve his life. Canterbury's enhancement has been reflected by its excellent performance according to the Prison Department's Key Performance Indicators in terms of regime, escapes and assaults; but refurbishment—plaster and paint—are only part of Canterbury prison's advancement and elevation into a modern prison. None of this would be realised if there was not the full co-operation of the staff and that is what Canterbury has. Many new roles have been taken on, especially with the Personal Officer Scheme. The resettlement unit still requires outside work for inmates to take up and they have produced good work as many written testimonials confirm.

PRISONERS' COMMENTS Requests and complaints are generally dealt with efficiently, there is the odd hiccup but that's human nature. Accommodation is very spartan, in-cell toilet is embarrassing to use because of the lack of privacy in shared cells. Canteen prices are very high, poor selection on offer. Visits tend to be very noisy, they take place in a converted workshed, small area for kids, but no toys for them to play with. Part time education only, excellent classes for non-English inmates. Poor work opportunities, wages average £6 per week, tasks are monotonous and have no sentence planning basis at all. Medical services are appalling. Punishments are reasonably light but little account taken of circumstances, fixed tariff for certain offences. Good gym facilities, but restricted to just 45 mins a day. There is a lack of card phones. Phoning home should not be the constant hassle it is, nor should it carry with it the risk of the black eye that is seen around the place from time to time because of it.

HM Prison Cardiff

Knox Road, Cardiff. CF2 1UG
Tel: 0222-491212 **Fax:** 02222-489079
Opened: 1827 **CNA:** 338 (HMP=253, RC=85) **Average Roll:** 407 **Category:** Male Local & Remand Centre

i **BACKGROUND** Cardiff is a Local Prison and Remand Centre (both with appalling conditions) situated in the centre of the Welsh capital city. Built in 1827 as a County Gaol, the former female wing (D.wing) became a Borstal after the Second World War but was closed in 1962. D.wing reopened in 1964 as a Remand Centre. The prison buildings remain largely as they were built, and over the years many ancillary buildings have been fitted in wherever space presented itself. Today the cell blocks are surrounded by this miscellany of smaller structures of various ages ranging from the late Victorian to the modern entry building and recently constructed kitchen. Neither the Governor nor BoV replied to our requests for information about the prison, and HMCIP published their latest inspection report in October 1993.

OFFICIALS
AREA MGR: John Wilkinson
CHAIR BOV:
GOVERNOR: N. Clifford
MEDICAL:
CHAPLAIN: Rev Kiddle
PROBATION: John Jones
EDUCATION:
LOCAL MP: Jon Owen Jones. Lab
STAFFING: Nine Governor grades, 7 Principal Officers, 28 Senior Officers and 162 Officers, not including specialist staff.

☞ **REGIME** *week days*: 0730 unlock. 0800 breakfast, treatments. 0830 work or main exercise. 1015 Remand exercise. 1120 cease labour. 1130 dinner. 1150 lock up. 1315 work. 1330 Rule 43 exercise. 1600 cease labour. 1625 tea. 1650 lock up. 1745–1930 association by rota, classes. 1950 lock up.

week ends: 0800 unlock. 0815 RC Mass (Sun). 0820 breakfast, treatments. 0910 Remand video. 0915 CE Service (Sun). 0915–1015 wing searching. 1015 main exercise. 1120 dinner. 1155 lock up. 1300 unlock, slop out. 1330 Remand association. 1400 Rule 43 exercise. 1545 tea. 1620 lock up. 1930 supper, no weekend evening association.

Out of cell: 6/24hrs weekdays and 4/24hrs at weekends. Remand Centre follows broadly similar timetable.

ACCOMMODATION & FACILITIES
Three living units in the main prison, A, B, D wings. A1=VPU & Segregation Unit, A2=adult Remands, A3/4=adult Convicted. B1–4 =adult Convicted. D=YO Remands. Cells filthy, cockroaches, rats and mice are rife, cell furniture in poor condition and recesses disgusting. Central bath house used for weekly shower despite three largely unused showers on each landing. Card phones in all wings (available 1000–1115, 1400–1600 and 1745–1930). Mail opened centrally and issued at dinner time—opened outwith the presence of the inmate. Appalling regime delivery with shortages of staff being blamed for constant cancellation of a wide range of activities. All meals eaten in cell.

VPU Located on A1 landing, the 15 cells in the VPU can hold a maximum of 30 inmates. Open access to the unit from main prison which HMCIP said should be boarded off. Conditions cleaner than the main prison but no servery and no washing up facilities other than the recess. Psychological and support work from probation, intended to act as a preparation for the Sex Offenders Treatment Programme at HMP Usk. Interviews, said HMCIP, 'literally took place in a broom cupboard, dustbins and brooms were removed before the interview began'. No large room for discussions, no evening association and only one session of PE per week. Poor regime which is often reduced further by staff shortages.

CANTEEN Situated in a room off the Centre, the canteen is very cramped and limits the stock to about 100 lines. In HMRC converted cell acts as canteen. Remands have access three times, and convicted once, per week. Local purchase facility and maximum of £15 private cash can be spent at any one time. Prices in accordance with Shaw's retail price list.

VISITS *How to get there*: Train to Cardiff Central, then bus to Dumfries Place. No Special Transport.
VISITING TIMES: Week Days: 1330–1515. Saturday: 1330–1515. Sunday: No Visits.

NOTES No staffed Visitors Centre. Canteen in visiting room, and Childrens Play Area on Tues, Thurs and Saturday. Wheelchair access and disabled toilet facilities and nappy-changing. Security stamp placed on all visitors' hands.

EDUCATION Located close to A.wing the education department consists of six well equipped classrooms. Two rooms on D2 converted as classrooms for HMRC inmates. Craft workshop. No PTE, FTE only. Subjects cover broad range, Open learning packs popular, evening classes three nights per week. High number of classes cancelled due to staff shortages. Library containing some 5,000 books with access for all inmates at least once per week.

WORKSHOPS Seven main employment parties: Tailors 1 (42 places), Tailors 2 (42), Tailors Training (14), Tailors Cutting (8), Laundry (14), Contract Services (35), Kitchen (27). Allocated to labour as part of induction process. Wages average £6. No work in HMRC apart from cleaners etc.

DISCIPLINE Segregation Unit A1 landing, nine ordinary cells and one strip cell. Adjudications properly conducted and awards appropriate to the offence. Remand Centre has no seg unit but has a number of cells on the first landing set aside for punishments. Number of adjudications in HMP (324) and HMRC (411) reasonable said HMCIP.

MEDICAL Full time SMO, 1×(f/t)MO, 1×(p/t)MO, 1×(G5)HC Manager, 1×HCPO, 2×HCSO, 12×HCO and 1×Nurse(HMRC). Visiting psychiatrist one sess/wk, Genito-urinary specialist 1×sess/wk. 'T' shaped HCC with 15 in-patient rooms with integral sanitation on the long limb of the 'T', one is a double room with bath & toilet en suite, other rooms have wash basin and toilet. 'Special Care Room' with cardboard furniture. Offices situated on the cross bar. HMRC medical facilities consists of just two rooms. Dental 2×sess/wk with two-week waiting list on average for non-urgent cases—when HMCIP inspected he found 'an offensive smell in the dental room . . . suspected to be due to rats which had died underneath the floor'. Optician 1×sess/mth. No pro-active health care team or health promotion. No HIV/AIDS team. No X-ray facilities. Drug counselling available (HMRC inmates referred to a Drug Throughcare Team). HMCIP was unable to find any Suicide Prevention Packs on the wings.

GYMNASIUM & SPORTS 1×PESO and 2×PEO. Large gymnasium allows for indoor soccer or basketball, but low ceiling prevents other ball games. Well equipped weights area and good shower facilities. Small grassed football pitch large enough for seven-a-side. PE at Cardiff unsatisfactory according to HMCIP because PE staff are regularly used for discipline duties. HMRC inmates are not receiving the compulsory periods of PE.

CHAPLAINCY Full time CE chaplain, p/t RC and Methodist ministers. Large chapel but no multi-faith room. Imam visits regularly. Team of 17 Prison Visitors serve the prison. Chaplaincy has a good relationship with inmates. Main services Sunday morning.

FOOD Staffing: 1×PO, 1×SO, 4×Officer (caterers), and an inmate work party of 11. Gone are the days when Cardiff's infamous PO Caterer (T.K. Davies) served up food the envy of most prisons. Food now served barely lukewarm according to HMCIP, though the four choices at dinner continues the 'TK' tradition of wide choice and good quality—at least when it left the kitchen. No pre-select menu. New £1.8m kitchen 1993. All meals dine in cell. Meal times far too close together.

ESTABLISHMENT REPORTS In a report (published October 1993) of an inspection in October 1992, HMCIP, said that the standards in the prison were unacceptably poor. Some staff and managers were trying hard to introduce changes, but this remains a prison with low standards and a bad regime. Living units with the exception of the HCC are filthy, graffiti is widespread and cockroaches are everywhere, both inmates and staff reporting sightings of rats in the wings. Food was left uncovered in the kitchen, arrangements for inmates clothing were exceedingly poor with only one pair of underpants and socks per week, inmates spent far too much time locked in their cells and not everyone received their entitlement to daily exercise. External court commitments resulted in attenuation of an already sparse regime. The governor and senior management team 'appeared tired and were fighting hard against a tide of outdated working practices'. There were pockets of good practice, the VPU and Pre-Release Unit for example, but generally there was too little constructive activity and there were clearly serious health risks which demanded radical change.

PRISONERS' COMMENTS **MAIN:** There is a pressing need for more telephones, one per landing is inadequate. Meal times are crammed together for the convenience of staff rather than the needs of inmates. Cells are dirty, difficult to clean with a lack of cleaning materials, and cockroaches and rats are prevalent. Association particularly at weekends is poor, education is unsatisfactory with a long waiting list for evening classes and a lack of staff resulting in many classes being cancelled. Visits are too short, particularly when families come from far away. Evening association on landings should be available every night rather than the once-in-a-blue- moon situation at present. **REMAND CENTRE:** Not enough PE available and no opportunity to kick a football about a yard. Exercise is inadequate, the library is not open sufficiently often and changing of kit is limited to a basic weekly change. Far too much lock up, and inadequate landing association. Canteen has inadequate stock and the limit on spending was particularly unfair to Remands. With some exceptions, staff are reasonably friendly. **VPU:** Frequent verbal abuse from inmates in main prison as a result of the VPU not being blocked off from the rest of A.wing. Food is often sabotaged, bread rolls are spat upon, cockroaches are put in the coffee and margarine is clearly marked 'For Nonces'. No hot water boilers in the VPU to make drinks, meal times are ridiculous with tea at weekends served at 1530. Education opportunities inadequate with perhaps no more than 30 mins during the morning and then only for those who do not work. No evening association at all and some staff left doors open for cell association while others locked them up: there is no consistency in approach. Only the recess for washing eating utensils, prison clothing is appalling with only one pair of underpants and invariably no socks at all. Cockroaches and rats are all over the prison. Inmate/staff relationships in the VPU are very good.

HM YOI Castington

Morpeth, Northumberland. NE65 9XG
Tel: 0670-760942 **Fax:** 0670-761188
Opened: 1979 CNA: 300 **Roll:** 286 **Category:** B YOI

i **BACKGROUND** HM YOI Castington is situated on part of a former RAF station close to the village of Acklington, about 25 miles north of Newcastle. Castington lies on the flat Northumbrian coastal plain about one mile inland and is exposed to the hard North Sea coastal weather. It was originally a satellite of HMP Acklington which it adjoins, though in 1979 it became a YOI in its own right. New accommodation and facilities have since been added and very little of the original RAF accommodation is present today. The institution comprises about six hectares enclosed by a security fence. It holds inmates aged between 17 & 21, serving a variety of sentences including life. The Governor provided detailed up-to-date information, though the Castington BoV did not reply to a request for a copy of their annual report. HMCIP published their latest inspection report on Castington in March 1994.

OFFICIALS

AREA MGR: A. Papps
CHAIR BOV: Mrs J. Haigh
GOVERNOR: C.R. Harder
MEDICAL: Dr T. White
CHAPLAIN: Rev Eltringham
PROBATION: P. Bennett
EDUCATION: E. Bell
LOCAL MP: John Thompson. Lab
STAFFING: 6 Governors + SMO, 8 Principal Officers, 24 Senior Officers and 107 Officers.

☞ **REGIME** *week days*: 0800 unlock/breakfast. 0830 work. 1200 dinner. 1330 work. 1645 tea. 1745–2000 association. No formal exercise period.

week ends: 0800 unlock/breakfast. 0930–1130 association. (Sundays: 0915–1000 inspection). 1200 dinner. 1345–1545 association. 1645 tea. No evening association. No formal exercise period.

Out of cell: 10.5/24hrs weekdays and 10.5/24hrs at weekends.

ACCOMMODATION & FACILITIES Five wings (A,B,C,D,E) each of 60 single cells with integral sanitation. Own light switch. No pets. Trainers, own socks, underpants permitted, radio cassette, CD-player. No home made tapes. Usual items allowed in possession, including cassette, curtains and bedspread. One of the few establishments still to insist on bedpacks. No VPU as such, but 'poor copers' section. Bail information & personal officer schemes, sentence planning and drug counselling. A card phone is available in each of the five living units, two cards allowed each week. Mail opened and checked outwith presence of the inmate, and given out at mid-day. All calls recorded. Castington has expressed an interest in joining the Sex Offender Treatment Programme, though does not have a group running at the moment.

CANTEEN Central canteen operated by two prison officers who, according to HMCIP, were 'handicapped by the lack of space which prohibited the holding of a large and varied stock'. Weekly turnover about £1500, new receptions can obtain an advance—repaid at 25p per week—and inmates had access to the shop once per week.

REQUESTS/COMPLAINTS On average 10 written R/C forms received each month, problems with property and adjudicatory awards 'featuring consistently'. Despite the small number of R/C, the seven-day target for replies was being met in less than half the cases. HMCIP found the logs and files to be completed correctly, 'but we found many of the replies given to prisoners somewhat perfunctory and impersonal'.

VISITS *How to get there*: Train to Newcastle upon Tyne. Metro to Haymarket, then bus X18 at 45 min past the hour. Takes 70 minutes. Special Transport from Cleveland, Leeds, S.Yorks & Cumbria, Manchester and Liverpool probation services. Contact prison probation.
VISITING TIMES: Week Days: 1330–1600 Tues, Wed, Thurs only. Saturday: 1330–1600. Sunday: 1330–1600.

NOTES Visitors Centre opened April 1993 for both Castington and Acklington—though closed on Saturdays. Canteen in visiting room (limited during week), Childrens Play Area. Prisoners report very good visits, normally of two-hour duration, though there are complaints that no extra PVO's allowed 'even when the visits room is empty (during) midweek'.

EDUCATION 'The Education building was one of the best we have seen' said HMCIP. Education open fifty weeks of the year with evening classes twice a week. Four full time teachers. Classes: (Day) General Education, Media Studies, Business Studies, 'A' levels, GCSE and Information Technology. (Evenings) Soft toys, Art, Yoga, Kart/Club, Woodwork, and Guitar. Five general-purpose classrooms along with woodwork, computer, wordprocessing and printing rooms. VTC in motor mechanics, light vehicle body repair and catering. Car-crime course won high praise from HMCIP.

WORKSHOPS Textiles (sweatshirts, boxer shorts, sheets and pillow slips). CIT bricklaying and painting & decorating. VTC in motor mechanics, light vehicle body repair and catering. The workshop was originally fitted out as an engineering shop but never used, then refurbished as a CIT plastering course but, again, never used. It is now once more an engineering shop. Labour allocation via SWIP, HMCIP said this should be replaced by a Labour Board, and work in the textile shop should be replaced with work 'better suited to training needs'.

DISCIPLINE HMCIP reported that since the last inspection adjudications had increased from 250 to 2,004. Examination of records revealed many were unnecessary and should have been dealt with under the Minor Reports procedure. Hearings were conducted in accordance with relevant procedures and inmates dealt with fairly. MO criticised for not visiting seg unit (and not passing inmates fit) on weekends.

MEDICAL Medical facilities at Castington were severely criticised by HMCIP. F/t MO divided his time between Castington and Acklington next door. HC staff for both establishments 1×HCSO & 5×HCO, none of whom are qualified nurses. HC staff 'did not seem to be much involved in general health promotion nor play any part in the HIV/AIDS prevention or suicide prevention programmes'. Drugs were issued in bottles which did not carry a name, nor the dosage or frequency. No specialist clinics in either establishment. Some 18 inmates report sick each day, medical interviews were 'conducted in great haste' in the presence of staff: 'the doctor should see the inmate in private'. Reception interviews were 'extremely brief with virtually no attempt made to assess feelings or emotional states, sometimes despite evidence of self-mutilation in the past'. Dentist surgery suffered from 'a faulty chair and unreliable unhygenic aspirator . . . only two amalgam carriers (there should be three), no X-ray apron . . . no ultra-sonic instrument cleaner, no liquid soap dispenser and no yellow bin liners for clinical waste'. After HMCIP published their report HM Prison Service promised 'comprehensive improvements in health care'.

GYMNASIUM & SPORTS Six staff in PE dept. Classes: fitness training, free weights, soccer squad, beginners weights, remedials, recreational basketball, four NVQ (sport & rec) sessions/week, and indoor soccer. Classes also for those in segregation unit and VPU. Programme: 0830–1000, 1000–1130, 1330–1500 and 1500–1615. PE is compulsory at Castington.

CHAPLAINCY Full time CE chaplain, part time RC, Methodist, Salvation Army, Muslim Imam. Communion Tues & Thurs. RC Mass Saturday, Ecumenical service Sunday. All welcome.

FOOD 'The kitchen had many defects and did not meet fully the current hygiene regulations'. A new kitchen is in the process of being built. Staff: 1×SO(Caterer), 4×Officer(Caterers) and work party of 14. Limited variety reported by prisoners, poor quality though there are reports of recent improvements. Three choices available at dinner six days a week and a three-week menu cycle in operation.

ESTABLISHMENT REPORTS
Castington has a solid reputation for containing YO's with histories of violent offences said HMCIP in a Report published 22 March 1994. However,

inmates were locked up on Wednesdays & weekends from tea-time until the following morning, offending behaviour programmes left much to be desired and there was a shortage of work training opportunities, although, overall, there was much more to admire than criticise'.

GOVERNOR'S COMMENTS In the year ahead the Governor of Castington seeks to build on the standards recognised by HMCIP, with the aim of achieving regime delivery coupled with financial prudence. Responding to HMCIP's report Castington's Governor, Chris Harder, said he was pleased the positive work done by staff at all levels had been recognised in the report, Castington has a difficult role to perform in developing a balance between security and progressive rehabilitation.

PRISONERS' COMMENTS
Requests/complaints now being dealt with quickly and efficiently, most staff are helpful. The accommodation requires decorating. Education highly praised with new courses being regularly offered by 'an extremely capable and dedicated staff'. Wages average about £6 with many opportunities for different jobs. The medical officer is occasionally unsympathetic: 'although this could be expected given the number of faked injuries to avoid compulsory PE'. Adjudication awards are 'on the heavy side', gymnasium and sports facilities are very good and (even) those who are not religiously active speak well of the chaplaincy team. The mail is opened outwith the sight of the prisoner and this is very much resented. Purchase of phonecards is restricted to £4 per week; all calls are recorded.

HM Prison Channings Wood

Denbury, Newton Abbott, Devon. TW12 6DW
Tel: 0803-812361 **Fax:** 0803-813175
Opened: 1972 **CNA:** 482(Main), 112(VPU) **Average Roll:** 486, 108 **Category:** C. Male

i **BACKGROUND** Channings Wood prison is situated deep in Devonshire countryside, about four miles from the town of Newton Abbot north east of Plymouth. The site passed to the prison authorities in 1970 and the first prisoners were received about two years later. The original hutted design has been replaced in the years since with newer buildings and the population has increased. Channings Wood is now a modern, purpose-built training prison for category C inmates serving short, medium and long term determinate sentences. The prison also holds a large number of lifers, and vulnerable prisoners allocated by Prison Service HQ, and operates the Core Sex Offender Treatment Programme. The Governor of Channings Wood, Mr Brandon, supplied up-to-date information about the establishment, though the prison's BoV declined our request for a copy of their annual report. HMCIP published their latest inspection report on Channings Wood in July 1993.

OFFICIALS
AREA MGR: John May
CHAIR BOV: Alison Murray
GOVERNOR: R. Brandon
MEDICAL: Dr J. Seale
CHAPLAIN: Rev I. Halliwell
PROBATION: G. Addison
EDUCATION: C. Brimcombe
LOCAL MP: Patrick Nicholls. Con
STAFFING: 9 Governor grades, 6 Principal Officers, 20 Senior Officers and 83 Officers, including specialist staff.

REGIME *week days*: 0745 unlock/breakfast. 0830 activities/work. 1130 lunch. 1215–1315 lock up. 1315 activities/work. 1630 tea. 1715–1755 lock up. 1755 association, 2100 lock up.

week ends: 0745 unlock/breakfast. 0830 activities/association. 11.30 lunch. 1215 lock up. 1315 activities/association. 1600 tea. 1645 lock up. No evening association.

Out of cell: 11.25/24hrs weekdays and 7.25/24hrs at weekends.

ACCOMMODATION & FACILITIES One (VPU) and four (Main) living units each housing 112 inmates in single cells with integral sanitation, sink, hot and cold water, light switch and integral light. Each living unit is self contained with optional dine in/out, two card phones, 2 TV rooms, 1 video room, games room, shower and bath facilities. 1 Cat D Unit housing 34, in single cubicles with own door key, access to night sanitation, communal washing and showering facilities, 1 TV room with satellite and video. Good in-possession list. Personal Officer scheme, drug counselling and Bail Information Scheme in operation. A card phone is available in each of the five living units, two cards allowed each week. Mail opened and checked outwith presence of the inmate, and given out at mid-day. All calls recorded.

CANTEEN Situated next to the Education department, the canteen supplies both the Main and VPU. Despite a large population there are only about 100 lines of stock. Local purchase facility for restricted items and only one visit per week allowed. Staffed by two Prison Officers who HMCIP said should be replaced by Prison Auxiliaries.

VISITS *How to get there*: Train to Newton Abbott, bus 189 from station to Denbury; alight half mile from Denbury. On Sun taxi from station—fare roughly £7. Special Transport: Coach from Cardiff, bookings: 0222-232999.
VISITING TIMES: Week Days: 1330–1530. Saturday: 1330–1530. Sunday: 0900–1115 & 1330–1530. VPU: 1330–1530 Tue, Wed, Sat, Sun.

NOTES No staffed Visitors Centre. Canteen in visiting room and creche available. Plenty of B&B's in the area. Picnic area. New long-term VPU with entrance and own car-park at rear of prison.

EDUCATION Education open 48 weeks of the year, seven full time teachers and evening classes three nights a week. Day classes: basic education; creative arts; maths; computers; cookery; biology; sign-writing; French; toymaking; English lit/ drama; Spanish; pottery; personal development; woodcraft; yoga; first aid; business studies. Evening classes (Main): VTC Catering, Ind. Cleaning. CIT Building Ops. Computers; French; Guitar; Art; Woodcraft; Cookery; Horticulture. VPU: yoga; cookery; computers; music appreciation; art; relationships; guitar; horticulture.

WORKSHOPS (VPU): Wood Machine Shop (cell furniture/speaker cabinets); Laundry; Education; Gardens and Cleaners. (Main):Tailors (Donkey jackets); Wood Assembly (cell furniture, speaker cabinets); Repair Charity Shop (tailors repairs, charity items); Gardens; Kitchen; Cleaners. CIT: Building Ops; Painting & Decorating. VTC: Catering; Industrial Cleaning; Horticulture; Computers. Labour Allocation Unit allocates labour from induction course. Minimum 3 months in workshops. Average employed wage: £6.86, top end: £9.60, lower level £5.50 .

MEDICAL Two local doctors cover part-time Medical Officer Mon–Fri. Dental Surgery (3 sess/wk); Optician (1 sess/mth). No visiting psychiatrist despite recommendations over a number of years by HMCIP that this service should be provided at Channings Wood. Hospital staffed by 1×PHCO; 1×SHCO; 2×HCO and a Nurse. Inmates report sick to the hospital at 0800 hrs.

GYMNASIUM & SPORTS Staffing: 1×PEPO, 2×PESO, 3×PEO. One hour classes start 0830 and end at 1700. Mon–Thurs inc, four one-hour PE Evening classes 1705–1805, 1805–1905 evening activity based programmes. Usual sports catered for with outdoor persuits in Map Reading & Navigation, courses taken day walking on Dartmoor every Wed 0830–1600. Six five-day courses including 3-day back packing expeditions.

CHAPLAINCY Staffing comprises full and part-time CE chaplains, p/t RC, Methodist. Other denominations covered by visiting ministers. Services (Main): Sunday am Holy Communion; Thursday evening RC service; Saturday am Pentecostal; Friday p.m. Muslim. Mon & Tues evening Fellowship meetings; Wednesday Bible Study. Services (VPU): Sunday am Ecumenical service (Unit); Tuesday evening, Ecumenical service (Chapel).

VULNERABLE PERSONS UNIT Of the same design as other living units, the VPU has a CNA of 112 and is a national resource. Wholly separate from the rest of the prison, surrounded by its own security fence and providing its own visiting room and entrance at the rear of the prison, all cells have integral sanitation and full employment for its inmates. Operates the Sexual Offender Programme.

FOOD Staffing: 1×PO, 3×Officer (caterers), and a work party of 16 inmates. Kitchen is a self-contained building at one end of the prison. Food is collected by inmates in heated trolleys and then transferred to hotplates in each living unit. Multi-choice menu on a two-week cycle, which HMCIP argued should be increased to a four- six-week cycle. Food was found to be 'perfectly acceptable'. There was a food complaints book in each unit but HMCIP reported that the PO(Caterer) never read its contents.

ESTABLISHMENT REPORTS In a report (published 14th July 1993) of an inspection in February 1993, Judge Stephen Tumim, HMCIP, said that at the time of the inspection there had been very little progress on the recommendations made at the full inspection in 1990: the fifth living unit was built with a flat roof contrary to experience; no psychiatric services were available; there had been little improvement in the time lifers waited for answers following parole assessment; the proposed extention to the VPU had not been proceeded with; and inmates in the VPU continued to be too closely controlled and a more serious approach to sentence planning was required. Channings Wood, however, had many positive features and was a properly managed establishment in which inmates were treated with humanity. An exciting (and unique?) scheme had been introduced to financially reward inmates who had successfully prepared themselves and achieved employment on release. Noticeably less tension in the prison than in other similar establishments, though training opportunities were not being co-ordinated effectively and departments lacked a common sense of purpose.

GOVERNOR'S COMMENTS Plans for 1995 include increasing regime delivery to provide 12 hours per day out of cell, introduction of more realistic meal-times and provision of multi-choice menu, and to 'maintain facilities in the face of dwindling resources'.

PRISONERS' COMMENTS **VPU:** Requests and complaints are dealt with speedily and staff are helpful. Canteen stock reported as good though with high prices, visits should improve when new visiting room is opened and education is excellent 'but only if you are willing to push yourself'. Working conditions are good though wages are restricted. Medical facilities are good 'in all aspects', adjudications fair and punishments even-handed. Food is 'very poor all round'. Gymnasium is 'very good with reasonable access'. Mail is censored 'rigorously' and given out at lunchtime.

MAIN: Request/complaints are dealt with 'reasonably quickly', accommodation is 'excellent', canteen has a good stock and local purchase facility. Visits room is large, clean and with space for children. Work conditions are good but poor wages, excellent medical facilities, 'atrocious' food. Excellent gym facilities, good religious services and good mail procedures and card phone access.

HM Prison Chelmsford

Springfield Road, Chelmsford, Essex. CM2 6LQ
Tel: 0245-268651 **Fax:** 0245-493041
Opened: 1828 **CNA:** 244 **Average Roll:** 334 **Category:** Local Male

i **BACKGROUND** Chelmsford prison was built in 1828 as the gaol for the County of Essex. It was taken over by the Prison Commissioners in 1877 and during the First World War it served as a military prison, closing in 1918. In 1931 the prison reopened to house male young offenders and during the following years was used as a local prison, a Borstal Recall Centre, a Corrective Training Centre and as a Central Prison for Preventive Detention prisoners. From 1963 it was used as a prison for adult males but was closed following a serious disturbance and fire in 1978. In 1980 Chelmsford reopened as a young offenders prison, and in 1988 it acquired its current function as a local prison for adult males. Neither the Governor nor the BoV at Chelmsford replied to our requests for information about the prison and HMCIP published their latest inspection report in February 1994.

OFFICIALS
AREA MGR: Tom Murtagh
CHAIR BOV:
GOVERNOR: Ray Reveley
MEDICAL:
CHAPLAIN: Rev Hayward
PROBATION: G. Chittenden
EDUCATION:
LOCAL MP: Simon Burns. Con
STAFFING: 6 Governor grades, 13 Principal Officers, 33 Senior Officers and 170 Officers, 7 Prison Auxiliaries, 6 Casual Prison Auxiliaries and 7 Night Patrols.

REGIME *week days*: 0800 unlock/breakfast. 0900 work, PE, education. 0930 visits. 1000 adjudications. 1145 lunch, lock up. 1400 work. 1615 cease labour. 1640 tea, lock up. 1800–2030 association by rota. 1945 lock up.

week ends: 0800 unlock. 0845 breakfast. 0900 association, church services (Sunday), canteen, cleaning, exercise. 1115 lunch. 1300 unlock, association by rota. 1545 tea, lock up. No weekend evening association. 1945 supper.

Out of cell: 5/24hrs weekdays and 3/24hrs at weekends.

ACCOMMODATION & FACILITIES Four main cell blocks (A,B,C,D). A.wing: segregation unit with CNA of 48, mainly used to hold vulnerable inmates. B.wing: 112 convicted places, dirty recesses and poor cell furniture with many two–ups. Out of cell 2 hours am and pm, lack of evening association. C.wing: 112 remand inmates, no work, association 0930–1130, 1400–1600 including exercise. No evening association. Poor cleaning standards and many cells with integral sanitation. D.wing: D1/D2 employed convicted inmates. D3/D4 Health Care Centre. Daytime and evening association Mon–Thurs.

CANTEEN Remands Tue/Fri. Convicted Wed. Earnings plus £5 private cash per week and

£10 for phonecards. Reasonable level of stock, clearly displayed prices and local purchase facility. Profit margin of 15% criticised by HMCIP as too high.

VISITS *How to get there*: Trains from Liverpool Street every half hour, then 20 min walk to prison. Eastern National buses from bus station: 53,55,56,91 & 92. Bus station in Duke Street, opposite BR station.
VISITING TIMES: Week Days: 1345–1545. Rem: Mon, Tues, Wed, Fri. Con: Thur. Saturday: 0930–1100 & 1345–1545 Rem only. Sunday: 1345–1545 Con only.

NOTES No Visitors Centre as yet, but Portakabin near gate with information. Canteen available Thursday and Sunday only. Visiting Orders required for all except Remand prisoners. No overnight stay but plenty of B&B locally.

EDUCATION Contracted out educational service provided by Community Education, contracted to deliver education for 48 weeks of the year, with 112 teaching hours from September 1993. No evening provision and a lack of skills training courses produce a poor rating for Chelmsford's education.

WORKSHOPS Laundry (12 places), domestic cleaners (38), gardens (4), kitchen (16) and works (8). No VTC or CIT Courses. Average wage £6.50.

MEDICAL Senior Medical Officer, assisted by local GP's, 1×HCPO, 2×HCSO, 8×HCO, 4×Nurses. HMCIP, who criticised the medical facilities at Chelmsford in his 1990 full inspection report, found refurbishment was under way and integral sanitation was being fitted. Dental waiting list very long and lack of facilities for visiting specialists.

GYMNASIUM & SPORTS 1×PEPO 1×PESO and 3×PEO. Small gymnasium comprising an indoor games area, adjoining weight training area and an outdoor sports field (Compound). Varied daytime programme—praised by inmates.

CHAPLAINCY Part time CE chaplain, RC and Methodist ministers. Small chapel prevents outside groups being invited but good attendances reported by inmates. Problems reported in vulnerable inmates being allowed to attend worship. Eight prison visitors available.

FOOD Staffing: 2×SO, 4×Officer (caterers) and an inmate work party of 16. Complaints by inmates that the food is repetitive and inconsistent in quality, meal times were too close together. No pre-select menu system. New kitchen opened 1992.

ESTABLISHMENT REPORTS In a report (published 1st February 1994) of an inspection in September 1993, HMCIP, said that the outstanding feature of Chelmsford was the quality of the relationships between inmates and staff which generated a relaxed atmosphere. Morale among staff appeared to be good and inmates seemed content to serve their sentences at Chelmsford. The regime for inmates on C.wing was to be developed with anger management and life skills groups. It remained a concern that there was a shortage of constructive activity, with consequences both for inmates while serving their sentences and society at large when they were released. There was little work experience and no work training opportunities. The education programme was not operating at the time of the inspection. The prison came to a halt at 1630 and no progress had been made since the last inspection in introducing PE and structured association in the evenings. Concern was also expressed about the shortage of space for visits. Work and training opportunities must be provided if Chelmsford is to provide anything more than a warehousing function.

PRISONERS' COMMENTS Adult inmates resented sharing with young prisoners who, because of a lack of activities, were generally disruptive. Card phones on each landing, though they can only be used during association in the mornings and evenings which was often inconvenient for speaking to relatives. No educational evening classes and cell hobbies were not encouraged. Lack of space for children to play in the visiting room with inadequate waiting facilities for visitors. Service from the prison shop was poor and convicted inmates can only visit once per week. Lighters were not allowed—though you can buy as many boxes of matches as you wish! Physical education was good, though there was too little time out of cell and not enough to occupy prisoners on association. Lack of cleaning and disinfectant liquids, some recesses lack toilet seats. Only trainers allowed in possession—no other civilian clothing. Prison issue of two vests, sock and underpants per week inadequate.

HM Prison Coldingley

Shaftesbury Rd, Bisley, Surrey. GU24 9EX
Tel: 0483-476721 **Fax:** 0483-488586
Opened: 1969 **CNA:** 222 **Average Roll:** 200 **Category:** C. Male

i **BACKGROUND** Coldingley is a purpose-built training prison on the site of a former Shaftesbury Home For Boys, situated seven miles south of Woking and nine miles west of Guildford in Surrey. The prison opened in 1969 as the country's first industrial prison, with the aim of providing a regime built around a 40 hour working week, though it has not lived up to expectations as a result of insufficient investment in new plant and the lack of realistic wages. HMCIP comment in their latest report that the hallmark of a sound regime, namely a range of purposeful activities and the involvement of staff with prisoners, is missing at Coldingley. In April 1993 the prison changed from a category B to category C trainer. Neither the Governor nor BoV replied to our requests for information about the prison and HMCIP, who published their latest inspection report on Coldingley in October 1994, commented that the inspection team was left in no doubt 'there were serious problems concerning the management of the prison'.

OFFICIALS
AREA MGR: A. de Frisching
CHAIR BOV:
GOVERNOR: T.A. Ward
MEDICAL:
CHAPLAIN: Rev Clarkson
PROBATION: John White
EDUCATION:
LOCAL MP: Michael Grylls. Con
STAFFING: 121 in unified grades.

REGIME *week days*: 0730 unlock. 0800 breakfast. 0825 work. 1200 dinner. 1300 work. 1730 tea. 1830 exercise. 1900–2100 association.
week ends: 0745 unlock. 0830 breakfast. 0900 association. 1200 dinner, visits, association. 1600 tea. 1630–2100 association.
Out of cell: 13.5/24hrs weekdays and 13.25/24hrs at weekends.

ACCOMMODATION & FACILITIES Four wings (A,B,C,D) each with 72 single cells, access to night sanitation via electronic unlocking. Ground floor contains offices and showers, with recesses on each landing. Cells have been fitted with power points but no TVs are allowed. Special Security Unit part of the segregation unit can hold three Cat As. Cage birds allowed. Card phones on all wings. Poor canteen facilities criticised by HMCiP. Personal officer scheme not working, no drug counselling or anti-addiction courses.

REQUESTS & COMPLAINTS Average of 35 per month being submitted, mainly for compensation regarding property lost in transit and complaints regarding home leave decisions. Time targets were being met both locally and at Area Manager level, though the system whereby the co-ordinating Governor allocated request/complaint forms to members of staff for them to answer was criticised by HMCIP, who said this should the task of the co-ordinating Governor.

CANTEEN Located in the education corridor, the canteen has very cramped conditions and a small range of stock. A pre-order system operates with orders being placed the previous week. Inmates complained prices were too high, but HMCIP found prices were fixed in accordance with Prison Service instructions and had a profit margin of 10%.

VISITS *How to get there*: Bus from Woking station every 30mins to Hen & Chickens pub, then half mile walk to prison down Shaftesbury Rd. Special transport: HALOW (London) bus service: 0171-793-7484.
VISITING TIMES: Week Days: 1400–1600 Tue & Thurs only. Saturday: 1000–1200 & 1400–1600. Sunday: 1000–1200 & 1400–1600.

NOTES No staffed Visitors Centre, canteen available in visiting room at weekends along with creche. Contact prison probation (extn 305) for details of local guesthouses. Wheelchair access but no disabled toilets. Large visitors car park.

EDUCATION Contracted out to Amersham and Wickham College. Open 46 weeks of the year, five days and three evenings per week. Three specialist classrooms for pottery, information technology and woodwork, and two general classrooms. Small library open weekdays but not weekends, no trained librarian and wages for inmates on education have dropped over the last four years.

WORKSHOPS No VTC/CIT courses. Three contract services industrial workshops employing 70 inmates each, laundry, machine shop and sign shop. Despite a work profile which claimed full employment, the reality is different—25% of the population had either not been assigned work or are regarded as unemployable. HMCIP said that in theory inmates in the contract services workshop (where the work is 'repetitive and boring') can earn up to £50 per week, but statistics show the average pay is just £6.49 per week.

DISCIPLINE Segregation Unit with six single cells and two strip cells located close to A.wing. About 750 adjudications in 1993, properly conducted and normally for minor breaches of the rules which are punished usually by stoppage of earnings. HMCIP found two documented examples where inmates had been segregated under Rule 43(GOAD) for six and four days respectively, where the BoV had not given authorisation.

MEDICAL Part time Medical Officer, 1×HCSO, 1×HCO. Morning surgery held at 0845 in the doctor's office, no appointment system in operation. Inmates report sick to landing officers at unlock and are called by tannoy when required. Between six and seven per cent of the population report sick each day, which is comparatively high. Medical Officer feels many complaints are an excuse to avoid work and this suspicion appeared to effect prescribing practice said HMCIP. The HCO remains in the room during examination, preventing a confidential interview with the doctor. Dental surgery lacks proper equipment. Dentist attends two sessions per week: in 1993 he saw 480 inmates and received £26,000—an average of £54 per inmate. Optician attends as required, normally once every two months. No drug anti-addiction programme, no generalised education on health matters, no multi-disciplinary HIV/AIDS team and no Listeners Scheme.

GYMNASIUM & SPORTS 1×PESO and 1×PEO. Very poor PE programme and wholly inadequate gymnasium, the size of a badminton court with a stage area for weights at one end. Small outside football pitch and a sloping tarmac area. Governor recently stopped daytime PE other than on Thursday and Friday afternoons. For a C category prison, Coldingley probably has the worst PE provision in the country.

CHAPLAINCY Part time CE chaplain who works four days of the week at Send and three at Coldingley, RC and Methodist ministers. Pool of four Prison Visitors. Good chapel and multi-faith room, with range of groups during the week. Main services Sunday. Imam visits weekly.

FOOD Staffing: 2×SO, 2×Officer (caterers), and an inmate work party of 11. Standard of meals good, three choices available for dinner, though no choice at tea. Choice of taking meals in cell or association. Breakfast 0800, Dinner 1230, Tea 1730. No menu cycle and no pre-select menu system. Initiatives are not encouraged.

ESTABLISHMENT REPORTS Coldingly is a prison in a muddle. It is not (and never has been) the industrial prison envisaged when the establishment was opened in 1969 said HMCIP in a report (published 20th October 1994) of an inspection in December 1993. The concept failed partly because it was not followed through with sufficient investment in new plant and equipment to keep pace with modern developments, and partly because there was insufficient motivation for inmates to work a forty hour week. It has been difficult to manage the industrial concept, given the unwillingness of the Prison Service to invest in suitable machinery and to offer more realistic wages to prisoners: staff are confused and lacking a clear sense of purpose. Inmates enjoy a good standard of accommodation in units of a manageable size, with access to night sanitation and electric power sockets. There is a relative absence of violence and prisoners appeared to feel reasonably safe. The conditions of the buildings are generally good and physical security was of a higher standard than found in many C Category prisons. Meals are served at sensible times with the opportunity for dining in association. The hallmark of a sound regime, however, namely a range of purposeful activities and the involvement of staff with prisoners, was missing. The kitchen, visiting facilities, canteen, reception and library all require investment to bring them up to a satisfactory standard. Sentence planning and personal officer work are underdeveloped. The needs of lifers and other long term prisoners were given insufficient attention, there was very little community work, or preparation for release. There were some positive features however, prisoners were unlocked for 13.5 hours per day and there were few complaints about food, but the Prison Service should make more effective use of Coldingley: it should be either a specialised industrial prison or a training prison which makes appropriate use of its robust cellular accommodation and good physical security. Whichever role is chosen, clear guiding principles should be established for staff. Investment to improve training opportunities will be necessary whichever option is chosen.

Director General, Derek Lewis, said in response to the report: 'Along with Full Sutton and its fashion clothing production, Channings Wood with its speaker cabinet production, Leyhill and Lindholme with their vegetable preparation schemes and many others, Coldingley has significant potential for the future. Judge Tumim's recommendation that Coldingley should be either an industrial prison or a training prison is therefore particularly pertinent'.

PRISONERS' COMMENTS Work is badly paid and there is little incentive to work. The idea that Coldingley is an industrial prison with work training opportunities is a myth which has become a cause of resentment. For a category C prison there is far too much security and though we have in-cell power points the governor says he has no authority to allow TVs—despite the fact that the Governors of Manchester, Winchester and Garth seem to have authority to allow them. The gymnasium is far too small and in some cases the amount of people using it creates a safety hazard, the Governor has stopped it being used for the vast majority of the week. There are no fire escapes from the landings and weekend activities are limited. The education staff provide an excellent service on limited resources. There is no pre-release scheme in operation, the personal officer and sentence planning systems are little more than a joke in reality, and there is no such thing at Coldingley as community work. Visiting time starts from the time when a visitor gets into the visits room—but only then do staff go and get the inmate, so the visiting time is running while staff are wandering around the prison. The Governor is not keen to embrace inmate views.

HM Prison Cookham Wood

Rochester, Kent. ME1 3LU
Tel: 0634-814981 **Fax:** 0634-82892
Opened: 1977 **CNA:** 120 **Average Roll:** 112 **Category:** Closed Female

i **BACKGROUND** Cookham Wood is a closed training prison for women over 21, situated some two miles south of Rochester in Kent. The establishment was planned and part-built as a remand centre for male young offenders, being erected on land adjacent to the then Rochester Borstal, now an adult male prison. Work started in 1972 but due to the shortage of suitable labour the first phase was not completed until late 1977. By that time the pressure of female prisoners within the penal system was such that the Prison Department decided in December 1977 to change Cookham Wood's role to that of a closed female prison. A further 60 places, making 120 in all, were completed towards the end of 1980. Cookham Wood has a reputation for being a tightly controlled establishment in which the women are given little freedom, a lack of responsibility and a poor regime. Neither the Governor nor the BoV at Cookham Wood replied to our requests for information, and HMCIP published their latest inspection report on the prison in March 1993.

OFFICIALS
AREA MGR: John Hunter
CHAIR BOV:
GOVERNOR: C. Ellis
MEDICAL:
CHAPLAIN: Rev King
PROBATION: John Sussex
EDUCATION:
LOCAL MP: Pegger Fenner. Con
STAFFING: 5 Governor grades, 2 Principal Officers, 6 Senior Officers and 39 Officers, including specialist staff.

REGIME *week days*: 0750 unlock. 0800 breakfast. 0830 exercise, association. 0900 Governors apps. 0930 work. 1125 cease labour. 1130 dinner. 1215 lock up. 1330 unlock, work. 1345 visits. 1545 visits cease. 1600 cease labour. 1605 tea. 1645 lock up. 1730–2000 association.

week ends: 0810 unlock. 0815 breakfast. 0900 work (pre–detailed) 0915 CE Service (Sun). 1000 Governors apps, stores & sheet change, association (all Sat only). 1015 RC Mass (Sun). 1030 exercise, adjudications (Sat). 1130 dinner. 1215 lock up. 1330 unlock, association (one wing Sat, other wing Sun). 1345 visits. 1545 visits cease. 1600 tea. 1645 lock up. No weekend evening association.

Out of cell: 7.5/24hrs weekdays and 5/24hrs at weekends.

ACCOMMODATION & FACILITIES Two main living units, North and South Wings. Each has three landings of 20 cells located each side of a narrow central corridor, making 120 cells in all. Low ceilings make for a claustrophobic feelings. All cells have integral sanitation. Both wings have large TV rooms and North Wing has facilities for both table-tennis and pool. Lifers have exclusive use of a small TV room. A well equipped hairdressing salon is available for all inmates. No facilities to buy and cook food. Bathing facilities are sufficient in both wings. No Personal Officer or sentence planning scheme—other than for lifers—and the once flourishing SWIP scheme has been abandoned.

CANTEEN Following a directive from Prison Service HQ, the canteen has been forced to charge retail prices and is now producing a profit of 10%. Very good service given to the women, daily access between 0900–0930 and, on Thursdays (pay day) the canteen was open from 12 noon until early evening. Large stock of over 200 lines and every effort made to cater for the large ethnic minority population. Local purchase facility, though limited to two items.

VISITS *How to get there*: Train from Victoria to Chatham, then bus (162,164,166) but check at station. No Special Transport. VISITING TIMES: Week Days: 0930–1100 Wed. 1400–1545 Mon–Fri. Saturday: 1345–1545 (60+ min visits w/e). Sunday: 1345–1545.

NOTES No staffed Visitors Centre. Canteen available at weekends and Wednesdays. Childrens Play Area and nappy-changing facility available in waiting area. For overnight stays contact prison probation. Ex-prisoners not permitted to visit for first 3 months.

EDUCATION Full time Education Officer, 1×Lecturer and 20 p/t teachers. Despite an enthusiastic education staff, places for 28 on FTE and some 30 more on distance learning, educational provision is very poor in Cookham Wood. F/t courses in business studies, art and craft skills, English as a second language, and adult basic education. No evening classes and no education on two afternoons per week as a result of funding cuts.

WORKSHOPS New receptions spend their first two weeks as wing cleaners and then are seen by the Labour Board which meets each Thursday. Main employment is the textile shop engaged in the production of kitchen whites for the Prison Service. EMC of 32 and open for only 22 hours per week. Kitchen, works, gardens, and orderly duties.

MEDICAL Part time (male) Medical Officer contracted for 15.75 hrs/wk, 3×HCO. HMCIP recommended, following complaints from inmates, that a female GP should be provided 'if reasonably possible'. No Well-Woman Clinic. Regular Gynaecological Clinics, weekly dental sessions and optical services as necessary. Five-bed cellular unit, including one strip cell which was being used (contrary to CI 3/87) without overnight staffing.

GYMNASIUM & SPORTS 2×PEO. Good gymnasium facilities open each morning during exercise time. Comprehensive programme praised by HMCIP which has encouraged many who had given up exercise to take part. Swimming and hiking (with security clearance) outside the establishment, and a group of people with disabilities use the gymnasium each Thursday. Wide variety of keep fit schedules and sports.

CHAPLAINCY Part time CE chaplain, RC and Methodist ministers. CE and RC services held each Sunday morning. Two evening groups held on a Tuesday—a fellowship meeting and a prayer meeting. Small chapel but well decorated and very clean.

FOOD Staffing: 1×SO, 1×Officer (caterer) and an inmate work party of 12. Full and varied menu with choices for dinner and tea. Dining room next to the kitchen is used by one of the two wings each weekend—the other dining in cell. No cooking facilities on the wings. Food reasonable but the menu is too predictable.

ESTABLISHMENT REPORTS In a report (published 25th July 1993) of an inspection in July 1992, HMCIP, said that Cookham Wood was almost entirely a containing prison with very few of the elements necessary for delivering an acceptable regime as described in the Prison Service document *Regimes form Women*: 'It must not continue this way'. While first impressions are of well-kept grounds and flower beds, the impression was deceptive. There was little encouragement for the women to be responsible for themselves, instead they felt they were being treated like children. They were not being treated as individuals said HMCIP, their needs were not being addressed and there was little preparation for release—and far too much time spent locked in a cell. Cookham Wood has it within itself to change this, Judge Tumim said. Many of the younger staff want to be involved and more should be asked of them. If staff were to use more flexibility then much more could be achieved at Cookham Wood within existing resources. Lack of pre-release and evening classes, unsatisfactory access to the library, poor gymnasium access due to staff shortages, lack of cooking facilities in the wings, no formal induction programme in operation and appalling time out of cell were other areas the Chief Inspector criticised—and had done so in his previous inspection report without any subsequent progress: and often a deterioration.

PRISONERS' COMMENTS Far too much time is spent locked in our cells, particularly at weekends when the day has finished at half past four. The food is reasonable but the menu is too predictable. Probation department slow to respond to inmates, and eating in cell results in food that is cold by the time you have got it back there. There is no mixing between wings and friends can only be seen by application. Wages are very poor, staff treat us like children and supervision on visits is oppressive. Women who complain feel they are subjected to emotional bullying by staff.

HM Prison Dartmoor

Princetown, Yelverton, Devon. PL20 6RR
Tel: 0822-89261 **Fax:** 0822-89679
Opened: 1809 CNA: 619 **Roll:** 561 **Category:** B.Trainer

i **BACKGROUND** By the year 1805 the many French prisoners captured during the Napoleonic war were becoming difficult to accommodate in the hulks at Plymouth. In November 1805 prisoners were marched 16 miles from Plymouth to start building Dartmoor prison, completing the task in February 1809. Three months later the first prisoners walked through the gates and, within four weeks, Dartmoor contained 5,000 prisoners. The prison was closed in 1812 and reopened in 1850: it has remained in use ever since. In 1979 Lord Justice May called for Dartmoor's closure saying it was 'nowadays simply against nature', and Lord Justice Woolf in 1990 adjudged the prison should either undergo radical changes quickly or be closed—a statement reiterated in 1992 by HMCIP. The Governor did not reply to a request for up-to-date information and the BoV, who did reply, declined to provide a copy of their annual report. Dartmoor also operates as an Assessment Centre for the Sex Offender Treatment Programme.

OFFICIALS

AREA MGR: John May
CHAIR BOV: G. Evatt
GOVERNOR: J. Lawrence
MEDICAL:
CHAPLAIN: Rev Bird
PROBATION: P. Lockett
EDUCATION: S. McCaffrey
LOCAL MP: Emma Nicholson. Con
STAFFING: 11 Governor grades, 7 Principal Officers, 24 Senior Officers, 148 Officers, 6 Night Patrols, 12 Prison Auxiliaries and 5 casual Prison Auxiliaries.

☞ **REGIME** *week days*: 0800 unlock. 0815 breakfast. 0915 exercise. 0930 labour, visits. 1130 cease labour, dinner. 1200 lock up. 1300 unlock/slop out. 1315 labour. 1400 visits. 1545 tea. 1630 lock up. 1745 unlock, association (except Friday). 1800 evening classes. 2000 lock up.

week ends: 0800 unlock. 0815 breakfast. 0845 RC service (Sunday). 0930 exercise/gym, visits. 1000 CE service (Sunday). 1130 dinner. 1200 lock up. 1300 unlock. 1330 association, visits. 1545 tea. 1615 lock up. No evening association.

Out of cell: HMCIP found that hours out of cell were not recorded at Dartmoor contrary to regime monitoring procedures. Figures of 21.7 hours of purposeful activity per week/prisoner (20.12 for VPU) was 'reasonably satisfactory' if accurate.

ACCOMMODATION & FACILITIES Seven living units (A,B,C,D,F,G,Pheonix wings). G.Wing=VPU, Pheonix Wing =Induction Unit. All single cells. Plans for integral sanitation well underway. Central bath-house 'was in a deplorable state' and was shut following the inspection. Work in hand to install showers on the wings. Comprehensive i/p list, and redecoration of cells by inmates allowed. Recreational facilities: TV, darts, pool table and table tennis. Personal officer scheme and drug counselling available. Induction wing for first two weeks, culminating in sentence plan—HMCIP reported the induction programme had been suspended due to staff shortages. Censorship had been abolished and the content only was inspected—though not in the presence of the prisoner to whom it was addressed. Card phones have been installed and access to them is reported as heavy with long queues forming at peak periods—due in part to the isolated location of the prison and the long distance some prisoners are away from their home areas.

CANTEEN Situated in a passageway leading to A.wing, the canteen opens once per week and carries some 200 items of stock. Operated by two prison officers and an auxiliary, HMCIP recommended the prison officers should be given work more suitable to their training. Outside purchases with private cash limited to toiletries. G.wing and Segregation Unit have their goods bagged & delivered.

REQUESTS/COMPLAINTS HMCIP said the statistics showed 'that ample use was made of the Request/Complaint procedures by inmates at Dartmoor'. Time targets were being met with replies, and the contents of those examined by HMCIP were 'full and helpful'. The performance of replies from the Area Manager (ex-Dartmoor Governor John May), however, 'was less good, with delays of two or three months being not uncommon'.

VISITS *How to get there*: Train to Plymouth and then either taxi to prison (17 miles) or bus (83,84,84A) to Yelverton and then taxi to prison (6 miles). Buses run only 2 hourly on Sundays. Special Transport: from Portsmouth,

Tel: 0705–871441 for mini-bus details, HALOW (London) bus service: 0171-793 7484.
VISITING TIMES: Week Days: 0930–1100 & 1400–1545 Tue–Fri only. Saturday: 0930–1100 & 1400–1500 (1 VO covers both). Sunday: 0930–1100 & 1400–1500 (1 VO covers both).

NOTES Staffed Visitors (Wesley House) Centre. Canteen and Childrens Play Area in visits. Three local pubs offer good B&B. Outside waiting area with toilet and baby changing facilities. Two reserved parking places on forecourt for disabled. Inform prison if wheelchair access required. No disabled toilets at present. No visits on Monday.

EDUCATION Education accommodation is spread around the prison. Open for 48 weeks of the year, with 38 weeks of evening classes. Daytime programme for 90 minutes in the morning and three hours in the afternoon. Evening classes operate for 90 minutes. Seven f/t lecturers, three VTC instructors and a panel of 15 p/t teachers. Business studies, computers, English, maths, OU, open learning, craft centre. VTC welding (16wks); Sheet metal fabrication (16wks) and micro-electronics (16wks). Cell study available. Education officer ex-prison officer and VTC instructor. 'A lively department keen to take a full part in offering good quality education to as many prisoners as possible'.

WORKSHOPS Labour Board meets every Tuesday and allocates work and party changes. Three CIT courses: Plastering; Painting & Decorating; Building Operatives. Carpenters (speakers). Textile shop (VPU). Average wage £7. Farm party look after livestock (144 dairy cows, 460 ewes, 780 lambs, 150 sucker cows & calves, and a small herd of Highland cattle). Farm making a loss, 'not surprising' said HMCIP 'given its dependence on beef and sheep'.

DISCIPLINE Average of five adjudications per day, 'high but not excessive' said HMCIP. Punishments were 'realistic and reasonable' and both the body belt and strip cell have declined from their previous high use. Segregation unit has a chequered reputation, there have been improvements, but they were 'fragile and capable of being easily reversed'.

MEDICAL SMO supported by three GP's from Tavistock. GPs cover daily surgeries, night calls and weekends. SMO covers Seg Unit, saw receptions and prepared reports: though 'it would be preferable' said HMCIP, 'if these reports were completed by a psychiatrically qualified practitioner'. 1×HCPO(RGN), 2×HCSO and ten HCO's. X-ray room, dentist (2 sess/wk) and optician & chiropodist (1 sess/mth). Between 2 and 27 inmates reported sick each day, with a further 20–50 reporting special sick throughout the day. Procedures for the dispensing of drugs involved 'bad practice' that increased 'the risk of inmates receiving the wrong medication'. Segregation of HIV positive inmates because staff would not allow them on the Wings was abolished after HMCIP condemned the practice, though 'it was encouraging . . . to find Dartmoor setting the pace in the introduction of [sex offender] treatment programmes'.

GYMNASIUM & SPORTS
'Opportunities for organised recreation and physical education were the worst we have seen in a Category B training prison and akin to those in some of the poorest local prisons' said HMCIP. The gym, a former wing burnt out in the early 1960's, was 'a fundamentally inhospitable place'. Low staffing, 1×PEPO, 1×PESO and 1×PEO resulted in only two evening classes a week and none on weekend afternoons. The staff were keen to make progress but 'felt limited by the prison, which does not promote opportunities for inmates'. Outside facilities 'were even worse', with no grassed area and a Red-gra area that was destroyed by the elements: 'no sooner was red gravel laid than the elements washed and blew it away'.

CHAPLAINCY 'The chapel was one of the few welcoming buildings in the prison' said HMCIP. Well decorated and with a chaplaincy team that was well respected. F/t CE chaplain, p/t RC, Methodist, Church Army, Salvation Army and Quaker. Twenty Muslim inmates held a weekly prayer meeting. Sixteen prison visitors were available through the chaplain.

FOOD A new kitchen was in the process of being built when HMCIP inspected Dartmoor, however existing standards of hygiene were 'very poor'. Food samples were not being collected in accordance with CI 28/86, inmates changing room was 'a shambles', the food barrow was 'filthy' and when food was served it was only 'lukewarm'. Three choices provided at dinner but only for ordinary diets. HMCIP, who tasted the food, thought it 'met basic needs' but was 'not appetising or well presented and we received many complaints from inmates about the general standard'.

ESTABLISHMENT REPORTS Over nearly two centuries Dartmoor has developed as a prison FOR punishment rather than as a place where prisoners serve their time AS punishment said HMCIP in a report (published June 1992) of an inspection in June 1991. No prison has a more melancholy or chequered history, nor is located more remotely from the homes of the prisoners it currently holds. The prison should be divided into smaller units and become a community prison as recommended by Lord Justice Woolf. Dartmoor should no longer be treated as a dustbin to hold prisoners no other institution wants to take. There is a need for profound changes in staff culture and this must be achieved within two years. If a training ethos is not developed within that period, Dartmoor should be closed. HMCIP was adamant: This must be a last chance for Dartmoor.

PRISONERS' COMMENTS Requests and complaints are invariably late, no connected power points and the canteen is poor compared with other establishments. Visits are good—when people can manage to get here—but the work opportunities are a disgrace. Inmates who are disabled spend all day locked in their cells because they can't work. Adjudications haven't changed in the decade since I was last here: they find you guilty no matter what you say. Inmate/staff relationships on the surface are OK, but its very much them and us. Mail is distributed at 1745, opened off-wing. Poor access to phones.

HM YOI Deerbolt

Bowes Rd, Barnard Castle, Co Durham. DL12 9BG
Tel: 0833-37561 **Fax:** 0833-31736
Opened: 1973 CNA: 450 **Roll:** 366 **Category:** Closed YOI

i **BACKGROUND** Located on high ground overlooking the historic town of Barnard Castle in County Durham, the site contained a hutted camp when it was sold to the prison authorities by the Army in 1971. The site opened as a Borstal in 1973 and changed to its current YOI function in 1988. The original army camp has now been replaced with purpose-built accommodation. The Governor of Deerbolt, Mr Ginn, supplied up-to-date information about his institution, though the BoV did not reply to our request for a copy of their latest annual report. HMCIP published its latest inspection report on Deerbolt in March 1992.

OFFICIALS
AREA MGR: Maurice Codd
CHAIR BOV: I. Black
GOVERNOR: W. Ginn
MEDICAL: Dr A. Lewis
CHAPLAIN: Rev Attley
PROBATION: T. Farrier
EDUCATION: C. Helroyd
LOCAL MP: Derek Foster. Lab
STAFFING: 5 Governor grades, 8 Principal Officers, 20 Senior Officers and 90 Officers, excluding specialist staff.

REGIME *week days*: 0800 unlock, breakfast, sick parade. 0830 work. 1115 cease labour. 1130 dinner. 1230 lock up (excl F.Wing who have association). 1330 work. 1615 cease labour. 1630 tea. 1700 lock up—excl F.Wing). 1800–2015 association.

week ends: 0800 unlock, breakfast, sick parade. 0830 cell/wing cleaning work. 1000 association. 1130 dinner. 1200 lock up -2 hrs. 1300 searching. 1400 association. 1630 tea. 1700 lock up—shared cell association max 2 per cell. 1945 supper. 2015 lock up.

Out of cell: 10/24hrs w/days: 6/24hrs w/ends. F.wing=12hrs.

ACCOMMODATION & FACILITIES Seven cells blocks: A,B,C,D,E,F,I Wings. A,B,I Wings: 58 singles cells, one double. C,D Wings: 52 single cells, four double. E,F.Wings 58 single cells, four doubles. Integral sanitation, h/c water and own light switches in all cells—only E&F Wings however have low voltage in-cell power. Due to refurbishment only 23 single and five double cells available in E. wing. Functions: A,B,E,F Wings used as residential YOI. C.wing for inmates who are inadequate or unable to cope. D.Wing for juveniles. I.wing for inductions. Personal Officer scheme, sentence planning, drug counselling. Comprehensive in-possession list. Routine censorship abolished June 1992, all letters opened outwith the presence of the respective addressee to check for enclosures. Card phones in all living units, all calls recorded and limited in duration to ten minutes.

CANTEEN Staffed by two Prison Auxiliaries it provides a good range of stock for purchase from either private cash or earnings. Prices clearly displayed and inmates paid on a credit transfer system. One visit per week.

VISITS *How to get there*: Train to Darlington. Hourly bus (75) to Middleton-in-Teeside, passes the prison—takes about 60 mins. Coaches from Rotherham, Doncaster, Barnsley and Sheffield. Book via home area probation.
VISITING TIMES: Week Days: 1400–1545 M–F. Saturday: 1400–1545. Sunday: 1400–1545.

NOTES No staffed Visitors Centre, canteen and Childrens Play Area in visiting room. Numerous B&B's in the town. Weather conditions can be severe, so warm clothing is required for the long walk from Barnard Castle in the winter.

EDUCATION Dept open 46 weeks of the year and staffed by seven f/t teachers. Wide-ranging curriculum. Full day programme and evening classes three nights of the week: basic education, English, maths, information technology, adult literacy, carpet fitting, horticulture, woodwork, parenthood, computing, catering.

WORKSHOPS All workshops at Deerbolt are for training purposes and result in the relevant VTC/CIT qualification. Bricklaying, Carpentry, Catering, Domestic Heating, Electrical Installation, Floor-laying, Furniture Craft, Industrial Cleaning, Motor Mechanics, Multi-skills, Office Skills, Painting & Decorating, Plastering. Labour allocated on I.wing as part of induction process and after educational assessment. Average pay £5.75, top end £10 and UB40 £2.50.

DISCIPLINE Segregation unit consists of 18 single cells in total. Two strip cells, four dry cells, 12 with integral sanitation, h/c water. Own light switches except specials. Regime affords two hours per day out of cell.

MEDICAL Medical services provided by area practice, located approx 14 miles from establishment. Six doctors visit 2 hours daily Mon–Fri, on-call weekends. Health Care Centre contains six single cells and two 6-bed wards. Staffing: Nurses (grades:1×G,1×E,4×D), 1×HCSO, 3×HCO. Dental surgery held Tuesday and Thursday morning, other visiting specialists as required.

GYMNASIUM & SPORTS 1×PEPO, 1×PESO and 6×PEO. Comprehensive programme catering for all levels and complying with Prison Service's 'Vision and Goals' policy. Classes 0900–1600 each day, evening classes five nights of the week. Gymnastics, football, special needs, induction training, weights, basket ball, trampoline, fitness, BAWLA, volleyball, life-saving, rugby training.

CHAPLAINCY Full time CE chaplain and p/t RC and Methodist ministers. Main church service Sunday morning, RC Mass Friday evening or Saturday morning. Chaplain will contact Imam for Muslims as requested.

FOOD Staffing: 1×SO and 4×Officer (caterers), and there is a work party of 15. Plans to introduce hygiene and food handling training. Mealtimes 0800, 1130, 1630. Inmates complained about both the quality and quantity of the food to HMCIP. No menu system in operation.

ESTABLISHMENT REPORTS In a report (published 31st March 1992) of an inspection in April 1991, Judge Stephen Tumim, HMCIP, found the regime at Deerbolt to be generally good and with a strong emphasis on education, purposeful training courses, physical education and community activities met the needs of inmates. Among recommendations to the Governor, Judge Tumim called for a reduction in the use of strip cells; evening classes to be increased to four times a week; library should be open in the evening at weekends, and its stock should be improved to meet the requirements of Deerbolt's population.

GOVERNOR'S COMMENTS In 1995 Deerbolt plans to continue to expand the regime and time out of cell for all its inmates.

PRISONERS' COMMENTS Reasonable requests and complaints system, normally get an answer within 24 hours. Good accommodation with internal light switch and sockets. No local purchase facility in the canteen and the prices are high. Good education with wide variety of subjects. The disciplinary system here is the worst I have seen in four years. You never get a fair hearing, the word of the officer is always accepted before yours and the punishments are heavy-handed. Food is reasonable, but the portions are far too small. PE is very good with access four times a week. Good religious activities. Mail opened elsewhere and handed out at dinner time. Phones are available every day but they cost a fortune.

HM Prison Doncaster

Off North Bridge, Harshgate, Doncaster, West Yorks. DN5 8UX
Tel: 0302-760870 **Fax:** 0302-369102
Opened: 1994 **CNA:** 771 **Average Roll:** 651 **Category:** Male Local & Remand Centre

i **BACKGROUND** Doncaster, the third prison to be privatised in the UK, has been contracted out for five years to: Premier Prisons Ltd, Lincoln Way, Sunbury on Thames. TW16 7HW. under a five year contract. Known as 'Doncatraz', the prison has been built on the site of a former power station in the city centre. The prison is located on an island, sitting between two rivers, with access to the establishment via a newly erected bridge. The prison became operational in June 1994 and has been the subject of much critical press comment alleging inadequate staffing and a lack of control—criticisms not always balanced against the teething troubles to be expected in a new establishment, and the difficulties of determining the exact staffing complement required by an establishment, even before it has taken its first prisoners. Accommodation consists of individual two-storey living units for 60 inmates that are built one on top of the other, providing four-storey self-contained living units. All cells have integral sanitation. Bullying and taxing are said to be endemic with staff allegedly losing control at times. HM Prison Service has recently agreed to pay the costs of importing public sector staff to complement those Premier Prison employees already on site. HMP Doncaster had two suicides in its first three months. Neither Kevin Rogers, the Director (Governor) of Doncaster nor Michael Gander, the managing director of Premier Prisons Ltd, replied to our requests for information about the establishment. As a result of its recent opening, the lack of response from Premier Prisons, and the fact that neither the BoV nor HMCIP have yet had an opportunity of reporting on the establishment, this entry will be brief, with full details next year.

OFFICIALS
AREA MGR: Joe Mullens
CHAIR BOV:
DIRECTOR: Kevin Rogers
MEDICAL: Dr
CHAPLAIN: Rev
PROBATION:
EDUCATION:
LOCAL MP: Harold Walker. Lab
HOME OFFICE CONTROLLER: J. Forster

VISITS *How to get there*: Train to Doncaster and then walk to prison. No special transport.
VISITING TIMES: Domestic visits 7 days per week. Start 1230. Last entry at 1915. Legal visits mornings only. Pre-book on 0302 342413.

NOTES Visitors Centre, canteen in visits room with childrens' play area. Nappy changing facilities.

HM Prison Dorchester

7 North Square, Dorchester, Dorset. DT1 1JD
Tel: 0305-266021 **Fax:** 0305-267379
Opened: 1881 **CNA:** 136 **Average Roll:** 191 **Category:** Male Local

i **BACKGROUND** Dorchester prison, which occupies a small site on the northern edge of the town centre, was built as the County Gaol for Dorset on the site of another prison between 1878 and 1881. It now operates as a local prison receiving both remand and convicted adult males from Dorchester, Taunton and Bournemouth Crown Courts and their associated magistrates' courts. Despite a lack of resources to provide a regime for young offenders, Dorchester accepts YO remands, though this function is due to be taken over by Guys Marsh. Neither the Governor nor BoV replied to our requests for information, and HMCIP published their latest inspection report on Dorchester in March 1994.

OFFICIALS
AREA MGR: John May
CHAIR BOV:
GOVERNOR: R. Walker
MEDICAL:
CHAPLAIN: Rev Sim
PROBATION: M. Thomas
EDUCATION:

LOCAL MP: James Spicer. Con
STAFFING: 3 Governor grades, 6 Principal Officers, 17 Senior Officers and 80 Officers, including specialist staff.

REGIME *week days*: 0745 unlock, breakfast. 0900 work. 1130 dinner. 1330 work. 1615 cease labour. 1615 tea. 1700–1900 association.

week ends: 0745 unlock/breakfast. 0900 association. 1145 dinner. 1400 association. 1615 tea. 1900 Supper. No weekend evening association.

Out of cell: 10/24hrs weekdays and 7.5/24hrs at weekends.

ACCOMMODATION & FACILITIES Four wings: A(**CNA:**67, Remands), B(126, Convicted), C(15, Cat D Convicted), D(21, VPU Remand & Convicted). Overcrowded, most single cells house two inmates. Most have integral sanitation further reducing space. Clean and tidy wings. Good shower and toilet facilities on the wings with good access to them. Good association facilities include satellite TV, videos, table-tennis, pool. Well developed Personal Officer and Sentence Planning schemes. Drug counselling. Bail Information Scheme. Card phones in all wings, mail uncensored (but opened outwith the presence of the prisoner) and handed out at dinner time. CABx provides monthly surgeries for inmates.

REQUESTS & COMPLAINTS There were 94 RC forms submitted in the eight months before the inspection. High proportion relate to complaints about health care matters. Time targets were generally being met and replies examined by HMCIP 'were clear and in plain English'.

BAIL INFORMATION SCHEME HMCIP described the BIS arrangements at Dorchester as the best he had found. All officers involved had received full legal aid training and advice can be provided immediately on reception. Application to see the Legal Aid Officer gets the Bail Information ball rolling.

CANTEEN Located in a large room close to the kitchen, the canteen has ample space and operates a local purchase facility for items not stocked. Profit of 10% and prices in accordance with Shaw's Guide. Open three times per week.

VISITS *How to get there*: Train to Dorchester and then ten minute walk to the prison. Special Transport: coaches run by Reading, Oxford, S.Glam, Gwent, W&M Glam and Hants Probation.
VISITING TIMES: Week Days: 1345–1530 (Con: Mon, Wed, Fri only). (Rem: Mon–Fri inc). Saturday: 1330–1530 (Con & Rem). Sunday: 1330–1530 (Con & Rem).

NOTES No staffed Visitors Centre, no canteen, no Childrens Play Area. Contact prison probation for details of local B&B.

EDUCATION Contracted out to Bristol University September 1993. Education Officer, 2×f/t tutors, 3×p/t lecturers. Open 50 weeks of the year with classes five days and five evenings per week. Classes from 0845–1215 & 1330–1630 Evening classes: 1800–2000. Basic skills, numeracy, information technology, woodwork, yoga, art, modern society, DTP, computing, craft, open learning, survival sewing, health and hygiene.

WORKSHOPS Largest employer Textile workshop with complement of 45 inmates, operating for 25–30 hours per week—commendable for a local. Production of tea-cloths, inmate towels and mailbags, average wages £7 per week. Other employers FTE, kitchen, orderlies and cleaners. One of the few locals able to provide full employment for remands. VPU inmates given cell work, the mundane placing of documents in envelopes, but allows for £2.50 per week on top of unemployed rate. C cat inmates cover small outside working party, limited to a few gardening projects.

DISCIPLINE Number of adjudications remarkably low for a local prison, HMCIP found the correct procedures being followed and consistency in awards given which were even-handed and broad based. Only four inmates placed on Rule 43(GOAD) in the eight months before the inspection and only six transfers out in the same period.

MEDICAL Part time Medical Officer, 1×HCPO, 1×HCSO, 1×HCO. HCC located in a group of cells on the ground floor of B.wing. No visiting consultants. Dentist 1×sess/wk, optician as required but usually monthly. HCC clean and welcoming, inpatient accommodation comprises three ordinary cells and a strip cell.

GYMNASIUM & SPORTS 1×PESO and 1×PEO. Former workshop converted into gymnasium, volleyball and badminton court (formerly largest part of the chapel), weights room with multi-gym and an all-weather surfaced yard. Classes 0845–1200 & 1330–1630 Mon–Fri. Evening classes 1700–1900 Mon–Thurs. Sat & Sun mornings. Classes mainly volleyball, football or weights. VPU classes three times per week. Certificated BAWLA centre.

CHAPLAINCY Part time CE chaplain, RC and Methodist ministers. RC Mass Saturdays with RC pastoral visits Thurs & Fri. CE Service Sunday. Small ethnic minority population catered for by visiting ministers. Prison Fellowship members visit regularly and Prison Visitors Scheme now in pipeline.

FOOD Staffing: 1×SO, 2×Officer(caterers), 1×Civilian Cook, and an inmate work party of 7. Wide and imaginative menu with three choices at dinner and tea—the latter being the main meal of the day. Extensive salad bar and ice cream in Summer (Wednesdays). HMCIP described the food as 'excellent'.

ESTABLISHMENT REPORTS In a report (published 10th March 1994) of an inspection in September 1993, HMCIP, said that management deserve credit for the achievements at Dorchester. However, evening association was limited to a few days a week, the regime for vulnerable prisoners is restricted, and that for YO's is not sufficiently active. Education staff did not understand the syllabus should be related to needs of inmates as identified through their respective sentence plan. Living conditions had been enhanced by integral sanitation and extra showers. Plans to convert recesses into launderettes. HMCIP shared inmate concerns that cells were too small for double occupancy with integral sanitation. Steady progress was being made towards a regime that matches as far as possible the model regime for local prisons. The senior management team deserved considerable credit for what they had achieved.

PRISONERS' COMMENTS CONVICTED: Visiting conditions are very poor, cannot sit next to visitors. Lack of space for association, cells are too cramped now integral sanitation has been fitted and the health care service at Dorchester is extremely poor. No medication available if anyone falls ill during the night and the HCO sifts all applications to see the MO with the effect that not many get through [HMCIP was left with a feeling that staff were over-zealous in this task]. No slippers are issued at Dorchester so you are stuck with smelly second-hand shoes. Inmate development courses here are really first class and the probation department is particularly helpful. Sentence planning and personal officer scheme have led to good inmate/staff relationships, and the inmate Listener Scheme appreciated.

REMANDS: Mixing remand and convicted inmates in the same wing does not work. Staff are trained in the needs of the majority and had little understanding of the minority. Space for association is lacking, tea is served too early in the day and no privacy screen had been fitted around the cell toilets which is embarrassing in shared cells. The Visitors Centre is too small and there are problems getting a pram up and down the steps. There is no restriction on the length of phonecalls and it would be fairer to introduce a booking system which gives everyone equal access to the phones.

VPU: Relationships with staff are generally good, but one or two staff resent working with sex offenders and tended to place all VPU inmates in that category regardless of their offence. Dorchester has improved significantly over the last few years, it is now cleaner and there is a more progressive attitude to inmates' rights and privileges. VPU regime too restricted, no evening association, and daytime activities are often curtailed because of adjudications. Employment and education opportunities are very limited and access to the main library is denied to VPU inmates.

D CATS: It is difficult to get access to the Governor, staff rarely visit C.wing and sharing a cell with integral sanitation is not right. Doctors prescribe a sedative for almost every ailment, inmate development course is good, batteries are very expensive in the canteen and we should be allowed to have them handed in on visits.

HM YOI Dover

Western Heights, Dover, Kent. CT17 7DR
Tel: 0304-203848 **Fax:** 0304-215165
Opened: 1952 **CNA:** 316 **Roll:** 278 **Category:** Closed Male YOI

i **BACKGROUND** The site of HM Young Offender Institution Dover occupies the site of a former military citadel that was built in Napoleonic times to repel any French invasion. The completed fortress, overlooking Dover harbour, was capable of housing hundreds of men in its many underground casements which were interconnected with tunnelling. The fortifications were developed and improved during the nineteenth century and they are listed as an ancient monument. In 1952 the site was acquired by the then Prison Commissioners and it has since then been a Corrective Training Centre, a closed Borstal, a closed Youth Custody Centre and, since 1988, a closed Young Offender Institution. Dover accepts male young offenders serving between four months and five years. Neither the Governor of Dover, nor the BoV, replied to our requests for information about the establishment. HMCIP published their latest inspection report on Dover in January 1993.

OFFICIALS
AREA MGR: John Hunter
CHAIR BOV:
GOVERNOR: B. Sutton
MEDICAL:
CHAPLAIN: Rev Stares
PROBATION: David Coupland
EDUCATION:
LOCAL MP: David Shaw. Con

REGIME *week days*: 0730 unlock. 0810 breakfast. 0845 work. 1200 Dinner. 1225 lock up. 1335 work. 1620 tea. 1650 lock up. 1830–2045 association.

week ends: 0730 unlock. 0800 breakfast. 0900 unit/cell cleaning. 0930 CE Service(Sun). 1030 RC Mass(Sun). 1130 lunch. 1155 lock up. 1305 association. 1400 visits. 1600 tea. 1640 lock up. 1830–1930 association.

Out of cell: 10/24hrs weekdays and 8/24hrs at weekends.

ACCOMMODATION & FACILITIES Five 'House' living units. RYE House with 50 two-man cells used for those felt to be potentially disruptive or capable of bullying. DEAL House with 58 single cells is used for vulnerable or weak inmates. SANDWICH House with nine single cells and seven 6-man dormitories is used as induction unit. ROMNEY House with nine single cells, one double cell and seven 6-man dormitories, and HASTINGS House with 10 single cells and seven 6-man dormitories, are used as the general residential units. All living units have integral sanitation and internal light switches. Personal Officer Scheme, drug counselling, card phones on all units and sentence planning in operation. Routine censorship abolished in June 1992, though all mail is opened outwith the presence of the prisoner concerned. card phones installed on all living units other than segregation block, calls are limited in duration and all calls are recorded.

CANTEEN Located in the general stores complex, the canteen is operated by two storemen. Pre-order system in operation, to prevent bullying, and goods are delivered to the Houses for collection by inmates on Thursdays and Fridays. Private cash can be spent on toiletries and all goods are clearly marked with prices. Adequate stock and local purchase facility.

VISITS *How to get there*: Train from Charing Cross or Victoria. Walk or taxi from station—one mile uphill. No Special Transport.
VISITING TIMES: Week Days: Only by arrangement with Governor. Saturday: 1400-1545. Sunday: 1400–1545.

NOTES No staffed Visitors Centre or Childrens Play Area. Canteen in visiting room. Telephone prison probation for details of local B&B. Easy access for wheelchairs.

EDUCATION Severe cut backs in funding result in restricted educational service. Day and Evening classes only operate four days of the week. Maths, English, Business Studies, Cookery, Woodcraft, Art, Soft toys, Open Learning, Computers, Prison Fellowship, English for Improvers.

WORKSHOPS Labour Board meets weekly to decide labour change applications. Five VTC Courses: Welding, Information Technology, Motor Mechanics, Mechanical Services (Plumbing), and Micro-engineering. CIT Courses: Painting & Decorating, Building Operatives, Plastering, Electrical Wiring, and Bricklaying.

DISCIPLINE Purpose built segregation unit comprising ten ordinary cells with integral sanitation, two strip cells equipped with drains for easy cleaning and two special cells. Poor regime which centres around meals, exercise and adjudications. Rule 46 Segregation authorisation by the BoV was sloppy, with forms not being signed and completed within the statutory 72 hours. In the four months prior to HMCIP's inspection, there had been 522 adjudications. In 42 cases the charges had been dismissed, 31 received cautions and of the remainder half received immediate loss of remission, while the other half received suspended loss of remission awards. HMCIP was satisfied that procedures were followed and awards were consistent and appropriate.

MEDICAL P/t Medical Officer, 1×HCSO and 3×HCO. Health Care Centre located on two floors of the main administration block. The upper floor contains two 3-bed wards and a 2-bed isolation unit. Ground floor contains dental surgery, X-ray room, opticians room and remedial gymnasium. HMCIP recommended closure of the HCC. Dental surgery tatty, with insufficient sterilisation equipment. Dentist visits once per week.

GYMNASIUM & SPORTS HMCIP highlighted the deficiencies of the poor gymnasium in 1990 and new sports hall is planned for 1994/5. Full PE programme from 0845 1945 Mon–Thurs, 0845–1600 Fridays. Classes 0800–1600 weekends. In Winter the rugby team plays on a Saturday afternoon and the soccer squad on Sunday mornings. Weights, basketball, football, table-tennis, jogging, remedials, fitness/circuit training, BAWLA, rugby squad training.

CHAPLAINCY Full time CE chaplain and p/t RC and Methodist ministers. Other faiths all catered for as appropriate and necessary. Main church services Sunday morning. Imam visits regularly for Muslim population.

FOOD Major fire in 1989 resulted in complete refurbishment of the kitchen at Dover. The food was satisfactory according to HMCIP, though he criticised the unimaginative menus which were lacking in variety. Main meal of the day is taken at tea time.

ESTABLISHMENT REPORTS In a report (published 14th January 1993) of an inspection in April 1992, Judge Stephen Tumim, HMCIP, said that Dover had undergone significant changes since their last inspection in 1990. The opportunities through VTC and CIT courses were extensive and well used. Improvements had been made to the out of cell hours, increasing association from four nights a week to seven. However the regime in the segregation unit needed to be improved said HMCIP and the design faults in the building rectified. Meals should be eaten in dining areas not cells and the timing of the meals should be more evenly spread throughout the day. Consideration should be given to providing midweek visits and to extending visiting times.

HM Prison Downview

Sutton Lane, Sutton, Surrey. SM2 5PD
Tel: 081 770 7500 **Fax:** 081 770 7673
Opened: 1988 **CNA:** 286 **Average Roll:** 281 **Category:** C.Male Trainer

i **BACKGROUND** HM Prison Downview, located alongside HM Prison High Down and a short distance from HM Prison Send, at Sutton in Surrey, comprises part of the site and some of the buildings of the former Banstead Mental Hospital. It was acquired by the Prison Service in the 1980s, originally being intended for use as a B Category training prison in order to ease the pressure on police cells which, at the time, held 1600 prisoners in the London area alone. As these prisoners began to be absorbed Downview's role changed to that of a C Category prison for adult males serving medium and long term sentences. Downview has recently begun an internal initiative to become the first 'Substance-free' prison in the UK. The Governor of Downview, David Lancaster, provided useful information about the prison, though the BoV did not reply to our request for a copy of their latest annual report. HMCIP published their latest inspection report on Downview in August 1994.

OFFICIALS
AREA MGR: Alan Rayfield
CHAIR BOV: Frank Foxwell
GOVERNOR: David Lancaster
MEDICAL: Dr Bill Bellenger
CHAPLAIN: Rev Paul Newman
PROBATION: Ian Smith
EDUCATION: Margaret Weller
LOCAL MP: Archie Hamilton. Con
STAFFING: 5 Governor grades, 7 Principal Officers, 18 Senior Officers and 22 Officers, including specialist staff.

REGIME *week days*: 0800 unlock/breakfast. 0945 work. 1130–1215 dinner. 1215–1330 lock up. 1330 unlock. 1345 work. 1630–1715 tea. 1715–1745 lock up. 1745–2045 association.
week ends: 0800 unlock/breakfast/association. 11.30–1215 dinner. 1215–1330 lock up. 1330–1630 association. 1630–1715 tea. 1715–1745 lock up. 1745–2100 association.
Out of cell: 11.25/24hrs weekdays and 11.25/24hrs at weekends.

ACCOMMODATION & FACILITIES
A.wing 44 single cells, B.wing 47 single cells and C.wing 196 single cells all with integral sanitation. Progression system in operation, from C.wing to A.wing—inmates on A&B Wings and the top landing of C.wing have signed drug-free compacts and there are plans to purchase a £20,000 drug testing machine which will serve Downview and provide a costed service to other establishments. Sentence planning, drug counselling, card phones (one card is issued to all receptions on arrival at Downview and repaid back at 50p.p/w over four weeks). Personal officer scheme in operation.

CANTEEN Situated just inside C.wing, though there are plans to move it further into the Wing. Staffed by Prison Auxiliaries. Purchases available from private cash (max £30 per week subject to an annual maximum £190). Local purchase facility.

VISITS *How to get there*: Train to Sutton then bus (280/380) to Belmont. Underground to Morden then bus (80) to Belmont. Ten minute walk uphill to prison; 80 bus stops outside the gate during visiting hours.
VISITING TIMES: Week Days: 1400–1600 daily except Wed. Sunday: 1400–1600. Sunday: 1400–1600.

NOTES Portakabin available for shelter, but no staffed Visitors Centre. No Childrens Play Area. Canteen in visiting room. Baby changing facilities and level access for wheelchairs. No overnight stay.

EDUCATION Open 50 weeks of the year, two full-time teachers and four industrial officers. No provision for evening classes at present. Day time classes in: English as a second language; home maintenance; C&G woodwork; C&G hairdressing; Cambridge Certificate in information technology; foundation studies; return to study—word/number power; art; NVQ business studies; open learning; cookery; OU; current affairs; French; German; sociology; English for mature students; maths; pottery and sculpture; adult basic education.

WORKSHOPS FTE (57 places at £5.25–£7pw). VTC: Hairdressing (10 at £5.25), Home Maintenance (10 at £5.25), 2×Computer courses (12 at £5.25 on each). Works (15 at £5.25–£7). Farm & Gardens (20 at £5.25–£7). PSIF: Light Assembly, Woodwork, Concrete (45 at £5–£10). Cleaners (32 at £5.05). ADT (12 at £5.25–£12). Inductions (12 at £4).

DISCIPLINE Total of 810 adjudications last year, a reduction of 19% on the year before but still high for a C Category prison. Punishments appropriate to offences according to HMCIP, who found minor errors in disciplinary documentation and on occasions the records of hearings are too brief.

MEDICAL Part time Medical Officer, 1×HCPO, 1×HCSO and 4×HCO's—two with nursing qualifications. Dentist visits weekly, though waiting list of up to six months for non-urgent cases. Report sick to landing officer at unlock, seen by MO during morning. HMCIP said medical examinations were good, but the prisoner and doctor should see each other in private—without the presence of the HCO. HCC with four inpatient rooms ,each with integral sanitation. Open from 0745-2100. Senior Psychiatric Registrar visits monthly, as does optician. 'Well Man' clinic in operation. See below for ADT course details.

ADDICTIVE DISEASES TRUST COURSE Substance abuse programme, the first specialised, dedicated residential addiction programme in a British prison. Complete abstinence from all mood-altering chemicals is the foundation for a new positive lifestyle. Majority of staff support ADT, and the policy of No Disclosure by the ADT counsellors (all ex-addicts themselves) towards inmate drug taking. Entry to the waiting list (usually about a dozen strong) is by application in the first instance to the probation officer in your home prison or write to the ADT Tutors, HMP Downview for further information about this important course.

GYMNASIUM & SPORTS Five PE Officers. Classes from 0845 to 2000. Applications for classes must be made on appropriate form, signed by the work party officer and handed into the PE Dept no later than Thursday prior to the week of commencement. Classes for remedials and over-35's each morning. Classes in: weight training; badminton; circuit; volleyball; power lifting; football; basketball; swimming/hiking; BAWLA.

CHAPLAINCY Part time CE chaplain who also serves High Down (contrary to S.9 Prison Act 1952 according to HMCIP!), p/t RC and Methodist minister, other faiths visited by Imam, Rabbi and Buddhist visitor regularly. Attractive Chapel and multi-faith room. RC Mass Saturday, CE Service Sunday. Weekly programme of groups for discussion, exploration and prayer.

FOOD Contracted out catering service. Staffing: 1×Catering Manager, 10×Chefs and 10×Kitchen porters—no inmates work in the Downview kitchen. HMCIP said the kitchen was one of the cleanest he had ever seen in a prison. Pre-select menu (a week in advance), and kitchen operates a three week menu cycle. Two choices at dinner and three at tea. Food is tasty but not hot enough, tea bags should be issued to replace the 'diesel', a Catering Committee with inmate representatives should be set up, and toasters in the wings should be considered said HMCIP.

ESTABLISHMENT REPORTS In a report (published 4th August 1994) of an inspection in January 1994, HMCIP, said that it was to the credit of management and staff that once the decision had been taken to alter Downview into permanent cellular accommodation, the necessary adjustments had been made promptly and sensibly. Inmate/staff relationships and basic amenities are good, though there is a lack of space for association. Time out of cell averages nearly 12 hours per day, arrangements for visitors, and health care services, are satisfactory. Education curriculum is impressive, though evening classes should be provided. The progressive regime works well, having the support of both inmates and staff, though lifers cannot take advantage of it. Sentence planning is not as effective as it could be and the absence of a Sentence Planning Board is an obvious weakness that should be put right. The ADT programme is well administered with clear therapeutic goals, though the two biggest dilemmas facing the ADT are future funding and an adequate research and evaluation programme. Despite the lack of qualitative data, a significant proportion of inmates have benefited from it and further funding and study should be made available.

GOVERNOR'S COMMENTS The regime will be enhanced by a longer working week for prisoners and the provision of evening classes.

PRISONERS' COMMENTS The progressive regime does not apply to lifers who experience a reduced regime as a result. There is a lack of meaningful occupation, no evening classes, a lack of space for dine out and association. Education is limited in scope and it is difficult to study ordinary subjects such as English. Unnecessary lock ups at dinner and tea times, no cooking facilities on the wings and nothing to eat after 1630. Food is repetitive and often only lukewarm. The canteen provides a poor service, there are long delays in receiving private cash from sending establishments and the card phones in the wings need acoustic hoods to afford some privacy. Only two visits per month compares unfavourably with other similar establishments, there are no inmate representatives on regime committees and the clothing issued from the CES is often dirty: cleaning materials are difficult to come by.

HM Prison & YOI Drake Hall

Eccleshall, Staffs. ST21 6LQ
Tel: 0785-850621 **Fax:** 0785-851931
Opened: 1958 **CNA:** 262 **Average Roll:** 139 **Category:** Female Open

i **BACKGROUND** Drake Hall is a combined prison and YOI located in a rural setting two miles north of the village of Eccleshall and nine miles north west of Stafford. The accommodation at Drake Hall was erected in 1941 to house upto 1,000 workers for the nearby munitions factory at Swynnerton, and was one of eight similar hostels in the locality. After the war the buildings housed US personnel for a time and, in 1957, Drake Hall housed the now largely forgotten group of Jewish and Maltese refugees, all British passport holders, deported from Egypt during the Suez crisis. In 1959 the site was purchased by the then Prison Commissioners and used as an open training prison for 450 adult males. By 1974 restrictive acceptance criteria made it increasingly difficult to find inmates suitable for open conditions and the prison was closed. In October 1975 Drake Hall reopened as an open female establishment with a CNA of 100. In 1976 the CNA was increased to 150 and in 1980 to 250. When Moor Court closed in 1982 a small Borstal unit opened at Drake Hall and, in 1988, the establishment became an open prison and Young Offender Institution—'open' though now surrounded by a fence to keep prowlers out after dozens of nocturnal incidents. Neither the Governor nor BoV replied to our requests for information about the establishment and HMCIP published their latest inspection report in November 1994.

OFFICIALS
AREA MGR: Dai Curtis
CHAIR BOV:
GOVERNOR: G. Hughes
MEDICAL:
CHAPLAIN: Rev Withers
PROBATION: Terry Probert
EDUCATION:
LOCAL MP: William Cash. Con
STAFFING: 127 Staff in Post, 64 in unified grades.

REGIME *week days*: 0745 roll check, breakfast. 0845 work. 1145 dinner. 1300 work. 1615 cease labour. 1645 tea. 1700–2030 association.

week ends: 0745 roll check, breakfast. 0900 association. 1145 dinner. 1400 visits, association. 1630 tea. 1700–2030 association.

Out of cell: 24/24hrs weekdays and 24/24hrs at weekends.

ACCOMMODATION & FACILITIES Three House blocks: Blythe, Columbus and Drake including 29 young offenders. Drake House has been refurbished and divided with half becoming a fourth House, Dylan which is used to accommodate long term and life sentence inmates. All inmates have privacy keys to their rooms and access to sanitation 24hrs. Limited association facilities, except in Dylan House.

Accommodation laid out in H-shape, with central bar being association area and offices. Good standard of cleanliness. Only one card phone per House, which HMCIP said was inadequate, and inmates often have to queue for two hours to make a call. Sentence planning erratic and with inappropriate targets. Personal officer work under-developed.

CANTEEN Staffed by two Prison Auxiliaries and open once per week. Large stock, well laid out and prices clearly displayed. Inmates attend on a rota basis to make purchases from earnings and spend £10 private cash once per month. No local purchases.

VISITS *How to get there*: Train to Stafford, then taxi—£12 return. No Special Transport available.
VISITING TIMES: Week Days: 1400–1530 Tue, Wed, Thursday only. Saturday: 1400–1530. Sunday: 1400–1545.

NOTES No staffed Visitors Centre. Canteen but no Childrens Play Area. Four visits per month each for 90mins. Easy access for wheelchairs. Eligible prisoners receive local town visits twice per month, 1000–1600 on licence—Sat & Sun only. Visits room, which can accommodate 30 visits, is rather bare and institutional. HMCIP has questioned the practice of strip searching after visits: in an open prison it became incongruous.

EDUCATION Concerns expressed about the educational provision at Drake Hall, a contracted out service to Dudley College of Technology. Claims that inmates are being required to pay £17 for Wordpower Certificates was confirmed by HMCIP to the embarrassment of education staff. F/t Education Officer. Core programme in basic skills, English as a foreign language, maths, drama, cookery. Beauty therapy course, hairdressing, office skills. There is a need for more basic home craft courses.

WORKSHOPS Painting & decorating course. Two PSIF Workshops (sewing machines, leather work and light assembly), a laundry and garden party make up the main employers. Wages average £6.50.

DISCIPLINE Segregation Unit comprises six cells one of which is a strip cell, little used and medical centre utilised for most segregations. Increasing number of adjudications with almost 500 in the year to April 1994 and 68 absconds in the same period.

MEDICAL Part time Medical Officer, 4×f/t Nursing Sisters. HCC located in separate building next to Blythe House. Two double rooms and an eight bed dormitory. No visiting specialists, inmates escorted in groups to local dental practice—many complaints about delays in treatment. Considerable scope for improvement of medical facilities.

GYMNASIUM & SPORTS 1×PESO and 2×PEO. Gymnasium located in converted assembly hall, floor marked out for various team games. Stage area contains weights. Induction includes 60mins PE for the first five days often (wrongly) claimed to be compulsory. Open seven days and evenings. Outside activities include jogging, canoeing, camping, outward bound. Full time CSLA course.

CHAPLAINCY Part time CE chaplain, RC and Methodist ministers. No internal church services, inmates are escorted to local churches in the community each Sunday. Ministers of other faiths visit the establishment weekly and there are fortnightly visits from a Muslim teacher. Four Prison Visitors.

FOOD Staffing: 2×SO, 1×Officer (caterers), and an inmate work party of 15 who work six and a half days a week for £4.15—and that includes 80p overtime! Plans for NVQ Caterbase course. No preselect menu system, three week menu cycle planned. Inmates state the food is tasteless and full of stodge. HMCIP reports recent improvements, though the metal trays should be withdrawn from use and replaced with ceramic plates. The food committee should be re-established and more inmates should have the opportunity of cooking their own meals.

ESTABLISHMENT REPORTS In the last report (published 27th August 1991) of an inspection in January 1991, HMCIP said that Drake Hall was an establishment trying to provide good training in a positive and caring way. There was much to appreciate in the individual training, the workshop, Painting and Decorating course, pre release groups and active community involvement—but there were also areas of concern. Catering standards were inconsistent and the work of the education department and the provision of dental care required attention: a total of 27 recommendations were made. In a report (published 8th November 1994) of a short inspection conducted in May 1994, HMCIP said the majority of the recommendations contained in the 1991 report had been implemented or were no longer relevant. There had been improvement in the management of the catering service and there was a greater awareness of the dangers of fire. It was disappointing however that the Amenities Committee did not appear to have met for almost a year. The problem of intruders entering the prison has resulted in Drake Hall being the only 'open' prison to be surrounded by a security fence. The strength of Drake Hall lay in the quality of relationships between inmates and staff, not just friendliness but involving practical advice and help. There has been significant progress in developing a balanced range of activities, a wide range of offence focused courses were being offered by enthusiastic and committed staff. Sentence planning and personal officer work was under-developed. Since the last inspection the accommodation had begun to be replaced, the new units would be a great improvement when eventually occupied. The base has been laid for a very good establishment. The induction programme was impressive and the compacts among the best HMCIP had seen. The working-out scheme provided more than a dozen women with the chance to earn realistic wages. Industrial enterprises inside the establishment should be further developed to allow inmates and staff to take part in constructive activities. The most important element however, namely the good relationships between inmates and staff, was already present in abundance.

PRISONERS' COMMENTS Requests and complaints seem to be passed from person to person, archaic blocks with eight power points between 100 women. There have been serious problems with meals but a small improvement has taken place recently. Canteen prices are too high and there is little opportunity to buy cheaper brands. Inmate/staff relationships are good. The introduction of town visits was welcome though the restrictions in the houses at lunch times and at night—sitting in the dining room—is deeply resented. Long waiting time for dental treatment, lack of opportunity for washing after work and there are inappropriate restrictions on personal clothing. Although only a small lifer population at Drake Hall, a lifers group is needed. deportees are deprived of the full regime in being excluded from certain activities—open visits, home leaves, unsupervised activity in the community. Health and beauty course failed to address the needs of ethnic minorities, restrictions are placed on private cash for toiletries—£30 per month—and there is a need to provide better work opportunities. Visiting facilities are in desperate need of improvement, particularly for those with families and young children.

HM Prison Durham

Old Elvet, Durham. DH1 3HU
Tel: 091 386 2621 **Fax:** 091 386 2524
Opened: 1840 **CNA:** 403 **Roll:** 574 **Category:** B, Local Male & Female

i **BACKGROUND** Durham prison occupies a site of approximately 2.8 hectares less than one mile from the city centre. The prison first opened in 1819 but was rebuilt in 1881. Since then it has maintained its primary role of a local prison serving courts in the north-east. In 1974 H.wing, a wing formerly used to accommodate male category A and E.List inmates, was converted for use by high security female prisoners. In September 1994 the prison was at the centre of media attention when a firearm was discovered inside the prison, following the discovery of live ammunition on two visitors. The Governor of Durham, Mr Mitchell, provided information about the establishment, though the BoV did not reply to our request for a copy of their latest annual report. HMCIP published their latest inspection report on Durham in April 1993.

OFFICIALS
AREA MGR: Al Papps
CHAIR BOV: W. Locke
GOVERNOR: R. Mitchell
MEDICAL: Dr R. Mitchell
CHAPLAIN: Rev Dixon
PROBATION: J. Leishman
EDUCATION: N. Leight
LOCAL MP: G. Steinman. Lab

REGIME *week days*: 0740 unlock/breakfast. 0830 work. 0850 education. 0910 exercise. 1200 dinner. 1330 work. 1355 education. 1410 exercise. 1700 tea, association (dependent on location). 2045 lock up.

week ends: 0815 unlock/breakfast. 0900 exercise, visits(Sat), church(Sun). 1030 exercise. 1200 dinner. 1345 visits or association. 1700 tea. 1800 association (dependent on location). 2045 lock up.

Out of cell: at best 10/24hrs weekdays, 11/24hrs at weekends.

ACCOMMODATION & FACILITIES Main prison: A,B,C,D,E Wings, segregation unit and security unit varying in capacity from 32 to 200 inmates. H.wing for high security females—see below. Full integral sanitation, though poor gymnasium facilities. Bail Information Scheme, VPU, Sentence Planning, Drug Counselling, card phones, Personal Officer Scheme. In-possession list quite extensive for a local, CD, radio, sound system options, max size including speakers 24"×8"×8", and earphone is mandatory. Home recorded cassettes must be in transparent cases, watches not more than £40 in value, and no pets.

H.WING (FEMALE) Recently refurbished H.wing, with four landings, caters for 48 high security female prisoners in single cells, all of which have integral sanitation and h/c water. 13.5 hours out of cell weekdays and weekends. All inmates engaged on purposeful activities: Textile workshop employs 30; Activity Centre, soft toys, DTP, pottery, knitting £7->£10. Education classes held on wing and programme has recently been improved: Mon–Fri 0845–1645, evening classes Mon–Thurs 1800–2045: Art, design, information technology, soccer scene, discussion, music, Indian cookery, typing, machine knitting, needlecraft, English and maths. Separate gym with good facilities, though only open twice per week. Outdoor exercise 30mins morning & afternoon, plus 2hrs in evening. Prisoners Council meets with staff to regularly improve regime and privileges etc. Separate visiting room with visits each afternoon for 90 minutes; refreshments provided by inmates themselves.

CANTEEN The main prison has a central canteen, with a satellite on H.wing. Staffed full time by two 2×SO and 4×Officers, the canteen is open each day from Saturday to Wednesday, though inmates are only permitted one visit per week. 'Impressive' range of stock and small number of items for ethnic minorities. Prices clearly displayed. Remands can spend private cash once per week.

VISITS *How to get there*: Train to Durham then 20 minute walk. Special Transport: coaches from Carlisle (0228–22333). Coaches from Doncaster, Barnsley, Sheffield and Rotherham (0709–64774). From Liverpool (051–920–9201) last Wednesday in the month.
VISITING TIMES: Week Days: 1330–1500. Saturday: 1330–1500. Sunday: 1330–1500 Con only.

NOTES Staffed Visitors Centre adjacent to prison. Creche facilities Mon–Fri and a canteen available in the visiting room. Phone prison probation for details of local B&B. Disabled access and toilet in visits waiting room. Note all visitors are searched by X-ray machine.

EDUCATION Open 50 weeks of the year with 5 f/t teachers and evening classes Mon–Fri. Timetable being revised as we went to press.

WORKSHOPS Three workshops (two textile shops one making fishing nets). Labour Board allocates work party, average wage £7 pw.

ADJUDICATIONS Segregation unit A1 landing. HMCIP reported a 77% increase in the number of adjudications at Durham over a three year period. The documentation appeared satisfactory and awards consistent in the circumstances.

MEDICAL 1×SMO, 2×MO, 2×HCPO, 4×HCSO & 16×HCO. Residential 36-bed hospital with full range of clinics and mental health team. Dental/Optician waiting list short. X-ray machine and dark room.

GYMNASIUM & SPORTS Staffing: 1×PEPO, 1×PESO and 2×PEO, which HMCIP said was inadequate. Gym located in converted workshop, its design prevents most games and is used mainly for weights, table tennis and darts. Three showers. Redevelopment plans include provision for new gym. PE programme being revised as we went to press.

CHAPLAINCY Two f/t CE chaplains, f/t RC, p/t Methodist and other faiths. All services available and regular bible classes/ chaplains hour.

FOOD Staffing: 1×PO, 1×SO and 5×Officer (caterers), and there is a work party of 30. Kitchen was too small said HMCIP, some parts were a hazard to health/safety. Meals transported in heated trolleys to each wing and dine-in is the order of the day—other than H.wing. HMCIP said meals were 'consistently good and varied' though there was an absence of halal meat for those on pork-free diets.

ESTABLISHMENT REPORTS In a report (published 28th April 1993) of an inspection in September 1992, Judge Stephen Tumim, HMCIP, said that the regime in Durham had improved since the last inspection in 1989, more time out of cell was allowed and facilities had been improved. H.wing as a national resource for female prisoners was questioned, however, as it often meant female prisoners were held hundreds of miles from their home areas.

GOVERNOR'S COMMENTS Hope to increase social skills and offending behaviour courses.

PRISONERS' COMMENTS Requests and complaints forms are dealt with fairly and within 24 hours. The wings differ considerably, D.Wing is the most modern with integral sanitation and light switches—no power points though. Basic range of goods held in the canteen, expensive 'but then it has no competition', and poor idea of priorities, 'one brand of cigarettes but eight varieties of hair gel'! Visits are very fair with a visitors centre for people to relax in before and after the visit, average selection in snack bar. Good standard of basic education with opportunities to attend college plus GCSE and OU facilities, evening classes four nights a week. Wages are as per other establishments, some jobs have bonus opportunities, work conditions vary depending on job. Wages vary between £2.50 UB40 and £10 top end employed rate. Average medical facilities and adjudications. Sometimes the food is good, 'at other times its an ulcer factory, where the quality and amount are never on the same level'. There is plenty of opportunity to visit the gym and the facilities are very extensive. All religious denominations are catered for, 'even the obscure ones'. The mail is checked but is not opened in front of the prisoner. Access to card phones is good.

HM Prison & YOI East Sutton Park

Sutton Valence, Maidstone, Kent. ME17 3DF
Tel: 0622-842711 **Fax:** 0622-842636
Opened: 1945 **CNA:** 81 **Roll:** 75 **Category:** Female Open

i **BACKGROUND** East Sutton Park is a YOI and an Open Prison for women, situated some seven miles south of Maidstone in Kent. It is reached by a narrow winding lane which climbs from the village of South Valence. To the left of the entrance gate is a small area of quarters and former mess/club building now used as an admin block. Behind the main Elizabethan Manor house are farm buildings, a stable block, a former indoor riding school now used as a gymnasium and a large walled garden. It was held as a family residence until 1939 when it was requisitioned by the War Department. In 1945 the house and estate, totalling some 36 hectares was sold to the then Prison Commissioners for the sum of £13,500. It was first used as a girls Borstal, but since 1977 has contained women both over and under 21. Neither the Governor of East Sutton Park, nor the Board of Visitors replied to our requests for information. HMCIP published their latest inspection report on East Sutton Park in June 1994.

OFFICIALS
AREA MGR: John Hunter
CHAIR BOV:
GOVERNOR: C.J. Galbally
MEDICAL:
CHAPLAIN: Rev Waters
PROBATION: Nigel Andain
EDUCATION:
LOCAL MP: Ann Widdecombe. Con
STAFFING: 2 Governor grades, 2 Principal Officers, 4 Senior Officers, 19 Officers, including specialist staff.

☞ **REGIME** *week days*: 0730 breakfast. 0805 house cleaning work. 1030 mail. 1200 lunch. 1300 work. 1615 cease work. 1645 tea. 1715 education classes. 2300 cease association.

week ends: 0800 breakfast. 0800 home visits depart. 1100 open visits. 1200 lunch. 1300–1600 visits. 1630 tea. 1730(Sat) RC Mass. 1800 open visits return. 1900 home visits return. 2000 supper. 2300 cease association.

Out of cell: 24/24hrs weekdays and 24/24hrs at weekends.

ACCOMMODATION & FACILITIES All accommodation sited in main house, consisting of 15 dormitories of different sizes housing between three and nine inmates. Space provided is small and HMCIP has called for larger lockers and wardrobes. Nine showers, three baths, eight toilets located on one side of the house—access to sanitation 24 hours a day. Main complaint is the lack of privacy the dormitory accommodation affords. Association area provides TV, video, table tennis and pool. Association until 2300. Pre-release hostel holds a maximum of 12 inmates. Routine censorship abolished. Mail opened by House Officer who removes any cash and then hands letter over to inmate unread. Three card phones (two without hoods) and management are investigating fitting a fourth. HMCIP criticised the Governor of East Sutton Park for restricting inmates to one £2 phone card per week from earnings.

CANTEEN No personal visits to canteen. Inmates complete written order forms which are collected on Wednesday mornings. Storekeeper runs canteen and bags items for collection on Thursday. Local purchase facility. Canteen is a reasonable size but poorly sited.

REQUESTS/COMPLAINTS Between April–September 1993 a total of 31 formal R/C forms had been issued—of which only 10 had been returned. The most frequent complaint being compensation for lost property.

VISITS *How to get there*: Bus or train to Maidstone, then bus (11,1,59) to Sutton Valence, then 1.5 mile walk (uphill) to the prison. No Special Transport.
VISITING TIMES: Week Days: No visits. Saturday: 1300–1600. Sunday : 1300–1600.

NOTES Open Town Visits for most prisoners every weekend 1300–1800, on licence restricted to 20 mile radius. No staffed Visitors Centre or Childrens Play Area. Canteen in visiting room. No overnight stays or disabled facilities, though wheelchair ramps available. Home visits 0800–1900 Sat & Sun for those who qualify, open local visits 1100–1800 weekends.

EDUCATION Contracted service provided by Canterbury College. 1×Education Officer, 1×D/Education Officer, 2×p/t Teachers, 2×VTC instructors and a panel of five p/t Teachers. Only open for 36 weeks of the year, poor programme, no art or craft classes, though the two VTC courses (Furnishings and Home Economics) are well equipped. Evening class four nights a week.

WORKSHOPS Nine designated work parties: Farm (£8.75–10), Gardens (£5.25–5.75), Education (£5.25), Works (£5.50), Kitchen (£7.50), House Inductions (£5.25), Laundry (£7.50), Community Work (£5.25) and Orderlies (£6.50–7.50). Pioneering Cheese Production Plant in operation and due to make a 'sound profit' according to HM Prison Service. However HMCIP wondered whether this took into account the £250,000 that was now needed to upgrade the sewerage plant because of cheese fats!

DISCIPLINE No Segregation unit. Adjudications averaged less than one per day, mainly for breach of licence conditions. HMCIP examined the records and found the procedures were correctly followed and awards were reasonable.

MEDICAL Part time Medical Officer provided by local GP practice, assisted by nursing cover provided by 1×f/t RGN and 2×p/t RGN's. Report sick in mornings and doctor attends Mon–Wed–Fri lunchtimes: urgent cases in the meantime will see a doctor in the local village. Average of 30 report sick each week—a high figure for such a prison said HMCIP. Dental and optical services reportedly good. No HIV/AIDS management team. Multi-disciplinary suicide awareness group met regularly.

GYMNASIUM & SPORTS Staffed by 1×PEO and 2×Sports/Games Officers. No PE programme for weekends or weekday evenings—though unsupervised activities are allowed during these periods. PE facilities generally good, light and airy gymnasium, though the toilet and shower area was unheated. PE facilities available to staff during lunch on weekdays.

CHAPLAINCY Part time CE chaplain attends for 10 hours per week. Part time RC and Methodist ministers attend as necessary. No church in the prison and inmates attend the local churches in the community if they wish. The library is also used as an in-house chapel when necessary.

FOOD Staffing: 1×Officer (caterer), 1×civilian caterer and there is an inmate work party of six. Five week menu cycle in operation and most inmates expressed their satisfaction to HMCIP about the food. Meals taken in dining room, which HMCIP said was 'drab and uninviting'.

ESTABLISHMENT REPORTS In a report (published 15th June 1994) of an inspection in November 1993, Judge Stephen Tumim, HMCIP, said that East Sutton Park fostered good staff/inmate relationships. The 'drawback' with the prison was the lack of privacy for inmates. The education department should make a 'greater contribution to the regime' said HMCIP, and though the HCC provided good medical cover there was concern at the lack of information about inmates on drug withdrawal programmes on arrival. Attendance system for staff 'was wasteful and did not make optimum use of hours available'.

HM Prison Elmley

Eastchurch, Sheerness, Kent. ME12 4OZ
Tel: 0795-880808 **Fax:** 0795-880118
Opened: 1993 **CNA:** 607 **Average Roll:** 448 **Category:** Male Local, C Cat Trainer & VPU

i **BACKGROUND** Opened by Lord Justice Woolf in June 1993, this 'community prison' on the Isle of Sheppey has two units which act as a local prison, serving Kent magistrates courts and Maidstone Crown Court. Elmley also has a VPU and Cat C Unit. Each cell has integral sanitation and each house block of 155 prisoners has shower facilities, group rooms and TV rooms. In addition to standard accommodation, there is a 29 bed inpatient medical facility which provides 24 hour care. Inmates enjoy on average 10.5 hours out of cell per day. Elmley has strong links with the local Kent community, provides a positive and varied regime and a Personal Officer Scheme which is being developed to improve dynamic security and help inmates with their problems. Sentence planing is also in operation. Offence focused group work deals with anger control, alcohol and drug abuse. A separate therapeutic unit exists for VPU inmates and a special education course preparing remand prisoners for court. Legal aid officers and a Bail Information Scheme are run by the prison's Probation Unit. Neither the Governor nor BoV replied to our requests for information about the prison, and HMCIP will conduct their first inspection of Elmley in February 1995. The next edition of the Handbook will carry full details of Elmley, but due to the lack of official information that has been provided, and the forthcoming HMCIP inspection, this entry will provide only basic information.

OFFICIALS
AREA MGR: John Hunter
CHAIR BOV:
GOVERNOR: W.J. Cooper
MEDICAL:
CHAPLAIN: Rev Williams
PROBATION: Nick James
EDUCATION:
LOCAL MP: Roger Moate. Con

VISITS *How to get there*: Train to Sheerness, bus to Eastchurch then one mile walk. Special Transport: ABBA Coaches leaves Victoria 1100 on Saturdays and Wednesdays, adult £10 children £5 return, other pick up points can be arranged if on route, contact Mr O'Toole: 081-859-1808/8708.
VISITING TIMES: Week Days: 1345–1545. Saturday: 1345–1545. Sunday : 1345–1545.

NOTES Staffed Visitors Centre, Childrens Play Area and canteen. B&B available locally. Disabled access.

PRISONERS' COMMENTS
Requests/Complaints are dealt with promptly, but they rarely go in the inmate's favour and some have even been misplaced. Accommodation is a mixture of singles and doubles, internal light switch but no power points. A fair canteen that has a varied selection, no limit on private cash, though some items are overpriced. Visiting facilities are excellent with two hour visits and a really good visiting room. The education department offers a wide variety of courses and staff make an effort. Poor work opportunities, low wages which average £5–6. The prison is kept very clean and no one gets on your case to do the work as long as its done. The doctor is 'useless' according to one prisoner, whereas another respondent thought the medical staff were 'very understanding and helpful' and to see the SMO, the inmate first has to make a Governor's application! Poor adjudications with very heavy handed awards for minor offences, the governor follows no guidelines, has no consistent policy and appears to decide matters on whim. The food is the best in the region, though chips every day with everything is too much. Portions could be a bit more generous, but its good and wholesome. Good PE facilities which are available seven days a week. Religious needs are catered for and there is a wide variety of visiting ministers. Mail is not opened in front of inmate, handed out at dinner time. Phone cards are plentiful and access is very good.

HM Prison Erlestoke

Devizes, Wiltshire. SN10 5TU
Tel: 0380-813475 **Fax:** 0380-818663
Opened: **CNA:** 206 **Average Roll:** 205 **Category:** C. Male

i **BACKGROUND** Erlestoke prison is situated in a quiet rural location on the northern edge of Salisbury Plain about seven miles from the town of Devizes and approximately the same distance from Westbury. There are references going back to a manor house built in 1791, and this was acquired by the War Department in 1940: serving as the Combined Services Senior Officer's Training School until a fire destroyed the centre of the house and rendered much of the remainder unsafe in 1948: today only one wing of the original manor house is left and in use. The site was taken over by the then Prison Commissioners in 1960 for use as a Detention Centre, it became a Young Prisoners' Centre in 1977, changing to its current role as a Category C adult male trainer in 1988. The Governor of Erlestoke did not reply to our request for information, but the BoV at the prison kindly provided a copy of their 1993/4 Annual Report. HMCIP published their latest report on Erlestoke in October 1993.

OFFICIALS

AREA MGR: John Wilkinson
CHAIR BOV: L.G. Francis
GOVERNOR: Alison Gomme
MEDICAL:
CHAPLAIN: Rev G. Baker
PROBATION: Reg Burgin
EDUCATION:
LOCAL MP: Michael Ancram. Con
STAFFING: 5 Governor grades, 6 Principal Officers, 21 Senior Officers, 86 Officers, 8 Prison Auxiliaries, 3 casual Prison Auxiliaries and 9 Night Patrols.

REGIME *week days*: 0730 unlock, 0800 breakfast, 0830 labour, 1120 cease labour, 1130 lunch, 1200 lock up, 1315 unlock for labour, 1625 cease labour, 1640 tea meal, 1700 lock up, 1800 unlock, evening classes, association, 2000 lock up.

week ends: 0800 unlock, 0830 breakfast, 0900 cell cleaning, library, landing cleaning, 1145 lunch, 1215 lock up, 1330 unlock, visits, association, sports, 1620 tea, 1650 lock up, 1800 unlock, association, 2000 lock up.

Out of cell: 10.25/24hrs weekdays, and 9.5/24hrs at weekends.

ACCOMMODATION & FACILITIES Four cell-blocks, two of which are of modern design with good facilities. A third, is of 1960's 'spur' design and the fourth unit has recently been completed. Single cells, most with privacy locks and access to Night-San. Showers, toaster, boiler and card phones in each unit. Washing machines will be installed in near future.

CANTEEN Located opposite reception and operated by three storemen. Very small size results in a small stock. Open Thursdays all day.

VISITS *How to get there*: Train to Warminster South, then taxi (Tel 83098) to prison. Contact Portsmouth Probation Service for details of minibus service: 0705-871441.
VISITING TIMES: Week Days: 1330–1530. Saturday: 1400–1530. Sunday : 1400–1530. Legal etc: 0930–1130 weekdays.

NOTES No staffed Visitors Centre, but waiting room with facilities adjacent to visitors car park. Childrens Play Area and canteen within visiting room. For B&B contact prison probation. Fortnightly visits, level access.

EDUCATION Contracted out service to Trowbridge College. Forty-five inmates on FTE and 65 attending day classes. Computer course and Art & Design course, both to A level GCSE. Catering class, business studies both v.popular; 70% of inmates on day or evening classes. Programme suitably balanced between basic education, advanced courses, art and practical work. Despite a loss of £1000 in budget there has been no reduction in education provision. Excellent library.

WORKSHOPS Sewing machine shop, gardens, domestics, works & CIT courses, education, engineering, Drawing Office Skills VTC.

MEDICAL P/t Medical Officer contracted for seven hours per week, and assisted by 2×HCO. Health Care Centre with strip cell, two single cells and a dormitory with eight beds. Dental sessions twice per week. Average of eight report sick each day.

GYMNASIUM & SPORTS HMCIP commended PE programme. Facilities for weight-training and indoor and outdoor sports. SOPEI and two PEI's are assisted by six trained uniformed staff. Soccer and rugby teams from outside community play regular fixtures with prisoners. All inmates, except those on Kitchen and Works, are allowed 3 hrs a week in the gym without loss of pay.

CHAPLAINCY Part time CE, RC and Methodist chaplains. Chapel bright and modern, good size and well furnished. RC Mass Saturday morning, CE Service Sunday morning. Weekly bible classes and Muslim prayers on a Friday.

FOOD Staffing: 1×SO and 32×Officer (caterers), and there is a work party of 10. Catering staff have been criticised for a lack of imagination, breakfast is 'meagre' and food trolleys dirty. Breakfast at 0800, lunch 1130 and tea at 1630. Plans for pre-select menu and continental breakfast.

ESTABLISHMENT REPORTS In a report (published 5th October 1993) of an inspection in April 1993, Judge Stephen Tumim, HMCIP, said that the treatment of prisoners in Erlestoke was impressive. Basic facilities were good. Cells were of a fair size with no shared occupancy. Men had ready access to showering facilities, sufficient clothing and space within the wings. Most had their own keys to privacy locks on their cells doors. 'Visiting facilities were welcoming, albeit the prison's isolated location made for difficult travelling for visitors . . . The programme of activities was equally impressive . . . Relationships are the strength of Erlestoke and with the implementation of sentence planning and an inmate development unit men have a good chance of tackling offending behaviour and preparing themselves for release'.

BoV'S COMMENTS Eleven members in post with one vacancy. Main problems in Erlestoke stem from drug related issues, three dog-searches in 1993 produced small amount of cannabis and smoking implements. Good discipline maintained by staff with a relaxed regime. All cells to have privacy locks and integral sanitation by the end of 1994. Sentence planning introduced for those serving over 12 months. No restraints, serious incidents or applications for Rule 43(OP) in the last year.

PRISONERS' COMMENTS Good accommodation, single rooms give privacy, are warm and reasonably sized with access to showers and night sanitation. Lack of materials prevents better standard of cleaning. Poor food is the main complaint at Erlestoke, with repetitive menus and small portions—especially at breakfast. Visits at weekends last only 90 minutes and there are only limited refreshments available. No town visits allowed. Good staff relationships generally, education is very good and the excellent PE facilities are marred only by the fact that they frequently closed due to staffing problems particularly at weekends. Last year of the 322 applications for home leave, 286 were approved—with a return failure rate of less than ten per cent.

HM Prison Everthorpe

Brough North Humberside. HU15 1RB
Tel: 0430-422471 **Fax:** 0430-421351
Opened: 1956 **CNA:** 228 (in use) **Average Roll:** 219 **Category:** C. Male

i **BACKGROUND** Everthorpe Prison lies between the villages of North and South Cave, some 15 miles west of Kingston-Upon-Hull in North Humberside. Everthorpe Hall and the surrounding Home Farm were purchased by the then Prison Commissioners as penal estate in 1953. Everthorpe was the first complete new prison to be built in England and Wales since Victorian times. The buildings are of simple traditional design with inmates living in four blocks set out in a H-shaped formation. Everthorpe was originally designated as a prison, but it opened in March 1956 as a closed Borstal. It retained that role until May 1983 when Everthorpe became a Youth Custody Centre and remained as such until 1991; when Everthorpe saw no less than three changes of function in less than 12 months: first to a Young Offender Institution, then a Remand Centre and, in October 1991, a C category adult male trainer. Neither the Governor nor BoV at Everthorpe replied to our requests for information, and HMCIP published their latest inspection report on the prison in August 1993.

OFFICIALS
AREA MGR: Maurice Codd
CHAIR BOV:
GOVERNOR: R. Smith
MEDICAL: Dr
CHAPLAIN: Rev Rathbone
PROBATION: Ian McNichol
EDUCATION:
LOCAL MP: David Davies. Con
STAFFING: 5 Governor grades, 7 Principal Officers, 15 Senior Officers and 72 Officers, 99 staff in post including specialists

REGIME *week days*: 0745 unlock. 0755 treatments, breakfast. 0830 work. 1145 cease labour (1130 Wednesdays). 1150 treatments. 1200 dinner. 1330 work (1400 Wednesdays). 1400–1600 visits. 1635 cease labour. 1640 treatments. 1645 tea. 1725 lock up. 1800 unlock, PE, evening classes, association, sports field (Summer). 2030 association ends. No work Friday afternoon, used for canteen, kit-change, Muslim service (1345) and association until 1615.

week ends: 0745 unlock. 0800–0830 treatments, breakfast. 0845–0945 wing and cell cleaning. 0845–0930 CE Service (Sun). 0900–0930 RC Mass (Sat). 0945–1145 association. 1200 dinner, lock up. 1340 unlock. 1345–1600 association. 1605 tea, lock up. No weekend evening association.

Out of cell: 10/24hrs weekdays and 7/24hrs at weekends.

ACCEPTANCE CRITERIA Everthorpe accepts C cat adult males serving no more than six years and with no less than six months left to serve on arrival.

ACCOMMODATION & FACILITIES Four cell blocks, A, B, C, D, each with four identical living units of 76 single cells majority with integral sanitation. One wing closed for refurbishment provides reduced CNA (304) to 228. Internal light switch and power points. Sentence planning, personal officer scheme, drug counselling. Card phones with unrestricted access on each wing during non-patrol states, one phone per 76 inmates however makes for long queues. Max two phonecards/wk, max of five i/p.

CANTEEN Carries stock of 175 items and manned by f/t storeman and PA. Open from 0845–1200 and 1330–1630 on Thursdays and Fridays. No canteen committee.

VISITS *How to get there*: Limited bus service, 155 Hull–Goole bus passes Brough station. For details telephone 0482-27146. Probation service coach each month: contact prison probation officer for details.
VISITING TIMES: Week Days: 1400–1600. Saturday: 1400–1600. Sunday : 1400–1600.

NOTES No staffed Visitors Centre, but heated shelter outside gate. No Childrens Play Area, vending machine in visiting room (coins). Visits area flat, disabled access not a problem but visiting conditions are poor.

EDUCATION Poor educational provision at Everthorpe, with poor attendance at classes. F/t education officer. Open 46 weeks of the year, with classes five days a week but no evening classes. Computing, information technology, Art & Design course, law, business studies, sociology, psychology, book-keeping, history, geography. French and German. Basic educational skills.

WORKSHOPS Five VTC/CIT courses: bricklaying, carpentry, industrial cleaning, multi-skills, painting & decorating. Farm with large pig unit and dairy herd. PSIF woodmill and assembly shops. Average wages £7.00.

DISCIPLINE The 164 adjudications in the three months prior to HMCIP inspection was high for a C cat establishment and some could have been dealt with without formal disciplinary hearings. Staff complained the Governor was unduly lenient, but Judge Tumim rejected the criticism totally after examination of the records.

MEDICAL Part time Medical Officer, 1×HCSO, 2×HCO. Two psychologists attend weekly, ENT clinic and dermatologist as required. Dentist 1xsess/wk with 3 week waiting list. Optician 1×sess/8wks. Single storey HCC located close to main gate. No inpatient X-ray and psychiatric services — provided by HMP Hull.

GYMNASIUM & SPORTS 1×PESO and 3×PEO. Classes 0830-1545 Mon–Thurs, no classes Friday. Evening classes Mon–Wed 1800–2000. Weights, fitness training, over 35s, basketball, remedials, volleyball, football, rugby, BAWLA, badminton and jogging.

CHAPLAINCY Part time CE chaplain, RC and Methodist ministers. RC Mass Saturday morning, CE Service Sunday morning. Visiting ministers for ethnic faiths. Fellowship meetings. Pool of five Prison Visitors.

FOOD Staffing: 1×SO, 4×Officer (caterers), and an inmate work party of 15. Four week menu cycle in operation, meals at 0800, 1200 and 1645 (1600 at weekends). Many complaints by inmates, catering staff reluctant to visit serveries at meal times and HMCIP said consideration should be given to privatising the catering service at Everthorpe.

ESTABLISHMENT REPORTS In a report (published 5th August 1993) of an inspection in March 1993, HMCIP, said that staff at Everthorpe had been poorly prepared for the change from young offenders to an adult population, and particularly in the adjustment of their own attitudes. Education provision is poor and does not meet the needs of prisoners fully. The Board of Visitors were almost alone in thinking the food at Everthorpe was good, HMCIP felt it was, at best, just average. Pre-release work had been abandoned because of alleged staff shortages, sentence planning still in its infancy, and Judge Tumim was concerned that race relations were given a very low priority. The new Governor and senior management team have the abilities to make good any inadequacies of the past.

PRISONERS' COMMENTS Food is very poor, it lacks flavour and variety. Shortages of cleaning materials make it difficult to keep the wing clean and food trays are often dirty because the tray cleaning machine has been broken for months. Own denims are not allowed, and no outside videos allowed to be donated to the prison and weekend association is non-existent. Plans for in-cell television. Canteen articles are expensive, there is not enough counselling available and access to the sports field is very restricted. Visits are dingy and dirty with no play area for children. Apart from the Art and Design course the education suffers from a general lack of interest in running appropriate courses and there are no launderette facilities on the wings. Access to PE is restricted, some staff treat inmates like young offenders and there is a lack of daily newspapers.

HMP & RC Exeter

New North Road, Exeter, Devon. EX4 4EX
Tel: 0392-78321 **Fax:** 0392-422647
Opened: 1854 **CNA:** 317 **Average Roll:** 372 **Category:** Adult Male Local & Remand Centre

i **BACKGROUND** Exeter Prison, standing high on a sloping hillside above the city, was opened in 1854 as the County Gaol for Devon. The prison, comprising an area within the perimeter wall together with a few houses in the local district, is located a few minutes walk from the city centre and directly opposite Exeter Central (NOT Exeter St.David's) Railway Station. The current population consists of adult males in the main prison, and young offenders who are located in the Remand Centre built to one side of the establishment. Exeter also has a small female unit within the main prison for emergency use only. The Governor did not reply to our request for further information about Exeter, and the Chairman of the BoV refused us a copy of their latest annual report. HMCIP published their latest report on Exeter in July 1994.

OFFICIALS

AREA MGR: John May
CHAIR BOV: R.F. Lloyd
GOVERNOR: Toby Newth
MEDICAL:
CHAPLAIN: Rev Birdwood
PROBATION: A. de Costa
EDUCATION:
LOCAL MP: John Hammam. Con
STAFFING: 6 Governor grades, 7 Principal Officers, 22 Senior Officers and 156 Officers, including specialist staff.

REGIME *week days*: 0745 unlock, inmates on report to A1, breakfast. 0900 work, exercise (0900–1000 exercise Rule 43. 0915–1015 Convicted main exercise. 1100–1200 E.List inmates; Remand main exercise). 0915–1130 official visits, bathing. 0945 classes. 1120 Governors Apps B2 landing. 1200 lunch, lock up. 1330–1630 domestic and official visits, work. 1630 tea. 1730–2015 activities, association by landing rota, slop out, supper.

week ends: 0745 unlock, inmates on report to A1, breakfast. 0845 slop out. 0900 exercise (0900–1000 exercise Rule 43. 0915–1015 Convicted main exercise. 1100–1200 E.List inmates; Remand main exercise). 1120 (approx) Governors Apps B2 landing. 1145 lunch, lock up. 1330–1630 domestic visits. 1345 unlock for video. 1615 tea. 1730–2015 association by landing rota, slop out, supper.

Out of cell: 8/24hrs weekdays and 6/24hrs at weekends.

ACCOMMODATION & FACILITIES Five accommodation areas: A.wing (118), B.wing (closed for refurbishment apart from one landing holding Rule 43's), C.wing (94), HCC (29), Remand Centre (52—see separate entry below). A.wing has integral sanitation, showers on landing though in-cell toilet shared. C.wing refurbished seven years ago, but no integral sanitation. Both A&C wings hold both remand and convicted inmates. Card phones in each wing, though no privacy hoods fitted and long queues develop. Mail opened centrally and issued at lunchtime—not opened in the presence of the prisoner.

REMAND CENTRE Located at the front of the prison, the Remand Centre has a CNA of 52, though an operational maximum of 75. Staffed by a PO, 2×SO and 20 Officers, the atmosphere is relaxed with open and constructive relationships between inmates and staff. Classes, cleaning, work or PE in the morning followed by association, videos and visits in the afternoon provides a short programme, and there is a great deal of boredom reported by inmates of the Remand Centre.

CANTEEN Operates from a very cramped location in two cells on C.wing for the main prison, and a single cell in the Remand Centre where the facilities are no better. Canteen open daily including weekends and profit margin of 10–20% determined by prison staff. No price list of items is held or displayed. The canteen system needs to be reviewed said HMCIP.

VISITS *How to get there*: Bus or train to Exeter and then short walk. No Special Transport. VISITING TIMES: Week Days: 1330–1530. Saturday: 1330–1530. Sunday : No Visits.

NOTES Little that is good can be said about visiting facilities at Exeter said HMCIP. No staffed Visitors Centre but waiting room opposite main gate with vending machines and nappy-changing facilities. WRVS canteen in visiting room and supervised creche facilities. Visits on ground floor, access not a problem. Visiting room is a converted workshop which provides a depressing atmosphere of plain white walls and gantried ceilings. New visits facility due to be built in 1994/5.

EDUCATION Contract for educational provision at Exeter has been awarded to Bristol University. The programme provides classes in basic skills, social development, and information technology. Open learning. Classes also for those on Rule 43 and young offenders. Operates 48 weeks of the year for three hours a day. Evening classes Mon–Tues–Thurs. Library on C2 and open every day. Library in RC, open two mornings a week.

WORKSHOPS Kitchen, works, reception, hospital, stores, orderlies, workshop—operating both full and part time working systems: lose your job in Exeter and you return to p/t workshop work, with consequent loss of pay. Labour Board each Thursday.

DISCIPLINE Segregation Unit located on A1, nine cells and a staff office doubling as an adjudication room. HMCIP witnessed adjudications in progress, and inspected records of past adjudications. Correct procedures were being followed and awards were consistent and appropriate to the offence.

MEDICAL Senior Medical Officer, p/t MO 1×HCPO, 2×HCSO, 12×HCO (four SEN's) and 1×Nurse (RGN,RMN). HCC old and single storey building with many faults. No integral sanitation. Dental sessions weekly, waiting list in non-urgent cases of four weeks. Optician as required. Inpatients can use day-room for approx five hours per day. SMO aims for 12 hours per day out of cell.

GYMNASIUM & SPORTS 1×PESO and 4×PEO. reasonable facilities for a local prison, comprising external hard surface playing area, a large and oddly shaped gymnasium, weight training and activity rooms. Exeter participates in external weekly volleyball league. Evening classes twice per week for both Remand Centre and main prison.

CHAPLAINCY Full time CE chaplain, p/t RC and Methodist, Quaker, Pentecostal and Salvation Army ministers. Large chapel, completely refurbished in the mid 1980s and has undergone recent redecoration. Jewish and Muslim inmates catered for by visiting Rabbi and Imam as appropriate.

FOOD Staffing: 1×PO, 4×Officer (Caterers) and an inmate work party of 17. Kitchen undergoing major refurbishment, despite which good quality food is being prepared., though Rule 43 inmates think their food is routinely tampered with.

ESTABLISHMENT REPORTS In a report (published 21st July 1994) of an inspection in September 1993, HMCIP, said that though Exeter incurred a good deal of overcrowding most inmates spent a good deal of time out of their cells. Initiatives to develop the regime were under constant review and there was a well-established ethos of inmate/staff respect and co-operation. Exeter is suffering from a massive rebuilding programme. A new education contractor has just taken up responsibility and HMCIP was impressed by their enthusiasm. The regime for those on Rule 43 is very limited, lacking in association opportunities and a shortage of offence-focused groups—the regime for young offenders in the Remand Centre was little different, with little work or other out of cell activities. Though Exeter was struggling with recent changes HMCIP felt there was an underlying expectation that things were improving. A new Governor, who took up post just a few days before the inspection, and the agreement to match staff attendance to the work that needs to be done, will help fulfil this expectation.

HM Prison Featherstone

New Rd, Wolverhampton. WV10 7PU
Tel: 0902-790991 **Fax:** 0902-791843
Opened: 1974 **CNA:** 599 **Average Roll:** 548 **Category:** C Male Trainer

i **BACKGROUND** Featherstone prison is located on the outskirts of Wolverhampton in the West Midlands. HM YOI Brinsford is on adjacent land. The Governor of Featherstone refused to complete the questionnaire we sent him, on the basis that he did not have the time, and the BoV did not reply to our request for a copy of their latest annual report. HMCIP published their latest inspection report on Featherstone in January 1993.

OFFICIALS
AREA MGR: Jim Blakey
CHAIR BOV:
GOVERNOR: C. Scott
MEDICAL:
CHAPLAIN: Rev Rumbold
PROBATION:
EDUCATION:
LOCAL MP: Patrick Cormack. Con
STAFFING: 7 Governor grades, 12 Principal Officers, 23 Senior Officers and 122 Officers, including specialist staff.

REGIME *week days*: 0745 unlock. 0755 breakfast. 0820–1120 activities. 1120 dinner. 1255–1640 activities. 1640 tea. 1745–2000 association.

week ends: 0745 unlock. 0755 breakfast. 0900–1120 activities. 1120 dinner. 1300–1630 activities. 1630 tea. 1745–2000 association.

Out of cell: 9.5/24hrs weekdays and 9.5/24hrs at weekends.

ACCOMMODATION & FACILITIES Five main living units, four of which provide room for 116 inmates in single cell accommodation, all with integral sanitation, power points and internal light switch. Association areas with TV, table-tennis, darts and pool. No cooking facilities but boiler for hot drinks. Fifth wing opened in 1992 and accommodates 100 inmates in fifty double rooms. Apart from underwear and trainers, no civilian clothing. No washing machines or clothes drying facilities. Large number of cell thefts and restricted internal movement to reduce mugging incidents. Large number of escapes.

CANTEEN Open once per week for earnings and private cash orders. reasonable stock and effort made to cater for ethnic minorities. Only one phone card from private cash every two weeks.

VISITS *How to get there*: Bus (872) Mon–Sat from Wolverhampton bus station. 870 service on Sunday. Special Transport: Probation coaches from Nottingham and Derby.
VISITING TIMES: Week Days: 1400–1600 VO's & PVO's. Saturday: 1400–1600 No PVO's at weekends. Sunday : 1400–1600.

NOTES No staffed Visitors Centre. Canteen in visiting room and Childrens Play Area. No smoking. Large visits room allows for 2hr visits.

WORKSHOPS VTC/CIT courses: Industrial Cleaning; Fashion & Design; Machine Setter Operator; Precision Engineering; Welding. Textile shop (employing 145) unpopular, large PSIF workshop based employment.

DISCIPLINE Hooded gangs once used freedom of movement to carry out muggings, but restricted movement has reduced this. Total of 380 adjudications in the six months before the inspection. Proceedings fairly conducted, adjudication room well furnished.

FOOD Inmate food committee meets monthly. Pre-select menu system introduced for both dinner and tea meals, the latter of which is the main meal of the day. Varied menu offers Afro-Carribean dishes, though portions on the small side.

ESTABLISHMENT REPORTS In a report (published 19th January 1993) of an inspection in June 1992, HMCIP said that he had received no complaints from prisoners about clothing despite a poor laundry service from Stoke Heath. The canteen was seen to give a good service with a reasonable range of stock. The pre-select menu system for meals had proved popular, though washing eating utensils in toilet recesses was unsatisfactory. Cell accommodation and cleanliness were of a high standard, though the fabric of the buildings was showing serious signs of wear and tear. Though drugs were said to be easily available, they were not dominating the prison, the level of escapes was not unduly alarming and searching schedules have been improved. Featherstone has a positive training culture, born of its healthy traditions. It is a matter of both surprise and regret that not all places at Featherstone were being used, to do so would enable more prisoners to take advantage of its excellent regime, and reduce the numbers held elsewhere.

PRISONERS' COMMENTS Requests dealt with but tend to be slow at times, but the general quality of replies is OK. Excellent accommodation with toilet, power points and light switch, though large number of cell thieves roaming around. Visiting facilities are good, though duration varies from day to day with an average of about an hour. Pretty good education with plenty for everyone and a wide variety on offer—the art class is particularly good. Wages average about £6. Average medical facilities with no inpatient facilities. Adjudications are fair, but the governor is too lenient on persistent offenders who continue to cause problems in the wing. Excellent gym facilities, can be used every day and has to be booked. Governor grades tend to fade into the paint work, and the senior management team are hardly ever seen around the place. Outgoing mail is OK, but incoming mail is subject to delay quite often. Mail is opened in front of the inmate. Shortage of card phones.

HM YOI & RC Feltham

Bedfont Rd, Feltham, Middx. TW13 4ND
Tel: 081-890-0061 **Fax:** 081-844-1551
Opened: 1983 **CNA:** 874 **Average Roll:** 697 **Category:** Closed YOI & Remand Centre

i **BACKGROUND** Feltham is situated two miles West of Feltham railway station and about a mile from Ashford C Category training prison. The original Feltham was built in 1854 as an Industrial School and was taken over in 1910 by the Prison Commissioners as their second Borstal Institution. Ashford prison also started life as as a school and in 1961 was made into a Remand Centre: soon acquiring a reputation for poor industrial relations. In 1975 there were plans for a new Borstal at Feltham, and serious concerns were voiced about the security at Ashford: the two merged and it was decided to build a new Borstal and Remand Centre at Feltham. In August 1983 the new Borstal was completed and old Feltham was demolished. In 1986 the new Remand Centre was ready, but industrial action prevented it opening until March 1988. In recent years there has been considerable media focus on inmates at Feltham: CCTV cameras have been installed to prevent bullying and there were four suicides in the six months to March 1992. Feltham has pioneered 'Radio Feltham', operated by inmates who broadcast to the institution five hours a day under the control of Team Leader Jackie Evans. The Governor of Feltham did not reply to our request for information, though the BoV provided a copy of their Annual Report. HMCIP published their latest report on Feltham in December 1993.

OFFICIALS

AREA MGR: Peter Kitteridge
CHAIR BOV:
GOVERNOR: Vacant
MEDICAL: Dr
CHAPLAIN: Rev Brundle
PROBATION: D. Upcott/S. Watts
EDUCATION:
LOCAL MP: Alan Keen. Lab
STAFFING: 14 Governor grades, 21 Principal Officers, 63 Senior Officers and 306 Officers, including specialist staff.

REGIME *week days*: 0745 unlock, 0815 breakfast, 0845 labour, 1120 cease labour, lunch & lock up, 1320 labour, 1605 cease labour, 1630 tea and lock up, 1800 unit based activities, association, 2030 association ends, 2045 lock up.

week ends: 0745 unlock, 0815 breakfast, 0845 domestic activities, 0930 association, 1045 association ends, 1115 lunch served and lock up, 1345 association, 1530 association ends, 1615 tea served and lock up, 7.00 supper served. No weekend evening association.

Out of cell: 9.8/24hrs weekdays and 6.5/24hrs at weekends: a behavioural points system means these figures are averages, and Remand Centre inmates may not enjoy even this limited regime.

ACCOMMODATION & FACILITIES Inmates accommodated in 18 Houses each designed to aid a therapeutic regime. In the YOI each of the living units consists of two connected wings each designed to hold 32 inmates on two landings. With the exception of a small 4-bed dorm on the first landing, all inmates have single cells with integral sanitation. The nine Houses in the RC are similar except for some double occupancy cells. Cells in the YOI are clean, whereas those in the RC suffer from graffiti and vandalism. Showers on all living units—each fitted with CCTV to prevent bullying. Card phones on all living units, though their use is strictly controlled. All mail is opened outwith the presence of the inmate, though it is claimed it is not read. Feltham has expressed an interest in joining the Sex Offender Treatment Programme, though does not have a group running at the moment.

CANTEEN Two separate canteens, one in the YOI and another in the RC: both equipped with CCTV to prevent bullying. Remands canteen open once a week, no delay in canteening receptions, well stocked though more attention needed for ethnic minorities. YOI canteen totally lacking in space, items set out on a table! Limited stock and open on Friday's only. No local purchase facility.

VISITS *How to get there*: Train to Feltham, then bus (117,237) to Three Horseshoes pub, then 15 min walk. No Special Transport.
VISITING TIMES: Week Days: 1400–1600 (Rem). Saturday: 0900–1100 (Rem) & 1400–1600 (Con). Sunday : 1400–1600 (Con).

NOTES Staffed Visitors Centre, canteen in visits (Sat/Sun p.m. only). Convicted visits fortnightly. Middlesex Area Probation Service provide excellent facilities, including a children's play area, refreshments, a 'Help Desk' and a bus service to and from Feltham railway station.

EDUCATION Education department closed at time of inspection. Library open Mon–Thurs evenings—but remands have no access. No evening classes and poor access for remands has resulted in education at Feltham being the subject of much criticism by HMCIP: 'the education unit was closed and there had been no evening classes for over a year . . . there should be a 50 week provision of daytime education together with some weekend and evening classes'.

WORKSHOPS Considerable emphasis on domestic work (141 places). Kitchen, works, gardens and orderlies. Work allocated from a Job Centre in the YOI. Three VTC/CIT courses: Bricklaying; Industrial Cleaning; Machine Setter Operators, providing just 32 places—unsatisfactory according to HMCIP, who recommended a motor mechanics/car body repair course.

DISCIPLINE A behavioural modification 'Points' system in place, working concurrently with formal disciplinary adjudications for serious breaches of the rules. Each inmate starts day with 300 points and staff can deduct points for misbehaviour—however the fairness of its operation has been criticised by HMCIP who felt it was inconsistent and removed the procedural safeguards applicable to formal disciplinary charges. The inspection team could glean little explanatory detail about why points had been deducted—'For fucking about' was one example cited, while others contained nothing more than the number of the rule allegedly breached!

MEDICAL 1×SMO, 1×P-Psych, 5×S-Psych, 3×MO, 2×HCPO, 4×HCSO, 24×HCO, 2×Nurses. HCC located on Bittern Unit, effective inpatient facility with 25 single rooms with integral sanitation and 2 rooms for segregation. Garden outside used daily with inpatients being out of cell 0800–1155, 1315–1600, 1700–1930. Poor transfer rate to NHS hospitals for mentally ill. Receptions see MO following morning, but the rapid examination and lack of appropriate medical testing was criticised by HMCIP for not meeting Directorate of Health Care's standards in assessing all the health care needs of inmates. Sick parade inmates filtered by HCO—of the 60-odd who report sick each day about three get to see the MO. Poor documentation on HCC strip cell use.

GYMNASIUM & SPORTS 1×PEPO, 2×PESO, 8×PEO. YOI/RC inmates both have access to PE seven days a week—four evening classes in YOI but none in RC. Programme also developed for juveniles. HMCIP found the PE dept was consistently exceeding its planned target of hours for inmate involvement and the work with juveniles was first class. Weights, basketball, volleyball, football. CSLA, DoE, hiking, camping.

CHAPLAINCY Full time CE chaplain and p/t RC and Methodist ministers. Strong ecumenical commitment and mutual support between a wide-ranging chaplaincy team. CE Service Sunday 0900 for YOI, and 0945 for RC. RC Mass at 1045 for both YOI & RC.

FOOD Staffing: 1×PO, 1×SO, 6×Officer (caterers), and work party of 20. Food improved as a result of menu consultation with inmates. Dine in association on some units only. HMCIP said though the standard of food was satisfactory, the dinner portions were too small and the timing of meals unsatisfactory. No pre-select menu system.

ESTABLISHMENT REPORTS In a report (published 10th December 1993) of an inspection in August 1993, Judge Stephen Tumim, HMCIP, said that measures taken to improve family ties had been welcomed. The inspectors saw the beginnings of a positive programme, the reception procedure was more civilised but the treatment of young prisoners still gave cause for concern. The basic lifestyle was unsatisfactory, too many prisoners spent too much time in cells which were barren of furniture and devoid of stimulation. Sentence planning was at best mediocre and the involvement of personal officers patchy. The attitudes of some staff seemed to be offhand and uninterested. During August 1993 no educational classes took place at all and there had been no evening classes for the previous 12 months. The shortage of suitable training opportunities was lamentable—training courses offered a total of 32 places for a population of almost 800.

PRISONERS' COMMENTS The points level system causes resentment because staff apply it inconsistently. Little organisation to the PE programme and access to the gym is limited to once or twice per week. No education at all for those on remand. The standard of the food was inconsistent, vegetables were of poor quality and not washed properly. There are no racial problems at Feltham. Inmates can see a doctor, and Family Days are much appreciated. Some of the young prison officers had an attitude problem. Feltham does little to help prepare inmates for release.

HM Prison Ford

Arundel, West Sussex. BN18 0BX
Tel: 0903-717261 **Fax:** 0903-726060
Opened: 1960 **CNA:** 536 **Average Roll:** 449 **Category:** D. Male Open

i **BACKGROUND** Ford prison is an adult male open establishment situated about four miles south of Arundel in West Sussex. The land on which the prison now stands first passed into public ownership in 1917 when it became an airfield during the latter stages of the First World War. In 1939 the Royal Navy took over and further developed the site until 1960, when it was purchased by the then Prison Commission. Unwanted land comprising most of the former airfield was sold, much of it becoming an industrial estate which adjoins the prison, while the rest reverted to farmland. Today Ford prison comprises a few structures from the pre-war years, many buildings built during the war and a small number built by the Prison Service. Neither the Governor nor BoV at Ford replied to our requests for information about the prison, and HMCIP published their latest inspection report on Ford in December 1993.

OFFICIALS
AREA MGR: Alan Rayfield
CHAIR BOV:
GOVERNOR: D. Godfrey
MEDICAL:
CHAPLAIN: Rev Barnes-Ceeney
PROBATION: Tom Dixon
EDUCATION:
LOCAL MP: Michael Marshall. Con
STAFFING: 5 Governor grades, 5 Principal Officers, 10 Senior Officers and 47 Officers, including specialist staff.

REGIME *week days*: 0745 unlock. 0800 applications & breakfast, 0830 sick parade 0900 labour, 1150 cease labour, 1200 lunch, 1300 roll check, 1315 labour, 1650 cease labour, 1700 tea, 1800 roll check, association, 2100 roll check, 2300 lights out.

week ends: 0745 unlock, 0800 breakfast & treatments, 0915 town visits commence, 1000 cleaning, 1140 roll check, 1145 lunch, 1400 domestic visits, 1700 tea. 1730 roll check, 1745 association, 2100 roll check, 2300 light out.

Out of cell: 24/24hrs weekdays and weekends.

ACCOMMODATION & FACILITIES Accommodation divided into two parts, known as A and B Blocks. A.Block is a two-storey building holding 256 in a mix of single and double rooms, and also contains the kitchen, dining hall, library and Health Care Centre for the prison. B.Block is a collection of 20 wooden huts, 16 men in each. Full-time access to sanitation. Snooker hall with seven full-size tables and upgraded television rooms. Cooking, showering and card phone facilities available.

CANTEEN Access 5 days a week. Run by two Storemen it carries 300 lines of stock. No limit on the number of phonecards that can be purchased. Amalgamation of earning and private cash with no limit on spending. Prices, in accordance with Shaw's Guide to Retail Prices, are clearly displayed. Local purchase facility.

REQUESTS & COMPLAINTS According to HMCIP the Requests/Complaints system was working properly, very few men had to wait more than seven days for a local response and the Area Manager usually met his 6 week target.

VISITS *How to get there*: Train to Ford then half mile walk to prison. Littlehampton three miles, taxis available. Special transport: HALOW (London) bus service: 0171-793-7484.
VISITING TIMES: Week Days: 1400–1600 PVO's and VO's. Saturday: 1400–1600 No PVO's at weekends. Sunday : 1400–1600.

NOTES No staffed Visitors Centre. Canteen and Childrens Play Area in visiting room. Visitors can purchase toiletries from canteen for prisoner. B&B available in Littlehampton. Disabled access and nursing-mothers room.

EDUCATION Staff part of Northbrook College and an educational year of (only) 44 weeks. Full-time courses in basic skills, open learning, business, computing and Open University. VTC courses in catering and information technology. All computers are networked but security controlled. Classes in art, pottery, painting and drama—Ford has a playwriter-in-residence. Max roll of 60 on classes. Large library in A.Block, 5000 books, study cubicles and open 7 days.

WORKSHOPS VTC Courses in catering and computing. CIT Courses in painting & decorating, general building and carpentry. Full and daytime education. Workshops: engineering, fire dummies, light textiles and laundry. Farms and gardens, kitchen, cleaners, and usual orderlies. Average wages £7.

DISCIPLINE There were 176 adjudications in the first five months of 1993 and HMCIP repeated in its most recent Report a criticism about 'minor infractions' of the rules that it first criticised in 1988. Adjudication room unintimidating, and perilously close to Reception! Ghosting is common and often seen as without reason: HMCIP reviewed 92 cases of Ghostings but concluded that 'without a close investigation of each individual case it was impossible to draw firm conclusions about whether transfer to closed conditions was used excessively'.

MEDICAL Medical care provided by a part-time Medical Officer and his GP colleagues. Emergency cover provided and daily (Mon–Fri) surgery at 0830. Visiting psychiatrist, dentist (twice a week) and optician (once a fortnight). Report sick at morning 'unlock'. Health Care Centre staffed by one HCPO, one HCSO and two HCO's—inmates report a good service. HMCIP recommended abolition of HCPO post and installation of civilian clerk to handle appointments system. HIV+ inmates guaranteed confidentiality.

GYMNASIUM & SPORTS 1×PESO and 2×PEO. Main sports hut is poorly ventilated and large enough only to provide a low-ceilinged weights area. No indoor games possible but but free weights, multi-gym and exercise bicycles available. Main visits room is used in the evenings for badminton. V.good outside amenities, cricket pitch, soccer and rugby fields, bowling green and putting course. A new gym had been promised for 8 years but never materialised. HMCIP suggested up-rooting the gymnasium from the now defunct Northeye!

CHAPLAINCY Chaplaincy team consists of f/t CE chaplain, and p/t RC and Methodist priests. RC midweek communion service. Regular visits from Sikh and Hindu ministers and from the local Rabbi—whose facilities, said HMCIP, 'rank among the best multi-faith areas we have seen'.

FOOD Kitchen staffed by a PO, SO and four Officer Caterers. Max of 26 on Kitchen party. Meals taken in large dining hall situated next to kitchen. Four week menu system in operation and during the week there are four choices at both lunch and tea meals. Few complaints received and HMCIP reports the food 'tasted good'. Breakfast 0800, lunch 1145, and tea 1645.

ESTABLISHMENT REPORTS Ford did not have a clear purpose said HMCIP in a Report (published 13 December 1993) of an inspection in June 1993. 'The Governor's idea that the regime prepared inmates for release was not shared in practice by a large number of staff, many of whom had been at Ford for far too much of their service. It was impossible to escape the feeling of inertia in the living units. Sentence planning and personal officer work had not really taken off, nor had staff been given suitable incentives for close involvement with inmates. . . . There were pockets of good practice being pursued by individuals unsupported, and in some cases they thought hindered, by other staff'.

PRISONERS' COMMENTS There are no courtesy locks on room doors. There is a shortage of detergent and cleaning materials of all kinds. Lifers experience (and resent) inferior conditions to other prisoners in that they have less opportunity for community work outside and have to wait longer for town visits. Service in the canteen entails queuing for an hour, conditions of sale are too complicated and bureaucratic, simpler arrangements are needed. More female officers would be welcome. Boredom is the big problem in Ford, not helped by PE staff who insist that even the most casual game of football has to be supervised by a member of the PE staff! There is little room for objections here, the smallest complaint seems to be met with threats of a transfer back to closed conditions. Too many staff are young and inexperienced.

HM Prison Frankland

Brasside, Durham. DH1 5YD
Tel: 091-384-5544 **Fax:** 091-384-9203
Opened: 1962 **CNA:** 432 **Roll:** 383 **Category:** Dispersal

i **BACKGROUND** Frankland is located about three miles from Durham city centre. Design work for Frankland, the first purpose-built dispersal prison, began in 1966 but the project was held over for many years and building work did not begin until 1977. In October 1980 the prison was almost built when industrial action by the POA over Continuous Duty Credits caused the opening of three temporary prison camps: one of which was Frankland. Three months later, when the industrial action collapsed, the prison was closed to enable the final building and security work to take place. Frankland finally opened as a dispersal in April 1983. Since then it has suffered a number of serious disturbances—often seen by the many London prisoners it holds as a punishment allocation. The Governor did not reply to our request for information about Frankland, and the chairman of the prison's BoV refused us a copy of their annual report. HMCIP published their latest inspection report on Frankland in November 1992.

OFFICIALS

AREA MGR: Al Papps
CHAIR BOV: B.S. Millwater
GOVERNOR: P. Buxton
MEDICAL:
CHAPLAIN: Rev Bindoff
PROBATION: A.M. Price
EDUCATION: Mrs A. Smith
LOCAL MP: Gary Steinberg. Lab
STAFFING: 11 Governors and 405 in unified grades.

REGIME *week days*: 0800 unlock/breakfast in cell. 0840 work. 0930 visits. 1115 cease work/exercise. 1200 dinner in cell. 1345 unlock/work. 1400 visits. 1545 cease work. 1600 tea in cell. 1730–2000 association.

week ends: 0800 unlock/breakfast in cell. 0930 association. 1145 dinner in cell. 1345 unlock/association. 1400 visits. 1600 tea in cell. 1730–2000 association—except Sunday.

Out of cell: 8/24 hours weekdays and 8/24 hours weekends.

ACCOMMODATION & FACILITIES
Each of the four wings holds 108 inmates in single cells all with integral sanitation. Showering and bathing facilities available at all unlock times. Cooking facilities available on each wing, and small recreational areas provide snooker, pool and darts. Personal officer scheme, drug counselling, card phones. Extensive dispersal i/p list. VPU. Frankland has expressed an interest in joining the Sex Offender Treatment Programme, though does not have a group running at the moment. 'Contrary to the popular belief expressed by many prisoners, we were assured that only letters to and from Category A prisoners were subject to full censorship' said HMCIP. Mail for others is opened and checked, not in the presence of the prisoner though, and only a random five per cent sample censored. Card phones in each wing.

CANTEEN Located centrally and provides an excellent service. Staffed by a Senior Officer and 2 PA's, it is open seven days a week and there are four shopping periods each day. Extensive stock includes meat, vegetables, fresh fruit, milk and cereal. Prices are posted on all notice boards and selling prices are kept low: the shop's net profit is five per cent.

REQUESTS/COMPLAINTS HMCIP said there had been 784 R/C forms issued in the nine months prior to the inspection, a high number 'as might be expected in a dispersal prison'. The majority of requests were receiving answers at a local level within fourteen days, 'but those requiring a response from Headquarters were often waiting longer than the six weeks laid down for a substantive reply.

VISITS *How to get there*: Train or bus to Durham. United Bus Service (62,62A and some 65) from bus station (weekdays only) at 30 min intervals. No.63 departs at 16 mins past the hour on Saturdays. Special coaches from Manchester (061-236-7621), South Yorks (0709-364774) & Merseyside (051-920-9201) and HALOW (London) bus service: 0171-793-7484.
VISITING TIMES: Week Days: 0930–1130 (except Mon) & 1400–1545. Saturday: 1400–1545. Sunday : 1400–1545.

NOTES No staffed Visitors Centre. Canteen and Childrens Play Area in visiting room. Contact prison probation for B&B. Disabled access. Two visits every four weeks. Special visits by appointment only.

EDUCATION Nine f/t teachers supported by a panel of 20 p/t teachers. Three discipline staff supervise the department. Sixty f/t education places and a 47 week year was operated with 36 weeks of evening classes—Tues/Thurs main prison, Wednesday for Rule 43. Caters for all levels from remedial to degree. Small business course and 12 month course in furniture craft. Catering course to NVQ level.

WORKSHOPS Industrial work centres on the manufacture of furniture for the Prison Service and private sector. Inmates from the VPU operate the woodmill and spray shop. Employed for less than 20 hours a week. Laundry with workforce of 30 does a weekly total of 5,500 kilos of washing for Frankland and Durham. CIT in painting & decorating—under used. Dispersal wage scheme gives average earnings of £8 per week.

DISCIPLINE Segregation Unit with 24 cells, an observation room, and 2 strip cells 'that had been used on more than 60 occasions in nine months'. G4(Ops) in charge of Segregation Unit Staffing: G5, PO, 4×SO and 20×Officers. Two exercise yards. No figures available for number of adjudications, but awards 'sensibly reflected the seriousness of offences'.

MEDICAL Health Care Centre with two six-bed wards, eight furnished rooms and two unfurnished rooms. Staffing 1×HCPO, 2×HCSO & 12×HCO—five HCO's are qualified nurses. Senior Medical Officer conducts morning sick parade. Mobile X-ray machine installed to reduce trips to outside hospitals. Dentist 2 sess/wk with a waiting list in non urgent cases of about a month.

VULNERABLE PRISONER UNIT
Seventy-two VP's were located in the VPU at the time of the inspection, some 30% were believed to be due to non-payment of debts, while the remainder were as a result of their offences. HMCIP recommended proper records be kept of these details. Regime is kept as normal as possible with inmates shielded from the hostility of other prisoners. Education takes place in the VPU daily and, on Wednesday, evening classes and access to the sports field are available. No pressure applied to return to normal location. Religious services held in the Unit. Employment in the spray paint shop.

GYMNASIUM & SPORTS 1×PEPO, 1×PESO, 4×PEO. Good gymnasium. Weights room well equipped though small. Adjoining fitness area, containing multi-gym and a punch-bag. Hard surface area outside for basketball, soccer, tennis and volleyball. Huge tarmac area rear of D.Wing offers good facilities for 7-a-side, large sports field enclosed by security fence has full size soccer and rugby pitches. Full daytime programme based on work location—max of 45 in gym at any one time. HMCIP received no complaints from prisoners or staff about the PE Dept.

CHAPLAINCY F/t CE chaplain, RC priest, p/t Methodist and minority faiths. Good chapel with spacious buildings. Friday prayers for Muslims. Buddhist and Sikh ministers visit regularly.

FOOD Staffing: 1×PO, 1×SO, 4×Officers and 18 inmates. Good standards of hygiene in n kitchen. Four week menu system in operation—including diets. Prisoners complained about the quality and quantity of food to HMCIP: 'The food we sampled was satisfactory but bland and presented unimaginatively'. Catering staff should visit serveries at meal times.

PROBATION/PSYCHOLOGY Senior Probation Officer and five main grade officers serve the prison. Groups: Sex Offender; Addiction; Lifers. Counselling available. Team of psychologists with Principal, 2×Seniors, 2×Higher and 2×Assistant psychologists. This team also covers Durham, Castington, Low Newton, Deerbolt and Kirklevington Grange.

ESTABLISHMENT REPORTS HMCIP last inspected Frankland in September 1991. The prison has a number of valuable facilities for long-term prisoners, offering out of cell routines for most of each day—together with evening association except on Sundays. HMCIP was 'concerned that after nearly ten years as a dispersal prison, the security of Frankland needs considerable repair and improvement'. HMCIP also raised issues of the need for better control of disruptive prisoners and the need to restore staff training but, all in all, HMCIP found the regime at Frankland 'encouraging'.

PRISONERS' COMMENTS Average request complaints system. Single cells, no power points. Pathetic canteen always looks as if it's just been burgled. Poor visits and work opportunities. Medical facilities are good and the Medical Officer is fair. Good PE facilities, especially weights. Religious needs catered for with many visiting ministers. Mail is censored and handed out at 1500 each day. Only one card phone per landing.

HM Prison Full Sutton

Moor Lane, Full Sutton, York. YO4 1PS
Tel: 0759-372447 **Fax:** 0759-371206
Opened: 1987 **CNA:** 604 **Average Roll:** 438 **Category:** Dispersal

i **BACKGROUND** Full Sutton Prison is built on land that had previously been an RAF Bomber Command base and missile site, acquired from the Ministry of Defence in 1963. Uncertainties about the size of the prison estate caused the building of Full Sutton to be shelved on a number of occasions, and it was 1983 before building work finally got under way. The prison sits inconspicuously at the southern edge of the Vale of York, about 11 miles east of York and it has operated since its opening in 1987 as one of the six current maximum security establishments in the Dispersal System. The prison also operates as an assessment centre for the Sex Offender Treatment Programme. The Governor of Full Sutton (and Editor of the Prison Service Journal), John Staples, provided information about the prison, though the BoV did not reply to our request for a copy of their latest annual report. HMCIP published their latest inspection report on Full Sutton in June 1994.

OFFICIALS
AREA MGR: Al Papps
CHAIR BOV: Ms D. Hurst
GOVERNOR: John Staples
MEDICAL: Dr A. Kumar
CHAPLAIN: Rev I. Gommersall
PROBATION: D. Goldring
EDUCATION: Ms V. Foster
LOCAL MP: David Davis. Con
STAFFING: 13 Governor grades, 23 Principal Officers, 73 Senior Officers and 441 Officers, including specialist Staff. In excess of 7,000 hours TOIL owed to staff.

REGIME *week days*: 0745 unlock. 0805 breakfast. 0900 work, education. 1045 AD cease work, exercise or association. 1100 BCEF cease work, to wing association or exercise. 1145 dinner. 1230 lock up. 1330 unlock, trays out, lock up. 1350 AD to work. 1400 BCEF to work. 1545 AD cease labour to exercise or association. 1600 BCEF cease work to exercise or association. 1625 EF tea, lock up. 1630 ABCD tea, lock up. 1745 trays out. 1750 association, evening classes, canteen, gymnasium. 1930 activities cease. 2000 lock up.

week ends: 0745 unlock. 0805 breakfast. 0855 unlock association and church services. 0930–1115 sports field. 1130 lock up. 1135 dinner, lock up. 1330 unlock, trays out. 1340 unlock, association, gym. 1400 visits. 1500 gym ceases. 1600 visits cease. 1625 association ceases. 1630 tea, lock up. 1740 trays out. 1745 association. 2000 lock up.

Out of cell: 8.5/24hrs weekdays and 8.5/24hrs at weekends.

ACCOMMODATION & FACILITIES Seven living units, A,B,C,D,E,F, and Special Secure Unit. A.wing, holding up to 108 vulnerable inmates separated for their own protection. B,C,E and F wings house normal dispersal inmates. D.wing houses all sex offenders, regardless of length of sentence, and offers ongoing sex therapy courses which deal with offending behaviour. F.wing is split into two with half being used as a Segregation Unit and the other half housing normal dispersal inmates.

VISITS *How to get there*: Train to York. Weekdays 'Ingleby' coaches (0904-37620) from station to Full Sutton village. Special Transport: from Manchester (061-236-7621) and Liverpool (051-920-9201).
VISITING TIMES: Week Days: 1400–1600. Saturday: 1400–1600. Sunday : 1400–1600.

NOTES No staffed Visitors Centre. Canteen and, at weekends only, Childrens Play Area. Contact prison probation (ext 3028) for details of B&B. Hand luggage, pushchairs or prams to be left at visiting room gate. No food and drink to be brought into visiting room. Limited disabled access. Nappy changing facilities.

EDUCATION Large and spacious Education Unit, well equipped classrooms with facilities for art, cookery, woodcraft and information technology. Craft Design Technology, business studies, Leeds Course (mature students), creative writing, food technology, Open University, foreign languages. Open 52 weeks of the year with classes five days and three evenings a week. Excellent 35-page education booklet locally produced for inmates gives good, clear details of all education facilities on offer at Full Sutton. CIT: Bricklaying, Plumbing, Painting & Decorating. Motor Cycle Maintenance.

WORKSHOPS Education: FTE(77 places), PTE(48), VPU(50). VTC(24). CIT(36). Works(2). PSIF Shops: Textile 1 (making bib and brace overalls) and Textile 2 (making inmate shirts): wages for textile 1&2 from zero to £8 with average of £7.

Textile 3 (making bib and brace overalls and fashion wear for a private sector company) and Textile 6 (making fashion wear for private sector company): wages for Textile 3&6 from zero to £11—average of £10. Contract Services Workshop assembling ball bearings for private sector company, wages from zero to £12 with average of £10. Farm & gardens (33 inmates). Kitchen(18). Cleaners & orderlies (91). Induction(4). Employment Board sits weekly. No restrictions on time in party before labour change.

DISCIPLINE Adjudications reached 1500 in 1992 and dropped to around a thousand in 1993. Incidents included 18 assaults on staff, 10 assaults on inmates, 17 drug finds, 5 attempted escapes, 16 home leave failures, 17 incidents of food refusal, 7 fires, 6 acts of concerted indiscipline, 2 demonstrations, 5 attempted suicides, 1 suicide. C&R methods had been used on 107 occasions, and on 22 occasions a body belt had been used: HMCIP discovered several occasions when the Medical Officer had not given authority for its use.

MEDICAL Full time Medical Officer assisted by local GP. 1×HCPO, 1×HCSO, 11×HCO. Health Care Centre with a 12 bedded inpatient dept. Surgery Mon–Fri afternoons. Weekly clinics held by Optician, Physiotherapy, Chiropodist and Radiographer (X-ray). Dentist and psychiatrist visits twice weekly. HIV/AIDS counsellors. Group Therapy available via MO. Health Promotion Clinic offers a simple check and general advice on leading a healthier lifestyle.

GYMNASIUM & SPORTS 1×PEPO, 2×PESO and 5×PEO. Classes 0845–1145 & 1350–1600 Mon–Fri. Evening classes 1750–1950 Mon–Thurs. Classes cater for remedials, CSLA, BAWLA, soccer, weights, volleyball, basketball, badminton, hockey, among others.

CHAPLAINCY Four f/t and p/t CE chaplains, p/t RC and Methodist ministers. Visiting ministers for minority faiths. Two main CE Services on Sunday at 0900(main) and 1430(VPU). RC Mass Saturday 0900 and Pentecostal service Friday afternoon. Monthly Methodist communion. Muslims led in prayer by Imam Friday afternoon and Sikh minister visits once a fortnight. Religious evening classes Monday and Tuesday consisting of worship, bible study and religious videos.

FOOD Staffing: 1×PO, 1×SO, 6×Officer Caterers, and an inmate work party of 16. Meal tasted by HMCIP was of acceptable quality and the size of the portion was reasonable. HMCIP repeated a criticism first made in 1990 that dinner should not be served before noon and tea not before 1700.

ESTABLISHMENT REPORTS In a report (published 3rd June 1994) of an inspection in November 1993, HMCIP said that impressive progress had been made on all but a handful of the 122 recommendations in the 1990 full inspection report, some exceptions being that meals times were still too early, butchery in kitchen difficult to supervise and there was no store for dirty linen. The reputation for disorder was gradually receding, staff were seen to be regaining control and confidence and morale was improving. Conditions for prisoners were good, not least for vulnerable prisoners although they had fewer opportunities to use available facilities. The range of work, education and training opportunities was adequate for the needs of the majority of inmates although vulnerable prisoners felt unsafe out of their wings. Textile design and marketing project was applauded though the poor take up rate of some opportunities led HMCIP to question whether the situation was likely to improve 'while inmates can rely upon private cash which they do not have to earn'.

PRISONERS' COMMENTS
Request/complaints system almost non-existant. Single cells,tends to be very noisy, good standard of cleanliness. Above average canteen, local purchase facility in theory but hopeless in practice. Good education, visits are a bit oppressive and wages average about £6.00 per week. Poor medical provision, many of the guys in here walk about doped up quite legally. Adjudications are not fair, block has a bad reputation. Menu system for food which consists of variations on the stew/stodge theme.. Good gym facilities, PE staff have the right attitude, though there is a waiting list for spaces. Mail opened in front of prisoner. Good access to card phones.

HM Prison Garth

Ulnes Walton Lane, Leyland, Preston. PR5 3NE
Tel: 0772-622722 **Fax:** 0772-622276
Opened: 1988 **CNA:** 512 **Average Roll:** 498 **Category:** B. Male

i **BACKGROUND** Garth prison, located alongside Wymott prison, is situated about three miles from Leyland and some ten miles from Preston in Lancashire. The establishment was purpose-built as a B category training prison for adult males serving four years and over and was opened in 1988. Neither the Governor nor BoV at Garth provided information about the prison, and HMCIP published their latest inspection report on the prison in February 1992.

OFFICIALS
AREA MGR: Ian Lockwood
CHAIR BOV:
GOVERNOR: W. Rose-Quirce
MEDICAL:
CHAPLAIN: Rev Ainsley
PROBATION: S. Fiddler
EDUCATION:
LOCAL MP: Den Dover. Con
STAFFING: 8 Governor grades, 8 Principal Officers, 28 Senior Officers and 144 Officers, excluding specialist staff.

☞ **REGIME** *week days*: 0730 unlock. 0750 breakfast. 0830 exercise or locked in spurs. 0900 work. 1115 cease labour. 1120 dinner. 1320 work. 1615 cease labour. 1625 tea, lock up. 1750–2000 association.

week ends: 0730 unlock. 0750 breakfast. 0830 cell cleaning. 0845 RC Mass (Sun). 0930 exercise. 0945 CE Service (Sun). 1000 association. 1100 lock up. 1115 dinner. 1315 visits start. 1400 association. 1550 tea. 1650 lock up. 1750–2000 association.

Out of cell: 9.5/24hrs weekdays and 9.5/24hrs at weekends

ACCOMMODATION & FACILITIES
Four identical wings (A,B,C,D) each with a CNA of 128 and all with integral sanitation and power points. Showers and toilets on each landing. Two TV rooms, launderette facilities but no drier, and general room for ironing etc. Cooking facilities on each wing. Personal officer scheme, sentence planning, drug counselling and two card phones in each living unit. Television allowed in-cell. Garth holds around 100 lifers with G5 Residential Manager designated LLO. Inmate Council meets with management to discuss relevant issues—see **Prisoners' Comments** below.

ENCOUNTER GROUP Unique scheme in which young offenders without custodial experience are brought into the prison to speak with inmates and hopefully be deterred from offending in the future. The impact is considerable according to HMCIP who witnessed a session.

CANTEEN Located off the main link corridor the canteen is staffed by three storemen and an inmate canteen committee meets quarterly. Open once per week, 10% profit margin and 160 lines of stock including fresh Fruit, milk and cereals. Local purchase facility. Private cash spends on toiletries and hobbies only.

VISITS *How to get there*: Train to Leyland then bus (110) from Queens Hotel to prison at 1309 Mon–Sat, return journey 1625. Sun 1238 from Queens Hotel. Return journey 1550 from outside prison. Probation coaches from W.Yorks (0532–40601); S.Yorks (0709–364774); Tyneside (091-266-7801) and Merseyside (051-920-9201).
VISITING TIMES: *week days*: 1330–1530. Saturday: 1330–1530. Sunday: 1330–1530.

NOTES Staffed and well equipped Visitors Centre (0772-622756), canteen and Childrens Play Area. Contact prison probation for details of B&B. Disabled access good, baby-changing facilities and public telephone available.

EDUCATION Well attended department which HMCIP described as excellent. Ten f/t teachers. All inmates given a clear explanatory booklet on arrival. Space for 40 on FTE and 60 on PTE. Classes five days and three evenings per week. Foundation studies ranging from basic skills to C&G/RSA examinations. Open learning and higher education in wide variety of subjects. Leisure subjects covered on evening classes. Good library with 5,600 books changed regularly by library authority. Six books at any one time and two hours per inmate per week—those on classes can attend more often.

WORKSHOPS VTC/CIT: bricklaying, motor mechanics, multi-skills, plastering, painting & decorating. PSIF contract services workshop, light textiles, tailors, weavers and gardens. Average wage £6.30. Labour Board allocates employment as part of induction process. Minimum of 12 weeks in shops before attending education.

DISCIPLINE Segregation Unit with 20 cells and two strips. Three separate exercise yards. Not an excessive number of disciplinary reports, and those witnessed by HMCIP were properly conducted with awards consistent with the offence.

MEDICAL Full time Medical Officer, 1×p/t MO, 1×HCPO, 2×HCSO, 4×HCO and two agency nurses. Regular clinics by dentist, chiropodist, genito-urinary and optician. HCC with 5-bed ward, strip cell, and eight single rooms. Only two rooms have integral sanitation. No health promotion, report sick at unlock.

GYMNASIUM & SPORTS 1×PEPO 1×PESO and 4×PEO. Large gymnasium and well equipped weights room. Outside sports fields well maintained with space for a rugby field and two soccer pitches. Hard surface area for tennis. Each inmate allocated two one-hour daytime sessions and two evening sessions per week. Activity based programme with options for both morning and afternoon. CSLA and BAWLA.

CHAPLAINCY Full time CE chaplain, p/t RC and Methodist ministers. Shared chapel and spacious meeting rooms. Muslim Imam visits for prayers each Friday. Church services Sunday morning. Chaplains group each Friday.

FOOD Staffing: 1×PO, 1×SO, 5×Officer (caterers), and an inmate work party of 20. Three choices at dinner, two at tea and choices for vegetarian diet. Plans to introduce a pre-select menu system. Choice of dine in or out (most dine in).

ESTABLISHMENT REPORTS In a report (published 11th February 1992) of an inspection in April 1991, HMCIP, said that a solid employment base had been laid with industries, an imaginative use of the the education department encouraged inmates to partake in a wide variety of courses and the general quality of life for inmates was very reasonable. Cells were warm and benefited from h/c water and sanitation. During the twelve months preceding the inspection progress in developing the regime with personal officers and sentence planning had been cancelled, the morale of staff had declined because of disputes over manning levels. As long as the dispute remains unresolved it risks damaging the stability and potential of this training prison.

PRISONERS' COMMENTS Inmates Council, comprising representatives from each wing, meet with management to raise issues of general importance. Issues raised when HMCIP visited: pre-release course had not been operating and should be brought back into use; concerns at lack of medical cover after 2000, and long delays in seeing the dentist, optician and other medical specialists was further adding to the general dissatisfaction with medical services. Food was allowed to remain in trolleys for too long on the wings before serving; lifers were concerned that not enough priority was being devoted by staff to the writing of reports for Review Boards and there is a lack of trained legal aid officers.

HM Prison Gartree

Market Harborough, Leics. LE16 7RP
Tel: 0858-410234 **Fax:** 0858-410808
Opened: 1966 **CNA:** 360 **Average Roll:** 271 **Category:** B. Male

i **BACKGROUND** Gartree prison is located in open countryside close to the village of Market Harborough in Leicestershire. The prison opened in 1966 and following additional security became part of the dispersal system in 1969. In April 1992 Gartree was removed from the dispersal system and became a B category establishment holding inmates serving in excess of five years: Gartree is a first-stage lifer centre and 80% of the inmate population are lifers. The Governor provided information about the establishment, though the BoV did not reply to our request for a copy of their latest annual report. HMCIP published their latest report on Gartree in August 1993.

OFFICIALS
AREA MGR: J. Blakey
CHAIR BOV: Mrs S. Spence
GOVERNOR: R.J. Perry
MEDICAL: Dr C. Berry
CHAPLAIN: Rev M. Phillips
PROBATION: Ms M. Sanderson
EDUCATION: J. Whittington
LOCAL MP: Edward Garnier. Con

REGIME *week days:* 0745 unlock/breakfast. 0840 work. 1145-1215 exercise. 1230 dinner. 1335 work. 1640 tea, lock up. 1755 association. 2045 lock up.

week ends: 0800 unlock/breakfast. 1000 exercise. 1145 dinner. 1220 lock up. 1335 unlock, association, visits. 1630 tea. 1705 lock up. 1750 association. 2045 lock up.

Out of cell: 12/24hrs weekdays and 11/24hrs at weekends.

ACCOMMODATION & FACILITIES Four 83-cell blocks (A,B,C & D wings), each with three landings of cells (TV/dining room on each landing) and a ground floor with no cells. Two card phones, one cooker, grill, washing machine and drier on each wing. Each cell has integral sanitation and there are showers on each landing. Each cell has a power point. All cells have privacy lock for which the prisoner holds the key. E.Wing, segregation, maximum of 12. Gartree Therapeutic Community (GTC) takes up to 21 occupants based on referrals from within Gartree. Based very much on the 'Grendon Model'—and run by ex-Grendon psychologist Roland Woodward—it provides a challenging regime of group work and therapeutic counselling.

VISITS *How to get there*: Train to Market Harborough, then taxi (approx £6 ret). Prison minibus meets train at weekends. Special Transport: Minibus from Wolverhampton alternate Wednesdays (0902-710621) and HALOW (London) bus service: 0171-793-7484.
VISITING TIMES: Week Days: 1400–1615 Tues–Fri. Saturday: 1400–1615. Sunday: 1400–1615.

NOTES Staffed Visitors Centre, canteen and Childrens Play Area. Contact prison probation for details of B&B. For disabled access contact prison.

EDUCATION Open 49 weeks of the year, with five full time teachers and evening classes Tues, Wed, Thurs. Daytime classes in Urdu; GCSE maths & English; cookery; information technology; drama; art; current affairs; French; German; Catering studies. Evening classes: band music; drama; Asian video; soft toys; yoga; computing; debating society; Gaelic; music theory.

WORKSHOPS VTC/CIT courses: Furniture Craft and Precision Engineering. PSIF Workshops, Textiles, Footwear, Plastics. Average wage £7. Kitchen (£10), Full-time education £5.

MEDICAL Full time Medical Officer. Health Care Centre with 10-beds.

GYMNASIUM & SPORTS Classes from 0840 to 1915 each weekday, 0840–1615 weekends. 1×PEPO; 1×PESO; 4×PEO's. Main gymnasium used for tennis, weights, remedials, aerobics, badminton, hockey, circuit, basketball, soccer and volleyball. Astro-turf used for soccer, hockey and cricket. Inter wing competitions at weekends.

CHAPLAINCY Full time C/E chaplain, p/t RC and Methodist ministers.. Main church service Sunday morning. Visiting Buddhist minister and Sikh service Fridays. Christian bible class Sunday pm.

FOOD Spacious kitchen, well equipped and spotlessly clean said HMCIP. Pre-select menu for main meal of the day with four choices. No halal meat available at time of inspection. Food was of a good quality and conveyed to wing serveries in heated trolleys. Cleaning standards in wing-based cooking facilities need to be improved.

ESTABLISHMENT REPORTS In a report (published 5th August 1993) of an inspection in September 1992, HMCIP said that the atmosphere at Gartree, which improved when the establishment became a first-stage lifer centre, had improved further since the prison was removed from the dispersal system in April 1992. The refurbishment of the living units had been coupled with an improvement in the relationships between inmates and staff. Staff were right to be cautious, though the supervision in some areas appeared unnecessarily high in comparison with other Category B establishments. There were clear signs that inmates welcomed the opportunity to work in partnership with staff to further develop the prison. Staff were committed, ably led by the Governor and keen to maintain the momentum: the future for Gartree holds much promise.

PRISONERS' COMMENTS Though the request/complaint system functions very well it does not always produce the desired answer. Very good accommodation with power points and night-san. Recent large improvements in canteen stock. Visiting room has recently been refurbished and provides a relaxed atmosphere for visits. Education is excellent with provision for all levels from remedial to degree. Wages in general are very poor, and full-time education is the lowest with about £5 per week. Disciplinary adjudications are well conducted and the Governor 'often gives inmates the benefit of the doubt—not a punitive attitude'. New £500,000 Gym provides excellent facilities and with helpful staff who are keen to see you progress. Mail is opened in the presence of the prisoner, no censorship. Four phone cards allowed per week, and there is an urgent need for another phone box per wing.

HM YOI Glen Parva

Tigers Road, Wigston, Leics. LE8 2TN
Tel: 0533-772022 **Fax:** 0533-477679
Opened: 1975 **CNA:** 848 **Roll:** 820 **Category:** Closed YOI

i **BACKGROUND** Glen Parva is situated in a pleasant residential district about a quarter of a mile west of a road linking Leicester with Glen Parva. It is a multi-functional closed establishment for Young Offenders, incorporating a Young Offender Institution (CNA 480), Remand Centre and Allocation Unit (CNA 332 but agreed operational capacity of 464). Much of the accommodation was planned and designed in the 1960's and constructed in the 1970's as a single phase project to the then applicable standards for Borstals: half the buildings were built by inmate labour, the other half by contractors. In 1990 two 'Bedford' residential units were added as well as a new kitchen. The Governor of Glen Parva, C.J.Williams, supplied comprehensive information about the establishment, though the BoV did not reply to our request for a copy of their annual report. Glen Parva was last inspected in September 1991 and HMCIP's subsequent report was published in July 1992.

OFFICIALS
AREA MGR: J. Blakey
CHAIR BOV: Mr M Clutton
GOVERNOR: C.J. Williams
MEDICAL: Dr A. Timmins
CHAPLAIN: Rev H. Dodhia
PROBATION: Mr D Kemp
EDUCATION: Mr G Young
LOCAL MP: Andrew Rowbathan. Con
STAFFING: Fourteen Governor grades, 27 Principal Officers, 56 Senior Officers and 247 Officers, including specialist staff.

REGIME *week days*: 0745 unlock/breakfast. 0830 work. 1145 lunch. 1230 lock up. 1330 work. 1615 tea. 1645 lock up. 1730–2030 association. No formal exercise period but built into PE programme min 2 hrs/week.

week ends: 0745 unlock/breakfast. 0830 unit/cell cleaning. 0900 association. 1145 lunch. 1230 lock up. 1330 Governor's Inspection of Units. 1400 association. 1615 tea. 1645 lock up. No weekend evening association.

Out of cell: 11.25/24hrs weekdays and 11.25/24hrs at weekends.

ACCOMMODATION & FACILITIES
Convicted: four units designed to hold 100 inmates, comprising 48 single cells and three 4-man dormitories. VPU is of same design and capacity but has mixed population of remand and convicted. **Remand:** two units each designed to hold 100 in double cells, and three units each holding 90 inmates in double cells. All units have showers, servery, association area and equipment. All sleeping accommodation has integral sanitation and wash basins. Personal Officer and Bail Information Schemes and drug counselling. Routine censorship abolished at Glen Parva in 1992, letters are now checked for illicit enclosures and then passed to the inmate unread—though the envelope is not opened in the presence of the inmate. Card phones have been fitted in each of the living units, together with wards in the HCC. Calls limited to ten-minute duration and have to be booked in advance.

CANTEEN Two shops for inmates in Glen Parva, one at the north end (serving Units 1–5) and the other at the south end of the establishment, (serving Units 8 & 10): both 'operated in different ways' and 'neither was entirely satisfactory' said HMCIP, who called for a central canteen to be built, and the poor range of goods and items for ethnic minorities to be extended. Bagging and delivery of goods should be replaced with an across-the-counter service.

REQUESTS/COMPLAINTS The G4 Residential oversees R/C system. Average of fourteen a month, procedure was well-publicised and known by inmates. Inmates state that some forms take longer than others to come back and HMCIP noted that most were dealt with within fourteen days. Delays at Headquarters were commonplace.

VISITS *How to get there*: Train (Mon–Sat) to South Wigston (from Leicester) then 10 min walk. Sundays train to Leicester then Midland Fox bus (42) from Grand Hotel, Belvoir St, Leicester—5 min walk from BR Station. Midland Fox bus (42) daily from St. Margarets Bus Station. No Special Transport.
VISITING TIMES: Week Days: 1345–1515 (Con). Saturday: 1345–1515 Saturday only (Rem). Sunday: No Visits.

NOTES No staffed Visitors Centre or Childrens Play Area. Canteen in visiting room. Contact prison probation for details of B&B. Wheelchair access quite easy.

EDUCATION Comprehensive education programme. Staffing of 12 f/t and 40 p/t teachers. Education housed in two separate sites, north and south, each had good accommodation and satisfactory equipment levels. Linked to Charles Keene College of Further Education. VTC: Machine Setter/Operator, Motor Mechanics, Industrial Cleaning and Maintenance. CIT: Painting and Decorating, Carpentry, Bricklaying. Day classes: home economics, IT, maths, English, computers, numeracy, art, marketing, open learning, skills training.

WORKSHOPS Plastic moulding, bricklaying, carpentry, painting and decorating, machine operator & setters, motor vehicle maintenance, horticulture, laundry, industrial cleaners and orderlies, kitchen. Work allocated by personal officer as part of sentence plan. Maximum pay £11.40, UB40 £2.50, average £7.

DISCIPLINE Segregation unit in Unit 7, on the southern part of the establishment, comprises 20 cells, four of which are holding cells and two special cells. Staffing: 1×SO and 3×Officers. Inmates on report normally located in seg unit on morning of hearing. HMCIP's scrutiny of adjudication documents found all procedures were being 'carefully and thoughtfully followed'.

MEDICAL Senior Medical Officer, two f/t MO's and two p/t MO's. Visiting psychiatrists in mental handicap, individual psychotherapy and forensic psychiatry. Visiting consultant in genito-urinary medicine. Dentist (2 sess/wk), optician (1 sess/mth), speech therapist (1 sess/wk), physiotherapist (6 sess/wk), art therapist (4 sess/wk). Primary Health Care Clinic by local GP (3 sess/wk). Staffing: 1×HCPO, 4×HCSO's and 25×HCO's. Hospital contains six wards: 1&2 used for inmates unable to cope on ordinary location due to 'low intelligence, limited social skills, immaturity or chronic mental illness'. Wards 3&4 operates as a therapeutic community with 20 places—referrals from YOI's in England and Wales. Wards 5&6 provide 15 places for acute admissions—medical and psychiatric. Report sick to unit staff by 0800.

GYMNASIUM & SPORTS Gym staffed by 1×PEPO, 1×PESO and 9 PEO's. Strong emphasis on developmental courses: C&G Rec/Leisure; Community Sports Leaders Award; Life Saving; First Aid at Work; Treatment of Injuries; Football Leaders Award, Soccer Skills Award; English Basketball Assoc' Star Awards; English Volleyball Assoc' Proficiency Award; RFU Proficiency Award; Duke of Edinburgh Awards; BAWLA (weight training, power-lifting and Olympic lifting awards). In addition internal basic skills courses are run in table-tennis, trampoline, cricket, minor games and outward bound. Full day and evening gym programme.

CHAPLAINCY Full time CE chaplain and 10 part-time visiting ministers from other faiths. Imam visits fortnightly and the Sikh priest visits weekly. Sunday service 0845, communion 1800 Thursdays. Mass for RC's Saturday 0930. Chaplain's hour 1400 Sunday, Chapel group ('watch videos, read the bible, meet and talk with Christian people over a cup of tea or coffee') 1600 Mon–Wed–Fri. Baptism & Confirmation classes held as requested. Muslim & Sikh prayers 1800 Friday.

FOOD Staffing: 1×PO, 2×SO and 6×Officer (caterers), four further catering officers have been agreed and there is a work party of 25. Inmates complain the food is cold when served, poorly presented and meal times are unrealistic. HMCIP recommended that private contractors should take over the catering at Glen Parva. Five choices at main meal.

ESTABLISHMENT REPORTS In a report (published 16th July 1992) of an inspection in September 1991, Judge Stephen Tumim, HMCIP, said that Glen Parva is a large and modern establishment, 'which does not necessarily benefit from either of these features'. The institution was run in a caring and concerned way with most staff anxious to do their best. There are a number of areas which require scrutiny. No set periods for exercise, evening association in the units was limited, the need and value to strip search all inmates after visits was questioned and there was no evening association at all at weekends, with a particular lack of opportunity to attend evening classes for those on remand. Judge Tumim also expressed concern about the failure to use some hospital accommodation, the quality of the dental service provided and the lack of funds for providing psychiatric care and support.

GOVERNOR'S COMMENTS During 1994 it is not envisaged that Glen Parva will change its role from a Remand Centre and YOI. However, the pressure of ever-increasing numbers of young remand prisoners could compel us to alter the remand/convicted ratio within the establishment. Glen Parva is committed to developing and expanding its regimes and to providing more prisoner-centred activities. We also see a need for ourselves and our establishment to be more open and accessible to the 'outside world' through strong community links. Much of Glen Parva's work during 1995 will be concerned in these areas.

PRISONERS' COMMENTS Sometimes requests and complaints take longer than they should at Glen Parva. Visits are 'getting a lot better' and there is no reported delay in the receipt of mail or problems with access to telephones, though time limit on calls is resented and should be redressed by supplying more phones. Education and gymnasium very well regarded.

HM Prison Gloucester

Barrack Square, Gloucester.. GL1 2JN
Tel: 0452-529551 **Fax:** 0452-310302
Opened: 1792 **CNA:** 209 **Roll:** 237 **Category:** B. Local

i **BACKGROUND** Gloucester prison was first built in 1792 and was used initially as the County Gaol for Gloucestershire. The prison was rebuilt in 1840 and although some of the original structure remains, the present buildings are either Victorian or of modern design. Following the disturbance at Pucklechurch Remand Centre in April 1990 the prison has also been holding young offenders though mainly operates as a Category B local prison with a training wing (C.Wing). The Governor of Gloucester, Mr Winckley, provided some information about the establishment, though the BoV did not reply to our request for a copy of their annual report. HMCIP published their latest inspection report on Gloucester in September 1993.

OFFICIALS
AREA MGR: J. Wilkinson
CHAIR BOV: C. Price
GOVERNOR: P. Winckley
MEDICAL: Dr B. Zaidi
CHAPLAIN: Rev V. Godden
PROBATION: J. Wiseman
EDUCATION: B. Vicary
LOCAL MP: Douglas French. Con
STAFFING: 4 Governor grades, 5 Principal Officers, 18 Senior Officers and 84 Officers, excluding specialist staff.

REGIME *week days*: 0800 unlock/breakfast. 0900 work, exercise, education. 1130 dinner. 1330 work, visits, education. 1600 tea. 1800–2030 association.

week ends: 0800 unlock/breakfast. 0900 canteen, chapel, exercise. 1130 dinner. 1300 visits, association, canteen, exercise. 1800–2000 association.

Out of cell: 8.5/24hrs weekdays and 7.5/24hrs at weekends.

ACCOMMODATION & FACILITIES
Three wings. A=adult convicted, B=adult remands, C=YO remands. Card phones on each wing. Night-san on C.wing. No segregation unit. Central canteen and three association rooms. Bail Information Scheme, sentence planning, drug counselling, Personal Officer scheme. Some cells with integral sanitation. Battery-operated televisions allowed in possession, along with radio-cassettes, home-made tapes, trainers etc, but no pets. Probation dept run Help & Advice Shop last Wednesday every month with input from DSS, CABx, APEX, Job Club, Drug/Alcohol Agencies among many others: an excellent initiative that should be available in all establishments. Routine censorship abolished in June 1992, each wing deals with its own mail but all mail is opened and examined outwith the presence of the inmate. Card phones and hoods fitted in all wings and access reported as good.

CANTEEN Situated in a passageway between A&B wing, the canteen is staffed by two prison officers, prices are clearly displayed, and it is well stocked. Convicted one visit per week, remands Mon–Wed–Fri.

VISITS *How to get there*: Train to Gloucester then 15 min walk to prison. No Special Transport.
VISITING TIMES: Week Days: 1330–1530. Saturday: 0930–1130 (Rem). Sunday: No Visits.

NOTES No staffed Visitors Centre. Canteen and Childrens Play Area. No overnight stay. Baby-changing facilities and wheelchair access. Convicted three visits per month.

EDUCATION Education open 50 weeks of the year. Four f/t teachers and evening classes held twice a week. Mainly caters for English and maths but good art classes, drama and self-catering studies. OU students catered for and room for 19 inmates on FTE.

WORKSHOPS Motor mechanics course (12 places), Education (12), Horticulture Course (8), Works (10), Craft Shop (10), Barber (1), Kitchen (10), Servery (5), Wing Painters (4), Stores (5), Yards (4), Mess (3), Cleaners (18), Orderlies (9), Community Party (6)—total of 136 places for a prison that has a baseline CNA of 209 and which often operates well above that figure.

MEDICAL Full time MO, no night cover. 1×HCPO, 1×HCSO and 1×HCO. Dental surgery. Located on first floor of B.wing, 14 cells and one protected room. Daytime association for in-patients if staff available. Plans to introduce agency nurses to provide night cover, and introduce substance abuse groups.

GYMNASIUM & SPORTS Four PE staff. Reasonably sized gymnasium and sports yard. Weights area. volleyball, basketball, football, circuit training, fitness, remedials and range of evening classes five nights of the week.

CHAPLAINCY Part time CE, RC, Methodist, Quaker, Salvation Army and Muslim ministers. Large chapel accessible from B.wing in which all services are conducted. RC Mass 0830 Sunday, followed by an 'All Comers' service at 0940. Holy Communion Saturday 0940. Weekly bible study classes and Chaplain's Hour Wednesday evenings. Extra Chaplain's Hour on Thursday for vulnerable inmates.

FOOD Staffing: 1×SO and 2×Officer (caterers), and there is a work party of 11 inmates. Kitchen recently refurbished to a high standard, new equipment has been installed. No health/hygiene training given to inmates. Choice of five meals available each lunchtime, and three choices available for tea. Inmates complain about poor quality of vegetables, poor presentation and little or no choice of meal for those on Vegan diets. No pre-select menu system.

ESTABLISHMENT REPORTS In a report (published September 1993) of an inspection in February 1993, Judge Stephen Tumim, HMCIP, said that Gloucester was a small prison trying to fulfill a complex role with limited resources. Most inmates found it convenient for visits and were generally content to be there. HMCIP was criticial of the regime but the governor was aware of the shortcomings and was willing to consider improvements. More multi-disciplinary groupwork should be undertaken, carpets should be fitted to the association area, a choice of morning or afternoon visits should be given, and health checks on admission should take place in the HCC not the reception.

GOVERNOR'S COMMENTS New gymnasium and hospital in pipeline.

PRISONERS' COMMENTS Requests and complaints dealt with slowly: 'it took four days to be given a form after application'. No power points in cells but internal light switch. Canteen provides a good service with local purchase facility, though prices tend to be on the high side. Three 'good visits per month', though no town visits allowed even for D Cats. Work is scarce, wages are poor and there are 'far too many unemployed inmates'. Adjudications reported as 'fair'. Good menu system for food in operation with varied diets. Mail is no longer censored only 'checked for cash then handed out at 11.30am, card phone facilities are excellent'.

HM Prison Grendon

Grendon Underwood, Aylesbury, Bucks. HP18 OTL
Tel: 0296-770301 **Fax:** 0296-770756
Opened: 1962 **CNA:** 235 **Roll:** 181 **Category:** B. Adult Male Only (Therapeutic)

i **BACKGROUND** In 1939 Sir Norwood East and Dr Hubert presented a paper to the Home Secretary on the psychological treatment of offenders, recommending that a therapeutic prison should be developed. Grendon Hall, a Victorian country house taken over in 1953, became and remains Spring Hill Open Prison. Grendon prison was built in the grounds of Spring Hill and opened in 1962. Grendon is a Category B prison which only takes adult males—sadly there remains no 'Grendon' for either YO's or female prisoners. Grendon also contains a pre-release unit with 10 bed-sits operated by Officer Joe Chapman. The Governor of Grendon and Spring Hill, Tim Newell, provided an abundance of information about Grendon, and a short amount about Spring Hill), and the BoV (who also cover both establishments) provided a copy of their latest annual report. HMCIP published their latest report on Grendon in October 1993. Adult male inmates wishing to apply for a place at Grendon should contact the Medical Officer in their current establishment, or write to Dr Jack Wright, Medical Officer at Grendon.

OFFICIALS
AREA MGR: Amy Edwards
CHAIR BOV: Lady Slynn
GOVERNOR: Tim Newell
MEDICAL: Dr. Jack Wright

CHAPLAIN: Rev K. Pounds
PROBATION: Jack Cordery
EDUCATION: Bev Turner
LOCAL MP: David Liddington. Con
STAFFING: 9 Governor grades and 176 uniformed staff—including specialist grades—for *both* Grendon and Spring Hill. Staffing for Grendon: 3×PO, 4×HCPO, 5×SO, 13×HCSO, 61×Officers, 22×HCO, 11×PA, 2×PA(Cas), 9×NP. Total of 107 in unified grades.

☞ **REGIME** *week days*: 0745 unlock/breakfast. 0830 Group Therapy or work, dependent on wing. 11.30 dinner. 1300 exercise. 1400 Group Therapy or work. 1630 tea. 2100 lock up.

week ends: 0745 unlock/breakfast. 0900 sports field. 1130 dinner. 1300 visits. 1600 tea. 2100 lock up.

Out of cell: 13/24hrs weekdays and 13/24hrs at weekends.

ACCOMMODATION & FACILITIES

Five 40-man therapy wings, one assessment unit, a pre-release and pre-transfer unit. All cells have internal light switch, power point and access to night sanitation. Extensive i/p list, usual long term privileges and possessions including caged bird. All electrical equipment must be examined by works dept. and bar-coded before issue. Sentence planning, drug counselling, card phones & personal officer scheme. According to HMCIP in October 1993: 'bright colours had been used to decorate the wings and there were plants on the landings and condiments on the dining room tables'. Central canteen. One visit per week. Local purchase facility, though local prices tend to be on the high side. Mail usually arrives at the establishment each day at 1100. After being sorted in the General Office it goes to the Centre, where it is sorted into wing batches. Wing staff are notified and generally collect it within 15 minutes. Inmates can witness the opening of their mail if they wish.

THE GRENDON WAY OF DOING THINGS Each therapeutic wing is an autonomous community. It selects its own officials, including an inmate-Chairman who presides over all meetings of the community. Each wing consists of four or five small inmate-groups who collectively comprise the community. Grendon is a robust and proven regime that challenges the criminal way of life: it should not be under estimated. Success requires constant hard work and a resolute desire to lead a crime-free life—both in Grendon and after release. Each community sets its own rules, though there are three policies which cover the prison as a whole: **No Drugs, No Sex, No Violence**—breach **any** of these and you will probably return to your prison of origin on the next bus—if not sooner. Acceptance is dependent on medical agreement, in addition to the successful completion of an assessment period that requires a level of intelligence and rationality rarely associated with Grendon by those ignorant of what it really does. Work is allocated by a Labour Board staffed entirely by inmates. Cleaners are answerable to an inmate Foreman-cleaner, who controls the wages of those for whom he is responsible. Applications for education, home leave, temporary release etc have to be supported by the community to stand any realistic chance of success. You are free to leave at any time (though not literally!) and it takes perseverance and commitment to stay the course: but the rewards are there for those who *want* to succeed. The Editor of the book you now hold in your hands is an ex-Grendon inmate who went there from the strip cells of Dartmoor, and emerged from the Grendon experience with a completely different outlook on life: see **'A Product of the System'**, by Mark Leech, (Gollancz 1992. ISBN: 0-575-05571-5) which can be loaned via the prison library or purchased (£6.99) from any good bookshop.

✍ **REQUESTS/COMPLAINTS** Little resort to formal requests/complaints procedure as most problems are resolved by the therapeutic community—each wing is a 'community', headed by an inmate Chairman who has been elected (usually for a three-month non-renewable period) by both staff and inmates.

VISITS *How to get there*: 1225 Bus (Red Rover) from Aylesbury. Only one bus connects with visits. No public transport on Sundays. Special transport: HALOW (London) bus service: 0171-793-7484. The prison is investigating the use of its own transport to collect visitors.
VISITING TIMES: Week Days: 1315–1500 Wednesday only. Saturday: 1315–1500. Sunday: 1315–1500.

NOTES Staffed Visitors Centre. Canteen in visiting room, creche supervised by volunteers. Contact prison probation for details of B&B. Wheelchair access quite easy. Three visits allowed per month and management plans to increase this to four. Family visits every six months and held in each wing. Isolated location not easy to reach.

EDUCATION Education Unit at Grendon is open 48 weeks of the year, seven full time teachers and three evening classes per week. Education at Grendon is given to those who can persuade their group and Wing Tutor that it is justified on a therapeutic basis: therapy comes first, academic education second at Grendon. **Wing tutors: Bev Turner (B); Michael Dillow (C); vacant (D); Anne Wilson (F); Annette Tyler (G)**. C&G numeracy, Word power; Health & Hygiene; GCSE English, maths, psychology and others. Open learning in psychology, law, human biology, business studies, history and sociology. OU students catered for. Evening classes. All classrooms non-smoking areas.

WORKSHOPS Apart from the Kitchen and Laundry, workshops now in operation: Grendon is a therapy-based establishment with the emphasis on tackling offending behaviour rather than mailbags. The plethora of jobs that are available within each community are normally granted by a labour board, which is headed by the inmate Chairman of the community and one member from each small group within it.

DISCIPLINE Formal disciplinary hearings at Grendon are almost unheard of on the therapeutic wings, those that do occur tend to emanate from the Acute Psychiatric Unit. Confronting behaviour which offends against the principles of the establishment is a matter for each community unless it consists of a major offence, drugs, sex or violence, in which case a transfer back to prison of origin is almost as inevitable as it will be swift. In the six months prior to the 1991 full inspection by HMCIP there had been 34 reported offences against discipline—in five of which the inmates had been found 'unfit to plead'.

MEDICAL Staffing: 1×SMO, 5×Psychiatrists, 4×HCPOs, 13×HCSOs and 22×HCOs. Morning sick parade held each day and report sick at other times via wing staff. HCC now Pre-Release Unit.

GYMNASIUM & SPORTS Six staff: 1×PESO, 5×PEO's who have to cover both Grendon and Spring Hill. Small gymnasium dating from 1961, multi-gym, large weights room. Outdoor facilities: very large sports field encompassing soccer and rugby pitches, running track, athletics track, assault course, Red-gra area. Classes: badminton, volleyball, basketball, football, padder tennis, circuit training and remedials. Evening classes Mon–Thur 1800–2000.

CHAPLAINCY Full-time chaplain (CE) and part time RC & Methodist ministers. Visiting ministers of other faiths. Active chaplaincy who play a part in much of the establishment, assisting with prison visitors, social events and religious study.

FOOD The main meal of the day is taken at 1630 and there are plans to reschedule this to 1715. Pre-select menu system in operation. The kitchen was found to be in a very poor state by HMCIP when an inspection was conducted in May 1993: at the full inspection in 1991 HMCIP had recommended catering should be contracted out to a private contractor but this was not accepted by the Home Office and, in 1993, HMCIP reported 'the kitchen should not be used any longer in its present state'.

ESTABLISHMENT REPORTS The ethos of Grendon continues to flourish said HMCIP in a Report (published 5th October 1993) of an inspection in May 1993. Prisoners were taking the opportunity to confront underlying problems assisted by committed and skilful staff. HM Chief Inspector was impressed by the quality of the therapy programme, saying it was 'refreshing' to find inmates exercising personal responsibility and choice. Judge Tumim also greeted with cautious optimism the recent study of reconviction statistics: of 214 men covered by the study, 33.3% were reconvicted within two years of release, compared with a national reconviction rate for adult males of between 42% and 47%.

GOVERNOR'S COMMENTS Sanitation facilities are now completed for all the prison, art therapy and allied therapies are now in place. Landscaping of gardens should be completed to help create a more pleasant environment. Research into the effectiveness of therapy will be widely promoted to other prisons.

PRISONERS' COMMENTS As far as requests and complaints are concerned, the general impression is that locally the system works when put into operation but, beyond the establishment, time limits are not being respected and 'the Home Office take forever'. Accommodation is regarded as very good and visits are 'excellent'. Work opportunities are small and the wages are considered very poor. Medical facilities are said to be 'excellent' and the food has seen recent improvement with the introduction of a menu system. Gym access has been improved with 'something on every day'. Religious needs are catered for and 'every denomination is treated very well'.

HM YOI Guys Marsh

Shaftesbury, Dorset. SP7 OAH
Tel: 0747-853344 **Fax:** 0747-851584
Opened: 1960 **CNA:** 300 **Average Roll:** 290 **Category:** Closed YOI

i **BACKGROUND** Guys Marsh, situated near Shaftesbury in Dorset, is located on the site of small wartime camp of mainly single-storey timber buildings that had been used as a military hospital. The Prison Commissioners purchased the site for the penal estate in 1960 and shortly afterwards purchased the adjoining farm to provide work for the inmates. The establishment opened in 1960 as an open Borstal for male trainees. In 1983 Guys Marsh became an open Youth Custody Centre and, in 1988, a Young Offender Institution. In December 1992, following the erection of a security fence around the site, the establishment became a closed YOI (with a small juvenile unit) taking inmates from the West Country who would otherwise have been detained considerable distances from their homes in the YOI at Feltham, Middlesex. Neither the Governor nor BoV at Guys Marsh responded to our requests for information about the establishment and HMCIP published their latest inspection report in August 1993.

OFFICIALS

AREA MGR: John May
CHAIR BOV:
GOVERNOR: P.B. Tucker
MEDICAL:
CHAPLAIN: Rev Liston
PROBATION: A. Yelling
EDUCATION:
LOCAL MP: Nicholas Baker. Con
STAFFING: 6 Governor grades and 105 other unified grades, including specialist staff.

REGIME *week days*: 0730 unlock. 0815 breakfast. 0830 work. 1115 adjudications. 1200 dinner. 1300 work. 1655 cease labour. 1700 tea. 1730–2100 association.

week ends: 0730 unlock. 0815 breakfast. 0830 house and room cleaning. 0900 CE Service (Sun). 0915 RC Mass (Sun). 0930 inspection (Sat). 1015 association. 1150 dinner. 1215 lock up. 1315 unlock. 1330 association. 1700 tea. 1730–2100 association.

Out of cell: 10.25/24hrs weekdays and 10.25/24hrs at weekends.

ACCOMMODATION & FACILITIES
Five separate accommodation blocks. Wessex, Cumbria and Dorset Houses are identical and were built in 1983. Each houses 60 inmates (58 single rooms and one double room). Mercia and Anglia Houses, which opened in 1992, provide for 60 inmates in single cells with integral sanitation. Blocks have communal areas for association and a dining room.

CANTEEN Canteen, located on the ground floor of the shared services building, is open Monday and Tuesday evenings for private cash and Fridays for earnings. Carries about 150 lines of stock, private cash can be spent on any items other than tobacco. Guys Marsh enforces the annual private cash limit. Canteen and Catering Committee meets regularly.

VISITS *How to get there*: Train to Gillingham or bus to Shaftesbury. Minibus pick up service from prison meets train at Gillingham at 1305. Portsmouth probation run minibus service: 0705-871441.
VISITING TIMES: Week Days: 1330–1530. Mon, Tues, Wed only. Saturday: 1330–1530. Last admission 3.15. Sunday: 1330–1530.

NOTES No staffed Visitors Centre. Canteen and Childrens Play Area. Contact prison probation for details of local B&B. Wheelchair access easy, baby-changing facilities available. Three visits allowed every 28 days, one of which must be taken mid-week.

EDUCATION Located in the shared services building, which also contains the library, kitchen and chapel, the education facilities are very good but underused because all education is part time and does not attract a rate of pay. Curriculum includes YO Induction Programme (15 hours/wk) and YO Pre-Release Programme (5 hours/wk).

WORKSHOPS Average pay: Orderlies £6.25; Cleaners £5.10; CES £5.55; Laundry £6.35; Kitchen £7.75; VTC/CIT £5.30; Farms/Gardens £5.50; Works £6.45.

DISCIPLINE Segregation unit not brought into use, inmates who cause undue problems frequently transferred to Portland or Feltham YOI's. Total of 2.6 reports per inmate compares favourably with an average of 5.2 reports per inmate for similar establishments. Examination of 52 adjudication records showed 37 lost (or suspended loss) of remission, nine loss of earnings, three cautions and three other awards.

MEDICAL Part time Medical Officer, 1×HCSO, 1×HCO. Very good medical facilities, average of 12 report sick each day between 0745–0815 and are seen by MO later in the day. No visiting specialists as all requirements are dealt with by local hospital or practices. Dentist visits 3×3hr sess/wk. No no-smoking policy other than on visits. HIV/AIDS counsellors and drug counselling available.

GYMNASIUM & SPORTS 1×PEPO, 1×PESO and 3×PEO. Good PE facilities, new large gymnasium, no weights room but hut due for conversion. Ten acre sports field divided into two football pitches, a full size rugby field and grass and artificial cricket wickets. New sports field also has a pavilion and toilet facilities. Three new porous tarmac areas would add to the facilities. Open seven days and four evenings a week, Guys Marsh has also cultivated an excellent relationship with the local community and runs CSLA courses.

CHAPLAINCY Part time CE chaplain, RC and Methodist ministers. RC Mass and CE Service both held on Sunday morning. Imam visits as required, as does Buddhist minister. Multi-faith facilities available.

FOOD Staffing: 1×SO, 2×Officer (Caterers), and an inmate work party of 8. Three week menu cycle, though no pre-select system. Tea is the main meal of the day. No NVQ caterbase in Guys Marsh, though plans for future introduction. Kitchen old and does not conform to current standards. CI.9/92 requires that a food-infection outbreak control team be set up in every establishment: no such team existed at Guys Marsh.

ESTABLISHMENT REPORTS In a report (published 5th August 1993) of an inspection in October 1992), HMCIP said that the problems facing the Governor at Guys Marsh were those which came from managing any multi-functional establishment. The change of role to closed conditions, the additional juvenile population with their needs and plans to take unconvicted young inmates from Dorchester prison, all presented a multitude of problems. Cells are dominated by the sanitation. The need for a farm at Guys Marsh needs to be reviewed. The establishment had an excellent and long-standing reputation for providing training opportunities for young men and it was not possible to see how this would be effected with the change of role. Inmate/staff relationships are good and inmates see staff as being helpful and positive, this was particularly evident among those who had been transferred from other establishments.

Haslar Holding Centre

Dolphin Way, Gosport. PO12 2AW
Tel: 0705-580381 **Fax:** 0705-510266
Opened: 1864 **CNA:** 136 **Average Roll:** 111 **Category:** B. Immigration Detainees

BACKGROUND Used as an immigration detention centre but designated as a prison, Haslar is located on the Hampshire coast a short distance from the centre of Gosport and short ferry ride from Portsmouth. It stands on the seafront, overlooking Spithead and the Isle of Wight. Haslar was built in 1864 as an army barracks, providing accommoddation for soldiers who guarded the Haslar Naval Hospital next door and it was used as such until 1953. The establishment was acquired by the Prison Commissioners in 1960 and opened as a Senior Detention Centre in 1962. In 1988 it became a Young Offender Institution and, in June 1989 as a result of consistently low numbers, Haslar became an Immigration Detention Centre and continues in the role today. There is a small convicted population to fulfil essential domestic tasks, but the vast majority of the Haslar population have been neither charged nor convicted of any offence; their detention is wholly immigrational in nature. This led to a call from HMCIP that Haslar should no longer be called 'HM Prison' and the Home Secretary announced a change of name in January 1993. Neither the Governor nor Board of Visitors replied to our requests for information. HMCIP published their latest report in Janaury 1993.

OFFICIALS
AREA MGR: Alan Rayfield
CHAIR BOV:
GOVERNOR: J.R. Duvell
MEDICAL:
CHAPLAIN: Rev Sutton
PROBATION: Helen McDuff
EDUCATION:
LOCAL MP: Peter Viggers. Con

REGIME Haslar operates a 24 hour unlock regime in which there is unlimited access to association areas and sanitation.

ACCOMMODATION & FACILITIES Four dormitories, no cellular accommodation. Bedspaces separated by privacy screens but no properly partitioned cubicles. Clean and tidy accommodation areas with no evidence of vandalism or graffiti. Two association rooms, each with two card phones for outgoing calls and one line for incoming calls. Good sanitation facilities, including squat toilet. HMCIP's population survey (by nationality) revealed: Algeria (8%); Angola (5%); Bangladesh (2%); Chile (1%); Columbia (3%); Egypt (1%); Ghana (9%); India (12%); Iran (3%); Israel (1%); Ivory Coast (1%); Lebanon (5%); Malaya (1%); Morocco (2%); Namibia (1%); Niger (1%); Nigeria (18%); Pakistan (8%); Saudi Arabia (1%); Sierra Leone (2%); Turkey (3%); Zaire (12%). Of the 109 on the roll, 105 had been in custody up to nine months, one upto 12 months, two up to 15 months and one up to 18 months. Local CABx used to visit Haslar twice per week but this was cancelled after temporary funding from the Home Office was withdrawn. UKIAS representatives visit once per week. No censorship of mail officially, but detainees complained to HMCIP that as it was not opened in their presence, they had no way of ensuring that it wasn't read. Two outgoing card phones and one incoming line in each association room.

CANTEEN Situated in the main corridor and staffed by two Prison Auxiliaries, the canteen is open 0845–1130 & 1330–1545 Mon–Fri and simoetimes on Sunday. Reasonable stock, including freshly made rolls, non-alcoholic lager, small articles of clothing and phonecards.

REQUESTS/COMPLAINTS Formal R/C system rarely used as most issues are resolved between detainees and staff informally. Most issues relate to the delays in being informed about their cases from the immigration authorities.

VISITS *How to get there*: Train to Portsmouh Harbour, then Gosport ferry (5 mins), 15/20 min walk to the prison. No Special Transport.
VISITING TIMES: Week Days: 0930–1130 & 1330–1630. Saturday: 1330–1630. Sunday: 1330–1600.

NOTES No staffed Visitors Centre. Canteen on weekends only. No overnight stays, no Childrens Play Area. Wheelchair ramp into the visting room.

EDUCATION Education plays a significant part in the regime at Haslar, and takes place in a series of small classrooms close to the dining room, which operate from 0915–1130 & 1345–1615 Mon–Fri. Evening classes 1800–1945. Two f/t & six p/t teachers. All detainees interviewed on arrival by education officer. Core education mainly on languages and basic education, but business studies and computing particularly favoured.

MEDICAL P/t Medical Officer, 1×HCSO and 1×HCO. Three bed ward and isolation rooms in Health Care Centre. Detainees visit dentist and optician locally under escort.

GYMNASIUM & SPORTS Small gymnasium, with good floor marked out for ball games. Outside tarmac area for volleyball etc. Staffed by 1×PESO and 1×PEO. Well involved in the regime and access to inmates each day.

CHAPLAINCY Part time CE, RC & Methodist chaplains who visit two or three times a week. Chapel on first floor and rooms for other faiths to practice their religion. HMCIP recommended appointment of multi-faith assistant to the Chaplain.

FOOD Staffing: 1×SO and 1×Officer (caterers), and there is a work party of 5 convicted prisoners. Catering staff have a hard task catering for so many different nationalities and cultures, but the well rounded menu, with plenty of rice dishes, makes the best of a difficult situation—orange juice offered each day at lunchtime. Three choices at dinner and two at tea.

ESTABLISHMENT REPORTS In a report (published 19th January 1993) of an inspection in June 1992, Judge Stephen Tumim, HMCIP, came away from Haslar having been impressed with the civilised and caring atmosphere that existed in the Centre. There were however areas of concern: CABx visits should be reintroduced immediately (rejected by the Home Secretary in June 1992); the name should be changed to 'HM Remand Centre Haslar' (rejected on legal grounds by the Home Secretary who authorised the name 'Haslar Holding Centre' instead); improved funding was required for catering (not addressed by Home Secretary).

HM YOI Hatfield

Thorne Road, Hatfield, Doncaster. DN7 6EL
Tel: 0405-812336 **Fax:** 0405-813325
Opened: 1954 **CNA:** 180 **Average Roll:** 160 **Category:** Open YOI

i **BACKGROUND** In 1954 the RAF camp at Hatfield in Yorkshire was purchased by the then Prison Commissioners who redeveloped the site, completing the work in the early 1980s. The nearby Tudworth Hall farm and a small former Land Army camp some 22 miles away at Gringly were acquired to provide additional facilities for the inmates. Gringly was completely redeveloped by about 1960 to house some 70 inmates. Misterton Carr farm, some 20 miles from Hatfield, was also purchased to provide inmate labour. Gringly, a former Detention Centre, was closed in 1988. Hatfield is a Young Offender Institution for males aged between 17 and 21. Neither the Governor nor the BoV replied to our requests for information, and HMCIP published their latest inspection report on Hatfield in August 1993.

OFFICIALS
AREA MGR: Maurice Codd
CHAIR BOV:
GOVERNOR: J.W. Clark
MEDICAL:
CHAPLAIN: Rev Tomlinson
PROBATION: Alan Furness
EDUCATION:
LOCAL MP: Kevin Hughes. Lab
STAFFING: 4 Governor grades, 5 Principal Officers, 12 Senior Officers and 44 Officers, including specialist staff.

REGIME *week days*: 0730 roll check. 0800 breakfast. 0830 Misterton Farm party to work. 0845 labour parade. 1130 cease work. 1200 dinner. 1255 work. 1610 cease labour. 1645 tea. 1745 evening classes, roll check, association. 2045 association ends. 2200 lights out.

week ends: 0730 roll check. 0800 breakfast. 0830 Misterton & Tudworth Farm parties to work. 0845 association, gymnasium open. CE Service (Sun). 0945 Accompanied Visits (Sat), library open. 1130 dinner. 1200 association. 1330–1530 visits. 1545 Accompanied Visits return. 1600 gymnasium closes. 1630 tea. 1700 association. 2030 association ends. 2200 lights out.

Out of cell: 13/24hrs weekdays and 13/24hrs at weekends.

ACCOMMODATION & FACILITIES Three main accommodation blocks: A,B,C units. Each contains 60 single rooms and were built in the late 1980s. Each unit has three landings with 20 rooms on each, very clean communal areas. Privacy keys to all rooms but many are broken into. TV, association and quiet room on all units, free access to showers. No facility for making hot drinks. Sentence planning and personal officer schemes. Drug counselling. Card phones in all living units.

REQUESTS & COMPLAINTS In common with many YOIs, the formal RC procedure is rarely used and is viewed with some suspicion by inmates, averaging three per month. Time targets are being met.

CANTEEN Open every Friday morning, inmates can spend pay and private cash. Located close to the living units but too small for its purpose. Limited stock list with 51% of all purchases at this YOI being on tobacco, 13% on phone cards and 10% on biscuits and cola. Tea, coffee or other hot drinks are not stocked.

VISITS *How to get there*: Train to Doncaster and then bus, stops half mile from prison. Enquiries South Yorks Transport (0302-329666) for buses and BR Doncaster for trains (0302-340222). Special Transport from Newcastle/Durham: 091-284-2585, also from Leeds probation.
VISITING TIMES: Week Days: No visits. Saturday: 1330–1530. Sunday: 1330–1530.

NOTES No girlfriends under 18 admitted without parents. No staffed Visitors Centre or Childrens Play Area. Canteen in visiting room. No more than three adults admitted. Nappy-changing facilities.

EDUCATION Almost all inmates at Hatfield spend their first week in the Education Department undergoing an induction course, with the overriding aim of identifying inmates' needs. All education part time. Open for 51 weeks of the year, five days and four evenings per week. Classes: basic education, English, maths, general and computer studies. Excellent child care course. Also provides basic food-handling course, information on STDs, first aid course and information on exercises and diet. Evening classes in cookery, woodwork, art, toymaking and pottery. HMCIP recommended addition of anger management course and more full time education courses.

WORKSHOPS There are no workshops at Hatfield. Farm and Gardens is the main employer, taking upto 40 inmates. VTC/CIT: Bricklaying; General Con Ops; Industrial Cleaning; Motor Mechanics; Painting & Decorating. Usual domestic, catering and orderly jobs.

DISCIPLINE Most adjudications at Hatfield are for infringements of the Hatfield rules and for fighting. Verbal abuse to staff is infrequent. Average of 2.9 offences per inmate per year. HMCIP said the new Segregation Unit should enable greater use of awards other than the loss of remission which has dominated adjudications to date.

MEDICAL Part time Medical Officer, 1×HCO, 1×Nurse. HCC with one three-bedded and one four-bedded ward, generally clean and well decorated. Report sick in the morning and seen by MO at lunchtime. Small number reporting sick each day, mainly sports injuries and infections. Dentist 1 sess/wk and waiting list of 7–14 days.

GYMNASIUM & SPORTS 1×PESO and 2×PEO. Large purpose-built gymnasium and a very large and well equipped weights room. Outdoor facilities comprise rugby pitch, cricket wicket and two football pitches. All inmates receive minimum of two hours of PE per week with football and weights being the most popular activities. Other sports: basketball, volleyball, fitness training and swimming in a nearby pool. External one-day hikes and one-week camps quite frequent, 10km road race, weight-lifting displays and sponsored football matches make for a well rounded PE programme.

CHAPLAINCY Part time CE chaplain, RC and Methodist ministers. Small chapel for CE services. RC Mass at local church in the community. No multi-faith room, group room or vestry. Bible study class Thursdays 1745.

FOOD Staffing: 1×SO, 2×Officer (caterers), and an inmate work party of 15. Lack of quantity rather than quality is the main complaint at Hatfield, one slice of bread at dinner despite the strenuous manual work. Three choices at dinner with meals popular with the young inmates, fish, curries, pies and chips with everything other than the duff.

ESTABLISHMENT REPORTS In a report (published 10th August 1993) of an inspection in September 1992, HMCIP, said that Hatfield appeared to be an impressive establishment which had been involved in training young men for over a quarter of a century. Throughout the establishment there were numerous examples of a continuing commitment to training from staff. Community work and links were well established. The PE department and Education Centre provided a good service and work training opportunities were sound. There was a good range of vocational and construction industry training courses. The two farms and the internal grounds were the main employers of inmate labour, though there are reservations about the value of the work experience available to inmates on the farm parties. Staff expressed concern about bullying, taxing and absconding. The Governor was seeking ways in which weaker members of the inmate population could be made to feel more confident and secure and planned to develop an anti-bullying strategy. Some parts of the regime had a traditional feel to them and more uniformed staff should be involved in the induction and pre-release programmes.

PRISONERS' COMMENTS Hatfield is generally regarded as a good place with education and health care receiving praise. Food has too little variation and all religious diets are converted to vegetarian. Highly suspicious of the complaints request procedure. Trainers are the only items of civilian clothing allowed in use. Involvement in the community is good and should be developed further. Inmate committees should be established for relevant areas such as regime, canteen, visits, food etc. There is a lack of full time education. Staff on the whole are quite good though there are a small minority who are well known for making life difficult.

HM Prison Haverigg

Millom Cumbria. LA18 4NA
Tel: 0229-772131 **Fax:** 0229-772561
Opened: 1967 **CNA:** 405 **Average Roll:** 329 **Category:** C. Male

i **BACKGROUND** Haverigg prison is situated on the coast about two miles south of Millom in West Cumbria. In 1939 the Air Ministry purchased the land and built an aerodrome for wartime use. In 1966 it passed to the Prison Department who converted the site to a C Category training prison, the first inmates arrived in 1967. Most facilities including inmate accommodation is in the former RAF huts or in temporary buildings of a similar style. In recent years a new Health Care Centre, kitchen, sports hall and temporary wing have been added. A minor disturbance occurred in October 1993 but was contained to one wing and brought under control by Haverigg staff. The prison has acquired media prominence for its drug culture, and the prison must be the only C category establishment in England and Wales to possess its own drug detection dog. Neither the Governor nor BoV replied to our requests for information about the prison and HMCIP published their latest inspection report in July 1994.

OFFICIALS
AREA MGR: Ian Lockwood
CHAIR BOV:
GOVERNOR: Bernard Wilson
MEDICAL:
CHAPLAIN: Rev Ian Smith
PROBATION: D. Hart
EDUCATION:
LOCAL MP: John Cunningham. Lab

REGIME *week days*: 0730 roll check, applications MUST be handed in before breakfast. 0750 breakfast. 0805 sick parade. 0825 work. 1140 cease labour. 1200 dinner. 1300 work. 1620 cease labour. 1715 tea. 1730–2030 association. Lights out midnight.

week ends: 0730 roll check, applications (Sat) MUST be handed in before breakfast. 0800 breakfast. 0805 sick parade. 0820 association. 1130 cease association. 1200 dinner. 1230 association. 1630 cease association. 1715 tea. 1730–2030 association. Lights out midnight.

Out of cell: 13/24hrs weekdays and 13/24hrs at weekends.

ACCOMMODATION & FACILITIES
Living accommodation divided into three zones, known as Residential 1 (A&B wings, 101 inmates), 2 (C&D wings, 114) and 3 (E.wing, 86). A–D wings former RAF huts, each capable of housing 18 inmates in single and double rooms. Huts in poor state of repair, dirty toilets and discarded items of property and clothing litter the grounds. Considerable vandalism, privacy locks on doors broken open by cell thieves and the huts are a haven for bullying and trafficking primarily in drugs according to HMCIP. E.wing comprises five new living units of temporary construction, each costing £120,000 and housing 18 inmates in 14 single and 2 double rooms. Association facilities in four prefabs, provide snooker, pool. Induction programme lasting three days for all new arrivals.

VPU Discrete accommodation close to the Segregation Unit provides for a maximum of 21 VPs. Their conditions are even worse than the main prison, being cramped and spartan. The regime was impoverished, no work opportunities but education staff helped to alleviate the boredom. HM Prison Service commented on publication of the HMCIP Report that conditions for VP inmates would improve at Haverigg when the 'proposed new house block opens'.

VISITS *How to get there*: Train to Millom. Bus (15) from Market Square. Special Transport: Liverpool (051-920-9201); Manchester (061-236-7621) and Carlisle probation.
VISITING TIMES: Week Days: 1315–1515. Saturday: 1315–1515. Sunday: 1315–1515.

NOTES (Still) no staffed Visitors Centre at Haverigg but nappy-changing facilities now available. Contact prison probation for details of local B&B. Easy wheelchair access to the visiting room. All inmates serving six years or over, including lifers, are entitled to apply for family visits which take place every four weeks and last from 1000–1600 on Saturdays and 1000–1400 on Sundays—inmates can attend on both days if they wish. Comfortable room allows cooking facilities and watching TV with family with limited supervision.

WORKSHOPS Textile based industries with about 180 inmates employed either in the production of textile goods or on sewing machine repairs. The former weaving industry has been removed and replaced with a PSIF Contract Services shop which employs 30 inmates. Two CIT courses in Bricklaying and Painting & Decorating, and two VTC courses in Electronics and DIY each provide 12 places. other work includes farms and gardens (23 places), kitchen (6), stores (17), works (14), orderlies and cleaners (23). Average wages in shops £6.50.

DRUGS In 1993 there were 154 drug finds at Haverigg, recent finds include syringes indicating that hard drugs are circulating the establishment in addition to the more common cannabis.

FOOD 'Inmates had described the conditions under which food was cooked, served and eaten as disgusting' said HMCIP, adding 'there was evidence to support many of their complaints'. Kitchen was dirty, staff did not wear protective clothing and the dirt on the floor had accumulated over several weeks. Food was of an acceptable standard and reasonably presented, but the conditions in which it was eaten, said HMCIP, were both 'unpleasant and unhygienic'.

ESTABLISHMENT REPORTS In a report (published 13th July 1994) of an inspection in January 1994, HMCIP, said that the threat of closure had hung over Haverigg for some years. If the prison is to remain part of the penal estate, further investment is needed and the proposed new cell blocks to replace the huts were welcome. Trafficking in drugs was still a major problem at Haverigg and inmates with convictions for drug dealing should be allocated elsewhere. The atmosphere in the prison is relaxed, employment opportunities more than matched the inmate population though inmates resented the monotonous tasks they were required to perform. The regime for the VPU inmates needs to be improved, Haverigg has neither the resources nor accommodation to cater for them effectively and they should be sent elsewhere. The conditions under which food was prepared, served and eaten were very poor and a serious cause for concern.

Responding to the report HM Prison Service undertook not to transfer any more drug dealers to Haverigg and revealed the prison is shortly to have its own drug detection dog. Catering problems are a legacy of the RAF origins but they are being tackled and a new kitchen is already being built. Those who serve or prepare food now wear the appropriate clothing and regular cleanliness inspections are being carried out by the senior catering manager.

GOVERNOR'S COMMENTS Judge Tumim rightly recognises the hard work put in by staff to make inmates' experiences of custody as positive as possible. We are aware of the problems highlighted in the report and we are constantly endeavouring to improve and expand the service we provide.

PRISONERS' COMMENTS Large numbers of inmates transferred to Haverigg with only weeks to serve treat the place badly. Inmate/staff relationships generally good, though some of the younger staff are a little aggressive and tend to treat people like young offenders. Good gym, canteen and education facilities, but not enough training courses. Pay rates are too low for the hours and work required. A great deal of cell thieving goes on with doors being broken open most days. There is some bullying in the huts and association facilities were poor.

HM Prison Hewell Grange

Redditch, Worcestershire. B97 9QQ
Tel: 0527-550843 **Fax:** 0527-550178
Opened: 1949 **CNA:** 136 **Roll:** 136 **Category:** D. Male

i **BACKGROUND** The Hewell Grange Estate passed into the hands of the Windsor family about 400 years ago. Improvements and developments were carried out over the years, including the construction in 1890 of a three-storey Elizabethan style mansion in soft red sandstone brought from Runcorn in Cheshire. The house is surrounded by formal gardens and a deer park. The Estate was a family seat until it was purchased by the Prison Commissioners in 1947, and it opened as a Borstal shortly afterwards. Hewell Grange became a Youth Custody Centre in 1986, and a Young Offender Institution in October 1988. In October 1991 Hewell Grange became an open prison for adult males. It has a CNA of 136, but authority has been obtained from the Area Manager to exceed the CNA to reduce per capita costs. Neither the Governor nor Board of Visitors replied to our requests for information about the prison. HMCIP published their latest inspection report on Hewell Grange in September 1993.

OFFICIALS
AREA MGR: Dai Curtis
CHAIR BOV:
GOVERNOR: D. Bamber

MEDICAL:
CHAPLAIN: Rev Lodge
PROBATION: Richard Charles
EDUCATION:
LOCAL MP: Roy Thomason. Con
STAFFING: 4 Governor grades, 1 Principal Officer, 4 Senior officers and 23 Officers, including specialist staff.

REGIME *week days*: 0745–0815 breakfast. 0830 work. 1200 dinner. 1330 work. 1700 tea. No formal lights out time, nor formal closure of association rooms.

week ends: 0745–0815 breakfast. 1200 dinner. 1700 tea. No formal lights out time, nor formal closure of association rooms.

Out of cell: 24/24hrs weekdays and 24/24hrs at weekends.

ACCOMMODATION & FACILITIES
Dormitory accommodation each with between five and 12 beds—no single rooms. There are 17 dormitories on the second floor, a further three on the first floor, and what is known as the 'Hostel' is located in an annexe to the main house. Toilet and showering facilities on each floor are barely adequate for the population. The shower room in the annexe is dirty, paint is peeling off the ceiling, tiles are ingrained with mould, shower heads are too low, and there are no shower curtains said HMCIP. Association space is large, with TV rooms, snooker, bowls, darts and table-tennis. A first floor balcony was used for board games. Hewell Grange acceptance criteria exclude serious sex offenders, lifers, inmates who cannot climb stairs and those who require f/t medical cover. Arsonists only by prior agreement. Excellent Job Club—see below. Routine censorship abolished, mail sorted by staff and opened in main office—handed out at lunchtime. Cardphones on all floors and access reported as easy, though queues of considerable length can build up at peak times.

REQUESTS/COMPLAINTS There were 33 formal R/C forms issued in three months prior to inspection. Eight of these had been withdrawn subsequently. The majority were appeals to the area manager against a decision of the governor. Forms requiring a local reply related to such things as town visits, food, parole: queries about remand time, adjudications and medical records were replied to within fourteen days, and all were answered personally, in detail, by the Governor.

VISITS *How to get there*: Bus (147) Birmingham to Redditch every half hour. Bus (145) Birmingham to Bromesgrove hourly. Bus 318 Redditch–Bromesgrove passes gate hourly. No Special Transport.
VISITING TIMES: Week Days: 1330–1530 1 hr visits weekdays. Saturday: 1330–1530 2 hr visits weekends. Sunday: 1330–1530.

NOTES Visitors Centre outside the prison is shared with HMPs Blakenhurst and Brockhill. No Childrens Play Area. Canteen in visiting room. Poor facilities.

EDUCATION Located in a modern purpose-built education block, eight classrooms, including three furnished for cookery, art and computer studies. Education Officer assisted by two f/t lecturers and 14 sessional staff. Twenty-eight on FTE, with waiting list. Three courses: one for basic education, one set at a higher educational level offering scope for individual programmes, and one in business skills. Evening classes only operate one night a week—covering gardening, computers, art, maths and soft toy making. Library open each evening.

WORKSHOPS Labour Board meets every Thursday to allocate work. Large farm and gardens party, usual cleaners and kitchen, with remainder on external work placements or FTE.

JOB CLUB Created in 1989 the Job Club has the aim of helping inmates to secure employment or training on release. The working out scheme started with one inmate in March 1992, today there are almost two dozen inmates who earn realistic wages, contribute to their keep, pay their own fares to work and home at the weekends. The Club is located in an impressive room, it contains ample space and numerous advice leaflets. Job Club staff currently negotiating with British Rail and local farms in relation to employment. Almost 30 inmates have been successfully placed in f/t employment on release. It deserves every possible encouragement and ought to be copied at all other establishments.

DISCIPLINE Average of three a week , mainly for breach of licence conditions. Half of all cases heard by the Governor with the remainder shared by other governor grades. Records well kept but awards were a little inconsistent. Serious offences result in ship-out.

MEDICAL P/t Medical Officer, and five other GP's on call 24 hours a day. Four-bed ward. No dental surgery as inmates visit local dentist/optician on licence.

GYMNASIUM & SPORTS 1×PEPO, 2×PESO and 4×PEO serve both Hewell Grange and Brockhill. Gymnasium consists of converted Real Tennis court which together with adjacent weights room and large sports field provide good PE facilities. Other than one class in the afternoon for the kitchen workers, activities in the gym were mainly confined to evenings and weekends.

FOOD Many recommendations by HMCIP in 1989 have been acted on and the kitchen is now well equipped and clean. Problems however since the CNA was exceeded in that the kitchen was too small for such numbers. Pre-select menu system in operation for ordinary and special diets. No complaints received about food at Hewell Grange and HMCIP found the meals to be appetising.

ESTABLISHMENT REPORTS In a report (published 29th September 1993) of an inspection in May 1993, Judge Stephen Tumim, HMCIP, said that Hewell Grange had made the transition from YOI to adult prison with apparent ease. The regime places emphasis on education or work during the day, and PE or leisure during the evenings. The Job Club was outstanding. As a small prison Hewell Grange had been under the threat of closure for many years and the Governor had cut back on staffing, increased the CNA and rewritten attendance systems in an effort to make the establishment less costly to operate. HMCIP opposed any further increase in the inmate population, stating that inmates currently had insufficient privacy and several dormitories were clearly overcrowded.

PRISONERS' COMMENTS It has taken me seven weeks to obtain a complaint and request form. The conditions here are filthy, for a D Category establishment this place is the pits. The canteen is very good, however, and education is excellent, though wages here are really poor with an average of about £6 per week. Visits take place in the dining hall with a steady flow of prisoners walking past. Medical facilities are excellent. Disciplinary adjudications result in punishments that are always very heavy-handed. Food is a disgrace. Very small gym and its open on a 'pot luck' basis. Religious services are very good. Regardless from where inmates come in the UK you are only allowed two phonecards a week—if you want to buy a third you have to see the Governor! Mail opened before we get it and its dished out at dinnertime.

HM Prison High Down

Sutton Lane, Sutton, Surrey. SM2 5PD
Tel: 081-643-0063 **Fax:** 081-643-2035
Opened: 1993 **CNA:** 485 **Average Roll:** 208 **Category:** Male Local

i **BACKGROUND** Situated opposite HMP Downview in Sutton, HMP High Down is a Category B local prison opened by Chad Varah, the 83 year old founder of The Samaritans. Built on the site of a former mental hospital at Banstead, the establishment runs a comprehensive package for preparing prisoners for resettlement in the community, and serves the Crown Court at both Guildford and Croydon. The establishment has had a chequered history in the short time it has been open, being the scene of a hostage incident in February 1993, the inmate involved died of 'Adult Respiratory Distress Syndrome' when later transferred to HMP Belmarsh. There was also a death of an inmate in the Health Care Centre in December 1993, apparently from heart disease. The prison has a rigid canteen system which has come in for criticism from the BoV, who have also called for an Inmate Listener Scheme: though creation of a suicide suite has been rejected. Neither the Governor nor BoV replied to our requests for information about the prison, and HMCIP conducted their first inspection of High Down in November 1994. Their report has yet to be published: full details next edition.

OFFICIALS
AREA MGR: Alan Rayfield
CHAIR BOV: L.E. Rogers
GOVERNOR: S. Pryor
MEDICAL:
CHAPLAIN: Rev Boddy
PROBATION: Peter Sturge
EDUCATION:
LOCAL MP: Archie Hamilton. Con

VISITS *How to get there*: Train to Sutton, then bus to prison, or one and a half mile walk. No Special Transport.
VISITING TIMES: Week Days: 1400–1600 Last admission 1530. Saturday: 1400–1600. Sunday: 1400–1600.

NOTES Staffed Visitors Centre, but no Childrens Play Area. Canteen in visiting room. Contact prison probation for details of B&B.

HM Prison Highpoint

Stradishall, Newmarket, Suffolk. CB8 9YG
Tel: 0440-820611 **Fax:** 0440-820303
Opened: 1977 **CNA:** 679 **Roll:** 482 **Category:** C. Male

i **BACKGROUND** Highpoint prison lies deep in Suffolk countryside, some 13 miles from Bury St.Edmunds and on what was originally a RAF airfield. The site, split in two by a main road (A143), was acquired in 1973 with the intention of building TWO establishments: a Detention Centre on what is now 'North' and a B Category prison on what is now the 'Main'. Much of this work was to have been carried out by C Category inmates and, in May 1977, the first draft of C Cats arrived . . . followed by a second draft . . . then a third . . . Intentions gave way to lethargy and Highpoint became (and remains) the large Category C prison that it is today. The establishment had a bad start, has earnt for itself a shameful record of escapes and has suffered a number of serious disturbances—the last of which occurred in September 1994. Neither the Governor nor the BoV replied to our requests for information about Highpoint. HMCIP inspected the prison in December 1990: they made almost 200 recommendations. Their latest report on Highpoint, published in August 1993, said while improvements had been made the work done on the 1990 recommendations remained 'inadequate'.

OFFICIALS
AREA MGR: Tom Murtagh
CHAIR BOV:
GOVERNOR: D. Sherwood
MEDICAL:
CHAPLAIN: Rev Godfrey
PROBATION: Roger Dennis
EDUCATION:
LOCAL MP: Richard Spring. Con
STAFFING: 8 Governor grades, 15 Principal Officers, 39 Senior Officers, 153 Officers, 16 Night Patrols, 12 Prison Auxiliaries, two Casual Prison Auxiliaries, 43 industrial staff, 10 probation/education and 75 non-industrial staff.

☞ **REGIME** *week days*: 0810 unlock. 0815–0845 breakfast. 0845 work. 0900 sick parade. 1115 cease labour. 1130 dinner. 1200 Muslim Service (Fri), mail issue. 1245 work. 1615 cease labour, tea, association. 1745 evening classes. 1900 supper. 2045 lock up.

week ends: 0810 unlock, breakfast. 0815–0830 applications (Sat), P/cash letters (Sun). 0930 CE Service (Sun), cell inspection, induction interviews. 1100–1115 dinner. 1200 mail issue, association. 1420 (Sun: HIV/AIDS video for inductions). 1600 tea, 1645 lock up. 1800 association. 1845 supper. 2100 lock up.

Out of cell: 12/24hrs weekdays and 12/24hrs at weekends.

ACCOMMODATION & FACILITIES Accommodation consists of two separate sites, Main and North. Thirteen separate and widely varying units. The East and West Wings of the Main site comprise five former airmens' billets, with narrow and claustrophobic corridors and crowded four-man rooms. Toilet and shower facilities poor. In sharp contrast South Wing has good modern accommodation, single cells with integral sanitation. North Wing accommodation is in three H-shaped airmens' billets. Each housed 60 men in two 30-men rooms. Two television rooms, access to sanitation. No launderette facilities. Routine censorship abolished though all mail is opened outwith the presence of the inmate. Card phones on all living units with access reported as good. All calls susceptible to being monitored/recorded.

CANTEEN Separate canteens for each unit, good range of stock reported though prices not displayed and are said to be high. Local purchase facility. One visit per week to spend private cash and earnings. Verified reports of muggings after visiting the canteen call for vigilance and safety in numbers.

VISITS *How to get there*: Bus 933 from Bury St.Edmunds, Check with Eastern Counties Buses for times: 0284-766171. Special Transport: ABBA Coach from All Saints Church, New Kent Road SE14, Thurs & Sun, adults £10, children £5 return. Bookings: 081 859 1808, Mon–Fri 0900–1700.
VISITING TIMES: Week Days: 1345–1545. Saturday: 1345–1545 No PVO's. Sunday: 1345–1545.

NOTES No staffed Visitors Centre, but cafe outside prison. No Childrens Play Area but canteen in visiting room. Highpoint is a prison on both sides of a main road; check beforehand which side the prisoner is on. If using public transport, go to Bury St.Edmunds or Cambridge, not Newmarket.

EDUCATION Large education department, staffed by 1×f/t Education Officer, 2×Deputy EO, 5×f/t teachers, 3×IO, and 30 p/t teachers. Split into two sites: good facilities in

North, poor and cramped conditions above a dining hall in Main. 46 week year with full daytime programme, English, maths, art, computing, languages etc, and evening classes three evenings a week: Art, craft, woodwork, music/guitar, computing, drama, CIT/VTC theory classes.

WORKSHOPS Large workshop recently opened for contract services. VTC Motor Mechanics, Information Technology and Engineering Skills. Normal other occupations, works, kitchen, farms and gardens, stores, cleaners, orderlies, and party that works at Hollesley Bay.

DISCIPLINE Segregation unit newly opened. HMCIP reports 2,165 adjudications in the 12 months prior to his inspection. Of these 24 were of assault—8 of which were on staff—and 46 were drug related: 34 findings of cannabis, four of cocaine, two of heroin and six of other drugs. HMCIP reports that adjudication procedures were being followed and awards were consistent and appropriate.

MEDICAL F/t Medical Officer, with oversight provided by Senior Medical Officer at Norwich. 1×HCPO, 1×HCSO and 7×HCO. Hospital well equipped with good X-ray facilities, five-bed ward, and two dental surgeries. Two dentists visit each week. Optician visits as appropriate though often lengthy delays in being seen. No chiropody service.

GYMNASIUM & SPORTS 1×PEPO, 1×PESO and 6×PEO. Very good sports facilities, purpose-built sports hall opened in 1990, excellent changing/showering facilities (Main). Older facilities available in North, lacks a weights room and has limited changing facilities. Classes each day in both sections from 0830 to 1615. Badminton, volleyball, football, weights, gymnastics, remedial PE, Over-40's. Evening classes two one-hour sessions four days a week (Mon–Thurs). CSLA courses run regularly, also GCSE Physical Education available. Staff use facilities Friday evenings and at all other times when inmates are not rostered to use them.

CHAPLAINCY Full time CE chaplain and p/t RC and Methodist Ministers. other faith representatives visit regularly as requested. Services: CE Sunday 0900, RC Monday 1830. Bible classes Thursday 1830. Inmate prayer Group Tuesday dinnertime. Active Prison Visitors scheme.

FOOD Staffing: 1×PO, 2×SO and 6×Officer (caterers) to run two separate kitchens. Inmate work party of 26, who start at 0700–1230 & 1430–1745 with one full or two half days off each week. Separate menus for each half of the prison, based on four-week menu cycles. Food said to be very good by HMCIP, though Halal meat was not available because of difficulties with a local supplier.

ESTABLISHMENT REPORTS In a report (published 5th August 1993) of an inspection in January 1993, Judge Stephen Tumim, HMCIP, said that Highpoint had made many physical improvements since their 1990 inspection. Though time out of cell had been increased and training opportunities had been improved, the best use was still not being made of them. In 1990 HMCIP had recommended that research be conducted into the high level of adjudications, this had not been done and the level was still high. Pre-release training was at best sporadic, the increased drug counselling called for in 1990 had not materialised, nor had the recommended Deportation Liaison Officer been appointed, and there was little notable development towards focusing the regime on individualism, relationships and activities. On the staff side, unformed officers should be more involved in developing inmate compacts, linking activities to throughcare, preparing inmates for release, and an effective personal officer scheme should be introduced. The Director General of HM.Prison Service, Derek Lewis, said in reply to the report that a draft redevelopment plan was being drawn up to build Highpoint on one site. Accommodation on the Main site will be increased to take prisoners tranferred from North, the scheme will take eight to ten years to complete. It is unlikely that Highpoint will get a new Visitors Centre in the foreseeable future, but money will be found for updating living accommodation and kitchens.

HM Prison Hindley

Gibson St, Wigan, Lancs. WN2 5TH
Tel: 0942-866255 **Fax:** 0942-867442
Opened: 1961 **CNA:** 267 **Average Roll:** 287 **Category:** Male Local

i **BACKGROUND** Located about four miles south-east of Wigan, mid-way between Manchester and Liverpool, Hindley prison occupies a spacious flat site. Though Hindley has had a number of roles in its 34 year history, from a Borstal to closed Youth Custody Centre, closed Young Offender Institution, Remand centre and latterly a prison, the establishment has always catered for inmates under 21 since it first opened in December 1961. Today the prison holds young men remanded in custody for trial, and those who have recently been sentenced. Inmates sentenced to four years or more are transferred directly from Hindley to Castington, but the majority of other inmates are transferred to Stoke Heath—some convicted inmates being retained at Hindley for essential domestic work. The prison also has a VPU. The Governor of Hindley, David Roberts, provided helpful information about the prison, though the BoV did not respond to our request for a copy of their latest annual report. HMCIP published their latest inspection report on Hindley in January 1993.

OFFICIALS
AREA MGR: Ian Lockwood
CHAIR BOV: S. Simmons
GOVERNOR: D. Roberts
MEDICAL: Dr Farouque
CHAPLAIN: Rev Rennie
PROBATION: R. Griffiths
EDUCATION: D. Nash
LOCAL MP: Lawrence Cunliffe. Lab

REGIME *week days*: 0745 unlock, breakfast, cell inspection. 0840 work. 1145 cease labour. 1200 dinner. 1330 work. 1600 cease labour, tea. 1745 classes, gymnasium. 1945 lock up.

week ends: 0745 unlock, breakfast, cell inspection. 0900 gym, RC Mass (Sat), activities, association. 0915 VPU exercise. 1200 dinner. 1330–1600 cell cleaning. 1600 tea. 1800 slop out and supper. No weekend evening association.

Out of cell: 7.5/24hrs weekdays and 6/24hrs at weekends.

ACCOMMODATION & FACILITIES
Four identical wings, A(CNA: 78), B(70), C(84), D(24). C.wing has integral sanitation, D.wing partial integral sanitation. VPU top landing of B.wing. Very small cells, suitable only for one inmate despite the fact that many are two'd up. Graffiti, lack of cleanliness and vandalism in most wings. Three landings of spurred accommodation in each wing. Ground floor TV rooms, dining area and offices. Bail Information Scheme. Sentence Planning, Personal Officer Scheme. Inmate/staff relationships good.

VISITS *How to get there*: Train to Wigan then bus (658) from bus station or Market Square to Gibson Street. No Special Transport.
VISITING TIMES: Week Days: 1330–1530. Saturday: 1330–1530. Sunday: 1330–1530.

NOTES Staffed Visitors Centre with canteen. No Childrens Play Area or overnight stay facilities, though B&B in Wigan quite plentiful.

EDUCATION Excellent educational provision, contracted to City College, Wythenshawe, Manchester M23 9BQ. Large number of inmates attend education each day, though there is a lack of evening classes. CIT Painting and Decorating, Carpentry. Classes in basic education, information technology, art, ceramics, parent craft, independent man. NVQ business studies.

WORKSHOPS FTE (94 places). CIT Painting and Decorating (3. Carpentry (11). Concrete workshop (22). Textile (20). Seamstress Shop (8). Stores (5). Kitchen (21). Works (5). Farms & gardens (5). Orderlies (7). Red Bands (1). Wing Cleaners (100). Non-wing Cleaners (6). Wages average £6.00.

DISCIPLINE High number of adjudications with average of five reports per day: mostly for fighting, using abusive language and possession of unauthorised articles—there were 20 drug finds in the six months prior to the HMCIP inspection. Segregation Unit located next to workshops, 10 ordinary cells with integral sanitation, 2 strip cells. There were two suicides in one day in the Seg Unit in 1992. Hindley does not operate a Minor reports system.

MEDICAL Full time Medical Officer Dr Farouque Head of Health Care. HCSO, 2×Enrolled Nurses, 2×Registered Mental Nurses, visiting dentist, optician and chiropodist. Surgery times: 0800–0900 Monday to Friday. On weekends and Bank Holidays emergencies only. Medications: 0800–0830 each morning. Report sick by arranging an appointment to see Doctor with landing officer. Counselling sessions in HIV/AIDS and Substance Abuse. Suggestions to improve the health care service at Hindley to any member of the HC staff.

GYMNASIUM & SPORTS 1×PEPO, 1×PESO, 4×PEO. large gymnasium situated off main (M1) corridor, large sports field and number of tarmac areas. Classes seven days a week 0800–1200 and 1315–1700. Evening classes Mon–Fri. BAWLA (Friday afternoon). Swimming.

ESTABLISHMENT REPORTS In a report (published 14th January 1993) of an inspection in July 1992, HMCIP, said that Hindley fulfils a complex role, holding a disparate range of inmates many of whom feel they have little to lose by vandalising their surroundings. The population contains inmates who, either individually or in gangs, seek to impose their will on others by threatened or actual violence or extortion. Bullying and taxing have been accepted as particular problems and it is imperative that action be taken to re-educate the bullies rather than simply protecting their victims. Standards of cleanliness in the wings is unacceptable: the smell from one recess pervaded the whole wing and rubbish from cell windows litters the prison's yards. The refuse disposal service should be improved and steps should be taken to improve the control and issue of kit. Many unconvicted inmates choose to work and there are good employment opportunities, though there is a shortage of training courses: HMCIP suggested an Industrial Cleaning course. Overall, despite the lack of cleanliness and questions about some of the training that is on offer at Hindley, HMCIP thought the prison had a lot to offer young men on remand. They suggested a number of ways in which the regime could be improved (more time out of cell for all inmates, increased evening association and evening classes on four nights per week) but it was basically sound and well supported by staff. What was needed was an investment to improve living conditions and, shortly after publication of the report, refurbishment of Hindley got under way.

HMP & YOI Hollesley Bay Colony

Woodbridge, Suffolk. IP12 3JS
Tel: 0394-411741 **Fax:** 0394-411071
Opened: 1887 **CNA:** 511 **Average Roll:** 266 **Category:** Open & Closed Male YOI

i **BACKGROUND** Hollesley Bay Colony (HBC), which comprises the original open establishment and the more recently built closed YOI at Warren Hill, started life in 1887 as a fee paying college for young men wishing to learn husbandry before starting careers in all reaches of the empire. By 1905 HBC had become a training centre for London's unemployed with a probability of resettlement locally on successful completion of the one month residential course. HBC became a part of the prison estate in 1938 when it was purchased by the then Prison Commissioners—HBC remains the largest penal holding in HM Prison Service with the whole site occupying about 630 hectares. Since the last inspection in October 1990 adult male inmates have occupied some of the open units. Neither the Governor nor BoV at HBC replied to our requests for information. HMCIP published their latest inspection report on HBC in June 1994.

OFFICIALS
AREA MGR: Tom Murtagh
CHAIR BOV:
GOVERNOR: M. Clarke
MEDICAL:
CHAPLAIN: Rev Clarke
PROBATION: Bob Burlinson
EDUCATION:
LOCAL MP: John Gummer. Con
STAFFING: 325 staff in post, 179 in unified grades.

REGIME *week days*: (Open units) 0730 applications. 0815 breakfast. 0845 work. 1145 cease labour. 1200 lunch. 1315 work. 1645 cease labour. 1715 tea. 1800–2045 association. (Closed units) 0730 unlock, applications. 0800 breakfast. 0845 work. 1130 cease labour. 1145 dinner. 1345 labour. 1615 cease labour. 1630 tea. 1815 unlock. 1900 association. 2030 lock up.

week ends: (Open units) 0745 applications, sick parade. 0815 breakfast. 0845 unit cleaning. 1000 inspection. 1200 dinner. 1400 visits. 1630 tea. 1800 association. 2045 lock up. (Closed units) 0730 unlock, applications. 0800 breakfast. 0830 cell cleaning. 0845 PE. 1145 dinner. 1330 trays out. 1400 unlocked p.m. activities. 1545 lock up. 1615 tea. No evening weekend association.

Out of cell: **(Open)** 24/24hrs both weekdays and weekends. **(Closed)** 10/24hrs weekdays and 7/24hrs weekends.

ACCOMMODATION & FACILITIES

OPEN: Six living units in the Open section: Stowe, Wilford, Special, Hoxon, Cosford and Hartsmere—two closed because of low inmate roll. Units of modern design with single rooms and appropriate shower and association facilities in each. Access to sanitation 24 hours. Card phones in each unit. **CLOSED:** Warren Hill has four living units each holding 45 young offenders: Deben, Gipping, Orwell and Alde. Card phones on each unit, integral sanitation, single cells with internal light switch and plans for in-cell power. Sentence planning, personal officer scheme, drug counselling.

CANTEEN Each living unit has its own canteen, serviced from a central stock located in the admin block. Price lists regularly updated and displayed. Inmates have been issued with ID cards to prevent fraud. No local purchases allowed and the canteen subject of much criticism by inmates.

VISITS *How to get there*: Train to Woodbridge or Melton station from Ipswich. Check with Eastern Counties Bus Ltd (Ipswich 53734) as bus service is infrequent—No service on Sundays. No Special Transport.
VISITING TIMES: Week Days: No Visits. Saturday: 1400–1540 check in holiday periods. Sunday: 1400–1540.

NOTES No staffed Visitors Centre. Check the VO to make sure which part of the prison you have to go to. HBC is isolated and very difficult to get to on public transport. Canteen in visiting room and only closed part of prison has a Childrens Play Area. No overnight stay and local B&B difficult. Town visits if eligible once per month.

EDUCATION Contracted out to Norwich City College. Nine f/t staff with 29 p/t teachers. Excellent facilities reported but shortage of staff often prevents use—no classes at all on a Friday. VTC Motor Mechanics, Mechanical Engineering, and Industrial Cleaning.

WORKSHOPS Estate and farm party (30 places), works (8), orderlies (17), kitchen (16), officers mess (3), veg-prep shop (14), motor mechanics (8), industrial cleaning (8), packing shed (19), mechanical engineering (8). Wages average £4. Everyone works at HBC, no radios in shops and labour allocation system which many inmates criticise as unfair.

DISCIPLINE Segregation unit in constant use, strip cell used frequently though MO has not always signed authority. HMCIP was disappointed to find five occasions where staff had used the strip cell for incidents or threats of self-harm. Average of around 100 adjudications a month, not including the 70 per month dealt with in each unit by minor report system, mainly for petty offences of failure to make a bed pack or be out of bed at unlock. HMCIP criticised the documentation in which '"Yes" was often and unsatisfactorily the only record of the hearing'. Awards appeared reasonable and not excessive. There were signs of recognition of the need for a dynamic training approach, allowing individual development which would also offer staff other opportunities to control behaviour said HMCIP.

MEDICAL Two part time Medical Officers, 1×HCPO, 1×HCSO, 4×HCO. HCC with 30-bed inpatient facility, two dental sessions per week with waiting list of about 20.

GYMNASIUM & SPORTS 1×PEPO, 3×PESO and 8×PEO. New gymnasium and extensive facilities for PE. Gym, opened in June 1989 is spacious and has a weights room and full supporting facilities. Fibre-glass sports dome. Former living unit turned into a 50 bed outdoor pursuits centre, outdoor unheated swimming pool and extensive playing fields. Brand new gym in Warren Hill, rugby and football pitches and an all-weather 60×40m playing surface.

CHAPLAINCY Full time CE chaplain, RC and Methodist ministers. Two separate chapels for open and closed regimes. Only rarely are services of minority faith ministers required. Chaplaincy not well supported by inmates, Chaplain provides no Prison Visitor Scheme.

FOOD Staffing: PO, SO, 6×Officer (Caterers), and an inmate work party of 16. Kitchen built in 1979 proved too small and has been extended. Food is acceptable though unimaginative according to HMCIP. Inmates repeated to the *Handbook* complaints they made to HMCIP: portions are too small.

ESTABLISHMENT REPORTS In a report (published 29th June 1994) of an inspection in December 1993, HMCIP, said that all but a handful of the recommendations set out in the 1990 FIR had been accepted and the Governor reported progress on them all and some sensible decisions had been taken. The introduction of adults to fill vacancies in the open units was commended, although the institution was barely half full and there was still a wasteful under-use of training opportunities. The regime in the closed section was not as oppressive as it had been at the time of the 1990 inspection, staff were more optimistic and fewer inmates segregated for their own protection. The design of the four living units in Warren Hill was 'an expensive blunder', providing insufficient space for inmates and difficult working conditions for staff. The food was reasonable but the size of the portions given to growing young men met with understandable criticism said HMCIP. Far too much idleness was seen, bullying was still a significant problem and too much emphasis was placed on formal methods rather than on using activities such as work, education and PE to control behaviour. The abilities of many staff were not yet being fully tapped and HMCIP found many staff lurking in offices rather than interacting with young offenders. The Governor has started improvements, it would be improved if staff had a clear sense of purpose in developing a dynamic training regime.

PRISONERS' COMMENTS Closed Unit: Requests and Complaints take too long to be dealt with, the problem is usually long gone by the time a reply arrives. No power points yet in cells. Canteen is small but OK and we have been issued with ID cards. Visits last two hours, though there is no smoking. Good education service with large number of courses. Poor wages in the workshops which have no radio to improve the monotony. Medical facilities are poor, you only get a paracetamol unless you are seriously ill. Adjudications are very unfair, you are guilty long before you walk into the room and getting Added Days or losing remission is the norm, rarely suspended. Food is quite bad, there's never enough of it and people always complain but it makes no difference. Brand new gym, good instructors and well set out. Religious services held every Sunday. Mail normally given out about 1030, having been previously opened elsewhere.

Open Unit: Speedy answers to formal RC forms, though far too many find their way to the Governor when they could be dealt with far sooner by wing staff. Accommodation is excellent, single room, own light, though no power points yet. Very poor choice in the canteen, normal prices, no local purchase and run according to traditions in vogue when the dinosaurs were around. Good visits, weekend only, town visits once per month. Fantastic education facilities, only one problem: no staff! Excellent medical facilities, but mediocre staff. Very petty, nickings for everything, lose days with ease and hearings very unfair, they just don't want to listen, more concerned with sending a signal to staff than doing justice to the inmate. No problems with the mail, not censored, arrives in wing mid-morning, plenty of phones and phone cards with good access.

HM Prison Holloway

Parkhurst Road, Holloway, London. N7 ONU.1
Tel: 071-607-6747 **Fax:** 071-700-0629
Opened: 1851 **CNA:** 517 **Average Roll:** 452 **Category:** Female Local

i **BACKGROUND** In the early part of the 19th century, prison conditions within the City of London were very much a cause for concern. As space within the City was at a premium, the Corporation purchased ground in the nearby countryside at Holloway on which a single replacement prison was built. Holloway prison opened in 1851 for both men and women, though in 1903 it changed its role to a prison for women only. The Victorian Holloway was replaced by phased construction between 1975/85, no trace of the former jail is now left. Holloway is the largest prison for women in Great Britain. The prison serves as a remand centre for the South of England and the Midlands, including the whole of Greater London. The prison's massive catchment area extends as far as the Staffordshire Potteries and Leicestershire to the north, Norfolk to the east and Oxfordshire, Hampshire and the Isle of Wight to the south: Holloway serves more than 240 different courts. As a result of the Female High Security Unit at Brixton being recently closed for refurbishment, Holloway now (temporarily) takes Category A inmates. To describe Holloway as a 'local' is really to understate its true role. In addition to serving the courts, Holloway acts as a training prison for sentenced inmates, has a Mother and Baby Unit and facilities for treating mentally disturbed inmates. The Governor did not reply to our request for information about the prison, though the BoV at Holloway kindly provided a copy of their latest annual report. HMCIP published their latest inspection report on Holloway in March 1992.

OFFICIALS
AREA MGR: Amy Edwards
CHAIR BOV:
GOVERNOR: Ms J. King
MEDICAL:
CHAPLAIN: Rev Burgess
PROBATION: E. Hogarth
EDUCATION:
LOCAL MP: Jeremy Corbin. Lab
STAFFING: 11 Governor grades, 16 Principal Officers,

41 Senior Officers and 243 Officers, including specialist staff.

REGIME *week days*: 0730 unlock, breakfast, treatments, applications. 0815–0900 exercise. 0915 free flow gym, education, workshop, activities centre. 0915–1100 visits. 1015 adjudications. 1125 free flow back to units, dinner. 1315, free flow as 0915. 1530 free flow back to units, tea. 1700–2000 association by rota.

week ends: 0800 unlock, breakfast, treatments, applications. 0830–0915 exercise. 0930–1130 visits, association by rota. 1030 adjudications. 1130 dinner. 1300 association. 1500–1530 tea. 1700–2000 association by rota.

Out of cell: 10.5/24hrs weekdays and 10/24hrs at weekends.

ACCOMMODATION & FACILITIES Four five-storey cell blocks, A,B,C,D. each divided into units holding approx 32 inmates with own servery and dining facilities. Convicted located: A4/5, B4/5, C4/5 and D4. Total of 275 single cells, ten doubles and 232 in four-bedded rooms. Each unit has two showers and four baths, one card phone and two association rooms. Three hairdressing salons on each of the three main accommodation levels. Good laundry facilities but no cooking facilities on units. Listeners Scheme. Extensive list of articles allowed in possession. High turnover of staff at Holloway inhibits sentence planning and personal officer schemes. First class Activity Centre provides: induction course, HIV/AIDS awareness, Narcotics Anon, relaxation courses, guest speakers, staff training, three day business course, quiz nights, Question Time (quiz the Governor) and pre-release training.

BAIL UNIT 1×SO, 2×Officers, all trained legal aid officers who have undergone specialist Bail Unit training. Located in the remand wing it is open from 0715 to 1630 Mon–Fri. Designed to help all eligible women to be released on bail, provide information to the courts or other agencies, reduce the time spent in custody, make bail more accessible and prevent detention of women inmates in police cells.

CANTEEN Located on the ground floor, the canteen is too small to hold stock and display goods, plans to relocate it to D4. Large range of stock, including fresh fruit and 25 lines for ethnic minorities. Open for earnings once per week, bagging system for seg unit. No canteen committee. Local purchase facility.

VISITS *How to get there*: Underground to Caledonian Road. Bus (29,253,14,17,259 & 221) passes prison gate. No Special Transport. VISITING TIMES: Week Days: 0915–1100 (except Wed), 1315–1500. Saturday: 0915–1100 & 1330–1630. Sunday: 1330–1630 Con only.

NOTES Despite the enormous catchment area of Holloway there is still no Visitors Centre, people come long distances, often with children and there is nowhere in the immediate vacinity to wait. Childrens Play Area supervised by a f/t worker from the Save The Children Fund. No overnight stay facilities. Disabled access. Appointments system for visits in operation and 'No Smoking' policy now in force in the visiting room.

EDUCATION Well equipped Education Centre located in purpose-built accommodation with 17 classrooms, and a bright and welcoming library with a large stock and good access. Open for 49 weeks of the year with classes five days and four evenings a week. Basic education, English, computer studies, full time courses in art, pottery, crafts, music, maths, sociology, psychology, current affairs and yoga.

WORKSHOPS VTC/CIT: Office Skills, Catering, Hairdressing, Beauty Therapy, Skills Training, Craft, Painting & Decorating. Farms & Gardens party. One workshop, textile based employing up to 40 remand and convicted inmates. In 1993 Reed Re-Start was set up in Holloway to help with work experience prior to release. Reed Re-Start is a secretarial service, at commercially competitive rates, dealing with word-processing and telephone sales. Usual essential employment in domestics, orderlies and kitchen.

DISCIPLINE Level of reports markedly lower at Holloway than other female establishments, most offences are relatively minor and HMCIP said some of them should have been dealt with informally. Most serious reports are for breach of temporary release licence. HMCIP was 'impressed' with the way adjudications are conducted at Holloway. Segregation Unit on D1 landing with 11 single cells and one strip cell.

MEDICAL Full time SMO, 3×MO, G4 Health Care Manager, HCPO, Senior Sister, 84×Nurses. Numerous visiting consultants. Large HCC with 91 beds. Used principally for psychiatric cases. Beds located in two units D1 (50 beds, mainly detox) and C1 (41 beds, mainly psych). Single rooms and four-bed dorms, all with integral sanitation. Regime for inpatients greatly improved in recent years from one hour per day out of cell, to around ten hours per day at present.

MOTHER & BABY UNIT Facilities for 23 pregnant women mainly in four-bed rooms, and a dozen mothers and their babies in 12 single rooms.

Ante natal care provided by MO and trained midwives within the M&BU. Ultrasound scans performed on all pregnant women, and high risk pregnancies go to Whittington Hospital for consultant opinion. Amniocentesis test offered to all women over 38. No machine for measuring foetal heartbeat. All babies born in the labour ward of Whittington Hospital, average stay of 72 hours. Breast feeding is encouraged and though the diet given to pregnant women is largely the same as for the rest of the prison, extra fresh fruit, milk, iron and vitamins are provided. Mother and baby separated when child is nine months old.

GYMNASIUM & SPORTS 1×PEPO, 2×PESO and 4×PEO. Excellent purpose-built indoor facilities, very large sports hall, large separate weights room and a heated swimming pool. Outdoor facilities limited by small site to one small grassed area used for rounders. Good showering facilities. Open daily 0930–1530, one evening class only.

CHAPLAINCY Full time CE chaplain, RC priest, and p/t Methodist minister. Purpose-built chapel divides in two with curtains, one side used for CE, other for RC. Multi-faith room with regular services 20–30 strong. Comprehensive programme of weekly meetings and religious groups. RC Mass and CE Service, Sunday. Pool of 23 Prison Visitors.

FOOD Staffing: 1×PO, 1×SO, 4×Officer (caterers), and an inmate work party of 28. HMCIP was concerned that the kitchen had become the the preserve of one racial group (West Africans) though could detect no deliberate discrimination. Food is reasonably varied and traditional prison fare in choice. The quality of vegetables (supplied by Hollesley Bay YOI) was very poor. No pre-select menu system, three choices at dinner, two at tea.

ESTABLISHMENT REPORTS In a report (published 11th March 1992) of an inspection in April 1991 HMCIP, said that there had been great improvements in the treatment of inmates at Holloway in the past few years. Inmates were unlocked and engaged in structured activities for 10 hours each day. The Education Department in particular offered a wide range of both practical and creative courses. There was some local concern over the imbalance of men to women in senior management posts at Holloway (6:1). The visits area is too small for the purpose, badly designed, offers few facilities, is poorly laid out and has no natural light or ventilation. The delays in transferring mentally ill offenders to secure hospitals must be reduced. Some of the conditions in the Mother and Baby Unit are to be deplored, it is dark and gloomy, infested with cockroaches and ants, resulting in frustration and squalor. Holloway is a developing establishment where staff are dealing with inmates as individuals. The prison is moving in the right direction but there is an enormous task still to be done.

BoV Annual Report 1993/4. BoV requested a formal response from the Minister of State on the following: when a Visitors Centre is likely to be provided; the date when all the polycarbonate windows in the establishment will be replaced; to be reassured that encouraging women to apply for managerial posts at Holloway will receive greater priority in the future; and the BoV sought a reply about the delay in receiving the report from the Social Services Inspectorate.

PRISONERS' COMMENTS Visits room is very small for the size of the prison, it's ill-equipped and badly ventilated. Meal times are perverse with tea at weekends being served at 1500, and 1530 during the week. Pay and private cash restrictions are pitched too low. There is no in-cell power in Holloway. Medical staff try to filter out too many inmates who wish to be seen by a doctor, there is a lack of information given on reception, and the Bail Unit was hardly known about. Access to Probation and Psychology departments is difficult. The Mother and Baby Unit is dirty and infested with cockroaches, though inmates are not locked up at night in the M&BU, permission is needed before leaving the room, and the regime is too rigid and rushed.

HM Prison Holme House

Holme House Rd, Stockton-on-Tees. TS18 2QU
Tel: 0642-673759 **Fax:** 0642-674598
Opened: 1992 **CNA:** 649 **Average Roll:** 353 **Category:** Male Local

i **BACKGROUND** Holme House prison was officially opened by prisons minister Peter Lloyd in April 1993. Built to relieve prison overcrowding in the north-east the establishment serves courts throughout Teeside. The prison was one of the fastest ever built, with identification of the site to final completion taking just four years. The establishment is based on a design originally developed for Bullingdon prison, but now used at half a dozen new prisons around the country. Excellent probation department which runs a number of offence-focused groups that last anything from half a day, to three weeks or more: Alcohol Education; Drug Awareness; Keeping Your Cool, courses, along with half day seminars explaining parole and home leave for example. Contact Antonia Town or Derek Horner at the prison's probation department for details. Accommodation in small self-contained living units with integral sanitation. Holme House takes mainly adult males, though there is a small Young Offender section. Neither the Governor nor BoV replied to our requests for information about the prison. HMCIP conducted their first inspection of Holme House in October 1994: their report was awaited as we went to press—full details next edition.

OFFICIALS
AREA MGR: Al Papps
CHAIR BOV:
GOVERNOR: A.K. Rawson
MEDICAL:
CHAPLAIN: Rev McCarthy
PROBATION: Mike Waddington
EDUCATION:
LOCAL MP: Frank Cook. Lab

VISITS *How to get there*: Train to Stockton or Middlesborough, then bus to prison. No Special Transport.
VISITING TIMES: Week Days: 0915–1130, 1315–1630. Wed only 1800–1930. Saturday: 0930–1130, 1330–1630. Sunday: 1330–1630.

NOTES Staffed Visitors Centre, canteen and Childrens Play Area. Disabled access. Contact prison probation for details of local B&B.

HM Prison Hull

Hedon Road, Hull. HU9 5LS
Tel: 0482-20673 **Fax:** 0482-229018
Opened: 1870 **CNA:** 328 **Roll:** 430 **Category:** Male Local

i **BACKGROUND** Hull prison, which opened in 1870 holding both men and women, is situated two miles east of the city centre. In 1939 the establishment was used as a military prison and later a Civil Defence Depot. In 1950 it reopened as a closed male Borstal, and became a training prison a decade later. In 1969, after extensive security work, Hull became one of the first maximum security 'Dispersal' prisons. On August 31st 1976 the prison erupted in an orgy of violence and destruction which lasted five days and closed the jail for the best part of a year: 8 officers were convicted at York Crown Court of assaulting inmates after the riot and, for the first time too, 7 prisoners (inspired by the Canadian Ronald St.Germain) challenged the prison disciplinary system in the courts—and won. In February 1986 Hull was removed from the Dispersal system and took its current role as a male local prison and Remand Centre. Under its current Governor, Rannoch Daly—who provided an abundance of information—Hull has made much progress in recent years. Stephen Hare, Chairman of the Hull BoV, kindly supplied their latest annual report. HMCIP published their latest report on Hull prison in February 1992.

OFFICIALS
AREA MGR: Maurice Codd
CHAIR BOV: L.S.C. Hare
GOVERNOR: Rannoch Daly
MEDICAL: Dr Prasad
CHAPLAIN: Rev C. Dick
PROBATION: Mr V. Scargill
EDUCATION: Mrs D. Turner
LOCAL MP: John Prescott. Lab
STAFFING: 9 Governor grades, 17 Principal Officers, 30 Senior Officers, 218 Officers and 11 Prison Auxiliaries, including specialist staff.

REGIME *week days*: 0730 unlock, breakfast, applications. 0800 discharges to reception. 0815 bathing, canteen. 0830 education, work. 0900 exercise, reception board, call ups, sentence planning. 1100 cease labour. 1200 lock up, roll check, unlock, serve dinner, association. 1330 kit changes, bathing, canteen, work, education. 1400 exercise. 1645 cease bathing, canteen, education work, lock up, roll check, searching. 1730 tea. 1830 association, evening classes, telephones (evenings only). 2030 lock up, roll check.

week ends: 0730 unlock, breakfast, applications. 0900 bathing, church (Sun), canteen, exercise, 1000 letter issue. 1200 serve dinner, lock up, roll check. 1330 unlock, trays out, bathing, canteen. 1345 association, telephones. 1700 lock up, roll check, searching. 1800 unlock, serve tea. 1830 association, telephones. 2030 lock up.

Out of cell: 12/24hrs weekdays and 10.5/24hrs weekends.

ACCOMMODATION & FACILITIES
Three main wings B,C,D, with a total population of upto 307. B.Wing: all single cells with electronic access to night san. C.Wing: local wing for both remand and convicted CNA 163, takes overspill from The Wolds. D.Wing: local wing mainly convicted with CNA of 135 with integral sanitation. Four card phones on each wing. No cooking facilities in B,C or D. No in-cell power. Samaritans hold counselling session on Thursdays. Vulnerable inmates held in the segregation unit; a sparse regime and sometimes, temporarily, on nothing more than a mattress on the floor due to lack of space. V.good i/p list. Routine censorship abolished though mail is not opened in the presence of the prisoner. Card-phones on all wings but poor access limits use to weekday evenings only—though all day at weekends. No outgoing mail reported on a Saturday.

SPECIAL UNIT The Control Review Committee's Special Unit at Hull, which opened in November 1988, is designed to complement those in operation at Parkhurst (C.Wing) and Lincoln: though the CNA is 20, average roll in the Unit is seven and has dropped as low as one inmate in recent times. The function of the Unit is seen as retraining, with the object of facilitating re-entry into the normal prison system. Very relaxed atmosphere, unlocked throughout the day except for staff meal breaks—and no association weekend evenings. All food cooked by Unit inmates. Small discrete visiting room. No work is available. Highly publicised escape in 1989 lead to increased security. Selection for the Unit via the Special Unit Selection Board. Hull BoV recommended to the Home Secretary in their 1993 annual report that the Special Unit should be closed.

CANTEEN Located under the Centre, the canteen at Hull is well stocked. Convicted can visit once per week and remand inmates twice a week. Local purchase facility.

VISITS *How to get there*: Train to Hull then bus (78,76,24) from opposite BR Station. Special Transport: Coach from Barnsley, Doncaster, Rotherham & Sheffield. Booking essential (0709–376761) 10 days in advance of travel date.
VISITING TIMES: Week Days: 0900–1115 (not Tue/Thur) & 1315–1615. Evening visits 1815–2000 Tue & Thur. Saturday: 0900–1115 Rem & 1315–1615 Con. Sunday: 0900–1115 Rem & 1315–1615 Con.

NOTES No smoking. Last admission 30 mins before end of each session. Evening visits (both remand and convicted) MUST be booked **at least 24 hours in advance** by the visitor—book on 0482-20673 extn 286 between 1400–1600 each day. Staffed Visitors Centre at 13 Newtown Ct (opp. Prison) open daily. Canteen only for convicted visits. Supervised Childrens Play Area on Tues and Thurs. Contact prison for details of local B&B. Good disabled access. New visits facilities early 1995.

EDUCATION Contracted out service to the Humberside County Council Adult Education Services. New education block due to be built in 1995. 1×f/t Education manager (Denise Turner), 4×Academic Staff. Dept open 50 weeks of the year and for both day and evening classes, caters for all levels from remedial education to Open University with comprehensive curriculum. Dept also produces Hull's well supported prison magazine 'Doing Time'. In addition to running courses in the dept, education also provided to Special Unit, HCC, Seg Unit and on the wings. The dept ethos challenges sexist and racist behaviour, yet encourages self-empowerment and accountability.

WORKSHOPS Textile shop producing towels and gym shorts. Contract Services workshop producing socket wiring, light assembly work. Two new workshops June 1994: Tailors shop and further Contract Services shop with varied assembly work. Realistic wages scheme being considered at present. Average wage £6.00, top end £6.35, UB40 £2.50. Party change only after three months in shop. CIT Painting & Decorating and Electronic Wiring Courses opened April 1994, VTC Multi-skills courses due to open early 1995.

DISCIPLINE Total of 1077 adjudications in the year ending 31st December 1993 consisting, among others, of 92 cases of assault, 96 of intentionally endangering health or safety of others, 29 of fighting, 44 escapes or absconds, 113 unauthorised possession and 333 cases of disobeying orders. There were also 121 GOAD segregations in 1993.

MEDICAL Two f/t and 1xp/t Medical Officers, assisted by 1×HCPO, 1×HCSO, 10×HCO, 8×Nurses (1×G, 1×F 6×D/E grades). Accommodation for 19 patients—7 bed ward and 12 single rooms. Daily sick parade, weekly clinics with psychiatrist, dentist, optician, STD/HIV. Report sick at central surgery when unlocked for breakfast at 0800 and collected to see doctor at 0900.

GYMNASIUM & SPORTS
Comprehensive PE programme with activities ranging from remedial PE to BAWLA. Classes from 0900 to 2000 Mon-Fri, with separate periods set aside for Rule 43's, Special Unit inmates and

kitchen workers. minor games, weight training, circuit, keep tit, football. swimming on Friday and outside activities as staffing permits.

CHAPLAINCY Full time CE chaplain and p/t RC and Methodist ministers assisted by a team of some ten others. Chapel services: 0900 Sunday CE, followed by RC Mass. Weekly Muslim service on a Friday. Chaplaincy Groups Monday–Thursday each week. Prison Visitors available—see chaplain.

FOOD New kitchen has been open since January 1993, and floor drainage already been condemned as faulty. Four civilian caterers have been added to the staff. Though inmates rate food quality as very poor, BoV comment that some nonetheless manage to be served twice! NVQ Catering Course for kitchen inmates.

ESTABLISHMENT REPORTS In a report (published 11th February 1992) of an inspection in May 1991, HMCIP said that there had been substantial improvements to the regime at Hull for young offenders in B.wing. Time out of cells had increased during the day on activities including exercise, education, PE and association. Unfortunately there were some inmates still locked up during the day and there was no provision for evening association or activities on Saturday afternoons. The quality of life for adult inmates is poor and will remain so until resources are made available. Rule 43 inmates are held in conditions which give cause for concern. HMCIP was disappointed at the lack of data on the Special Unit and was concerned by the low numbers and staffing levels.

BOARD OF VISITORS Mr Hare; Mr Jewitt; Mr Bradley; Mrs Christon; Mrs Doyle; Mrs Eggleston; Mr Kirk; Mrs Lucas; Ms Sexton; Ms Shaw; Mrs Staite; Mrs Thomas; Mr Wroot. Cover provided by duty member 52 weeks of the year. In addition to rota visits, each member of the BoV has a designated area of responsibility in the prison. The Board referred four matters to the Home Secretary for a response in their 1993 Annual Report: Overcrowding was a serious problem which must be reduced; the CRC Special Unit was too costly and should be closed; mentally disturbed offenders should not be held in the Health Care Centre, and the prison's uncertain future created low morale among staff.

GOVERNOR'S COMMENTS Hull in 1995: We hope to move to being a Community Prison serving Hull and the Humberside area. Young Offenders will be taken on remand and held in one of the existing wings. Building work will commence on a new education block and a new wing in 1995. The existing sports compound will be resurfaced and a new reception/visits block will come on stream late 1994, greatly improving the visiting facilities.

PRISONERS' COMMENTS
Requests/complaints are dealt with speedily when it comes to local issues, but there are delays at Area Manager level. Average accommodation with many two-up cells. Good canteen and reasonable prices. Visits are poor at the moment but the new visits room will much improve things when it opens. Education is pretty progressive and provides a lot more than basic education. The wages are bad though work conditions and opportunities are improving. The HCC is small but treatment is good for those genuinely in need of it. Fairness of adjudications is generally good, though it depends on what governor you get, the Governor and Deputy do the job properly, but some G5's seem to be punishment-mad. Food is average but getting better, gymnasium facilities are good and you can use it every day. Religious needs are catered for and mail is handed out about 1100. No outgoing mail on a Saturday.

HM YOI Huntercombe

Nuffield, Henley-on-Thames. RG9 5SB
Tel: 0491-641711/5 **Fax:** 0491-641902
Opened: 1945 **CNA:** 240 **Average Roll:** 229 **Category:** Closed YOI

i **BACKGROUND** Huntercombe is a closed Young Offender Institution situated halfway between Henley and Wallingford in Oxfordshire, some 40 miles north-west of London. The site was developed in 1941 as an interrogation centre for prisoners of war and internees and, immediately after the war, Huntercombe became an open Borstal. It was converted to a closed Borstal in 1963 and has provided secure accommodation for young offenders ever since. It is linked to HM YOI Finnamore Wood Camp, an open YOI that is currently non-operational: Derek Lewis, Director General of HM Prison Service, announced in October 1994 that Finnamore Wood would reopen in the next year. The Head of Custody, Mr Strong, provided information about Huntercombe. HMCIP last inspected the establishments in March 1994 and their report was published in October 1994.

OFFICIALS

AREA MGR: A. de Frisching
CHAIR BOV: Mrs Needham
GOVERNOR: Ms A. Hair
MEDICAL: Dr Lee Jones
CHAPLAIN: Rev Sutherland
PROBATION: John Clarke
EDUCATION: Mrs C. Swann
LOCAL MP: Michael Heseltine. Con

REGIME *week days*: 0750 unlock/breakfast. 0830 activities, work. 1200 dinner. 1220 lock up. 1335 unlock. 1340 activities, work. 1630 cease labour. 1650 lock up. 1735 tea. 1800–2030 association (Mon–Thurs only at present).

week ends: 0750 unlock/breakfast. 0845 lock up, house cleaning. 0900 church service. 0915 PE. 1000 association. 1150 dinner. 1200 lock up. 1330 visits. 1400 association. 1700 tea. 1720 lock up. No weekend evening association.

Out of cell: 10.6/24hrs weekdays and 6.45/24hrs at weekends.

ACCOMMODATION & FACILITIES

Four house blocks, each holding 60 inmates in cellular accommodation. All cells have integral sanitation, sink and h/c water. No power points. Each house has two card phones. Full list of own clothing allowed in possession, washing and drying facilities on each House with extensive list of privileges. All mail is opened outwith the sight of the inmate and, on outgoing letters, inmates are required to print their last home address—for reasons which remain unclear and which inmates at Huntercombe have written to complain about.

CANTEEN The canteen and the service it provides to inmates is disappointingly poor said HMCIP in his latest report . . . the result of the canteen having been built *outside* the prison! Inmates cannot visit the canteen as a result and a pre-order system is in operation. Poor range of stock with just over 100 lines, though there is a local purchase facility to supplement it. Private cash spends only once per month.

VISITS *How to get there*: Oxford coach from Victoria Coach Station, London, stops 50 yds from prison. No Special Transport
VISITING TIMES: Week Days: 30–45 min by special arrangement. Saturday: 1330–1630. Sunday: 1330–1630.

NOTES No staffed Visitors Centre or Childrens Play Area. No overnight stay facilities. Canteen in visiting room. No smoking. Several steps into visits room, severely disabled should notify prison before arrival. Special visits 0900–1100 weekdays. One 90min domestic visit every fortnight. Poor quality visits room: 'The impression given by this visits room' said HMCIP, 'is one that neither Huntercombe nor the Service would wish to give'.

EDUCATION New Education department due to open shortly giving much improved facilities, staff from Amersham & Wycombe College. Currently open five days and three evenings for 50 weeks of the year. Six f/t teachers. Day classes: word power, number power, English, information technology, screen printing, offending behaviour, psychology, geography, drama, maths, wood skills, French, parent skills, basic cookery, book keeping, painting, business studies, textile crafts, general studies. Evening classes (1800–1930, Mon, Tues, Wed): computers, yoga, craft, music, art, woodwork, board games, alcoholics anon.

WORKSHOPS VTC/CIT courses: Painting & Decorating, Bricklaying, General Construction Operators, Industrial Cleaning. Kitchen, Farm, Inside Gardens, Education, Project Work, usual cleaners and orderlies. Average wage £6.50. Labour Board meets weekly. A motor mechanics course should be provided said HMCIP.

DISCIPLINE Fairly high level of adjudications with 684 in 1993. Awards are generally consistent and the discretion to suspend awards was exercise frequently. Bullies were identified said HMCIP through a regular flow of intelligence information and the atmosphere in the living units was orderly and relaxed as a result. Unused accommodation in the HCC to become new segregation unit. Few incidents of C&R and no records of mechanical restraints in 1993/94.

MEDICAL Part time Medical Officer part of local practice, currently attends three mornings per week soon to be increased to five. 1×HCSO, 1×HCO, 1 Nurse. Dentist 2 Sess/wk, Psychiatrist 1 Sess/wk. Report sick at unlock 0750 to house office.

FOOD 1×SO, 1×Officer (caterer), 2×Civilian Cooks and work party of 12 inmates. Kitchen has many design faults and generally untidy. Despite this the food was of a good standard with a four week menu cycle and pre-select menu system. Tea is the main meal of the day and meals served at sensible times: 0800, 1200, 1730 (1700 weekends). Beverage packs issued with meals instead of 'diesel' tea, comprising sachets of tea, coffee, milk and sugar. All meals taken in association, and HMCIP said the plastic plates ought to be replaced with earthenware or ceramic plates, and consideration should be given to allowing inmates to have their own plates in possession.

ESTABLISHMENT REPORTS There was considerable apprehension about the future of Finnamore Wood at the time of the inspection said HMCIP in a report (published 25th October 1994) of an inspection in May 1994. It was also a matter of regret that the major redevelopment programme started in 1986 at Huntercombe had come to a halt, leaving education, administration, visits and the chapel still housed in poor and inappropriate buildings and on a site that is extremely untidy. There was a sound management structure, and a sensible and mature staff showed a caring approach to their work and their relationships with inmates were good. Education staff are required to work in sub-standard accommodation and though the work profile showed a reasonable spread of work, more emphasis should be placed on skills training. The absence of weekend evening association is unsatisfactory. Meals are of a good standard and served at sensible times. The inmate development and pre-release courses are currently being reviewed, though considerable progress has been made in these areas in a relatively short time and it was clear the majority of staff were committed to developing effective throughcare strategies.

BOV Report 1993/94: Tendering for prison education at Huntercombe has been 'a disaster', said the BoV in their Annual Report, which 'has radically lowered the morale of education staff'. An enormous amount of time was spent by staff in dealing with the upheavals arising from it. The result is that an external college with no previous experience of handling prison education is 'struggling' at Huntercombe. The Board is concerned about the long delays in getting replies to requests and complaints, from the area manager. It 'condemns' the Prison Service for refusing to release its report of an investigation into an assault by prison staff on a prisoner being transferred to another prison. It is also concerned at the Crown Prosecution Service's failure to prosecute offences committed by prisoners, and claims such actions are sending the wrong message to prisoners. The Board is also concerned about the future of Boards of Visitors following the Home Secretary's decision not to appoint a President of Boards of Visitors. In order to take on the task of monitoring the performance of the establishment contracts in the future, the Board believes that there is a need to reorganise the structure and leadership of the Boards in order to prevent their demise. From April 1st 1994, Finnamore Wood became an open prison, though at the current time is not operational.

GOVERNOR'S COMMENTS Plans to improve time out of cell in 1995 to 11 hours per day, increase of evening association to five nights per week, along with improved access to the gym and an improvement in activity hours.

PRISONERS' COMMENTS Requests and complaints are dealt with fairly swiftly, sometimes you have a reply within a couple of days and normally within a week in any event. There are no power points in the cells, but they would only be abused in this prison. Canteen orders are taken from a list of items and later delivered to the houses which is unpopular with inmates, prices are very high and only expensive brand names are available—local supermarket brands would enable us to buy much more for our money. Education is good considering the current facilities, though a new education department is due to open soon and this will improve matters. Plenty of work and training opportunities are available. Medical facilities are quite good, but the cover provided is poor as the medical staff are only available at certain times. Adjudications here are not fair, though you have to be an idiot to get placed on report because the staff are quite laid back and only react when forced to do so. There is never enough food and not much variety. Portion sizes are really small considering the work that we do and the age of population. Normal diets seem to fare much better than vegetarians for example, both in variety and quantity. Gym facilities are good and will be even better after a new gym has been built, it can be used three times a day during the week, but only once at weekends. Mail is already opened by the time we get it at dinner time. Card phones are available and phonecards can be bought from either private cash or earnings with no limit being set.

HM Prison Kingston

Milton Road, Portsmouth. PO3 6AS
Tel: 0705-829561 **Fax:** 0705-871241
Opened: 1877 **CNA:** 104 **Average Roll:** 94 **Category:** B.(Male Lifers Only)

i **BACKGROUND** Kingston prison, situated about 2 miles from Portsmouth city centre, opened in 1877 and was originally used as a local prison for the Portsmouth area. In the years immediately preceding the Second World War it held preventive detainees, who were transferred to Parkhurst prison at the outbreak of the war in 1939. During the next five years Kingston was used by the Royal Navy as Naval Detention Quarters. In 1945 the establishment closed and it stood empty until 1948 when it was used as a Recall Centre for Borstal trainees, remaining in that role until 1969 when, following alterations, it became a B category training prison solely for life sentence prisoners—to this extent Kingston was (and remains) unique in being the only establishment to cater exclusively for life sentence prisoners. Kingston was once exclusively for domestic lifers (those who have killed someone known or related to them), but now over half the inmates are serving life for other than domestic homicides. Neither the Governor nor BoV at Kingston replied to our requests for information about the prison and HMCIP published their latest inspection report on the jail in August 1994.

OFFICIALS
AREA MGR: Alan Rayfield
CHAIR BOV:
GOVERNOR: John Dovell
MEDICAL:
CHAPLAIN: Rev O'Connor
PROBATION: Corrine Skinner
EDUCATION:
LOCAL MP: David Martin. Con
STAFFING: 3 Governor grades, 5 Principal Officers, 11 Senior Officers and 60 Officers, including specialist staff.

REGIME *week days*: 0750 unlock. 0815 breakfast. 0900–1230 work. 1240 Dinner. 1305–1405 exercise 1415–1700 work. 1710 tea, evening association. 1800 outside exercise. 1815–1945 evening classes. 2100 lock up.

week ends: 0800 unlock. 0800 applications (Sat). 0815 breakfast. 0830 RC Mass (Sun). 1030 CE Service (Sun). 1030–1145 outside exercise. 1145 dinner. 1220–1330 lock up. 1340 association. 1545 tea. 16.20 lock up. 1710–2100 evening association.

Out of cell: 11.25/24hrs weekdays and 10.5/24hrs at weekends.

ACCOMMODATION & FACILITIES Three wings (A, C, D), each with two landings, radiate from the Centre. All cells are of a good size and have integral sanitation. Showers on each landing and a bath house at the end of D.wing. Snooker, pool, darts, and each of the four TV rooms has a 'hearing loop' for the hard of hearing. Personal officer and sentence planning schemes. Extensive i/p list.

CANTEEN Located to one side of C.wing the canteen is woefully inadequate according to HMCIP and plans for new location are well advanced. Open three times per week. Profit margin of 12%, complaints of high prices and restricted stock. Local purchase facility.

VISITS *How to get there*: Train to Portsmouth & Southsea. Turn right out of station for bus (16a, 16b) to St.Mary's Hospital—across the roundabout from the prison. No Special Transport. VISITING TIMES: Week Days: 1345–1545 Mon,Tues,Wed Only. Saturday: 1345–1545. Sunday: 1345–1545.

NOTES No staffed Visitors Centre, canteen on weekends only. Childrens Play Area, supervised at weekends. Contact prison probation officer for details of local B&B. Disabled visitors contact prison before arrival. Two VO's per month though exchange for PVO's allows one weekday visit per week. No family visits. Normally two hour visits, but recent increases in population have caused problems at peak periods.

EDUCATION Contracted out since September 1993 to Highbury College, Cosham, there is a f/t Education Co-ordinator, deputy and 19 p/t teaching staff. Five places on FTE and 68 on PTE. Core programme of English, maths and computing, and inmates can suggest topics for educational provision. Day classes in history, cookery, life skills, general studies, music, two language classes and a discussion group. Open Learning and OU catered for along with GCSE O and A level studies. Evening classes four nights a week with emphasis on recreational topics. Small library but well stocked and reasonably up to date, professional librarian available seven hours per week.

WORKSHOPS Three large workshops providing upto 59 places in the printing and book binding industry. NVQ provided in printing and drawing office offers training and practical experience. Poor wages range from £4.15–£6.60—average pay for shops £6.02. Needs more training opportunities.

DISCIPLINE Segregation unit of five cells in the basement of A.wing which are not used and the unit remains unstaffed. In 1993 there were just 14 disciplinary reports at Kingston, none serious, and no instances of C&R or mechanical restraints.

MEDICAL Part time Medical Officer, 1×HCSO, 2×HCO. Forensic psychiatrist 2 sess/wk, genito-urinary as required and psychologist available. Dental 1 sess/wk, waiting list 3–4 weeks and 6 monthly checking system. Optician visits every 6 weeks. No HIV/AIDS management team, and health promotion poorly developed. HCC located on spur off the Centre, clean and compact it has four rooms with integral sanitation.

GYMNASIUM & SPORTS 1×PESO and 2×PEO. Classes seven days and four nights a week. Small gymnasium, good sized weights room and multi-gym area for indoor activities. Good showering facilities. Outside football pitch, tarmac area used for tennis and volleyball, an area covered with Astro-turf for bowling and hockey and a small putting green. Good community contacts with several teams visiting for football, volleyball and cricket.

CHAPLAINCY Part time CE chaplain, RC and Methodist ministers. Visiting ministers of other faiths attend regularly. RC Mass 0830 Sunday. CE Service 1030 Sunday. Third Wednesday/month 1800 Pentecostal Service. Fourth Wednesday/month 1800 Quaker Service. Monday evening Methodist Minister's Hour. Friday evening RC Priest's Hour.

FOOD Staffing: 1×SO, 2×Officer (Caterers) and an inmate work party of 7. New kitchen very clean—catering staff received an award from Portsmouth City Council for high standards of cleanliness and hygiene matters. Four week menu cycle with two choices at dinner and tea. HMCIP found the food to be appetising, hot and well presented. No pre-select menu system.

ESTABLISHMENT REPORTS In a report (published 4th August 1994) of an inspection in February 1994, HMCIP, said that Kingston had now changed from its once 'domestic lifer only' policy to take those sentenced to life for crimes other than domestic homicides. There was evidence that a large number of inmates had problems and needs beyond those suggested by the main offence—in possibly 30% of cases criminality was linked to some form of sexual difficulty. Expertise in the probation department could be better utilised in sentence planning and throughcare, HMCIP had concerns about the low numbers in the workshops and said more should be involved in FTE. The practice of transferring from Kingston those recategorised from B to C should not be so automatic. There are no tensions in the prison, a good standard of cleanliness is maintained in the wings and inmates were informed of their rights and privileges on reception. There is a need for a further VTC/CIT course. The roofs of the cell block have come to the end of their useful life and need to be replaced.

PRISONERS' COMMENTS Rates of pay are seriously lower than average in other prisons, and work is of a poor quality. Morning and afternoon visits should be allowed and an open day for families would be a good thing. Stock in the canteen needs to be extended, in-cell power should be installed and there is not enough art in the curriculum. Female Prison Visitors (as arranged by the Chaplain) are restricted to association rooms and there is a shortage of community contact. The segregation unit should be used as a *Time Out* facility enabling inmates to get away for a few days. Card phones should be more private and not located next to the pool tables. The print shop is not being adequately used, and the influx of Vulnerable Prisoners is changing the tone of the prison, with the danger that everyone could be labelled a VP. Lifers here do not receive enough information about the changes in legislation effecting them. There is a need for more training, including NVQ's, in such trades as plumbing in which employment prospects on release may present themselves. All cheques sent in for prisoners must be made payable to 'The Governor'.

HM Prison Kirkham

Preston. PR4 2RA
Tel: 0722-684343 **Fax:** 0722-682855
Opened: 1941 **CNA:** 644 **Roll:** 471 **Category:** D. Male

i **BACKGROUND** At the beginning of the Second World War the RAF built a number of temporary airfields and camps. Kirkham was at that time a large depot without an associated airfield, but with hutted accommodation and large hangars. In 1962 Kirkham passed into the control of the prison authorities. Many of the buildings originally constructed by the RAF remain, the additions being a recently completed kitchen, some greenhouses and two vegetable stores. Kirkham is a large open prison for adult males, serving sentences that range from less than four months to over ten years. The prison occupies about 40 hectares of rich, flat, low-lying farming country some three miles from the Ribble estuary. Neither the Governor nor the Board of Visitors responded to requests for information. The information in this entry is drawn mainly from the HMCIP who published their latest inspection report on Kirkham in August 1993.

OFFICIALS
AREA MGR: Ian Lockwood
CHAIR BOV:
GOVERNOR: A. Jennings
MEDICAL:
CHAPLAIN: Rev Rose
PROBATION: Marjorie Sedgwick
EDUCATION:
LOCAL MP: Michael Jack. Con.
STAFFING: 5 Governor grades, 7 Principal Officers, 16 Senior Officers, 58 Officers.

REGIME *week days*: 0730 rise. 0740 breakfast. 0815 labour. 1150 cease labour. 1210 dinner. 1300 labour. 1310–1540 visits. 1650 cease labour. 1710 tea. 1730 association. 1800 evening classes. 2000 classes finish. 2100 association ends. 2105 roll check.

week ends: 0730 rise. 0800 breakfast/inspection. 0900–1115 visits. 1210 dinner. 1300 classes/recreation. 1330–1530 visits. 1630 tea. 1700 association. 2100 association ends. 2105 roll check.

Out of cell: 24/24hrs weekdays, 24/24hrs weekends.

ACCOMMODATION & FACILITIES
Twenty-five single storey huts dating from 1941. One further purpose-built unit, also single storey, was completed in 1990. Huts laid out in two parallel lines (North and South Wings respectively). The new self-contained unit, C1, has 14 double rooms, a TV room, washing and toilet facilities. HMCIP said that apart from C1 and A2 units 'the living accommodation was unsatisfactory'. New living units now under construction. Limited i/p list, restricted civilian clothing list and far short of what most long-termers will be used to. Personal officer scheme. No VPU. Drug counselling available. Access to sanitation 24hrs. No lifers at Kirkham. All in-coming mail is sorted by Prison Auxiliaries and issued from windows in North and South Wing offices. Inmates collect their letters on their way back from dinner. Only Registered and Recorded Delivery items opened in front of the inmate. Eight card phones for inmates, all situated together in eight kiosk-like boxes. Eight phones are 'insufficient' for a prison with a population that could reach over 600. A bid for four more phones had been made by the Governor said HMCIP.

CANTEEN Recently refurbished after criticisms of HMCIP. Inmates say provides an excellent service now. Large range of stock, prices reasonable and local purchase facility available.

REQUESTS/COMPLAINTS Average of a dozen R/C forms a month submitted, most frequent issues being compensation for lost property, parole decisions, transfers and home leave. Of 22 that were dealt with in the establishment, only 15 received a reply within seven days, and three still remained to be answered after a fortnight.

VISITS *How to get there*: Train to Kirkham from Preston then 193 (30 mins service) bus from Kirkham Mkt Sq—stops by prison. Taxi to prison from station, approx £2. Special Transport: coaches from Humberside and W.Yorks probation.
VISITING TIMES: Week Days: 1310–1540. Saturday: 0900–1115, 1315–1515. Sunday: 1315–1515.

NOTES No staffed Visitors Centre or Childrens Play Area. Canteen in visiting room but not during official (legal etc) visits. Contact prison probation for details of local B&B. No town visits at Kirkham, though HMCIP have called for their introduction. According to HMCIP the waiting room for visitors is 'about the size of a bus shelter'. Poor visits room furnishings but helpful staff. New visits facility is planned.

EDUCATION Open for 48 weeks of the year, with evening classes Mon–Wed–Fri (1800–2000) for 42 weeks of the year. Five f/t teachers, 20 p/t staff. All inmates must work for three months in the workshops before being allowed access to education—other than those adjudged after testing to have a reading age under 12. Space for 47 on f/t education, three foundation courses concentrate on the three R's. Ad hoc Business studies courses. Two six-week computer literacy courses and IT also available. OU. HMCIP agreed with Education Officer who believed the balance at Kirkham 'was too heavily weighted in favour of the prison's industry'.

WORKSHOPS Allocation to employment at Kirkham is done each Tuesday by a Labour Board, chaired by the Head of Inmate Activities and attended by the Education Officer, Industrial Manager, Farm Manager and Works SO. Range of industrial workshops: weaving (33 inmates, 31.5 hours/wk); weaving II (14, 32.5); laundry (18, 33.3); woodwork (32, 35); contract services (29 ,31.8) involving metal recovery, packing medical items, paper strips and marking toggle ropes: 'The shop was profitable but provided poor quality work with no training value' said HMCIP, who expressed 'serious doubts about the suitability of this type of work for inmates'. Average wage £7 but pilot enhanced wages scheme in operation for some. Large farm party, employing over 150 inmates on such things as: veg prep, dairying, glasshouses, polythene tunnels, pigs, potatoes, rare breeds, storage and dispatch.

DISCIPLINE HMCIP who studied the records of adjudications at Kirkham said the standard was 'generally satisfactory', though some records of hearings were 'too brief'. Latest statistics show Kirkham as having 0.6 offences per head of average inmate population; only two establishments rate lower. No complaints were made by inmates about adjudications. Governor monitored awards and trends, advising his management team as appropriate. Segregation unit with four cells, integral sanitation. Only used to hold inmates prior to transfer to closed conditions.

MEDICAL P/t Medical Officer, 1×HCSO and 1×HCO, agency nurse covers for leave etc. MO attends for one hour each weekday morning and Wednesday afternoons (reception day). HMCIP noted the MO's 'managerial functions were being neglected'. Dentist provides three or four sessions a fortnight, dental surgery in a poor state, modern hygiene standards not being met and equipment needed either replacing or upgrading. Optician attends twice a month.

GYMNASIUM & SPORTS 1×PEPO, 1×PESO, 2×PEO's. Another department which suffers from Kirkham's heavy emphasis on industry. 'The day programme was sparse but accompanied by full evening programmes' said HMCIP. Large gym (once the training base for Prison Service PEO's) with weights room, remedial room, two squash courts and a large field containing a cricket square, two soccer pitches and a putting green. Evening programme similar to that found in community centre and includes fishing and indoor/outdoor bowls.

CHAPLAINCY Two chapels, one for CE the other for RC. Both ministers have their own offices. CE Service of Holy Communion Fridays and Sunday mornings and the Catholic Mass is at the same time—0900 Sundays. Mens Fellowship meeting Friday and religious videos on Saturday. Two visiting Rabbi's attend Jewish inmates. Minority religions can make use of the 'Other Faith's Room'.

FOOD Three separate dining rooms adjacent to the kitchen. Poor decoration in all of them. Recent improvements reported in the food, five-week varied menu, with three choices for dinner and good quality. New kitchen operated by PO, SO, 3× Officer Caterers and work party of 22.

PROBATION Senior Probation Officer and six main grade officers seconded from Lancashire Probation Service. Good working relationship with Governor and staff reported by the Senior, who also 'expressed considerable frustration' that his staff were dealing with problems of a practical nature that could be more usefully dealt with by prison officers, leaving probation staff free to deal with offending behaviour work etc. No SWIP scheme in operation. A fortnightly evening group and a session during the pre-release programme were the only behavioural groups provided. HMCIP found 'few activities devoted to offending behaviour or the emotional disturbances associated with it'.

ESTABLISHMENT REPORTS Though the prisoners' accommodation at Kirkham was poor, said HMCIP in their latest inspection report (published 4th August 1993), inmates were being treated fairly and the regime available to them covered a range of constructive and positive experiences. The military-camp style of Kirkham however did not lend itself well to a large open prison. The allocation criteria were such that there was always a shortage of inmates. Kirkham was well-managed, but its future development was being constrained by poor living accommodation, a heavy emphasis on industrial work and by the restrictions placed on the type of individual allocated to Kirkham. Responding to the Report Derek Lewis, Chief Executive of HM Prison Service, said all new facilities sought by the Chief Inspector, including an enlarged visiting room and new accommodation for administration, education and library, were now in the prison's development plan. Mr Lewis supported HMCIP's view that D Category lifers should be held at Kirkham, but in the past this has caused local opposition: 'The residents and the town council' said Mr Lewis, 'take a keen interest in the type of prisoners held at Kirkham, the prison is situated on the edge of a housing estate and in the interests of good community relations, prisoners convicted of sexual offences are not sent to Kirkham. We would not alter that without local consultation.

HM Prison Kirklevington Grange

Yarm. Cleveland. TS15 9PA
Tel: 0642-781391 **Fax:** 0642-790530
Opened: 1992 **CNA:** 74 **Roll:** 68 **Category:** C, D. Male

i **BACKGROUND** Kirklevington Grange was built in the latter half of the 19th century, a compact country house typical of that period. It subsequently passed into the hands of the Prison Service. a long corridor was added to one end of the house with four accommodation blocks protruding from it. The facility was brought into use as a detention centre in 1963. Separate blocks were added at various times to house the gymnasium, education department and farms and gardens department. In October 1992 the establishment changed its role to that of a resettlement prison for Category C adult males. The prison is situated near the town of Yarm, about 10 miles from Middlesborough and Darlington. The Governor of Kirklevington Grange provided an abundance of information about the prison, though the BoV did not reply to our request for a copy of their annual report. The Grange was last inspected by HMCIP in November 1993 and their report was published on 19th May 1994.

CRITERIA Males serving 2+ yrs with <12mths to go. Cats C&D only. No sex offenders, arsonists, lifers, appellants or those with further charges.

OFFICIALS
AREA MGR: Mr Papps
CHAIR BOV: Mrs Merrit
GOVERNOR: Mrs Midgely
MEDICAL: Dr Waters
CHAPLAIN: Rev Moore
PROBATION: Mrs Kendal
EDUCATION: Mr Dougherty
LOCAL MP: Tim Devlin. Con
STAFFING: 2 Governor grades, 3 Principal Officers, 7 Senior Officers and 32 Officers including specialist staff.

REGIME *week days*: 0745 unlock/breakfast. 0900 work/education/Job Club. 1215 dinner. 1330 work/education/Job Club. 1630 cease work. 1715 tea. Gym, education, association till 2000. Return to rooms 22.30, lock up.

week ends: 0745 unlock/breakfast/town visits/gym/association. 1215 dinner. 1330 association until 2230.

Out of cell: 16.5/24hrs weekdays and 16.5/24hrs at weekends.

ACCOMMODATION & FACILITIES Single rooms with own keys. Large list of in-possession items allowed, usual carpet, curtains and duvet etc, and £15 per week maximum may be used each week for personal possessions and hobby materials. Caged budgie or canary (only) allowed. On arrival inmates receive two letters at public expense. There is no censorship, mail is given out at the hotplate at midday, or left in reception for those working outside the prison. Three card phones were fitted with access throughout the day and no limit on phonecards. There is an opportunity to obtain a phonecard shortly after reception.

CANTEEN Sited to one side of the main prison corridor, the shop holds 138 different lines, contains a fridge for perishables and has a local purchase facility. Open Mon (1430–1700 & 1730–1830); Tues, Wed (0800–1200 & 1300–1630); Thurs: 0800–1000. Inmate-staff canteen committee meets monthly.

REQUESTS/COMPLAINTS Very little reference to formal Request/Complaint system at the Grange. Since re-opening in October 1992, HMCIP reported in May 1994 that only 16 forms had been submitted—five of these were later withdrawn and all request/complaint forms were dealt with 'adequately within seven days'.

VISITS *How to get there*: Train to Eaglescliffe then infrequent bus, or taxi to Yarm. No Special Transport.
VISITING TIMES: Week Days: 1345–1600 Tues, Wed, Thur only. Saturday: 1345–1600. Sunday: 1345–1600.

NOTES No staffed Visitors Centre or Childrens Play Area. Canteen in visiting room. Contact prison probation for details of local B&B. Disabled access. No smoking in visiting room. Property but not monies accepted on visits. Very few visits at the Grange as town visits, allowed once induction completed and D Cat status achieved, renders them superfluous.

EDUCATION Education open 50 weeks of the year with two full time teachers and five nights of evening classes a week. All prisoners' educational needs are assessed as part of induction and action plan drawn up. Courses in Information Technology; Home Management; Textiles Design and Craft; Humanities; Basic Skills; Driving (CPC); Multi-Skills (DIY). Well appointed Education Centre, facilities include IT Centre with laser, colour and dot matrix printers, and a library with 1500 books.

WORKSHOPS No workshops as such, kitchen and cleaning parties with average wage of £7 per week. Most inmates at Kirklevington Grange attend outside college courses or inside education, or are otherwise employed outside the prison during the working day. Expectation that first month will be spent as cleaners. Labour Board held each Friday. Wages average a basic of £6.50 per week.

DISCIPLINE Since the Grange reopened in October 1992 there have been 70 adjudications (as at 19.10.93: HMCIP). Seven were dismissed, 18 resulted in cautions, 15 prisoners had been transferred out and there had been only one case of Rule 43 segregation.

MEDICAL Local GP acts as part-time Medical Officer, assisted by a full time Health Care Officer and an Agency Nurse. A doctor is in attendance every morning at 0845 hours Monday to Saturday. National scheme of proactive health care has been in place at the Grange since July 1993 which runs courses in stopping smoking, diet, exercise, heart disease and provides counselling for a wide variety of problems. Criticised by HMCIP for inadequate approach to HIV/AIDS.

GYMNASIUM & SPORTS Two full-time PE staff. Weight and fitness training, badminton, padder tennis, carpet bowls, hiking, swimming, cycling and visits to sports centres. Football matches with external teams are a regular feature. Good relationship with local disabled groups, the prison holds a Certificate of Merit for its work with handicapped people. Plans to introduce courses leading to qualifications for those in the leisure industry. A 'common sense' attitude is expected from prisoners who use the PE facilities.

CHAPLAINCY There is a small chapel within the prison, offering a choice of services. part time chaplains—Anglican, RC, Methodist—are appointed and visit regularly, as does a Salvation Army visitor. Visits by representatives of all other religions can be arranged. A range of activities is offered by the chaplaincy team, including: Sunday services both within and outwith the establishment, confidential counselling and evening classes giving a choice of instruction classes, discussion groups and videos.

FOOD The kitchen is staffed by an SO Caterer, 2 Catering Officers and 6 kitchen workers. Breakfast at 0815 is typically traditional porridge or cornflakes and a hot savoury. Dinner at 1215 is kept fairly light with a choice of main dishes. Tea, at 1700 is the main meal of the day with a choice of main courses and a sweet pudding. Every kitchen worker has to undergo a certificated Food-handling Course.

ESTABLISHMENT REPORTS Relationships between prisoners and staff were at the heart of the peaceful environment at Kirklevington Grange said HMCIP in a Report (published 19th May 1994) of a full inspection in November 1993. HMCIP was most favourably impressed with Kirklevington and what is being achieved there, and had very few recommendations for improvement. Essentially it is one of those prisons, such as Blantyre House, Latchmere House and North Sea Camp, where selected inmates are carefully prepared by experienced staff and outstanding Governors for resettlement in the community. The whole process seemed to the inspectorate to be a proper discharge of the duty of the Prison Service to help them lead law abiding and useful lives in custody and after release. 'We commend it'.

GOVERNOR'S COMMENTS We are committed to a regime which will assist inmates to resettle in the community and to avoid risks of reoffending on release. This will be achieved by a realistic programme for challenging offending behaviour, structured training and activity sessions relevant to their needs. In all aspects of our work with inmates we are committed to a policy of racial equality and to the elimination of discrimination. All inmates and staff will be treated without prejudice on the grounds of colour, race or religion. A relaxed but positive regime will operate in a safe and stable environment. We aim to expand our activities in 1995 and broaden our criteria to take men serving longer periods. Kirklevington Grange only takes men in the last 6–12 months of their sentence at present.

PRISONERS' COMMENTS On arrival at Kirklevington entry is via the Reception Unit, the walkway is enclosed by a fencing structure which appears intimidating. The reception procedure is conducted in a civil and friendly manner, reassuring new arrivals that communication with staff is both natural and genuine. Once over the [7 day] induction period you will be engaged in activities in the community. In contrast to larger establishments, in general everyone greets you in passing—the politeness and courtesy of staff is consistent to the point of being uncomfortable! The efficient manner in which the regime operates soon becomes a comfortable change and in a short period of time characteristics long since disposed of are restored to second nature—in short the civility rubs off. Joining a regime where everyone is motivated and in a positive frame of mind is infectious and welcome. Free of petty restrictions and intimidating presence in living areas, a welcome feeling of self responsibility and privacy is soon established.

HM Prison Lancaster

The Castle, Lancaster.. LA1 1YL
Tel: 0524-68871 **Fax:** 0524-62593
Opened: 1458 **CNA:** 186 **Average Roll:** 250 **Category:** C. Male

i **BACKGROUND** Lancaster is reputed to be the oldest prison in Europe and has walls in parts over five feet thick! It is situated within Lancaster Castle which occupies a hill-top site above the lowest crossing of the River Lune. Remnants of the original fortification survive alongside an Elizabethan tower and many 15th, 18th and 19th century additions. The Castle's history as a place of confinement is too extensive to detail but was punctuated only by a variety of other uses between 1916 and 1955. The prison is leased from the Duchy of Lancaster, but in 1992 the lease was extended for only four years and there is a great deal of uncertainty about the future of Lancaster Castle as a prison: there is much local pressure to turn it into a tourist attraction. Neither the Governor nor BoV replied to our requests for information about the prison. HMCIP published their latest inspection report on Lancaster in October 1994.

OFFICIALS
AREA MGR: Ian Lockwood
CHAIR BOV:
GOVERNOR: D. McNaughton
MEDICAL:
CHAPLAIN: Rev Clemence
PROBATION: George Mayne
EDUCATION:
LOCAL MP: Elaine Kellett-Bowman. Con

REGIME *week days*: 0745 unlock. 0815 breakfast. 0830 work. 1115 exercise (except Friday). 1200 dinner, lock up. 1315 work. 1330–1545 visits. 1545–1615 exercise (Friday). 1615 cease work, exercise. 1700 tea. 1715 association. 1800 classes, unlock, gym. 2030 lock up.

week ends: 0745 unlock. 0815 breakfast. 0830 CE Service (Sun). 0930–1130 visits. 1145 lock up. 1200 dinner. 1215 association. 1330–1545 visits. 1645 lock up. 1700 tea, association. 2030 lock up.

Out of cell: K/A=11.75/24hrs G=7/24hrs weekday/weekends.

ACCOMMODATION & FACILITIES Three wings: A.wing comprises three landings of cells and two landings each of two 6-bed dormitories; G.wing comprises seven dormitories, each housing 12–14 inmates; K.wing was built as a tower and has five semi-circular landings of large wedge-shaped cells most of which are in double occupancy. All cells have integral sanitation and low voltage power points and showers on landings. Inmates have access to association for two hours every alternate weekday evening, G.wing one day, K.wing the next. Dormitories have satellite TV. Card phones on each wing, mail opened outwith the presence of the inmate and distributed at dinner time.

VISITS *How to get there*: Train or bus to Lancaster, prison 5 min walk from BR Station and 10 min walk from Bus Station. No Special Transport.
VISITING TIMES: Week Days: 0915–1115 & 1415–1615 Tues, Fri only. Saturday: 1315–1515. Sunday: 1315–1515.

NOTES No staffed Visitors Centre. Childrens' Play Area available weekday afternoons only. Canteen in visiting room. Contact prison probation for details of local B&B.

EDUCATION Four f/t and 14 p/t teachers. Open five days and three evenings 50 weeks of the year. Three classrooms and four workshops. Basic education, RSA Continuing Education, Social Studies, Return To Study, Computing, Business Studies.

WORKSHOPS VTC/CIT courses: Painting & Decorating; Electronic Wiring, Information Technology; Welding. Two textile workshops, one making boxer shorts, the second mailbags.

DISCIPLINE Reports average 30 per month, hearing fairly conducted and documentation properly completed. Segregation Unit, part of A.wing, seven ordinary cells with integral sanitation, one strip cell.

ESTABLISHMENT REPORTS In a report (published 25th October 1994) of an inspection in June 1994, HMCIP said that local management had long been conscious of the serious limitations of Lancaster as a modern prison and as recently as two years ago had plans to close it. It was only the rise in the prison population which caused this to be postponed. Lancaster is unable to fulfil several parts of the Service's Statement of Purpose. Conditions in the dormitories of G.wing are deplorable, there is hardly any space for association or purposeful work and constructive activities. Relationships between inmates and staff , and management and staff, are impressive. If Lancaster is to remain in the penal estate, conditions for prisoners must be improved. There must be a substantial reduction in the population in order to make space available for humane containment and for more activities designed to help prisoners address their offending behaviour and acquire work skills necessary for them to lead law abiding lives on release.

PRISONERS' COMMENTS Though Lancaster is a C Category prison, there are too many locked gates and its security is more appropriate to B.Cat prisons, and with a wall of more than sixty feet in places it is unnecessary. There is a lack of showers and the frequency of kit changes is poor. No space exists for laundry facilities on the wings and this makes the kit change situation worse. There are too many restrictions on privileges and canteen purchases. The wing card phone is situated close to the association room and is available during association times only, the wing phone can only be used in an emergency. Poor quality food, despite a fairly recent kitchen, though there are prisons with worse. Lack of space for education, a department held in high regard, limits the regime.

HM YOI Lancaster Farms

Queensmore Road, Lancaster. LA2 3JX
Tel: 0524-848745 **Fax:** 0524-848393
Opened: 1993 **CNA:** 372 **Average Roll:** 372 **Category:** Closed YOI

i **BACKGROUND** Lancaster Farms was originally conceived as a C Category training prison but shortly before it opened it was redesignated as a closed YOI, and later began to take remand prisoners in addition to its convicted population. The institution is located alongside the M6 motorway on farmland that formerly belonged to Kirkham prison. There were two escapes from Lancaster Farms in 1993, one through the visits and a second slipped his cuffs at court. Neither the Governor nor BoV replied to our requests for information about the prison, and HMCIP conducted their first inspection of Lancaster Farms in November 1994. Publication of their report was awaited as we went to press: full details 1996 edition.

OFFICIALS
AREA MGR: Ian Lockwood
CHAIR BOV:
GOVERNOR: D. Waplington
MEDICAL:
CHAPLAIN: Rev Geen
PROBATION: Kevin Brown
EDUCATION:
LOCAL MP: Elaine Kellet-Bowman. Con
STAFFING: 8 Governor grades, 6 Principal Officers, 28 Senior Officers and 110 Officers, including specialist staff.

ACCOMMODATION & FACILITIES Three House blocks, Coniston, Derwent & Windermere, divided into two mirror image units.

Each of the six units has its own function and can house 60 inmates in a mixture of single and double cells. All cells have integral sanitation. Average of 13 hours per day out of cell drastically cut recently to as little as two or three hours for remand prisoners at weekends.

VISITS *How to get there*: Train to Lancaster then bus to prison. No special transport. VISITING TIMES: Weekdays: 1330–1615—see Notes. Saturday: 1330–1615. Sunday: 1330–1615.

NOTES All weekday visits MUST be booked in advance—contact Booking Office on 0524-848779. Very good Visitors Centre, though at peak times baby-changing facilities are inadequate.

WORKSHOPS VTC/CIT courses: Cookery; Industrial Cleaning; Parenting—which has won wide acclaim in the press.

DISCIPLINE Large number of disciplinary adjudications. In its first nine months of operation there were almost 1,000 adjudications, leading to more than 3,700 Additional Days, including 66 cases of assault, 149 for fighting, and 163 for unauthorised possession.

GOVERNOR'S COMMENTS Annual Report March 1994: Two escapes in 1993, which have resulted in tighter security procedures, can be classed as the prison's failures. The successes in the first twelve months are more numerous: the prison opened ahead of time, there was only one assault on a member of staff, no use of the C&R Team, no suicides and there is no VPU or Rule 43(OP) inmates. The Handling Adolescents Training Course developed by Lancaster Farms has been adopted nationally. Our Parenting course has received wide media attention and there have been a number of letters from the families of ex-inmates, commenting upon the effect Lancaster Farm had on improving behaviour. The private catering contract has been a success with an excellent standard of food being delivered within budget. Many prisoners on Education have won awards and certificates, the PE department has developed a varied programme to occupy large numbers of energetic inmates, and we have quickly developed a high quality of Trade Training. We have established the beginnings of an anti-bullying culture, prisoners feel safer at this prison than most others. We are well advanced with planning courses addressing car crime and drug abuse. In 1995 our main aim will be to improve efficiency and effectiveness in every department, with specific measures set out in our Business Plan 1994/95.

PRISONERS' COMMENTS Requests and Complaints are normally dealt with on time, but there are times when they can take ages to get back to you. No power points in the cells, though internal light switch and toilet—which are very noisy at nights. Canteen is OK, prices are good, but the range of stock is too limited. Visits are excellent with a relaxed atmosphere. Education is very good, staff are keen to help. Wages average about £5. There is not much interest shown by the medical officer, though the nurses are genuinely interested in what they're doing. Reports are even handed, though the block is a bit on the rough side. BoV are worth a mention, they are better here than I've seen at other prisons, will help solve problems and they do get back to you when they say they will. Good gym facilities with rota system giving good access. The food is a poor subject, its not varied enough and the quality is poor. Church services are good, but most of the lads go to take the piss and this disrupts the service, though the staff don't seem to do anything about it. Mail is not opened in front of the inmate, card phones in all houses.

HM Prison Latchmere House

Church Rd, Richmond, Surrey. TW10 5HH
Tel: 081-948-0215 **Fax:** 081-332-1359
Opened: 1948 **CNA:** 145 **Roll:** 142 **Category:** D. Male

i **BACKGROUND** Latchmere House prison is located between Richmond and Kingston-upon-Thames in a residential area close to Richmond Park. Since 1948 it has been a Borstal Allocation Centre, a Junior Detention Centre, Remand Centre for Juveniles, a Place of Detention for Foreign Nationals held under the Immigration Act and as a Remand Centre for adults. In 1991 it became a resettlement prison and, apart from one exposé in The Sun in May 1994, it has kept a low profile. The Governor of Latchmere, Sean O'Neil, provided information about the establishment, though the BoV did not reply to our request for a copy of their annual report. HMCIP published their latest inspection report on Latchmere House in July 1992.

OFFICIALS
AREA MGR: Peter Kitteridge
CHAIR BOV: Terry Medcalf
GOVERNOR: Sean O'Neill
MEDICAL: Dr Jeffries
CHAPLAIN: Rev D. Gamble
PROBATION: Mr. J. Martin
EDUCATION: Nil on Site
LOCAL MP: Jeremy Hanley. Con

REGIME *week days*: 0745 unlock/breakfast. 0830 college, work, day release. 1200 lunch. 1800 evening meal. Association throughout excepting minimal domestic work. Open (internal) conditions no lock up.

week ends: 0745 unlock, no breakfast, instead Brunch at 1200, evening meal 1700. Association throughout excepting minimal domestic work.

Out of cell: 24/24hrs weekdays and 24/24hrs at weekends.

ACCOMMODATION & FACILITIES Two houseblocks with single cubicles or three bed dormitories. A.wing is in effect a Pre-Release Hostel. All men progress to A.wing if at Latchmere House long enough. In-cell sink, h/c water, light switch, night-san giving access to toilet, showers, boiler & toaster. Extensive in-possession list. Poor facilities, just one TV on each spur, no pool, table-tennis, darts or snooker, reported by inmates, and HMCIP recommended 'a sensibly equipped association area should be provided'. No canteen facilities on site, purchases from local shop. Very little recourse to formal request/complaint procedure, most requests dealt with by officers on site. Uncensored mail, opened to check for enclosures and handed to prisoner. No restrictions on phone calls.

VISITS *How to get there*: Train or tube to Richmond, then bus (371) to Cardinal Tudor Drive, then short walk. No Special Transport.
VISITING TIMES: Week Days: Town visits 1000–1500. Saturday: Town visits 1000–1500. Sunday: Town Visits 1000–1500.

NOTES No staffed Visitors Centre, no canteen or Childrens Play Area. Prisoners do not normally have visits in the prison, but are able to go into the town each day. Local B&B. HMCIP queried why town visits had to end at 1530 when inmates would be out of the establishment much later were they at work or college.

EDUCATION No day education facilities on site but local college open 50 weeks of the year. Evening classes Mon–Thurs, cookery and post-release survival.

WORKSHOPS 1×Plastics workshop, 2×Assembly shops and 1×Computer IT shop. Much work in the community, though HMCIP received complaints about working conditions: 'Community workers . . . were paid only 8p per hour while the employer was expected to pay the prison 98p per hour for their services . . . this was particularly galling when they were working for Prison Officers in their homes'. HMCIP agreed that the packed lunch given to community workers was too small.

DISCIPLINE HMCIP examined the records of 40 adjudications and found that loss of remission was being awarded far too often. Thirty of the records examined related to breach of temporary release licence, with wide variations in the level of awards.

MEDICAL Local GP and agency nurse 0800–1000 Mon–Fri and 1800–2000 Monday evenings. Emergency cover and call out facilities. Report sick to wing staff or Health Care Centre on A.wing.

GYMNASIUM & SPORTS One PEO from local college. No PE at weekends and only about one hour during the working day on weekdays. Inmates told HMCIP that anyone working outside the establishment has little chance of using the gymnasium, and they had to stand and watch it being used by staff at weekends.

CHAPLAINCY Part-time chaplaincy team for all religions, prisoners attend religious services externally, plus social evenings Sundays within Latchmere House.

FOOD Well regarded by prisoners who report it as being: 'well prepared and presented'. HMCIP received no complaints about he standard of food at Latchmere.

ESTABLISHMENT REPORTS In a report (published 23rd July 1992) of an inspection in January 1992, Judge Stephen Tumim, HMCIP, said that he welcomed the introduction of Latchmere House as a resettlement prison, allowing inmates the opportunity to address the 'crucial areas of employment, accommodation and relationships from within a supportive structure'. An induction unit should be provided however for new arrivals, and HMCIP questioned the necessity of a 17 foot security fence (and two coils of razor wire) in a prison from which most inmates wondered in and out each day. However, Latchmere House was a 'sound base' from which to move forward, 'the direction and quality of advancement will depend on the type of inmates received, their relationships with staff and the development of mutual trust and a sense of community'.

GOVERNOR'S COMMENTS Numerous plans. Increase prison population numbers, improve general appearance and facilities, especially real wage work and much investment in staff development courses arranged.

PRISONERS' COMMENTS Most requests are dealt with by officers on site. Single cells, no power points and poor sanitation facilities. No canteen, day education or visits—allowed home weekends—on site, but all facilities in Kingston. Wages £35 per week. Gymnasium during evenings, and adjudications are few and far between—most resulting in ship-outs.

HM Prison Leeds

Armley, Leeds. West Yorks. LS12 2TJ
Tel: 0532-636411 **Fax:** 0532-790151
Opened: 1847 **CNA:** 591 **Average Roll:** 846 **Category:** Male Local & Remand Centre

i **BACKGROUND** Leeds prison, otherwise known as Armley Gaol and designed as a fortress, sits on a hill overlooking the city and was built in 1847. It is of radial design with four large wings and occupies a site of nearly four hectares. The wings, centre, tower block entry gate and associated buildings are all Grade II listed buildings. When first opened the prison had 334 cells, but additional accommodation has been provided over the years. Leeds accepts a wide variety of inmates, ranging from civil prisoners to those in Category A. The prison serves more than 50 courts and allocates to Acklington, Castington, Everthorpe, Hatfield, Kirkham, Lancaster, Lindholme, Northallerton, Rudgate and Wymott to name but a few. The Governor did not reply to our request for information about the prison, though the BoV kindly supplied a copy of their 1993/94 annual report. HMCIP conducted a full inspection of Leeds in June 1994 and their report has not been published as we went to press. The last inspection at Leeds took place in 1990 and was scathingly critical, though as the BoV make clear, there have been some improvements since then. Due to the forthcoming HMCIP Report this entry will be brief with full details in the 1996 edition.

OFFICIALS
AREA MGR: Terry Bone
CHAIR BOV: Mary Denton
GOVERNOR: A. Fitzpatrick
MEDICAL:
CHAPLAIN: Rev Theobald
PROBATION: Paul Marsh
EDUCATION:
LOCAL MP: John Battle. Lab

VISITS *How to get there*: Train or bus to Leeds. Buses (40,44,80) from BR Station. Bus (72,508) from bus station. No Special Transport.
VISITING TIMES: *week days*: 1230–1515 (Rem) 1330–1515 (Con). Saturday: As above + 0915–1115. Sunday: No Visits.

NOTES No staffed Visitors Centre or Childrens Play Area. Canteen available. Remand prisoners are only allowed visits on alternate days, but Saturday is a 'free day' 0915–1115. Wheelchair access can be arranged with prior notice. Plans to introduce all day visits, so check with prison.

ESTABLISHMENT REPORTS In a report of an inspection in March 1990, HMCIP said that Leeds was overcrowded. The introduction of integral sanitation had been given no priority in redevelopment plans. Inmates lacked proper and full occupation, although some of the convicted sewed garments for a while each day, other inmates cleaned and others attended some classes. On B.wing, where those under 21 were held, the regime was seriously inadequate, there had been a number of suicides and a very large number of cases of self-harm. HMCIP said that some of the self-harm cases resulted from personal problems or were an attempt to influence the court to grant bail, but the vast bulk were committed by young people on remand in circumstances where they were locked up 23 hours a day, two or three to a cell, with a bucket for a toilet, no work, and frequently no answer to cell bells rung during the day for attention or to visit the toilet. Inmates subject to such conditions felt neglected, insecure and became as individuals unbalanced. Reception was appalling and quite unsuited to its task. Staff struggled to deal with 200 inmates on Rule 43, who received no PE, limited education, work and association. The regime for remand inmates on normal location was sparse. Inmate/staff relationships were amicable, adjudications fairly conducted and the segregation unit was not over-used for punishment. Applications system worked effectively though the number one Governor rarely if ever saw any inmates. There needs to be shared working involving probation and prison staff. Limitations on the number of letters should be removed, visiting facilities were reasonable but capable of improvement and there was a lack of pre-release or social skills courses despite the presence of trained staff. The chaplaincy provided a good service to inmates and staff, education was impressive but grossly under-used. Physical education was some of the worst HMCIP had seen and workshops were under-used while inmates remained locked up. Food was generally good but more choice is necessary and meal times need amendment: inmates should not go more than 16 hours without food. Canteen services were good but there was a lack of space, clothing for convicted inmates was inadequate and should be increased. The prison Hospital was clean but grossly understaffed, it was too difficult to see the doctor and there was a lack of regime for inpatients. A major rebuilding programme was underway, the Governor was aware of the shortcomings and was intent on improving matters.

BoV ANNUAL REPORT 1993/94 It has been a busy and eventful year at Leeds, new facilities have been successfully commissioned and some of the older accommodation has been refurbished. Additional features have been added and some positive moves made to improve the regime in line with recommendations in the Woolf report. Two new wings were opened by HRH The Princess Royal (E&F), along with a new kitchen and PE facilities. A temporary Visitors Centre was opened in September which has proved to be a success, though the lack of air conditioning in the visiting room is causing problems but a No Smoking policy is highly unlikely. New security screening facilities have already revealed illegal substances being brought into the prison. B.wing has completed its integral sanitation programme, though other wings have been put on hold while a decision is made about the size and role of Leeds in the future. Despite a concerted campaign by the BoV rubbish is still being thrown from cell windows and making the yards unsightly. Management at Leeds has suffered from prolific changes that saw five Governor grades move to new posts. New Health Care Centre came into operation in December. Education contracted out to South Manchester College, and an entirely new education team moved into the prison with first indications being that the previous high standards are being at least maintained. In November, due to intelligence received, all locks in the prison were replaced, being completed throughout in nine days and with critical areas being achieved in 48 hours. Due to the insufficient number of card phones a booking system has been introduced which places a greater burden on wing staff and only marginally reduces the hassle factor. There were three suicides at Leeds during the year, one in March and two in July. Two attempted suicides were resuscitated by staff though both suffered serious injuries.

HM Prison Leicester

Welford Road, Leicester. LE2 7AJ
Tel: 0533-546911 **Fax:** 0533-471753
Opened: 1825 **CNA:** 194 **Average Roll:** 319 **Category:** Male Local + SSB

i **BACKGROUND** Leicester prison, which presents the external appearance of an impressive and strong medieval fortress, is situated in a commercial and residential district about half a mile from the city centre. The large gatehouse and cellular accommodation are the oldest parts of the prison having been built in 1825. Further construction took place in 1874, which used up the bulk of the space inside the secure perimeter wall, and in 1990 a new visits and admin block were built adjoining the gatehouse. Today the prison appears very much as it must have done at the end of the Victorian era, though what was once the Governor's Quarters close to the main gate has been converted into a staff mess. Leicester operates as a local prison for adult males, and also contains a Special Security Block (SSB) for Exceptional Risk Category A inmates. Neither the Governor nor BoV at Leicester replied to our requests for information about the prison, and HMCIP published their latest inspection report on Leicester in October 1992.

OFFICIALS

AREA MGR: Jim Blakey
CHAIR BOV:
GOVERNOR: G. Ross
MEDICAL:
CHAPLAIN: Rev Stark
PROBATION: John Chalmers
EDUCATION:
LOCAL MP: James Marshall. Lab

STAFFING: 6 Governors, 258 other staff in unified grades.

REGIME *week days*: 0745 unlock. 0800 breakfast. 0845 convicted exercise, work. 0900 sick parade, Rule 43 exercise. 0915 classes. 0930 (Mon & Wed) Rule 43 classes. 1015 reception board. 1045 remand exercise, adjudications. 1100 Governors' applications. 1115 dinner lock up. 1315, unlock, slop out. 1330 convicted exercise, work. 1400 (Mon & Wed) Rule 43 association. 1415 remand exercise. 1455 remand association by rota. 1600 tea, lock up. 1745 unlock classes, B1 association, film (Fri). 1800 slop out starts. 1930 supper. 2000 lock up.

week ends: 0800 unlock. 0815 breakfast. 0845 RC Mass (Sun), 0900 convicted and Rule 43 exercise. 0915 sick parade. 0920 CE chapel (Sun), CE Service (Sat). 1000 reception board. 1015 remand exercise. 1115 dinner, lock up. 1315, unlock, slop out. 1330 remand film (Sun). 1400 remand association. 1415 Rule 43 bathing. 1530 tea, lock up. 1630 SSB association. 1715 B1 association. 1930 supper. 2000 lock up.

Out of cell: 6.5/24hrs weekdays and 4/24hrs at weekends.

ACCOMMODATION & FACILITIES The main living accommodation at Leicester is a long rectangular cell block with four landings, the north end of the block holds convicted inmates and is called, A.wing, the south end holds trials and remands and is called B.wing. Partial integral sanitation. Most cells have two occupants, some have been converted to dormitories. Part of B2 is securely sealed off from the rest of the wing and houses the Special Security Block (SSB). Landing recesses due to be converted to showers when integral sanitation completed. Good inmate/staff relationships despite the austere conditions. Impoverished association facilities and all meals dine in cell. Sentence planning and personal officer scheme, but both undeveloped. VPU. Drug counselling available. Association for remands 1455-1600 alternate days, convicted association restricted to inmate orderlies and key workers only, 1745–2000. Card phones on A2, B1, HCC, Seg, VPU.

SPECIAL SECURITY BLOCK Set up in 1967, in response to the escapes of Great Train Robbers Wilson and Biggs, the SSB at Leicester is one of four around the country (others at Durham, Parkhurst and Whitemoor). The SSB has 11 cells on either side of B2 landing though only eight have been kept as inmate accommodation. Electronic entry control system and both internal and external areas of SSB monitored by CCTV. Separate secure visiting room, exercise yard covered with anti-helicopter wires, all cell walls have built-in tamper alarms and the eight inmates are supervised by 2×SO and 30×Officers split into two shifts: there have been no escapes since it opened. Education classes, wing laundry, weights area and cooking facilities. Association and TV room double as dining room. Whole unit cramped and should be moved said HMCIP. Open from 0745–2000 with lock up only at staff meal times. Full dispersal privilege list and inmate/staff relationships are good. Far too many staff doing too little said HMCIP.

CANTEEN Canteen located in two converted cells on A2 landing. Very small serving area though good stock, well laid out and prices clearly displayed. Remand earnings paid on the day after reception, trial earnings paid each Friday. Private cash may be spent on Tuesday, Thursday and the day after reception. HMCIP cites 1990 annual canteen turnover as £83,000 and a profit margin of 9%. No local purchase facility.

VISITS *How to get there*: Train or bus to Leicester and then 15 min walk. No Special Transport.

VISITING TIMES: Week Days: 1330–1530. Saturday: 1330–1530. Sunday: 1330–1530.

NOTES Staffed Visitors Centre (**Tel:** 0533 544706) open Mon–Fri 1030–1530, Sat 1130–1430. Canteen Mon–Sat. Childrens Play Area in visits room, and also in VC Tues, Thurs and Saturday. Disabled access good. Baby-changing facilities in visits room, and child-minding in the VC.

EDUCATION 3×f/t and 23 p/t teachers. Housed in converted production workshop, provides three classrooms, two offices and two small resource areas, one of which doubles as a classroom. HMCIP said the accommodation was inadequate and squalid. Open four days and evenings per week, 0930–1130, 1400–1600 and 1745–1930. Core subjects, English, RSA information technology and arts. Small library holds a max of 8 inmates at any one time, open 0900–1000 and 1345–1600 weekdays. No weekend or evening opening.

WORKSHOPS No VTC/CIT courses. Lack of work opportunities with about 150 unemployed inmates. Textile production workshop closed down to improve educational provision. Employment centres around Contract Services shop (makes toy pushchairs and candle holders), education, kitchen, domestic cleaners and works. Average employed pay £6, UB40 £2.50.

DISCIPLINE HMCIP examined a total of 86 adjudications and found minor errors in recording and more serious errors in relation to the wording of charges. High level of adjudications though awards are not on the heavy side.

Segregation unit located in the basement. Five ordinary cells, toilet/shower area and separate exercise yard. One strip cell.

VPU Area adjacent to Seg Unit used as VPU, with 12 cells frequently holding in excess of 30 inmates. Partial integral sanitation. All meals dine in. Impoverished regime for VPU inmates, exercise daily (weather permitting), but little else available. Association 1400–1600 Mon & Tues.

MEDICAL Full time SMO, 1×p/t GP (18hrs/wk), HCPO, 2×HCSO, 10×HCO, one of whom is female and another a Registered General Nurse. HCC located in two-storey building, lower floor containing offices and examinations rooms etc, top floor comprises a dormitory, 5-bed ward, 4-bed ward and six single cells. A2 landing used as HCC overflow. Strip cell used on 19 occasions in the six weeks prior to the inspection, the relevant paperwork failed to record use of body-belt, and there had been occasions when hospital officers had allowed discipline staff to use the strip cell to locate a disruptive inmate without any prior authority from a doctor and in cases where there was no emergency. Dental treatment 1 sess/wk, short waiting list, but optician 1 sess/8wks and long waiting list. Four visiting psychiatrists each 1 sess/wk.

GYMNASIUM & SPORTS 1×PESO and 3×PEO. Very poor PE facilities, converted workshop used as gym, low ceiling restricts use and concrete walls and floor causes abrasions. PE programme 0830–1130, 1330–1530, 1700–1900 Mon–Fri. No weekend PE programme at all. Programme category based, with identified sessions for Cat A and Rule 43 inmates, remands, convicted and remedials. New sports hall planned for 1996/97.

CHAPLAINCY Full time CE chaplain, p/t RC and Methodist ministers. Minority faiths catered for by pool of visiting ministers. Chapel located on top floor of rotunda, access restricted but conditions reasonable. RC Mass 0845 Sunday, followed by CE Service at 0930, average attendances of 10 and 50 respectively. Sikh worship Wednesday, Muslims and Chaplains Hour both on Saturday. United service held on A1 landing for VPU inmates.

FOOD Staffing: 1×SO, 4×Officer (caterers), and an inmate work party of 18. Plans for NVQ Caterbase course for inmates in kitchen. Five week menu cycle in operation, though no pre-select system due to high turnover. Delayed plans for new kitchen now due to open in 1995. Food reasonable in terms of both presentation and taste.

ESTABLISHMENT REPORTS In a report (published 21st October 1992) of an inspection in November 1991, HMCIP, said that three problems face Leicester: overcrowding, lack of facilities and the effects on staffing and resources of the SSB. There are few facilities for inmates to exercise, associate or take part in PE. The main exercise area is inadequate, the gymnasium a converted workshop and the association space is limited to parts of A2 and B2 landings. The state of the kitchen gives cause for concern, staff facilities throughout the prison were of poor quality and insufficient to meet their needs.

PRISONERS' COMMENTS The lines of communication are ill-defined and there appears to be little staff interest in resolving problems. Accommodation is usually two'd up, internal light switch and recently installed radio adapter but no power points. Canteen prices are expensive, choice is poor and access is restricted. Visitors are kept waiting far too long for admission because of the slow processing system. Education is very good considering the facilities and the staff are committed to their work. Very basic work opportunities, mundane tasks and poor wages. Average medical facilities for a local prison. Disciplinary adjudications are reasonably fair, and better than experienced in other locals and awards are even-handed for the most part. The food is overcooked and dull—there's certainly enough of it, bit its not worth eating half the time. Gym facilities are adequate, but access is difficult if you are on education or have a job. Religious provision is very poor, as a Buddhist I have have great difficulties. Mail is opened long before we receive it, limited access to card phones which makes life difficult; as a remand prisoner I can only use the phone in the morning, I have a solicitor to act for me, but others who are conducting their own defences are severely hampered in preparation of their cases.

HM Prison Lewes

Brighton Rd, Lewes, East Sussex. BN7 1EA.
Tel: 0273-477331 **Fax:** 0273-483042
Opened: 1867 **CNA:** 258 **Average Roll:** 347 **Category:** Male Local

i **BACKGROUND** Like many county towns in England, Lewes acquired a new prison in the middle of the last century, planned on a radial system and surrounded by a high wall. The prison was outside the town when it was built and a generous amount of land was enclosed within the perimeter wall which has allowed for in-filling over the years with additional buildings. It stands today at one end of the High Street about half a mile from the town centre. The prison has a well-known reputation for appalling conditions and an impoverished regime. Neither the Governor nor BoV replied to our requests for information about the prison, and HMCIP published their latest inspection report on Lewes in November 1992.

OFFICIALS
AREA MGR: Alan Rayfield
CHAIR BOV:
GOVERNOR: J.F. Dixon
MEDICAL:
CHAPLAIN: Rev Powe
PROBATION: David Royce
EDUCATION:
LOCAL MP: Tim Rathbone. Con
STAFFING: 7 Governor grades, 13 Principal Officers, 33 Senior Officers and 171 Officers, including specialist staff.

REGIME *week days*: 0745 unlock, breakfast. 0845 wing routines commence, inmates to labour. 1100 dinner. 1330 wing routines commence, inmates to labour. 1600 tea. 1730 commence wing routines, slop out. 1900 supper. 2000 lock up.

week ends: 0745 unlock, breakfast. 0840 wing routines commence. 0900 RC Mass (Sat), CE Service (Sun). 1100 dinner. 1315 wing routines commence. 1530 tea. 1715 commence wing routines, slop out. 1900 supper 2000 lock up.

Out of cell: 7/24hrs weekdays and 5/24hrs at weekends.

ACCOMMODATION & FACILITIES
Four main wings, A,B,C,F, and two pseudo wings: G and K wings. A.wing (102 cells with 190 places) houses young offenders and adult remands. A1 landing, sealed off and known as K.wing (16/32), is used as a VPU. C.wing (121/180) houses convicted inmates. C1 landing, sealed off and known as G.wing (18/27), is used to house inadequate inmates unable to survive on normal location for reasons other than the nature of their charge or offences. B(40) & F(88) wings recently reopened after refurbishment and fitting of integral sanitation. HMCIP said the regime was unsatisfactory and association should be moved from afternoons to evenings, and a community centre should be provided. Bail Information Unit and Drug Therapy Group. Card phones on each wing.

CANTEEN located on the Centre. Lack of space restricts stock, reasonable variety of goods held, including tinned fish, meat and fruit. Canned soft drinks, fruit juices in cartons and some dairy products kept in two fridges. One visit per week with bagging service for inmates not on normal location. Clear prices but no local purchase facility.

VISITS *How to get there*: Train or bus to Lewes, then 10 or 15 min walk from station to prison up steep hill, or taxi service available. Special Transport: minibus from Crawley, weekly: 0293-512450.
VISITING TIMES: Week Days: 0900–1100 & 1330–1500. Saturday: 0900–1100 & 1330–1500 Con only. Sunday: 0930–1100 & 1330–1500 Con only.

NOTES Staffed Visitors Centre, canteen and Childrens Play Area. No overnight stay facility, but plenty of local pubs do B&B, though expensive. Disabled access not good, but special arrangements can be made if prisoner applies in advance for a 'flat visit'. Remands one visit per day and no visits Sat & Sun afternoons.

EDUCATION Contracted out to Lewes Tertiary College. Education Centre located on the first floor above the kitchen, with space for 65 inmates and comprises four double classrooms divided by folding partitions to provide six general classrooms, art room and pottery room. Poor take up rate of only 50%. Open 50 weeks of the year, five days and four evenings per week. Broad range of subjects from remedial education to Open University.

WORKSHOPS VTC/CIT: Painting & decorating; Bricklaying; Skills Training; Craft. Main employment centres education (44 places), VTC/CIT (32), Contract Services workshop (4), works (14), domestic services including kitchen, gardens, orderlies, cleaners and stores (92).

DISCIPLINE Segregation unit basement of F. wing. HMCIP examined adjudication records and found errors, omissions, variation in awards and a tendency for the record of the hearing to be too brief. Most adjudications conducted by G5's, HMCIP said this task was one for a member of the senior management team.

MEDICAL Full time SMO, 1×f/t Medical Officer, 1×HCPO, 4×HCSO, 14×HCO. HCC with six-bed observation ward, ten cells, and four-bed ward. Good dental facilities and two week waiting list, optician as required. HCSO trained HIV counsellor. Report sick at unlock, escorted to HCC later in the morning.

GYMNASIUM & SPORTS 1×PEPO, 1×PESO and 4×PEO. Two gymnasiums, neither purpose-built, and two weights areas. One gym provides good facilities, three badminton courts, second gym located in converted workshop is in poor condition and used for minor games. Classes from 0900–1130, 1315–1630 and 1745–1845. CSLA.

CHAPLAINCY Full time CE chaplain, p/t RC and Methodist ministers. CE Service 0900 Sunday, RC Mass 0945 Saturday and 1400 Wednesday. No multi–faith facilities, Imam has refused to come to the prison until a suitable room is available. Various religious groups and meetings through the week.

FOOD Staffing: 1×PO, 1×20,4×Officer (caterers), and an inmate work party of 16—paid >£10. Four week multi-choice menu cycle now in operation, with food of a good standard. All meals dine in cell.

ESTABLISHMENT REPORTS In a report (published 25th November 1994) of an inspection in June 1994, HMCIP said that Lewes was improving but very slowly. There are marked differences in the regimes and attitudes of staff: the newly refurbished B&F wings had a progressive regime with good staff attitudes, while those on C.wing 'were old fashioned and restrictive'. Staff deployment contained features of the pre-Fresh Start days and seemed to be a compromise 'between what was needed and what staff with deeply entrenched outdated attitudes were prepared to accept'. The last full inspection was critical of the cleanliness of the prison, progress had been made but Lewes still remained 'very grubby'. HMCIP was encouraged by the progress that was being made with the adoption of the Prison Service's operating standards and development of the strategic plan, both of which involved a cross section of staff. These initiatives 'should provide the vehicle to move Lewes more quickly towards the standards expected of a modern local prison'.

PRISONERS' COMMENTS I've never had a reply to a Request/Complaint form, getting a Request/Complaint form in the first place is like getting blood out of a stone. Accommodation is grotty, but a reasonable amount of space. As a remand prisoner I think we should be able to 'go shopping' to the canteen more than once a week. Many innocent items not allowed in on visits more for convenience of reception staff than any realistic security objection. No remand visits weekend afternoons. Average education, poor work opportunities and medical facilities are extremely poor; if your ailment requires anything stronger than a Paracetamol, you're wasting your time. Adjudications are arbitrary and inconsistent at times with heavy-handed awards. Reasonable access to the gym, and my religious needs are more than met—I'm a confirmed atheist and the vicar insists on speaking to me each time he comes into the wing! Mail and phones are a real problem, all letters are opened before we get them and the phone is restricted and monitored.

HM Prison Leyhill

Wotton-under-Edge, Glos. GL12 8HL
Tel: 0454-260681 **Fax:** 0454-261398
Opened: 1946 **CNA:** 410 **Average Roll:** 395 **Category:** D. Male Open

i **BACKGROUND** Leyhill open prison is situated one mile from Junction 14 of the M5 motorway, between Bristol and Gloucester. Originally it was a collection of temporary buildings erected during World War II to provide shelter and treatment for wounded American servicemen. Leyhill opened in 1946 as the first independent minimum security prison and has earned a reputation for leading the way in the treatment of prisoners, though of late that reputation has slipped: in

August 1994 the prison was given a month to get its act together or it would be considered as a candidate for privatisation. Leyhill operates the Core Sex Offender Treatment Programme. Neither the Governor nor the BoV replied to our requests for information, and HMCIP published their latest inspection report on Leyhill in July 1992.

OFFICIALS

AREA MGR: John Wilkinson
CHAIR BOV:
GOVERNOR: D.T. Williams
MEDICAL:
CHAPLAIN: Rev Swann
PROBATION: Keith Lane
EDUCATION:
LOCAL MP: John Cope. Con
STAFFING: Total of 179 staff in post, 78 in unified grades.

REGIME *week days*: 0730 roll check. 0740 breakfast. 0800 sick parade. 0815 labour, CE Service (Wed). 0830 gym opens. 0930 canteen as designated Wed & Thurs only. 1100 call ups. 1140 cease labour. 1200 dinner. 1300 work. 1640 cease labour. 1655 tea, association. 2100 return to rooms.

week ends: 0730 roll check. 0800 breakfast. 0900 inmate activities, association, PE, clubs, CE Service (Sun). 1130 roll check dinner. 1330 roll check. 1345 visits. 1650 roll check, tea, association. 2100 return to rooms.

Out of cell: 24/24hrs weekdays and 24/24hrs at weekends.

ACCOMMODATION & FACILITIES

Two main living units, A & B, each containing 192 single rooms with internal light switch but very spartan and no power points. Open access to showers and toilets. Three card phones in each unit. Personal officer scheme and sentence planning. Many restrictions on clothing and petty rules on items allowed in possession. Cooking facilities on each unit. Good standard of cleanliness. Leyhill theatre first class but not used as much as it could be.

CANTEEN Located in B.Unit association room, open Wed and Thurs for pay and private cash. Local purchase facility, prices clearly displayed and reasonable stock—serving area is cramped with space for only two inmates at a time.

VISITS *How to get there*: By rail to Bristol, then bus (309) at 1220 to Tortworth School. Prison one mile from J.14 M5. Special Transport: From Bristol BR every Tues at 1220, calling at Bristol Bus Station. Coaches from Cardiff and Portsmouth probation—contact prison for details.
VISITING TIMES: Week Days: 1330–1545. Saturday: 1330–1545. Sunday: 1330–1545.

NOTES Open Day each year. No staffed Visitors Centre. Canteen and Childrens Play Area in large comfortable visiting room, small coffee tables and soft chairs, Smoking/non-Smoking sections. Overnight stays in Family Centre located in Bristol. Contact prison probation.

EDUCATION Good education department with first class computer room. Education classes five days of the week, but weekend education is also available for some. Evening classes three nights per week with mainly leisure based subjects. Numeracy, basic education, literacy, business technology, information technology, p/t lifer course and OU. No smoking in Education Unit.

WORKSHOPS VTC/CIT Horticulture; Computing; Industrial Cleaning. FTE, Woodmachine shop, Carpenters, Laundry, Print shop. CES, Farms & gardens, Kitchen and community workers. Long hours, hard work in shops or on farm with poor wages for both. Labour Board held weekly in the Library Office.

MEDICAL Part time Medical Officer, 1×HCSO, 2×HCO. Purpose-built HCC, good facilities. Sick parade each morning by visiting GP. Dentist and optician clinics monthly, very few other visiting specialists as most cases referred to local hospitals.

GYMNASIUM & SPORTS 1×PESO and 2×PEO. Very good PE facilities, large gym three years old, with excellent sports field facilities including rugby and football pitches and a cricket wicket. Open seven days a week.

CHAPLAINCY Part time CE chaplain, RC and Methodist ministers. Main church services Sunday. Multi-faith room with cooking facilities. Excellent system of visiting ministers of ethnic faiths.

FOOD Staffing: 1×SO, 2×Officer (caterers), and an inmate work party of 11. Large kitchen and two dining halls attached to it are located close to the living units. Inmates can either dine in or out. Four week menu cycle. Many complaints in the past about the standard of the food at Leyhill but vastly improved in recent years with a consistently high standard now being produced.

ESTABLISHMENT REPORTS In a report (published 9th July 1992) of an inspection in December 1991, HMCIP, said that the design, layout and quality of accommodation provide every opportunity for staff to run a regime suitable for those coming to the end of very long sentences. Variety of offence-focused initiatives had been introduced while the range and quality of community links was impressive. HMCIP was seriously concerned however at the lack of resources particularly for psychiatric assessment and treatment available to men with histories of very serious offending. Overall Leyhill is a vibrant prison which manages to be civilised and good humoured.

PRISONERS' COMMENTS Requests and complaints are usually dealt with very quickly, accommodation is very bare and borders on the spartan. Canteen prices are moderate and there is a good local purchase facility. Visits are excellent though education could be better used—good facilities are put to less use than might be the case were they not located in what is effectively a penal labour colony. Working conditions vary and there is widespread favouritism, wages are poor for the work required. Medical facilities are reasonable. Adjudications themselves are fairly conducted, but the system is very trivial and there is no consistency at all. Food is very good all round and there are excellent facilities in the gym. Religious activities are average, new church opened not long ago and a fortune appears to have been spent on what is a very underused building. Three phones per unit, mail given out at 1100, it is opened in the wing office, though not in front of the inmate concerned.

HM Prison Lincoln

Greetwell Rd, Lincoln. LN2 4BD
Tel: 0522-533633 **Fax:** 0522-532116
Opened: 1872 **CNA:** 444 **Average Roll:** 574 **Category:** Male Local & Remand Centre

i **BACKGROUND** There has been a prison at Lincoln since medieval times, though the current prison stands on the outskirts of the city and was opened in 1872. In the last ten years a new admin block and wing have been added, and the perimeter wall has been considerably strengthened. Neither the Governor nor BoV replied to our requests for information about the prison, and HMCIP published their latest inspection report on Lincoln in August 1993.

OFFICIALS
AREA MGR: Joe Mullens
CHAIR BOV:
GOVERNOR: D. Shaw
MEDICAL:
CHAPLAIN: Rev Duce
PROBATION: Tony Connell
EDUCATION:
LOCAL MP: Kenneth Carlisle. Con
STAFFING: 8 Governor grades, 9 Principal Officers, 35 Senior Officers and 186 Officers, including specialist staff.

REGIME *week days*: 0735 unlock, slop out, applications, kit change, breakfast. 0835 unlock classes. 0900 unlock wings. 0910 sick parade. 0920 canteen (Friday). 1000 gym, bath house. 1030 exercise. 1130 dinner, lock up. 1315 unlock, slop out, classes, remainder association. 1630 tea. 1700–1930 association (Mon–Thurs, classes, gym.

week ends: 0800 unlock, slop out, breakfast. 0845 unlock, slop out, trays out. 0900 A1/2 association, gym, exercise A.yard (Sun). 1000 church (Sun) 1120 dinner. 1300 unlock, slop out, trays out. 1315 association A1/2 landing. 1545 tea, lock up. No weekend evening association on any wings.

Out of cell: 24/24hrs weekdays and 24/24hrs at weekends.

ACCOMMODATION & FACILITIES Four main wings: A(Remands, 172 inmates), B(YOs & Adults, 126), C(VPU, 92), E(convicted adults, 105). Two pseudo wings, F(Pre-release Unit, 4) and G(Yard Cleaners, 3). E.wing opened 1992, integral sanitation with showers in former recesses, launderette facilities, TV rooms, pool and table-tennis. All other wings are Victorian in both era and conditions: majority still slopping out, communal bath house, association limited on ground floor, cells dirty. Civilian clothing limited to trainers. Bail Information Scheme and VPU. No sentence planning or personal officer scheme, though plans for both in the pipeline. SWIP. Card phones on each wing. Mail opened before delivery at midday.

BAIL INFORMATION SCHEME
Established in 1987, Lincoln's BIS has a f/t Bail officer who sees all new remand receptions. Scheme works well, with good success rate in granting bail at subsequent hearings. Apply by wing application system.

CANTEEN Three canteens in the prison, the largest being in A.wing. lack of space prevented large stock and only 100 lines are carried, with no cereals or fruit. C.wing canteen in converted cell and its stock is contained in a cupboard. E.wing has a good canteen.

VISITS *How to get there*: Train to Lincoln Central. Bus (5) to Queensway and then 5 min walk to prison—or any County Hospital bus. No Special Transport.
VISITING TIMES: Week Days: 1315–1515 Tues–Fri. Mon 1.45–3.15. Saturday: 1315–1515. Sunday: 1315–1515 No remand visits.

NOTES No staffed Visitors Centre, but small waiting room outside main gate that opens at 1300. Canteen and Childrens Play Area. For overnight stays (B&B) please contact the prison probation officer. WRVS shop in visits for remands. Wheelchair ramps and nappy-changing facilities available.

EDUCATION Education officer, 5×f/t and 39×p/t teachers. Converted workshop provides six classrooms, additional places available in E.wing, domestic skills block and HCC. Basically drab but serviceable with space at a premium. Open 50 weeks of the year, with classes four days and evenings per week. Wide range of topics from basic education, business studies and languages, to arts and crafts. About 50% of the inmate population involved in education, with just over 30% remands.

WORKSHOPS No formal labour board, work assigned by wing SO. Two textile workshops making T-shirts and vests, one shop for VPU. Laundry, education, kitchen works and domestics make up the bulk of other employment places. Wages upto £9pw (kitchen), £2.50 UB40.

ADJUDICATIONS Hearings average four or five per day, correct procedures are followed said HMCIP and awards were suitable. Charges were not always brought under the right section however and there should be regular meetings between adjudicating governors to ensure consistency of operation. Seg unit, which once had a poor reputation, is better today with no complaints being made about treatment. 10 ordinary cells and one strip cell.

MEDICAL Full time SMO, 1×MO, 1×HCPO, 4×HCSO, 16×HCO. HCC in two-storey building, 11 single rooms without integral sanitation, two strip cells, 8-bed ward, 3-bed ward and day room. Regime being developed for inpatients with no complaints received about treatment. GUC 1×sess/wk. Dentist 2×sess/wk with no waiting list. Consultant Psych 1×sess/wk. Optician 1×sess/mth. treatment rooms in main prison deal with medication issue. Report sick to landing officer at unlock.

GYMNASIUM & SPORTS 1×PEPO, 1×PESO and 4×PEO. Inadequate indoor facilities for PE, particularly for an overcrowded local with a large number of young offenders. Missing tiles on gym roof result in large puddles of water on floor. Large area for weights, tiny shower area, multi-gym. Large fenced sports field with rugby and soccer pitches, no changing area or toilets. Yard used for basket ball. VPU, and Seg Unit have dedicated sessions. Day and evening classes. CSLA.

CHAPLAINCY Full time CE chaplain, p/t RC and Methodist ministers. Main church services Sunday, Imam visits weekly for Muslims with visitors also from Salvation Army and Quakers. Well integrated and interested Chaplaincy Team at Lincoln, out and about in the prison each day with regular meetings and groups.

FOOD Staffing: 1×PO, 1×SO, 4×Officer (caterers), and an inmate work party of 11. Kitchen, refurbished late 1980s, located under Centre with central serving point for whole prison. Impressive six week menu cycle in operation, three choices at dinner and tea. No pre-select menu system.

ESTABLISHMENT REPORTS In a report (published 23rd November 1993) of an inspection in July 1993, HMCIP, said that the main concern at Lincoln was the level of overcrowding and the presence of young offenders. The prison has neither the space nor the resources for young offenders, their regime is 'threadbare', with evidence of bullying. They have few work opportunities, limited education and PE access. Though 'association' is allowed each weekday afternoon and Mon/Wed evening, it means 100 are crammed into the basement of a small wing to watch a video. Convicted regime improving with association and work opportunities. Remand inmates have a regime geared to meeting very basic needs only. No personal officer scheme. Daily exercise, showers three times a week and one weekly visit to the canteen. If the momentum for change is to be maintained the prison should have fewer prisoners, improved facilities for education and physical education and better leadership from middle managers.

PRISONERS' COMMENTS Canteen is too small and has very limited stock, convicted inmates cannot use private cash to buy food or tobacco and association facilities are poor with cell association being forbidden. Library facilities are very limited, video machines in constant need of repair, limited phone cards, shortage of phones and access very restricted. Visits are dreadful, inmates have to wear coloured bibs, visiting time is too short in duration, the visits room is very noisy and there is no reasonable waiting area for visitors. Medical services suffer from a presumption of malingering. The food is generally reasonable, though the timing of meals is ludicrous: at weekends tea in B.wing for example is served at 1430! Inmates in the VPU feel threatened when visiting the HCC and at the close of visits when they are not separated securely. Young Offenders are not allowed cell hobbies and the segregation unit, which has recently been refurbished, suffers from badly fitting windows.

HM Prison Lindholme

Bawtry Rd, Doncaster. DN7 6EE
Tel: 0302-846600 **Fax:** 0302-843352
Opened: 1986 **CNA:** 622 **Average Roll:** 640 **Category:** C. Male with D. Unit

i **BACKGROUND** Lindholme is a converted RAF station which opened as a Category C training prison for adult males in 1986. Many of the original RAF buildings remain in use, including the residential units. The hangars and other ancillary buildings are now used as workshops or stores. The Governor did not reply to our request for information about Lindholme and the BoV refused a copy of their latest annual report. HMCIP published their latest inspection report on Lindholme in July 1994.

OFFICIALS
AREA MGR: Joe Mullens
CHAIR BOV: J.M. Ozanne
GOVERNOR: P.J. Leonard
MEDICAL:
CHAPLAIN: Rev Tarleton
PROBATION: Sandy Shaw
EDUCATION:
LOCAL MP: Richard Body. Con
STAFFING: 200 staff in unified grades, 365 staff in post including specialists such as works, medical and catering staff.

REGIME *week days*: 0745 unlock, breakfast, treatments. 0830 work, education, PE, reports to Seg Unit. 1100 adjudications. 1130 cease labour, education etc, lunch. 1230 lock up. 1330 work. 1345 visits. 1630 cease labour, education etc, tea. 1730 lock up. 1800 unlock, association and activities. 2045 lock up.

week ends: 0745 unlock, breakfast. 0800 treatments. 0845 reports to Seg Unit (Sat), wing cleaning. 0900 association (Sun), CE Service (Sun). 0930 wing inspection (Sat). 1000 association (Sat). 1100 adjudications. 1115 cease association. 1130 dinner. 1230 lock up. 1330 unlock. 1340 association. 1345 visits. 1400 special sick. 1545 cease visits. 1600 cease association, tea. 1700 lock up. 1740 association, RC Service (Sun). 2030 cease association. 2045 lock up.

Out of cell: C Cats 10/24hrs both weekdays and weekends. D cats 24/24hrs both weekdays and weekends.

ACCOMMODATION & FACILITIES Category D inmates located in G.wing—formerly the RAF Officers Mess—which consists of a number of small dormitories containing between two and four beds. Facilities include two TV rooms, large pool room, squash court and on-wing launderette. Category C inmates located in a series of two-storey brick buildings which had provided dormitory accommodation but are in the process of being converted into single and double rooms. H.wing (formerly a Sergeant's Mess) holds 143 inmates mainly in two-man rooms. E & F wings recently completed conversions provide 40 two-man rooms, remaining conversion work completed July 1994. Personal officer scheme, and card phones on each unit—though inmates report long queues. Lindholme suffers from a serious drug problem: in the 12 months to February 1994 there were 47 finds of cannabis, 14 of other controlled drugs, 26 of hypodermics and needles and 85 of smoking and other drug implements. In confidential medical screening 150–200 inmates admitted to being drug users. Drug counselling available via probation/medical officers.

REQUESTS & COMPLAINTS Only 90 of the 200 R/C forms requiring a local reply in 1993 received one within the time target of seven days—and almost 80 were still waiting after a fortnight. Many replies were 'terse and impersonal' according to HMCIP.

VISITS *How to get there*: Infrequent bus (188) from Duke St, Doncaster at 1300—arriving prison 1335 and leaving 1607. Coaches from Hull and Leeds, Manchester and Preston: please contact prison probation department for booking details.
VISITING TIMES: Week Days: 1345–1610—average of 25 visits. Saturday: 1345–1530—average of 60 visits. Sunday: 1345–130.

NOTES Staffed Visitors Centre, canteen and (Wed, Sat) supervised Childrens Play Area with television and videos. Facilities for bottle-making and nappy-changing. Good access for disabled. No smoking in visiting room. Town visits for D Cats limited to half a day. Domestic visits: C Cats twice per month, D Cats one per week.

EDUCATION VTC/CIT Courses: Bricklaying; Painting & Decorating; Plumbing; Carpentry; Computing; Catering; Horticulture; Furniture Craft. Good educational provision catering from remedial to degree.

WORKSHOPS Job Club allocates inmates to labour and a Job Club officer is available each day. Inmates complete a form giving their first, second and third choices—most inmates get their first choice according to HMCIP, who said the work allocation system at Lindholme was among the best they had seen.

DISCIPLINE Segregation unit was found by HMCIP to be 'clean, well organised and in no way oppressive'. The total of 1671 adjudications in 1993 was high for a Category C establishment, though many of the charges related to refusals to work or inmates absenting themselves from the work place without permission. HMCIP examined recent adjudication forms and found the awards to be compatible with offences proven.

FOOD Staffing: 1×PO, 2×SO, 3×Officer(Caterers), and an inmate work party of 28. Meals taken in association, three-week menu cycle offering three choices at dinner and two at tea—for both ordinary and diets. All meals are ordered in advance with pre-select menu system.

ESTABLISHMENT REPORTS In a report (published 21st July 1994) of an inspection in March 1994, HMCIP said that Lindholme had improved markedly since the last inspection. The conversion of inmate accommodation from large, impersonal dormitories to pleasant rooms was progressing well. A personal officer scheme and sentence planning were in place and contributed to good staff/inmate relationships. The lifer management unit and Job Club provided examples of the investment of time and effort by staff being put to good effect. HMCIP, however, remained concerned that Cat D inmates continue to be held in what are effectively closed conditions. H.wing is dirty, smelly and in need for major refurbishment. In general though, HMCIP was 'heartened' by much of what they found at Lindholme. A sensible regime development plan and sound inmate/staff relationships supported by compacts provide a good basis for further progress.

PRISONERS' COMMENTS Probation staff seemed only interested in running groups; they did not want personal contact with inmates. A lack of continuity in staffing SWIP posts limited the amount of time personal officers could spend helping inmates. Town visits for D Cats began at 1230 which was inconvenient for many relatives. Inmates have little understanding of the procedure for gaining transfer to G.wing (D Cat Unit) and a feeling that decisions on applications for this transfer were made arbitrarily. The formal Request/Complaint procedure was unsatisfactory: replies took far too long to arrive and were rarely helpful. The wing application was no better, with forms being often 'lost' or delayed. There are not enough card phones and a lack of privacy as a result of no hoods and the phones being located immediately beside each other. There are no proper association facilities. Televisions were removed whenever there was an act of vandalism which was unfair to those not responsible—as one Lindholme inmate put it: 'its a pretty poor system which punishes the innocent because it can't get a grip of the guilty'. Lifers felt staff expected them to act as wing policemen and do their job for them. The pay structure penalises those who attend education.

HM Prison Littlehey

Perry, Huntingdon, Cambs. PE18 OSR
Tel: 0480-812202 **Fax:** 0480-812151
Opened: 1988 **CNA:** 574 **Roll:** 552 **Category:** C. Male

i **BACKGROUND** Littlehey has a brief history. The prison, which is modern and purpose-built, received its first inmates in February 1988. HMCIP first inspected Littlehey in November 1990, he praised it for its imaginative regime and it has since earnt a reputation for effectively integrating those convicted of sexual offences with inmates convicted of non-sexual crimes: a process started almost as soon as the establishment was opened by its first Governor, Stephen Twinn, who is today in charge of prisons for Group 4. Littlehey operates the Core Sex Offender Treatment Programme. The current Governor of Littlehey, Mr Knight, provided detailed information about his establishment and the BoV kindly provided a copy of their latest annual report. HMCIP published their latest inspection report on Littlehey in May 1994.

OFFICIALS

AREA MGR: Amy Edwards
CHAIR BOV: Shona Johnstone
GOVERNOR: M.L. Knight
MEDICAL: Dr F. O'Sullivan
CHAPLAIN: Rev L. Master
PROBATION: Mr D. Wallace
EDUCATION: Mr C. Swan
LOCAL MP: Tony Grant. Con
STAFFING: 8 Governor grades, 11 Principal Officers, 24 Senior Officers and 112 Officers, including specialist staff.

REGIME *week days*: 0800 unlock. 0830 work. 1200 dinner in association. 1330 work. 1630 cease labour. 1700 lock up. 1730 tea in association. 2045 roll check, lock up.

week ends: 0800 unlock. 0830 kit exchange. 0930 exercise/association. 1145 dinner in association. 1215 lock up. 1345 association. 1400 visits. 1700 lock up. 1730 tea in association. 2045 roll check, lock up.

Out of cell: 10.75/24hrs weekdays and 10.45/24hrs at weekends.

ACCOMMODATION & FACILITIES Six residential wings all with integral sanitation. A–D are of identical design with 112 single cells on two floors. E.wing, built in 1990, is of traditional design and holds 90 in double cells on three landings—suffers from poor heating. F.Wing is the smallest block housing 36 inmates, mostly Cat D, in a more relaxed environment with privacy locks allowing 24hr access to wing facilities. All wings have the usual servery, shower, toilet, TV and interview rooms. Drug counselling available. Sentence-planning and personal officer scheme in operation. Extensive i/p list—covers 15 pages! Routine censorship abolished, mail opened outwith presence of inmate. Cardphones on all living units and maximum of 8 cards allowed in possession.

SEXUAL OFFENDER TREATMENT PROGRAMME Littlehey was selected as one of the establishments for the core sex-offenders programme, managed by a Governor 5 and with input from a visiting psychologist based at Whitemoor. Eleven Prison Officers and one Probation Officer have undergone national training in working with sex offenders and the target is to run eight courses per year—each consisting of 14 core elements. Inmates taken from all other establishments and progress on the course is used to determine such issues as home leave and/or decategorisation. Courses are wing based. Other courses in Human Growth & Development, Drug/Alcohol Awareness, and Personal Achievement Courses. HMCIP reported the group work at Littlehey 'was among the best we have seen'.

CANTEEN Inmates do not visit the shop at Littlehey but place written orders which are subsequently delivered to the wing. Good canteen with 230 lines of stock—and probably the only one to have copies of Standing Orders on display for sale! Local purchase facility. Inmates report high prices. Bi-monthly canteen committee meeting with inmate reps reviews stock held and lines carried.

VISITS *How to get there*: Train or bus to Huntingdon or St.Neotts, then 7 miles taxi journey (approx £7.50 each way). Bus available from Huntingdon Station on Sat/Sun. Special Transport: coaches from Birmingham (monthly); Leicester (2nd/4th Wed of month).
VISITING TIMES: Week Days: 1400–1600 except Tues & Fri. Saturday: 1400–1600. Sunday: 1400–1600.

NOTES No staffed Visitors Centre, though waiting room with facilities for changing and feeding babies. Canteen and Childrens Play Area in visiting room, Play Area only supervised at weekends. Prisoners can have one visit a week if on weekday, or 2 visits per month if taken at weekends. Stairlift for disabled.

EDUCATION Education block, open 50 weeks of the year and every weekend, provides a library, specialist classrooms for art, music and computing, along with offices for staff. Some workshop spaces are used by the education department to provide specific courses in vehicle maintenance, body repair, painting and decorating, brickwork and industrial cleaning. Day classes: Life skills, literacy—word power—English & Communications, German, Business studies, A.Level design, History, Open Learning, Small Business, Numeracy—number power—home economics, Computing, Science, Geography, Law, Information Technology. Evening classes: Painting, Open Learning, Creative Writing, Sugar-craft, Computers, Afro-Caribbean Group, Sculpture, Asian Group, Soft Toys, Motor Mechanics, French, Gardening, Pottery, Guitar.

WORKSHOPS Workshops 1 and 2 are the main employers at Littlehey, producing such items as T-shirts and underpants, shoes and electronic timing equipment and repairing Braille machines. Farm and gardens party along with usual kitchen workers, cleaners and works. Average wage: £7pw.

DISCIPLINE Ten-cell seg unit, centrally located, eight cells with integral sanitation. Regime is deliberately sparse, comprising little more than cleaning, serving food and one hour's exercise per day. No recorded use of mechanical restraints.

BOV report they are very concerned at the discipline problems created for the Governor since they lost their disciplinary powers. There were 39 absconds in 1993 (compared with 28 in 1992) and the BoV attribute this to their loss of disciplinary function.

MEDICAL Hospital provides the usual treatment rooms, and accommodation for up to 12 inmates, with integral sanitation. Littlehey's regional hospital unit treats inmates from other establishments. New SMO took up post in 1993. Suicide Prevention Committee meets quarterly—no inmate members. Telephone box to allow private access to Samaritans set up in one wing. Full time medical resources.

GYMNASIUM & SPORTS 1×PEPO, 1×PESO and four PEO's. Comprehensive and well thought-out PE programme. Sports hall, weights room, changing rooms and showers. Outdoors two full size football pitches, rugby pitch, cricket square and 100m x 50m tarmac area. Activities: badminton, basketball, bowls, camping/outdoor persuits, cricket, fitness training, football, over 35's, over 50's, padder tennis, remedial PE, rugby, swimming, table tennis, volleyball and weights. External award courses run in a large number of subjects including FA Referees, GCSE Physical Education and Community Sports Leaders.

CHAPLAINCY Full-time C/E chaplain, part time RC and Methodist, but all religious denominations catered for with visiting ministers.

FOOD Staffing: 1×PO, 2×SO and 6×Officer (caterers), and there is a work party of 25. 'When the meals are good, they are excellent, when they are bad they are very bad and are one of the main causes of complaint at the fortnightly applications clinic' said the BOV. Standard reported as 'improving' and a catering committee of staff and inmates meets every two months. Inmates on the farm are provided with pre-cooked frozen meals and have access to microwave/farm dining room.

ESTABLISHMENT REPORTS In a report (published 4th May 1994) of an inspection in January 1994, Judge Stephen Tumim, HMCIP, said that prisoners at Littlehey spoke well of the work, training and educational opportunities at the prison. The two main criticisms, that there should be a visitors centre, and Littlehey should become an assessment centre for the sex-offender treatment programme, were both accepted in principle by the Home Secretary and will be put into effect as soon as resources permit.

BOV Annual Report 1993. Published in May 1994. BoV commended the Governor and staff on a 'positive year' despite many changes which had lead to uncertainty. Board made particular reference to the work carried out by inmates in the community, though they remained concerned that the procedures for dealing with offences against discipline allowed serious charges of assault to go untried because of a perceived reluctance on behalf of the police/CPS to prosecute. Three other 'Points of Chief Concern' were the need for a visitors centre; the lowering of staff morale by agency status, and the prospect of privatisation. The BoV further reported a lack of breathing apparatus and appropriate staff training in its use.

GOVERNOR'S COMMENTS Many offending behaviour group initiatives, Job Club and Pre-Release Courses.

PRISONERS' COMMENTS There is a slight delay with requests and complaints, but nothing too serious. Accommodation is reported as excellent with single cell, internal light switch, but no power points yet. The canteen is very expensive and with a limited local purchase facility. Visits tend to be very noisy but are otherwise good. Education is top class with a wide range up to degree level. On the work front conditions and opportunities are said to be good, but wages felt to be less than adequate. Medical facilities are average. Disciplinary punishments are criticised for being far too heavy. There is a varied menu for food, though the quality leaves something to be desired. Gymnasium and sports are described as excellent and with access seven days a week. Religious services cater for all relevant needs, mail is uncensored and a maximum of eight phone cards can be held i/p at any one time.

HM Prison Liverpool

68 Hornby Road, Walton, Liverpool. L9 3DF
Tel: 051 525 5971 **Fax:** 051 525 0813
Opened: 1855 **CNA:** 931 **Average Roll:** 1,204 **Category:** Male Local and Remand Centre

i **BACKGROUND** The prison at Walton was constructed in 1855 to replace a much older and more cramped establishment in the centre of Liverpool. Much of the original hospital and cellular accommodation remains though it has been extended over the years. In common with many Victorian prisons, Walton was originally fitted with a simple and effective in-cell sanitation system of which traces remain. After an interval of about a century integral sanitation is now being fitted once again. Bombing during the Second World War destroyed much of the centre of one cell block and this has since been replaced with little attempt made at matching. Neither the Governor nor BoV at Walton replied to our requests for information about the prison. HMCIP published their latest report on the prison in November 1993.

OFFICIALS
AREA MGR: Terry Bone
CHAIR BOV: Vacant
GOVERNOR: M. Jacques
MEDICAL: Dr. Tucker
CHAPLAIN: Rev Tony Ball
PROBATION: Martin Evans
EDUCATION: Mr Mackintosh
LOCAL MP: Peter Kilfoyle. Lab
STAFFING: 16 Governor grades, 27 Principal Officers, 73 Senior Officers and 487 Officers, including specialist staff.

☞ **REGIME** Liverpool is a multi-functional establishment catering for a a number of different prisoner groups. Convicted are mainly in full-time employment with association on the ground floor of each wing two or three evenings a week. Unconvicted have little if any work opportunities. Most of the unconvicted inmates spent more than 20 hours a day locked in their cells said HMCIP, and while the convicted population fared better, all inmates at Liverpool were locked up for far too long. Liverpool also has a VPU (H.Wing) with limited association facilities. Meals at 0800, 1230 and 1730.

ACCOMMODATION & FACILITIES
Seven cell blocks (A, F & G Wings for convicted, I,J & K Wings for remand and trials, H=VPU & Seg) are in the process of completing their integral sanitation programme and HMCIP reports it to be on course for completion by end 1994. Facilities very limited. Most prisoners are housed two to a cell and a small number three to a cell. Forty card phones—each inmate allowed 10 mins maximum to complete all calls.

CANTEEN The siting of the shop is not ideal and choice is restricted. neither fresh fruit nor cold drinks are offered, and no private cash spends are allowed on food items. No local purchase facility. 'Better facilities should be found to provide more than the present very basic service. A full review of the shop service is required, the arrangements we saw were well below standard' said HMCIP.

REQUESTS/COMPLAINTS A snapshot of a month showed that 49 Requests/Complaints were submitted by prisoners which in view of the size of the population, said HMCIP, suggested that most matters had been dealt with satisfactorily by the wing application system. Most referred to lost property (10), followed by allocation or transfer (7), shop/wages (5), visits (4), food/catering, health care and mail (3 each). All had been answered by a Governor grade. Replies were full, sympathetic and clear.

VISITS *How to get there*: Train to Liverpool Lime Street, then underground via Central to Rice Lane or Walton Junction Stn (Merseyrail) which is about ten minute walk from prison. Bus (68) runs near the prison. No Special Transport.
VISITING TIMES: *week days*: 0850–1105 & 1310–1615. Saturday: 0910–1100 & 1300–1515. Sunday: 1300–1515.

NOTES No staffed Visitors Centre, but waiting room with luggage lockers. Canteen, Childrens Play Area and nappy-changing facilities available. No overnight stay facility, but plenty of local B&B. Provision for wheelchairs. Visiting room reinforced 'the feeling of claustrophobia and clutter . . . poorly ventilated . . . hot and noisy'. said HMCIP

PROBATION Probation team headed by Senior Probation Officer Martin Evans. Four major group programmes in operation. Three-day courses in: Alcohol Awareness; Anger Management; Drug Awareness; and Domestic Violence. Applications for entry via wing probation officer in first instance.

EDUCATION Seven general classrooms, woodwork, book-binding, computer and desk-top publishing rooms. Rooms are small and in a poor state of decoration. Education officer, p/t deputy, 3 p/t lecturers and 30 sessional teachers. Full-time education. Classes in: art, business studies, engineering, foundation studies (OU). Cell study also provided. Evening classes (Mon–Thu) Bible class, woodwork, soft toys. art, AA Group, chess, CIT Brick laying and Painting & Decorating, keyboards, maths, computers, tailors, RC Group.

WORKSHOPS Wages between £2.50(UB40) and £8(Kitchen). Labour allocation board day after reception: An average of 40–50 receptions were dealt with in a space of about 90 minutes each day. . . a mechanical process said HMCIP. Seven production workshops (tailoring, laundry, leatherwork & wood-machining) operating 24.3 hrs per week. Works, FTE, CIT Courses, kitchen, gardens and cleaners.

DISCIPLINE 'We saw the adjudication room and examined the records of the 50 adjudications that had taken place in the last month . . . We found that with the exception of a few recording omissions, the adjudication records were completed properly . . . award of cellular confinement used sparingly' said HMCIP.

MEDICAL Health Care provision was heavily criticised by HMCIP, who argued for radical improvements or a new HCC. Staffing of 1×SMO, 4×MO, 2×HCPO, 8×HCSO and 36×HCO—<50% HC discipline staff are qualified nurses. Dentist (6 sess/wk), Optician (fortnightly), good X-ray equipment, ENT/GUC 1 sess/week. Report sick at unlock. HIV/AIDS awareness poor. 'A good deal of the work in the Health Care Centre concerned psychiatric care' said HMCIP 'Medical Officers and the SMO, who were not qualified psychiatrists, did half the psychiatric reports . . . [these] should be written only by qualified psychiatrists'.

GYMNASIUM & SPORTS 1×PEPO, 1×PESO and 5×PEO. Very poor conditions. The gymnasium 'leaked, which was potentially dangerous, and in protracted cool weather green mould formed on the floor . . . there were no toilet or shower facilities for inmates . . . despite the inadequate facilities, the commitment of the PE staff enabled a varied programme of activities to take place'. Weight training room, small five-a-side football pitch and all-weather sports field.

CHAPLAINCY The 21 strong chaplaincy team headed by Rev. Tony Ball delivers a well-rounded programme. Main worship 0900 Sunday (CE,RC,Meth) with VPU services an hour later. Daily Mass at 0845 and Evensong at 1530. Chaplain also holds Bible class, Chaplain's Hour and arranges for Prison Visitors. Application ensures chaplaincy interview.

FOOD 'The main meal was the mid-day meal when a pudding was offered. There was no formal menu cycle. We were told that the rota was "a loose" four-week cycle with odd changes for variety. The mid-day meal was tasted, there was one choice for each diet: meat & potato pie for normal diets, vegetable pie for vegetarians, vegetable curry for vegans . . . all with mashed potato and cabbage. It was followed by semolina with raisins. The food was hot and, with the exception of the vegetable pie which had little flavour, quite tasty' said HMCIP.

ESTABLISHMENT REPORTS In a report (published 23rd November 1993) of an inspection in May 1993, HMCIP said that as a result of an extended catchment area following the riot at Strangeways, Liverpool had become a severely overcrowded prison. It was 'impossible' to have a meaningful induction programme for new inmates; sentence planning and the proper assessment of inmates was severely inhibited and, because of the overcrowding, there was insufficient space to allow much association on the wings. Relations between management, staff and inmates appeared sound and relaxed. Card phones have been fitted, with 40 throughout the establishment. 'Few of the expected problems (e.g. trafficking or vandalism) had materialised, calls were allowed during association times from Monday to Friday, Saturday morning and all day on Sunday, limited to ten minutes duration. This was a source of complaint, but in the circumstances we felt it reasonable' said HMCIP. All inmates are allowed two cards in possession, except for those in Cat A or on the E List. Inmates are virtually unrestricted in use of postage stamps whether purchased or sent in. There is no censoring, even for Cat A & E List prisoners, unless required by the Governor. 'Prisoners were advised to tell their relations not to send in cash because of a history of "losses" through the postal system'. The Inspectors, however, found Liverpool to be: 'in most respects a well-managed and well-run establishment'.

PRISONERS' COMMENTS Requests and Complaints dealt with when it suits them. No internal light switches, almost all two'd up and some are four to a cell. Not all wings have integral sanitation at the moment. The canteen is OK, visits are a bit cramped though they have a facility for kids. There is a good education department with good teachers who have good attitudes. Applications needed to go sick, wages and work conditions leave much to be desired, food seems to consist of mash spuds with every meal and we are limited to calls of ten minutes on the phone. Adjudications go on every day, they don't seem very fair and punishments are often very heavy handed. Staff on the whole are good, there are one or two well known ones who go out of their way to wind people up, but mainly the staff are quite helpful. Governors are a bit mysterious as they are hardly ever around, and always seem to hold conversations on the hoof when you do collar one.

HM Prison Long Lartin

South Littleton, Worcs. WR11 5TZ
Tel: 0386-830101 **Fax:** 0386-832834
Opened: 1971 **CNA:** 362 **Average Roll:** 346 **Category:** Dispersal

i **BACKGROUND** Long Lartin is situated about six miles from the town of Evesham in Worcestershire and one mile from the village of South Littleton. The prison, which occupies the site of a former War Department Ordnance Depot, was purpose-built as a C category prison and opened in January 1971. The following year additional security features were introduced and it has since operated as part of the Dispersal system. In February 1994 one inmate was murdered at Long Lartin, followed by a second inmate-murder seven months later in September. Neither the Governor nor BoV replied to our requests for information about the prison, and HMCIP published their latest inspection report on Long Lartin in December 1992.

OFFICIALS
AREA MGR: Jim Blakey
CHAIR BOV:
GOVERNOR: P. Atherton
MEDICAL:
CHAPLAIN: Rev Brace
PROBATION: Terry Bottomly
EDUCATION: C. Tanner
LOCAL MP: Michael Spicer. Con
STAFFING: 346 staff in post.

REGIME *week days*: 0740 unlock, breakfast. 0800 treatments. 0820 work, sick parade, remedials. 0900 gym, education, visits. 1115 treatments. 1130 cease labour, exercise, governors applications. 1145 dinner. 1215 lock up. 1340 unlock, work, gym, education, visits. 1630 cease labour, tea. 1700 lock up. 1800–2100 association.

week ends: 0800 unlock, breakfast. 0830 treatments. 0900 gym, canteen. 1115 treatments. 1145 dinner. 1215 lock up. 1340 unlock. 1400 visits. 1415-1545 outside association. 1630 tea. 1700 lock up. 1800–2100 association.

Out of cell: 10/24hrs weekdays and 9.5/24hrs at weekends.

ACCOMMODATION & FACILITIES Six main wings, A,B,C,D,E,F each capable of holding 72 inmates in single cells with access to night sanitation. Very poor standards of cleanliness in all wings, landings are festooned with washing and rubbish, cigarette ends and food remains litter the floor said HMCIP. Very small cells, no power points, Dispersal i/p list means cells are cluttered. Cooking facilities on all wings. 135 lifers.

CANTEEN Central location close to kitchen. Open Tues, Fri & Sat with private cash being allowed to supplement earnings. Extensive stock and local purchase facility. Freezers hold meat and perishables. Inmates paid in cash, though HMCIP has recommended a credit transfer system be introduced.

VISITS *How to get there*: Train to Evesham. Van picks up visitors at 1.30. No Special Transport.
VISITING TIMES: Week Days: 1400–1600 VO's & PVO's. Saturday: 1400–1600 No PVO's. Sunday: 1400–1600 No PVO's.

NOTES Staffed Visitors Centre. Canteen and Childrens Play Area (supervised on Fri,Sat,Sun only). Overnight stay at The Woolpack public house, Evesham (0386-47047). Disabled access to both VC and visiting room.

EDUCATION Education Officer, 5×f/t and 20×p/t teachers. Open 46 weeks of the year for five days, and two evenings per week (for 25 wk/yr). Wide range of subjects ranging from basic English to foreign languages, history, and 27 inmates are on OU. Tuition in music and art. Good library, large, well stocked but no civilian librarian.

WORKSHOPS VTC/CIT: drawing office skills, micro-engineering, welding and woodcraft. Laundry, textile workshop, weavers, and engineering shops main employers, kitchen, education, works and domestics making up the rest. Average wages £7.50.

DISCIPLINE Seg unit with 24 single cells with integral sanitation, 2 strip cells and enclosed exercise yard. Frequently full with majority on Rule 43(GOAD). Seg Unit has four gym sessions per week. Teacher visits twice a week, daily visits from doctor, chaplain and governor. Adjudications average about a dozen per week, awards even-handed.

MEDICAL 1×f/t MO, 1×p/t MO, 1×HCPO, 1×HCSO, 5×HCO—none were trained nurses at the time of the inspection. HCC located on single floor of main prison, six-bed ward, three single rooms and a strip cell. Dentist 5×sess/wk, with waiting list about a month long. Unsatisfactory X-ray service said HMCIP, with inappropriate delays. Visiting consultants: orthopaedic, gastro-enterology, dermatology and ENT.

GYMNASIUM & SPORTS 1×PEPO, 1×PESO and 3×PEO. Main gym small by modern standards with space for just three badminton courts. Weights area on stage. Two ancillary rooms with punch-bag and fitness training. Large, flat well drained sports field with ample space for soccer and rugby. Filthy toilet block. Tarmac running track and large artificial surface for soccer, hockey etc.

CHAPLAINCY Full time CE chaplain, p/t RC and Methodist ministers. Two well decorated chapels with lounge areas, well decorated and clean. CE and RC services Sunday morning simultaneously. Group of 55 Prison Visitors. Full programme of services, meetings and events. Two-hour Sikh service Wed evening, music class and choir rehearsal Tues.

FOOD Staffing: 1×PO, 1×SO, 4×Officer (caterers), and an inmate work party of 15. Kitchen given a major refurbishment in 1990. No regular menu cycle, two choices at dinner. Lack of vegetables, poor quality and small portions.

ESTABLISHMENT REPORTS In a report (published 18th December 1992) of an inspection in January 1992, HMCIP said it had been disappointing to find Long Lartin at such a low ebb. Workshops had been closed for some months confining inmates to the wings. There were a number of areas of concern, but most worrying was the tilt in the balance of control away from staff towards a few very influential prisoners. There was much anecdotal evidence pointing to the easy availability of drugs and alcohol, staff confidence is low. The recently appointed Governor had recognised the problems, and had set out a strategy to tackle them and should be given every possible support.

HMRC Low Newton

Brasside, Durham. DH1 5SD
Tel: 091-386-1141 **Fax:** 091-386-2620
Opened: 1965 **CNA:** 199 **Average Roll:** 245 **Category:** Remand Centre

i **BACKGROUND** Low Newton Remand Centre, situated about four miles from Durham, was purpose-built in 1965 with accommodation for 65 males and 11 females. Additional accommodation was provided in 1975 and the Centre now has a CNA of 199, though is normally overcrowded. Low Newton accommodates both male and female young persons and adult women remands and JR's. Neither the Area Manager, Governor or BoV replied to our requests for information about the Remand Centre and HMCIP published their latest inspection report on Low Newton in February 1990. Surprisingly, HMCIP say there has been no inspection since that date and, as much of the information will be long out of date, only a brief entry will be given here to avoid inaccurate information. Are you in Low Newton? Write to us to obtain a questionnaire you can complete about the establishment for the next edition.

OFFICIALS
AREA MGR: Al Papps
CHAIR BOV:
GOVERNOR: A. Holman
MEDICAL:
CHAPLAIN: Rev Cummings
PROBATION: H. Robson
EDUCATION:
LOCAL MP: Gerry Steinberg. Lab

ACCOMMODATION & FACILITIES Male population housed in five wings, two of which have integral sanitation. Females are housed on two wings, one of which has integral sanitation. Both male and female sections have high standards of cleanliness. No VTC/CIT courses, good education unit, though cramped at the time of the inspection with plans for a new unit. Food is reasonable and eaten in association in both male and female sections. Part time Medical Officer, separate medical facilities for male and female inmates.

VISITS *How to get there*: Bus (65) from Durham bus station, hourly service on the half-hour. Special Transport: coaches from Cumbria, S.Yorks and W.Yorks probation.
VISITING TIMES: Week Days: 1330–1530 M–F. Saturday: 1330–1530. Sunday: 1330–1530.

NOTES No staffed Visitors Centre or Childrens Play Area. Canteen in visiting room. B&B information available from prison probation. Wheelchair access can be arranged with advance notice.

ESTABLISHMENT REPORTS In a report (published 1st February 1990) of an inspection in May 1989, HMCIP said that Low Newton was carrying out its function as a Remand Centre to a high standard. Staff were well in control of inmates and the young men were responding well to the firm but fair treatment they were receiving. There was justifiable pride in the way Low Newton discharged its responsibilities. There was very little evidence of graffiti or vandalism and levels of noise and behaviour were healthy and reasonable. Even in the best run establishments there are opportunities for improvement ands Low Newton is no exception but essentially it requires fine tuning rather than radical change. At the time of the inspection it was assumed that a major redevelopment of Low Newton was to begin in the Autumn of 1989 to build a new living unit to hold 96 additional inmates and extend existing shared facilities. It is essential that a proper chapel was part of that development. It was also essential that the provision of other ancillary services such as the library and kitchen be enlarged and improved.

HM Prison Maidstone

County Rd, Maidstone, Kent. ME14 1UZ
Tel: 0622-755611 **Fax:** 0622-688038
Opened: 1819 **CNA:** 549 **Roll:** 539 **Category:** B. Male

i **BACKGROUND** Maidstone prison was built between 1810 and 1819, close to the town centre, it has been in service as a penal establishment ever since. The prison houses a national VPU (Thanet Wing), a Pre-Release Hostel, and Maidstone also operates as an Assessment Centre for the Sex Offender Treatment Programme. Neither the Governor nor the BoV at Maidstone replied to our requests for information about the prison. HMCIP published their latest report on Maidstone in March 1993.

OFFICIALS
AREA MGR: John Hunter
CHAIR BOV:
GOVERNOR: H. Bagshaw
MEDICAL:
CHAPLAIN: Rev Ghinn
PROBATION: Normal Marshall
EDUCATION:
LOCAL MP: Anne Widdicombe. Con
STAFFING: 204 in unified grades.

REGIME *week days*: 0800 unlock/breakfast. 0845 work. 1115 cease labour. 1145 lunch. 1215 lock up. 1345 work. 1615 cease labour. 1630 tea. 1700–1745 lock up. 1745–2000 association.
week ends: 0800 unlock/breakfast. 0900 association. 1000–1100 sportsfield. 1130 lunch. 1215–1330 lock up. 1330 association. 1400 visits. 1630 tea. 1700–1745 lock up. 1745–2000 association.
Out of cell: 9/24hrs weekdays and 9/24hrs at weekends.

ACCOMMODATION & FACILITIES Four main wings: Kent=[CNA]166, Medway=171, Weald=99 and Thanet=102. Each wing has large dining room/association area. Medway wing holds mainly lifers. Kent and Weald (the latter of which is the only surviving wing from the original prison) hold medium–long termers and Thanet is a national VPU. Personal officer scheme and drug counselling available. Routine censorship abolished June 1992, mail is sorted in wing office and handed out at lunchtime. All wings have card phones and access is reported as easy though long queues develop at peak times.

THANET WING VPU Operates as a national VPU with inmates allocated to it by Headquarters. Four-storey building with own visiting and dining facilities. Cells on three floors all with integral sanitation. Groups for sexual offenders operate almost constantly and other offending behaviour groups available. Enjoys the same regime as the rest of the prison as far as association is concerned and VPU inmates operate the prison laundry. Atmosphere regarded as relaxed, though usual verbal abuse from other inmates continues.

PRE-RELEASE HOSTEL Operates from a purpose-built eleven-room hostel in the prison grounds. There is direct access through a separate service door in the outer wall, well equipped and very clean. Managed by a Principal Officer and a small team of auxiliaries. The rules are 'not onerous' according to HMCIP, but they do ensure good order and discipline. Half the inmates were in regular employment. A deduction is made for board and lodging as well as compulsory savings.

CANTEEN Centrally located in a single storey building operated by civilian staff. Holds some 300 lines of stock though this had been criticised by auditors who felt it was too large. Local purchase facility available and widely used. Prices are on the high side according to inmates and HMCIP, in their 1990 report, found the profit-margin had crept up to 18%.

VISITS *How to get there*: Train to Maidstone East Station (from London Victoria), then five min walk to prison. No Special Transport. VISITING TIMES: Week Days: 1400–1600. Saturday: 1400–1600. Sunday: 1400–1600.

NOTES No staffed Visitors Centre. Canteen and Childrens Play Area. Contact prison probation for details of local B&B. Stairs to visiting hall, but wheelchair access can be arranged with advance notice. Inmates can have four visits per month providing 1×VO exchanged for 2×PVO. Maximum of 44 visits at any one time.

EDUCATION Headed by f/t education officer, deputy and 5×f/t teachers. Department is part of Mid-Kent College which is responsible for education in six other prisons. Open for just 38 weeks of the year with some 60 inmates engaged on FTE. Classes: basic skills, English, maths, computers, art & craft, media studies, French and cookery. Evening classes on Tuesday only—computing, yoga, music, German, and English.

WORKSHOPS Tailors, laundry, bookbinding and printing workshops. Works, grounds, gardens, kitchen, cleaners, wing serveries, orderlies, stores and Braille unit. CIT Bricklaying and Painting & Decorating.

DISCIPLINE Segregation unit located next to the hospital but separate from other accommodation. A total of 16 cells on two floors. HMCIP examined the records of 50 adjudications—and saw three more in action—all were found to be well conducted and awards were fair and consistent. Fairly high level of disciplinary reports.

MEDICAL F/t Senior Medical Officer, assisted by f/t MO and p/t MO who had a contract for ten hours. 1×HCPO, 1×HCSO and 5×HCO. Two agency nurses also on duty during the day and a third provides night cover. Wide range of specialists attend on a regular basis—two consultant psychiatrists provide 30 sess/wk. Ten-bed ward, six individual rooms and a strip cell. HMCIP found 'very poor' X-ray facilities.

GYMNASIUM & SPORTS 1×PEPO, 1×PESO and 3×PEO. Facilities: gymnasium (30m×12m) purpose-built in 1961, heated, covered swimming pool (20m×10m), Redgra pitch (70m×45m), tarmac tennis court (30m×25m), and a weight training room (25m×12m) in a converted workshop. Good use is made of the facilities and a comprehensive programme offered to all including Thanet VPU.

CHAPLAINCY Full time CE chaplain and p/t RC and Methodist ministers. Minority faith ministers visit regularly. Prison has purpose-built church and all services are held within it. CE Service 1000 Sunday, with RC Mass an hour before at 0900. Average of 40 attend services. Evening Services Wednesday (CE) and Thursday (RC) 1800 hours. Midweek communion service on Thursdays 1110 hours.

FOOD Staffing: 1×PO, 2×SO and 4×Officer (caterers), and there is a work party of 20 inmates. Though Maidstone was probably the first prison to introduce pre-select meals, in 1978, this had been stopped during the 1980's and HMCIP recommends it be reintroduced. Food committee on which inmates are represented meets monthly. Only inmates in the VPU dine in association, others are locked in their cells during meal times. Kitchen requires much refurbishment and £400,000 is being spent to upgrade its facilities.

ESTABLISHMENT REPORTS In a report (published 25th March 1993) of an inspection in July 1992, Judge Stephen Tumim, HMCIP, said that the 'unusual openness' between prisoners and staff at Maidstone was to be seen everywhere in the prison. However HMCIP was concerned that though the traditional ethos of the prison was in place, the erosion of activities, together with insufficient time for staff to spend with prisoners, could jeopardise its continuance: 'Maidstone meets two-thirds of the prison Service's Statement of Purpose, it successfully holds category B prisoners in custody, albeit with difficulty, and it undoubtedly looks after them with humanity. However not enough is being done to assist them to lead law-abiding and useful lives. In particular we drew attention to the unexplained cuts in Education, which appear to be the norm in South-East England'.

On publication of the report the Home Secretary remarked that HMCIP's criticism of educational cuts was was based on a 'misconception, as no cuts have been made'.

HM Prison Manchester

Southall St, Manchester. M60 9AH
Tel: 061-834-8626 **Fax:** 061-834-0443
Opened: 1868 **CNA:** 971 **Roll:** 750 **Category:** Male Local

i **BACKGROUND** Manchester's Strangeways Prison is situated one mile north of the city centre. It was opened as Salford Prison in 1868 with two living units: 744 cells in A,B,C,D,E wing for males, and 315 cells in G,H,I,J,K wings for females. In 1963 the females moved to Styal prison and their accommodation became a Borstal Allocation Centre and remand facility. With the opening of Risley Remand Centre in 1965 the remand population was moved out, though in 1980 overcrowding at Risley led to Strangeways once again taking on a remand function. In April 1990 the prison exploded in a 28-day orgy of violence and destruction, which led to other serious disturbances around the country and, ultimately, to the Inquiry chaired by Lord Justice Woolf. The prison has been substantially rebuilt, integral sanitation has been completed and in July 1993 the in-house bid for management of the prison was successful after a process of private tendering. The Governor of Strangeways, Robin Halward, supplied very helpful information about the prison, though the chairman of the BoV felt unable this year to provide a copy of their latest annual report. HMCIP published their latest inspection report on Manchester Prison in August 1992.

OFFICIALS
AREA MGR: Terry Bone
CHAIR BOV: Stuart Whelpton
GOVERNOR: Robin Halward
MEDICAL: Dr Wils Walker
CHAPLAIN: V/Rev Noel Proctor
PROBATION: Shirley Johnson
EDUCATION: Paul Dennerley
LOCAL MP: Bob Litherland. Lab

REGIME *week days*: 0730 unlock. No lock up until 2145 throughout day except for 30 mins at tea-time. Lock up 21.45.

week ends: 0730 unlock throughout day except for 30 mins at tea-time. Lock up 21.45.

Out of cell: 13/24hrs weekdays and 13/24hrs at weekends.

ACCOMMODATION & FACILITIES Two Victorian radial blocks (A,B,C,D,E & G,H,I,J) with mixture of single and double cells all with internal light switch, in-cell power points and integral sanitation. F.wing Hospital. VPU. Television rental scheme—see below. Sentence planning, personal officer scheme. Card phones on each wing but not enough of them according to inmates. Daily canteen facilities for remands and weekly for convicted.

TV RENTAL SCHEME Cells at Manchester have mains electricity supplies and TV aerial points. Televisions are not provided as of right, but they can be rented through the prison canteen. A deposit of £10 is required and the weekly rental is £3. There are enough TVs to meet demand. 'TV rental means that inmates have to make choices about how they use the money they have earned and they are required to show a level of responsibility in managing their budget as well as a responsibility for the equipment. Any abuse of the scheme can lead to the facility being withdrawn for a particular inmate or group of inmates' says the Governor, whose experience to date is that the TV Rental Scheme 'is working well'.

VISITS *How to get there*: Train to Manchester Victoria, then bus or 5 min walk to prison. No Special Transport.
VISITING TIMES: Week Days: 0845–1115 & 1415–1600 & 1900–2030. Saturday: 0845–1115 & 1415–1600. Sunday: 1415–1600 & 1900–2030.

NOTES All evening visits are only for inmates who are working through the day. All legal visits MUST be booked at least 24 hours in advance. Staffed Visitors Centre, canteen and Childrens Play Area. B&B locally, please contact prison probation for details.

EDUCATION Full range of subjects covered by flexible learning. Facilities are excellent, though inmates report no education on either the induction wing or remand wing. Those who are convicted report excellent classes and a staff who are keen to take ideas on board. Others, however, report having to wait a couple of months or more for a place.

WORKSHOPS Computer Aided Design. Upholstery. Wheelchair Assembly. Contract Work. Laundry. Kitchen. Cleaners and Orderlies. Wages average £9pw—for those who have a job.

MEDICAL Senior Medical Officer. HCC with room for 49 inpatients. Report sick to wing treatment room in the morning or report special sick to HCC during day.

GYMNASIUM & SPORTS Excellent gymnasium facilities, with comprehensive PE programme and helpful staff. Classes 0800–1915 Mon–Thurs and 0800–1615 Fri. Volleyball, weights, basketball, multigym, exercycles, soccer, BAWLA.

CHAPLAINCY Full time CE chaplain and p/t RC Methodist ministers. Comprehensive religious programme, including counselling, prayer and bible meetings, sing-along etc. All welcome to this vibrant and brand new chapel.

FOOD The clear message here from Manchester prisoners was 'Could do better'. Despite a new kitchen and qualified chefs to staff it, inmates complain that the food is often cold, portions are not large enough, there is no menu system in operation and the quality is poor. Breakfast 0745, dinner 1105 and tea 1605.

ESTABLISHMENT REPORTS In a report (published 13th August 1992) of an inspection in March 1992, Judge Stephen Tumim, HMCIP, said that although there had been a measurable improvement in inmates' living conditions since the riot, he was not convinced that there had been an equivalent improvement in the regime. The prison still lacked the necessary facilities for association and security limits had been placed on the number of inmates allowed to participate in evening activities. The physical security of the prison was awesome and needs to be managed in a way which minimises the disruption caused to daily activity. HMCIP was deeply concerned about the long term effects of these security measures, but was encouraged by what he had been told about the quality of inmate/staff relationships—stressing it was important to ensure that their development was not inhibited by the high profile security.

GOVERNOR'S COMMENTS In the next year we intend to continue the expansion of the first market-tested prison, anticipating active regimes and offending behaviour programmes.

PRISONERS' COMMENTS
REMAND: Complaints can take a while to be resolved, accommodation is good, but not enough time is given to keeping the wing clean. Visits are excellent and would be even better if the room was divided for non-smokers. Long education and work waiting lists. Medical facilities are good, the food is often cold but edible and the gymnasium is excellent. I've had a couple of reports and I was dealt with fairly—though firmly. The card phones are insufficient for the numbers, it causes endless hassle and disputes: we need more phones.

VPU: I have a double cell with power points, I have daily canteen facilities but no local purchases possible. Education for VP's is non-existent. Though visits are good they would be better if there was a toilet in the visiting room. Work, like education, is not open to VP's. Why can't we have work and education opportunities like the rest of the prison? On the medical front there is a long waiting list for the dentist, though medical staff are very helpful and deal with problems without undue delay. Chapel services are excellent, really uplifting. We can get phone cards each day and mail is not given out until 1710.z

CON: Requests and complaints depend on whether my personal officer is on duty, if not it can take a while. I am in a double cell and not had an option of a single. The canteen is good but you cannot use money-off coupons—why? Visits are good, though my family are often kept waiting a while. I would like more opportunity to go on education classes, but they're few and far between. It's a fair walk to the HCC but you are seen very quickly when you get there. The food is OK, though people on diets do not get a choice like others. Mail is opened in front of me though it is always late in the day.

HMRC & YOI Moorland

Bawtry Road, Doncaster. DN7 6BW
Tel: 0302-351500 **Fax:** 0302-350896
Opened: 1992 **CNA:** 641 **Average Roll:** 604 **Category:** Remand Centre & Closed YOI

i **BACKGROUND** Moorland consists of a Remand Centre, holding unconvicted and unsentenced inmates under 21, a separate closed Young Offender Institution for sentenced under 21s, and is located about ten miles east of Doncaster. The establishment, which is built on land adjacent to HMP Lindholme, was intended as a Category B closed training prison for adult males but, shortly before it opened, its role was changed to that of a Remand Centre and YOI in response to public anxiety about conditions in which young inmates were then held on remand and awaiting sentence at Hull and Leeds prisons. The Prisons Board decreed that 75% of the places at Moorland should accommodate young inmates on remand, and 25% should hold sentenced young offenders. The prison was completed in 1991. Moorland has a Juvenile Unit (Block 2, C.Wing) holding 48 remanded 15&16 year olds—who transfer to Wetherby on sentence. Neither the Governor nor Chairman of the Board of Visitors replied to our requests for information about Moorland, and HMCIP published their latest inspection report on the establishment in October 1994.

OFFICIALS
AREA MGR: Joe Mullens
CHAIR BOV:
GOVERNOR: C. Griffiths
MEDICAL:
CHAPLAIN: Rev Bonney
PROBATION: Michael Eastwood
EDUCATION:
LOCAL MP: Ann Taylor. Lab
STAFFING: 9 Governors, 16×PO, 45×SO and 219 Officers, 6×Night Patrols. A total of 394.5 staff in post, 281 in unified grades.

REGIME *week days*: 0730 unlock, roll check, treatments, applications. 0830 work. 1210 dinner. 1325 work. 1715 tea. 1730–2000 association.

week ends: 0730 unlock. 0800 breakfast. 0900 cell searching, Samaritan & Probation Clinics, gym, exercise, inspection. 1130 dinner. 1320 association, visits. 1715 tea. 1800–1945 association.

Out of cell: 10/24hrs weekdays and 10/24hrs at weekends.

ACCOMMODATION & FACILITIES Four house blocks, each identical in design and capable of holding up to 155 prisoners. Each house block contains three wings (ABC) each of three landings providing a total of 42 double cells and 71 single cells. All cells have integral sanitation. House block 1 mostly young remands; House block 2 induction and Juvenile Unit; House block 3 convicted/sentenced young offenders; House block 4 Vulnerable Prisoners Unit in A Wing, remand inmates in B&C. Each wing has: cardphones (phonecards, which are held by staff, are issued immediately before the call, and returned directly after it); launderette facilities; association rooms with pool and table tennis tables. Poor cleanliness standards, graffiti, smelly vandalised toilets and all cell furniture is bolted to the floor. Bail Information Scheme. Very good anti-bullying scheme in operation. VPU has a full regime with work and association opportunities.

ANTI-BULLYING INITIATIVE Three stage procedure in operation. When a bully has been identified by staff, either as a result of observation or reports from inmates, the prisoner is placed on *Stage One*, this involves no sanction but a strong oral warning from the group Manager and Senior officer responsible for the Anti-Bullying Initiative is given. If the bullying continues *Stage Two* comes into operation which involves full and regular audits of all the prisoner's property in his cell, including goods bought in the canteen. Prisoners on Stage Two are not allowed to visit the canteen but have to pre-order their goods in writing. If the bullying persists, *Stage Three* effectively removes the prisoner from areas where bullying could occur: this involves not only the restrictions of Stage Two, but also no association, exercise taken separately from other inmates, and they are frequently moved to another house block to prevent bullying by proxy. The initiative is effective from the victim's point of view, but does little to help the bully realise the problem, and could be open to abuse if bullying claims are accepted without full and fair inquiry.

REQUESTS & COMPLAINTS Total of 177 complaint forms had been issued in 1993. One third had been withdrawn or not proceeded with, the majority received answers within a reasonable time but not always within time targets. The majority concerned loss of personal property or appeals against adjudications.

VISITS *How to get there*: Train to Doncaster then bus (188) comes to Moorland via

Lindholme prison, leave Doncaster 1300 arrives Moorland 1332. Special Transport: Coaches from Leeds (Pat Ranskill 0532-430601) and Hull (0482-223072) probation services.
VISITING TIMES: Week Days: 1330–1530 M–F. Saturday: 1330–1530 No PVO's weekends. Sunday: 1330–1530.

NOTES Staffed Visitors Centre (0302-351500 exn 287), open noon to 1600, light refreshments, toilets and baby-changing facilities available. Canteen. Childrens Play Area available part of week. No overnight stay facilities. No Smoking in visiting room. Con: 2×VO & 2×PVO per month.

EDUCATION Contracted out to Doncaster College. Total of 90 daytime places with an average uptake of 55. Open five days for 50 weeks of the year—and three evenings (Mon–Wed) for 40 weeks. Remand inmates receive 17.5hrs and convicted 16.5hrs per week. Good educational facilities with spacious education unit. Adequate library, though much of the stock was destroyed during a disturbance at Moorland when it first opened and has yet to be replaced. Official publications well displayed and listed.

WORKSHOPS VTC/CIT courses: Computers, Catering, Multi-skills, Painting & Decorating. Contract services workshop making electrical transformers, Tailors, Education, Stores, Works, Book-binding, Farms & Gardens. Wages average £6.50.

DISCIPLINE 1×PO, 1×SO, 3×Officers. Extremely high level of disciplinary adjudications, with 3082 (almost ten a day) in 1993. In the same period there were 120 drug finds, though all but a few were cannabis. Segregation unit with 25 single cells and two strip cells (used 39 times in 1993). Bleak regime with spartan cells and bare cages for exercise. C&R techniques had been used on 87 occasions and a lack of information prevented HMCIP from being satisfied C&R was used only as a last resort.

MEDICAL Senior Medical Officer, 2×f/t MO, 4×p/t MO, 1×HCPO, 4×HCSO, 11×HCO, 9×Nurses (1×G, 7×E, 1×B grades). Dentist 2×Sess/wk, four week non-urgent waiting list. Very poor regime for psychiatric patients in the HCC, and lengthy delays in arranging transfer to external secure units. X-ray unit with weekly visit from radiologist. Primary health care (sick parade) interviews with the MO criticised for lack of privacy and undue haste. Multi-disciplinary addiction group and HIV/AIDS counselling. Moorland has a high rate of self mutilation incidents.

GYMNASIUM & SPORTS 1×PEPO and 2×PESO, 5×PEO. Large gymnasium with gallery for spectators, well equipped weights room. Full size soccer pitch, rugby pitch and Astroturf. Good changing and showering facilities. Four 90 minute periods through the day, each allocated to a separate house block. Prison soccer team plays in local league, but rugby team banned for three years after a collective assault on a visiting squad. CSLA.

CHAPLAINCY Full time CE chaplain and Church Army Captain, p/t RC and Methodist ministers. Imam visits once per week and Sikh minister twice per week. Main church services Sunday with average attendance of 50 at CE and 15 for RC. Blanket policy of preventing those on punishment from attending services criticised by HM.Chief Inspector. Pool of five Prison Visitors attend regularly.

FOOD Staffing: 1×PO, 1×SO, 6×Officer (caterers), and an inmate work party of 23. Four week menu cycle with two choices at dinner and tea. No pre-select menu system. HMCIP said the standard of food was good and the portions adequate—a view prisoners at Moorland do not agree with.

ESTABLISHMENT REPORTS In a report (published 20th October 1994) of an inspection in February 1994, HMCIP said that Moorland was in most respects impressive. The treatment of prisoners was on the whole satisfactory and in parts outstanding. Staff had done well to establish a positive regime in a comparatively short time. Facilities for sports and physical activities were very good, classroom accommodation was adequate and arrangements for visitors, including the Visitors Centre outside the establishment, was as good as HMCIP has found in any closed prison. Judge Tumim paid particular attention to the serious concerns about bullying, suicide prevention and attitudes of staff that had been expressed in the media and elsewhere. Though a rigorous anti-bullying strategy was in place, the inspection took place shortly after two apparent suicides which had occurred within a few days of each other. There was a serious rift in the HCC, between a minority of Health Care Officers and trained nurses who were trying to improve standards, and HMCIP said it was surprising that in an establishment which held so many disturbed and disordered adolescents there were neither psychiatrists nor psychologists on the permanent staff. Repairing vandalism at the prison was costing £100,000 per year, insufficient use was being made of the space in the wings and prisoners did not have enough to occupy them during association periods. The Personal Officer system worked well, there were a number of good offence-focused groups but more were needed. In its short history the establishment had learned some important lessons and HMCIP found Moorland a refreshing experience overall. Responding to the Report HM Prison Service said the 'rift' between HCO's and trained nurses had been dealt with. Derek Lewis, Director General, said Moorland is now fulfilling an important role within the Prison Service, there is always room for improvement and the recommendations by HMCIP provide a valuable pointer for future development.

PRISONERS' COMMENTS Still waiting for an answer to my request/complaint after two weeks, accommodation is very good, canteen is nothing special and I would say average. Visits are pretty good, though the amount of time visitors are kept waiting is unreasonable. Education has a wide range of courses available and average wages are £4–5. We have a new hospital, though it takes ages to see a dentist, and black inmates suffer from a lack of proper skin cream. There are too many adjudications, far too many petty rules, no long term privileges and not enough to do in the evenings. The food is OK, but nothing special and the Gym is good with regular use by all. No water boilers and the prison library has a stock that has been heavily vandalised. Good religious provision. Mail is given out after dinner and there is only one phone per wing with cards being held by staff.

HM Prison Morton Hall

Swinderby, Lincoln. LN6 9PS
Tel: 0522-868151 **Fax:** 0522-868068
Opened: 1985 **CNA:** 168 **Average Roll:** 154 **Category:** D. Male Open

i **BACKGROUND** Morton Hall is located outside the village of Swinderby in Lincolnshire, some two miles from the A46 main Newark to Lincoln trunk road. The building from which the establishment takes its name was built in 1901 and was occupied as a family residence until 1942, when it was taken over by the RAF. New single-storey hutted accommodation was added in the gardens of the Hall and the site was acquired by the then Prison Commissioners in 1958. Morton Hall opened as a Borstal in 1959, inmates lived in the hutted accommodation while the Governor occupied the Hall. The establishment was closed for a decade between 1975 and 1985, when it was reopened as a D Category open establishment for adult males. In 1989 a serious fire gutted the Hall, reducing it to an insecure smoke-blackened shell. The original RAF huts have been augmented by the addition of prison buildings. The Governor, Charles Bushell, provided very helpful information about Morton Hall, though the BoV did not reply to our request for a copy of their latest annual report. HMCIP published their latest inspection report on Morton Hall in December 1992.

OFFICIALS

AREA MGR: Joe Mullens
CHAIR BOV: R. Wright
GOVERNOR: Charles Bushell
MEDICAL: Dr P. Dennis
CHAPLAIN: Rev Rennard
PROBATION: Trevor Cartwright
EDUCATION: C. Fisher
LOCAL MP: Douglas Hogg. Con
STAFFING: 3 Governor grades, 2 Principal Officers, 7 Senior Officers and 21 Officers, including specialist staff.

REGIME *week days*: 0800 breakfast. 0830–1145 labour. 1200 dinner. 1400–1600 visits (Wed only). 1300–1645 work. 1700 tea, association. 1800–1930 evening classes (Mon–Wed). In rooms 2300.

week ends: 0800 breakfast. 0930 Governor's Inspection (Sun). 1200 dinner. 1400–1600 visits, association. 1700 tea, association. In rooms by 2300.

Out of cell: 24/24hrs weekdays and 24/24hrs at weekends. Roll check six times per day plus ad hoc checks.

ACCOMMODATION & FACILITIES Inmates housed in 84 two-bedded (glass-fronted) rooms: there are no single cells. No communal areas and accommodation spartan. Association area in large Nissen hut provides TV rooms, table tennis and pool which HMCIP said was inadequate both in size and facilities available. Good external facilities with sports field, nine hole pitch and putt course and an artificial lake recently stocked with fish. Three card phones in living unit. Sentence planning, drug counselling, personal officer scheme and night sanitation. Two day induction course for new admissions. Holds about a dozen lifers. SWIP Officer office hours Mon–Fri.

REQUESTS & COMPLAINTS Applications taken on a daily basis (except Sun) by Head of Residence, good inmate/staff relationships keep formal RC to a minimum. In the three months prior to HMCIP inspection, only seven forms had been issued, of these two had been returned and the one requiring a local reply was responded to within seven days. System is properly administered and working satisfactorily said Judge Tumim.

CANTEEN Canteen sited close to the main gate with reasonable display and plenty of room for inmates. Attendance linked to employment, main pay day Tuesday. Open 1215–1315 Mon–Thurs, and Fri 1215–1300. Canteen opening clashes with dinner. Approx 100 lines of stock carried, local purchase facility and clearly displayed prices.

VISITS *How to get there*: Train from Lincoln or Nottingham to Swinderby. Bus (17) from Lincoln or Newark (16 or 17). No Special Transport.
VISITING TIMES: Week Days: 1400–1600 Wednesday only. Saturday: 1400–1600. Sunday: 1400–1600.

NOTES No staffed Visitors Centre. Canteen and Childrens Play Area. Baby-changing facilities available. Local guest house does B&B, contact prison probation. New visiting centre on ground floor. Maximum three adults and children allowed at any one time. Town Visits every 28 days after three-month qualifying period: taken 0930–1800 Sat or Sun, inmates can go home if they live reasonably close, or spend the day with family in Newark or Lincoln. Home leave also operated. Visits every 14 days.

EDUCATION Principal employer of inmates, f/t classes from 0815–1145, 1315–1615 five days a week for 50 weeks of the year. Evening classes on three nights of the week. Two f/t teachers and various p/t staff. Operates from two Nissen huts which are small and out of date. Comprehensive curriculum ranges from basic education to Open University. HMCIP particularly praised the educational provision at Morton Hall. Library with 3,500 books, though no easy chairs, display areas, tables for note-taking or study booths. Open 1800–2000 Mon–Thurs.

WORKSHOPS VTC/CIT Courses in Micro-engineering and home economics. Principal employers farms & gardens, occupying more than half of all work places. Works, kitchen, and domestics make up remainder. Wages on the low side with average of £6.10. Work allocated as part of induction course and party change via sentence planning. Eligibility for outworkers in community after three months at Morton Hall.

DISCIPLINE Segregation Unit self-contained beside HCC comprising four cells with integral sanitation, toilets and exercise yard. Unit staffed only when occupied. Total of 21 adjudications in the 12 months prior to the inspection, heavy reliance on loss of remission.

MEDICAL Part time Medical Officer, 2×Nurses. One bed HCC. Very few visiting specialists with most inmates transferring to Lincoln County Hospital and dental treatment provided by a Lincoln dental practice. Health services well organised, efficiently run and representing good value for money said HMCIP. Report sick to Unit Officer 0745.

GYMNASIUM & SPORTS 1×PESO and 1×PEO. Gym small by modern standards, one badminton court, though marked out for volleyball, basketball and soccer. Small weights room, grassed sports field marked out for three soccer pitches and cricket wicket. Weights room too small for numbers using it. Open 0830–1130 and 1330–1630 Mon–Fri, 1800–200 Mon–Thurs. Five daytime sessions.

CHAPLAINCY Part time CE chaplain, RC and Methodist ministers. CE Services Sun 1800 and Tues 1815. RC mass Fri 1815. Good size chapel well cared for though in need of carpeting. Small ethnic faith population. Imam appointed and able to visit Muslims, and Rabbi based in Nottingham able to visit Jewish inmates. Wide-ranging discussion group Thurs 1330–1500.

FOOD Staffing: 1×SO, 1×Officer (caterers), and an inmate work party of 12. All meals eaten in large, bright dining hall beside kitchen. All kitchen inmates complete food hygiene course. No NVQ Caterbase. HMCIP said food both in taste and presentation was very acceptable.

ESTABLISHMENT REPORTS In a report (published 3rd December 1992) of an inspection in March 1992, HMCIP, said that it was a pleasure to be able to record Morton Hall as a thoroughly well administered establishment. The prison needs better accommodation and facilities and there is a long-term plan for development. The prison is well governed and the staff have a high morale. Imaginative features of the regime include the use of information technology, the excellent education and PE programmes, the approach taken to sentence planning and to the performance of prison tasks by staff and inmates: these outstanding features deserve recognition said Judge Tumim. The co-operation that existed between senior managers and the commitment they displayed to the regime and its further development was exemplary. The long list of recommendations should not cancel the fact that Morton Hall was found to be essentially in good shape.

GOVERNOR'S COMMENTS We run regular pre-release courses, and courses addressed specifically at drink or drug abuse, drink driving and burglary—all courses prison officer led. Sentence planning procedures in place and operate reasonably well, with all inmates serving over six months being seen every 12 weeks. Special arrangements made for lifers. Inmates who have carried out the appropriate preliminary work at Morton Hall may qualify to spend some time in their home areas prior to release, attending offending behaviour courses and furthering their employability. Those reading the *Prisoners' Handbook* need to be aware that Morton Hall is by no means a holiday camp. Inmates will be expected to work seven hours per day, and abide by the rules of the establishment. Those who fail to do so may continue their sentences in more secure surroundings.

PRISONERS' COMMENTS Requests and Complaints generally good, not many complaints and the facility to complain is sometimes denied by staff. Poor accommodation, no single rooms or power points and no privacy due to glass-fronted rooms [new accommodation blocks being built 1994/5 with single rooms]. Canteen is generally poor, times clash with meals and there is general dissatisfaction with lots of complaints. Visits generally oppressive, too many staff in visiting area. Very basic education, does not cater for variation with too much emphasis on art. Low wages compared with other prisons, no pay if sick. No complaints of excessive punishments, but many of inconsistency in awards. Menu system in operation for food, reasonably varied, good quantity, though quality spoiled by bad cooking. Good PE facilities, open every day with good access. All religious faiths catered for at Morton Hall. Mail handed out at midday, recent complaints of mail being opened without notification, routinely censored. Good access to card phones.

HM Prison The Mount

Bovingdon, Hemel Hempstead, Herts. HP3 ONZ
Tel: 0442-834363 **Fax:** 0442-834321
Opened: 1987 **CNA:** 484 **Average Roll:** 406 **Category:** C. Male

i **BACKGROUND** The Mount prison was designed as a C Category training prison and built on the site of a former RAF Station on the outskirts of Bovingdon village in Hertfordshire. Following changes in the prison population and despite its design, The Mount opened in 1987 as a Youth Custody Centre, later becoming a YOI. In December 1990 the urgent overnight closure of HMP Grendon caused a hurried reappraisal of the prison estate with the consequence that a large number of young offenders were moved out of The Mount to make way for C Category adult prisoners from Grendon. Although Grendon reopened in September 1991, the young offenders did not return and today The Mount fulfils the C Category adult training role for which it was originally designed and built. Neither the Governor nor BoV replied to our requests for information about the prison, and HMCIP published their latest inspection report on The Mount in November 1992.

OFFICIALS
AREA MGR: Arthur de Frisching
CHAIR BOV:
GOVERNOR: M. Donnelly
MEDICAL:
CHAPLAIN: Rev Crichton
PROBATION: Jim Adams
EDUCATION:
LOCAL MP: Richard Page. Con
STAFFING: 6 Governor grades, 10 Principal Officers, 27 Senior Officers and 101 Officers, including specialist staff.

REGIME *week days*: 0745 unlock, breakfast. 0845–1140 work. 1200 dinner, lock up. 1330 work. 1415 visits. 1610 cease labour. 1630 tea, lock up. 1745–2000 association.

week ends: 0745 unlock, breakfast. 0900 RC Mass (Sat), cell cleaning. 0940 CE Service (Sun). 0930–1130 association, exercise, gym. 1145 dinner, lock up. 1330 unlock, association, gym. 1400 visits. 1630 tea, lock up. No weekend evening association.

Out of cell: 9.5/24hrs weekdays and 7.5/24hrs at weekends.

ACCOMMODATION & FACILITIES Four identical cell blocks, Brister, Fowler, Lakes and Ellis Houses, each with 112 single cells with integral sanitation. Very good bathing and showering facilities in each House. Large central area of each House used for association, dining room and servery—though all meals eaten in cell. Three card phones in each House, max of 10 cards/mth. Pre-

Release Unit with 36 places in separate block. Houses inconsistent in regime policy. The Mount was selected for in-cell TV on trial basis, though it lacks credibility said HMCIP with no power points and battery operated sets only. Personal Officer scheme, sentence planning. Extensive i/p list. Two-week Pre-release Course.

REQUESTS & COMPLAINTS Poor system at The Mount with many delays—an examination of the records by HMCIP showed that at 155 Requests/Complaint forms were still outstanding at the end of one three month period. High number of RC forms issued, indicating a lack of inmate/staff relationships with complaints being pushed up to governor level.

CANTEEN Located opposite the education department it is some distance from the Houses. Around 170 lines of stock carried, though small space limits display. Canteen Committee meets monthly. One visit per week to spend earnings, private cash allowance transferred monthly.

VISITS *How to get there*: Train (Euston) to Hemel Hempstead and bus from Station to prison. Metropolitan Line to Chesham, bus from tube Station to prison. No bus service on a Sunday from London Victoria, Hemel Hempstead or Chesham Bus Stations. No Special Transport.
VISITING TIMES: Week Days: 1345–1600 Mon, Thur, Fri only. Saturday: 1345–1600. Sunday: 1345–1600.

NOTES No staffed Visitors Centre. Canteen and Childrens Play Area. No overnight stay facilities. Lift available for disabled visitors. Baby-changing facilities and pay phone available.

EDUCATION Modern and purpose-built Education Centre, located close to the Houses. Large employer of inmates with 115 on f/t courses, with eight OU students. Open 50 weeks of the year with day classes four and a half days of the week, and evening classes two days of the week for a 25 week year. Classes 0900–1130, 1400–1630. Very broad range, including cookery, computing, basic education, numeracy, languages, soft toys, information technology, sciences, drama and art. Very good library with computer access to local library outside: inmates can borrow up to six books for up to three weeks.

WORKSHOPS VTC/CIT courses: Bricklaying, Painting & Decorating, Motor Mechanics, Light vehicle Body Repairs, Industrial Cleaning. PSIF workshop. Kitchen. Works. Gardens. Cleaners. Orderlies. Average pay £5.50.

DISCIPLINE Seg Unit part of admin block with eight ordinary cells, seven with integral sanitation, one unfurnished cell and two strip cells. there were 437 adjudications in the six months prior to the inspection, over 60% of which were for unauthorised possession, use of abusive language or refusing to comply with an order.

MEDICAL 2×p/t MOs, 1×HCSO, 3×HCO. HCC with inpatient facilities converted to provide discharge planning centre: inmates requiring inpatient care transferred to Littlehey. Three month waiting list for dental services, VD clinic every two weeks, no HIV/AIDS counselling.

GYMNASIUM & SPORTS 1×PEPO, 1×PESO and 6×PEO. Modern, purpose-built, gymnasium, large separate weights room. Outdoor facilities comprise tarmac area and a large grassed sports field with one rugby, two soccer pitches and a cricket wicket. Full programme with activities throughout the week including four weekday evening classes. Local teams visit to play league games, and prison football, cricket and volleyball teams play away games. Inmates also leave the establishment for swimming, hiking and helping the handicapped.

CHAPLAINCY Full time CE chaplain, p/t RC and Methodist ministers. Main church services Saturday (RC) and Sunday (CE) morning. Good chapel, attractive and clean. Religious meetings four nights a week, with one non-religious debating group run by Chaplaincy. Muslim prayer meeting 1400–1600 Friday and 0900–1115 Sunday. No multi-faith room. Sikh service 1400–1600 Friday.

FOOD Staffing: 1×SO, 4×Officer (caterers), and an inmate work party of 15. Tea is the main meal of the day, all main courses were good though limited variety of vegetables makes for meals that are predictable. No pre-select menu system. No NVQ Caterbase, though kitchen inmates complete hygiene course.

ESTABLISHMENT REPORTS In a report (published June 1992) of an inspection in February 1992, HMCIP said that the change of role from YOI to C Category prison, resulted in a 19% drop in staff and a change of culture from the one developed for young offenders to one capable of handling more sophisticated and challenging adult inmates. There are three areas of concern: staffing; type of inmate allocated to The Mount and, thirdly, the development of the training regime. Too few staff were at The Mount to meet the external commitment or provide weekend evening association. Control of the incoming population was unclear and should be monitored, as objective information of sentence length, age and the numbers received after recategorisation would enable the Governor to focus the regime on the type of inmate actually received. Opportunities for purposeful, quality, work were severely limited with less than half the available workshops being in use. The establishment needs a regime that does not rely on its proximity to London but had other features which would make it worthwhile in the eyes of the inmate population. HMCIP made a total of 114 recommendations.

PRISONERS' COMMENTS Difficult to obtain answers to applications, time targets for Request and Complaint forms were not being met. Restricted inter-wing movement, lack of access to sports field, too little community work and an absence of town visits make The Mount a C Cat prison in name only. Limited educational opportunities, with no evening classes. Good VTC/CIT courses. Food is of variable quality, short menu makes meals predictable and the issue of toiletries can only be described as erratic. Shortage of cleaning materials, little consistency between the wings in the way the rules are applied and the wages are low in comparison to other C Category establishments. Very few offence-focused groups, with a need for more counselling services to deal with drink, drugs, anger control and other offence related behaviour. The televisions-trial was designed to fail, each set requires its own licence, no power points nor facilities for recharging batteries.

HM Prison & YOI New Hall

Dial Wood, Wakefield, W. Yorks. WF4 4AX
Tel: 0924-848307 **Fax:** 0924-840692
Opened: 1961 **CNA:** 122 **Average Roll:** 135 **Category:** Female Closed

i **BACKGROUND** New Hall, situated near Wakefield in West Yorkshire, was originally a military camp that began life in 1900 and remained as such until it was acquired by the then Prison commissioners in 1933 to become the first open prison in England operating as a satellite of Wakefield. In 1961 New Hall was converted from open prison to Detention Centre but with little development of the site. In 1987 the establishment closed and, after a very short period of limited refurbishment, was reopened in August 1987 as a secure local prison for women and girls. The most striking feature of New Hall is the huge new security block that has been built in the grounds with security equipment equal to that in any dispersal prison and of a design identical to that in Full Sutton: it is now being fully used as a B category unit. Neither the Governor nor BoV replied to our requests for information about the prison, and HMCIP published their latest inspection report on New Hall in February 1992.

OFFICIALS

AREA MGR: Terry Bone
CHAIR BOV:
GOVERNOR: D. England
MEDICAL:
CHAPLAIN: Rev Smith
PROBATION: James Bryan
EDUCATION:
LOCAL MP: Ann Taylor. Lab
STAFFING: 3 Governor grades, 4 Principal Officers, 12 Senior Officers and 86 Officers, including specialist staff.

REGIME *week days*: 0730 unlock, treatments. 0800 breakfast. 0825 exercise, classes, work. 0930 sick parade. 1030 adjudications. 1145 dinner. 1340 gym, classes, 1545 cease labour, tea. 1620 lock up. 1800–2030 association.

week ends: 0730 unlock, treatments. 0800 breakfast. 0825 reception board. 0900 CE Service (Sun). 0930 sick parade. 1000 adjudications. 1045 association after inspection. 1140 dinner, lock up. 1345 association. 1540 treatments. 1545 tea, lock up. 1700 showers, association. 1800 RC mass (Sat). 2030 lock up.

Out of cell: 9.5/24hrs weekdays and 9.5/24hrs at weekends.

ACCOMMODATION & FACILITIES

Main accommodation in three small two–storey cell blocks with a total of 78 cells with integral sanitation, well decorated and in good condition. One small hut with 15 cubicles and a second with dormitory accommodation for 23 inmates. Good showering facilities. Large dining hall doubles as association room with TV. Second association room for table tennis and pool. Sentence planning, personal officer scheme. card phones in each unit.

VPU Ground floor of one unit used as VPU with 13 cells holding women who had chosen segregation because of the nature of their crimes. Regime very impoverished with too much time spent locked in cell: lack of association, intimidation and abuse from other inmates, food was tampered with and weekday visits restricted to 30 mins.

CANTEEN Small canteen located off central corridor. Small stock, though fresh fruit available, about a dozen items for ethnic minorities are stocked and there is a fridge for perishables. Local purchase facility. Restricted opening hours.

VISITS *How to get there*: Train to Wakefield Westgate or Huddersfield. Hourly bus (263) on the hour from Wakefield or from Huddersfield (231 every 2 hrs), then one mile walk to prison. No Special Transport.
VISITING TIMES: Week Days: 1330–1515 Tues–Thurs only. Rem/Con. Saturday: 0930–1130 & 1330–1515. Sunday: 1330–1515.

NOTES Convicted visits: 30min. Remand visits: 15 mins. No staffed Visitors Centre, but Portakabin for shelter. Canteen and Childrens Play Area. Plenty of B&B in Wakefield or Huddersfield, contact prison probation.

EDUCATION Five f/t teachers, 4×p/t and 30 p/t assistants. Eight classrooms which range from the very good to the small and dim. Combined art and pottery room, good range of computers, three TVs, two video cameras and a home economics room fitted with washing machine, fridge, freezer, cookers and microwave. Good hairdressing salon with NVQs available. Operates 52 weeks of the year, 0830–1140 & 1330–1540 & 1800–1930 five days and four evenings per week. Library located in a PortaKabin with about 1500 books of which inmates can borrow four books for any length of time and special orders taken.

WORKSHOPS No VTC/CIT courses. Main employers, Farms & Gardens, Kitchen, Works, Education, Textile workshop, Cleaners. Average wage £5.50. Difficult to obtain labour change before completion of eight weeks in shop.

DISCIPLINE High number of reports with over 700 a year. hearings conducted in recreation room, well conducted though disparity and inconsistency of punishments and records were too brief. Seg Unit with four cells off main corridor—HMCIP said they were unsuitable by virtue of both construction and location.

MEDICAL 1×F/t MO, 1×p/t MO, 1×SNS, 1×HCSO, 3×NS, 5×HCO. HCC with one three-bed ward, five single cells and one strip cell. Lack of integral sanitation and poor regime for HCC inpatients. Dentist 1×sess/wk, Psych 2×sess/wk, Optician 1×sess/mth.

GYMNASIUM & SPORTS 3×PEO. Purpose-built gym marked out for badminton, basketball and volleyball. Circuit training, jogging, badminton and aerobics most popular classes. Special classes for over 35s and pregnant inmates.

CHAPLAINCY Part time CE chaplain, RC and Methodist ministers. Main CE Service 0830 Sunday with Holy Communion 1700. RC Mass Saturday 1800. Very little multi-faith activities and no programme of weekly groups, discussions or meetings apart from one meeting of Christian Fellowship.

FOOD Staffing: 1×SO, 2×Officer (caterers), and an inmate work party of 12. No pre-select menu system, but wide variety of meals offered, HMCIP found the food to be well cooked and appetising. All meals eaten in dining room. Meal times however are perverse and should be reorganised.

ESTABLISHMENT REPORTS In a report (published 20th February 1992) of an inspection in February 1991, HMCIP, said that the regime at New Hall was more relaxed and open than in other local prisons. The key was the induction programme that deals with inmates as individuals, identifies needs and provides a structure which enables those needs to be dealt with. The overall result was an atmosphere more akin to a semi open prison than a local. The problems facing the establishment are more national than local, its future is in doubt with a falling female population and the addition of the new secure block perhaps indicates a direction though the long term thinking is not clear. In terms of treatment of inmates New Hall has not only demonstrated that a local prison can operate a training oriented regime but also that such a regime can be offered equally to convicted and unconvicted adults and young offenders.

PRISONERS' COMMENTS Visits room is too small, lacks a creche and refreshments. Mother and baby Unit planned and will be welcome. Medical facilities however are inadequate, too many mentally disturbed inmates in the HCC and too little room for association though inmate/staff relationships are generally good. Association facilities restricted to dining rooms with just one TV and no open association, Showers are not cleaned properly, older inmates resent presence of young offenders and private cash limits need to be increased. There are no ironing or launderette facilities on the wings, the library is too small and opening times are very limited. Lockable lockers for those in dormitory accommodation should be provided and a general purpose party that could tidy up the prison would be an asset.

HMRC Northallerton

East Rd, Northallerton, N.Yorks. DL6 1NW
Tel: 0609-780078 **Fax:** 0609-779664
Opened: 1785 **CNA:** 146 **Average Roll:** 141 **Category:** Remand Centre

i **BACKGROUND** Northallerton Remand Centre occupies a site close to the town centre and includes some buildings constructed in 1785 as the North Yorkshire House of Correction. The principal buildings which remain in use were built in the mid 19th century. The prison was taken out of use in the 1930s and was used as a store during the Second World War, after which it was used as a military prison for three years. It held adult male inmates until 1983 when it became a Youth Custody Centre and, later, a Young Offender Institution. it continued to hold only sentenced inmates until October 1983, when the primary role changed to that of a Remand Centre. The Governor provided information about the establishment, though the Northallerton Board of Visitors did not respond to our request for a copy of their latest annual report. HMCIP published their latest report on the Remand Centre in September 1994.

OFFICIALS
AREA MGR: M. Codd
CHAIRMAN BOV: Mrs Blythman
GOVERNOR: D. Appleton
MEDICAL: Northallerton Hosp
CHAPLAIN: Rev B. Mayne
PROBATION: R. Allen
EDUCATION: A. Lyman
LOCAL MP: William Hauge. Con

REGIME *week days*: 0800 unlock, applications, breakfast. 0845 half inmates to work, other half to canteen, PE, exercise (0915–1015 or 1030–1130) 0900 visits commence. 1145 cease labour, dinner, lock up. 1330 unlock. 1345 visits commence, half inmates to work, other half to canteen, PE, exercise (1415–1515 or 1530–1630). 1645 cease labour, tea, lock up. 1800 unlock, education, association. 2000 association ends, lock up.

week ends: 0800 unlock, applications, breakfast in cell. 0900 unlock for service. 1000 unlock for activity, PE, exercise (0940–1040). 1145 cease activity, dinner, lock up. 1345 visits commence. 1400 unlock, activities. 1630 cease activities, tea, lock up. 1800 unlock, association. 2000 association ends, lock up.

Out of cell: 6.75/24hrs weekdays and 5/24hrs at weekends.

ACCOMMODATION & FACILITIES
Main wing 85 double cells, all with integral sanitation. Light switch in all cells but no power points. Shower facilities within the wing, available daily throughout association periods. Two card phones on ground floor. C.Wing 45 single cells all with integral sanitation and facilities as above. Seg Unit 9 single cells, five with integral sanitation. Bail information scheme, sentence planning, drug counselling, personal officer scheme.

REQUESTS & COMPLAINTS HMCIP reports that the formal R/C system is working effectively at Northallerton. Landing Officers record all applications and attempted to resolve issues without recourse to the formal system: only 10 formal R/C forms had been submitted in the two months prior to the inspection.

CANTEEN Open five hours a day during the week. Convicted inmates pay and private cash on Thursday afternoons. Remand visit according to labour allocation. Stock of 108 items with a large selection of confectionery. Local purchase facility but no provision for fresh fruit. HMCIP was told prices were set according to Shaw's retail guide, but canteen staff could not produce a copy when asked to do so . . .

VISITS *How to get there*: Train or bus to Northallerton station and then short walk to prison. Special Transport: coaches from Manchester or Sheffield probation.
VISITING TIMES: Week Days: 0900–1145. 1345–1530 Tuesday only. Saturday: 1345–1530. Sunday: 1345–1530.

NOTES No staffed Visitors Centre or Childrens Play Area. No canteen, though vending machine is available (coins). Contact prison probation or casework officer for details of local B&B. No wheelchair access.

EDUCATION Education open 50 weeks of the year, during the core day and for 29.5 hours per week. Evening classes do not operate at present. Programme offers places for 100 inmates working on a part time basis (morning or afternoon attendance option). Six open-ended courses are available each session from the following: Adult basic education—word and number power; computer literacy; art; craft; woodwork; personal development; individual studies; business studies; creative writing; special needs individual tuition. Cell studies for those segregated. Comprehensive offending behaviour courses in car crime, drugs, substance abuse, budgeting accommodation, offending, citizenship, parenting, health and relationships.

WORKSHOPS No VTC/CIT courses. Only one workshop open at present, textiles. Large gardens party for extensive horticultural activity, and kitchen party with usual cleaners. Though a remand centre, Northallerton provides all prisoners with the opportunity to work and earn , on average, £7 per week. Labour Board allocates work party weekly.

DISCIPLINE There were 850 reports at Northallerton in 1993, HMCIP examined the records of 50 hearings and found they were well completed with some reports being dismissed for lack of evidence or due to incorrect framing of the charge. Little use made of cellular confinement, due in part to the fact that the nine-cell segregation unit is usually full with inmates on protection—most two to a cell. Use of C&R within acceptable bounds said HMCIP, 17 inmates had been placed in C&R locks, and one recorded in a body-belt, in 1993.

MEDICAL Twenty-four hour medical cover provided by Northallerton Health Trust. Internal facilities covered by HCSO, 2HCO's and agency nurse. Cover available 0745–2030 seven days a week. Dental surgery (1 sess/wk) and Optician (1 sess/mth). Psychiatrist only available if required to prepare reports for court. Report sick to treatment room at mealtimes. All receptions seen by doctor within 24 hours unless an emergency.

GYMNASIUM & SPORTS 1×PEPO, 4×PEO. Gymnasium open 0830–1945 Mon–Thurs and 0830–1630 Fri & weekends. Limited PE facilities at time of inspection but new sports hall recently completed. Small weights room and tarmac yard account for current PE facilities. Five staff provide a full programme over seven days and three evenings a week. No PE for R.43 inmates.

CHAPLAINCY Chaplaincy Team: Brian Mayne and Angela Richardson (C/E), Fr. Joe Brennan (RC) and Keith Parr (Meth). Visits from Home Minister can be arranged. Though all Chaplaincy Team are part-time, a chaplain is available every day. Church services: Sat 0915 RC, Sun 0915 United C/E, Methodist. Bible study, chaplains hour, chaplains library and prison visitors available on request. Chaplaincy print explanatory leaflet.

FOOD Kitchen located close to main gate, female civilian cook and two catering officers assisted by work party of 8. Current meal times due to change under 1994/95 to comply with model regime for remand centres: breakfast 0730–0900, dinner 1200–1400 and tea 1700–1930. HMCIP asked to see the Food Complaints Book, after complaints from inmates, but it could not be found. HMCIP recommended inmate representation on a catering committee would be valuable.

ESTABLISHMENT REPORTS In a report (published 9th September 1994) of an inspection in March 1994, HMCIP said that at the time of the inspection Northallerton was struggling to recover from the effects of a change of role to which the establishment's physical resources were not well suited. The management structure was inappropriate and ineffective, and the quality of communications within the establishment was inconsistent. Arrangements for receiving visitors to the establishment were most unsatisfactory, and the need for a new visits complex was obvious and pressing. Accommodation was satisfactory although grubby, but association facilities were limited and there were structured activities on offer during the evenings. The majority of inmates are only offered part-time work and insufficient use was being made of the education and physical education facilities largely because of the inappropriate staff attendance system. Health care services were being adjusted to meet the requirements of the change of role but the process was being hampered by delays in appointing the necessary staff. The segregation unit was not a satisfactory place for inmates who were ill and it was particularly disturbing to find that inmates who were considered suicidal were also located there. Control is being exercised firmly but fairly and inmate/staff relationships are good. Though the education department has taken the lead in re-establishing some courses designed to aid inmates' resettlement, throughcare was uncoordinated and had been thrown into disarray by the change of role: the personal officer scheme had all but died out.

PRISONERS' COMMENTS Requests and Complaints forms do not meet time targets and accommodation suffers from a lack of adequate heating. Canteen provides little choice and the prices are far too expensive. Education is well attended and plenty of choice available. Not enough variety in the work place and average medical facilities. The Governor always seems to take the staff side in adjudications. Food is described as rubbish, with poor quality and insufficient quantity. Good sports facilities with new gym which can be visited each day. Mail is handed out before dinner, but not opened in front of the prisoner, and there is no difficulty in obtaining phone cards.

HM Prison North Sea Camp

Freiston, Boston, Lincs. PE22 OQX
Tel: 0205-760481 **Fax:** 0205-760098
Opened: 1935 **CNA:** 204 **Average Roll:** 103 **Category:** C. Male

i **BACKGROUND** In 1935 a party of young inmates and officers from Stafford prison walked across England pushing handcarts that were loaded with building and camping equipment. At a point six miles east of Boston in Lincolnshire they pitched their tents and began to build permanent accommodation for themselves. With construction well under way the inmates and staff then started to reclaim land from the sea by forming an earth rampart, backfilling behind with the rich alluvial soil from the Wash Saltings. The reclamation process continued over the years and, by 1985, the size of England had increased by more than 1000 acres as a result of their endeavours. From these industrious beginnings came North Sea Camp, first an open Borstal, changing in 1963 to a Senior Detention Centre, and assuming its current role as an Open Prison for adult males in July 1988. Neither the Governor nor Board of Visitors at NSC replied to our requests for information about the establishment, and HMCIP published their latest inspection report in November 1993.

OFFICIALS

AREA MGR: Joe Mullens
CHAIR BOV:
GOVERNOR: Ray Reveley
MEDICAL:
CHAPLAIN: Rev M. Rennard
PROBATION: Amanda Cooke
EDUCATION:
LOCAL MP: Richard Body. Con
STAFFING: 3 Governor grades, 3 Principal Officers, 7 Senior Officers and 27 Officers, including specialist staff.

REGIME *week days*: 0745 unlock/breakfast. 0900 work. 1215 lunch. 1330 work. 1615 cease labour. 1700 tea. 1730–2030 association.

week ends: 0745 unlock/breakfast. 0900 association. 1215 lunch. 1400 association. 1700 tea. 1730–2030 association.

Out of cell: 24/24hrs weekdays and 24/24hrs at weekends.

ACCOMMODATION & FACILITIES
Two living units (North and South) with dormitory accommodation holding upto 22 inmates. Both living units have adequate showering facilities and access to toilets 24 hours a day. Card phones on each unit located in windowed rooms, calls limited to ten minute duration and maximum of two phonecards per week. Replacement accommodation is to be phased in shortly, £750,000 has been allocated for 1994/5. Subject to the approval of the Chief Executive £2m has been earmarked for rebuilding in 1995/6 and a further £2m in 1996/7. This will replace all inmate accommodation and increase the CNA to 250. Until then however, inmates will have to live in conditions which HMCIP described as 'tatty and long past their useful life'.

CANTEEN Operated by two storemen and located in a small room adjacent to the library. Open for three hours per week (Wed pm and Thurs am). Private cash and earnings, though PC only on toiletries. Profit margin of 10%. Limited local purchase facility.

VISITS *How to get there*: Train to Boston which is some six miles from North Sea Camp. The prison provides transport Sat & Sun only from Boston BR Station at 1400 and returns after visits cease at 1545. Taxi available at station. No Special Transport.
VISITING TIMES: Week Days: 1400–1545 Wednesday only. Saturday: 1400–1545. Sunday: 1400–1545.

NOTES No staffed Visitors Centre. Canteen weekends only—though vending machine (coins) available. Childrens Play Area. Contact Tourist Office in Boston for details of B&B (0205-356656). Wheelchair access possible. Baby changing facilities. Visits advised at weekends. Town visits except for lifers.

EDUCATION Full time Education Officer, Deputy, Civilian Instructor and 13 p/t teachers. Located in series of PortaKabins and single storey buildings open for 46 weeks of the year: Computers, soft toys, bridge & chess club, business studies, art workshop, food hygiene, first aid, photography, AA, model engineering, film club, English, maths, basic education.

WORKSHOPS VTC Painting & Decorating Course. Farm and Gardens party of 44 inmates working a 34 hour week. Works party of 30. Domestic cleaners and Orderlies with 23 places. External community work schemes.

DISCIPLINE Segregation unit containing five ordinary cells but no integral sanitation. Not normally manned except when inmates are located in it. Incidents are extremely rare and adjudications few and far between.

MEDICAL Part time Medical Officer, contracted for 21 hours per week, there are no visiting specialists: all such cases (optical, dental and psychiatric etc) are referred to the local hospital.

GYMNASIUM & SPORTS 1×PESO and 2×PEO. No complaints noted by HMCIP from inmates. Gym of 1960's design and about the size of a badminton court with a small weights area at one end. Large sportsfield but exposed completely to the wind from the sea which often makes ball games difficult. Two hours PE per inmate per week and at least one coaching course run each month. A condition of external community work is that inmates must first prove their attitude in the gymnasium.

CHAPLAINCY Part time CE chaplain, RC and Methodist ministers. Discussion group Tuesday evenings and prison visitors arranged. Main church service Sunday morning in small discrete chapel used by all denominations.

FOOD Staffing: 2×Civilian Caterers, and an inmate work party of 11. No complaints recorded about the food, choice of eight different vegetables at dinner and two choices of meals at both dinner and tea. Civilian caterers well motivated. New kitchen opened in 1991.

ESTABLISHMENT REPORTS In a report (published 23rd November 1993) of an inspection in July 1993, HMCIP, said that North Sea Camp was establishing a positive training experience for prisoners. Since the last inspection in 1990 more inmates convicted of serious offences had been accepted including those serving life. Problems associated with the remote location had been offset by imaginative use of town visits and temporary release but these are not yet extended to lifers. The food was excellent. Replacement of the original huts was long overdue and HMCIP supported the planned rebuilding of a prison which gives practical assistance to prisoners, helping them to avoid reoffending when they are released.

PRISONERS' COMMENTS Inmates complained that the old accommodation was draughty in the winter being buffeted by the winds which come straight from the sea. The hardboard partitions separating the cubicles did not greatly reduce noise and there was little privacy—lifers in particular did not like sharing accommodation. Inmates praised the food quality although those working in the community were only allowed sandwiches. Visiting arrangements were generally satisfactory although those who lived some distance from the prison (and the inmate home-area profile shows that only a very small proportion come from Lincolnshire) suggested that home visits should start on Friday nights rather than Saturday mornings. The prison should hold a maximum of 12 lifers but held 16 at the time of the inspection and there was discontent at the regulations which prevent them from working in the community.

HM Prison Norwich

Mousehold, Norwich. NR1 4LU
Tel: 0603-37531 **Fax:** 0603-300867
Opened: 1887 **CNA:** 429 **Average Roll:** 454 **Category:** Male Local, Remand Centre & C/D Annexe

i **BACKGROUND** Norwich prison, situated on the eastern outskirts of Norwich at Mousehold, is an establishment located on three separate sites. The Local prison, with a CNA of 179, opened in 1887. The Britannia training prison annexe with a CNA of 150, located next to the local prison, originally formed part of the Royal Norfolk Regiment's depot but was converted in 1972 to provide C Category accommodation. The Remand Centre, with a CNA of 120, is located outside the main prison wall in a compound with the HCC, which has a CNA of 49. Norwich had three suicides in the HCC in 1993—two within eight days of each other. Joesphine Fowler, the Governor of Norwich, did not reply to our requests for information about the prison, though the Chairman of the BoV kindly provided a copy of their latest annual report. HMCIP published their latest inspection report on Norwich in July 1993.

OFFICIALS
AREA MGR: Tom Murtagh
CHAIR BOV: Thelma Paines
GOVERNOR: Ms J.M. Fowler
MEDICAL: Dr Khan
CHAPLAIN: Rev Noblett

PROBATION: Ray Bayles
EDUCATION:
LOCAL MP: Patrick Thompson. Con
STAFFING: 7 Governor grades, 8 Principal Officers, 32 Senior Officers, 189 Officers, 15 Prison Auxiliaries, and 16 Night Patrols including specialist staff.

☞ **REGIME** *week days*: **LOCAL:** 0800 unlock, slop out, applications, breakfast. 0845 Rule 43s to labour. 0914 convicted exercise, sick parade. 1000 remand exercise. 1030 adjudications. 1100 Rule 43 exercise. 1115 dinner. 1300 Rule 43s to labour. 1330 unlock, slop out. 1340 remand exercise. 1400 visits. 1415 canteen, library, kit change. 1500 convicted exercise. 1600 tea. 1730–2030 slop out, serve supper.

week ends: **LOCAL:** 0800 unlock, slop out, applications, breakfast. 0900 reception board (Sat), CE/RC Services (Sun). 0930 remand exercise. 1000 convicted exercise. 1030 adjudications. 1100 Rule 43 exercise. 1115 dinner. 1330 unlock, slop out. 1400 visits. 1530 tea. 1730–2030 slop out, serve supper.

Out of cell: 9.5/24hrs weekdays and 9.5/24hrs at weekends.

ACCOMMODATION & FACILITIES

LOCAL PRISON A.wing with four landings, has integral sanitation, showers in former recesses and a mixture of remand and convicted separated by landings. Daily PE sessions, all new arrivals screened for education and induction process with HIV video. Very little work other than cleaning and kitchen. Association on weekly rota system, meal times cause problems. All kitchen inmates located in C.wing dormitory. Mail opened centrally and issued at dinner time. Only three card phones results in long queues.

VPU Located in D.wing with CNA of 21 in 13 single cells and four-man dorms. Good separation apart from visits. Very limited regime, education and work opportunities and time out of cell less than five hours per day.

REMAND CENTRE Two wings, North and South, both with integral sanitation and holding adult and young offenders respectively. North wing serves as overspill from A.wing operating much the same regime apart from a slightly later tea meal (1615). South wing houses young offenders on remand, flourishing personal officer scheme (in both North and South). PE sessions daily Mon–Sat, reasonable education provision and small library. Norwich has no Bail Information Scheme. Remand Centre offers upto 9 hours per day out of cell. No card phones.

BRITANNIA ANNEXE Dormitory conditions in this C/D Cat Trainer and a few single rooms for lifers. No PE during the day, all training courses have vacancies and print shop unable to attract sufficient prisoners. Spartan educational facilities, classes weekdays and Saturday. Job Club. No sentence planning, personal officer scheme or offence-focused work, though non-individual compacts being used. Good visiting facilities with three visits per month. Card phones on ground floor, mail issued dinner time. Britannia was earmarked for closure in 1993, but it has since been decided to keep it open, refurbishment is planned—and not before time.

CANTEEN Main canteen in A.wing operates satellite canteens in Britannia and Remand Centre. carries around 120 lines of stock, prices clearly marked but lack of space limits display. Profit margin of 10%. Open each weekday in A.wing, twice a week in Britannia and four times a week in the Remand Centre/HCC.

VISITS *How to get there*: Train to Norwich. Bus (18,19,20) to Vincent Road. Walking: prison 1.5 miles from BR Station, 2 miles from Bus Station. No Special Transport.
VISITING TIMES: Week Days: 1400–1600 M–F. Saturday: 1400–1600. Sunday: 1400–1600.

NOTES Remand visits on Sunday by prior application only. No hospital visits Thurs or Sun. No visits to Britannia Annexe Thurs/Sun. Staffed Visitors Centre with light refreshments available and Childrens Play Area. Canteen in visits room.

EDUCATION Seven f/t staff and 32 p/t teachers all from Norwich City College. Comprehensive mix of educational opportunities with strong emphasis on basic education or foundation courses, open learning, information technology, employment skills training and arts and crafts. Weekend education being pursued. Six separate libraries with the largest in the Local prison and Britannia, opening times need improvement.

WORKSHOPS VTC/CIT courses: Bricklaying, Carpentry, General Construction, Welding. Printing and bookbinding (Britannia inmates only). Laundry, kitchen, and usual domestic jobs, for many inmates no work is available. Labour Board on Tuesdays. Wages average £6.50 for employed but drop to £2.50 for UB40.

DISCIPLINE Special Care Unit has returned to its former title of Segregation Unit. Turnover of inmates quite high. Adjudications in Remand Centre and Britannia modest, but larger numbers in Local prison. Main charges threats, fighting, abusive language, unauthorised possession and vandalism. Procedures were correctly followed said HMCIP.

MEDICAL Full time SMO, 2×MO, 1×G5 Health Care Manager, 1×HCPO, 4×HCSO, 21×HCO and two agency nurses. Report sick 0800 to landing officer. HCC on two floors, nine single rooms with integral sanitation and ten-bed ward on ground floor, 15 single rooms and ten-bed ward on first floor. Norwich HCC acts as backup medical facility for Blundeston, Wayland, Highpoint and Hollesley Bay Colony. Visiting psychiatrists 3×sess/wk, monthly asthma and GUC clinics, optician fortnightly, dentist weekly and monthly chiropodist clinic. HCC operates drug detox programme. No blood or urine testing on reception. Holds large number of psychiatric inmates, HMCIP commented the single cells have exposed bars and are not suitable for potentially suicidal inmates—in 1993 there were three suicides in the HCC at Norwich.

GYMNASIUM & SPORTS 1×PEPO, 1×PESO and 4×PEO. Small gymnasium in local prison, converted workshop but put to good use with stage area at one end for weights. Remand Centre gymnasium also in converted workshop, though conditions barely satisfactory. Britannia gymnasium larger than others but no showers. Small remedial room in HCC. Local prison inmates have access each day to PE, Remand Centre inmates do not have enough PE sessions provided, and there is a complete absence of daytime PE in Britannia.

CHAPLAINCY Full time CE chaplain, p/t RC and Methodist ministers. No regular Imam for Muslims. Chapels in each part of the prison. Local prison has large chapel, upper room serves as chapel in Britannia and small chapel in Remand centre. RC Mass in local prison Saturdays, Britannia and Remand Centre Thursday evening. CE Services Sunday all sites.

FOOD Staffing: 1×PO 2×SO, 4×Officer (caterers), and an inmate work party of 15. Three separate kitchens, all meals dine in cell except Britannia and South Wing. No pre-select menu system, two choices at dinner and tea. Good quality food said HMCIP, with good presentation and quantity. NVQ Caterbase course in local prison.

ESTABLISHMENT REPORTS An outstanding feature of Norwich prison is the quality of relationships which exist between staff and prisoners, said HMCIP in a report (published 14 July 1993) of a brief inspection in September 1992. This is born of a tradition in which staff do not unnecessarily confine prisoners in their cells. The relaxed atmosphere within its local prison is replicated in its remand centre and the training prison, Britannia. The special care unit, 'the best of its kind we have seen, has already created a tradition of providing personal attention to difficult prisoners and a flexible approach to their needs'. However there was a shortage of suitable activities for prisoners in the local prison. Its visiting room is 'cramped and shabby', the reception 'cramped, ill-designed' and 'squalid'. The quality of prisoner programmes was 'patchy'. Work training opportunities were 'generally unsatisfactory' and there was a concern among both prisoners and staff over an increase in violence, almost always over drug-dealing.

PRISONERS' COMMENTS **ADULTS:** Lack of occupation, education classes often cancelled at short notice without reason. printing shop should operate a proper course if it wants to attract inmates. New Visitors Centre is good, though the visiting room in the main prison is inadequate, drab and dirty. No hot water boilers to make drinks, lack of privacy in Britannia, particularly for lifers, no washing machines or driers on wings and low pay for those on classes discourages education—FTE inmates are paid less than cleaners.

YOUNG OFFENDERS: Showers are limited to two per week, associations is on a rota basis and consists of playing pool, watching TV or playing table tennis. Wages are low, canteen prices are high and kit is poor both in allowance and quality. No card phones and a lack of information. Education and PE are good, but sessions conflict with each other—choose either but not both.

HM Prison Nottingham

Sherwood, Nottingham. NG5 3AG
Tel: 0602-625022 **Fax:** 0602-603605
Opened: 1891 **CNA:** 245 **Roll:** 258 **Category:** B. Male (mostly Lifers)

i **BACKGROUND** Nottingham prison opened in 1891, three miles from the centre of the city and it has largely retained its Victorian character. The prison comprises 202 single cells in B & C wings, plus 16 places in a Pre-release Hostel and 27 dormitory places in D.wing. The Governor of Nottingham did not reply to our request for up to date information about the prison, and the BoV refused our request for a copy of their latest annual report. HMCIP published their latest inspection report in August 1993.

OFFICIALS

AREA MGR: Joe Mullens
CHAIR BOV: Mr C. Day
GOVERNOR: P. Bennett
MEDICAL:
CHAPLAIN: Rev Fitzgerald
PROBATION: J. Burr
EDUCATION:
LOCAL MP: John Hepple. Lab
STAFFING: 6 Governor grades, 7 Principal Officers, 18 Senior Officers, 93 Officers, including specialist staff, 11 Prison Auxiliaries and 6 Night Patrols.

REGIME *week days*: 0750 unlock/breakfast. 0845 work. 1130 cease labour. 1200 dinner. 1215–1315 lock up. 1330 work. 1700 tea. 1745–2000 association.

week ends: 0750 unlock/breakfast. 0830 cell cleaning. 0900 association. 1200 lunch. 1215 lock up. 1315 association. 1700 tea/association. 2000 lock up.

Out of cell: 12/24hrs weekdays and 12/24hrs at weekends.

ACCOMMODATION & FACILITIES B & C wings form the main accommodation and run parallel to each other. B.wing holds 180 on four landings of (mainly) single cells. C.wing holds 21 on two landings. All cells have integral sanitation. Showers, launderette and cooking facilities on all wings. All meals dine in. Association annexe with two TV rooms and pool table. Prisoner Support Unit provides a range of offence-focused groups. Personal Officer scheme in operation. Routine censorship abolished and card phones installed on all wings. Mail opened and examined outwith the presence of the prisoner and handed out at dinner time.

PRE-RELEASE HOSTEL Former Governor's quarters opposite main gate was converted in 1982 to provide PRES Hostel, holding 16 men in six rooms of various sizes. Lounge, kitchen, launderette and association area. Large garden. Most work provided by local employment agency, though generally work is mundane in nature.

CANTEEN Located in two converted cells on the ground floor of B.wing. Open all day Monday and Tuesday morning. Local purchase facility. Average stock range of about 120 lines. Two fridges hold perishables and soft drinks.

VISITS *How to get there*: Train to Nottingham. Bus (700) from Broad Marsh Rd (v.close to BR Station) to Victoria Centre. Then Bus (15,16,17,19) from Trinity Sq (opp.Victoria Centre) to Perry Road. No Special Transport.
VISITING TIMES: Week Days: 1330–1545 M–F. Saturday: 1330–1545 No PVO's weekends. Sunday: 1330–1545.

NOTES No staffed Visitors Centre. Canteen and Childrens Play Area. Contact prison probation for details of overnight stays. Arrangement can be made for disabled visitors to visit in the welfare dept.

EDUCATION Five f/t and 14 p/t teachers. Seven classrooms: four general purpose, 1 cookery, 1 computing and 1 Open University. Department open 50 weeks of the year, though evening classes only operate for 36 weeks of the year and on just two nights of the week. Department poorly decorated and inadequately heated. Two VTC Radio/Television Servicing courses.

WORKSHOPS Three PSIF workshops employ a total of 105 on interlock machining, knitwear and contract services. Gardens, Works, Kitchen, Yards, Outside Mess, Stores, Domestic, Redbands, FTE, VTC/CIT and Pre-release employ remainder.

DISCIPLINE Segregation unit located beneath C.wing with 8 ordinary cells and one strip cell. Staffed by 1×SO and 2×Officers. Adjudications take place in converted office, HMCIP reports documentation is correctly completed, hearings are in accordance with the official procedure. Awards were appropriate and consistent.

MEDICAL P/t Medical Officer contracted to provide 12 hours per week. HCC staffed by HCSO and 2 HCO, and provides accommodation for a maximum of 8 in-patients. Dentist visits each week and there is a short waiting list. HMCIP found no HIV/AIDS training nor suicide prevention work. Optician once per month. Visiting psychiatrist most weekends.

GYMNASIUM & SPORTS 1×PESO and 2×PEO. Small gymnasium and weights area. Outdoor sportsfield, uncovered/unheated swimming pool and small tarmac exercise yard. Day and evening classes in most sports, including CSLA course.

CHAPLAINCY Full time CE chaplain and p/t RC and Methodist ministers. Main CE Service 0930 Sunday average attendance of 25. RC Mass 0845 Sunday with attendance of one or two. Small Muslim population visited by Imam. Christian Fellowship on Tuesday and Thursday evening. Bible study alternate Monday evenings.

FOOD Staffing: 1×SO and 3×Officer (caterers), and there is a work party of 14. Incentive earnings scheme in operation for kitchen workers. General inmate discontent with the standard of food, no menu system was in place but one was being planned.

ESTABLISHMENT REPORTS There is much to admire in Nottingham prison, said HMCIP in a report (published 5th August 1993) of an inspection in November 1992. Traditionally friendly staff/prisoner relationships in the training prison 'were being used to good purpose, and staff appeared receptive to the need for change'. The change to lifer-only population had prompted plans for the creation of an appropriate regime, such as twelve hours a day out of cell and meals at sensible times, as well as a range of offence-focused training groups.

HM YOI Onley

Rugby, Warwickshire. CV23 8AP
Tel: 0788-522022 **Fax:** 0788-522260
Opened: 1968 **CNA:** 456 **Average Roll:** 400 **Category:** Closed YOI

i **BACKGROUND** Onley Young Offender Institution is located about six miles south of Rugby in Warwickshire, close to the village of Dunchurch. Onley was designed and purpose-built as a penal establishment and opened as a Borstal recall centre in 1968. In 1973 its function changed to that of a training Borstal and, early in 1975, it became a Young Prisoner Centre holding male inmates aged 17–21 years. In 1983 Onley was redesignated a Youth Custody Centre, and in 1988 the Young Offender Institution that it remains today. Neither the Governor nor BoV replied to our requests for information about the Onley, and HMCIP published their latest inspection report on the establishment in June 1991. Since then, there has been no further inspection and, given the lack of co-operation from management at Onley, much of the information available may be out of date. An inspection of the establishment is due shortly and full details will be given when the report is published. In the meantime a brief entry will be given and inmates at Onley are invited to write for a questionnaire to complete about the establishment for the next edition.

OFFICIALS
AREA MGR: A. de Frisching
CHAIR BOV:
GOVERNOR: J. Brooke
MEDICAL:
CHAPLAIN: Rev Darvill
PROBATION:
EDUCATION:
LOCAL MP: Tim Boswell. Con

ACCOMMODATION & FACILITIES All inmates located in single cells with slopping out the order of the day in five of the seven wings.

VISITS *How to get there*: Train to Rugby station. Mon–Sat Geoff Amos Bus Service from BR Station 1330. Return 1515. No Sunday bus. Coach from W.Midlands and Wolverhampton contact local probation office.
VISITING TIMES: Week Days: 1415–1530 M–F No entry after 1500. Saturday: 1400–1600. Sunday: 1400–1600.

NOTES No staffed Visitors Centre. Canteen and Childrens Play Area. Overnight stays in Rugby or Dunchurch, contact prison probation. Baby-changing room and wheelchairs can be accommodated.

ESTABLISHMENT REPORTS In a report (published 20th June 1991) of an inspection in July 1990, HMCIP said that there was much to admire at Onley. It was very well ordered and routines were effectively organised. Staff were happy and trying hard to achieve high standards. The cells were of a reasonable size but only G&H wings had integral sanitation. As in all YOIs there was a degree of bullying but it did not appear to be any more extensive than anywhere else. The inmates at Onley looked dull and anonymous and HMCIP was forced to wonder whether their offending behaviour was being challenged at the establishment. The quality of life for inmates had deteriorated significantly, especially in respect of time out of cell. Community and sporting activities had increased. On officer with 16 years service, however, told Judge Tumim that when he joined the service inmates at Onley had been unlocked from 0645 to 2145 every day of the week, whereas now there was no evening association on any of the wings at weekends at all. HMCIP said this was a decline in standards and as such was unacceptable.

HM Prison Oxford

New Road, Oxford. OX1 1LX
Tel: 0865-721261 **Fax:** 0865-722420
Opened: 1994 **CNA:** 106 **Average Roll:** 68 **Category:** C/D Resettlement Prison

i **BACKGROUND** Like much of the beautiful city that surrounds it, HM Prison Oxford is steeped in history. The oldest prison in the United Kingdom, its tower dates back to 1071 and the room in which John Wesley, the founder of Methodism preached in the mid 18th century is still there for all to see. The prison, known locally as The Castle because of its design, has had a number of roles over the years. For many years it operated as a local prison, then more recently as a satellite of Wormwood Scrubs. It ended its operational role completely in January 1993 when it was closed temporarily. The establishment reopened as a Resettlement Prison in April 1994, specialising in preparing inmates for resettlement on release in the Thames Valley area—essentially, the three counties of Oxfordshire, Buckinghamshire and Berkshire. The prison fosters strong links with the local community, using the resources of the outside probation areas and operates a working out scheme for selected individuals with the co-operation of business and services in the local area. The Manager of Oxford Resettlement Prison Jim Gommersall, and his Deputy Martin Crabbe, provided information about the establishment, and the BoV supplied us with a copy of their latest annual report. HMCIP has not as yet published a report on Oxford as a Resettlement Prison, which operates as a satellite of Bullingdon prison.

OFFICIALS
AREA MGR: A. de Frisching
CHAIR BOV: J. Twynam
MANAGER: Jim Gommersall
MEDICAL: Dr Lloyd
CHAPLAIN: Rev Dupree
PROBATION: Mary Faulk
EDUCATION: Jo Donachie
LOCAL MP: John Patten. Con
STAFFING: total of 36 staff in post.

SELECTION CRITERIA & COMPACTS
Adult male inmates, serving any sentence other than life and with a maximum of two years left to serve. Those with past or present convictions for sexual offences will be excluded, while those with a current or past record for arson, or who are home leave failures, will be considered but their admission will be by negotiation only. Applicants must be fit Labour Grade one or two, but those requiring on-going dental treatment or who have a current medical or psychiatric condition will NOT be accepted. Inmates must be free of major disciplinary reports for six months and wish to settle in the Thames Valley area. All inmates are expected to sign a Compact, which includes their willingness to participate in random urine testing for drug misuse. Inmates must NOT have a history of drug/alcohol problems currently requiring medical treatment, and must not be receiving night sedation or psychotropic medication. Apply in the first instance through your OCA or Wing Manager. Compliance with the terms of the Compact is STRICTLY enforced: you've been warned.

REGIME *week days*: 0715 unlock. 0730 breakfast. 0815 work. 1215 lunch. 1330 work. 1715 cease labour. 1730 tea, evening association. 2045 lock up.

week ends: 0715 unlock. 0730 breakfast. 0815 work/activities. 1215 lunch. 1330 work/activities, town visits for those eligible. 1715 cease labour. 1730 tea, evening association. 2045 lock up.

Out of cell: 13.25/24hrs weekdays and 13.25/24hrs at weekends.

ACCOMMODATION & FACILITIES One main wing which currently accommodates up to 106 people, mainly in single cells but there are some two and three man rooms. Access to night sanitation is by request through the cell bell system. During 1995 the prison intends to move to courtesy locking with free access to sanitation. Cells are roomy but no washing facilities, though there are modern shower and toilet facilities accessible at all times. Three card phones are installed and there are plans for three more. Sentence planning, personal officer scheme, drug counselling if required. Small prison shop on the wing offers the same sort of items and local purchases that would be available in an open prison. Large and comprehensive i/p list but NO TVs.

VISITS *How to get there*: Both the train and bus stations are within a few minutes walk of the prison. No Special Transport.
VISITING TIMES: Week Days: 1400–1700 M–F. Saturday: 1400–1700. Sunday: 1400–1700.

NOTES Staffed Visitors Centre. Canteen and Childrens Play Area. No overnight stay but local B&B. Disabled visitors can be accommodated with prior notice. Visiting hall, and garden for summer visiting.

EDUCATION A division of the North Oxfordshire College in Banbury. Policy of revising and enhancing skills acquired elsewhere with a view to finding work after release. Daytime: industrial cleaning course, computer skills workshop, wood-skills workshop (pm only) and general and basic education (am only). Also offers one-to-one educational guidance, arranges college interviews, adult education and training placements. Evening classes with emphasis on leisure and entertainment.

WORKSHOPS Much community work done for charities etc. Internal work includes kitchen, cleaning, industrial cleaning course, wing laundry, works. Plans for recycling plant, computer recycling, desk top publishing, electrical piece-work, joinery workshop. All inmates prior to discharge are expected to have found themselves a job and be working out five days a week by the time of release. Pay for internal work ranges from £3.50–£10, though piecework in the shops could increase this considerably. Job Club and Work Allocation Board dedicated to serving the combined needs of both the individual and the establishment.

MEDICAL Part time Medical Officer and f/t agency nurse. Treatments only, all other medical cases dealt with at HMP Bullingdon. Report sick to agency nurse at Centre.

GYMNASIUM & SPORTS 1×PEO. Limited gymnasium facilities. One evening of yoga, another of weights and a weekend slot which can be used for a variety of activities is about your lot.

CHAPLAINCY Part time CE chaplain, RC and Methodist ministers. Main services—RC Saturday morning, CE Sunday morning. Other faiths as required.

FOOD Private caterers in post. Food reported as excellent by inmates: 'Better than any other jail I've been in and I've seen the inside of 16'.

MANAGER'S COMMENTS We aim to increase our capacity by some 25% within the next twelve months, but will ensure that this is done gradually and with the necessary extra facilities.

PRISONERS' COMMENTS Wing meeting every week in which problems are usually resolved takes place of formal R/C system. Accommodation is average to very good, canteen is very small, though there are weekly town shopping trips. Visiting hall and garden for summer visits is good, though the wages and work opportunities are quite poor due to budget restrictions. Medical care is very basic. Adjudications are very fair, though the rules are strictly enforced. Staff here are not vindictive, though if you're going to behave in that way that gets you placed on report you shouldn't be thinking about coming to Oxford anyway.

HM Prison Parkhurst

Newport, Isle of Wight. PO30 5NX
Tel: 0983-523855 **Fax:** 0983-524861 Main Prison 0983-822540 Hospital
Opened: 1838 **CNA:** 286 **Average Roll:** 205 **Category:** Male Dispersal + SSB

i **BACKGROUND** Parkhurst prison, situated close to Newport on the Isle of Wight, started life as a Military Hospital in 1805. In 1835 a Select Committee report revealed the appalling conditions experienced by young convicts awaiting transportation in the hulks moored off Portsmouth—one of whom was just six and a half years old. The Parkhurst Prison Act was passed in August 1838, allowing the Hospital to be transformed into a prison and, on Boxing Day 1838, the first draft of boys from the hulk 'York' moored at Portsmouth moved in. During the next 30 years, in what was perhaps the CIT Bricklaying Course of its day, the boys dug the clay, baked the bricks and built a new cell block (C Wing) which remains in use today and is a tribute to their hard work. In 1863 Parkhurst became a female prison, but in 1869 it was again taken over by male prisoners and a new block (A&D Wings) opened in 1886. In 1968 Parkhurst became one of the first dispersal prisons for maximum security prisoners. It contains a Special Security Block and a hospital fully equipped with surgical theatres. Neither the Governor nor BoV at Parkhurst replied to our requests for information, and HMCIP published their latest inspection report in June 1992.

OFFICIALS
AREA MGR: Peter Kitteridge
CHAIR BOV:
GOVERNOR: D.M. Morrison
MEDICAL:

CHAPLAIN: Rev Anderson
PROBATION: Dudley Delannoy
EDUCATION:
LOCAL MP: Barry Field. Con
STAFFING: 367 staff in unified grades.

REGIME *week days*: 0800 unlock, breakfast. 0845 work. 1045–1145 exercise. 1200 lunch. 1230 lock up. 1330 unlock. 1350 work. 1630 tea. 1700 lock up. 1800–2100 association. Summer months: outside compound, Tues, Wed, Thurs 1800–2000, and exercise changes to 1530–1630.

week ends: 0800 unlock, breakfast. 0845 random cell search routine. 0900 sick parade. 0930 exercise. 1030 CE Service (Sun). 1115 exercise cease. 1145 lunch. 1230 lock up. 1330 association. 1630 tea. 1700 lock up. 1800–2100 association.

Out of cell: 12/24hrs weekdays and 12/24hrs at weekends.

ACCOMMODATION & FACILITIES
B.Wing is the main accommodation block with a CNA of 120. C.Wing (Special Unit) is therapeutic wing with a CNA of 20. M.Wing has a CNA of 40 and is situated within C.Wing. Single cells, integral sanitation and showers on each landing. Cooking facilities on all wings. Comprehensive i/p list, including caged birds. No sentence planning. SWIP scheme in operation. All Category A correspondence is censored. Other correspondence is subject to censoring where there is reason to believe the contents require it. Card phones in all wings. All calls recorded and Category A calls, which have to be booked in advance, are additionally monitored throughout their duration.

SPECIAL SECURITY BLOCK (SSB)
Opened in 1966 in response to the escapes of Charlie Wilson from Birmingham and Ronnie Biggs from Wandsworth. The SSB was intended to prevent escapes by those judged to present a special risk to national security or public safety, complements a second unit at Leicester. Less than a dozen inmates held in the unit with high staff-inmate ratios. Relaxed regime, large outdoor exercise/sports yard and separate visiting facilities. Allocation by Headquarters.

C.WING SPECIAL UNIT The unit first opened in 1970 to cater for difficult inmates in a therapeutic environment, it closed in 1979 as a result of a riot in the prison. The unit reopened in 1986 and is staffed by HCPO, HCSO, 2×HCO and 28 discipline staff. Relaxed regime with 12 hours per day out of cell. Workshop. Very rare for recourse to disciplinary reports. All staff volunteers.

CANTEEN Located in same building as library, education and kitchen. Wide variety of stock and the needs of ethnic minorities are catered for. Local purchase facility. Large freezer permits sale of meat and veg for cooking on the wings. Limited opening hours.

VISITS *How to get there*: Train to Portsmouth or Southampton, then ferry to Ryde or Cowes respectively. Hovercraft from Southsea to Ryde takes 10 mins. Bus (1,1A) from Ryde Esplanade to Parkhurst. From Cowes bus 1 or 1A to prison gate. Special Transport: Every Sunday ABBA Coaches leaves Goldsmiths College, New Cross, at 0900. Adults £17, children £9—inclusive of ferry fares. Booking in advance crucial: 081 859 1808/8708 Mr O'Toole.
VISITING TIMES: Week Days: 1015–1115 & 1400–1600 M–F. Saturday: 1015–1115 & 1400–1600. Sunday: 1015–1115 & 1400–1600.

NOTES New visits facility 1991, though no staffed Visitors Centre. Canteen and Childrens Play Area (w/e 1400–1600 only). Overnight stay contact prison probation for details of local families centre. Visitors should expect to be searched on arrival: though this practice was condemned by HMCIP who felt that blanket searching of visitors was only justified for SSB visitors. Easy access for disabled, except for High Risk Cat A visits.

EDUCATION Housed in barely adequate accommodation and a new building is planned. Open 43 weeks of the year, 24 places on FTE and a waiting list usually a dozen. Business studies, basic skills, general education, OU. Evening classes Mon–Thurs.

WORKSHOPS VTC/CIT Welding, Painting & Decorating, Information Technology, Occupational Therapy. Three PSIF workshops. Textile (much resented) making cooks whites. Light assembly and laundry. Usual cleaners, orderlies, kitchen, works and gardens.

DISCIPLINE Adjudication room, split down the middle by a steel grille, was unacceptable said HMCIP: 'In our view the arrangements for adjudications at Parkhurst were not conducive to a relaxed and just inquiry'. Awards are 'severe'. Segregation unit end of B.Wing with 14 punishment cells on the ground floor and 19 Rule 43 cells on the first floor.

MEDICAL Principal Medical Officer, 1×SMO, 3×MO. Purpose-built and well equipped surgical 3-theatre complex. Two surgical wards, E2 & E3. Two further wards: F2 for the 'tight control of deranged inmates', and F3 which offers a more relaxed regime. Drug Testing Unit in pharmacy: 'Urine tests of inmates considered by the Medical Officer to have some drug related symptoms, showed approximately 40% positive results'. Dentist visits weekly and optician once per month.

GYMNASIUM & SPORTS New gymnasium 1992, good facilities for all indoor sports. Good changing and showering facilities. Weights, basketball, volleyball, football. Programme of day and evening classes seven days a week.

CHAPLAINCY Full time CE chaplain and p/t RC and Methodist ministers. Other faiths visited regularly by appropriate minister. Main CE Service Sunday 0900, RC Mass Sunday 1030.

FOOD Staffing: 1×PO, 2×SO and 4×Officer (caterers), and there is a work party of 12 who each have one full day off per week. Pre-select menu system operates a week in advance. Four choices at dinner. Has a history of discontent: an inmate was murdered in the kitchen in 1986, and a black prisoner successfully brought a case against the prison authorities in 1988 having been denied a job in the Parkhurst kitchen because he was black.

ESTABLISHMENT REPORTS In a report (published June 1992) of an inspection in June 1991, Judge Stephen Tumim, HMCIP, said that although Parkhurst had been a difficult prison to get into focus, he was favourably impressed by the atmosphere despite a major refurbishment programme which had just started. The staff/inmate relationship at Parkhurst was very good, had been fostered over many years, and was a permanent and valuable feature. Lack of internal facilities was compensated by staff allowing as much use of external facilities as possible. HMCIP was 'heartened' to note the plans to convert the wings into smaller self-contained units of 60 or 70 men.

HM Prison Pentonville

Caledonian Road, London N7 8TT
Tel: 071-607-5353 **Fax:** 071-700-0244
Opened: 1844 **CNA:** 695 **Average Roll:** 721 **Category:** Male Local

i **BACKGROUND** Pentonville prison, the prototype for radial design where wings sprout from a Centre likes spokes from a wheel, was designed by Major Jebb—after whom the avenue on which Brixton prison stands was named. The prison was completed 150 years ago and has remained in use ever since as a local prison with its original perimeter wall. Though much in-filling of the site has taken place over the years, with buildings being either erected or demolished, the radial cell blocks remain much as they were when the prison first opened its gates in June 1844. The Governor did not reply to our request for information about Pentonville. The prison's pro-active and highly respected BoV kindly supplied a copy of their latest annual report, and HMCIP published their latest inspection report on Pentonville in March 1994: both disclosed serious shortcomings.

OFFICIALS
AREA MGR: Amy Edwards
CHAIR BOV: Annie Anderson
GOVERNOR: W.J. Abbott
MEDICAL:
CHAPLAIN: Rev Collins
PROBATION: Brenda Ball
EDUCATION:
LOCAL MP: Chris Smith. Lab
STAFFING: 14 Governor grades, 20 Principal Officers, 44 Senior Officers and 302 Officers, including specialist staff.

REGIME *week days*: 0745 unlock/breakfast. 0900 work. 1145 dinner. 1330 work. 1615 cease labour. 1715 tea. 1730–2030 association by rota.

week ends: 0745 unlock/breakfast. 0900 association by rota. 1215 dinner. 1400 association. 1700 tea. No weekend evening association.

Out of cell: Pentonville has a multi-faceted regime in which time out of cell depends on remand/convicted status and location in prison: most inmates spend about 5/24hrs OOC.

ACCOMMODATION & FACILITIES Four main wings: A,B,C,D. Three pseudo wings: E wing derived from A.wing, F&R wings derived from C.wing, which reopened in 1993 after major refurbishment. B.wing being refurbished, A/E wings still to be refurbished. Cellular accommodation generally clean and tidy, toilets and showers available on wings, no hot water boilers for hot drinks, card phones in each wing but no acoustic hoods. Two former workshops converted to well equipped association areas, one remand the other convicted use, each with multi-gym facilities.

CANTEEN Separate canteens for remand and convicted. Remand canteen in D.wing association area. Convicted canteen in C.wing. Limited range of stock, no local purchase facility.

VISITS *How to get there*: Train to Kings Cross, tube to Caledonian Rd. Buses 14,17,45,168a,221,259 to prison. No Special Transport.
VISITING TIMES: Week Days: 0915–1030 M–F + 1330–1530 Mon & Wed.
Saturday: 0915–1030 (Surnames A–J), 1315–1445 (K–Z). Sunday: 1330–1445 Con only. Evenings: 1815–2015 Mon & Wed (Con) 1845–2015 Tue & Thu (Rem).

NOTES No Convicted visits Monday, Wednesday or Saturday. No Remand visits Sunday. **All visits have to be booked in advance by phoning 'visits booking clerk' at Pentonville.** No staffed Visitors Centre. On Wednesday morning, visits end at 10.15. No Childrens Play Area. Canteen in visiting room.

EDUCATION Service contracted out to Kingsway College. Operates from two main sites next to C and D wings. Open for an impressive 52 weeks of the year, with a 42 week evening programme: no pay for attendance at education classes by remand inmates. Spacious library with plenty of seating and 5,000 books.

WORKSHOPS No VTC/CIT courses. Work for remands limited to cleaning, orderlies and education. Textile workshop for convicted, closed Wed afternoons. Wages average £6 for employed, £2.50 UB40. Poor work opportunities.

DISCIPLINE Segregation Unit located on C1, with 13 single cells and three strip cells. Very limited regime though little punishment-use made of seg. Adjudications fairly conducted, total of 564 adjudications in the six months prior to the inspection, average of four per day. Reports to Seg Unit morning of adjudication. In 1991 an inmate died in the Segregation Unit while subject to Control and Restraint techniques: inquest decided he had been 'unlawfully killed', though the CPS decided there was insufficient evidence to prosecute. Between 1st Jan & 20th Sept 1993, ratchet handcuffs used 17 times in taking inmates to the Seg Unit: C&R wrist/head locks applied 49 times and, on a further 20 occasions, both C&R and ratchet handcuffs were applied in the same period.

VPU Inmates on Rule 43 (OP) are located in the segregation unit due to a lack of alternative accommodation, and in a regime that is unsuitable and at best impoverished.

IMMIGRATION DETAINEES An average of 60 detainees are held at Pentonville and the BoV have made representations to the Home Office about their plight for several years without any effect. Immigration Department holds regular surgeries at Pentonville, but for many the regime is austere and unwarranted given they have not committed any criminal offence. BoV comment such inmates 'Put huge demands on time and emotions of staff and they frequently display suicidal tendencies'.

MEDICAL Full time SMO, 4×f/t MO's, 1×HCPO, 4×HCSO, 16×HCO and 14×Nurses. In August 1993 HCC moved from the totally unsuitable prison hospital to 'temporary' accommodation on two landings of the newly refurbished R.wing. Plans to build a new hospital have been deferred and this temporary location could become permanent without vigilance. R.wing provides improved regime for inpatients with more time out of cell, therapy and counselling, association on top landing and access to card phones. Segregation Unit used as HCC overspill! Dentist weekly, optician monthly, and other visiting specialists as necessary.

GYMNASIUM & SPORTS For a local prison Pentonville has quite good indoor PE facilities. Large gymnasium and nearby weights room with multi-gyms in each association room. PE programme Mon–Fri with Sports & Games Officers supervising weekend activities. Each inmate can attend a weights and a gym session each week. Sessions include circuit training, volleyball, CSLA, basketball and indoor football. Evening classes for squad training. No outdoor facilities.

CHAPLAINCY Full time CE chaplain and RC priest, p/t Methodist minister. Imam visits regularly for Muslims though no multi-faith room despite large ethnic population. Pool of 12 Prison Visitors. CE Service and RC Mass Sun 0915. Holy Communion for remand inmates Wed 0845 and group meetings 1800. Bible class Thurs and Fri 1800. Choir practice and bible study Sat.

FOOD Staffing: 1×G5, 1×PO, 2×SO, 7×Officer (caterers), and an inmate work party of 30. Survey of kitchen in 1993 by local EHO identified 8 breaches of food hygiene regulations, 6 in the kitchen, 2 in the wing serveries: refurbishment now underway. Short three-week menu cycle, no pre-select menu. Without exception the food is described by inmates as 'awful' and all meals dine in cell. Continental breakfast has proved successful.

ESTABLISHMENT REPORTS 'Despite the bleak and spartan surroundings' in which prison officers and prisoners at this local prison worked and lived, the inspectors were impressed by their general cheerfulness. The report (published 22nd March 1994) of an inspection in July 1993 said that many of the prisoners were prepared to accept the limitations of the regime because of the prison's proximity to their homes. They also seemed to have a genuine appreciation of the efforts of the Governor and his staff to make improvements to their quality of life.

BoV 1993/4 Annual Report: There has been positive progress at Pentonville in the last twelve months, however we continue to be concerned at the immigration detainee population who we feel should not be in an inner city prison, but in a properly equipped detention centre with hospital facilities. We are anxious that building works are completed in their entirety and would like to see an increase in useful activity for all inmates. A response from the Secretary of State is requested on the following major concerns. Immigration detainees should be moved to proper accommodation; a new purpose-built Health Care Centre should be built, refurbished cells should be designed in such a way that suicide and self-harm are not possible. Pay and private cash for inmates should be computerised, cell lighting should be improved, staff facilities require improvement and the complete building programme should be carried out.

PRISONERS' COMMENTS Atmosphere relaxed with good inmates/staff relationships. Limited canteen with no fruit and restricted private cash use. Visits room very spartan, all visits have to be booked in advance by visitor: new Visits Committee does not include inmate representatives! Poor dental services with huge waiting list, remand prisoners cannot use the library, shortage of phones and those installed have no acoustic hoods fitted. There is no personal officer scheme and some staff mask racial remarks in humour. Immigration detainees lack contact with family, are unaccustomed to the food and cannot cook their own. Home Office delays in dealing with cases creates injustice, Limited showers offend against religious beliefs, Little Embassy contact. Foreign language dictionaries available only in the library, which some detainees cannot attend, no reference books on immigration matters and there are difficulties in using the telephone. Low wages restrict contact with home, no-one in the prison is really interested in detainees' position or plight. HMCIP did not agree, but said it was true no-one knew what to do with these inmates who have committed no crimes at all].

HM YOI Portland

Easton, Portland, Dorset. DT5 1DL
Tel: 0305-820301 **Fax:** 0305-823718
Opened: 1848 **CNA:** 424 **Average Roll:** 380 **Category:** Closed YOI

i **BACKGROUND** Standing high above the English Channel on the island of Portland, the original prison had been constructed in the 1840s and took its first prisoners in 1848. Extensive rebuilding took place in 1910 followed by the acquisition of land and buildings (now demolished) from the Admiralty, which doubled the size of the establishment. Two additional cell blocks were added in 1968 and 1974, a new administration block, kitchen, dining block, boiler house and laundry have been major recent additions to the site. In 1921 Portland changed from convict prison to a Borstal, remaining in that role until 1983 when it became a Youth Custody Centre and, in 1988, it became the Young Offender Institution which it remains today. Neither the Governor nor BoV replied to our requests for information about the Institution, and HMCIP published their latest inspection report on Portland in April 1993.

OFFICIALS
AREA MGR: John May
CHAIR BOV:
GOVERNOR: D. Brisco
MEDICAL:
CHAPLAIN: Rev Steer
PROBATION: S. Christie
EDUCATION:
LOCAL MP: Ian Bruce. Con
STAFFING: 6 Governor grades, 11 Principal Officers, 26 Senior Officers and 119 Officers, including specialist staff.

REGIME *week days*: 0730 unlock. 0800 breakfast. 0900 work. 1200 dinner. 1330 work. 1615 cease labour. 1630 tea. 1800-2000 association. No association Wednesday evening.

week ends: 0730 unlock. 0800 breakfast. 0900 association. 1130 dinner. 1400 association. 1545 tea. No weekend evening association or fixed exercise times.

Out of cell: 10/24hrs weekdays and 8/24hrs at weekends.

ACCOMMODATION & FACILITIES Seven House blocks: Benbow (CNA 72), Raleigh (80), Drake (74), Nelson (76), Grenville (72), Rodney (72), Hardy (72). Total of 502 single cells and eight double cells. Partial installation of electronic unlocking to provide access to night san. Each House has association rooms on the ground floor and accommodation on three landings above. Facilities generally adequate, card phone in each House. Personal officer scheme, sentence planning, drug counselling.

CANTEEN Extremely poor canteen facilities. Each House has its own canteen in an empty cell, the 60-70 items of stock carried was among the lowest in the country. No local purchase facility, a basic skeletal service which Portland's management have ignored for far too long and must now address.

VISITS *How to get there*: Train to Weymouth. Bus weekdays and Sat from Kings Statue, Service 'J' at 1320 to YOI gate. Sunday 12.32,1.32,2.33 to Grave Corner and then 1 mile walk. Special Transport: Coaches from W.Glam, S.Glam, Gwent, Avon, Plymouth, Portsmouth & Southampton—**Tel:** 0705 871441.
VISITING TIMES: Week Days: 1400–1545 Wednesday only. Saturday: 1330–1545. Sunday: 1330–1545.

NOTES No staffed Visitors Centre despite inmates from a wide variety of areas. Canteen and Childrens Play Area in visiting room. For overnight stays, please contact: 0305-204797. To book special transport, please contact local probation office. Disabled access with advance notice. Inmates complain that the tables in the visiting room are at ankle height and make visiting uncomfortable.

EDUCATION Located in a self-contained block next to Drake, Benbow and Raleigh Houses, the education centre has poor conditions and the programme has five main components: induction course; special needs; further education; vocational training and evening classes. Basic education very good with validated courses being followed. Evening classes restricted to just one night per week. Library has high volume of visits from inmates, refurbishment is needed, open every weekday and Wednesday evening. Inmates allowed four books, with special orders catered for.

WORKSHOPS VTC/CIT courses: Bricklaying, General Construction, Painting & Decorating, Plastering, Carpentry, Mechanical Engineering, Motor Mechanics, Welding, and an Industrial Cleaning course which is particularly popular. Laundry, woodwork shop (making pallets), farm & gardens, kitchen, works, cleaners, orderlies and education. Wages average £6.50, with around 40 each day UB40 (£2.50).

DISCIPLINE Segregation Unit, E.Hall, located in a separate Victorian cell block close to the education block. E.Hall operates a robust regime, HMCIP describes a 'no nonsense' approach to both the operation of E.Hall and adjudications: of which there were 969 in the twelve months before the inspection, an increase of 239 on the previous year. A total of 901 had been found proved, excessive use of loss of remission said HMCIP with 65% receiving this award, 17% received loss of association, 9% stoppage of earnings and 2% a caution—7% had been dismissed. The frequent use of strip cells, application of C&R techniques and the robust 'no nonsense' approach does not mask official bullying.

MEDICAL Full time Medical Officer, 1×HCSO, 3×HCO. Small HCC with six furnished rooms with integral sanitation and nine-bed ward. Inpatient regime requires improvement with association often cancelled through shortages of staff. No drug, alcohol, substance group. Three dental sessions per week with waiting list of 7–14 days. Optician visits monthly. All new receptions seen by MO, have blood and urine tested. Conditions for inmates at risk of self harm require improvement, no observation ward and such inmates are often located in E.Hall overnight. Portland does not operate a Sex Offender Treatment programme, though at any one time the establishment holds between 30 and 45 sex offenders. Anger management courses operated four time per year and six-week course in parenting.

GYMNASIUM & SPORTS 1×PEPO 1×PESO and 4×PEO. Two gymnasiums, both small, unheated open-air swimming pool, two large tarmac areas, small weights room and two large sports fields in former quarries. All inmates receive two hours PE per week based on occupation. Evening programme Mon, Tues, Thurs 1800–2000. weekend PE 0930(1030 Sun)–1130, 1345–1545 Sat & Sun. The swimming pool should be covered as at Maidstone.

CHAPLAINCY Full time CE chaplain, p/t RC and Methodist ministers. CE Service 0915 Sunday. RC Mass 0915 Saturday. Muslim inmates meet monthly with their Imam, a multi-faith room exists in the chapel. Bible class Mon. Prison Visitors on Wednesday.

FOOD Staffing: 1×PO, 1×SO, 4×Officer (caterers), and an inmate work party of 11. Large purpose-built dining rooms very close to the kitchen not used and all meals dine in cell. No preselect menu system and HMCIP, who sampled the food, found the cooked potatoes left much to be desired.

ESTABLISHMENT REPORTS In a report (published 21st April 1993) of an inspection in July 1992, HMCIP said that there were examples of excellent work being carried out at Portland. These included the work of the induction unit in providing information, setting standards and developing sentence plans. The safe and healthy environment that had been created provided a secure base on which to develop throughcare and sentence planning. There was a need to transfer to suitable NHS hospitals those patients who were mentally ill. There was also a need to increase psychiatric and psychological services and matters relating to the supply of drugs. A total of 142 formal recommendations were made by HMCIP, ranging from expansion of educational provision to giving consideration to the establishment of a sex offender treatment programme. Portland or its regime was not oppressive or over-restrictive.

PRISONERS' COMMENTS Portland needs more staff, when all staff are duty there is evening association, but bed-watches in local hospitals result in evening association being cancelled in some Houses. Kit supply is a real problem, particularly jeans, but also wide-fitting shoes—the only items of personal clothing allowed are underpants! House canteens very poor, very small stock, no variation, no local purchase facility, and 310 per month private cash spends. Education is very good, work is average, medical services really quite bad, the staff just don't believe what you tell them; your leg would have to fall off before they took any notice: an absolute disgrace. Requests and complaints depend on what is being complained about, some can take ages to be answered. Adjudications are so unfair, almost always found guilty no matter what evidence is given, punishments are very heavy-handed, the Governor just goes through the motions. Food is OK, but variation leaves a lot to be desired, its boiled spuds every day and cabbage with everything. Gym and sports facilities are excellent with an outdoor swimming pool, and religious services are very good. Mail is not a problem, letters are opened in front of you. Phones are not so good, only two phone cards a week which is OK if you're phoning local, but when you live in Liverpool its hardly gives time to say anything.

HMP & YOI Prescoed

Coed-y-Paen, Pontypool, Gwent. NP5 1XP
Tel: 0291-672231 **Fax:** 0291-673800
Opened: 1939 **CNA:** 120 **Average Roll:** 71 **Category:** Open Adult Male & YOI

i **BACKGROUND** Prescoed is a purpose-built hutted camp erected by inmate labour and opened in 1939 as an open Borstal. Prescoed continued as a Borstal until 1964 when it became a Detention Centre. In 1983 it became an open Youth Custody Centre, changing to a open Young Offender Institution in 1988. It is a satellite of HMP Usk a short distance away. Prescoed now takes adult male inmates in addition to young offenders. Neither the Governor nor BoV replied to our requests for information and HMCIP published their latest report on Prescoed in August 1993.

OFFICIALS
AREA MGR: John Wilkinson
CHAIR BOV:
GOVERNOR: N.J. Evans
MEDICAL:
CHAPLAIN: Rev Mark John
PROBATION: Monica Sabor
EDUCATION:
LOCAL MP: Roger Evans. Con
STAFFING: 5 Governor grades, 7 Principal Officers, 14 Senior Officers and 78 Officers, including specialist staff and those at Usk.

REGIME *week days*: 0730 roll check, breakfast. 0900 work. 1215 lunch. 1330 work. 1615 cease labour. 1700 tea. 1730–2030 association.

week ends: 0730 roll check, breakfast. 0900 association. 1215 lunch. 1400 association. 1700 tea. 1730–2030 association.

Out of cell: 24/24hrs weekdays and 24/24hrs at weekends.

ACCOMMODATION & FACILITIES Six detached living units each with 20 single rooms. Units are modern, purpose-built compare favourably with student accommodation on a campus according to HMCIP. Access to sanitation 24 hours. Association areas in buildings known as Ancillary 1 & 2: the former for young offenders, the second for adults. Sentence planning, card phones, personal officer scheme, drug counselling. Bullying not as extensive at Prescoed as in other YOIs, though still seen as a potentially serious problem.

CANTEEN A small area close to the dining room serves as the canteen, comprising a counter and some racking secured by a shutter. Fewer than 100 lines of stock carried, largely consisting of sweets, biscuits and tobacco. Open Thursdays for both earnings and private cash.

REQUESTS & COMPLAINTS Only seven formal RC forms submitted by inmates at Prescoed in the 12 months prior to the inspection, none of them requiring confidential access. Most concerned loss of property and were dealt with inside the time targets.

VISITS *How to get there*: Train to Newport, Gwent. No bus service to Usk. Free bus service from HMP Usk to HMYOI Prescoed—50p at weekends.
VISITING TIMES: Week Days: No visiting. Saturday: 1330–1530. Sunday: 1330–1530.

NOTES No staffed Visitors Centre or Childrens Play Area. Canteen available. Local B&B. Wheelchair access. Visits take place in carpeted area of dining hall. Two visits every 28 days, and average of 35 visits each weekend. All inmates rubbed down after visit, and about 10% strip searched. Town visits allowed within three months of release.

EDUCATION Poor quality education building but surprisingly extensive. Main building with classrooms, computer room, discussion/video room. Second unit contains library, training kitchen and craft room. A third building houses the art room, woodwork room and motor vehicle room. Broad range of education covered, open learning courses.

WORKSHOPS Farm party main employer at Prescoed which has a 420 acre pig and dairy farm a short distance from the establishment. Part time education and domestic work accounts for all other employment opportunities at Prescoed. Successful Job Club in operation.

DISCIPLINE High number of adjudications, attributable to the immaturity of the young offenders and the temptations of an open regime, HMCIP examined the records and found them to be in order with the frequent use of suspended awards.

MEDICAL Part time Medical Officer, HCSO and HCO cover both establishments. Average of 7 report sick each day dealt with by HCO or MO. Dental session weekly seeing about 10 inmates each time. Optician once per month.

GYMNASIUM & SPORTS 1×PEPO, 1×PESO and 2×PEO serve both Usk and Prescoed. Statutory requirement of two hours PE per week to young offenders being met by activities based programme. Gym located in a Nissen hut which limits many activities, though soccer and rugby teams play both home and away matches.

CHAPLAINCY Part time CE chaplain, RC and Methodist ministers serve both Prescoed and Usk. Attractive chapels but no permanent minority faith room, Imam happy to visit from Cardiff for Muslim inmates when necessary. Main services Sunday morning and weekly programme of religious groups and meetings.

FOOD Staffing: 1×SO, 1×Officer (Caterers), 1×Prison Auxiliary, operate the kitchens at both Prescoed and Usk. No pre-select menu system in operation, nor fixed menu cycle. Continental breakfast served three days a week, and tea is the main meal of the day.

ESTABLISHMENT REPORTS In a report (published 5th August 1993) of an inspection in January 1993, HMCIP said that both Prescoed and Usk had a historical link which no longer existed. Both establishments were well run. Staff were very supportive of the Sex Offender Treatment Programme at HMP Usk and HMCIP disagreed with the suggestion that all inmates at Usk should be in the sex offenders programme. The population at Prescoed had dropped so low that the establishment was hardly financially viable and thought should be given to turning it into an open establishment towards which inmates from Usk could progress.Prescoed was a valuable asset and should not be lost.

HM Prison Preston

2 Ribbleton Lane, Preston. PR1 5AB
Tel: 0772-57734 **Fax:** 0772-556643
Opened: 1790 **CNA:** 324 **Average Roll:** 413 **Category:** Male Local & Remand Centre

i **BACKGROUND** Preston prison is a local prison situated near the city centre. It was originally built in 1790. The prison was rebuilt and substantially enlarged in mid-Victorian times. since that date the smaller buildings housing ancillary activities have been replaced and altered as and when required. The radial cellular block remains as it was when first built. The prison has remained in continuous use since 1790, except for the period 1931–9 when it was closed. it reopened in 1939, first as a civil defence centre, then as Naval Detention Quarters until 1945. Preston had been a training prison for C Category inmates until 1990 when it assumed its current local prison role. Preston has become renowned for its bitter industrial relations, and the consequent result that reforms long since the norm at other establishments are only now getting through the gate at Preston. The Governor of the prison, Ray Doughty, did not complete the questionnaire we sent to him and the BoV failed to reply to our request for a copy of their latest annual report. HMCIP published their latest inspection report on Preston in July 1994.

OFFICIALS
AREA MGR: Ian Lockwood
CHAIR BOV:
GOVERNOR: Ray Doughty
MEDICAL:
CHAPLAIN: Rev Spratt
PROBATION: Ms Lesley Thompson
EDUCATION:
LOCAL MP: Audrey Wise. Lab
STAFFING: 7 Governor grades, 307 staff in post.

REGIME *week days*: 0745 unlock, breakfast, treatments. 0830 work. 0845 remands to work (ABD Wings). 0900 special visits, sick parade, remand exercise (AB Wings). 1015 remand exercise D.wing. 1110 remand dinner. 1125 remand shop 4 cease labour, dinner. 1145 Rule 43(OP) and S1 dinner. 1215 roll check. 1315 visits commence. 1330 remands to shop 4 (ABD Wings), convicted exercise, labour, education (C.wing & A4). 1340 remand visits commence. 1345 ABD Wings association, video. 1350 punishment exercise. 1455 Rule 43(OP) exercise. 1530 Visits (convicted and R.43) cease. 1600 remand tea. 1615 cease labour, tea. 1700 roll check. 1730 gymnasium. 1745 unlock, classes. 1945 classes, chapel cease. 2000 cease association, lock up.

week ends: As above, but no: work, remand visits, education or evening association.

Out of cell: 6/24hrs weekdays and 4/24hrs at weekends.

ACCOMMODATION & FACILITIES
Four normal location living units, radiating from a Centre, A,B,C,D wings. A&B house remands, C.wing holds the convicted population and D.wings held remand inmates mainly from Manchester. Almost all cells are double occupancy, and only B.wing has integral sanitation—though no privacy screens. Cells v.small, HMCIP felt all B.wing cells were unsuitable for two prisoners and integral sanitation. Cells on A,C,D wings poorly decorated, few have picture boards, floors are cracked and some windows will not shut and are so small that the cells are perpetually gloomy said Judge Tumim. Three phones on each wing, but in noisy locations and some have no hoods. Central bath-house, no laundry facilities on wings. Sentence planning, personal officer scheme, VPU, Bail Information Scheme.

CANTEEN Open twice per week. Situated between the two gates that lead to A.wing, the rooms are small and badly designed. Despite this a reasonable range of stock is held including greeting cards and ethnic minority cosmetics. No local purchase facility.

VISITS *How to get there*: Train to Preston then walk half mile to prison, or bus from BR to bus station and walk quarter mile to prison. No Special Transport.
VISITING TIMES: Week Days: 1330–1600 M–F. Saturday: 1330–1600. Sunday: 1330–1515 No Rem visits.

NOTES Visitors Centre, but dispute with POA has prevented it being manned. Canteen and Childrens Play Area for convicted only. B&B available in Preston, contact prison probation. Wheelchair access to convicted visits only. No visits Sunday for remand prisoners.

EDUCATION Contracted out to Blackpool and Fylde College. Three main grade lecturers and a panel of 14 p/t teachers. VTC course for remands in multi-skills (electrical and plumbing skills). 5 days of the week education allocated to remands, 2.5 days convicted.

WORKSHOPS Two workshops: Heavy textiles (3A Shop, convicted) and Light textiles (4 Shop, remands). Operating for 26.15 hours per week. No refreshment facilities and no tea-break, pay ranges from £6.60–£8.15. Kitchen (18 places), education (70p per session).

DISCIPLINE Segregation unit located on S1 landing (sub-basement of C.wing), and operated by 1×SO and 6×Officers. Ten ordinary cells, 2 strips, 2 reinforced strips (E.List etc) and a double cell used for witnesses at adjudications. 1993: Strips used 112 times, no recorded use of body belt, 156 requests for Rule 43(OP) and 27 placed on GOAD. Average of five adjudications per day, many petty reports.

MEDICAL Senior Medical Officer, f/t MO, p/t MO, 1×HCPO, 2×HCSO, 16×HCO—of whom seven have general, and one has psychiatric, nursing qualifications. Three dental sessions per week (apply through landing officers), chiropodist as required, no physio-therapist, optician once per fortnight, X-rays at local hospital. E.wing (sub-basement of A.wing) used as psychiatric centre, upgraded substantially since inspection in 1991, good atmosphere now and very good inmate/staff relationships, though facilities still did not meet hospital standards, cells are very small and badly lit.

GYMNASIUM & SPORTS 1×PESO and 4×PEO. Described by HMCIP as one of the bright spots of Preston prison, the PE department provides a good service to inmates in every part of the establishment. Old gymnasium with sprung wooden floor and used for indoor ball and racquet games. Old workshop converted into a weight and circuit training area and is well equipped. Time allocated to both HCC patients (3 sess/wk) and inmates in VPU (2 sess/wk). BAWLA training centre. Disabled group use gymnasium facilities Wednesday am. A well organised, well motivated department making a significant contribution to the regime. HIV/AIDS multi-disciplinary team, but virtually no health promotion.

CHAPLAINCY Full time CE chaplain, p/t RC and Methodist ministers. Imam visits weekly. Main CE Service and RC Mass, Sunday morning. Limited activities due to resistance of local branch POA who object to remand inmates taking part in evening activities.

FOOD Staffing: 1×PO, 2×SO, 4×Officer (caterers), and an inmate work party of 18. HMCIP criticised the tea drink ('diesel') which was barely acceptable. No halal meat for Muslims. Six week menu cycle not in operation and a two choice menu system was said to cover inmate needs. The best that could be said for the food at Preston was that it was 'adequate'.

ESTABLISHMENT REPORTS In a report (published 23rd November 1993) of an inspection in July 1993, HMCIP said that with few exceptions, conditions for prisoners at Preston were unsatisfactory. Convicted inmates lodged in dirty cells with nothing more than a bed, mattress and bucket—better cells were available, but the POA had successfully argued for remand use only. Food was bland and some of it less than satisfactory. Although card phones were on all wings, inmates could only use them twice per week and had to book in advance. No attempts made to challenge offending behaviour, only two pairs of socks were allowed each week and slopping out for the majority of Preston inmates would continue for the whole of 1995. Despite these conditions staff gave a professional service to inmates, physical education and chaplaincy departments are worthy of special mention said HMCIP, while OCA and legal aid were thorough and competent in their work. The prison has a history of acrimonious industrial relations with the POA, but the bottom line remains that the conditions and regime at Preston must be improved—by one means, or another.

GOVERNOR'S COMMENTS The Chief Inspectors Report deals with a number of issues on which considerable advances have already been made. We are very much aware of the deficiencies which have dogged Preston. For the first time in recent years, we now have a very real opportunity for improvement. We are committed to resolving the difficulties and taking forward the essential changes. progress has been difficult and at times disappointing. But we will not be deterred from achieving the changes at Preston which are required to improve the regime and physical conditions for prisoners.

PRISONERS' COMMENTS Requests and complaints can take forever to be dealt with and cell bells are rarely answered [HMCIP found that the Cell Bell indicator board, located in a very public place immediately outside the Wing PO's Office, had been unscrewed and the wires wrenched out of the sockets] and the accommodation is a disgrace. There were two toilets for 70 men, the place is in a mess and there is far too much bang up. Each man has only one session of evening association per week and association on a Saturday morning. Health care is poor with a 'Paracetamol Rules OK' approach, and it is not possible to get urgent dental treatment. Food is poor in quality and insufficient in quantity—despite the fact that trays of extra food are thrown away. Some cells are freezing, the gymnasium is good with use six nights a week, but unless we go to the gym we can only have one shower a week.

Inmates in the **VPU** did not feel secure in their surroundings; staff on the whole were good, though other inmates frequently gave them dirty towels when they went to the bath-house. Life in the VPU was extremely boring and too much time locked up. Work and educational opportunities were extremely limited. There were bullying problems when inappropriate inmates were allocated to the VPU. On occasions VPU inmates receive only one slop out per day.

HMRC Pucklechurch

Pucklechurch, Bristol, Avon. BS17 3QJ
Tel: 0272-372606 **Fax:** 0272-372729
Opened: 1967 **CNA:** 56 **Average Roll:** 51 **Category:** Female Closed

i **BACKGROUND** Pucklechurch Remand Centre is situated eight miles north-east of Bristol, on an industrial estate in the village of Pucklechurch five miles off Junction 18 of the M4 motorway. When it was opened in 1967 it had accommodation for 53 males and 31 females, but additional accommodation in 1975 increased the CNA to 103 and 56 respectively. Pucklechurch was used as the National Escort Transfer Centre, where vehicles on the weekly inter-prison transfer run could drop off (usually for lunch) those inmates they had brought, and later collect those they were due to take with them. In April 1990 Pucklechurch was largely burnt to the ground during a serious disturbance later inquired into by Lord Justice Woolf as part of his 'Strangeways' inquiry, and the male population was moved out. Today the establishment holds only female inmates in two wings. Neither the Governor nor BoV replied to our requests for information about Pucklechurch, and HMCIP published their latest inspection report in September 1989. Much of the available information is out of date and, given the lack of co-operation from management/Bov at Pucklechurch, the fact that most of the establishment is closed and the inspection that must shortly be due, brief details only will be given.

OFFICIALS
AREA MGR: John Wilkinson
CHAIR BOV:
GOVERNOR: S.J. Swift
MEDICAL:
CHAPLAIN: Rev Wills
PROBATION: Roger Perry
EDUCATION:
LOCAL MP: John Cope. Con

ACCOMMODATION & FACILITIES
Two wings house female inmates all in single cells with integral sanitation. Good standard of cleanliness.

VISITS *How to get there*: Train to Bristol Parkway then taxi, or train to Temple Meads and bus to Pucklechurch—10 miles. No Special Transport.
VISITING TIMES: *week days*: 1330–1530 M–F. Saturday: 1330–1500. Sunday: No Visits.

NOTES No staffed Visitors Centre, canteen or Childrens Play Area! Overnight stay at Family Centre, Gloucester Road, Bristol (0272-425994). Less crowded during week but small visiting room makes visiting cramped. Nappy-changing and wheelchair access.

HM Prison Ranby

Retford, Notts. DN22 8EU
Tel: 0777-706721 **Fax:** 0777-702691
Opened: 1971 **CNA:** 331 **Average Roll:** 312 **Category:** C. Male

i **BACKGROUND** Ranby prison was an army camp before opening as a prison in 1971. It is a Category C prison for adult males, situated about three miles from Retford in Nottinghamshire and adjacent to Thorp Arch prison with which it is due to amalgamate in April 1995. A Health Care Officer at Ranby pioneered the Care & Support Unit, replacing the strip cell with a tastefully furnished bed-sitting room for inmates who are suicidal, though as neither the Governor nor BoV at Ranby replied to our requests for information about the CSU and prison in general, details of this important development have not been made available. HMCIP published their latest inspection report on Ranby in July 1993.

OFFICIALS

AREA MGR: Joe Mullens
CHAIR BOV:
GOVERNOR: T.J. Williams
MEDICAL:
CHAPLAIN: Rev Hirst
PROBATION: S. Aveyard
EDUCATION:
LOCAL MP: Richard Alexander. Con

REGIME *week days*: 0745 unlock/breakfast. 0845–1145 work. 1200 dinner. 1330–1635 work. 1700 tea. 1800–2030 association.

week ends: 0745 unlock/breakfast. 1000 inspection. 1030 association. 1145 dinner. 1400–1630 association. 1700 tea. 1800–2030 association.

Out of cell: 10/24hrs weekdays and 10/24hrs at weekends.

ACCOMMODATION & FACILITIES

Two main wings: A.wing, a two-storey building with spurred single cell accommodation completed in July 1988, has places for 192 inmates. B.wing consists of a collection of nine old army huts and a PortaKabin complex, with conditions in stark contrast to A.wing. Only recorded or registered mail is opened in the presence of the inmate.

CANTEEN Located in the kitchen/dining room complex, the canteen operates a credit payment system and has a stock of about 120 lines. No canteen committee. Local purchases once per week.

VISITS *How to get there*: Train to Retford from Sheffield. Walk up Queen St to Babworth Road (5 mins) and catch any bus going to Worksop from opposite Catholic Church. Special transport: coaches from Birmingham, Coventry, Chesterfield & Grimsby, contact prison probation.
VISITING TIMES: Week Days: 1400–1600 M–F. Saturday: 1400–1600. Sunday: 1400–1600.

NOTES No staffed Visitors centre or Childrens Play Area. Canteen. VO MUST be taken otherwise strictly 'No Access'. Weekends v.busy. Baby-changing facilities available.

EDUCATION Strong on basic educational skills, 24 inmates on FTE and the same number on p/t courses. Open Learning and OU available. Open five days and three evenings per week.

WORKSHOPS VTC/CIT courses: Bricklaying; General Construction. Wood shop, Plastics and Contract Services shop with poor quality work making potato boxes for the Prison Service.

DISCIPLINE Segregation Unit with ten cells, each with integral sanitation and rectangular wooden blocks in place of a bed. Adjudications running at about 700 a year which is not excessive, but not low either: most were minor and relate to attendance at work, behaviour or attitude in the workshops.

CARE & SUPPORT UNIT Devised by a HCO at Ranby to treat and prevent suicidal crisis in inmates, the CSU replaced the old strip cell, with a bed sitting room and an inmate carer who had been trained after interview by five separate senior managers. HMCIP said that Ranby could be highly influential in developing further strategies for suicide prevention—though unless the prison's management are prepared to inform others about it, the prospects of development appear bleak.

ESTABLISHMENT REPORTS In a report (published 9th July 1993) of an inspection in October 1992, HMCIP said that the physical environment of the establishment had not improved to any great extent since the last inspection in 1989. In 1993, the new kitchen and dining hall will represent a significant improvement, though they will also serve to emphasise the poor quality of some of the inmate living accommodation. Drug taking and bullying emerged as significant and linked problems, the relaxed atmosphere and free movement creating numerous opportunities for drug suppliers to operate. Not all control problems could be attributed to the drug culture however, the mix of inmates by age and sentence length created friction that has the potential to be disruptive. The absence of a Visitors Centre did little to convince inmates that the prison service cared. The outstanding achievement seen at Ranby was the Care & Support Scheme which makes a statement about the underlying philosophy of the establishment.

HM Remand Centre Reading

Forbury Rd, Reading. RG1 3HY
Tel: 0734-587031 **Fax:** 0734-591058
Opened: 1844 **CNA:** 182 **Roll:** 161 **Category:** Male (YO) Remand

i **BACKGROUND** Reading Gaol, situated half a mile from the town centre, opened in 1844. Oscar Wilde was imprisoned at Reading in 1895, the experience of which lead to his later writing his powerful 'Ballad of Reading Gaol'. Of a design familiar from the period, Reading has four wings radiating from the Centre and served as the County Gaol for Berkshire until 1914. In 1946 it was taken back into the prison system and served variously as a Borstal correctional and recall centre and a local prison until September 1992, when it became a Remand Centre for Young Offenders, holding untried and recently convicted inmates. On Boxing Day 1992 the Remand Centre suffered a serious disturbance. The Governor of Reading, John Petherick, supplied up-to-date information about the establishment, though the Reading BoV did not reply to our request for a copy of their annual report. HMCIP published their latest inspection Report on Reading in August 1993.

OFFICIALS
AREA MGR: A. de Frisching
CHAIR BOV: Mr Boulter
GOVERNOR: J. Petherick
MEDICAL: Dr Jackson
CHAPLAIN: Rev Derbyshire
PROBATION: Mrs A. Palk
EDUCATION: Mrs Shaw
LOCAL MP: Gerard Vaughan. Con
STAFFING: 5×Governor grades, 8×PO, 24×SO, 114 Officers including specialist grades.

REGIME *week days*: 0800 unlock/breakfast. 0900 activities. 1145–1345 lunch. 1345 activities. 1630–1830 tea. 1830–2030 association, education, games, groupwork. 2030 lock up.

week ends: 0800 unlock/breakfast. 0900 activities. 1145–1345 dinner. 1345 activities, association, visits. 1630–1830 tea. 1830–2030 association, education, games, groupwork. 2030 lock up.

Out of cell: 9.4/24hrs weekdays and 8.1/24hrs at weekends.

ACCOMMODATION & FACILITIES Main accommodation in three wings (A=74,B=33,C=63) which have double and single accommodation with integral sanitation. Central canteen. Bail Information Scheme, sentence planning, drug counselling, personal officer scheme. Despite the Remand Centre status in-possession list better than average. New receptions spend first 24hrs in E wing where support staff are available and comprehensive local information pack issued. Routine censorship abolished, but mail opened outwith sight of inmate and checked for illicit enclosures. Handed out dinner-time. Card phones on each landing, but calls restricted in time and only two phone cards allowed each week.

CANTEEN Very small canteen with an inadequate stock of about 100 items—predominantly sweets and biscuits. Purchases from earnings on Tuesdays and private cash on Fridays. Operated by SO and three officers.

REQUESTS/COMPLAINTS Average of 20 formal R/C submitted each month, most concern property or quality of food and a few related to adjudications. HMCIP who examined the records found that most had received replies within the time targets and the quality of replies was 'helpful and detailed'.

VISITS *How to get there*: Train to Reading then 5 min walk from station. No Special Transport.
VISITING TIMES: Week Days: 1330–1700—last admission 1600. Saturday: 1330–1700. Sunday: 1330–1700.

NOTES No staffed Visitors Centre. Canteen available in visits with Childrens Play Area. No overnight stay, but local B&B. Baby changing facilities in waiting room. Access for disabled visitors. Governor introduced experimental visiting system in 1994 which does not distinguish between remand and convicted status and which aims to give all inmates 1×60min visit per day—see ***Governor's comments***.

EDUCATION Open 49 weeks of the year, two f/t teachers and evening classes five nights of the week. Classes: IT; Health Education; English; Maths; Art; Cookery; Social Issues; Problem solving; Craft; Survival Skills; Communications; Sewing Skills; Woodwork; Drama; Ecology; Parent Craft; Improve Your Chances; Current Affairs.

WORKSHOPS No workshops at all. Cleaners £4.62, Reception £7.14, UB40 £2.50.

DISCIPLINE Segregation unit, situated at the end of C.wing, contains mainly Rule 43 inmates and none made any complaints about treatment to HMCIP. Upper landing used as association area for own-protection inmates, while ground floor used for punishments. Average of one adjudication a day. HMCIP who observed adjudications found 'impeccable observation of the rules'.

MEDICAL The Medical Officer is a local GP who is contracted for 11 hours per week. Nine bed hospital with 1×HCPO, 1×HCSO, 5×HCO (3 with nursing qualifications) + Agency Nurse. Hospital occupies semi-basement of A.wing but HMCIP found it 'bright, well lit and spotlessly clean'. 1xPsych sess/wk. Visiting dentists see an average of 20/wk. No HIV/AIDS multi-disciplinary team.

GYMNASIUM & SPORTS Staffing: 1×PESO, 3×PEO and 12 Sports and Games officers. Good range of activities with converted workshop acting as gymnasium. 'Grossly inadequate' external facilities with just two tarmac yards. Comprehensive daytime programme from 0800–2030 seven days a week. Classes: weights, basketball, volleyball, badminton, football, minor games, multi-gym, BAWLA.

CHAPLAINCY F/t CE chaplain, p/t RC, Methodist, Muslim and other faiths. RC Mass Saturday morning, CE Service Sunday morning.

FOOD Staffing: 1×Chef Manager contracted in with additional chefs ad hoc, and party of 6 inmates who 'appeared to do little other than cleaning and serving—neither particularly well' according to HMCIP. Kitchen refurbished in 1990. Four week menu cycle in operation 'few of the meals seemed to appeal to the inmates'.

ESTABLISHMENT REPORTS In a report (published 10th August 1993) of an inspection in February 1993, Judge Stephen Tumim, HMCIP, said that Reading was remarkably clean and free of graffiti despite the fact that the prison had suffered a serious disturbance on Boxing Day 1992. This had lead to a restricted regime where inmates are now locked up for longer than before and the establishment is still in the process of developing its regime. HMCIP praised the prison for the operation of its personal officer scheme which had created good relationships with inmates. However not enough was being done to develop a programme of structured activities inside and there was 'a clear lack of adequate outdoor exercise'.

GOVERNOR'S COMMENTS We have recently begun a three month experiment whereby we do not differentiate between Remand or Convicted visits—everyone can have one visit per day and we are guaranteeing a minimum 1 hour visit. The experiment is going well but I am reluctant to predict its outcome at this time! We also hope to introduce evening visits (on an appointment basis) at the end of the year or early 1995.

PRISONERS' COMMENTS There have been improvements at Reading since it changed from a local prison to a YO remand centre [in September 1992]. Requests/complaints are dealt with quite quickly though there is a delay sometimes in getting the form issued. Accommodation is good with many single cells, internal light switch, toilet etc. The canteen has a wide choice and the visiting is good. It takes a bit of time to get a job because you have to wait for someone to leave and some of the wages are a bit low. The food is not very good at all, only about 30 per cent of it is edible. Good gym facilities with local handicapped children coming in once a week. Mail is given out about 1115. Access to phones is OK, but it's wrong that we are restricted to just two phonecards a week—particularly as it's a remand centre and I need to phone my lawyers quite regularly. Staff are generally very helpful and will go out of their way to help solve genuine problems.

HM Prison Risley

Warrington, Cheshire. WA3 6BP
Tel: 0925-763871 **Fax:** 0925-764103
Opened: 1965 **CNA:** 692 **Average Roll:** 464 **Category:** C. Male + Female Remand Unit

i **BACKGROUND** Risley opened in 1965, purportedly as an example of the 'New Generation' Remand Centre. From its earliest days however it experienced many disturbances and incidents of suicide. Though the accommodation had a CNA of 500, it frequently held in excess of a thousand; the nickname 'Grisly Risley' was the result. In 1988 HMCIP strongly criticised the absence of measures to prevent suicide, and the 'barbaric and squalid' conditions in which inmates were forced to live. Less than a year later the Remand Centre was torn apart by a riot, and a subsequent inquiry recommended Risley's closure. Instead it was decided to retain the female remand wing (where facilities remain appalling) and develop a new training prison for men: by 1997 Risley should be a well resourced prison for 750 inmates. Risley operates the Core Sex Offender Treatment Programme. Neither the Governor of Risley, nor the prison's BoV, replied to our requests for information about the prison. HMCIP published their latest inspection report on Risley in June 1992.

OFFICIALS

AREA MGR: Terry Bone
CHAIR BOV:
GOVERNOR: Brendon O'Friel
MEDICAL:
CHAPLAIN: Rev Gibbard
PROBATION: Sue Macmillan
EDUCATION:
LOCAL MP: Doug Hoyle. Lab

REGIME *week days*: 0730 unlock/breakfast. 0830 work. 0900 education. 0915 special visits. 1130 lunch. 1200 lock up. 1300 work. 1515 admit last visitor through gate. 1540 cease labour. 1645 tea. 1730–2015 association.

week ends: 0730 unlock/breakfast. 0830 activities. 0915 CE Service (Sun). 1015 RC Mass (Sun). 1135 lunch. 1200 lock up. 1300 association. 1600 lock up. 1645 tea. 1730–2015 association.

Out of cell: 10/24hrs weekdays and 10/24hrs at weekends.

♂ **MALE ACCOMMODATION & FACILITIES** Three living units (A,B,C Wings) with around 100 in each wing. Recently refurbished, single cells, showers on all landings, purpose-built serveries and association facilities. Personal officer scheme, sentence planning, and integral sanitation. Routine censorship abolished but mail not opened in presence of the prisoner. Card phones on all units and access reported as good.

♀ **FEMALE ACCOMMODATION & FACILITIES** One living unit (E.wing), a tour of which was a 'depressing experience' according to HMCIP. Baseline CNA of 91 but the roll has topped 200 at times. Though a few single cells exist on E1 and E2 landings, the majority of women are housed in three dormitories, double-bunked and overcrowded: 'Too many people living together in to little space, there was also very little space for association and education, with the dining room doubling up as a classroom'. (HMCIP). Inmates complained to HMCIP of almost everything at Risley other than the attitudes of the staff. Chief complaints: poor medical services, no drug detoxification programmes, lack of vitamins, exercise and mental stimulus, food poorly presented, too much stodge and too little variety. Final meal of the day a little after 1500 on weekends. Life in single cells freezing, unhygienic and frightening.

VISITS *How to get there*: Train to Warrington, bus to prison. No Special Transport.
VISITING TIMES: Week Days: 1300–1530 Mon–Fri (both sexes). Saturday: 0900–1100 (Fem) 1300–1500 (both). Sunday: 1300–1500 Male only.

NOTES Staffed Visitors Centre. WRVS canteen available Mon–Fri. Toys available in visits room. Contact prison probation for details of local B&Bs. Prisoners at Risley are often transferred with little notice, so check before visiting. Mid-week visits less crowded. Reasonable access for disabled visitors.

EDUCATION Housed in former reception building, operates three (12 week) courses in Foundation Studies; Art and Design; Individual Learning. Six f/t staff and 32 p/t teachers. No central library.

WORKSHOPS Seven VTC/CIT (16 week) courses in converted former hospital block: Painting & Decorating; Electrical Installation; Information Technology; Technical Storekeeping; Industrial Cleaning; Hairdressing—all courses have waiting lists. Light assembly shop (electric plugs), laundry, PE Course, Community Service.

DISCIPLINE Segregation Unit located on C1 landing and consists of 11 ordinary cells and one special cell. Poor standards of record-keeping, insufficient details of inmates located in the Unit and no lists were available to HMCIP to check restraints or the records of their use. Study of ajudication records showed correct procedures were being followed, and natural justice respected. Fewer reports than expected, some fighting and few assaults.

MEDICAL 1×SMO, 1×f/t & 2×p/t Medical Officers, 12 single rooms—only with integral sanitation—three protective rooms. 2×HCPO, 6×HCSO, 26×HCO plus agency nurses. Purpose-built hospital block. Poor recreational facilities for in-patients. Dentist and optician visit regularly, though both have waiting lists.

GYMNASIUM & SPORTS 1×PEPO, 1×PESO, 4×PEO, 5×SGO. Converted chapel used as gymnasium and caters for gymnastics, circuit training and small team games. Well equipped weights room, outside tarmac area. Under 21's have to participate under threat of punishment.

CHAPLAINCY Full time CE chaplain and p/t RC and Methodist ministers. Bible study classes, chaplain's hour and Prison Visitors scheme in operation. Main church services Sunday morning, both male and female attend.

FOOD Staffing: 1×PO, 1×SO and 4×Officer (caterers),work party of 16. Poor and cramped kitchen. Food quality suffers from being transported in open handcarts. Meal times unsatisfactory and too close together—at weekends gap of almost 17 hours between tea and breakfast. Inmate consultative committee.

ESTABLISHMENT REPORTS In a report (published 2nd June 1992) of an inspection in September 1991, Judge Stephen Tumim, HMCIP, said the decision to close Risley as a Remand Centre was to be applauded, the redevelopment underway provides satisfactory single cell accommodation for Category C inmates. The large hospital, which had been the root of so much criticism had been developed into a workshop complex. In view of past conflicts between inmates and staff, HMCIP said it was particularly pleasing to find very high quality relationships. Staff are to be congratulated in successfully integrating 100 VPU inmates into the normal life of the prison, though the male side of the prison was to be contrasted with the 'grossly inadequate' conditions experienced by the female remand inmates. Their dorms were overcrowded, the reception gave cause for concern, the visiting room was far too small and neither facilities for children nor refreshments were available. On the whole the female regime was 'lack lustre with too much emphasis on unnecessary supervision at the expense of quality activities'.

HM Prison Rochester

Rochester, Kent. ME1 3QS
Tel: 0634-830300 **Fax:** 0634-826712
Opened: 1874 **CNA:** 303 **Average Roll:** 214 **Category:** Male Local

i **BACKGROUND** Rochester prison is situated about two miles south of Rochester city centre in Kent. Built originally as a convict prison and completed in 1874, the establishment was named 'Borstal' prison after the nearby village of the same name. At the turn of the century part of the establishment was given over to accommodating young offenders separately from adults. Following the Prevention of Crime Act 1908, the establishment was devoted solely to the custody of young offenders and became the first-ever Borstal institution. In September 1988 Rochester changed from a Young Offender Institution to a local prison and Remand Centre. The future of Rochester is very unclear at present, plans are in the pipeline for a change of role, but no details are available as we go to press. The Governor declined to provide information because of the uncertain future of the prison, and the BoV did not reply to our request for a copy of their annual report. HMCIP published their latest inspection report on the prison in September 1993.

OFFICIALS
AREA MGR: John Hunter
CHAIR BOV:
GOVERNOR: R.A. Chapman
MEDICAL:
CHAPLAIN: Rev Burton
PROBATION: David Coupland
EDUCATION:
LOCAL MP: Pegger Fenner. Con
STAFFING: 6 Governor grades, 12 Principal Officers, 27 Senior Officers and 132 Officers, including specialist staff.

REGIME *week days*: **Remands:** 0745 unlock. 0820 breakfast. 0900–1030 exercise, PE. 1030–1100 association. 1130 dinner. 1150 lock up. 1300 slop out. 1330–1530 Activities Centre. 1630 tea. 1650 lock up. 1745 association (for Cat C/D on A.wing only). 1900 card phones, supper, treatments. 2005 lock up.

week ends: **Remands:** 0745 unlock. 0830 breakfast. 0840 RC Mass (Sun). 0900 slop out. 0915–1100 PE (alternate Saturdays). 0940 CE Service (Sun). 1000 exercise. 1130 dinner. 1150 lock up. 1300 controlled unlock. 1315 visits, cell association. 1630 tea. 1650 lock up. 1745 (association for Cat C/D on A.wing only). 1800 begin slop out by landings. 1900 serve supper drink, treatments. 2000 prison locked up.

Out of cell: 6/24hrs weekdays and 5/24hrs at weekends.

ACCOMMODATION & FACILITIES Five detached cell blocks: A(CNA:60, Cat C/D Adults), B(87, YO Remands), C(64, VPU), D(85, closed refurbishment), E(82, YO Remands) wings. ABDE wings part of the original prison, C.wing added in 1970. BCDE wings all single cells with integral sanitation, A.wing combination of dormitories. Rochester has expressed an interest in joining the Sex Offender Treatment Programme, though does not have a group running at the moment.

CANTEEN Each wing has a room set aside for canteen—a relic of the Borstal days. No local purchase facility, open once per week and with limited stock.

VISITS *How to get there*: train to Chatham or Rochester and then bus to prison. No Special transport.

VISITING TIMES: Week Days: 1330–1515 Rem: Mon–Fri. Con: Tues & Thurs. Saturday: 1330–1515 Remand & Convicted. Sunday: 1330–1515 Convicted only.

NOTES No staffed Visitors Centre. Canteen and Childrens Play Area only available Tues, Thurs & Sat. Contact prison probation for details of local B&B. Midweek visits less crowded, Saturday visits very busy and time may be reduced to a minimum. Visiting room converted workshop, No Smoking policy in force, and a 1×VO=2×PVO exchange scheme allows for four weekday visits per month.

EDUCATION As part of an attempt to expand the regime, education building also provides recreational facilities. Those using the education centre can choose to attend a class or use the recreational facilities. Classes include: information technology, desk top publishing, cookery, art, and general education tailored to individual needs. No evening classes available for HMRC inmates. VPU inmates have restricted use of the education centre, attending just one evening class and a Wednesday afternoon only—though even this afternoon class is denied because many are working.

WORKSHOPS No employment for young offenders apart from cleaning. Gardens and works covered by adult inmates. Vulnerable inmates employed in the kitchen, on the farm and in the laundry. Average wages £6.50.

DISCIPLINE High number of adjudications, 80 in a four month period with an average population of 99 during this time. Exceptionally high number of reports incurred by young offenders, 218 in the same period with an average YO population of 82, caused HMCIP to recommend urgent attention be given to the problem. More time out of cell, more purposeful activities and greater use of personal officers. Segregation Unit with 19 cells. Restraints used five times in 1993.

MEDICAL Full time SMO, 1×p/t MO, 1×HCPO, 1×HCSO, 10×HCO. Two-storey HCC, each floor having 10 inpatient rooms (eight with integral sanitation) an eight-bed ward, four-bed ward and two strip cells, neither of which have proper ventilation. Dentist 3 sess/wk and no waiting list. Optician as required. Suicide Prevention group established after 15 attempted suicides in 1989.

GYMNASIUM & SPORTS 1×PEPO and 3×PEO. Medium sized gymnasium in need of refurbishment and flat grassed area suitable for five-a-side. Weights area and multi-gym. Outdoor swimming pool and large sport field with room for four full size football or rugby pitches. PE timetable being revised as we went to press.

CHAPLAINCY Full time CE chaplain, p/t RC and Methodist ministers. Minority faiths catered for by visiting ministers as appropriate. Main services Sunday, RC at 0845 and CE at 0945. Monthly mid-week communion service. If you wish to attend the Sunday service you MUST apply on Saturday, those registered as 'Nil Religion' are not allowed to attend.

FOOD Staffing: 1×SO, 3×Officer (caterers) and an inmate work party of 14. Kitchen in poor condition and requires refurbishment. Meals served in individual metal containers from which the food can be eaten or tipped onto a tray. Food reasonably hot and acceptable according to HMCIP. Four week menu cycle.

ESTABLISHMENT REPORTS Rochester 'lacked a unified sense of purpose' said HMCIP in a report (published 29th October 1993) of an inspection in April 1993. Category C and D prisoners were housed in 'poor quality dormitory accommodation' in A.wing, had 'a very restricted regime' in comparison with other similar establishments. Their freedom of movement within the grounds, employment opportunities, and use of the extensive facilities of the prison were limited by the need to keep them apart from other prisoners. Other groups were similarly deprived of regime. The 'establishment presented a picture of uncertainty; an unhappy series of compromises operating with an uneconomic use of resources'.

PRISONERS' COMMENTS **ADULTS:** High level of security and supervision. Dormitory accommodation is very unpopular. Most of the better jobs in the prison are allocated to VPU inmates. Staff tend to treat everyone as a young offender because of the history of the establishment.

YO: Canteen items are too expensive, particularly batteries, food is poor in quality, quantity and variety. Ethnic minorities receive little consideration and their different dietary needs are largely ignored. Visiting facilities provide little privacy. Inmate/staff relationships are good with help available when requested. Education staff particularly good with innovative ways of making education more attractive. Kit exchange system in disarray.

HM Prison Rudgate

Wetherby, W.Yorks. LS23 7AZ
Tel: 0937-844844 **Fax:** 0937-845862
Opened: 1959 **CNA:** 300 **Average Roll:** 268 **Category:** D. Male

BACKGROUND Situated alongside Thorp Arch Category C training prison, Rudgate occupies 6.7 hectares of countryside some three miles from the town of Wetherby. The site had previously been a part of a huge Royal Ordnance munitions factory that had been built in 1941 and closed in 1958, The Prison Commissioners bought 65 acres of the 650-acre site the same year and HM Prison Thorp Arch (as it was then known) opened in 1959. It was announced in July 1994 that Rudgate will join with Thorp Arch prison with effect from April 1995: the information below should therefore be treated with caution after that date. The prison was embarrassed in August 1994 when burglars broke into Rudgate by cutting through a security fence, taking thousands of pounds of inmates private cash and valuables from the cashiers safe! Neither the Governor nor BoV at Rudgate replied to our requests for information about the establishment, and HMCIP published their latest report on Rudgate in April 1992.

OFFICIALS
AREA MGR: Maurice codd
CHAIR BOV:
GOVERNOR: H. Jones
MEDICAL:
CHAPLAIN: Rev Rosheuval
PROBATION: Robert Ellis
EDUCATION:
LOCAL MP: Spencer Batiste. Con

REGIME *week days*: 0700 unlock/breakfast. 0800 work. 1200 lunch. 1300 work. 1635 tea. 1715–2045 association. Open regime.

week ends: 0800 unlock/breakfast. 0830 unit cleaning. 1000 association. 1145 lunch. 1230 lock up. 1330 association. 1615 tea. 1715–2045 association.

Out of cell: 24/24hrs weekdays and 24/24hrs at weekends.

ACCOMMODATION & FACILITIES Two main living units, North and South, large dormitories converted into rooms for between 2–5 inmates. Two new living units each holding 24 inmates in 12 double rooms. Good shower/toilet facilities, laundry on each unit. No formal induction programme, no sentence planning and no personal officer scheme except for lifers. Censorship of mail does not take place at Rudgate unless there is specific reason to do so. All mail is opened centrally and delivered to the living units—not opened in front of the inmate. All living units have card phones and ready access to them.

CANTEEN Located at the far end of the main living units the canteen is open every Tuesday, Wednesday and Thursday morning. Clearly displayed price lists, only a small selection of stock but fresh fruit can be ordered by local purchase. Does not cater for ethnic minorities, because 'the need has never arisen'.

VISITS *How to get there*: Train to Wetherby and then bus (760). From Leeds, bus (760) via Wetherby. Special Transport: Probation coach from Hull 1st Sunday in the month. VISITING TIMES: Week Days: 1330–1530 M–F. Saturday: 1330–1530. Sunday: 1330–1530.

NOTES No staffed Visitors Centre. Canteen and Childrens Play Area, supervised when busy. For details of B&B contact prison probation officer. Baby–feeding facilities. Disabled access possible with help.

EDUCATION Space is at a premium in the Rudgate education department, though sufficient for what is being attempted. Forty-five places on f/t education with wide range of classes. HMCIP in 1992 called for two VTC/CIT courses, but only General Construction Operators course is in place.

WORKSHOPS Laundry; winding; weaving; cutting; farms & gardens; kitchen; domestics; orderlies; yards/Wakefield Party; stores; works.

MEDICAL Part time Medical Officer who considers inmates to be a part of his General Practice and treats them as such. Six-bed ward and 2-bed isolation unit in hospital at Rudgate—HMCIP recommended its closure. Thorp Arch next door has a purpose-built hospital and will cover both establishments, apart from routine sick parades, from April 1995.

GYMNASIUM & SPORTS Housed in an old workshop complex, the gymnasium is 'dangerous' and only allows minimal indoor sports due to a girdered roof. Full PE programme during the day and evening. Remedial work and courses for over-35s. Multigym and weights room. Only one officer runs the gymnasium: when he is off duty the gymnasium is closed. This should improve when the prison joins with Thorp Arch.

CHAPLAINCY F/t CE, p/t RC and Methodist chaplains. Bible study class Monday, chaplain's hour and main services Sunday morning: CE 1000. Midweek Eucharist Wednesday, Chaplain dual post as chaplain of Thorp Arch.

FOOD Staffing: 1×SO and 2×Officer (caterers), and there is a work party of 8. Well organised kitchen produces high quality meals, inmates praised the catering staff and said they had no complaints about the food at Rudgate. No pre-select menu system, but three choices at dinner and two at tea. All meals dine in association.

ESTABLISHMENT REPORTS In a report (published 2nd April 1992) of an inspection in October 1991, Judge Stephen Tumim, HMCIP, said it was obvious that Rudgate had taken significant steps forward since the full inspection in 1988. The governor had initiated a full regime review, though inmates had not been invited to contribute to the process. Nevertheless some improvements had taken place and above all inmates appreciated the respect afforded to them by staff and a growth in trust and responsibility exemplified by day release and community work.

GOVERNOR'S COMMENTS [In April 1995 Rudgate will join with Thorp Arch prison next door. These comments are those of Mr Barnard who, while no longer the current Governor of the establishment, will be the Governor of the joint establishment when it opens].

The names of Thorp Arch and Rudgate will not be retained after the amalgamation in April 1995, though the new name has not been approved yet. The joint prison will have a C Cat half [the old Thorp Arch], and a D Cat half [the old Rudgate], with progression transfer through from C to D as part of the sentence planning process. The management structure has not been finalised yet. An additional 120-man cell block is also to be built in the C Cat half of the joint prison commencing in February or March 1995. Changes to the regime will be a major part of the amalgamation process though they have not yet been finalised. Though I am no longer the Governor of Thorp Arch, having left in order to lead the amalgamation implementation team, I will be the Governor of the joint establishment when it opens.

HM Prison Send

Ripley Road, Send, Surrey. GU23 7LJ
Tel: 0483-223048 **Fax:** 0483-223173
Opened: 1962 **CNA:** 151 **Roll:** 148 **Category:** C. Male

i **BACKGROUND** Send Prison lies in rural surroundings midway between Guildford and Woking in Surrey. Before passing to the prison authorities in the early 1960's it had been a small isolation hospital. In 1962 it opened as a Junior Detention Centre, later becoming a Senior Detention Centre. In 1986, following serious disturbances in a number of prisons, the pressure for additional places resulted in a change of role for Send to a Category C Training prison. The majority of the population are male convicted, serving between six months and four years. The Governor of Send, Tony French, supplied up to date information about the prison, and the Send BoV kindly supplied a copy of their 1993/4 Annual Report. HMCIP published their latest inspection report on Send in August 1993.

OFFICIALS
AREA MGR: Alan Rayfield
CHAIR BOV: Mr Wharton
GOVERNOR: Tony French
MEDICAL: Dr Barbour
CHAPLAIN: Rev Jeff Smith
PROBATION: Peter Spring
EDUCATION: June Pugh
LOCAL MP: Ian Taylor. Con
STAFFING: 2 Governor grades, three PO's, nine SO's and 43 Officers including specialist grades.

REGIME *week days*: 0800 unlock. 0810 treatments, breakfast. 0900 work. 1200 roll check, dinner. 1330 work. 1630 roll check. 1715 tea, association. 2030 lock up.

week ends: 0800 unlock, breakfast, association. 1145 roll check, dinner, association, visits. 1630 roll check. 1715 tea, association. 2030 lock up.

Out of cell: 12.5/24hrs weekdays and 12.5/24hrs at weekends.

ACCOMMODATION & FACILITIES No cellular accommodation. Much building work 1993/94, increasing CNA from 113 to 151. Three dormitories (A,B,C,) all with integral sanitation, now have extentions and B.Dormitory has been divided into rooms for six. Old kitchen, ablutions and quiet room have been transformed into dormitories. Standard i/p list, no pets, but reasonable list of civilian clothing. Sentence planning, drug counselling and personal officer scheme.

CANTEEN Located at the end of A.wing the shop is of a reasonable size but according to HMCIP is in need of redecoration. The shop opens every weekday morning except Fridays from 0815–0855 with each wing having its own allocated day. Local purchase facility and private cash spends on a Sunday. HMCIP was pleased to note an increase in the range of stock and 'the prices charged reflected the Prison Service requirement that shops should make around 10% profit.

REQUESTS/COMPLAINTS An average of six formal R/C forms issued each month as most matters are dealt with informally. Most complaints relate to the loss of property en route to Send. Despite the small numbers time targets were only being met in a handful of cases according to HMCIP, though the quality of replies being given 'appeared to be good and none of the cases had gone to appeal'.

VISITS *How to get there*: Train to Clandon then 1.5 mile walk, or train to Woking and then taxi—£12 return. No Special Transport.
VISITING TIMES: Week Days: 1400–1600 Tues, Wed only. Saturday: 1400–1600. Sunday: 1400–1600.

NOTES No staffed Visitors centre, but PortaKabin for shelter. October 1993 saw the introduction of a supervised Childrens Play Area and nappy changing facilities. Canteen in visiting room. Contact prison probation for details of B&B.

EDUCATION Education delivered by Amersham & Wycombe College of Further Education since August 1993. Day classes (0900–1200, 1330–1630): English, maths, computer studies, food studies, pottery, woodwork, social studies, business administration, art, soft toys, and silk screen printing. Evening classes, Mon & Wed 1800–2000: craft, yoga, pottery, guitar, woodwork and computers.

WORKSHOPS No workshops as such but large farm and gardens party with emphasis on gaining NVQ's in horticulture—in 1993/94 nine prisoners gained full Commercial Horticulture Certificates. Wages on average £7 with slightly more for kitchen workers.

DISCIPLINE Send does not have a Segregation Unit as such, adjudications are held in reception and two holding cells are available in the Health Care Centre where short term secure accommodation prior to transfer is necessary. Adjudications average about 20 per month and the punishments awarded are, according to HMCIP, 'modest and consistent'.

MEDICAL Staffing 1×HCSO and 1×HCO. Treatment times: 0810, 1230 & 1645. Small scale medical facilities, three-bed ward with integral sanitation, HMCIP found the HCC to be 'in good decorative order and generally very clean'. Report sick to HCC before 0800 and seen by MO after 0900. HMCIP found clinical audits, assessing HCC practices, were not being carried out. Dentist visits once per week, though HMCIP found the dental surgery was not fully equipped to 'modern dental standards'. Optician visits as required. Therapy groups for alcohol and drug abusers, though there were 'no regular programmes addressing good health practices or dealing with psychological problems such as anger management or offending behaviour; such programmes should be established'.

GYMNASIUM & SPORTS Two full time PE staff provide a balanced programme with classes from 0900–1200, 1330–1630 each day & 1800–2000 Mon–Thurs. Badminton, volleyball, football, weights, jogging, cricket, fitness training and circuit. Classes for CSLA and BAWLA.

CHAPLAINCY Part time C/E, RC and Methodist chaplains and visiting minister for Muslims. Other faiths catered for as appropriate. According to the Send BoV: 'It has been an unhappy year for the Chaplaincy as the number attending services are very low notwithstanding their regular visits to the establishment each week'. The chapel has been divided in half by a screen, enabling Alcoholics Anonymous to hold their meetings. 'The Chaplaincy feel that the sanctity of the chapel has been broken, however they appreciate the space has been used effectively: stoicism and patience describes the Chaplaincy team'.

FOOD Temporary kitchen staffed by SO Caterer, two Catering Officers and 10 inmates. HMCIP report very few complaints about the food, a two-week menu cycle was in operation and on some days only one main course is available. Dining room used for meals. In February 1992 the central kitchen was closed for enlargement and refurbishment and a small temporary kitchen was erected—so far the 'temporary' kitchen has been in use for over two years and, though both the BoV and HMCIP state it is well equipped, both also criticise it for being too small. The central kitchen is due to reopen in 1995.

ESTABLISHMENT REPORTS Board of Visitors in their Annual Report for 1993 (published

April 1994) detail two matters on which a response from the Secretary of State was requested. The temporary kitchen, which has been in place for two years, had a problem with rats which the staff dealt with during the year. But the need for a solid floor for the kitchen or a new dining hall and kitchen complex should be given very serious consideration. The increased CNA at Send means that the shortage of work/training for prisoners again needs most urgent consideration. Send had a very active and productive year of which the Board is proud.

HM Prison Shepton Mallet

Cornhill, Shepton Mallet, Somerset. BA4 5LU
Tel: 0749-343377 **Fax:** 0749-345256
Opened: 1821 **CNA:** 158 **Average Roll:** 187 **Category:** C. Male

i **BACKGROUND** Shepton Mallet prison is situated in the centre of the town of Shepton Mallet, 18 miles south-west Bristol in Somerset. The prison came into existence early in the 17th century as a House of Correction for men, women and children. It was rebuilt by inmates between 1817 and 1821 and eventually closed in 1930. The establishment was reopened in 1939 as a US Army military prison and operated as such until taken taken over by the Prison Department in 1966. The prison currently operates as a C Category training establishment. Neither the Governor nor BoV replied to our requests for information about the prison, and HMCIP published their latest inspection report on Shepton Mallet in July 1993.

OFFICIALS
AREA MGR: John May
CHAIR BOV:
GOVERNOR: P. O'Sullivan
MEDICAL:
CHAPLAIN: Rev Persson
PROBATION: David Child
EDUCATION:
LOCAL MP: D. Heathcoat-Amoury. Con
STAFFING: total of 89 staff in unified grades.

REGIME *week days*: 0730 unlock, breakfast. 0815–1115 work. 1155 dinner, lock up. 1330–1600 work (except Fri). 1605 tea. 1745–2030 association.

week ends: 0800 unlock, breakfast. 0830 domestic cleaning. 0915 association, RC Mass (Sat), CE Service (Sun). 1015 outside association, PE. 1125 dinner, lock up. 1300–1530 association, tea, lock up. 1800–2030 association.

Out of cell: 10.5/24hrs weekdays and 10.5/24hrs at weekends.

ACCOMMODATION & FACILITIES
Three main wings: A (VPU), B, C wings. Process of integral sanitation underway, a number of cells house two inmates, and two larger cells hold three, but cells are of a good size and integral sanitation should be completed throughout the prison by the end of 1994. Showering facilities and card phones on all wings, but association facilities are very limited.

REQUESTS & COMPLAINTS
Impressive Request and Complaint system said HMCIP with nearly 80% of all submitted forms being answered within seven days, the remainder within fourteen days. Replies to inmates are personalised, mostly comprehensive and easy to understand.

CANTEEN Recently moved to new accommodation and providing a much better service than previously. Stock was varied and included such items as pilchards, cereals, milk and coffee. All articles clearly priced and a profit of 10% is being made. Open three times per week, once for earnings and twice for private cash.

VISITS *How to get there*: Bus (376) leaves Bristol at 1055 or 1155 arrives Shepton 12.31 or 1331—change at Wells. Book straight through from Bristol. Special Transport: coaches from Portsmouth probation (0705 871441). Transport can be arranged from Bristol BR Station 1230 for visitors with special difficulties e.g. young children, those with ill health etc (except weekends). Phone prison probation officer one week in advance of visit.
VISITING TIMES: Week Days: 1400–1530 Mon Tues Wed only. Saturday: 1400–1530. Sunday: 1400–1530.

NOTES No staffed Visitors Centre. Canteen and Childrens Play Area. overnight stay at Bristol Family Centre (0272 425994). Refurbished visiting room with room for 26 visits. Baby-changing facilities available. Town visits introduced for those inmates who have successfully completed two home leaves. WRVS also operates a car service on behalf of the Probation Department for visitors with special needs.

EDUCATION Four f/t teachers and and 11 p/t staff. Good education department (part of Frome College) is situated in new buildings with six classrooms. Strong on basic skills, catering and computing. Business studies and OU. Space for 40 inmates on FTE. Evening classes three nights per week mainly art and craft subjects. Library at one end of the education department, good stock of 5,000 books. Max of six books can be borrowed every week. No music tapes for loan and very few talking books.

WORKSHOPS VTC/CIT courses: Painting & Decorating, Welding. Most of the contract services workshops have closed down with the exception of the tailors shop (making bib and brace overalls) which offers NVQ. Labour Board meets every Wednesday in the education dept. Poor work opportunities for all inmates at Shepton Mallet.

DISCIPLINE Segregation Unit with three cells in E.wing has no regular staffing and cell bells ring on A.wing. Shepton Mallet is seen by many as a dumping ground for difficult prisoners and a regular trade takes place with Dartmoor. Adjudications high, though properly conducted and awards not heavy handed.

MEDICAL Part time Medical Officer, 1×HCSO, 2×HCO. No inpatient facilities. Report sick to landing officer at unlock, seen by local GP later in the morning. GUC specialist visits as required, diabetes nurse attends but very few other visiting specialists. No multi-disciplinary HIV/AIDS team. Dental sessions twice per week and optician as requested. Good reception procedures with blood pressure and urine being tested. No positive health care programmes or general therapeutic activities.

GYMNASIUM & SPORTS 1×PESO and 2×PEO. Shepton Mallet is fortunate said HMCIP to have one of the best PE departments he had seen. Gym in converted chapel, upstairs a large sports hall provides for basketball, volleyball and racquet sports. Downstairs two excellent weights rooms, one for multi-gym and another for free weights. Good changing rooms, clean showers, though externally there was next to nothing apart from the tarmac exercise yard which is small, uneven and with dangerous protrusions such as a toilet block and open drains. Council owned football field about a mile from the prison can be used by inmates with D Category.

CHAPLAINCY Part time CE chaplain, RC and Methodist ministers. Chaplains Hour on Tuesday, occasional mid-week service. Main church services, CE Sunday, RC Mass Saturday. Chapel is well-looked after and is used on occasions by the education department for concerts and plays. Multi-faith room available.

FOOD Staffing: 1×SO, 3×Officer (caterers), and an inmate work party of 11. Cramped kitchen conditions and many complaints about the standard of the food. Three week menu cycle makes meals predictable, there is no pre-select system and kitchen workers do not receive any training in food hygiene. Two choices at dinner and sometimes a choice at tea. All meals dine in cell.

ESTABLISHMENT REPORTS Shepton Mallet is unsuitable as a Category C training prison, said HMCIP in a report (published 14 July 1993) of an inspection in December 1992. There was an unusual shortage of light, air and space which probably contributes to prisoners' lethargy. The prison is remote and awkward for visitors to get to. The families and friends of the 25% of prisoners from Wales face long journeys to see them. The quality of life for prisoners was variable. Prisoners enjoyed a lot of time out of cell but there was little in the wings to occupy them and they were not taking full advantage of the opportunities available in the education and PE departments. In the winter months prisoners had very little opportunity for exercise outside. The future for Shepton Mallet is not clear.

PRISONERS' COMMENTS **VPU:** A.wing acts as a VPU for inmates who are NOT sex offenders. The routine is good in that it keeps A.wing inmates quite separate from B&C wings, very good inmate/staff relationships, cells left unlocked all day other than for staff meal times. Work available in the light textile industry. The prison is very remote for visits, but the regime is getting better and visits are good. Food is not tampered with as far as we know, though the quality at times leaves much to be desired. No outside exercise in winter months, though there is PE for 45 mins every morning for those who want it. Very good personal officer scheme, inadequate wages leads to borrowing and baroning and the main complaint is the refusal of management to allow civilian clothing.

C & A wings: The prison had undergone a major painting transformation immediately before the inspection. There is plenty of time out of cell, but little constructive activities to fill the time. Poor public transport makes visiting difficult, cell furniture is in short supply, food is poor and sometimes served cold, meal times are too close together, particularly at weekends. Some cells are very cold, the Board of Visitors doesn't seem to come near the place from one month to the next. Gymnasium is quite small but the staff are first class and there is a very good programme with daily sessions available. Weekends are stagnant with nothing at all to do. Cell changes are very difficult to obtain because personal officers are allocated cells rather than individuals within them. Vast majority of staff are reasonable, there is evening association but confined to watching TV. Daily showers allowed if working. Avoid coming here if you can.

HM Prison Shrewsbury

The Dana, Shrewsbury, Salop. SY1 2HR
Tel: 0743-352511 **Fax:** 0743-356926
Opened: 1793 **CNA:** 168 **Average Roll:** 269 **Category:** Male Local

i **BACKGROUND** Shrewsbury prison, built on a hilltop half a mile from the town centre, first opened its gates in 1793. Much of the original building has long-since disappeared and the present establishment dates largely from the 1880s. Shrewsbury is a small local prison holding both remand and convicted prisoners, it serves the Crown Courts at Dolgellau, Shrewsbury, Stafford, Welshpool and Stoke-on-Trent. In addition 32 magistrates courts and 13 County Courts in are also served by the prison. Neither the Governor nor Board of Visitors replied to our requests for information about Shrewsbury. HMCIP published their latest inspection report in January 1992.

OFFICIALS
AREA MGR: Dai Curtis
CHAIR BOV:
GOVERNOR: D.J. Bradley
MEDICAL:
CHAPLAIN: Rev Biddle
PROBATION: J. Warren
EDUCATION:
LOCAL MP: Derek Conway. Con

REGIME *week days*: 0745 unlock/breakfast. 0830 work. 1145 lunch. 1230 lock up. 1330 work. 1615 tea. 1645 lock up. 1730–2030 association.

week ends: 0745 unlock/breakfast. 0830 unit/cell cleaning. 0900 association. 1145 lunch. 1230 lock up. 1330 Governor's inspection of units. 1400 association. 1615 tea. 1645 lock up. No weekend evening association.

Out of cell: 7.5/24hrs weekdays and 5.5/24hrs at weekends.

ACCOMMODATION & FACILITIES The majority of cells contained in two residential wings, double occupancy and integral sanitation. Bunk beds used in many cells. Central bath-house, though plans to convert recesses into showers in hand. Routine censorship abolished but mail not opened in the presence of the inmate. Card phones in all wings with access during association times.

REQUESTS/COMPLAINTS Average of 30 forms issued per month. Time targets at a local level were being met, but at Area Manager level there was delay beyond the six weeks prescribed for his reply. Forms submitted to the BoV were similarly not replied to within the time limits according to HMCIP.

VISITS *How to get there*: Train or bus to Shrewsbury then short walk to the prison.
VISITING TIMES: Week Days: 1330–1545 Rem. 1330–1515 Con. M–F. Saturday: 0930–1100 Rem. 1330–1530 Con. Sunday: No visits.

NOTES No staffed Visitors Centre or Childrens Play Area. Canteen in visiting room. Local B&B but can be full in summer months. Prisoners often moved at short notice, check before visiting.

EDUCATION The Education Centre comprises six classrooms on two floors. Staffed by an Education Officer, two f/t and 18 p/t teachers. Classes on five mornings and four afternoons per week, evening classes operate on two days of the week. Maths, computers, English language, cookery, technical drawing, art, general studies, first aid, job seeking, soft toys, model making, bible study and guitar.

WORKSHOPS Two textile workshops together employing 100 on production of vests and T-shirts. Usual mixture of cleaners and orderlies, FTE. No VTC or CIT courses.

DISCIPLINE Segregation unit consists of four cells on A1. In the six months prior to HMCIP's inspection there had been a total of 399 charges laid by staff. Procedures were followed and awards were if anything on the lenient side. A high number of dismissed charges lead HMCIP to call for an investigation into the level and accuracy of disciplinary charges brought against inmates.

MEDICAL P/t Medical Officer, HCPO and 2 ×HCO. Hospital consists of five cells on A2 landing. No night cover. Dental surgery once per week, optician once per month. Other specialists called as required.

GYMNASIUM & SPORTS PESO and 2×PEO. Gymnasium located off A.wing and in use for six hours a day and 90 minutes weekday evenings. Poor weekend regime as gym used for showing videos. BAWLA, volleyball, basketball, football, weights and fitness training.

CHAPLAINCY Full time CE chaplain and p/t RC and Methodist ministers. Visiting ministers of other faiths attend as and when necessary. Main church services Sunday morning. Bible study and Chaplain's hour. Prison Visitors scheme.

FOOD Staffing: 1×SO and 3×Officer (caterers), and there is a work party of 15. Kitchen cramped but clean, no menu system in operation. Food good quality and well presented. New kitchen on the drawing board.

ESTABLISHMENT REPORTS In a report (published 9th January 1992) of an inspection in February 1991, Judge Stephen Tumim, HMCIP, said that Shrewsbury was fulfilling its agreed functions and appears to have adapted well to the increased court commitment. The prison was soundly managed and the overall development plans show a firm commitment to improving standards. The quality of life for inmates was good, education caters for all classes of inmate irrespective of their length of stay and the inclusion of community activities into the PE programme will be worthwhile to both the prison and community. The pragmatic approach to improving production in the workshops provides a model which other establishments should consider adopting. Inmate/staff relationships appeared to be well developed, most noticeably in C.wing and HMCIP was in no doubt that the prison represented value for money.

HM Prison Spring Hill

Grendon Underwood, Bucks. HP18 OTJ
Tel: 0296-770301 **Fax:** 0296-770756
Opened: 1953 **CNA:** 210 **Average Roll:** 205 **Category:** D. Male Open

i **BACKGROUND** The prison began life in 1880 as Grendon Hall, a Jacobean red brick mansion sitting on top of a small rise (called Spring Hill) some ten miles west of Aylesbury in Buckinghamshire. It was used as a family residence until it passed to the War Department in 1939, when a small hutted camp was built in the grounds immediately behind the house. In 1953 Spring Hill was purchased by the then Prison Commissioners and has been used as an open prison for adult males ever since. The Governor provided information about the establishment and the BoV provided a copy of their latest annual report covering both Spring Hill and HMP Grendon (built in the grounds of Spring Hill in 1962). HMCIP published their latest inspection report on Spring Hill in January 1993.

OFFICIALS
AREA MGR: Amy Edwards
CHAIR BOV: Lady Slynn
GOVERNOR: Tim Newell
MEDICAL: Dr Peter Lewis
CHAPLAIN: Rev K. Pounds
PROBATION: Jack Cordery
EDUCATION: Jill Lewis
LOCAL MP: David Liddington. Con
STAFFING: Nine Governor grades and 176 uniformed staff—including specialist grades—for *both* Spring Hill and Grendon. Staffing for Spring Hill: 1×G4, 2×PO, 4×SO, 18×Officers. Total of 107 in unified grades.

REGIME *week days*: 0715–0745 rise, make bedpacks, treatments. 0745–0815 breakfast. 0815 roll check (all roll checks require you to be by your bed). 0830 work. 1130 Governor's application. 1130–1200 treatments. 1145 cease labour. 1200–1220 dinner. 1245 roll check. 1300–1600 work. 1645 roll check. 1700 tea. 2015 roll check. 2359 lights out—no movement out of huts after lights out until 0630.

week ends: 0715–0745 rise, make bedpacks, treatments. 0750–0805 breakfast. 0830 town visits out. 0845 roll check (all roll checks require you to be by your bed). 0830 activities. 0900 RC Mass (Sat, in Grendon). 0945 (and 1800) CE Service (Sun). 1130 Governor's application. 1130–1200 treatments. 1200–1220 dinner. 1245 roll check. 1300–1600 activities, visits. 1630–1700 tea. 1710 roll check. 1700–2015 activities. 2015 roll check. 2315 roll check. 2359 lights out—no movement out of huts after lights out until 0630.

Out of cell: 24/24hrs weekdays and 24/24hrs at weekends.

ACCOMMODATION & FACILITIES Inmates located in fourteen single-storey huts, providing singe and double occupancy rooms. Refurbishment of accommodation completed in December 1993 in response to highly critical report from HMCIP. Six card phones. No personal officer scheme. Sentence planning undeveloped. Incoming mail issued 1230, open outwith the presence of the inmate. pre-release courses suffer from staff shortages. Does not accept lifers, sex offenders, arsonists or deportees. ST inmates must have at least six weeks left, MT/LT inmates must be approaching their HLED or PED and be fit for full time work. SWIP officer and two probation staff. Inmates eligible for home leave every two months after PED/HLED.

REQUESTS & COMPLAINTS HMCIP examined records during a three month period. Of the 32 requiring local reply, 24 had received one with seven day, a further seven within fourteen days. Main subjects parole, transfer and adjudication. Area Manager not keeping to time targets.

CANTEEN Located on the first floor of the main house with about 150 lines of stock. Monthly private cash transfer to earnings of £15. Open twice per week, once on weekdays for earning and once at weekends for private cash phonecards and batteries.

VISITS *How to get there*: train to Aylesbury then bus (16) from bus station—no Sunday service. No Special Transport.
VISITING TIMES: Week Days: 1315–1515 Wednesday only. Saturday: 0915–1115 & 1315–1515. Sunday: 0915–1115 & 1315–1515.

NOTES No staffed Visitors Centre. Extremely poor visiting conditions have now been improved, visiting room recently refurbished. Canteen and Childrens Play Area. Contact prison probation for details of local B&B. Wheelchair access.

EDUCATION Housed on the first floor of Grendon Hall, open 49 weeks of the year, five days and two evenings per week. 3×f/t teachers + Instructor. Five classrooms with poor conditions: broken window sashes, leaking radiators, loose or missing floor tiles, collapsing ceilings. Open five days and three evenings per week, open learning, business studies course and print shop course. Inmate development course, new project consisting of induction programme, pre-release course, work project and community/charity projects.

WORKSHOPS No VTC/CIT courses. PSIF Workshop (assembly of weighing scales), kitchen, orderlies, laundry (in Grendon), farm & gardens (horticulture), FTE, cleaners, works, print shop, education. Polytunnels (36) producing salad crops, flowers and plants. Some NVQ opportunities.

DISCIPLINE No segregation unit at Spring Hill, when necessary Grendon is used to lodge inmates, usually overnight, before transfer or return to Spring Hill. G4 head of Spring Hill has authority from Area Manager (London North) to conduct adjudications, hearings properly conducted and awards appropriate to the offence.

MEDICAL Part time Medical Officer, 1×HCSO, 4×HCO. HCC with 3×four-bed wards, poor decoration. HCC staff filter all requests to see MO. Dental waiting list of three months. No medical cover after 1700 hrs.

GYMNASIUM & SPORTS No gym at Spring Hill, inmates use Grendon's facilities four times per week. PE programme includes many outdoor activities, cricket, canoeing and fishing. CSLA, Basic Expedition Training and Hanson Award courses. On site weights room.

CHAPLAINCY Part time CE chaplain, RC and Methodist ministers. Small but attractive chapel on the first floor of Grendon Hall. Multifaith room with own cooking facilities: Imam visits fortnightly. Buddhist shrine on main lawn. Bible study classes Mon & Wed evenings. Delightful Buddha Grove is on site offering a place for meditation and prayer.

FOOD Staffing: 1×SO, 1×Officer (PO at Grendon with overall charge), and an inmate work party of 17. Kitchen dates from 1977, reasonable size. All meals very good. No menu cycle and no pre-select menu system in operation (unlike Grendon). Tea is the main meal of the day, four choices (two for vegetarians).

ESTABLISHMENT REPORTS In a report (published 26th January 1993) of an inspection in May 1992, HMCIP said that some of the living conditions at Spring Hill were amongst the worst he had seen and should be replaced. The lack of facilities and the failure to maintain existing buildings are strong arguments in favour of separating the prison from Grendon. The reception is inadequate and the Health Care Centre poorly equipped and decorated. There was no gymnasium and the education was a collection of rooms on the first floor of the main house, a location it shared with the probation offices. No proper library or craft rooms exist and a purpose-built visiting room and Visitors Centre was also needed. In spite of these conditions there is a positive regime and a committed approach from the staff, Judge Tumim was impressed with the quality of work undertaken by staff and the relationships they established with inmates. The prison is relaxed with the concept of openness being developed through the regime. The Home Secretary, in response to the Report, rejected HMCIP's recommendation that Spring Hill should be independent of Grendon saying there are 'real advantages' in having a single managerial line for both establishments. A phased redevelopment plan is being made and inmates are now allowed to wear their own clothes.

GOVERNOR'S COMMENTS The main emphasis at Spring Hill will be to facilitate inmates to address offending behaviour.
Request/Complaints are fully investigated and inmates kept aware of any delays and the reasons. Education is predominately on site with special facilities for local college courses. Medical facilities are comprehensive but take many forms, no ward facilities on site. There are very few complaints regarding food.

PRISONERS' COMMENTS Spring Hill should be a separate establishment, it is the poor relation of Grendon. Direct access to Governor is difficult, staff screen all applications leading to delays and considerable inconsistency in approach. Education provision is too narrow, there is a need for more courses and offence-focused work. The mix of long and short term inmates needs careful examination, there are different needs which require different management responses: in Spring Hill both groups are poorly catered for. Long termers point to a number of C Cat establishments which gave more trust and responsibility than Spring Hill. No personal officer scheme or real induction programme. Cleaning materials are very difficult to obtain. Gym is too small. Excellent surgeries held by Citizen's Advice Bureau and Duty Solicitor scheme. High prices in the canteen, low wages levels, and the 'working out' scheme needs development. Long waiting lists for dentist and optician: why can't inmates attend local practices? BoV would be more effective if they held regular surgeries that are advertised. Timing of meals—with tea at 1530 at weekends—too close together. Muslim inmates complain that halal meat was not available.

HM Prison Stafford

54 Gaol Rd, Stafford. ST16 3AW
Tel: 0785-54421 **Fax:** 0785-49591
Opened: 1793 **CNA:** 532 **Roll:** 713 **Category:** C. Male

i **BACKGROUND** Stafford Prison is a closed training prison for Category C male inmates. It was first opened in 1793 as the new Staffordshire Gaol and although some of the original building remains, the present establishment is mainly Victorian (notably Main Hall and Crescent Wings). The prison was closed between 1916 and 1939, reopening at the outbreak of the Second World War to house both males and females. The female section of the prison closed within a few years of reopening, and for many years afterwards Stafford held young offenders as well as adults. Today the prison is a seriously overcrowded Category C trainer which takes inmates who, for various reasons, (e.g. disciplinary, emotional instability and inadequacy), would pose problems in other less secure and controlled Category C prisons. According to HMCIP, calling Stafford a Training Prison was 'something of a mockery . . . the prison is overcrowded, under-resourced and unsuitable in design for its current role'. Stafford is one of three prisons to operate a special Protected Witness Unit. Neither the Governor nor the BoV replied to our requests for information about the prison, and HMCIP published their latest inspection report in October 1992.

OFFICIALS
AREA MGR: Jim Blakey
CHAIR BOV:
GOVERNOR: R. Feeney
MEDICAL:
CHAPLAIN: Rev Dixon
PROBATION: Doug Handley
EDUCATION:
LOCAL MP: Bill Cash. Con

REGIME *week days*: 0730 unlock. 0800 breakfast. 0835 work. 1045–1115 UB40 exercise. 1145 cease labour. 1200 dinner. 1230 lock up. 1335 work. 1645 tea. 1645 lock up. 1800–2020 association.

week ends: 0730 unlock. 0800 breakfast. 0915 exercise commences, various groups until 1115. 1140 dinner. 1215 lock up. 1335 association. 1600 tea. 1615 lock up. 1715–1915 association.

Out of cell: 8/24hrs weekdays and 6/24hrs at weekends.

ACCOMMODATION & FACILITIES
Three cell blocks; Main (A,B,C Wings) & Crescent (F,G Wings) both with integral sanitation, and former recesses have been converted into showering facilities. D,E Wings, no integral sanitation and HMCIP reports plans for it have been shelved. Prison overcrowded with many living two to a cell. All three cell blocks reflect the era of their construction and do not provide proper association areas, nor facilities for dining out of cell. Routine censorship abolished though mail opened in a central office and then passed to the appropriate location. Card phones in all living units, access reported as restricted and queues at peak times.

CANTEEN Housed in a PortaKabin centrally sited at the time of the inspection but due to move into purpose-built accommodation that was then under construction. One visit to the canteen allowed each week, only 105 lines of stock carried, though displayed goods had clear price labels. No local purchase facility.

VISITS *How to get there*: Train to Stafford and then 15 min walk to the prison. No Special Transport.
VISITING TIMES: Week Days: 1330–1530 M–F. Saturday: 1330–1530. Sunday: 1330–1530.

NOTES Staffed Visitors Centre, open M–F from 1230 except bank holidays. Canteen and Childrens Play Area. For overnight stays contact prison probation. New visiting complex, baby-changing facilities, wheelchair access and refreshments.

WORKSHOPS PSIF have six workshops in the prison. In four of these the work is light assembly, electrical items, for a variety of private companies. The two remaining workshops produced laundry, catering and hospital jackets for prison staff and coveralls and PE shorts for the MoD. New workshop complex opened 1993. Four VTC/CIT: Electronic wiring; multi-skills; information technology; hairdressing.

DISCIPLINE Segregation unit located on E1.landing, which could accommodate 46 inmates. Impoverished regime found by Judge Tumim, no work, no education and few in cell activities for those (the majority) who were not on punishment. In the 9 months prior to the inspection there had been 1,007 adjudications, with awards which were appropriate to the offences committed. The special cell had been used 13 times in that period, including three occasions when an inmate had been restrained by a body-belt.

MEDICAL Headed by SMO, p/t MO, 1×HCPO, 2×HCSO, 12HCO—three were qualified nurses. Health Care Centre located in a converted granary with accommodation on three floors. Two seven-bed wards, double room, four single rooms and three protected rooms. Dentist visits 2 sess/wk. At time of inspection Stafford was still implementing Viral Infectivity Restrictions on those known (or considered) to be HIV+, located on G2 landing, it was a practice criticised by HMCIP.

GYMNASIUM & SPORTS Inadequate facilities appear to afflict Stafford and the gymnasium was no different. A small low ceiling sports hall permitted volleyball and basketball. PortaKabin with multi-gym. Best facility was the weights room which was well equipped and with good showering facilities.

CHAPLAINCY Full time CE chaplain and p/t RC and Methodist ministers. Other faiths visited by respective ministers as required. New church opened 1992—old one was a Nissen hut which Judge Tumim described looking like 'a relic of World War Two'. Main church services Sunday morning, bible study, Prison Visitors and Chaplain's Hour.

FOOD Following criticism of the poor kitchen conditions at Stafford in 1989 by HMCIP, the Home Office spent £43,000 on repairs and cleaning. The food was found to be of an overall reasonable quality, though the chips received most criticism. No pre-select menu system in operation and all meals dine in cell.

ESTABLISHMENT REPORTS In a report (published 21st October 1992) of an inspection in February 1992, Judge Stephen Tumim, HMCIP, said that little had changed since the previous inspection. Stafford is a training prison in name only. Both staff and inmates considered it to be a 'sin bin' which polarises attitudes, stifles initiatives and promotes inertia. The span of inmates held ranged from the dangerous aggressor to the chronic inadequate, and included the disturbed and borderline psychotic. There may well be a need for a place like Stafford, which accepts the more difficult and demanding inmate so that other prisons may function better, but such a prison requires more resources, not less, than those it relieves in this way. Stafford is receiving inmates with special needs and should be resourced to help them. Improvements to the regime, particularly the quality and quantity of employment and time out of cell, are essential prerequisites of any development. Stafford is far removed from the normal concept of a training prison and staff are preoccupied with control. This is not a criticism of management or staff, the prison is overcrowded, under-resourced and unsuitable in design for its present role.

HM Prison Standford Hill

Eastchurch, Sheerness, Kent. ME12 4AA
Tel: 0795-880441 **Fax:** 0795-760098
Opened: 1950 **CNA:** 384 **Average Roll:** 351 **Category:** D. Male Open

i **BACKGROUND** Standford Hill open prison is situated on a huge site, about one mile south of the village of Eastchurch, on the Isle of Sheppey. Its seven mile perimeter encloses an area of about 500 acres, most of which is farmed by the Prison Service. In 1909 Stonepits Farm, Eastchurch, was sold to an aero-club which, the following year, became the Royal Aero Club. During World War I the site was the base for the Royal Flying Corps. Between the wars it was an air-gunnery school. In World War II, the site was an RAF fighter station until put out of action and continued as an RAF Intelligence and debriefing centre. After brief use by the Army the site was acquired by the then Prison Commissioners in 1949. A working party from HMP Maidstone refurbished the accommodation and it opened as HMP Eastchurch in 1950. Over the years the prison has undergone a number of role changes: changing from YP Centre to 'Special' Local—an open prison with a closed unit in its grounds, and then a Centre for Preventive Detainees. Between 1966–67 the Preventive Detainees were phased out and Eastchurch—as it was still then known—became in effect a D Category prison with a C Category unit. In 1975 the name was changed to Standford Hill. In 1985 the semi-secure accommodation known as Shetland Unit was so badly damaged by fire that it was closed, leaving Standford Hill the open prison which it remains today. Neither the Governor nor BoV replied to our requests for information about the prison, and HMCIP published their latest inspection report on Standford Hill in July 1992.

OFFICIALS
AREA MGR: John Hunter
CHAIR BOV:
GOVERNOR: D. Twiner
MEDICAL:
CHAPLAIN: Rev D. Standley
PROBATION: Ian Taylor
EDUCATION:
LOCAL MP: Roger Moate. Con

REGIME *week days*: 0730 unlock. 0800 breakfast. 0840–1150 work. 1200 dinner. 1255–1650 work. 1700 tea, association. 2045 spur association until lights out at 2230.

week ends: 0730 unlock. 0800 breakfast. 0830–1110 activities. 1120 dinner, activities. 1600 tea, association 2045 spur association until lights out at 2300.

Out of cell: 24/24hrs weekdays and 24/24hrs at weekends

ACCOMMODATION & FACILITIES Two large three-storey rectangular accommodation units (Sunderland and Sterling) opened in 1986 with a traditional galleried style, providing excellent conditions which are free from vandalism and graffiti, and are well maintained. Total of 192 single rooms in each unit. Large open areas for association. Card phones and small canteen on both units.

VISITS *How to get there*: Train to Sheerness then bus (362) to Eastchurch then walk to prison. Special Transport: Coach from London—contact Abba Coaches 081-859-8708. VISITING TIMES: Week Days: 1330–1530 Tues, Wed, Thurs only. Saturday: 1330–1530. Sunday: 1330–1530.

NOTES No staffed Visitors Centre. Childrens' Play Area under review. Canteen in visiting room. B&B in Sheerness—contact home probation office. Strictly PVO's Tuesday & Thursday only.

EDUCATION Four f/t and two p/t teachers, open five days and three evenings for 47 weeks of the year. Good computer studies course, though department suffers from a lack of space.

WORKSHOPS VTC/CIT courses: Painting & Decorating; Bricklaying; Carpentry; General Construction. Main employer Farm & Gardens, Education. Textile shop, Tailoring and Contract Services assembly shops.

MEDICAL Part time Medical Officer. HCC has no inpatient facilities, such inmates being transferred to Swaleside. Sick parade each morning, report sick to unit office. Dental surgery was a professional disgrace said HMCIP when he last reported on it, and it was subsequently closed by the Governor: instruments that were rusty, were sterilised without being cleaned. The drill was sterilised(!) by soaking it in antiseptic and there were cigarette ends on the shelves.

GYMNASIUM & SPORTS 1×PEPO, 1×PESO and 2×PEO. Gymnasium located in old RAF hut with floor marked out for various indoor games. Excellent covered swimming pool, weight training room and comprehensive PE programme. Provides a valuable service to inmates.

CHAPLAINCY Full time CE chaplain, RC and Methodist ministers. Chapel in a dangerous condition with the altar subsiding as a result of tree roots! No inmate attends services in the community and HMCIP said this should be considered. No multi-faith room.

FOOD Staffing: 1×SO, 2×Officer (caterers), and an inmate work party of 11. The kitchen, which was severely criticised by HMCIP in 1988, had been demolished by the time of the 1991 inspection and a temporary facility built and plans for a new kitchen high on the list of priorities. Choice at tea meal only, with good quality and generous portions. No pre-select menu system.

ESTABLISHMENT REPORTS In a report (published 9th July 1992) of an inspection in November 1991, HMCIP said that the previous two inspection reports had concluded Standford Hill was a prison with pockets of good practice but unfulfilled potential. Though this inspection did not allow for complete inspection of the establishment, HMCIP saw evidence that there remain pockets of excellence in the establishment but its regime is still not fully developed. Since the last inspection improvements had been made to the catering and visiting arrangements and the quality of the meals was satisfactory. The greatest concern stems from the lack of training and preparation for release. No formal Personal Officer Scheme exists, except for a small number of lifers while HMCIP, quoting one member of staff, describes sentence planning at Standford Hill as 'farcical'. SWIP officers were in place but had received no formal training, and although the Probation Department organises some group work, the opportunities available for offence-focused work are not being exploited. Evening association had not been extended since the last inspection and allowing inmates TV sets in their rooms would be a welcome additional leisure activity. While staff need to be more involved with training work with inmates, relationships between inmates and staff were basically sound and the quality of life for inmates was satisfactory.

PRISONERS' COMMENTS Very good living conditions, but there is a lack of trust shown by staff. Inmates are locked in their spurs at 2045 each night which prevents access to the phones and recreational facilities, and is inconsistent with the regime at other open prisons. Little is done to address the needs of lifers and those serving long sentences, there are no town visits and the criteria for working outside the prison in the community are unnecessarily restrictive. Clothing issue scales are poor, menu is repetitive and wages are low. Work on the farm is back breaking and little more than slave labour. The canteen has only a limited stock, PE facilities are inadequate and education does not meet inmates' needs.

HM Prison Stocken

Stocken Hall Rd, Oakham, Leics. LE15 7RD
Tel: 0780-410771 **Fax:** 0780-410767
Opened: 1985 **CNA:** 396 **Roll:** 387 **Category:** C. Male

i **BACKGROUND** Stocken prison is located some seven miles north-east of Oakham in Leicestershire. The Hall and large estate, built on a greenfield site, were purchased in 1959. In 1980 the Hall itself, by then in a dilapidated state, and a small amount of surrounding land were sold. The prison was originally designed to hold 300 young offenders but eight months before the project opening date it was decided that the establishment would become an adult Category C prison. Stocken received its first prisoners in 1985. An additional 96 cell block, to the Director of Works linear design, was added and brought into use in 1990. Apart from this addition, and a small workshop, there has been little change in accommodation since the establishment opened in 1985. The Governor of Stocken supplied a good deal of information about the establishment, though the prison's BoV did not reply to our request for a copy of their annual report. HMCIP published their latest inspection report on Stocken in May 1994.

OFFICIALS
AREA MGR: Joe Mullens
CHAIR BOV: Mr Heath
GOVERNOR: D. Hall
MEDICAL: Dr. M. Campbell
CHAPLAIN: Rev M. Craddock
PROBATION: A. Gray
EDUCATION: A. Healey
LOCAL MP: Alan Duncan. Con
STAFFING: 5 Governor grades, 8×PO, 22×SO and 93 Officers, including specialist grades.

REGIME *week days*: 0735 unlock/breakfast. 0745 treatments. 0815 work. 0845 education. 1205 dinner. 1220 spur association. 1335 work. 1635 cease labour. 1715 tea, lock up. 1745 association. 2010 lock up.

week ends: 0735 unlock/breakfast. 0830 visits commence. 0930 sports field. 1140 dinner. 1200 lock up. 1315 unlock, association, visits. 1715 tea. 1745 association. 2010 lock up.

Out of cell: 12.35/24hrs weekdays and 12.35/24hrs at weekends.

ACCOMMODATION & FACILITIES Six residential blocks (A–F Wings). Five wings (A–E) each hold 60 inmates in single cells equipped with integral sanitation. F.Wing (1990) is of a different design, holding 96 in single cells with integral sanitation, power points, and allowing in-cell colour television for £1.75 per week. TVs also in A–E but no power points. Comprehensive (11 page) i/p list. Sentence planning, drug counselling, personal officer scheme. Large lifer population. Two card phones on each wing. Mail is opened but not censored and given out at dinner-time.

CANTEEN Recent improvements allow personal visits rather than previous pre-order system. A system of identification had to be introduced following impersonations. Small space and restricted stock. Local purchase facility and p/c can be used to supplement earnings.

REQUESTS/COMPLAINTS Between 45–50 request/complaint forms were issued each month and operation of the system was criticised by HMCIP: 'Prisoners . . . often waited two or three days before seeing a Governor . . . staff confirmed this complaint'. Only 12% of forms were answered within 7 days 'and over 50% were waiting more than 14 days for an answer'. HMCIP discovered half a dozen cases at HQ which were 'over six weeks old, replies given were variable in quality and often presented impersonally'.

VISITS *How to get there*: Train to Stamford 10 miles, Oakham 11 miles, Grantham 14 miles, then taxi. Special Transport: Minibus service from Birmingham, Coventry, Leicester, Chesterfield and Northampton, contact prison probation for details. VISITING TIMES: Week Days: 1345–1600 Wednesday only. Saturday: 1345–1600. Sunday: 1345–1600.

NOTES No staffed Visitors Centre, limited refreshments. Childrens Play Area. Only 2 visits per month, B&B in local towns. Ramp for wheelchairs at entrance—visiting area on ground floor.

EDUCATION Open 50 (29hr) weeks of the year, six full-time teachers and three evening classes a week. Operated by Mill Wharf Educational Services (Mill Wharf, Mill Street, Birmingham B6 4BU). Seventy full-time places. English, maths, psychology, sociology, biology, history, French, health & hygiene, home economics and word processing. Evening classes in sewing craft, music, African studies and social issues. Impressive art dept and six VTC courses: industrial cleaning, computing, light vehicle body repair, horticultural machine repair, information technology and painting & decorating. Library with 5000 volumes, well attended.

WORKSHOPS Two industrial workshops: sewing machine repair employs 26 and trains up to C&G level. Textile 46 on sweatshirts, sheets, face cloths. HMCIP found the tempo 'brisk and impressive, production targets were being exceeded'. Two 'cottage industries', packing Xmas cards etc—up to £12/wk. Five VTC courses—see above. Farm party for large dairy (new one for 1995), pigstock, beef cattle and lambs. HMCIP was cautious of new technology: 'A sensible balance needs to be struck between technical advances in pursuit of greater profit and work and training opportunities for prisoners'.

DISCIPLINE There had been 697 adjudications between 1.4.92 & 31.3.93, which HMCIP described as 'average' for such prisons. Adjudications were 'properly conducted' and 'awards appeared appropriate and consistent'—some staff thought punishments did not provide sufficient deterrence.

MEDICAL Part time medical officer, 1×HCO and 2×Nurses. Psychiatrist (2 sess/wk), Genito-urinary & orthopaedic when required. Optician (monthly) and psychologist (1.5 days/wk). HMCIP found evidence of low staffing levels. The pharmacy suffered from a lack of security. Inpatient care provided by Lincoln or Leicester prisons. Small supply of pain-killers (headache etc) held in each wing. Figures for reporting sick were below average said HMCIP, though sick parade was hurried and more time should be given to it. No health promotion. HIV/AIDS counsellors. Confidentiality was such that HMCIP was unable to discover the number tested or the results which 'were known only to the physician and the patient concerned'.

GYMNASIUM & SPORTS 1×PESO, 3×PEO's, 1×PEO(p/t). Though there were 'very good' PE facilities at Stocken said HMCIP, the 'quality and quantity of equipment in the weights area compared badly' with other prisons. Two football pitches and a rugby pitch. Good shower facilities. programme provided a good mixture of activities. Throughout the day weights alternated with sports and about 30 could attend each session. Evening programme for 2 hours Mon–Thurs, Fri=1hr. Once per month children can use sports facilities while visiting their fathers.

CHAPLAINCY F/t C/E chaplain, p/t RC and Methodist. Sikh, Muslim and Jehovah's Witnesses ministers visit regularly. HMCIP criticise the chaplaincy at Stocken for not being adequately involved in the induction process. Average RC Mass attendance 'was between 3 and 8, while 8 was the average congregation at the Anglican Sunday Service . . . the chaplaincy did not have a good name among some of the prisoners and many of the staff'.

FOOD 'We received many complaints from inmates about the cooking and presentation of meals' said HMCIP who 'had sympathy with the views expressed'. Food was left in trolleys for an hour before leaving the kitchen. 'The meals we saw served were poorly presented and those sampled were not very appetising'. A four week menu, 3 choices at dinner/tea. Dinner served an hour too early. MO visited the kitchen 'infrequently'

ESTABLISHMENT REPORTS Stocken had made good progress over the last eight years said HMCIP in a report (published 19th May 1994) of an inspection in October 1993. There was full employment and a wage structure which rewarded effort. Some aspects of throughcare were unsatisfactory, 'notably induction, sentence planning and training for staff in personal officer work'. The small living units, however, along with 'manageable work parties and space for purposeful activities, should serve as models for the design of training prisons in the future'.

PRISONERS' COMMENTS Average request complaints system, good accommodation with integral sanitation and power point. The canteen is too small for this prison. Poor visiting opportunities with visits on only three days a week—Wed, Sat & Sun. Excellent Education Department. Wages aren't too bad, with an average of £7. You require an appointment to see the doctor here. Staff aren't overly keen to place you on report and adjudications seem to be fairly conducted, though there is much inconsistency between adjudicators in the punishments they impose. Food is OK and we meet each month with the kitchen staff which helps to iron out any problems. Excellent gym facilities with good access, good religious provision. Mail is not opened in our presence. Good access to the card phone.

HM YOI Stoke Heath

Market Drayton, Salop. TF9 2JL
Tel: 0630-654231 **Fax:** 0630-638875
Opened: 1964 **CNA:** 300 **Average Roll:** 271 **Category:** Closed YOI

i **BACKGROUND** Stoke Heath occupies a spacious site amid farmland and adjacent to an Army Camp about five miles south of Market Drayton in Shropshire. The site was developed as a four wing prison in 1964 and was converted to a closed Borstal two years later. It has held male offenders under the age of 21 ever since, formerly as a Youth Custody Centre and becoming a Young Offender Institution in 1988. Stoke Heath has a major rebuilding programme underway and, at the time of the last inspection, had taken on an additional function as allocation and remand centre. Neither the Governor nor BoV replied to our requests for information about the prison, and HMCIP published their latest inspection report on Stoke Heath in July 1992. A full inspection of the Institution took place in July 1994, though no date for publication of the report had been set by the time we went to press. This will be a brief entry, to avoid publishing inaccurate data, and full details will be given in the next edition.

OFFICIALS
AREA MGR: Dai Curtis
CHAIR BOV:
GOVERNOR: J. Allridge
MEDICAL:
CHAPLAIN: Rev Cooper

PROBATION: T. Law
EDUCATION:
LOCAL MP: John Biffen. Con

ACCOMMODATION & FACILITIES Six four-storey wings. The four original wings (A,B,C,D) in a H-shape with the crosspiece housing central services, education, kitchen, gymnasium etc. Two new wings (E,F) of a similar design with integral sanitation. Cell windows meshed.

VISITS *How to get there*: Train to Shrewsbury, bus to Ternhill Crossroads, then one mile walk. Special Transport: coach from Liverpool & Manchester, contact probation. Saturday special bus leaves Crewe BR Station at 1300 returning at 1545—fare about £2.
VISITING TIMES: Week Days: no visiting. Saturday: 1330–1530. Sunday: 1330–1530.

NOTES No staffed Visitors Centre or Childrens' Play Area. Canteen in visiting room. Local B&B, contact prison probation. No steps to visiting area, good access by wheelchair. Narrow doorways make access to toilet difficult.

WORKSHOPS VTC/CIT courses: Painting & Decorating; Bricklaying; Welding. Education, engineering workshop, laundry, gardens, kitchen, cleaners, red bands and orderlies.

DISCIPLINE High level of bullying. Majority of reports are for fighting, refusing to work, using abusive language and assaulting other inmates. Discrete segregation unit located between B&D wings, with ten ordinary cells and two strip cells; used also as a VPU.

ESTABLISHMENT REPORTS In a report (published 25th July 1992) of an inspection in December 1991, HMCIP said that Stoke Heath offers a reasonable environment and good facilities in which to train young offenders and prepare them for release. The establishment's temporary additional role as an allocation centre is out of keeping with the primary training function but is containable. New kitchen and integral sanitation. The establishment also needs a new gymnasium, and its security requires up-grading. Inmate/staff relationships appeared good and steps had been taken to address the problems of bullying and taxing among inmates. The sound procedural change, placing equal emphasis on punishing the perpetrators and supporting the victims, needs to be underpinned by a greater readiness on the part of Prison Service Headquarters to reclassify if necessary, and transfer inmates who are disruptive or threatening. Stoke Heath should also be better supported in relocating inmates who require full time medical supervision.

PRISONERS' COMMENTS The food is bad. Even by comparison with other establishment, portions are sometimes small, the menu is repetitive, the food has little taste and poor presentation. There is no catering committee and meal times are perverse. Personal Officers have too many inmates to look after, quantity has been at the expense of quality, and there should be group meetings where inmates can meet with officers. There is a need for more work in the community. Kit change only allows two pairs of socks and underpants per week and blankets can only be exchanged every six months. Civilian clothing limited to trainers. Only two out of three landings can have association in the evenings at any one time. There is no reason why all inmates cannot be allowed association each evening. Generally, incidents are handled fairly but staff use C&R to remove inmates to the seg unit even when they have agreed to go quietly. Bullying is not too much of a problem. Staff control cell lights.

HMP & YOI Styal

Wilmslow, Cheshire. SK9 4HR
Tel: 0625-532141 **Fax:** 0625-548060
Opened: 1895 **CNA:** 189 **Roll:** 184 **Category:** Closed Female

i **BACKGROUND** Styal prison began life in 1895 as a home for children under the Victorian Poor Law Acts, and it continued as a children's home until 1956. Between 1956 and 1959 Styal was used to house Hungarian refugees. The Prison Commissioners purchased the 16 hectare site in 1960 and, three years later, it opened as a semi-secure prison for women. Styal is one of three female prisons to have a Mother & Baby Unit—the others are located at HMP Holloway and HMP Askham Grange. Neither the Governor of Styal, nor the BoV, replied to our requests for information about the prison, and HMCIP published their latest inspection report on Styal in July 1992.

OFFICIALS
AREA MGR: Terry Bone
CHAIR BOV:
GOVERNOR: G. Walker
MEDICAL:
CHAPLAIN: Rev Woodley
PROBATION: Michael Denton
EDUCATION:
LOCAL MP: Neil Hamilton. Con

REGIME *week days*: 0750 unlock. 0815 breakfast. 0840 work. 1000 tea break. 1215 cease labour. 1230 dinner. 1325 work. 1630 cease labour. 1700 tea. 1730–2100 association.

week ends: 0750 unlock. 0815 breakfast. 0840 cleaning. 0900 church services (Sun). 1230 dinner. 1330 visits. 1700 tea. 1730–2100 association.

Out of cell: 12/24hrs weekdays and 12/24hrs at weekends.

ACCOMMODATION & FACILITIES Accommodation is in 16 living units, known as Houses. Two Houses (Brown & Howard) have single rooms, one House (Fry) has mostly single rooms with a few doubles, one House (Righton) has four single rooms with the rest doubles or trebles; all other Houses have rooms or dormitories capable of housing between 2 and 8 inmates. Special Needs Unit takes up to a dozen inmates who have emotional or behavioural problems; SNU has very limited regime due to unco-ordinated staff approach. Mother & Baby Unit in Mellanby House, see below. Personal Officer Scheme, drug counselling, sentence planning and card phones in all living units. No smoking in living units after 2030. No hairdressing service. Regular (and much resented) room inspections. Poor facilities for lifers who are not allowed days out—unlike New Hall for example. Routine censorship abolished but all mail is opened outwith the presence of the inmate to whom it is addressed. Card phones on all living units, access is good, but queues develop at peak times. Calls from prisoners to their families overseas may be permitted from the prison phone—reverse charge only!

MOTHER & BABY UNIT Maximum of twelve mothers and their babies, who can remain together in Mellanby House until the child reaches 18 months. Relaxed, clean and peaceful atmosphere, though HMCIP was concerned with inadequate showering facilities during his last inspection. Takes inmates from around the country, application to be made to Governor of current establishment. In 1994 there was widespread criticism after an inmate at Styal was allegedly handcuffed while giving birth at an outside hospital.

CANTEEN Reasonable size, clearly displayed prices and a varied stock. Operated by three storewomen who were keen to increase stock and reduce the number of local purchases. Open once per week with inmates attending on a house-by-house basis. HMCIP found adequate provision had been made for ethnic minority stock.

REQUESTS/COMPLAINTS Average of 25 formal R/C forms submitted each month, and replies were of a variable quality said HMCIP. Subjects requiring local replies received them within fourteen days, but those requiring a response from the Area Manager seldom received answers within the six weeks prescribed for his reply.

VISITS *How to get there*: Train to Manchester Piccadilly, local train to Styal, then 10 min walk to the prison. No Special Transport.
VISITING TIMES: Week Days: 1330–1530 M–F (up to 2hrs Wed 1hr others). Saturday: 1330–1530 (up to 90 mins). Sunday: No Visits.

NOTES Staffed Visitors Centre, canteen available Wednesday and Saturday. Childrens Play Area. Local B&B v.difficult to find. Ramp for wheelchairs.

EDUCATION F/T Education Officer, 3×f/t & 20p/t teachers and four Instruction Officers. Located in one of the Houses which had been converted into classrooms, Styal has a well equipped education department. Full daytime programme including basic education, home economics, computing, communication skills, and soft furnishings. Open Learning, Open University, though mainly for long termers. Evening classes five nights of week with a range of subjects concentrating on recreational work.

WORKSHOPS Labour Board meets weekly. Textile PSIF Workshop, VTC Soft Furnishing, Multi-Skills, Home Economics. Farm & Gardens, Mess, Works, Orderlies, Kitchens, Domestic, Induction and Education.

DISCIPLINE Alderly House (the Segregation Unit) contains fourteen rooms and two protective cells. All the former are large and fitted with integral sanitation.

MEDICAL P/t Medical Officer, 1×PNS, 2×SNS, 10×NS, 3×EN. Five bed ward in HCC, along with three single rooms, an isolation unit and two epileptic seizure recovery rooms. GU Clinic. Good dental service with visits each week and short waiting list for treatment. Three psychiatrists visit weekly and Optician as required. Report sick at unlock. No 'Well Woman' clinic.

GYMNASIUM & SPORTS Good sized and well equipped gymnasium, staffed by 1×PESO and 1×PEO, and used for numerous ball and team games. Stage area used for weights. Swimming pool, but requires many improvements before use. Hiking/camping expeditions, but security clearance for inmates can take many months. No outdoor exercise other than for those on PE. Inadequate weekend PE regime with most women being confined to their House blocks.

CHAPLAINCY Full time CE p/t RC and Methodist chaplains. Main church services Sunday morning with very good attendance.

FOOD Catering is House based with a kitchen in each unit of accommodation except the Health Care Centre. Meals are cooked by prisoners on each House, they are given no training, menus are determined centrally and inmates complain they are unimaginative, offered no choice and contained too much stodge. Food sampled each day by catering staff and the Governor. All inmates, except those in the segregation unit, dine in association.

ESTABLISHMENT REPORTS In a report (published 16th July 1992) of an inspection in February 1992, Judge Stephen Tumim, HMCIP, said that he was impressed by the tidy layout of the prison, the conditions and suitability of most of the buildings and the absence of litter and graffiti. Though evidence of drug abuse was increasing HMCIP could not detect any serious tensions among inmates. Many of the recommendations contained in HMCIP's previous report had been implemented and improvements were self-evident. Although inmates were for the most part cared for satisfactorily, significant improvements need to be made to the balance of regime activities and to the standards of catering if the prison is to continue to move in a positive direction.

HM Prisons Sudbury & Foston Hall

Ashbourne, Derbyshire. DE6 5HW
Tel: 0283-585511 **Fax:** 0283-585736
Opened: 1942 **CNA:** 509 **Average Roll:** 436 **Category:** D. Male Open

BACKGROUND Sudbury open prison is situated 14 miles west of Derby and five miles east of Uttoxeter. Sudbury was built in 1942 as an American military hospital and many of the original structures, including the living accommodation, are still standing and in use. The site was acquired by the then Prison Commissioners in 1947 and opened in 1948 as an open training prison for adult males. Foston Hall, a Victorian country mansion, is situated two miles east of Sudbury. The Prison Department acquired the site from Derbyshire County Council in 1954 and opened it as a Junior Detention Centre in December 1955. In 1988 Foston Hall was redesignated as an education centre with open prison categorisation and has since been administered as a satellite of Sudbury. The Governor did not reply to our request for information about the prison and the BoV, though they declined to provide a copy of their latest annual report, did provide a press release. HMCIP published their latest inspection report on Sudbury/Foston in November 1992: the contents being far more critical than the BoV statement, set out in full below, which details no criticisms at all.

OFFICIALS
AREA MGR: Dai Curtis
CHAIR BOV: W.N.K Rowley
GOVERNOR: P. Salter
MEDICAL:
CHAPLAIN: Rev
PROBATION: Elizabeth Coe
EDUCATION:
LOCAL MP: E. Currie/P. McLoughlin. Con
STAFFING: 199 Staff in Post, 78 in unified grades.

REGIME *week days*: Details are for Sudbury, Foston denoted by (F:). Additional roll checks signalled by ringing of hand bell. 0730 (F:0720) roll check, breakfast, applications. 0815 (F:0840) work. 1215 (F:1200) dinner. 1300 roll check. 1315 (F:1300) work. 1650 (F:1645) tea, association. 1800 roll check 2045 (F:2045) roll check.

week ends: 0730 (F:0720) roll check, breakfast, applications. 0815 (F:0830) cleaning. 1015 (F:1015)inspection (both Sat & Sun). 1145 roll check. 1150 (F:1200) dinner, association. 1630 (F:1615) tea, association. 1800 (F:1800) roll check. 2045 (F:2040) roll check.

Out of cell: 24/24hrs weekdays and 24/24hrs at weekends.

ACCOMMODATION & FACILITIES
Sudbury: Dormitory accommodation located on each side of central corridor. Two other units

house kitchen and outworkers. All dorms have hot water boiler, toilets and showers. Three card phones, personal officer scheme and sentence planning. **Foston:** mainly dormitories although a small number of single rooms, cramped conditions but generally in a satisfactory state of repair. One card phone.

CANTEEN Well sited canteen in Sudbury off main corridor, open Thurs and Fri with attendance in rotation. Not a very wide stock carried, private cash restricted to toiletries, no local purchase scheme. Foston canteen sited off main hall, restricted stock and open once per week.

VISITS *How to get there*: Train to Burton on Trent, Tutbury or Uttoxeter. Stevenson bus 401 to Sudbury & Foston Hall. Trent Bus 104 from Derby to 'Salt Box' cafe then Stevenson bus 401 to Sudbury or Foston. No Special Transport.
VISITING TIMES: Week Days: 1330–1530. Saturday: 1330–1530 No PVOs weekends. Sunday: 1330–1530.

NOTES No staffed Visitors Centre, but limited facilities available. Canteen and Childrens Play Area. Local B&B. Baby-changing facilities and disabled toilet.

EDUCATION Ten f/t and 20 p/t teaching staff. About 75 places on education available at each establishment. Classes 0830–1145, 1315–1615, evening classes only two days per week for 36 weeks of the year.

WORKSHOPS VTC/CIT courses: Bricklaying, Painting & Decorating, Technical Store-keeping, Motor Mechanics, Horticulture. Heavy investment in PSIF workshops with laundry (serving ten establishments), wood working shop making cell furniture, boots and shoes, contract services and leather slipper manufacture. Farm & Gardens with NVQ and polytunnels producing salad crops: Sudbury won the Windlesham Trophy for the best kept prison grounds and gardens. Job Club with good reputation and well established track record.

DISCIPLINE Segregation Unit at Sudbury in an appalling condition and unsuitable for segregation. Conduct of adjudications thorough and fair, level of adjudications (about two per day) not excessive. Absconds from Sudbury/Foston running at about 90 per year.

MEDICAL Part time Medical Officer, 1×HCSO, 3×HCO. No records of blood or urine analysis on reception at time of inspection though now being carried out. HCC with six-bed ward and two single rooms. Good dental facilities.

GYMNASIUM & SPORTS 1×PESO and 3×PEO. Facilities very good at Sudbury, not so good at Foston. Sudbury has good sports hall and weights room, whereas Foston has a gym that is too small for organised games. Good external facilities in both establishments, two soccer pitches, large rugby field, artificial cricket pitch and bowling green.

CHAPLAINCY Full time CE chaplain, p/t RC and Methodist ministers. Pentecostal minister conducts mid-week service twice per month. Chapels at both Sudbury and Foston provide multi-faith rooms. Local villagers in Sudbury complain about where inmates may sit in outside churches.

FOOD Staffing: 1×SO, 5×Officer (caterers), and an inmate work party of 25. New kitchen December 1991 at Sudbury and refurbished kitchen at Foston. Meals though satisfactory were not very appetising nor well presented. No pre-select menu system. All meals in dining room.

ESTABLISHMENT REPORTS In a report (published 23rd November 1993) of an inspection in July 1993, HMCIP, said that Sudbury had the potential to become an excellent open training prison. First class training facilities are available to prisoners and HMCIP saw evidence of ability among staff. However, at the time of the inspection, the prison was falling well short of its capability. In the long-term it may be wise to develop the whole establishment at Sudbury. The closure of Foston Hall is not recommended until Sudbury incorporates the best elements of the Foston regime. There is a high level of activities at Sudbury. A sophisticated education department offers encouragement to improve learning skills. The general behaviour of inmates was satisfactory and relationships with staff were affable. The treatment of lifers and the quality of work in the community were commendable. Overall, life for inmates is reasonable although the prison lacks coherence and a purpose with which staff could identify. HMCIP received criticisms of senior management, who were said to be rarely seen and unsupportive. Judge Tumim was left reflecting how much more purposeful life for inmates and staff at Sudbury could—and should—be.

BoV PRESS RELEASE 29th MARCH 1994 The Board of Visitors of HM.Prison Sudbury has delivered its annual report on the establishment to the Home Secretary. In it the Board, whose function is to monitor the administration of the prison, welcomes the implementation of the Personal Officer scheme under which inmates are allocated to individual prison officers who are trained to deal with day to day welfare issues previously dealt with by the Probation Service. They have commented favourably on the conversion into a series of two-man rooms of the old open dormitories built as wards for an American Army Hospital in World War II. These improvements in the regime of the prison are seen as a major contributory factor in the reduction of absconds during 1993 from 106 to 72. The prison holds an average population of 426 D category inmates, for the most part coming to the end of their sentences. Rehabilitation is therefore a major aspect of the role of the prison. A Job Club established with the aid of the Employment Service has had spectacular success, placing 50% of candidates in employment upon release. The Board sees this as a reflection of the efforts put into education and training in trade skills and commends all those involved.

PRISONERS' COMMENTS The standard of hygiene and the quality of food are both very bad at Sudbury, with little or no variety in the diet and the system of choice at the hot plate instead of by pre-selection is unfair to latecomers. Foston should either be closed or receive a radical face-lift. There is little space for inmates and no TV after 2030. Meal time are too close together. PE favours a minority who engage in activities in which the PE staff are interested, and unsupervised cross country has ceased. Canteen prices are higher at Foston than Sudbury, lifers are restricted on numbers allowed in dorms and you can only get a straight answer from the No.1 Governor. Many staff have old fashioned attitudes, induction programme lacks information and visitors have to sit at tables instructed by staff which is unnecessary in an open prison. Long termers have to wait nine months before working outside the prison, SWIP office is not open often enough, there is a lack of continuity in the evenings at Foston Hall and it is very difficult to see the doctor.

HM Prison Swaleside

Eastchurch, Sheerness, Kent. ME12 4DZ
Tel: 0795-880766 **Fax:** 0795-880607
Opened: 1985 **CNA:** 504 **Average Roll:** 488 **Category:** B. Male

i **BACKGROUND** Swaleside is a new prison, built between 1985 and 1988, located in a cluster of prisons on the Isle of Sheppey in the Thames estuary. Sheppey is a featureless, low lying, island, Sheerness its only town of any size is at the western edge of the island. The prison estate, comprising HMPs Elmley, Standford Hill and Swaleside lie at the eastern edge some seven miles away. A road bridge across the tidal water is the only connection with the mainland. Swaleside is a B Category establishment and is said to be a dispersal prison in everything but name: analysis showed that half the 498 inmates come from London, 463 of them are serving over four years (72 were serving life), with almost two-thirds convicted of robbery. The Governor did not reply to our request for information about the prison, though the BoV kindly supplied a copy of their latest annual report. HMCIP published their latest inspection report on Swaleside in July 1994.

OFFICIALS

AREA MGR: John Hunter
CHAIR BOV: C.J. Jenings
GOVERNOR: R. Tasker
MEDICAL:
CHAPLAIN: Rev Green
PROBATION: Simon Penny
EDUCATION:
LOCAL MP: Roger Moate. Con
STAFFING: 218 Staff in Post including specialists grades.

REGIME *week days*: 0800 unlock. 0815 breakfast. 0910 work. 1000 adjudications. 1140 cease labour. 1200 dinner. 1230 lock up. 1330 unlock. 1345 work. 1610 cease labour. 1630 tea. 1700 lock up. 1800–2000 association.

week ends: 0800 unlock. 0815 breakfast. 0900 sick parade, CE Service (Sun). 1000 adjudications, RC Mass (Sun). 1200 dinner. 1230 lock up. 1330 unlock, visits, association, PE. 1345 sports field. 1415 half–time movement from sports field. 1620 medications. 1630 tea. 1700 lock up. 1730–2000 association.

Out of cell: 9.5/24hrs weekdays and 10/24hrs at weekends.

ACCOMMODATION & FACILITIES Four wings each with 126 single cells with integral sanitation. Each wing has three landings each with three short 14-cell spurs. Showers and bathing facilities discrete to each spur, a small launderette allows for personal washing and there are cooking facilities on each wing. Three TV rooms, dining rooms converted for snooker and pool. Cleanliness leaves much to be desired. Sentence planning and personal officer scheme of questionable effectiveness. Comprehensive i/p list.

REQUESTS & COMPLAINTS A member of the Swaleside BoV monitors request/complaint forms and gives a verbal report at monthly board meetings. According to the latest BoV Annual Report, the majority of R/Cs are dealt with successfully and on time and though most prisoners are using the system for genuine problems, 'there remains a small minority who have found yet another means of attention seeking'.

CANTEEN Canteen currently operated from one central unit and is managed by a canteen Manager, Storeman and Prison Auxiliaries. Carries a huge 350 lines of stock and each inmate spends an average of £6 from earnings and £12 private cash each week—the canteen manager buys £250 of fresh meat each week for cooking on the wings. Plans to resite the canteen and allow it to open Friday evenings and weekends.

VISITS *How to get there*: Train to Sheerness then bus (362) to Eastchurch, then 20 min walk to prison. Special transport: ABBA Coaches leaves Victoria 1100 on Saturdays and Wednesdays, adult £10 children £5 return, other pick up points can be arranged if on route, contact Mr O'Toole: 081 859 1808/8708.
VISITING TIMES: Week Days: 1345–1545. Saturday: 1345–1545. Sunday: 1345–1545.

NOTES Small Visitors Centre (opened 1994). Canteen (by outside contractor). Children's Play Area. No smoking. Contact home probation officer for details of B&B in Sheerness—difficult to find in the Summer. Baby changing room, visits room on first floor, no wheelchair access but special arrangements can be made with prior notice.

EDUCATION Excellent educational facilities, well stocked library and a good range of foreign language material. Open 50 weeks of the year but no evening classes. Daytime programme with full time places for 100 inmates (70 on general education and 30 on art and craft courses). Basic core education in English, maths and English as a second language. Open learning and OU catered for.

WORKSHOPS VTC/CIT: trade courses in Painting & Decorating, Industrial Cleaning (v.pop), Bricklaying and Micro-engineering, all of which are well supported. A new course in Hairdressing has proved very popular. Textile workshop (white cooks jackets). Contract Services workshop (plug and lamp assembly, bulkhead fittings, horse jumps, cell furniture and chipboard side tables). Plans to expand range of products resulted in separate wood machine shop being equipped and to involve inmates in the decision-making process, should make for better prisoner participation than has hitherto been possible at Swaleside.

DISCIPLINE HMCIP analysed the paperwork of adjudications in a six month period and was satisfied that hearings were carried out fairly and awards were consistent and appropriate. Rule 43 GOAD segregation was another matter felt the BoV: 'At the time of writing one man is in his ninth month of solitary confinement and two others in excess of four months . . . this may sometimes be the prisoner's own fault, but it remains inhumane and unacceptable'. The segregation unit contained 'far too many prisoners who should not be there'.

MEDICAL Full time Medical Officer and p/t MO, 1×HCPO, 1×HCSO and 6×HCO. Swaleside has a 24 hour inpatient hospital with fourteen beds, full out-patient facilities and clinics for Asthma/Epilepsy, Cardiac, and Diabetes. In conjunction with HMPs Elmley, Standford Hill and Blantyre House, blood screening for cholesterol levels is available—using equipment loaned free by a drug company—and counselling is available for those found to be at risk. Dentist has two sessions per week, a waiting list is used other than for emergencies.

PROBATION Swaleside is supplied with probation staff seconded from Kent Probation Service. The Senior Probation Officer is assisted by four main grade officers—one main grade to each wing, plus each officer's specialities available to the whole prison. Currently running Alcohol, Anger Management and Straight Thinking courses. Lifer Group.

GYMNASIUM & SPORTS 1×PESO and 2×PEO. Football, rugby, volley ball, basket ball, badminton, weight lifting are some of the activities offered in Swaleside. Externally the prison has participated in both inter-prison and external group competitions producing, according to the BoV, 'sides to be reckoned with'! Individual achievements include power lifting in which Swaleside has reached the National Standards. A CSLA Course for leadership helps prisoners foster links with life outside prison.

CHAPLAINCY Part time CE chaplain, RC and Methodist ministers. High percentage of ethnic prisoners and the Imam has successfully cultivated a group which now regularly has between 40 and 60 prisoners at each meeting. Prison operates a 'come and go' policy for the chapel, and there is little evidence of this system being abused. A party was organised at Christmas for prisoners and their children at which some 400 attended. Weekly Chaplains Group.

FOOD Much food now arrives ready-prepared, breakfast is a one-choice option. Both dinner and tea meals provide four choices—though for ordinary diets only. PO Caterer assisted by two SO caterers, two officer grades and four industrial cooks with a work party of 15 prisoners who all have to complete aninduction, Health & Hygiene course leading to an in-house Food-Handling Certificate. Similar courses run for those on wing hot plates. BoV report the planned refurbishment of the kitchen has been taken out of 1995/96 budget and now scheduled for 1996/97: 'Swaleside has only been open for five years, it is incredible that the kitchen was so ill-designed that £1m is now needed to put it in order'.

ESTABLISHMENT REPORTS In a report (published 23rd November 1993) of an inspection in July 1993, HMCIP, said that Swaleside continues to hold a 'hostile and difficult' population and it was to the credit of the discipline staff that they were not intimidated and were maintaining order and control in all areas of the prison. The rising number of assaults on staff (49 in 1993 and seven in the first month of 1994) was a major concern and could be the result of the high turnover of staff and the high ratio of inexperienced officers being posted to the prison. The daytime education programme and VTC courses were praiseworthy but the absence of evening classes could not be defended. The Governor told HMCIP that there 'was a possibility that Swaleside might become a dispersal prison'.

BOV Annual Report 1993/94: Four matters requiring immediate attention were identified. For the third year running the situation regarding mentally disturbed prisoners was raised. Inmates being confined in the segregation unit for 23 hours/day was inhumane and unacceptable. Transfers from Cat.C prisons without explanation may not be a punishment in theory but, to those at the sharp end it is most certainly seen and accepted as a punishment. An alleged assault by staff at Wandsworth had been promptly passed to that establishment for investigation. Five months elapsed and in spite of numerous determined efforts no explanation or investigation report has been forthcoming; a prevarication that was completely unacceptable.

PRISONERS' COMMENTS Initial Request forms are rarely dealt with satisfactorily. The cells are single, clean and in-cell power is being fitted at the moment. Canteen prices are very high. The visiting facilities are excellent, refreshments provided by private contractor of a very high standard. Medical staff treat you as a prisoner first and patient second, you really have to battle to get help. Adjudications can produce heavy-handed punishments depending more on the Governor than the offence committed. The food has deteriorated, same meals week in and week out, I could tell you the dinner three months ahead. Very good gym facilities and a PE staff who have a good attitude. No problems with the mail, but three phones between more than 100 inmates is just not adequate.

HM Prison Swansea

Oystermouth Road, Swansea, West Glamorgam. SA1 2SR
Tel: 0792-464030 **Fax:** 0792-642979
Opened: 1861 **CNA:** 208 **Roll:** 202 **Category:** Male Local

i **BACKGROUND** Swansea prison is situated about half a mile from the city centre, on the coastal road and directly beside Swansea Football Club. Building started in 1845 and was completed in 1861. It functioned as a prison for both male and female prisoners until 1922 when females were transferred to Cardiff prison. Swansea has since operated as a local prison, holding prisoners up to and including Category B. Swansea also holds and allocates young offenders and it was a spate of YO suicides at Swansea in the early 1980's which started the Samaritan-trained inmate Listener Scheme that is now developing into a national provision. The Governor provided an abundance of up to date information about the prison, and the BoV kindly provided a copy of their 1993/4 annual report. HMCIP published their latest inspection report on Swansea in May 1993.

OFFICIALS

AREA MGR: J. Wilkinson
CHAIR BOV: Mr A. Stewart
GOVERNOR: J. Heyes
MEDICAL: Dr. R.R. Jones
CHAPLAIN: Rev E. Hunt
PROBATION: Mrs G. King
EDUCATION: Ms A. McRae
LOCAL MP: Alan Williams. Lab
STAFFING: 5 Governor grades, 6 Principal Officers, 18 Senior Officers and 98 Officers: 146 in unified grades including specialist staff.

☞ **REGIME** *week days*: 0745 unlock/breakfast. 0830 work/activities. 1200 activities cease. 1215 lunch, roll check. 1245 lock up. 1315 activities. 1645 cease activities. 1700 serve main meal, roll check. 1730 lock up. 1800 association. 2045 lock up.

week ends: 0745 unlock/breakfast. 0845 work/activities. 1200 activities cease. 1215 lunch, roll check. 1245 lock up. 1315 activities. 1545 cease activities. 1600 serve main meal, roll check. 1630 lock up. 1700 association. 2045 lock up.

Out of cell: 12/24hrs weekdays and 11/24hrs at weekends.

ACCOMMODATION & FACILITIES
A.wing 91 cells for male convicted all with integral sanitation—waiting list for association and subject to min 14 days on wing; B.wing 24 cells for male remands no integral sanitation; D.Wing male young offenders (closed May 1994 for refurbishment). D.Wing to close for refurbishment early 1995. Segregation and VPU (01 landing) with 25 cells with integral sanitation. VPU, Sentence Planning, Drug Counselling, Bail Information, Listener and Personal Officer Schemes. Though Swansea is a local prison the list of in-possession articles is comprehensive, including record players etc, but no caged birds. All new arrivals are given a locally produced booklet providing essential information about the prison. Routine censorship abolished but examination takes place outwith the presence of the inmate. Swansea allows SAE to be sent in. Card phones located in the association areas and HMCIP criticised the lack of privacy hoods: 'It was almost impossible to conduct a telephone conversation against background noise'. Phonecards through earnings or private cash, maximum of two i/p at any one time.

CANTEEN 'The premises used for the prison shop' said HMCIP, 'resembled a dungeon'. There is no natural light or ventilation and the temperature frequently exceeded 80°F. About 130 items of stock are held and there are limited local purchase facilities. Price lists displayed in all wings. Remands visit twice per week and though convicted only once per week private cash can be used to supplement earnings. No limit applied on private cash spends.

REQUESTS/COMPLAINTS Dealt with every day other than Sunday. On average eight formal R/C forms issued each month. Notices about the R/C procedure were not displayed on notice boards in the wings said HMCIP, and revealed that one reason advanced for the low number of formal R/C was that prisoners perceived complaining as likely to provoke a transfer. 'Many were generally ill-informed about the complaints/requests system and a small number expressed an inherent lack of confidence in the system'. HMCIP examined the files of R/C forms and found the quality of the replies 'variable' though with the majority receiving replies within stated time targets.

VISITS *How to get there*: Train to Swansea, bus to Quandrant Bus Station, then five min walk to the prison. No Special Transport.
VISITING TIMES: Week Days: 1330–1530. Saturday: 1330–1530. Sunday: no visits.

NOTES Staffed Visitors Centre, canteen and Childrens Play Area. Contact prison probation for details of local B&B. Wheelchair access possible with prior notice. Baby-changing facilities available.

EDUCATION Contract for educational services at Swansea awarded to Bristol University. Education open 48 weeks of the year with full day-time programme and evening classes Mon–Fri. Four full-time teachers. Daytime: open learning, art, IT, maths, woodwork, English, cooking, guitar, AIDS/safe sex, lifeskills and foundation courses in drugs and suicide prevention.

WORKSHOPS Two workshops: joinery and textiles (VPU), with wages ranging between £7 and £12.

DISCIPLINE Adjudications at Swansea, according to the BoV Annual Report for 1993/94, are running at between 40 and 50 per month. BoV report no in-house procedure for making detailed breakdowns or analysis of adjudications and it is an area in which the Board would wish to extend its work.

MEDICAL Fourteen bed Health Care Centre built 1979. Part time Medical Officer and visiting consultants. BoV report that though the hospital now has a Principal Health Care Officer in post, 'it still remains a concern to the Board that there is no State Registered Nurse among the staff'. A recent drug research survey conducted by Dr J. Keene, University College Swansea, gathered from replies to questionnaires given to inmates at Swansea, indicates a high level of drug misuse among prisoners. Drug counselling is available at Swansea though the BoV report that 'increased searches, possible use of police dogs and voluntary urine testing' are among the measures currently being examined.

GYMNASIUM & SPORTS Inmates wishing to use the gymnasium should make application on the wing or see one of the PEO's. No scheduled gym classes as such.

CHAPLAINCY Part time C/E, RC and Methodist chaplains. Other faiths catered for as necessary. Main church service Sunday morning.

FOOD According to the Swansea BoV in their 1993/94 Annual Report, 'the kitchen is outdated and fails to meet present day expectations'. Despite this the kitchen staff have managed to introduce a new meal time pattern with the main meal of the day being served at tea-time, while a lighter meal is served for lunch.

ESTABLISHMENT REPORTS Last inspection report published by HMCIP May 1993.

BoV Annual Report 1993/94 records no matters on which the Board require a response from the Secretary of State: 'Progress, if somewhat slower than had been hoped, has been made on the refurbishment plan with A.wing re-roofing and integral sanitation. Whilst the necessary works have created noise, the "atmosphere" of the prison has been calmer and quieter than in some previous years with no major incidents or disturbances. Certainly that is a reflection on the good relationships between staff and inmates'.

GOVERNOR'S COMMENTS Plans to introduce an increased range of educational classes, complete refurbishment plans on time and increase the number of treatment groups.

PRISONERS' COMMENTS Accommodation yet to be refurbished is unfit for habitation, canteen is inefficient and requires computerisation. Visiting arrangements are too restricted with particular complaints in relation to legal visits. Only education comes away with a clean bill of health. Medical services are consistently rated 'poor' and the food quality is similarly described. Though card phones are available there are no hoods fitted and, particularly with refurbishment in progress, it is often difficult to hear what is being said.

HM YOI Swinfen Hall

Lichfield, Staffs. WS14 9QS
Tel: 0543-481229 **Fax:** 0543-480138
Opened: 1962 **CNA:** 167 **Roll:** 163 **Category:** Closed YOI

i **BACKGROUND** Swinfen Hall was built in part of the grounds of a house of the same name, and opened as a closed Borstal in 1962. Between 1967 and 1972 Swinfen Hall operated as a closed Detention Centre, then it began to receive young inmates. Swinfen Hall is now a Young Offender Institution holding inmates serving between four years and life. The establishment operates the Core Sex Offender Treatment Programme. Neither the Governor nor BoV replied to our requests for information about the YOI, and HMCIP published their latest inspection report on Swinfen Hall in December 1993.

OFFICIALS
AREA MGR: Dai Curtis
CHAIR BOV:
GOVERNOR: A.J. Davis
MEDICAL:
CHAPLAIN: Rev Fagan
PROBATION: Eric Brady
EDUCATION:
LOCAL MP: David Lightbown. Con

REGIME *week days*: 0745 unlock, 0805 breakfast. 0900 labour. 1145 cease labour. 1150 dinner, lock up. 1400 labour. 1645 cease labour. 1650 tea, lock up. 1805 association & Gymnasium. 1940 Gymnasium ends. 2010 association ends, 2015 lock up.

week ends: 0745 unlock, 0805 breakfast, 0900 cell cleaning and inspection. 1150 dinner, lock up. 1400 unlock, association, visits. 1640 association ends. 1650 tea, lock up. No evening association weekends.

Out of cell: 9.10/24hrs weekdays and 6.55/24hrs at weekends.

ACCOMMODATION Three Wings (A,B,C) each with 58 single cells and one 8-man dorm. All have integral sanitation—old recesses converted to association rooms, clean and tidy cell blocks with showering facilities, table-tennis, pool and table football. Stage system in operation, top landing (three's) of C.wing provides enhanced regime, separate TV rooms, more privileges, kettle and fridge. Cell searches every 8 weeks. Washing machine and dryer on each Wing. Swinfen (still) doesn't open the mail in front of the inmate, but does so at a central point and it is then distributed to the Wings. Letters to family are encouraged and there are very few restrictions on numbers. Four phonecards can be bought each week, these are held in Wing office, given out just prior to the call and retrieved by staff immediately afterwards; designed to reduce bullying and 'taxing'. All calls limited to maximum of ten minutes duration and have to be booked in advance.

CANTEEN Well situated off main corridor linking Wings. F/t storeman operates canteen which pays out on Thursdays. £10 per month private cash spends. Swinfen Hall operates a 'delivery service' to counteract bullying and allows access to canteen twice per week. Stock is very restricted due to shortage of space and is being revised with refrigerator being installed.

REQUESTS/COMPLAINTS Very little recourse to formal R/C system—5 or 6 a month—each sent direct to Governor who delegates reply, and checks that it has been done. Time targets being met. Main subjects tend to be loss of property from cells—privacy locks being considered. Wing Application system deals with most matters.

VISITS *How to get there*: Bus or train to Lichfield then taxi or Trent Valley bus (901) from Birmingham passes prison gate. No Special Transport.
VISITING TIMES: Week Days: 1400–1600 Mon–Thu. Friday 1430–1600. Saturday: 1400–1600. Sunday: 1400–1600.

NOTES Visitors Centre but closed for last three years, limited facilities. WRVS canteen and Childrens Play Area. Contact prison probation officer for details of B&B in Lichfield. Visits often last full two hours. Random sample of prisoners strip-searched after each visit. Maximum of 22 visits at any one time.

EDUCATION Ten rooms (7 classes, 3 special rooms for cookery, computing and business studies). Education staff part of Tamworth College who have recently been awarded a three year contract at the YOI. Yvonne Hurlow, Education Officer, assisted by f/t Deputy, 2 f/t lecturers, VTC Instructor and 26 p/t teachers. 50 week education year. Evening classes (2 nights a week 1815–1945) in: leisure computing, starting your own business, cookery, musical workshops, first aid, health & hygiene, car maintenance course planned. HMCIP was 'disappointed by lack of enthusiasm for education programme shown by many uniformed staff'.

WORKSHOPS Education, VTC Computing, CIT Bricks and Paints, works, farm, estates, kitchen, gardens, cleaners and orderlies. £2.50 (UB40) to £8.50 in kitchen. Employment Board deals with labour applications.

DISCIPLINE Average of 2–3 per day. Records show that most inmates plead guilty to charges but HMCIP, who examined the records of 194 adjudications at Swinfen Hall, was concerned that no proper scrutiny was made by adjudicator to discover if guilt was genuine or an acceptance of the inevitable: 'At the least there ought to have been a statement by the adjudicating officer that he was satisfied that the charge had been proved and that the inmate was guilty . . . the record of the proceedings generally seemed cursory'.

MEDICAL Health Care Centre clean and recently decorated. Three inpatient rooms but no integral sanitation. Dental and visiting specialists rooms. No X-ray equipment. Medical Officer p/t GP. Visiting psychiatrist—ex Prison Service PMO—5 sessions a week. 1×HCSO and 2×HCO's provide cover 0745–2015. Health Care staff seemed well motivated and had a positive therapeutic approach. Dentist: 1 sess/wk with large waiting list. Optician services provided by local hospital. HIV/AIDS video shown to all new receptions, who are seen on arrival by health care staff. Only YOI to have a Sex-Offender programme: 2×20 week courses a year, though lack of trained staff on wings to cope with after-effects.

GYMNASIUM & SPORTS Available 0900–1940 Mon–Fri and 0900–1630 weekends. 1×PESO and 3×PEO's. Weights, basketball, badminton, remedials. Tarmac area (closed for repair) and sports field for soccer, rugby, cricket, athletics and target-golf. Externally there is a cross-country course, canoeing, hiking and swimming for those who qualify on security and behavioural grounds. Gymnasium well attended and activities enjoyed by inmates.

CHAPLAINCY P/t CE Chaplain, assisted by p/t RC and Methodist ministers. Visiting ministers from Muslim and Sikh religions. Chaplain sees all new receptions. Bible study Monday and Discussion Group on Thursday. Counselling available on wide range of issues. Application to Wing Office.

FOOD Breakfast 0805, dinner 1150 and tea 1650. 1×SO assisted by 3 Officer Caterers and a kitchen party of 11 inmates. Choice of three dishes, four week menu system in operation. Catering Committee including inmates has resolved many grievances and produced a menu in-keeping with the majority of inmates. HMCIP who examined the menu thought there was a predominance of 'stew-type' meals.

ESTABLISHMENT REPORTS The regime at Swinfen Hall was constructive and forward looking and the training programme was well-regarded by prisoners said HMCIP in a Report (published 7th December 1993) of an inspection carried out in June 1993. Staff generally were well motivated and committed to the principle of challenging prisoners' behaviour. It was refreshing to find such a united and positive staff staff culture in the prison. More purposeful activity is required, however, and an urgent need for a group work area to be created. Work training opportunities should be expanded and the regime would benefit from the provision of more practical training rather than one dependent on education. The overall impression of Swinfen Hall was very favourable.

HM YOI Thorn Cross

Appleton Thorn, Warrington, Cheshire. WA4 4RL
Tel: 0925-602081 **Fax:** 0925-262153
Opened: 1985 **CNA:** 240 **Average Roll:** 176 **Category:** Open YOI

i **BACKGROUND** HM YOI Thorn Cross sits on the extreme northern edge of the Cheshire plain, just south of the River Mersey at Warrington. It is surrounded by open countryside, some two miles from the A49 main Warrington to Whitchurch road and has no security fence or gatehouse. The site, formerly a Royal Naval Air Station, passed to the Prison Department in 1970 and was used as an open prison for adult males (operating as HMP Appleton Thorn) until 1981. The entire camp was replaced between 1982–85 by a purpose-built open establishment for young offenders. Thorn Cross has been used for this purpose ever since with only minor additions or alterations, and holds inmates between 15 and 21 years. Neither the Governor nor BoV replied to our requests for information about the prison, and HMCIP published their latest inspection report on Thorn Cross in March 1994.

OFFICIALS
AREA MGR: Ian Lockwood
CHAIR BOV:
GOVERNOR: I. Windebank
MEDICAL:
CHAPLAIN: Rev Mellor
PROBATION: Gordon Carr
EDUCATION:
LOCAL MP: Michael Hall. Lab
STAFFING: 5 Governor grades, 7 Principal Officers, 13 Senior Officers and 53 Officers, including specialist staff.

REGIME *week days*: 0730 unlock, 0800 breakfast. 0845 work. 11.45 dinner. 1300 work. 1630 cease labour. 1655 tea. 1730–2030 association.

week ends: 0730 unlock, 0815. breakfast. 0830 cleaning, activities. 11.30 dinner. 1300 activities, association. 1600 tea. 1730–2030 association.

Out of cell: 13/24hrs weekdays and 13/24hrs at weekends.

ACCOMMODATION & FACILITIES Thorn Cross has accommodation for 300 inmates located in five Units (1,2,3,4,5) each holding 60 inmates. Unit 1 is currently closed giving a reduced in-use CNA of 240. Single rooms furnished with carpet, bed, table, and locker. Inmates have access to sanitation at all times and keys to their own rooms. Units 2&3 have laundry facilities. Dine out facilities, association rooms and good range of recreational facilities. Very clean and relaxed environment with good inmate/staff relationships. Good i/p list with combined sound system or equivilent alternatives, own shoes, trainers, socks and underpants—seven pairs of each. Personal Officer scheme, very little bullying confirmed by survey. Two card phones on each Unit, mail opened outwith presence of inmate and issued dinner time, and relatives/friends can send in stamps.

CANTEEN Open Friday afternoon only (Friday morning for Juveniles) for both earnings and private cash. Small room off main concourse, no fridge, stock of just over 100 items. Requires development.

VISITS *How to get there*: Train to Warrington and then bus (8) to prison. No Special Transport.
VISITING TIMES: Week Days: no visits. Saturday: 1315–1545. Sunday: 1315–1545.

NOTES No staffed Visitors Centre. Canteen and Childrens Play Area. No overnight stay facilities. Good wheelchair access. Special visits during the week may be restricted in duration. Meals or sandwiches available from Thorn Public House.

EDUCATION Contracted out to City College, Wythenshawe, Manchester. Nine classrooms on two floors, well equipped and in good condition. Special rooms for woodwork, handicrafts, information technology and catering. NVQ Business Studies. Computing, art study group and music among others. Large library next to education department, open Mon/Wed evenings, and Fri afternoons. Well attended and with local order facility.

WORKSHOPS VTC/CIT courses: Painting & Decorating, Plastering, Mechanical Engineering, Tailoring, Braille, and Caterbase. Parties: Kitchen, Gardens, Education, Works, Community Service, Cleaners, Orderlies, and Stores. Wages average £6.60, UB40 £2.50.

DISCIPLINE Segregation takes place in Unit 6, though little use is made of it. Unit has 14 cells, 12 with integral sanitation and two unfurnished. Total of 543 adjudications in the eight months prior to the inspection, properly conducted, minor errors in recording process and awards even-handed.

MEDICAL Part time Medical Officer, 1×HCSO, 2×HCO. HCC with five inpatient rooms, two with integral sanitation. Dentist visits weekly, with two week waiting list for non-urgent cases. Medical examinations on reception were conducted too briefly with an average of just 2 mins each! Multi-disciplinary HIV/AIDS, substance abuse team, with counselling skills.

GYMNASIUM & SPORTS 1×PEPO, 1×PESO and 4×PEO. Large indoor sports hall marked out for badminton, volleyball, five-a-side, basketball and indoor hockey. Weights gym with multi-gym facilities. Outdoor large tarmac yard, basketball court and five-a-side soccer pitch. Three grassed soccer pitches, one rugby pitch and two cricket wickets, one artifical. Extremely comprehensive sports programme, forward-thinking and committed PE staff who have developed excellent links with the community.

CHAPLAINCY Part time CE chaplain, RC and Methodist ministers. CE Service 0900 Sun. Chaplain's Hour 1730 Mon. RC Mass 1730 Wed. Bible Study 1730 Thurs. Religious Instruction class 1800 Fri. Large list of visiting ministers of non-Christian faiths.

FOOD Staffing: 1×SO, 3×Officer (caterers), and an inmate work party of 10. Three week menu cycle but revised every three months. Inmate food committee (2 reps from each Unit) meets every two months. NVQ Caterbase course. Food tasty and filling. very good hygiene in kitchen with staff keen about quality.

ESTABLISHMENT REPORTS Thorn Cross is clean with a cheerful prison population, said HMCIP in a report (published 10 March 1994) of an inspection in August and September 1993. Staff showed enthusiasm and they were clearly doing work they enjoyed and doing it well. The vocational training and construction industry training courses and physical education were good features, but formal education had suffered over the last year because of tension between the Home Office and teachers and the successors of local education authorities.

PRISONERS' COMMENTS Education is either for the academically good or those with learning problems, there doesn't seem to be any middle ground. There should be more courses in English, maths, history, geography and current affairs. General all round satisfaction with the institution, though resentment at not being allowed to smoke in the Units and being forced to go to bed early. Pre-release arrangements are vague. There needs to be weekly visits available rather than fortnightly and purchase of food from private cash would be welcome. There is very little bullying or taxing, food is generally good, portions are a bit on the small side, there are second helpings available—but you've got to be quick!

HM Prison Thorp Arch

Wetherby, West Yorkshire. L23 7AY
Tel: 0937-844241 **Fax:** 0937-845446
Opened: 1965 **CNA:** 166 **Average Roll:** 144 **Category:** C. Male

i **BACKGROUND** Thorp Arch is a purpose-built establishment, constructed on a greenfield site between 1963 and 1965. It opened in June 1965 as a Remand Centre for males under 21. An additional cell block and ancillary buildings were added to the site in 1975 and it has remained substantially unaltered since then. The establishment changed role from a Remand Centre to a C Category trainer for long-term adults males in March 1987. It continues to operate as such today though, from April 1995, the prison will join with the adjacent Rudgate open prison. The Governor,

Mr Barnard, provided information about the establishment, though the BoV did not reply to our request for a copy of their latest annual report. HMCIP published their latest inspection report on Thorp Arch in October 1994.

OFFICIALS

AREA MGR: Maurice Codd
CHAIR BOV: H. Rawnsley
GOVERNOR: Grenvil Barnard
MEDICAL: Dr D.W. Verity
CHAPLAIN: Rev Rosheuvel
PROBATION: P. Knight
EDUCATION: P. Granville
LOCAL MP: Spencer Batiste. Con
STAFFING: 4 Governor grades, 4 Principal Officers, 10 Senior Officers and 43 Officers, not including specialist staff.

REGIME

week days: 0750 unlock. 0815 breakfast. 0825–0855 exercise. 0900 work, education. 1000 adjudications. 1125 cease labour 1135 dinner. 1200 lock up. 1300 work, education. 1530 cease education. 1630 cease labour. 1640 tea. 1700 lock up. 1800–2045 association. Summer evenings: outside exercise except Mon & Wed.

week ends: 0745 unlock. 0805 breakfast. 0900–1120 association. 1130 dinner. 1150 lock up. 1300 unlock, association. 1615 lock up. 1640 tea. 1700 lock up. 1800–2045 association. Summer: outside exercise all day except lock up and meal times.

Out of cell: 10.75/24hrs weekdays and 11.75/24hrs at weekends.

ACCOMMODATION & FACILITIES

Three wings: A(CNA=27), B(67), C(72). All 166 cells have wash basins, toilet, light switch and low voltage (3v,6v,9v,12v DC) mains power. Card phones on each unit. Good sentence planning and personal officer schemes in operation. No VPU. Drug counselling available. Mail not censored and handed out before dinner. Showers on each wing. Phone cards six per month.

CANTEEN

Located off the central corridor, with only 70 lines of stock. Canteen open Tuesdays for private cash spends (max of £115 pa), and on Wednesdays for wages and private orders. Local purchase facility only operates fortnightly.

VISITS

How to get there: Bus from Leeds (760), or Harrogate (78). Special Transport: coaches from various areas, check with prison probation office.

VISITING TIMES: Week Days: 1400–1600 Tues and Thurs only. Saturday: 1330–1530. Sunday: 1330–1530.

NOTES

No staffed Visitors Centre. Canteen and Childrens Play Area. Contact prison probation for details of local B&B. Wheelchair access: with prior notice visits can be taken in prison hospital.

EDUCATION

Open 50 weeks of the year, five days and (only) two evenings per week. Very short day (0900–1120 & 1345–1545), HMCIP recommended in 1991 that it match the working day but this has not been done. Wide variety of subjects, remedial to degree education.

WORKSHOPS

FTE (40 places). VTC: Catering, Multi-Skills and CIT Painting & Decorating. Two workshops, Light Textiles and Tailoring. Wages average £6.50. Limited work opportunities. Party change after 3 months.

DISCIPLINE

HMCIP examined the records of 50 adjudications conducted in the six months prior to the inspection. Notice of Report usually served day before, prior segregation rarely practised and the hearings themselves were impeccably conducted according to Judge Tumim. Only two reports of the 50 had been dismissed, and there was a heavy predominance of loss of remission awards to the almost total exclusion of other punishments.

MEDICAL

Part time Medical Officer, 1×HCSO, 1×HCO. HCC with 10 bed ward, three strip cells, observation cell and seven ordinary cells. Dental session weekly, optician monthly, report sick to HCC by 0815 or attend through day as required.

GYMNASIUM & SPORTS

1×PEPO and 2×PEO. Large sports hall, weights room, sports field and all-weather pitch. No community based projects.

CHAPLAINCY

Full time CE chaplain, p/t RC and Methodist ministers. Imam visits on Saturdays. Two separate chapels for RC and CE and Multi-Faith Room in Chaplains Office. RC and CE services held 0900 Sunday, Bible reading class Sunday evening, discussion group Thursday evening including people from local community.

FOOD

Staffing: 1×SO, 1×Officer (Caterer), 2×Civilian cooks and an inmate work party of 11. Old kitchen was poorly equipped and in urgent need of refurbishment, now replaced by 'quick-build' construction. No pre-select menu system in operation, four week menu cycle, two choices at dinner and tea and plentiful in quantity. Breakfast normally continental other than at weekends. Infrequent visits to the kitchen by the Medical Officer.

ESTABLISHMENT REPORTS

In a report (published October 1994) of an inspection in April

1994, HMCIP said that all but a few of the recommendations in 1991 had been implemented, progressed or overtaken by changes in the Prison Service. The HCC which remains empty should be brought into use and redesignated. The prison shop should be civilianised. Thorp Arch emerges from this inspection with credit. The quality of services to inmates is good, with all men housed in single cells with integral sanitation. Favourable comments were made by inmates about food, and laundry facilities were available. There is full employment and a good education service. The probation department enjoyed a good working relationship with both staff and management and were involved in the training of staff in sentence planning and personal officer work. The absence of a Sex Offenders Treatment programme is to be regretted, given that such offenders make up 10% of the Thorp Arch population.

GOVERNOR'S COMMENTS There could be possible future expansion with a further wing of 98 cells, and a concomitant expansion of the regime. The names of Thorp Arch and Rudgate will not be retained after the amalgamation in April 1995, though the new name has not been approved yet. The joint prison will have a C Cat half, and a D Cat half, with progression transfer through from C to D as part of the sentence planning process. The management structure has not been finalised yet. An additional 120-man cell block is also to be built in the C Cat half of the joint prison commencing in February or March 1995. Changes to the regime will be a major part of the amalgamation process though it has not been finalised at this time. Though I am no longer the Governor of Thorp Arch, having left in order to lead the amalgamation implementation team, I will be the Governor of the joint establishment when it opens.

PRISONERS' COMMENTS Requests and complaints are dealt with on average within two weeks locally and six weeks at Area Manager level. Single cells, integral sanitation, own curtains, carpets, rugs, plates, cups and bowls allowed. Canteen has a good stock and fortnightly local purchase. Visits are good, excellent refreshments, regular visits allowed. Education has excellent staff, a good programme and a shortage of resources. Wages average £6.50, day time medical care quite basic, low level of adjudications which are fairly conducted and the food is OK with two choices at both dinner and tea. Religious facilities are good and there is no censorship of mail or difficulty with access to phones or purchase of phone cards.

HM Prison Usk

29 Maryport St, Usk, Gwent. NP5 1XP
Tel: 0291-672411 **Fax:** 0291-673800
Opened: 1844 **CNA:** 241 **Average Roll:** 194 **Category:** C. Male (VPU)

i **BACKGROUND** Usk has a long and varied history as a penal establishment, opening in 1844 as a House of Correction and in 1870, after the addition of other buildings, it became the County Gaol for Monmouthshire. It remained in that role until 1922 when it closed, reopening in 1939 as a closed Borstal and continuing in this role until 1964 when it became a Detention Centre. In 1983 Usk became a Youth Custody Centre and a Young Offender Institution between 1988 and May 1990, when it was designated as an adult C Category establishment for vulnerable prisoners. It continues in that role today And operates the Core Sex Offender Treatment Programme. Usk is linked to nearby Prescoed open prison. Neither the Governor nor BoV replied to our requests for information and HMCIP published their latest report on Usk in August 1993.

OFFICIALS
AREA MGR: John Wilkinson
CHAIR BOV:
GOVERNOR: N.J. Evans
MEDICAL:
CHAPLAIN: Rev Mark John
PROBATION: Monica Sabor
EDUCATION:
LOCAL MP: Roger Evans. Con
STAFFING: 5 Governor grades, 7 Principal Officers, 14 Senior Officers and 78 Officers, including specialist staff and those at Prescoed.

REGIME *week days*: 0730 unlock/breakfast. 0900 work. 1215 lunch. 1330 work. 1615 cease labour. 1600 tea. 1730–2030 association.

week ends: 0730 unlock/breakfast. 0900 association. 1215 lunch. 1300 association. 1530 tea. 1600 lock up. No weekend evening association.

Out of cell: 12.5/24hrs weekdays and 8.5/24hrs at weekends.

ACCOMMODATION & FACILITIES
Three wings (A: CNA 47), B(27), C(47), all single cells with simple integral sanitation. Former recesses have been converted into showers and the wings tend to be very clean. Sentence planning, card phones, personal officer scheme, drug counselling.

CANTEEN Located at the centre of the living accommodation the canteen is well sited, dealing with purchases from earnings on Wednesday and from private cash on Thursdays. Only 103 lines carried. Local purchase facility.

REQUESTS & COMPLAINTS There were only 23 submissions of RC forms in the 12 months prior to the inspection and one for confidential access. All had received replies within the time targets except for those sent to the Area Manager.

VISITS *How to get there*: Train to Newport. Infrequent bus service to Usk—free prison transport from Usk to HMYOI Prescoed at 1300—fare of 50p at weekends. Sunday: no bus service from Newport to Usk. No Special Transport.
VISITING TIMES: Week Days: 1330–1530 Tues, Thurs only. Saturday: 1330–1530. Sunday: 1330–1530.

NOTES No staffed Visitors Centre or Childrens Play Area with TV and videos, but no toys. Canteen in pleasantly decorated visiting room. Local B&B. Wheelchair access but not to main visits room. baby-changing facilities available. Average of 26–40 visits a week, all inmates rubbed down and small proportion given strip search.

EDUCATION Eleven classrooms in a two storey education block. Computer room with 12 terminals. Well equipped craft workshop producing high quality wooden goods. Large art room and training kitchen. Broad curriculum covering remedial to degree education, open learning courses and multi-skill courses provided.

WORKSHOPS Main employer is the Education department offering upto 34 places. PSIF concrete shop requires very heavy manual labour in making paving slabs and posts. CIT Plastering course but no VTC at all. Other employments meet the needs of the establishment, kitchen, cleaners etc.

DISCIPLINE There were only 20 adjudications at Usk in the 12 months prior to the inspection, leading HMCIP to call for the cell used for hearings to be returned to cellular use. No recorded uses of strip cells or body belt.

MEDICAL Part time Medical Officer, HCSO and HCO cover both establishments. Average of 10 report sick each day dealt with HCO or MO. Dental session weekly seeing about 10 inmates each time. Optician once per month. Usk operates the Core Sex Offender Treatment Programme, four officers and two probation staff have been trained for the task. 15 week course designed to cater for groups of eight inmates meeting formally on two half-days per week.

GYMNASIUM & SPORTS 1×PEPO, 1×PESO and 2×PEO serve both Usk and Prescoed. Reasonable sized gymnasium, well equipped and with an activity based programme designed for the older than average population. Outdoor facilities limited but running circuit had been established. Well maintained soccer pitch outside the perimeter—used more by locals than inmates. Well attended department, a total of 97 BAWLA awards in 12 months prior to inspection.

CHAPLAINCY Part time CE chaplain, RC and Methodist ministers serve both Prescoed and Usk. Attractive chapels but no permanent minority faith room, Imam happy to visit from Cardiff for Muslim inmates when necessary. Main services Sunday morning and weekly programme of religious groups and meetings.

FOOD Staffing: 1×SO, 1×Officer (caterer), 1×Prison Auxiliary, operate the kitchens at both Prescoed and Usk. No pre-select menu system in operation, nor fixed menu cycle. Continental breakfast served three days a week, and tea is the main meal of the day.

ESTABLISHMENT REPORTS In a report (published 5th August 1993) of an inspection in January 1993, HMCIP, said that both establishments had a historical link which no longer existed. Both establishments were well run. Staff were very supportive of the Sex Offender Treatment Programme at HMP Usk and HMCIP disagreed with the suggestion that all inmates at Usk should be sex offenders in the programme. The population at Prescoed had dropped so low that the establishment was hardly financially viable and thought should be given to turning it into an open establishment towards which inmates from Usk could progress. Prescoed was a valuable asset and should not be lost.

HM Prison The Verne

Portland, Dorset. DT5 1EQ
Tel: 0305-378282 **Fax:** 0305-823724
Opened: 1949 **CNA:** 552 **Average Roll:** 536 **Category:** C. Male

i **BACKGROUND** The Verne Prison opened in 1949 on the site of a former military barracks dating from the end of the 19th century. The prison, which sits high above the naval base on the island of Portland off the Dorset coast, is a Category C training prison for adult males. The majority of the population are aged 21-30, 80% of whom have less than three years to serve. Neither the Governor nor the BoV replied to our requests for information about The Verne, and HMCIP published their latest inspection report on 15th July 1994.

OFFICIALS
AREA MGR: John May
CHAIR BOV:
GOVERNOR: T.M. Turner
MEDICAL:
CHAPLAIN: Rev Bloomfield
PROBATION: S. Leadley
EDUCATION:
LOCAL MP: Ian Bruce. Con
STAFFING: 281 staff in post, 150 of whom in unified grades. One Senior Officer and two Officers were female, with no members of the ethnic minorities in unified grades.

☞ **REGIME** *week days*: 0730 unlock 0745 sick parade. 0750 breakfast. 0810 work. 0845 education. 1130 lunch, mail and newspaper issue. 1250 work. 1615 cease labour, tea, evening activities, association. 2050 return to rooms.

week ends: 0745 unlock/breakfast. 0815 treatments and association 1130 dinner, association. 1330 visits. 1545 tea and association until 2050.

Out of cell: 12/24hrs weekdays and 12/24hrs at weekends.

ACCOMMODATION & FACILITIES
Three accommodation blocks and ten dormitories built in 1970. Each of the three accommodation blocks divided into two, giving a total of six separate wings (A1,A2,B1,B2,C1,C2) each with 80 rooms on their second and third floors. Ground floors used as association, dining and staff office areas. All inmates have keys to their rooms, access to 24 hour sanitation/showering facilities, though lights are switched off by staff at 2200. The dormitory accommodation contained in 12 casements which make up D.Wing. Large cavernous rooms whose design makes difficult partitioning for privacy and HMCIP has repeatedly called for conversion into single room accommodation because of 'the absence of privacy and the prevalence of bullying'. Card phones on all living units.

CANTEEN Manned by a Prison Auxiliary from 0800 to 1630 Mon-Fri—but only open to inmates for 14 hours during this period. Private cash transfer (£15) per month. Local purchase facility. Prices decided by the officer who runs the shop with profit margin averaging 10%.

VISITS *How to get there*: Train to Weymouth then service bus from Kings Statue, Weymouth, to Victoria Sq, Portland. Taxi to prison. Special Transport: probation service coaches from S.Glam, Gwent, W.Glam, Bristol, M.Glam, Portsmouth and Plymouth. Contact prison probation officer for details of booking.
VISITING TIMES: Week Days: 1330–1530 Mon–Fri. Saturday: 1330–1530 No PVO's weekends. Sunday: 1330–1530.

NOTES No staffed Visitors Centre. Canteen and Childrens Play Area. For overnight stay facilities contact Mr Mott, Accommodation Officer: 0305-204827/204797. Arrangements for wheelchair access should be made with prison two weeks in advance of visit. No disabled toilets or facilities.

EDUCATION F/t Education Officer, deputy, 4xf/t and 6 p/t teachers. Open 48 weeks of the year for day (and 36 for evening) classes. Two and a half day induction course. Day: 0830–1130 & 1345–1615 Mon–Fri covering GCSE, Business Studies, Basic Education, Maths, OU and Private Study. Evening classes 1745–1945 Mon–Thurs: woodwork, soft toys, Spanish, pottery, guitar workshop, computer literacy and art.

WORKSHOPS Eight VTC/CIT courses: Bricklaying; General Construction Operators; Carpentry; Painting & Decorating; Plastering; Micro Electronics; Motor Mechanics; Welding; Electronic Wiring. Woodmill shop and assembly shops unpopular. Farms and Gardens, Works, Kitchen.

DISCIPLINE Three-fold rise in the number of assaults on inmates by inmates, a large increase in the number of adjudications and £15,000 worth of vandalism, all of which HMCIP attributes to the change in the type of inmate being sent to The Verne. The new Segregation unit recommended by HMCIP in 1990 has not been provided.

MEDICAL F/t & p/t MO's, 1×HCPO, 3×HCO. HCC with 5-bed ward, two single cells, and 1×Strip cell. Dentist one full session per week, no rota for calling up long-termers and lifers. Optician once per month. Report sick to HCC at unlock. Unsatisfactory appointments system which should be changed said HMCIP.

GYMNASIUM & SPORTS 1×PESO, 3×PEO. Gymnasium in converted cinema, small size and with rubberised flooring. Grass sports field for football, baseball and cricket, and two hard court areas used for five-a-side football. Six one-hour day sessions aimed at newly arrived inmates, cleaners and various work parties.

CHAPLAINCY Full time CE chaplain, p/t assistant CE, and p/t RC and Methodist ministers. Eleven visiting ministers of other faiths attend the prison regularly. The chapel is located in the former army officers mess, with main services on Sunday: 0830 RC; 0930 CE/Methodist. Multi-faith room. Regular religious meetings, including Pentecostal, Quaker, Christian Music group and RC discussion class.

FOOD Staffing: 1×PO, 1×SO and 2×Officer (caterers), inmate work party of 15. Food is a major cause of complaint at The Verne which saw serious disturbances in January 1994. HMCIP severely criticised the food in 1990 and, in 1994, Judge Tumim recorded 'the overall position was worse'. A three week menu cycle with little variety at weekends was in place and meal times were too close together: HMCIP suggests contracting out the catering service at The Verne.

ESTABLISHMENT REPORTS In a report (published 15th July 1994) of an inspection in February 1994, HMCIP said that there were factors present at The Verne which were similar to those which prevailed at Wymott prior to the disturbance there in September 1993. Design of the buildings placed severe limits on the level of control that staff could exercise to prevent bullying, racketeering and misuse of drugs. Vandalism was increasing and disciplinary sanctions were ineffective in controlling the behaviour of some disruptive prisoners. Staff relationships with inmates were generally good and certainly much stronger than at Wymott. Large numbers transferring into The Verne had created a destabilising effect. The types of inmate being allocated to The Verne were placed there as a result of their security category: a process that would continue to be flawed said HMCIP as long it took account of security requirements alone, and paid little heed to potentially serious control problems which those who do not pose a security threat could present. HMCIP recommended to the Director General that a secure wing with a more restricted regime should be built at The Verne, there should be an increase in the number of lifers allocated to the establishment and the dormitories should be replaced by single room accommodation.

HM Prison Wakefield

Love Lane, Wakefield, W.Yorks. WF2 9AG
Tel: 0924-378282 **Fax:** 0924-384391
Opened: 1849 **CNA:** 662 **Average Roll:** 645 **Category:** Dispersal

BACKGROUND Wakefield prison, situated about half a mile from the city centre, dates from 1849. It served as a convict prison and then a local prison until 1945 when it became a training prison for medium and long term prisoners. In 1975 Wakefield upgraded its security and became part of the dispersal system. It is a large establishment, the largest dispersal in the country and the Prison Service's main centre for lifers. Wakefield is built in dull red brick with four wings radiating from a Centre, and assorted buildings filling the spaces between them. The site is surrounded by a five metre high fence and, outside that, a reinforced concrete wall capped with anti-climbing devices and an intruder alarm system. The majority of staff at Wakefield do not comply with the Prison Board policy on wearing name-badges. The prison also operates as an assessment Centre for the Sex Offender Treatment Programme. Neither the Governor nor BoV replied to our requests for information about the prison, and HMCIP published their latest inspection report on Wakefield in May 1994.

OFFICIALS
AREA MGR: Terry Bone
CHAIR BOV:
GOVERNOR: R. Duncan

MEDICAL:
CHAPLAIN: Rev J. Lynn
PROBATION: L. Cameron
EDUCATION:
LOCAL MP: David Hinchliffe. Lab
STAFFING: 646 Staff in Post, 455 in unified grades.

REGIME *week days*: 0745 unlock. 0755 breakfast. 0830 work, sick parade, exercise. 1110 cease labour, dinner. 1145 lock up. 1310 unlock. 1350 exercise/work. 1400 education. 1600 cease labour. 1635 tea, lock up. 1740 unlock classes. 1745 association. 1915 classes end. 2000 lock up.

week ends: 0745 unlock, breakfast. 0830 CE service. 0845 games, exercise. 1045 cease games. 1110 dinner. 1145 lock up. 1310 unlock. 1330 visits, association. 1545 tea. 1615 roll check. 1945 lock up.

Out of cell: 10.5/24hrs weekdays and 10.5/24hrs at weekends .

ACCOMMODATION & FACILITIES
Four main cell blocks radiating from the centre: A (CNA: 156), B (126), C (158) and D (163). All single cells with integral sanitation programme partially complete. Cooking facilities on all wings, ready access to bathing and toilet facilities. personal Officer Scheme, sentence planning and card phones in all wings. Mail now moved onto wings, all Cat A mail is fully censored in and out, with less censorship for other categories: Governor states level of censorship is currently under review. No power points in cells, large i/p list.

REQUESTS & COMPLAINTS Average of 153 formal RC per month very high though seen to be diminishing. Substantial difference between number of forms issued and those returned—some inmates complained to HMCIP that forms critical of staff had disappeared after being handed in, whereas staff claimed prisoners had destroyed the forms themselves. Both accounts remain anecdotal as no system exists at Wakefield to establish the truth.

CANTEEN Located off A.wing near the Centre, carries around 220 lines of stock, though has no fridge for fresh food. Open once per week for earnings. Local purchase facility delivers Thursdays.

VISITS *How to get there*: Train to Wakefield Westgate station, then walk to the prison. Special Transport: coaches from Newcastle, Chester-le-Street, Durham & Darlington about once per month.
VISITING TIMES: Week Days: 1330–1530 Wed, Thurs only. Saturday: 1330–1530. Sunday: 1330–1530.

NOTES No staffed Visitors Centre because of claimed lack of suitable accommodation. Canteen and Childrens Play Area. No overnight stay facilities, but contact prison probation officer for details of B&B in Wakefield. Wheelchair access possible, no disabled toilet facilities.

EDUCATION Adequate if rather shabby department, said HMCIP in 1991, located at the end of C.wing. Excellent adult literacy and basic skills unit. Seven f/t and 30 p/t teachers. Open for only 42 weeks of the year with evening classes only three nights per week despite a huge waiting list for places. Broad range from remedial to OU students. Library located in clean and large room, stock of 12,000 books. Each wing allocated one evening per week. Library system lacks support from the management structure.

WORKSHOPS VTC/CIT courses: Painting & Decorating, Plastering, Mechanical Engineering, Tailoring and Braille Unit. Light and heavy textile shops making blankets and mail bags. PSIF Contract Services shops employed on light assembly work. Labour Board meets on Wednesday. Wages average £6.75 but new pay scheme can bring wages upto £25 with signed compact: see prisoners' comments.

DISCIPLINE Generally relaxed atmosphere within the prison. Adjudications totalled 909 for 1993, a marginal increase on the year before, though still low with an average of three per day. Many suspended awards, adjudications properly conducted. F.wing segregation unit houses Rule 43 (OP & GOAD) inmates. Strip cells are used sparingly said HMCIP.

MEDICAL Full time SMO, 1×MO, 1×G5, 4×HCSO, 17×HCO. HCC located in separate accommodation recently reopened after three year refurbishment programme. Inpatient facilities for 40 with integral sanitation. Many design faults and manning levels restricting operational capacity and leaving 50 mentally ill inmates located on the wings. Inpatients dine in association, teachers visit daily, waiting list for both dentist and optician now in excess of four months.

GYMNASIUM & SPORTS 1×PEPO, 1×PESO and 4×PEO. Poor PE facilities. Covered sports area offers large space for activities but its construction makes it unsuitable. Old gym, barely the size of a badminton court, provides inadequate alternative facilities. Outside, long narrow Redgra used for soccer and jogging needs replacement. Fenced in volleyball court. Despite these restrictions, good PE programme offered, with dedicated sessions for VP inmates, over 35's and medical remedials.

CHAPLAINCY Full time CE chaplain, p/t RC and Methodist ministers. New chapel opened 1992, after being in temporary accommodation for 14 years. Multi-faith facilities, visiting Imam, Sikh priest, Buddhist minister, Church Scientists, Quakers, Mormons, Jehovah's Witnesses and Jews all have support from visiting ministers. CE Service 0830 Sun, followed by RC Mass at 0930—average attendances 15/25 respectively. Service also Sunday afternoon from which Cat A's are excluded. Weekly programme of meetings and groups each day except Sat: Monday evening sessions range from 'Rock Gospel' to contemplation! Pool of about 60 Prison Visitors.

FOOD Staffing: 1×PO, 2×SO, 4×Officer (caterers), civilian cook and an inmate work party of 11. Food taken to wings by heated trolley. catering staff oversee serving on each wing. Meal times are unacceptable, though plans to move dinner and tea to 1215 and 1715. General standard of the food is satisfactory. Four week menu cycle, no pre-select system.

ESTABLISHMENT REPORTS While work to install integral sanitation was well advanced at Wakefield, said HMCIP in a report (published 10th May 1994) of a short inspection in December 1993, the decision to place two toilets in each small dormitory without any privacy screen was insensitive. Considerable progress had however been made since the last inspection, with the health care centre being completely refurbished and HMCIP were impressed by the calm, clean and safe environment the Wakefield offers both inmates and staff. Situated about half a mile from Wakefield city centre, the present prison dates from 1842 and is of radial design. Wakefield is the main centre for lifers and is strangely both the largest and cheapest to run dispersal prison in the system.

GOVERNOR'S COMMENTS
Management and staff at Wakefield are pleased that this inspection—which was totally unannounced—was able to report so positively on the developments taking place. This was an independent assessment of the motivation, commitment and achievement of those who serve at Wakefield. We do not intend to sit on our laurels, but will continue to move forward and will address the points raised in the Inspector's report.

PRISONERS' COMMENTS
Communications are poor in Wakefield, personal officer scheme spoiled by staff absences and lack of individual attention. Medical facilities are poor with long delays. Request /Complaint forms are sometimes refused. Cells have little ventilation with two small panes of glass. Canteen is too small to offer a good stock, no fridge means no fresh food is stocked and though there is a local purchase facility, no list exists of the items that can be ordered! Civilian clothing is not allowed at this dispersal. Visits room very cramped with limited facilities for the kids. Education is OK and you can organise your own course if necessary. Allocation to work is erratic, must sign blind contract or not allowed to work. Rules are often illogical or applied inconsistently—60 minute cassette tapes are allowed, but not 90 minute ones as these take too long to censor. No privacy when using in-cell sanitation, the Redgra pitch is unusable for four months of the year and visits are insufficient with just two hours on Wednesday, Thursday and weekend afternoons. Requests and complaints took too long, replies are stereotyped and many complaints that could be dealt with verbally are not. Adjudications depend on which Governor you get, though often the result is superfluous because you get unofficial punishments—like sack from work—whatever the outcome. High level of mail censorship/interference causes delays to both incoming and outgoing mail, three card phones on each wing is insufficient for the numbers, maximum of three cards in possession, and you have to hand in the old cards to get new ones! There is no formal induction course and the prison is run entirely for the convenience of prison staff rather than the care of inmates.

HM Prison Wandsworth

PO.Box 757, Heathfield Rd, Wandsworth, London SW18 3HS
Tel: 081-874-7292 **Fax:** 081-877-0358
Opened: 1851 **CNA:** 965 **Roll:** 923 **Category:** Male Local

i **BACKGROUND** Wandsworth Prison opened in 1851 as the County Prison for Surrey. The establishment, which stands on a 12 acre site, was designed in the Victorian radial style and provided two distinct accommodation areas. Five large cellular wings had originally formed the main prison for men and a separate and much smaller three-wing block accommodated female prisoners until 1945. Ronnie Biggs escaped from Wandsworth in July 1966, and it is the only prison to have a working set of gallows. Wandsworth has gained a reputation as a penal dustbin, taking difficult prisoners (and staff) from other jails and confining them in a regime which was at best brutally austere and at worst inhuman. Since the arrival of its present Governor, Graham Clarke, Wandsworth has been not so much steered as dragged in a more enlightened direction: encouraged by probably one of the most professional Boards of Visitors in the country. Many problems still remain as this entry shows, but the issues are at last being tackled—albeit slowly. Wandsworth also operates as an assessment centre for the Sex Offender Treatment Programme. The Governor provided up to date information about the prison, and the BoV supplied a copy of their (impressive) annual report. HMCIP published their latest inspection Report on Wandsworth in March 1993.

OFFICIALS

AREA MGR: P. Kitteridge
CHAIR BOV: M. Wall
GOVERNOR: G. Clarke
MEDICAL: Dr R. Burrows
CHAPLAIN: Rev P. Meadon
PROBATION: B. Elmes
EDUCATION: M. Williams
LOCAL MP: Tom Cox. Lab
STAFFING: 14 Governor grades, 23 Principal Officers, 56 Senior Officers and 302 Officers.

REGIME *week days*: 0745 unlock/breakfast. 0845 work, education. 1200–1300 dinner. 1315 work, education. 1630–1730 tea. 1800–2000 association and evening classes. 2000 lock up.

week ends: 0745 unlock/breakfast. 0845–1115 exercise, association. 1200–1300 dinner. 1315–1630 exercise association. 1645–1730 tea. 1800–2000 association. 2000 lock up.

Out of cell: 10/24hrs weekdays and 8/24hrs at weekends.

ACCOMMODATION & FACILITIES

Eight wings in total: A.Wing=Remands; B/D.Wings=Convicted; C/E.Wings=Closed; G/H/K.Wings=VPU. Bail Information Scheme, Personal Officer Scheme, sentence planning, part completed integral sanitation. Standard in-possession list, no pets and little civilian clothing, but trainers and sound systems allowed. VPU is a specialist centre for Sexual Offender Treatment Programme. Routine censorship abolished, mail opened centrally and not in the presence of the prisoner. Card phones installed on all wings, though access reported by prisoners to be easy.

REQUESTS/COMPLAINTS There were 1834 formal R/C forms issued—of which 1,111 were returned and dealt with as active complaints. Main areas of complaint were allocation, property and medical matters. The majority of complaints received replies within seven days, though the BoV recorded that they did 'not have the resources to judge whether the replies [were] of a consistently high standard'.

VISITS *How to get there*: Tube to Tooting Bec then bus (219) to County Arms, or tube to Clapham Junction then 77 to Heathfield Road. Trains to Earlsfield, or Wandsworth Common available but limited service. No Special Transport.
VISITING TIMES: Week Days: 0830–1030 (Rem) 1315–1515 (Con). Saturday: 0830–1030 (Rem) 1315–1515 (Con). Sunday: 0830–1030 (Rem) 1315–1515 (Con).

NOTES Visiting times above are those between which visitors should arrive at the prison to allow full visiting periods. VPU visiting times as above. Visitors Centre opened February 1994. Canteen and Childrens Play Area. No overnight stay facilities, but plentiful in London. Disabled access is not good but arrangements can be made.

EDUCATION Open 50 weeks of the year, contracted educational service from South Thames College. **Main Prison** day classes: Information Technology; Literacy/Numeracy; Music; Counselling Skills; BTEC modelling; Business RSA; Modern Languages; Art; Yoga; Sculpture; Psychology; Drama; English; NVQ; Social Studies; Criminal Justice; Meditation. Evening classes: Chess; IT; Woodwork; Drama; Design; Current Affairs. **VPU** classes: Business; Drama; Literacy; Current Affairs; Health Studies; English; Maths; Media Studies; Open Learning; Art; Music. Evening classes: Picture framing; Basic maths; Music keyboards; French; Model-making; Chess; Guitar; Black history.

WORKSHOPS Laundry (due to be refurbished in 1995), two textile shops, repair shop, brush shop and carpenters shop. BoV report that 97% of convicted inmates at Wandsworth are now allocated a job. Plans to introduce NVQ's in Laundry, Tailors and Textiles shops in 1995.

DISCIPLINE Segregation unit relocated to K1 landing from E1. Large complement of staff that once existed has been pared down without any deterioration in control. The body belt was used only once in 1993 according to the BoV 'the reduction in the use of this restraint is a commendable change in the prison over the last few years'.

MEDICAL Separate hospital facility, SMO and nursing grades, dental, X-ray, physio, psychiatrist and optician clinics. Report sick to wing staff.

The BoV has been 'increasingly concerned' about patient care in the Health Care Centre. In December 1993 the BoV took the unusual step of compiling a report on the most serious aspects of management of the Health Care Centre. They sent this to the Secretary of State, calling for an independent inquiry. Cells and recesses are dirty, a refurbished ward is out of use because it has no fire escape, a complete review is required of equipment levels and there are serious problems of accountability. Nurses are answerable to a Nurse Manager, whereas Health Care Officers report to a Governor who has no nursing qualifications at all. Two suicides at Wandsworth in December 1993, one in the Segregation Unit and another in the Health Care Centre: the BoV said the continued existence of ligature points in the Health Care Centre is a disgrace to the Prison Service.

GYMNASIUM & SPORTS Three gymnasiums, one devoted to weights and power lifting, a second for sports and games and a third equipped with exercise machines. Wandsworth has achieved international weightlifting success, with one prisoner travelling abroad to compete. 1×PEPO, 1×PESO and 4×PEO was 'insufficient' said HMCIP and should be increased. PE programme from 0830–1130 and 1345–1630 each weekday. Evening classes run from 1730–1930 Monday to Thursday inclusive.

CHAPLAINCY F/t CE and RC chaplains, p/t Methodist, Muslim, Buddhist, Sikh and Jewish ministers. Main Church services Sunday morning.

FOOD Staffing: 1×PO, 2×SO and 8×Officer (caterers), and there is a work party of 44 inmates. Civilian caterer appointed to complement prison service staff. Increased funding for food has been used to improve the menu at Wandsworth. The kitchen was extensively refurbished (at a cost of £1m) in 1988, despite which it has a number of shortcomings said HMCIP. Insufficient storage space, no staff showers and there was not enough room in the kitchen for those required to operate it.

BOARD OF VISITORS Membership of the Wandsworth BoV: Mr Akerman; Rev Clarke; Mr Dix; Mr Freeman; Mrs Gibbins; Mr Goldbold; Mrs Gordon; Mr Infield; Mr Kumar; Major Lowe; Lady Moore; Mrs Powell; Mr Powles; Mr Purcell; Mr Smellie; Ms Thomas; Mr Walburn; Mrs Walker; Mrs Wall.

Wandsworth BoV in their 1993/94 Annual Report requested a response from the Secretary of State on three matters: An assurance that plans to refurbish A and B wings will be restored in order to remove intolerable and uncivilised living conditions, and an adherence to the undertaking that integral sanitation will be complete by the end of 1994; An assurance that a full fire inspection will be carried out immediately; That all staff coming into contact with prisoners will be required to wear name badges. BoV report there was an average of 17 drug finds per month at Wandsworth, every month, for the whole of 1993—20 on visits and 182 on prisoners or within the prison—including two large finds, one of heroin and another of crack cocaine. Board hold weekly surgeries on Thursdays.

ESTABLISHMENT REPORTS In a report (published 16th March 1993) of an inspection in August 1992, Judge Stephen Tumim, HMCIP, said that 'few penal matters are more depressing than to see how little life at Wandsworth has progressed' since the prison underwent its last full inspection in 1989. 'There is completely inadequate work and education. PE facilities, sanitation, mealtimes and visiting conditions are unacceptable'. HMCIP remarked that a 'Visitors Centre and visits complex are still lacking, unemployed prisoners, perhaps the majority of prisoners, are locked up for nearly 23 hours a day. There is no evening or weekend association, and no association areas or quiet rooms. The Prison Service statement of purpose, in particular "to help them lead law-abiding and useful lives in custody and after release", does not seem to be generally applied in Wandsworth. As in all prisons, good work is being accomplished by staff'.

GOVERNOR'S COMMENTS The year ahead will be busy and demanding. Staff at all levels will continue to strive through new initiatives and prisoner participation to improve upon the regime for the benefit of all in Wandsworth.

PRISONERS' COMMENTS **(Convicted—D.Wing):** Requests/ complaints usually dealt with within 24 hours, fairly. The wings differ considerably, D.wing is the most modern with integral sanitation and light switches—no power points. A.wing is probably the worst, still in the dark ages over there. Basic range of goods in canteen, prices expensive 'but then it has no competition: one brand of cigarettes but eight varieties of Afro hair gel!' Visits are very fair, average selection in snack-bar and visiting time is variable dependent on pressure of space. Education provides good standards, wages in all cases are similar to other establishments.

(Remand—A.wing): I am out of my cell, on average, less than 5 hours per day, including exercise and slop out. Single cell, no internal light switch, squalid conditions. Average canteen but no local purchase. Education is fair, varied day and evening classes—if you can get on them, long waiting lists. Poor work opportunities for remands who are paid only £2.50, we can spend private cash, but I do not have any. Medical facilities are fairly good, appointment system works well and now we have nurses the service has improved. Adjudications are as they've always been at Wandsworth—they go through the patter and write down all the right words with one eye on the High Court, but nothing's changed, you're still guilty from the minute you step through the door. Gymnasium? What's one of those?

HM Prison Wayland

Griston, Thetford, Norfolk. IP25 6RL
Tel: 0953-884103 **Fax:** 0953-882248
Opened: 1985 **CNA:** 580 **Roll:** 538 **Category:** C. Male

i **BACKGROUND** Wayland is a modern, purpose-built Category C training establishment, opened in 1985, it sits in a rural setting between Thetford and Norwich in East Anglia. The Prison has a national VPU, a relatively large lifer population and operates the Core Sex Offender Treatment Programme. The Governor, Mr Duff, provided information about Wayland and the prison's Board of Visitors very kindly supplied a copy of their latest annual report. HMCIP published their latest inspection report on Wayland in July 1993.

OFFICIALS
AREA MGR: J. Murtagh
CHAIR BOV: Mr Simpson
GOVERNOR: W.S. Duff
MEDICAL: No Full Time MO
CHAPLAIN: Rev Peter Stell
PROBATION: Jenny Faulconbridge
EDUCATION: W. Sargeant
LOCAL MP: Gillian Shepherd. Con

REGIME *week days*: 0810 unlock/breakfast. 0850–1120 work. 1130–1150 dinner. 1200–1340 lock up. 1350–1620 work. 1630–1650 tea. 1700–1740 lock up. Association until 2030.

week ends: 0810 unlock/breakfast/association/exercise. 1130–1150 dinner. 1200–1340 lock up. 1340–1630 exercise/association. 1630–1650 tea. 1700–1740 lock up. Association until 2030.

Out of cell: 10/24hrs weekdays and 10/24hrs at weekends.

ACCOMMODATION & FACILITIES Five 112-cell blocks, A,B,C,D,E. A–D normal location, E.Wing=VPU. Pre-release Unit of 36 cells. Separate seg unit. All single cells, in-cell sink, h/c water, toilet and light switch. Each spur (28 cells) has its own showers. 2 phones, 3 TV rooms per wing. I/p: rad/cassette, walkman, duvet & cover, curtains, carpet and jewellery etc. All civilian clothing must be of one colour only. No pets. Routine censorship abolished. Mail opened out of sight and handed out at about 1015. Card phones on all units, though access is said to be hard with long queues at times.

CANTEEN No canteen visits. In an effort to reduce muggings, blank forms are given out Tuesday and goods delivered on Friday evening. The BoV confirmed in their 1993/4 annual report that the choice of goods offered is very restricted, and prices are generally more expensive than in the average supermarket. The policy of giving 50% of canteen profits to the Home Office was unsatisfactory.

REQUESTS/COMPLAINTS There were 950 requests and complaints in 1993—an increase of 33% on 1992 figures (708) despite the fact that in 1993 the roll for two thirds of the year was at least 20% lower than in 1992. Targets are being met for time limits. Main grievances were loss of property, home leave, transfer, canteen and food.

VISITS *How to get there*: Train to Thetford or Attleborough, then taxi booked in advance on 0953-881388. Special Transport: coach from London, to book (for Saturday) 071-237-8076, or (for Sunday) 071-237-2707.
VISITING TIMES: Week Days: 1400–1600 No visits Tues & Thurs. Saturday: 1400–1600. Sunday: 1400–1600 No PVO's Sunday.

NOTES No staffed Visitors Centre. Canteen and Childrens Play Area (with TV). Contact prison probation for details of local B&B. Arrangements can be made for wheelchair access if advance notice is given to prison. Room available for feeding and changing babies. Occasional lifer family days that last from mid-morning to mid-afternoon.

EDUCATION Well equipped and attended unit. Staff provided by Norwich City College. Broad spectrum from remedial to degree. Especially good classes in art, VTC computers and French. VTC classes: Welding, Painting & Decorating; Bricklaying; Roofing; Light-engineering; Vehicle body repair; Car mechanics; Electrical installation and Industrial Cleaning. The BOV have recommended that security tagging of books from the library be introduced to prevent 'losses'.

WORKSHOPS Only a laundry, pay averages £7. Wing cleaners £4 and UB40 £2.50. The BoV in their 1993 Annual Report state that all too frequently cynical disregard appears to have been paid to real training in 1993. Providing courses have been filled and the unemployed figures effectively massaged in the regime statistics and the relevant hours worked, this apparently has been enough.

DISCIPLINE There were 1,067 charges brought in 1993, with 82 being dismissed and 'a limited number' were overturned on appeal. Twenty assaults on staff and 32 assaults on other inmates were recorded. A total of 121 were placed on Rule 43 (41 GOAD & 80 OR), 32 prisoners were given cellular confinement, 1 medical restraint and 24 non-medical restraints were applied at Wayland.

MEDICAL The medical cover provided by the outside group practice was criticised by the BoV in their 1993 Annual Report: The local practice failed to meet the Governor's Contract, being only available for three morning sessions of 0830–1100 on 24 weeks out of 52. As a result prisoners were inadequately 'fitted' for adjudications and only received visits in the Segregation Unit on attendance days: the new cellular confinement initiative, which increases max cellular confinement from 3-28 days, cannot be implemented under these arrangements. Doctor attends normally Mon-Wed-Fri mornings. Report sick in mornings, first five inmates taken on each wing get to see the doctor—others see the Health Care staff.

GYMNASIUM & SPORTS Large sports hall used for badminton, softball tennis, football, volleyball and basketball. Separate weights room with good equipment. Allowed 2×90 min periods per week during working hours and also in the evening. Gym also open at weekends. One rugby, one cricket and two football pitches. BoV report that the gymnasium 'remained one of the two main torchbearers of progressive activity in 1993'; resulting in 'an entry into the *Guinness Book of Records* for continuous 24 hour weight lifting'.

CHAPLAINCY Full time CE chaplain. Regular services are held for all denominations, CE, Free Church, RC, Methodist, Muslim and Buddhist.

FOOD There were 44 Request/complaints regarding food in 1993, along with 23 formal complaints to the BOV. Diets were the main complaint and the kitchen staff (who are working within an inadequate kitchen designed for 480 inmates rather than 580) have not always shown appropriate sensitivity. Inmate NVQ catering course now in operation in the kitchen. Trials of hot soup and drinks dispensers proved successful but were withdrawn due to minority abuse. New kitchen is planned, though the cost of £850,000 is described as excessive by the BOV.

ESTABLISHMENT REPORTS In their Annual Report 1993/94 the BoV requested a response from the Secretary of State on seven points. Wayland needs a Drug Therapy Unit. Without such a unit there is little likelihood that the twin problems of assaults and violence will be addressed effectively. The Board sought immediate endorsement for the appointment of a f/t prison doctor; prompt confirmation that the entry criteria, reduced from 18 to 6 months in 1993, will be reintroduced by mid-1994; assurances of positive action to reduce the frequent movement of inadequate, vulnerable and mentally disturbed prisoners; and confirmation that funding will be made available in 1994/5 for the kitchen, the Visitors Centre, and tackling recidivism.

GOVERNOR'S COMMENTS With respect to the future we are looking at the feasibility of offering differing regimes in separate parts of the establishment. To this end we recently established a drug therapy unit on a discrete spur within one wing and from July 1994 we have introduced an induction spur with a new style induction programme. We want to move towards more effective use of sentence planning in conjunction with the use of prisoner compacts in order to create a better match of prisoners' needs and available resources and activities, specifically in the areas of work, vocational training, education, offending behaviour programmes and personal development programmes. This can only be achieved with the support of all staff in the prison and the active co-operation of the prisoner population.

PRISONERS' COMMENTS Major requests/complaints 'are usually acted on within a week, lesser ones often get ignored'. All cells have internal light switches, toilet and sink: no power points. The canteen 'seriously needs reviewing . . . poor choice of goods which are relatively expensive'. Visits were reasonable. Good education. Workshops quite good, but average pay £7 for 35 hours in the shops is the same amount paid to those in the prison library. No permanent doctor but medical staff are helpful. Punishments vary from governor to governor and 'seem to vary markedly' even for the same offence. Food is the main cause of complaint: 'very often it's not cooked properly, and a choice is only available for the first group or two . . . if last out there's no choice and quite often not enough left so small portions given'. Good gym facilities, 'but new system restricts access'. All religious denominations catered for. Mail is opened out of sight and given out at about 1015. No limit on phone cards, 'however, with only two phones per wing (1 for every 56 inmates) large queues form and a wait of 1–1.5 hours is quite common; especially at weekends'. Noisy location of phones makes conversation difficult.

HM Prison Wellingborough

Doddington Rd, Wellingborough, Northants. NN8 2NH
Tel: 0933-224151 **Fax:** 0933-273903
Opened: 1963 **CNA:** 284 **Average Roll:** 275 **Category:** C. Male

i **BACKGROUND** The prison lies just outside the town of Wellingborough in Northamptonshire, and was designed and commissioned as a closed Borstal when it opened in 1963. In May 1983 it became a Youth Custody Centre, changing to a Young Offender Institution in 1988. In January 1990 Wellingborough closed briefly and then reopened to take about 150 inmates from Grendon prison which had closed in December 1990 due to electrical faults. When those inmates returned to Grendon in September 1990, Wellingborough remained as a C Category male trainer and continues to operate in the role today. The Head of Custody at Wellingborough declined to complete the Governor's Questionnaire—see below. We received no reply from the prison's BoV when we requested information and, similarly, we received no reply from the Area Manager responsible for Wellingborough when we wrote to her about the establishment. HMCIP published their latest inspection report on Wellingborough in October 1993.

OFFICIALS
AREA MGR: Amy Edwards
CHAIR BOV:
GOVERNOR: J. Whettan
MEDICAL:
CHAPLAIN: Rev Dent
PROBATION: Mike Doel
EDUCATION:
LOCAL MP: Tim Boswell. Con
STAFFING: 7 Governor grades, 8 Principal Officers, 21 Senior Officers and 66 Officers, excluding specialist staff.

REGIME *week days*: 0750 unlock/breakfast. 0830 work. 1000 adjudications. 1130 cease labour. 1145 dinner. 1220 lock up. 1340 work. 1630 cease labour. 1635 tea. 1650 lock up. 1750–2000 association.

week ends: 0750 unlock/breakfast. 0830 cleaning. 0855 association. 0900 chapel. 0915 sports field. 1100 cease activities. 1120 dinner. 1155 lock up. 1330 unlock, association. 1615 tea. 1650 lock up. 1750–2000 association.

Out of cell: 9.5/24hrs weekdays and 9.5/24hrs at weekends.

ACCOMMODATION & FACILITIES Six wings: A, B, C, D, E, F, all with integral sanitation. Small cells, communal areas generally untidy, and all meals dine in cell. Hot water boiler, showers, toilets, two association rooms and card phones on ground floor. Generally relaxed atmosphere. Personal officer scheme, sentence planning.

CANTEEN Procedure for ordering canteen goods is cumbersome, all goods have to be ordered in writing and are brought to the wing the following day. Staff cannot deal with pay queries nor can inmates purchase alternative goods when those ordered are not available: a poor system that should be reviewed and simplified.

VISITS *How to get there*: Train to Wellingborough, then taxi to prison as no suitable bus service. Green buses run regularly from Northampton to Wellingborough town centre & coach runs from Marylebone to Wellingborough on Wed, Sat, Sun—approx £6 return. No Special Transport.
VISITING TIMES: Week Days: 1400–1600 Wed, Thurs, Fri only. Saturday: 1400–1600. Sunday: 1400–1600.

NOTES Staffed Visitors Centre. Canteen. No Childrens Play Area. Contact prison for details of local B&B. No wheelchair access. Arrangements can be made if advance warning is given to prison. Poor visiting facilities, particularly at weekends.

EDUCATION Northampton College were awarded the education contract at Wellingborough in April 1993. Open 50 weeks of the year for five lays and two evenings per week. Business studies, naths psychology, information technology, cook-ry, English, wordpower, accounting, English liter-ature, open learning, video skills, art, drama and computing.

WORKSHOPS VTC/CIT courses: Bricklaying, Carpentry, Painting & Decorating, Plastering, Micro-electronics, Welding, Motor Mechanics and Electronic Wiring. Laundry. Farms & Gardens. Kitchen. Cleaners. CES. CSV. Wages average £6.50 with good working conditions and broad opportunities reported.

DISCIPLINE Total of 293 adjudications in he six months prior to the inspection. Most eports are for wiring-up. Drug detection search eam with dogs visited the establishment but there vere no specific finds. Segregation Unit rarely sed for punishment and all documentation in rder.

MEDICAL Part time Medical Officer, ×HCSO, 3×HCO. HCC located in separate build-ig, two wards provide nine beds, seven single ooms and one strip cell. Weekly dental sessions ith ten day waiting list, and optical services as ecessary. Shortage of staff trained in suicide wareness.

GYMNASIUM & SPORTS 1×PESO and ×PEO. Small gym with space for one badminton ourt, stage area used for weights and large addi-onal weights area in back room which is the full ngth of the gym itself. Large fenced sports fields, asses daily 0830–1130 & 1345–1615. Weights, jog-ng, remedials, over 35's, badminton, basketball, occer, fitness training, volleyball and competitive pecial Olympics'.

CHAPLAINCY Full time CE chaplain, RC id Methodist ministers. CE Service 0900 Sun, RC lass 0900 Sat. Muslim prayers Fri. Weekly pro-amme of discussion, meditation and fellowship oups.

FOOD Four week menu cycle in operation ith two–week pre-select system. Dinner and tea eal times are perverse and need to be made uch later. Kitchen well equipped and spacious., ough general indication of lack of cleanliness, re and supervision. Food was left uncovered, cks were dirty and there was large pools of water d food debris: HMCIP said that hygiene stan-rds in the kitchen were unacceptably low.

ESTABLISHMENT REPORTS In a report ublished 5th October 1993) of an inspection in ne 1993, HMCIP, said that they were impressed see the improvements to the regime since the last inspection in February 1992. There was sound evidence of positive relationships between inmates and staff, despite the complaints of some staff who still perceived the subtler handling of adult prison-ers as appeasement. Inmates recognised that staff were in control, although a little too restrictive for a Category C establishment. The prison was never-theless free from tension. Buildings are in good order, refurbishment nearing completion, and the reception should be re-sited. HMCIP was con-cerned about catering arrangements which were generally unsatisfactory, and in some respects very poor. Difficulties in distributing the food, with it being manhandled down stairways, should be rec-tified as a matter of urgency and there should be better supervision of inmates working in the kitchen where hygiene standards were unaccept-ably low. Inmates should also dine in association and strong support is given to the building of din-ing rooms—something HMCIP last recommended in his previous report. Catering was the poorest of the functions seen during the short inspection, and spoils what is an otherwise encouraging picture. Wellingborough enjoys good educational and workshop facilities which form the core of a posi-tive regime. They are supported by a responsive work allocation system linked to sentence plan-ning. HMCIP was impressed by the high levels of co-operation between all departments, and it was clear that the establishment had the potential to provide an excellent therapeutic environment.

GOVERNOR'S COMMENTS I have come to the conclusion that the likely benefit to the establishment does not justify the necessary investment of resources to complete the question-naires. D.Yardwood, Head of Custody.

PRISONERS' COMMENTS Evening association terminates too early at 2000, causing long queues for the phones. The lunch time lock-up is wasteful and unnecessary. In-cell television is not allowed and the regime is too restrictive in comparison with other C Category prison regimes. The food is poor, too many stews, few variations and seemingly general absence of interest from those providing food. There are few salads or food for healthy eating, invariably the food is cold and greasy. Catering staff are not seen at wing server-ies. Visiting arrangements are poor, with no toilet for inmates. A request to use the toilet often leads to the termination of a visit. There are no facilities for children. At weekends the visits room is too small and sometimes visits have to be curtailed. This is likely to worsen when the refurbishment of F.wing is complete and there is a rise in popula-tion. Wellingborough is a dumping ground for other C Category establishments. It is more like a B Category establishment with very restricted facili-ties for lifers. Young offender regime attitudes still remained, and A.wing in particular is very restricted. Inmate/staff relationships on the whole are good, the prison was a good one, personal officers were generally good and the governors were well meaning although not very effective. There were no problems with female staff although objection is taken to being rubbed down by them. The potential of the establishment is good, especially the workshops and education. The prison is scruffy and could be improved by a better cleaning programme. Wing launderettes should be soundproofed.

HM YOI Werrington

Stoke-on-Trent, Staffs. ST9 ODX
Tel: 0781-303514 **Fax:** 0781-302504
Opened: 1895 **CNA:** 110 **Roll:** 104 **Category:** Closed YOI

i **BACKGROUND** Werrington is a small closed YOI situated on the edge of the Potteries on the outskirts of Stoke-on-Trent. The institution started life in 1895 as an Industrial School and was subsequently purchased by the Prison Commissioners in 1955. Two years later it opened as a Senior Detention Centre. Following implementation of the Criminal Justice Act 1982 it converted to a Youth Custody Centre in 1985, and in 1988 it became a Young Offenders Institution. Neither the Governor nor the Board of Visitors replied to our requests for information about the Institution. HMCIP published their latest report on Werrington in April 1992.

OFFICIALS
AREA MGR: Dai Curtis
CHAIR BOV:
GOVERNOR: B. Stanhope
MEDICAL:
CHAPLAIN: Rev Humphreys
PROBATION: Jeff Oxborrow
EDUCATION:
LOCAL MP: David Knox. Con
STAFFING: 3 Governor grades, 2 Principal Officers, 4 Senior Officers and 27 Officers, excluding specialist staff.

REGIME *week days*: 0715 unlock. 0745 inspection. 0755 breakfast. 0815 work. 1115 adjudications. 1200 applications/call ups. 1210 cease labour. 1230 dinner. 1330 work. 1610 cease labour. 1645 tea. 1745 evening classes. 1800–2045 association. 2200 lights out.

week ends: 0745 unlock. 0830 breakfast. 0900 PE. 1030(Sun) Gov's Inspection. 1130(Sat) RC Mass; (Sun) CE Service. 1215 dinner 1330 activities. 1600 tea. 1700–2045 association. 2200 lights out.

Out of cell: 12/24hrs weekdays and 12/24hrs at weekends.

ACCOMMODATION & FACILITIES Five main dormitories. Eight single cubicles for use prior to disciplinary transfer, and two detention rooms which appear to be rarely used. HMCIP described dormitories as having a 'workhouse atmosphere . . . clean, but bleak and bare'. No evidence of bullying. Routine censorship abolished but mail opened outwith presence of the prisoner and handed out at dinnertime. Card phones in association area, all calls monitored.

CANTEEN Very small shop with limited space, basic decor and metal shelving on which stock was displayed. Inmates served through small hatch, price list was displayed, though with only 50 lines being carried there was not a great deal of choice. Wages paid Friday, and £5 private cash.

VISITS *How to get there*: Train to Stoke-on-Trent, bus (54,47,215,218) to Hanley, then bus (16,232) or Moorland Minibus to Werrington. No Special Transport.
VISITING TIMES: Week Days: 1330–1530 Wednesday only. Saturday: 1330–1530. Sunday: 1330–1530.

NOTES No staffed Visitors Centre or Childrens Play Area. Canteen. Contact prison probation or unit manager for details of local B&B. Good access for wheelchairs. No under-18's unless accompanied by an adult. Visits presently allowed weekly for parents—2 hour visit weekends and Wednesday if at prison for 1330. Visits cannot normally be extended beyond 1530.

EDUCATION Three f/t and 30 p/t teachers. Five classrooms, including art and pottery room. Open 50 weeks of the year for both day and evening classes, both of which operate five days a week. Mainly devoted to basic education, but with a practical aspect (e.g. maths=budgeting) whenever possible.

WORKSHOPS VTC/CIT Bricklaying—16 week course with room for ten inmates, reportedly excellent instructor; Home Management—four week course giving basics of painting and wall-papering etc; Motor Mechanics—modular course after which employment in tyre/exhaust centre realistic possibility. Farm and gardens party and usual cleaners/kitchen workers etc.

MEDICAL P/t Medical Officer, 1×HCSO, 1×HCO. Four-bed dormitory/ward and single room serving as isolation room. Dentist visits regularly and optician once per month. Inmates report sick at unlock and are seen by the doctor later in the morning.

GYMNASIUM & SPORTS 1×PESO, 2×PEO. Poor PE facilities—small gymnasium dates from 1901! Very large grassed sports field, marked out for rugby and football. Two tarmac areas intended for ball games. Comprehensive day and evening programme, many external activities and all staff are qualified instructors in various sports. CSLA course.

CHAPLAINCY P/t RC, Methodist and CE chaplains. Good inmate relations developed. Main CE Service Sunday 1115, RC Mass Saturday 1115. Discussion groups held Wednesday evening. Ministers from other faiths visit as regularly as required.

FOOD Staffing: 1×SO and 1×Officer (caterers), and there is a work party of 5. HMCIP impressed with both quality and quantity of the meals and he received no complaints from inmates. Meals were served at realistic times. Kitchen was too small to cope properly and new extention is planned along with full refurbishment.

ESTABLISHMENT REPORTS In a report (published 2nd April 1992) of an inspection in September 1991, Judge Stephen Tumim, HMCIP, was impressed with the progress that had been made since his last inspection in 1988. additional work training places had been created and the farm continued to provide work and skill training. Sentence planning was well developed. However dormitories should be made more attractive, the main meal of the day should be served at tea time rather than mid-day, the range of goods stocked in the canteen should be increased, more frequent changes of underwear and socks should be allowed and the number of catering staff should be reviewed. Werrington continued to suffer from an uncertain future and this was having an effect on staff morale.

In reply to the report the Home Secretary announced that a decision had been taken to keep Werrington open: a decision reached, he said, because of the good inmate/staff relationships, the positive regime in which inmates had a full and busy day, and the Personal Officer Scheme which was particularly well developed.

HM YOI Wetherby

York Rd, Wetheby. LS22 5ED
Tel: 0937-585141 **Fax:** 0937 586488
Opened: 1958 **CNA:** 160 (120-Juv, 40-YO) **Roll:** 158 **Category:** Closed YOI

BACKGROUND Wetherby YOI sits less than a mile from the town centre of Wetherby in West Yorkshire. Originally a naval training establishment, it opened as a Borstal in 1958. In 1983, when the Criminal Justice Act 1982 introduced youth custody centres, Wetherby was redesignated in that role. In August 1985 Wetherby became a closed YOI following the opening of Thorn Cross YCC. It became a YOI on 1st October 1998, when the Criminal Justice Act 1988 introduced such institutions. In October 1992 the establishment began to take juveniles. The Governor of Wetherby, Mr Atkinson, supplied information about Wetherby, though the YOI's Board of Visitors did not reply to our request for a copy of their latest annual report. HMCIP published their latest inspection report on Wetherby in October 1994.

OFFICIALS
AREA MGR: M. Codd
CHAIR BOV: Mr Begley
GOVERNOR: P. Atkinson
MEDICAL: Dr Mates
CHAPLAIN: Rev Jackson
PROBATION: W. Burton
EDUCATION: J. Owen
LOCAL MP: Spencer Batiste. Con
STAFFING: 4×Governors, 7×PO, 14×SO, 55×Officer including specialist staff.

REGIME *week days*: 0730 unlock/breakfast. 0800 work. 0830 PE/education. 1200 dinner/lock up. 1330 unlock, work. 1700 tea, lock up. 1800 association. 2045 lock up.

week ends: 0800 unlock. 0830 breakfast. 0900 unit cleaning. 1030 Gov's inspection. 1200 dinner/lock up. 1330 unlock, association, visits. 1700 tea. 1800 association. 2045 lock up.

Out of cell: 12/24hrs weekdays and 11/24hrs at weekends.

ACCOMMODATION & FACILITIES Two Units (West, South) with 60 single cells and integral sanitation, h/c water. Two billets (North Unit) each providing 20 single rooms with free movement to ablutions at all times. I/p list of standard items, including computer (gameboy) games, sound system but no pets. Sentence planning began July 1994. Drug counselling, card phones and personal officer scheme.

CANTEEN Totally inadequate canteen, small size and limited stock with only 90 lines being carried. Plans to extend the premises have not materialised. Open from 1300–1530 each Friday, with receptions being given access on arrival. Phonecards limited to two per week and private cash restricted to £5. Clearly displayed prices, in line with Shaw's Guide, and a profit margin of 10%.

VISITS *How to get there*: Train to Leeds then bus (794,795,798 & 799) from W.Yorks bus station to Wetherby. Bus (795) Mon–Sat from Infirmary Street behind the Post Office in City Sq, 5mins past the hour until 1805, (796) 25 mins past the hour until 1753. Sundays 798/799 15 mins to the hour from Eastgate bus station. Special Transport: coaches from various areas, check with prison probation officer.
VISITING TIMES: Week Days: 30 min visits by prior arrangement only. Saturday: 1330–1530 120 min visits at weekends. Sunday: 1330–1530.

NOTES No staffed Visitors Centre or Childrens Play Area. Canteen (light refreshments). Wheelchair access.

EDUCATION Open 49 weeks of the year, seven f/t teachers (18 p/t) and evening classes Mon–Wed. Full day and evening programme: literacy, numeracy, computers, maths, English, life skills, art, communication skills, woodwork, basic cookery, HIV/AIDS, family planning, first aid, keyboards. Well attended.

WORKSHOPS VTC catering and VTC plastering—for juveniles. Two multi-skills shops. Pay rates range from £2.25 for UB40 and segregation, to a maximum of £7.40 and £8.65 on the farm and kitchen parties respectively. Juveniles on FTE start on £4.60 and could increase that to £5.60.

DISCIPLINE Excessive amount of disciplinary reports with 868 between April 1993 and January 1994. HMCIP examined the records of adjudications and, though he found them to be properly conducted, the level of awards were much too punitive: in the above ten month period inmates on West Unit alone had 1,458 days added to their sentences. Segregation unit with eight ordinary cells, all with integral sanitation, and one strip cell.

MEDICAL Four local GP's part time rota visits Mon-Sat, for one hour. On call Sundays and Bank Holidays. Five-bed ward. Staffing 1×HCSO, 1×EN. Visiting dentist, psychiatrist and optician as required. Report sick at unlock and receive appointment for evening. 'Special Sick' at any time.

GYMNASIUM & SPORTS With the exception of a large sports field and reasonable tarmac area, the PE facilities at Wetherby are poor. Small gym with low roof. Reasonably equipped weights room but the roof leaks badly. Staffing 1×PESO and 2×PEO's. Classes 0830–1530 Mon–Thurs. Weekend programme 1300–1930—afternoon sessions are compulsory for juveniles.

CHAPLAINCY Part time CE chaplain, RC and Methodist ministers. Imam visits weekly. CE Service 0900 Sunday, RC Mass 1100 Sunday—each attracting about 40 inmates. Religious instruction group Wednesday afternoon, and fellowship group in the evening. Pleasant chapel, though in need of decoration.

FOOD Staffing: 1×PO, 2×Officer (caterers), and an inmate work party of 10. All meals eaten in association. Breakfast 0800 (0830 at w/e), dinner at 12 noon and tea at 1700. Four week menu cycle with two choices at both dinner and tea. Food is tasty, well presented and sustaining said HMCIP. New kitchen just come into operation.

ESTABLISHMENT REPORTS Wetherby has a long and proud tradition of being an establishment in which individual needs of young inmates receive appropriate attention said HMCIP in a report (published 26th October 1993) of an inspection in March 1994.

However staff now have to deal with the challenge of juveniles, many of whom had been sexually or physically abused and who viewed kind acts by adult males with suspicion. There are many incidents of self harm, bullying and childish mischief. Managers believed inmates could benefit from their time at Wetherby through a combination of discipline, the opportunity to acquire skills and sound relationships with staff. The basic standard of amenities for inmates is satisfactory. Meals are reasonably appetising and all inmates are housed in single rooms with, in the case of juveniles, the benefit of integral sanitation. The accommodation in North Unit is however very poor, medical services are satisfactory, though the amount of self harm is worrying. The practice of locating suicidal inmates in the segregation unit overnight on 15 minutes observations is not satisfactory. A better induction programme is needed, and a workable sentence planning and personal officer scheme should be introduced. There is an urgent need for a new sports hall. Wetherby is one of only six establishments holding sentenced juveniles. The Prison Service has little experience of dealing with this section of the inmates population as a group, and no special provision has been made for their care. They require close supervision and demand constant attention. It is greatly to the credit of all Wetherby staff that the inmates appear to be relatively cheerful and confident.

GOVERNOR'S COMMENTS We have a new kitchen came into operation in June 1994, new planned outside activities programme and new incentive pay scheme in the pipeline. We also will be introducing new religious instruction classes. We operate an incentive regime on a number of fronts, with a range of sticks and carrots built into the system. Before we started taking juveniles there was no real scope for sentence planning, throughcare or personal officer schemes, as inmates were only here for an average of three weeks, I am pleased we are now able to begin developing these important aspects of our regime.

PRISONERS' COMMENTS
Request/complaints answered speedily. Accommodation scores highly other than an absence of power points. Canteen is good with fair prices and local purchase facility. Visits are average, though staff who show visitors in are perceived as 'not too friendly'. Education scores top marks at Wetherby and the unit consistently praised for its wide variety of appropriate courses. Wages and work are both considered 'good' and the incentive earnings scheme appreciated. 'Good' also describes the inmates' medical views. Adjudications on the other hand come under fire for 'heavy-handed' punishments. Food is 'reasonably varied, quality's not too bad but there isn't enough of it'. Very good sports and games facilities, religious needs are catered for. Access to phones is good, mail is opened outwith the presence of the inmate however and handed out after dinner.

HM Prison Whatton

Cromwell Road, Nottingham. NG13 9FQ
Tel: 0949-50511 **Fax:** 0949-50124
Opened: 1966 **CNA:** 217 **Average Roll:** 201 **Category:** C. Male (VPU)

BACKGROUND Whatton prison, built as a Junior and Senior Detention Centre in 1966, lies between the town of Bingham and the village of Whatton some nine miles east of Nottingham. Many of the facilities, such as dining halls and gymnasium, were duplicated during the building process to allow for separation of the Junior and Senior detainees it was designed to contain. Whatton became a Young Offender Institution in October 1988 and, in April 1990, was redesignated as a C Category adult male training establishment for vulnerable prisoners: 90% of inmates are sex offenders undergoing the Core Sex Offender Treatment Programme—see below. The Governor of Whatton did not reply to our request for information about the prison, and the Chairman of the prison's BoV refused a copy of their annual report. HMCIP published their latest inspection report on Whatton in June 1993.

OFFICIALS
AREA MGR: Joe Mullens
CHAIR BOV: C. Day
GOVERNOR: M.A. Lewis
MEDICAL:
CHAPLAIN: Rev Pulman
PROBATION: H.S. Dhindsa
EDUCATION:
LOCAL MP: Kenneth Clarke. Con

REGIME *week days*: 0745 unlock. 0815 breakfast. 0845 work. 1145 dinner. 1345 work. 1615 cease labour, tea. 1800–2030 association. Summer: sports field 1900–2000.

week ends: 0745 unlock. 0815 breakfast. 0900 association. 1145 dinner. 1400 association. 1615 tea. 1730–2030 association. Summer: sports field 1900–2000.

Out of cell: 10/24hrs weekdays and 10/24hrs at weekends.

ACCOMMODATION & FACILITIES
Two two-storey living units, each a mirror image of the other. Mainly dormitories, though a small amount of cellular accommodation is available. Integral sanitation fitted, card phones in each unit

and mail given out at dinner time—opened outwith the presence of the addressee. Poor i/p list and restricted civilian clothing allowed. Shower access v.good, association rooms average and no cooking facilities on the units.

ACCEPTANCE CRITERIA All applicants for a place at Whatton **Must**:-

i) have a C Category; ii) have been on Rule 43 for a period of at least six weeks; iii) have no record of institutional violence; iv) have at least six months left to serve; v) not require the services of a full time MO; vi) not be engaged in on-going psychiatric treatment; vii) not have a current appeal against conviction outstanding, or be involved in any legal process that challenges the conviction.

CORE SEX OFFENDER TREATMENT PROGRAMME Whatton operates the Core Sex Offender Treatment Programme with application for entry in the first instance being made to probation staff in your current establishment. The core programme has five aims: To undermine beliefs which offenders use to give themselves permission to offend; To increase offenders empathy with the suffering they cause their victims; To increase offenders awareness of offence cycles which lead to offending; To rehearse ways of avoiding these patterns; To prepare offenders to recover from failure of self-control. The programme is delivered in 14 separate blocks, consisting of half day units and is mostly done through group work; challenging offending behaviour and the distorted view of relationships that many sex offenders possess.

VISITS *How to get there*: Train to Nottingham, bus (25—unreliable) to Bingham, then bus (413) to Whatton, or taxi from Bingham, or bus from Nottingham to Aglockton then 20 min walk to prison. No Special Transport.
VISITING TIMES: Week Days: 1400–1600 Tues, Thurs only. Saturday: 1400–1600. Sunday: 1400–1600.

NOTES No staffed Visitors Centre or Childrens Play Area. Canteen. Wheelchair access.

EDUCATION Individual education programmes are devised for each inmate at Whatton from a number of key elements that include Information Technology, Art, Open Learning, Home Economics, and basic English and maths. Evening classes three nights per week and are well attended. Library on first floor of education unit, with some 4500 books and open weekdays between 0745–1930 or 2000. Closed at weekends. Professional librarian works 23 hrs/wk.

WORKSHOPS VTC/CIT Bricklaying, Plastering, Painting & Decorating. Community Craft Shop teaches basic woodworking skills and repairs prison furniture in addition to charity work in the community. Textile shop in what had previously been a gymnasium, manufactures pyjamas cut at HMP Rudgate and plans to introduce NVQs shortly. Wages average £6.50.

DISCIPLINE Whatton is generally a relaxed establishment, such tension as exists concerns new admissions adjusting to the regime. Vandalism is negligible and there have only been five incidents in two years—two home leave failures, two losses of tools and one assault. During the same period reports average less than four per month.

PROBATION Senior and two main grade probation officers seconded to Whatton from Notts Probation Service (NPS) nominally for two years but often longer. NPS has run sex offender treatment programmes for many years and has acquired considerable expertise, the probation staff at Whatton are deeply involved with the core programme and consequent group work. The core programme is only a small part of a larger picture, known locally as offence focused work and embracing all aspects of treatment including sentence planning, various modular courses and personal officer scheme. Probation staff provide relapse therapy for sex offenders.

MEDICAL Part time Medical Officer, 1×HCSO, 3×HCO. Large HCC with 15 bed unit (6 double cells and three singles). No X-ray, dental or optical facilities, inmates requiring emergency treatment escorted to Nottingham. No multi-disciplinary HIV/AIDS team, no pro-active health promotion.

CHAPLAINCY Part time CE chaplain, RC, Salvation Army Brigadier and Methodist ministers. Two chapels, though space is limited and there are no facilities at all for minority faiths. Wednesday evening Chaplaincy visits for informal discussions with inmates. Limited weekly programme of groups and discussions organised by Chaplain.

FOOD Staffing: 1×SO, 2×Officers and an inmate work party of 10. Two large, bright, dining rooms situated on either side of the kitchen provide dine out facilities for all inmates. Kitchen workers two shift system (0645–1215 & 1330–1700) six and a half days per week (£7.20 early shift, £6.20 late shift). No pre-select menu system, but food reported to be very good by inmates and no problem with quantity. Three choices for dinner and tea.

ESTABLISHMENT REPORTS In a report (published 7th June 1993) of an inspection in May 1992, HMCIP said that Whatton had made the transition from YOI to C Category VPU with remarkable speed and success.

PRISONERS' COMMENTS **Non core-programme inmates:** Inmates told HMCIP they felt safe in Whatton and appreciated being treated like human beings, in contrast to their experiences in segregation in local establishments. Self-confidence improves at Whatton, dignity is restored and inmate/staff relationships are excellent. Security is far too strict however for a C Category establishment, the high standard of behaviour warranted some relaxation [the Governor declined to reduce the high level of security pointing to the 'potentially catastrophic consequences of an escape']. Inmates at Whatton cannot wear their own clothes as security regulations prevent this, and access to PE—particularly of the remedial or less strenuous variety—is not provided often enough. There should be an open establishment to which sex offenders can progress after completion of the core programme.

Core-programme inmates: All but one inmate on the core programme believed they had benefited from the treatment they had received. Addressing their offending behaviour through understanding their victim's suffering had had a considerable effect on some inmates. There was, however, a feeling that the programme 'backed off' at various critical points, and two inmates thought it was too easy to avoid sensitive areas. The programme was too short in duration and not linked clearly enough to further treatment, particularly on release.

HM Prison Whitemoor

Longhill Road, March, Cambs. PE15 OPR
Tel: 0354-660653 **Fax:** 0354-50783
Opened: 1991 **CNA:** 534 **Average Roll:** 466 **Category:** Dispersal

i **BACKGROUND** Whitemoor, which operates as a dispersal prison and contains a VPU, Special Security Unit and Assessment Centre for the Core Sex Offenders Treatment Programme, occupies a 90 acre site covering part of a former railway marshalling yard at March in Cambridgeshire. Construction of the purpose-built prison began in February 1988 and the first inmates entered the establishment in September 1991. Exactly three years later Whitemoor was the scene of an armed breakout during which a prison officer was slightly injured. In the inevitable all-four-corners search of the prison that followed, 1lb of Semtex high explosive and six detonators were discovered which, experts claimed, was enough the demolish the gatelodge and most of the surrounding perimeter wall. These incidents are being investigated by Sir John Woodcock, ex-Chief Inspector of Constabulary, though it is still unclear whether the Home Secretary will publish the report—see below. Neither the Governor nor BoV replied to our requests for information about the prison. HMCIP inspected Whitemoor in January 1994 and their report was due to be published in September 1994 but has been delayed as a result of the Woodcock Inquiry. Information here will be brief with full details next edition.

OFFICIALS
AREA MGR: Amy Edwards
CHAIR BOV: Penny Lambert
GOVERNOR: Brodie Clark
MEDICAL:
CHAPLAIN: Rev Salmon
PROBATION: Matthew Ryder
EDUCATION:
LOCAL MP: Malcolm Moss. Con

ACCOMMODATION & FACILITIES
Four main wings, A,B,C,D, designed in a cruciform shape and each containing 126 single cells all with integral sanitation. Cooking, card phone, showering and laundry facilities on each wing. Large i/p list. No power points in cells. A/B.wings=VPU, C/D.wings=Dispersal.

VISITS *How to get there*: Regular train service from London and Midlands to March. Special Transport: buses laid on from London by HALOW (071-793-7484), and from Birmingham—contact probation at prison for details.
VISITING TIMES: Week Days: 1345–1615. Saturday: 1345–1615. Sunday: 1345–1615.

NOTES Staffed Visitors Centre with nappy-changing facilities. Canteen open daily from 1230–1700. Childrens Play Area supervised by childcare volunteers. Visits room contains 48 low tables with easy chairs. No overnight stay facilities, but contact probation for details of B&B. Tues visits reserved for children. Further information contact prison visits staff on extn 284.

ESTABLISHMENT REPORTS In a short report (published 5th August 1993) of an inspection in November 1992, HMCIP said that Whitemoor was well designed and offers good quality accommodation and facilities for prisoners. Office and storage space is inadequate and operation of the request/complaints system requires review. Whitemoor faces two distinct problems: having two population groups (VPU/Dispersal) who could not be allowed to mix, and a significant number of inmates who were determined to challenge the system and who sought confrontation. VPU inmates cannot use the Education Centre, and staff told Judge Tumim (2.02b) that there were double standards in that VPU inmates were placed on report if they refused to work, whereas dispersal inmates on C&D wings refused work with impunity. HMCIP also questioned whether it made sense to have a textile workshop in a prison where the inmates refuse to work or produce so little as to be ineffective. The inadequacy of pay rates and the reliance on private cash are magnified by dispersal prison privileges which bear no relation to prisoners' very limited spending power. It may be time, said Judge Tumim, for the Prison Service to review dispersal regime activities, and the applicable pay and private cash allowances allowed there.

PRISONERS' COMMENTS **VPU:** Complaints are actively discouraged. No smoking in any part of the visiting room and the block is always full. No religious facilities for Humanists. Good access to the card phones. It was a huge mistake to try and make two incompatible halves of a prison fit together. Whitemoor should be either a VPU or ordinary prison. VPU inmates are always taken to visits last and brought back first, while C & D wings get first choice at everything. Visitors are made to wait too long. There is no access to the Education centre and time out of cell is less than in the other half of the prison. Food is poor, service is slow and breakfast inadequate with little variety. No use using the Food Complaints Book, no one reads it and it's a complaint in itself. Whitemoor has not lived up to its expectations and sex offender treatment programmes have not materialised.

Dispersal: Request Complaints procedure did not work and cannot be trusted. When complaints against staff were followed up nothing happens, the procedure for disciplining staff is unknown to inmates and the authorities use this to hide lack of action. Food is appalling, quality inconsistent, presentation is poor and it is often inedible. Staff adopt the wrong attitudes, private cash rules forbid purchase of batteries or toiletries, there are never enough cleaning materials, and the prison operates for the convenience of VPU inmates who get preference on visits, activities and PE. Canteen is too small, prices are high and it is difficult to use the local purchase facility.

SSU: Unnecessary restrictions on telephone calls. Request/Complaint system is not working and those responsible for it need to address its obvious shortcomings. Irish inmates are being used as political scapegoats in the issue of repatriation. Education is very important to SSU inmates and there is a fear that it could be lost.

THE WOODCOCK INQUIRY On 10th September 1994 the Home Secretary announced that Sir John Woodcock, former HM Chief Inspector of Constabulary, had been appointed to carry out an inquiry into the attempted escape from Whitemoor prison on 9th September 1994. In his statement Mr Howard said:

> 'Sir John Woodcock's terms of reference will be to enquire into all the circumstances surrounding the escape of six prisoners from the Special Secure Unit of Whitemoor prison on the evening of Friday 9th September 1994, to report his conclusions to the Home Secretary and to make recommendations on any action that should be taken to avoid any recurrence'.

In a letter to *The Independent* and other newspapers on 12th September 1994, the former Chair of Whitemoor's BoV, Pat Seligman, warned that public opprobrium directed at prison staff would be unfair and uninformed. She said:

> 'Until March this year, I was a member of the BoV at Whitemoor . . . Required to report regularly to the Home Secretary our independent opinion as to the running of the prison, we aired our concern about excessive 'privileges' accorded to prisoners in dispersal prisons. Coupled with our concern about the sparsity of searching of visitors to prisoners due to staffing level restrictions, security is inevitably compromised. The decision not to body-search visitors to IRA prisoners was made not locally by management, but at Home Office level. The implications resulting from this decision are now obvious. If the resignation of anyone is called for, it should be that of the Home Secretary. Since the elimination of staff overtime, the gradual reduction in staffing levels, accompanied by the expectation of an enhanced regime for prisoners, has meant that routine duties such as cell-searching cannot be conducted in accordance with governors' contracts'.

Responding to the letter, also in a letter to *The Independent* and other newspapers, the Director General of the Prison Service, Derek Lewis, said:

> '. . . neither the Home Secretary nor the Prison Service has sanctioned any relaxation of security for IRA prisoners. or the provision

of special privileges. When the Special Unit that held the IRA prisoners at Whitemoor was reopened in July 1992, it was not general practice to conduct rub-down searches of visitors to prisoners in all such units. Following a review of policies, instructions were issued by Prison Service HQ, in May 1993, which required full rub-down searches for all visitors in all Special Secure Units. That applied at Whitemoor since the reopening of the Special Unit in June (sic) 1993. it will be a matter for the inquiry now under way, to confirm that this policy was being fully implemented. The Prison Service policy is that no special privileges are given to IRA prisoners that are in any way different from other prisoners of the same security category'.

It is expected that the Woodcock Inquiry will take some months to produce its report.

HM Prison Winchester

Romsey Rd, Winchester. S022 5DF
Tel: 0962-854494 **Fax:** 0962-842560
Opened: 1846 **CNA:** 262 **Average Roll:** 411 **Category:** Male Local + C Cat Annexe

i **BACKGROUND** Winchester prison is situated about one mile (uphill) from the city centre, sandwiched between the Hampshire Police Headquarters and the main entrance to the Royal Hampshire County Hospital. It was designed as the County gaol for Hampshire and opened in 1846. At the rear of the prison, in 1964, a Remand Centre for Young Offenders was built: once known as the 'Dolls House', it has since been converted for use by C Category prisoners and is today known as the 'Annexe'. Neither the Governor nor BoV replied to our requests for information about the prison, and HMCIP published their latest inspection report on Winchester in July 1993.

OFFICIALS
AREA MGR: Alan Rayfield
CHAIR BOV:
GOVERNOR: M.K. Pascoe
MEDICAL: Dr R. Ilbert
CHAPLAIN: Rev Guymer
PROBATION: Vernon Young
EDUCATION: D. Davies
LOCAL MP: Gerald Malone. Con
STAFFING: Total of 281 staff in unified grades.

☞ **REGIME** *week days*: **Main prison:** 0730 unlock, breakfast, lock up. 0800 sick parade C2. 0845 slop out, trays out. 0900 workshops, Remand association, Rule 43 exercise. 0915 education. 1035 Remand exercise. 1135 cease labour, dinner, lock up. 1320 unlock, slop out, trays out. 1330 Convicted exercise. 1400 Remand association. 1620 cease labour. 1625 tea, lock up. 1745 classes. 1800 convicted association (Mon–Thurs), choir practice (Wed), Methodist service (Fri). 2000 lock up.

Annexe: 0730 unlock, breakfast, no lock up. 0815–1130 workshops. 1140 dinner, no lock up. 1230 association by rota. 1315–1630 workshops (–1530 Fri). 1640 tea 1745–2000 association.

week ends: **Main prison:** 0800 unlock, breakfast, lock up. 0815 CE Service (Sun). 0845 slop out, trays out. 0900 RC Mass (Sat). 0915 Remand association, Rule 43 exercise. 0920–1020 convicted exercise. 1030 remand exercise. 1110 dinner, lock up. 1300 unlock, slop out, trays out. 1330 Convicted visits (Sun: Cat A only). 1350–1530 association on wings, R43 in 5 Shop. 1545 tea, lock up. Only the Annexe has weekend evening association, 1700–2000.

Annexe: 0800 unlock, breakfast, no lock up. 0900 kit change, cell cleaning. 1000 association. 1120 dinner, no lock up. 1300–1545 association. 1545 tea. 1700–2000 association.

Out of cell: **Main prison:** 5.5/24hrs weekdays and 3.5/24hrs at weekends.

Annexe: 12/24hrs weekdays and 12/24hrs at weekends.

ACCOMMODATION & FACILITIES
MAIN PRISON: Four main Wings radiating from a Centre. A.wing was closed for refurbishment at time of inspection. B.wing houses 75 convicted, C.wing houses 98 remands, D2/3=VPU, D1/Basement=kitchen and works parties. Main prison badly in need of cleaning and redecoration, graffiti abounds, few cells have lockers and several card phones are without acoustic hoods. Lack of plans to turn recesses into showers after integral sanitation was criticised by HMCIP. To qualify for convicted association inmates have to be serving six months or more and are required to have been in the prison for 28 days—even then only 25 are allowed out at any one time: very poor association facilities. R43 inmates only have association weekend afternoon. Bail Information Scheme. In cell television permitted, but battery operated only. No power points.

Annexe: Houses 63 C&D Cats, clean and tidy environment, no graffiti or vandalism. Single cells with access to sanitation. all inmates employed, personal officer scheme and sentence planning. Two card phones. Visits taken in main prison—complaints that all inmates are strip searched and made to squat, contrary to the Security Manual procedure, following visits. Good association facilities, outdoor exercise yard for football and (sloping?) grassed area for volleyball. C&D Cat home leaves.

REQUESTS & COMPLAINTS Average of 60–70 per month submitted. Examination of the records showed time targets locally were being met, and replies were mostly thoughtful and well constructed.

CANTEEN Located in the same building as the communal showers, the canteen is available to convicted once per week for both earnings and private cash, and twice per week for remands who have a spending limit of £30. Turnover of £4000 per week with a profit of 10% and prices set to Shaw's Retail Guide. Stock of 190 item and no local purchase facility.

VISITS *How to get there*: Train to Winchester then walk to prison (uphill), bus (22,24,25 or 66) to prison. Special transport arranged by Portsmouth PROBATION: 0705–871441. VISITING TIMES: Week Days: 1330–1530 M–F. Saturday: 1330–1530. Sunday: 1330–1530.

NOTES No smoking on visits. No staffed Visitors Centre. Canteen and Childrens Play Area. Overnight stay v.difficult, but cheap B&Bs in Southampton. There is a supervised creche in the visits room and information available from HALOW (see 'Useful Organisations' Section) on Tuesday and Saturday afternoon. Good access for wheelchairs.

EDUCATION Winchester's Education Department is a model for a local prison—and has been for at least a decade. Five f/t teachers and 12 p/t staff, all part of Eastleigh College in Southampton. Open 46 weeks of the year with classes five days and four evenings per week. Very good keyboard music class. Computing, cooking, art and information technology. Lots of ad hoc courses run for a month or so at a time. Really first class department. Library located in basement landing of C.wing, reached by the spiral stairs. All inmates can visit once per week and borrow upto six books at a time. Special orders taken for books and newspapers ordered.

WORKSHOPS Limited work opportunities, though better than other locals. No VTC/CIT courses. Tailors shop (Annexe inmates), and two Light Assembly shops, one for Main Prison convicted, the second for R43 inmates. Usual kitchen, yards, works, orderlies and cleaners. Incentive earnings scheme introduced at Winchester in 1991.

DISCIPLINE Good inmate/staff relationships and prison routines that tend to work to time, provides a relaxed and secure environment. Most incidents centre around the remand prisoners in C.wing, which is a wing vulnerable to disorder, with a number of passive demonstrations: informal agreement between the Governors of Lewes, Winchester and Dorchester facilitated disciplinary transfers as necessary. Narrow and claustrophobic basement landing of A.wing houses Segregation Unit of eight cells. Number of adjudications has fallen from four or five a day to one or two, and it is not uncommon for there to be none at all. Procedures are correctly followed and awards consistent and appropriate.

MEDICAL Full time SMO, 3×MO, 1×HCPO, 4×HCSO, 13×HCO. Appointments system in operation for sick parades, report sick night before and given an appointment to be seen by doctor following morning. medication issued from hatch on C2 three times per day. HCC closed for refurbishment during inspection, but it had a poor inpatient regime and required urgent improvements—inpatients were only allowed out of cell for two hours per day. Dentist attends weekly—no waiting list. Optician once per month.

GYMNASIUM & SPORTS 1×PEPO, 1×PESO and 4×PEO. Good gymnasium facilities with a good bunch of PE staff. Main gym marked out for indoor games, and weights and fitness centre on the stage. CSLA. Daily programme of classes with lunch time activities and evening classes three nights per week.

CHAPLAINCY Two f/t CE chaplains, p/t RC and Methodist ministers. Sun: 0815 CE Service, 0945 Morning Service, 1315 R43 Holy Communion, 1400 Bible Study. Mon: 1800 Study Group. Tue: 1800 R43 Bible Study. Wed: 1800 Choir Practice/Fellowship. Thur: 1800 R43 Chaplain's Hour. Fri: 1800 Methodist Service. Sat: 0915 RC Mass. Strangely, at Winchester, applications for PV have to be made via Wing PO—not Chaplain.

FOOD Staffing: 1×PO, 1×SO, 5×Officer (caterers), and an inmate work party of 18. No set menu cycle and a six-week one would be appropriate. Food said by HMCIP to be satisfactory and there was little adverse comments from inmates. Meals collected from serveries at the kitchen and eaten in cell: food is taken to the Annexe in heated trolleys arriving only lukewarm at times. 'Toy Town' meal times, as one inmate put it.

ESTABLISHMENT REPORTS In a preface to the Report (published 14th July 1993) of an inspection at Winchester in January 1993, the Chief Inspector said he was troubled by the prison's plan to turn modest cells for two into cramped toilets for two: 'At Winchester, with its reduced population and its very adequate ground space, there is no impracticality in adopting the three-cells-into-two method'. The quality of activities were of a high standard for a local prison, with pockets of excellence. Remand prisoners had the opportunity of work if they wished and the pace of industry in the workshops was impressive, though opportunities for association were disappointing. The kitchen requires urgent attention: despite recent improvements following a visit from the EHO, there was still a heavy infestation of cockroaches in the kitchen and, during an evening visit, cockroaches were found in the shutters of serveries with bread rolls and buns left uncovered immediately below.

PRISONERS' COMMENTS **Main prison:** Applications go unanswered, one shower a week was not enough, the recesses are foul-smelling and there is a lack of cleaning materials. Weekend exercise is often reduced to 30 mins despite the fact that the regime plan clearly shows it to be for 60 mins. No evening association for remand inmates and limited association on B.wing. Relationships with staff were a lot better than they had been in the past. The standard of food was satisfactory, though meal times are too early. It is difficult to obtain razors, power points need to be installed and the issue of kit is poor with just two pairs of socks per week. Cell lights are too bright. **Rule 43 (OP):** Inmates have to run a gauntlet of abuse from other prisoners, exercise is cancelled even if it remotely looks like it could rain in the next hour. PE is available, but you have to give up the chance of using the telephone in return. Only one shower per week, poor hygiene standards with only one sluice for 15 men. Shortage of disinfectant. Visits are shared with inmates on normal location, and some have chosen not to take visits at all, rather than have the threats and the hassle. Educational provision is insufficient.

Annexe: Closeness of main prison restricts development, Amenities committee has difficulty raising issues with staff. Waiting conditions are poor for visitors, evening education in the Annexe is little more than a gesture. Laundry facilities should be installed and there is a wide variation in wages. PE opportunities are poor and the food is worse than in the main prison, often only lukewarm.

Wolds Remand Prison

Everthorpe, Brough, N.Humberside. HU15 2JZ
Tel: 0430-421588 Prison 0430-421639 Controller **Fax:** 0430-421589
Opened: 1992 **CNA:** 368 (Baseline 320) **Roll:** 364 **Category:** Male Remand

i **BACKGROUND** The Wolds is a new prison designed and built in one phase for the Prison Service specifically to contain those held on remand. The Wolds is situated between North and South Cave in East Yorkshire, next door to HMP Everthorpe, and is operated under licence by Group 4 Remand Services Ltd, Farncombe House, Broadway, Worcs. WR12 7LJ. The establishment opened on 6th April 1992 with a baseline CNA of 320—increased temporarily to 368 in 1994 to relieve pressure on police cells. Nick Metcalfe, Human Resources Manager at The Wolds, supplied an abundance of information about the establishment, though the prison's BoV did not reply to our request for a copy of their latest Annual Report. HMCIP published their first (and to date only) inspection report on The Wolds in August 1993. HMCIP recommended that once Doncaster became operational The Wolds should hold convicted inmates: a change to convicted status is now imminent and will probably be completed early in 1995.

OFFICIALS

HOME OFFICE CONTROLLER: Stuart Mitson
AREA MGR: Maurice Codd
CHAIR BOV: Mrs Bentall
DIRECTOR: W. MacGowan
MEDICAL: Dr J. Ilargaratine
CHAPLAIN: Rev D. Casswell
PROBATION: Mr D. Jackson
EDUCATION: Mr R. Joad
LOCAL MP: David Davis. Con
STAFFING: 8 analogous 'govenor' grades comprise the Senior Management Team headed by the Director. There are three tiers of custody staff below senior management level: 9 Managers, 41 Prisoner Custody Supervisors, 58 Prisoner Custody

Officers, and 4 Security Guards who equate to Prison Auxiliaries. Prisoner Custody 'Supervisors' have no supervisory role in relation to staff, but carry more responsibility, have more contact with prisoners and are paid a higher salary.

THE HOME OFFICE CONTROLLER

Unlike public sector prison establishments, disciplinary adjudications and restraint authorisation in private sector prisons and remand centres are not functions discharged by the Director (Governor) or any member of his staff. Instead they are carried out by Home Office appointed 'Controller', Stuart Mitson, who visits the prison as necessary.

REGIME *week days*: 0730 unlock/breakfast. 0800 cell cleaning 0830 exercise period. 0930 induction briefing new admissions. 1130 briefing ends. 1145 lock up, roll check. 1200 dinner. 1230 exercise. 1330 SWIP, assessments, interviews. 1715 lock up, roll check. 1730 tea. 2130 lock up.

week ends: 0730 unlock. 0800 cell cleaning. 0830 breakfast. 0930 induction briefing new admissions. 1130 briefing ends. 1145 lock up, roll check. 1200 dinner. 1230 exercise. 1330 SWIP, assessments, interviews. 1715 lock up, roll check. 1730 tea. 2130 lock up.

Out of cell: 14/24hrs weekdays and 14/24hrs at weekends.

ACCOMMODATION & FACILITIES
Six housing units holding 50 prisoners in each (A,B,C,D,E,F), 156 single cells and 72 double cells. E.Unit closed VPU. Segregation Unit 18 cells. Health Care Centre 16 beds. All cells have integral sanitation, sinks and power points are in the process of being fitted. In-possession list comprehensive and including carpet, CD player, video games, paints, jewellery and flask among many others. The Wolds provides a Bail Information Scheme. First two days Induction Unit inmates are given information and go through risk assessment programmes. Inmates at the Wolds open their own mail in front of staff, first mail delivery 0930 and second at 1430. Four card phones on each unit with access all day. Fax facilities also available for urgent cases.

CANTEEN Shop with large stock open six days of the week—not Monday. Operated by Group 4 clerical staff, inmates can spend upto £30 per day from private cash—though HMCIP regarded this amount as excessive and also argued for a credit payment system. Stock range of 250 items and clearly displayed price lists. HMCIP received no complaints from inmates about the shop.

REQUESTS/COMPLAINTS Average of 40–50 formal R/C per month. Those requiring local response answered by records office staff, those requiring a response from elsewhere are sent to Custodial Contracts Unit. Almost all complaints requiring a local response received an answer within seven days, with a few taking 14 days said HMCIP, although those answered outwith the Wolds rarely received a response within the six week target.

VISITS *How to get there*: Train to Brough station, then Cottingham minicoach five miles to prison—coach details 0482.843585. East Yorks bus (155) from Hull to Goole stops at prison—details 0482.27146. No Special Transport. Prison sends travel leaflets on request.
VISITING TIMES: Legal: 0800–2200, 7 days. Weekdays: 1400–1700 & 1830–2100. Saturday: 1400–1700 & 1830–2100. Sunday: 1400–1700 & 1830–2100.

NOTES Legal visitors MUST book in advance. The length and frequency of social visits depends on (a) whether the prisoner is remand or convicted and, (b) whether he has agreed to participate in scheduled activities (i.e. 'opted in'), or has declined to do so (i.e. 'opted-out'). There is a minimum and maximum for each category:

Opt-in: Rem: 60–90min daily. Con: 60–90min 2 per/wk.

Opt-out: Rem: 30mins daily. Con: 1×60 mins every 14 days.

Unstaffed Visitors Centre, creche and refreshments. Wheelchair access and toilets available. Visits take place in a relaxed atmosphere around individual tables and contact is permitted. Property and money can be handed-in on a visit. All visitors and their belongings pass through a metal detection/X-ray system.

EDUCATION Education open 50 weeks of the year, one full-time teacher and many part-time. Service delivery sub-contracted the Humberside Educational Services for a period of four years. Day classes Mon,Tues,Thurs,Fri 0900–1130 & 1330–1600 in English, maths, computer workshop, pottery, and soft toys, guitar.

WORKSHOPS One small workshop repairing broken furniture and involved in light assembly. Maximum workforce of 20 earning an average of £10 per week. Kitchen party of 15 men work as assistants (£1 per day worked), and in addition there are unit cleaners, painters and a gardens party.

DISCIPLINE Adjudications conducted by the Home Office Controller. It was suggested to HMCIP that the Director of the Wolds should play a part in this process, but this was rejected by HMCIP: 'We preferred the safeguards offered within the present arrangements'. From 1st

January to 12th May 1993, there were 357 adjudications. An examination of the completed records of adjudication by HMCIP indicated that they were dealt with competently and awards were fair.

MEDICAL Health Care Centre with 16 bed. Medical service is contracted out to AMI who provide qualified nurses and registered medical practitioners. Staffing: F/t Medical Officer, Nurse Manager, D/Nurse Manager, 7 Nurses and 3 Nurse Assistants. HMCIP found 'a relaxed atmosphere with patients out of cell for 14 hours per day . . . inmates speak well of the service they receive'. All remand inmates at The Wolds have the right to consult their own GP though few do so as most GP's will only attend for a fee. Twelve trained HIV counsellors, Daily surgery and visiting dental and optical specialists. Inmates report sick by informing unit staff who then notify Health Care Centre staff.

GYMNASIUM & SPORTS 'Facilities for physical exercise were excellent and compared with the best amenities in the Prison Service . . . uniquely in our experience, sports facilities were available to inmates 365 day a year'. Staffing: Supervisor and three PEO's. PE programme largely unstructured giving maximum flexibility of gym use. Main sports hall was large enough to permit five a side football and facilities for badminton, volleyball, basketball and an indoor cricket net. A 'well appointed' fitness room equipped with multi gym, exercise bikes, rowing and running machines.

CHAPLAINCY Full time CE chaplain employed by Group 4. P/t RC, Methodist and Pentecostal ministers. Imam visits weekly. Despite access to chaplain being good, the attendance at church services is poor.

FOOD Catering contracted out to ARA. HMCIP received no complaints about the quality or quantity of food: 'The meals were as good as we have seen anywhere and they were served at sensible times and in civilised circumstances'. Preselect menu system in operation, three choices at dinner and tea and a separate menu provided for Muslims with Halal meat provided on four days of the week. The same food provided for prisoners was also provided for the staff mess. Budget for food at the Wolds is more than in public sector prisons because all food is bought on the open market rather than from Prison Service Farms & Gardens. STAFFING: Manager, Chef and a baker, assisted by work party of 16 who work on two-shift basis: 0630–12 noon, 1330–1900.

ESTABLISHMENT REPORTS Amenities for prisoners at the privatised Wolds are excellent said HMCIP in a Report (published 26th August 1993) of an inspection in May 1993. Prisoners had keys to their rooms, the meals were good, served at sensible times and in civilised circumstances. A daily visit of an hour's duration was allowed every day of the year and HMCIP found abundant opportunities for education and physical recreation. The sports centre and education department were impressive, the library was well-stocked, well-managed and offered good access to prisoners. There was free movement to exercise from early morning until last thing at night. But there was a clear need for more job training. Some prisoners were out of their cells for 14 hours a day, but only a quarter of them were availing themselves of the opportunities. The majority were lethargic, content to laze about in a state of inertia in which corruption could flourish.

DIRECTOR'S COMMENTS The regime at the Wolds is due to change in late 1994 to convicted prisoners of Category B status. This will result in more work, the availability of sentence planning and regime focus on offending behaviour, education and resettlement.

PRISONERS' COMMENTS
Request/complaints generally heard two days after submission of form, though if something is really pressing access is available to Unit Manager. The accommodation is rated as very good, with toilets, sinks and power points in all cells. Prices in the canteen are reasonable and staff are pleasant. Good visiting facilities with evening visits being especially welcome for relatives who work during the day. Adjudications are fair and punishments are minimal and certainly not heavy handed in my opinion having had harsh treatment in other prisons. The medical facilities are good but bad access is reported: the normal routine of know when you are going to be ill and book in the day before! Food is excellent, with salad meals always available and a varied menu, always a good portion of milk with breakfast, a huge bonus. Also welcome are the tea bags and coffee. Top marks go to the gymnasium both for content and access. All religious needs are catered for, the chaplaincy here work hard, every week bands, singers, talks etc. No problems reported with the mail: You open your own mail, no censorship, first mail 0930 in the morning and 1430 in the afternoon, fax facilities are available for urgent needs, access to card phones all day and evening.

HM Prison Woodhill

Tattenhoe St, Milton Keynes. MK4 4DA
Tel: 0908-501999 **Fax:** 0908-505417
Opened: 1992 **CNA:** 566 **Average Roll:** 493 **Category:** Male Local & Remand Centre

i **BACKGROUND** Woodhill, which opened in July 1992, is located on the south west edge of Milton Keynes in Buckinghamshire, about a mile from the city centre and main line railway station. It is a purpose-built establishment and, though it remains as built, a further living unit should be completed in 1995. The prison operates as a local/remand establishment and contains a special unit complex which houses a special unit, special assessment unit and protected witness unit. There have been two suicides at the prison in the last twelve months. Despite a number of letters, neither the Governor nor BoV replied to our requests for information about the prison. HMCIP, who inspected the establishment for the first time in April 1994, published their report on 20th October 1994.

OFFICIALS

AREA MGR: Amy Edwards
CHAIR BOV:
GOVERNOR: R. Clarke
MEDICAL:
CHAPLAIN: Rev Green
PROBATION: Pat Jameson
EDUCATION:
LOCAL MP: Barry Legg. Con

ACCOMMODATION & FACILITIES
Four main cell blocks each with 120 single cells which open onto landings overlooking dining/association areas on the ground floor. Cells have integral sanitation and the design gives angled windows to prevent swinging lines. Good standards of cleanliness with £5 bonus paid to best cleaning team each week. Each wing has launderette facilities and good association rooms. Special Unit complex—see below. Card phones in each wing, with max of five phone cards per week. Personal officer scheme and sentence planning. Good offending behaviour group work being conducted by probation dept. Woodhill operates the Concentrated Core Sex Offender Treatment Programme.

SPECIAL UNIT COMPLEX **Special Unit:** CNA 12. Designed to control recalcitrant prisoners usually from dispersal prisons, taking a total of 15 inmates in its first 14 months of operation. Only cleaning work required of inmates in Special Unit, all subject to a personal development plan reviewed at 10 weekly intervals—plans are tailored individually and allocate periods of education, PE, discussions with probation, personal officers and psychologists. Average length of stay five months.

Special Assessment Unit: CNA 9. Similar to Special Unit in the inmates it takes, but able to respond to requests from dispersals to take inmates much faster than the Special Unit is able to do. Reports are submitted to Special Unit Selection Committee (SUSC) as to whether a prisoner is suitable fro transfer to the special unit. average length of stay 45 days.;

Poor regime that needs development.

Protected Witness Unit: CNA 8. Designed to hold prisoners who are giving evidence or assistance to the police in cases of serious crime, requests for admission come from the respective police force and normally have to be supported by the CPS. All inmates in the PWU are known to staff simply as 'Bloggs' followed by a number, their identity and the reasons for being in the PWU are known only to senior management of the prison. PWU inmates meet no other prisoners and cook their own meals—as do those in both Special Units—consisting of basic prison rations and foodstuffs provided by police sources. HMCIP reports that police forces send in money for the use of PWU inmates, and states that in one case an inmate received £300 from the police.

CANTEEN Central canteen with unpopular pre-order system open once per week for both private cash and earnings. Reasonable stock with local purchase facility, all inmates limited to total of £60 spends per week—weekly canteen turnover £3,000 on goods and £2,000 on phonecards. One of the few canteens to use a bar-code reader linked to a cash till that produces itemised receipts.

VISITS *How to get there*: Train to Milton Keynes then bus or taxi to prison—bus times do NOT correspond to visiting times. No Special Transport.
VISITING TIMES: Week Days: 0930–1130 (Fri only), 1400–1600 (Mon–Fri) and 1815–2015 (Wed only). Saturday: 0930–1130 & 1400–1600. Sunday: 0930–1130 & 1400–1600.

NOTES Staffed Visitors Centre, Canteen and Childrens Play Area. Plenty of local B&B. Disabled access and nappy-changing facilities. Excellent visits room. No smoking. Ultraviolet hand stamping, and a £15,000 handprint machine recently installed to further prevent escapes: three attempts made by inmates to pass out as visitors in 1993—all failed.

EDUCATION Education staff of 6 f/t teachers part of Milton Keynes College. Open five days and two evenings for 50 weeks of the year. Classes from 0830–1130 & 1400–1645. Induction programme takes all new receptions to education dept. Waiting time for classes usually short, initially pay is £4 for attending five sessions (two and a half days), rising to £7 for 10 sessions (five full days). Classes strong on basic education, modern languages, information technology, printing and art. Good library facilities with computer link to local library.

WORKSHOPS VTC/CIT courses: Catering. Woodhill has been built without any workshops, work mainly of a domestic nature. The establishment has set itself a target of 25.4 hours per week per inmate on purposeful activities—higher than the Prison Service target. However, HMCIP reports that only half the inmates were involved when he examined the records. Wages range from £4.25 to £12.

DISCIPLINE Since Woodhill opened there have been well over 100 finds of illicit drugs or equipment. In the six months prior to the inspection there had been 29 uses of C&R and the strip cells had been used 25 times—HMCIP discovered the Medical Officer was not always verifying the appropriateness of the strip cell. Very high level of adjudications with well over 1500 cases being heard in 1993 alone. Hearings conducted properly said HMCIP and punishments were firm.

MEDICAL Full time Senior Medical Officer, 2×f/t MO, 3×p/t MO, Gv.Health Care Manager, 2×HCSO, 3×Sisters (2×RMN & RGN, 1×RGN), 10×HCO, 20×Nurses. HCC with two wings each with two landings (A1,A2,B1,B2). HCC badly designed, with no natural light, ventilation or space for activities. A1=acute psychiatric patients, A2=VPU, B1=primary health care, B2=non-acute psychiatric patients. All patients had a limited regime, some were out of cell for 11 hours per day, but the facilities are limited and education staff visit only once per week. Regular visiting specialists. Dentist 2xSess/wk with a waiting list of a month for non-urgent cases though not all urgent cases are being identified: HMCIP saw one inmate with a possible dental abscess who was not referred for urgent treatment because staff were not aware there was a system of quick referrals. Optician monthly. Well equipped X-ray room used 14–40 times per week. Average of 30 report sick each day, no proper appointment system; seen by MO (sometime) next day. HMCIP criticised HCC staff for staying in the room while the MO is seeing the patient: such interviews should be conducted with just the inmate and doctor present. No organised general health care promotion scheme.

GYMNASIUM & SPORTS 1×PEPO, 2×PESO, 8×PEO. Very large sports hall with extended weights area, complemented by three separate changing rooms. Outside floodlit tarmac area and Astroturf playing field. HMCIP said the daytime programme was the best he had seen in any prison and was produced after consultation with inmates. Inmates receive a booklet crammed with information about what is on offer, and courses lead to qualifications in CSLA, body-building, first aid, weight lifting, soccer, volleyball, basket ball, gymnastics and team building. Fitness testing, bowls and over 35's. PE staff also operate a motor cycle training course, helping inmates become legal road users, in many cases for the first time.

CHAPLAINCY Full time CE chaplain, p/t RC and Methodist ministers. Large chapel used by all denominations, with multi faith area. Main services 0830 (RC) 0930 (CE). Bible study classes on Monday evening, meditation group on Wednesday and choir practice on Friday. Imam visits Thurs & Fri for Muslims. Pool of 14 Prison Visitors arranged by the Chaplain.

FOOD Catering service contracted to private company who also cater for the staff mess at a total cost of £479,406 (1994/95). Meals: breakfast 0745, dinner 1315, tea 1730. Three week menu cycle with the main meal of the day being dinner during the week and tea at weekends. There have been a number of food refusals at Woodhill, though mainly concerning one wing.

ESTABLISHMENT REPORTS In a report (published 20th October 1994) of an inspection in April 1994, HMCIP said that the outstanding design and construction of Woodhill's buildings was matched by the quality of its regime and performance of managers and staff. The prison was full of good practice. The induction course attended by all prisoners was practical and there was a range of offence-focused group work. Inmates spent an average of 12 hours per day out of cell. Standards of primary health care were satisfactory, there were few complaints from prisoners, though the design of the HCC should not be repeated in any other prison, being gloomy and claustrophobic. The Visitors' Centre was a model of good practice, but arrangements were spoiled by the amount of time visitors were kept waiting. The special unit complex was under-used. The treatment of vulnerable prisoners needs improvement, inmates felt unsafe and HMCIP gained the impression that senior management had not really made up their minds about the purpose of the VP regime. The main criticism was the cost of the catering contract which compared unfavourably with the cost of prison officer manned kitchens. Woodhill is a credit to all those involved in its management, and there are many lessons for other governors to learn from this prison.

PRISONERS' COMMENTS Good accommodation with plenty of space and well heated. Excellent education and PE facilities and inmate/staff relationships good. Overall the health care arrangements are good, though it takes too long to see a dentist. The canteen is expensive and the ordering system inflexible. Young offenders suffer from a lack of facilities on the house blocks and a lack of clean bedding. Vulnerable prisoners feel unsafe when moving around the prison, there is a lack of meaningful activities for them and they are paid less than other prisoners when undertaking education.

HM Prison Wormwood Scrubs

PO Box 757, Du Cane Rd, London W12 OAE
Tel: 081-743-0311 **Fax:** 071-749-4685 (Inmate Matters) 071-749-5655 (General Matters) 071-740-1955 (Probation Matters)
Opened: 1890 **CNA:** 472 **Average Roll:** 667 **Category:** Male Local & Lifer Wing

i **BACKGROUND** Wormwood Scrubs was built between 1887 and 1890, using inmate labour from Millbank Prison and to the design of Sir Edmund du Cane: the first Chairman of the Prison Commissioners in tribute to whom the road outside the prison was named. The design of the four separate wings broke with the then traditional construction of cell blocks radiating from a Centre. Wormwood Scrubs was built largely under the direction of the prison's first Governor, Major Arthur Griffiths, an avid exponent of the establishment and later promoted to HM Inspector of Prisons. Unlike Major Griffiths, however, the current Governor of the prison was not forthcoming with any information, though the BoV kindly supplied a copy of their latest annual report. HMCIP published their latest inspection report on Wormwood Scrubs in February 1994.

OFFICIALS
AREA MGR: Amy Edwards
CHAIR BOV:
GOVERNOR: J.F. Perris
MEDICAL:
CHAPLAIN: Rev Westwood
PROBATION: Frances Ablitt
EDUCATION:
LOCAL MP: Clive Soley. Lab
STAFFING: 21 Governor grades, 43 Principal Officers, 77 Senior Officers and 350 Officers, including specialist staff.

REGIME Wormwood Scrubs is a large multi-functional establishment which provides differing regimes to the various groups of inmates located within it. There have been improvements recently, the majority of inmates average about eight hours a day out of cell during the week and six hours at weekends—no evening weekend association. Lifers in D.wing have 11 hours out of cell weekday and weekends.

ACCOMMODATION & FACILITIES Five cell blocks (A,B,C,D,E) all inter-connected by a massive link corridor at the north end—built at a cost of £50m it not only links the cell blocks, but provides new kitchen, sports hall, library and ample toilet and office facilities. A(Remand) & B(Local) wings offer dreadful conditions, filthy toilets and are due to close early 1995 for refurbishment. A.wing also houses the segregation unit and small VPU. C(Local) & D(Lifers) wings have to wait until 1996 at the earliest for their refurbishment, the roof of C.wing is in serious need of attention and D.wing is as depressing as ever: both have integral sanitation. E.wing newly built was opened 1994 and provides 145 cells with integral sanitation and good association facilities. New kitchen and hospital also opened in last 12 months. Card phones on each wing, mail is opened centrally and delivered for distribution at tea time. Wormwood Scrubs also provides an independent special unit, known as the 'Annexe', which provides a therapeutic regime—applications for entry to your prison probation officer in the first instance. All radios that have mains facility must have certificate from shop showing removal.

CANTEEN Each wing has it own canteen facility and opens according to locally publicised routines.

VISITS *How to get there*: Tube to East Acton or bus 72. Short walk down Du Cane Rd to

prison—next door to Hammersmith Hospital. No Special Transport.
VISITING TIMES: Week Days: 0930–1100, 1315–1530. Saturday: 0915–1045, 1315–1530. Sunday: 0915–1045, 1315–1530.

NOTES **Remand visits only:** Sun, Mon, Wed, Fri mornings and Sun afternoon. **Convicted visits only:** Tues, Thurs, Sat mornings, and Mon, Fri, Sat afternoons. **Both remand and convicted visits:** Tues, Wed, Thurs afternoon. One 15 min Remand visit allowed six days of the week. Clothes change weekdays only, cash can be handed in but only at the beginning of the visit. PVOs at W/Scrubs can be used weekdays and Saturday mornings. Convicted visits 30 mins. Staffed Visitors Centre 081-740-1511 for help and advice), WRVS canteen. No Childrens Play Area. Contact prison probation for details of local B&B. Wheelchairs can be accommodated but no special facilities. Luggage lockers in Visitors Search Area for items not permitted on visits—refundable £1 coin req.

EDUCATION Contracted to the Local Education Authority, education is open for 48 weeks of the year, evenings classes five nights of the week and (uniquely for a local) operates a day-time class on Saturday and Sunday. New education department with excellent facilities and library open seven days a week.

WORKSHOPS Large diversity of work available with manufacture of UPVC windows, a tailoring shop, cutting shop, some contract assembly work and laundry. New workshop complex just opened with good facilities.

DISCIPLINE Segregation Unit at the end of A.wing, very limited regime of exercise and slop out. 706 disciplinary hearings in 1993/4—a low figure when set against an average population of nearly 700.

MEDICAL & PHYSICAL EDUCATION FACILITIES Both these areas were in a state of flux at the time we went to press. New hospital and sports hall just come on stream and routines are uncertain. Full details next edition.

CHAPLAINCY Two full time CE chaplains and RC priest. P/t Methodist minister. Other faiths catered for by visiting ministers. Sikhs and Muslims use the RC chapel for prayer, and Jews have their own synagogue. Two chapels, CE and RC with main services Sunday 0930.

FOOD Staffing: 1×G5, 1×PO, 2×SO, ?×Officer and an inmate work party of 38. New kitchen just opened. Breakfast 0800, dinner 1130–1200 and tea at 1615. Impressive eight week menu cycle, with three choices at both dinner and tea. The food tends to be plain and simple, but there's plenty of it.

ESTABLISHMENT REPORTS
Wormwood Scrubs was marking time, said HMCIP in a report (published 1st February 1994) of an inspection in August 1993. Some staff, in anticipation of refurbishment, had lost interest in the appearance and maintenance of the wings for which they were responsible and had let its standards of cleanliness and hygiene slip Time out of cell had increased to 11 hours per day for lifers and eight hours per day for others—six hours daily at weekends. Most on A and B wings were accommodated two to a cell and still slopped out. The regime for vulnerable prisoners on Rule 43 was often curtailed.

PRISONERS' COMMENTS **Convicted:** Standards of hygiene are very poor, only four hand basins for 80 men and cutlery has to be washed in the toilet area. Health care is very poor, doctors are reluctant to do more than dispense tablets and plasters. Lack of vacancies in training establishments means we wait a year or more for a transfer, lunch and tea meals are too close together and leave a gap of 17 hours at weekends. Association on alternate evenings is appreciated but we have little to do other than sit and watch a telly.

Lifers: We cannot have visits on Sundays, though we are allowed four visits a month. Food is reasonable. probation staff are very good, but discipline staff view them with some suspicion. D.wing should be staffed by officers older and more experienced than the young team we have at present. Not all staff wear name badges and it is difficult to track down your personal officer at times. Reports suffer from factual inaccuracies and there have been complaints to HMCIP that some inmates had been refused disclosure of the contents of reports.

Remand: Hygiene is very poor, water pipes leak and toilets do not work properly. No in-cell sanitation and toilets massively over-subscribed at slop out and nauseating. Cleaning materials were very difficult to get hold of, we can only get one change of bedding and one shower a week. Staff contact was poor, lack of continuity led to a lack of interest, matters raised with one group were not being passed on to the other shift. Association is inconsistent, routines easily disrupted and facilities for association are poor. Facilities for attending court are poor, little time to shower and shave and there is no proper changing room. Lack of card phones on the wing.

HM Prison Wymott

Ulnes Walton Lane, Leyland, Preston. PR5 3LW
Tel: 0772-421461 **Fax:** 0772-455960
Opened: 1979 **CNA:** 432 **Roll:** 288 **Category:** C. Male (VPU)

i **BACKGROUND** Wymott continues to operate as a Category C prison catering for the north-west area of the Prison Service. It is a modern, purpose-built establishment, spread over 104 hectares which opened in 1979. From the outset it has operated as an industrial prison and the six workshops remain the biggest source of employment. In 1986 Wymott suffered a serious disturbance which caused considerable damage to the fabric of the living units. The Governor, Mr Mullen, supplied information about the prison, though the Wymott BoV did not respond to our request for a copy of their latest annual report. HMCIP carried out their latest inspection of Wymott in March 1992.

OFFICIALS
AREA MGR: I. Lockwood
CHAIRMAN: B. Grimshaw
GOVERNOR: J. Mullen
MEDICAL: Dr P. Sharma
CHAPLAIN: Rev S. Ritchie
PROBATION: R. Brotherstone
EDUCATION: Mrs E. Saunders
LOCAL MP: Den Dover. Con
STAFFING: 364 Staff in post, 174 in unified grades.

REGIME *week days*: 0800 breakfast. 0845–1145 work. 1200 dinner. 1230–1300 exercise. 1300–1645 work. 1730 tea. 1800–2000 association, exercise.

week ends: 0800 breakfast, activities. 1130 dinner, activities, visits. 1630 tea. 1800–2000 activities, exercise.

Out of cell: 24/24hrs weekdays and 24/24hrs at weekends.

ACCOMMODATION & FACILITIES Following a serious disturbance at Wymott in September 1993, the prison has been redesignated as a national VPU, numbers have been reduced and rebuilding work is underway. Two 192 room blocks and one 48 room unit. All single rooms with access to night-san & boiler. All inmates have privacy keys and low power voltage supply for sound systems etc. Launderette on each Unit. Sentence planning, drug counselling, personal officer scheme in operation. Possessions: no pets, no radio/cassette more than 10 watts output, own T-shirts, trainers, underwear, socks and sportswear allowed. Mail is usually given out once per day at lunch-time. Mail boxes emptied at the end of every day. Mail is said not to be censored but envelopes are opened outwith the presence of the inmate and outgoing mail has to be posted unsealed. Four phones available on each unit, at times there are the usual queues but nothing too serious. Maximum of 6 cards a week can be bought from private cash and the phones are available all day until 2045.

CANTEEN The canteen is small but caters well for the reduced inmate population. One trip per week dependent on place of work. Although some items are expensive, others like tobacco are reasonably priced. Plans for a new canteen are in the pipeline, £10 per month from private cash to supplement earnings, and £10 for toiletries.

VISITS *How to get there*: Train to Leyland then bus (110) from Queens Hotel to prison at 1322 Mon–Sat. Sunday service runs to prison at 1252, buses are infrequent Special Transport: coaches from Chester-le-Street, S.Yorks, W.Yorks, Manchester & Birkenhead once per month—book via probation.
VISITING TIMES: Week Days: 1330–1530. Saturday: 1330–1530. Sunday: 1330–1530.

NOTES Staffed Visitors Centre, including CAB office, baby-changing facilities and open 7 days a week. Canteen. Childrens Play Area Tue, Thur, Sat & Sun. Chairlift for disabled.

EDUCATION Open 50 weeks of the year, two f/t teachers (18 p/t) and evening classes five nights of the week. Education is not being allowed to run to its full potential because of post-riot building work and evening classes are held in living units. Classes: English, food science, maths, French, art & design, life skills, soft toys, model making, music, sociology, psychology, expressive art, yoga, learning support, wildlife, horticulture, creative writing, hygiene, IT, open learning, AA, and stress management.

WORKSHOPS Engineers (fences, gates, doors, stainless steel equipment); Tailors (denim trousers, jackets and shirts); laundry; weavers; gardens (greenhouse and ornamental); domestic cleaners. Average wages £7 but vary between £6-9. Enhanced wages scheme in Engineers and Tailors Core Sex Offender Treatment Programme. Cognitive Skills/Offending Behaviour Group

Programme. Community Sports Leaders Award Course, and Pre-release/Inmate Development Course.

MEDICAL Medical facilities at Wymott are reported as being poor by prisoners and the unit is shortly to close down completely and transfer 'over the road' to HMP Garth. One prisoner remarked he would 'dread being genuinely, seriously ill at Wymott'.

GYMNASIUM & SPORTS A fully equipped sports hall is available and in use most days and evenings, fully operational weights room and rowing machines. Three full size soccer pitches and also a cricket square during the summer. Plans for a running track.

CHAPLAINCY F/t C/E chaplain and Church Army Captain, p/t RC and Methodist ministers. Main church services Sunday morning, Muslim Prayers Friday afternoon. Bible study, religious films, singing group activities available mid-week evenings and Sunday afternoon.

FOOD Standard of food at Wymott is said to have improved markedly since the Sept 93 riot. There is a limited choice available at present because only a temporary kitchen is in use; a new kitchen is in the process of being built. Many 'burger-type' meals because of refurbishment, which become dull and predictable after a while say inmates.

ESTABLISHMENT REPORTS Anyone reading the report of HMCIP's inspection at Wymott in March 1992, would have recognised that a serious incident was just around the corner. There had been 1542 adjudications in the previous year, 192 inmates had been placed on Rule 43 (GOAD). There had been 104 injuries to inmates in 11 months requiring treatment at the local casualty, 16 separate discoveries of cannabis pipes had been made in a single month, while heroin worth £2000 had been discovered at the jail along with several hypodermic syringes. Staff sickness had increased to the point where it was 60% above the notional non-effective allowance, a third of the receptions at the prison had convictions for drug offences, and HMCIP found that wing occurrence books contained several accounts where prisoners had clearly been under the influence of drugs: in September 1993 the prison erupted. Following the regaining of control the Prison Service accepted HMCIP's recommendation that the prison should become a national VPU.

PRISONERS' COMMENTS 'I have been at Wymott for a little over three years and have seen the population change dramatically. Until the riot in September 1993 the type of inmate didn't really suit Wymott. Now however the prison is classified as a Vulnerable Persons prison and caters exclusively for Rule 43 inmates from around the country. This in my view makes for a much calmer regime and the inmate population has been halved. The staff here are all willing volunteers having been given the option of relocation and there is therefore a very worthwhile nucleus of interested staff and this in itself makes for a better prison. In my time at Wymott I have rarely encountered staff who are not prepared to sit and listen to inmate problems. The "new" Wymott has great potential, the only problem I see at present is that the management and staff are not quite in sync with each other over issues that will best serve the inmate population, this is a problem which I'm sure will be overcome in due course. Although Wymott is currently under reconstruction and is not the pleasantest place around. I can see that the new Wymott will serve better the inmate population as time passes, and in saying that I would gladly serve my sentence out at Wymott, alas being a lifer this will not happen'.

United Kingdom Penal Establishments

HM Prison Service HQ
Cleland House, Page Street, London. SW1 4LN. Tel: 071-217-3000.

HM Prison Service College
Love Lane, Wakefield. WF2 9FQ, West Yorkshire. Tel: 0924-371291. Fax: 0924-382970

i ENGLISH/WELSH PRISONS BY CATEGORY

Local prisons and Remand Centres

Bedford, Belmarsh, Birmingham, Blakenhurst, Brinsford, Bristol, Brixton, Bullingdon, Canterbury, Cardiff, Chelmsford, Dorchester, Durham, Elmley, Exeter, Gloucester, Haslar, Highdown, Holme House, Hull, Leeds, Leicester, Lewes, Lincoln, Liverpool, Manchester, Moorland, Norwich, Oxford, Pentonville, Preston, Rochester, Shrewsbury, Swansea, Wandsworth, Winchester, Wolds, Woodhill, Wormwood Scrubs

Dispersal Prisons

Frankland, Full Sutton, Long Lartin, Parkhurst, Wakefield, Whitemoor

Category B Training Prisons

Albany, Blundeston, Dartmoor, Garth, Gartree, Grendon, Kingston, Maidstone, Nottingham, Swaleside

Category C Training Prisons

Acklington, Aldington, Ashwell, Blantyre House, Brockhill, Camp Hill, Channings Wood, Coldingley, Downview, Erlestoke, Everthorpe, Featherstone, Highpoint, Kirklevington Grange, Lancaster, Lachmere House, Lindholme, Littlehey, The Mount, Ranby, Risley, Send, Shepton Mallet, Stafford, Stocken, Thorp Arch, Usk, The Verne, Wayland, Wellingborough, Whatton, Wymott

Adult Male Open Prisons

Ford, Hewell Grange, Kirkham, Leyhill, Morton Hall, North Sea Camp, Rudgate, Standford Hill, Sudbury/Foston

Closed YOIs

Aylesbury, Castington, Deerbolt, Dover, Feltham, Glen Parva, Guys Marsh, Hindley, Hollesley Bay Colony, Huntercombe/Finnamore Wood, Lancaster Farms, Low Newton, Northallerton, Onley, Portland, Reading, Stoke Heath, Swinfen Hall, Werrington, Wetherby

Open YOIs

Hatfield, Thorn Cross

Female Prisons

Askham Grange, Bullwood Hall, Cookham Wood, Drake Hall, East Sutton Park, Holloway, New Hall, Pucklechurch, Styal

Non-operational

Ashford
Buckley Hall opens 10/95
Campsfield House
Lowdham Grange

ii SCOTTISH PRISON SERVICE

HEADQUARTERS: Scottish Prison Service, Calton House, 5 Redheughs Rigg, Edinburgh EH12 9HW. Tel: 031-556-8400

COLLEGE: The Principal, Scottish Prison Service College, Newlands Road, Falkirk FK2 0DE. Tel: 0324-712847. Fax: 0324-714920

ABERDEEN: The Governor, HM Prison, Craiginches, Aberdeen AB9 2HN. Tel: 0224-876868. Fax: 0224-896209

BARLINNIE: The Governor, HM Prison, Lee Avenue, Glasgow. G33 2QX. Tel: 041-770-9691/9700. Fax: 041-770-9448

CASTLE HUNTLY: The Governor, HM Young Offender Institution, Castle Huntly, Longforgan, Dundee. DD2 5HL. Tel: 0826-22265 Fax: 0826-22510

CORTON VALE: The Governor, HM Prison, Corton Vale, Stirling. FK9 5NY. Tel: 0786-832591 Fax: 0786-833597

DUMFRIES: The Governor, HM Young Offender Institution, Terregles Street, Dumfries. DG2 9AX.
Tel: 0387-61218 Fax: 0387-64144

DUNGAVEL: The Governor, HM Prison, Strathaven, Lanarkshire. ML10 6RS.
Tel: 0357-40371 Fax: 0357-40225

EDINBURGH: The Governor, HM Prison, Saughton, Edinburgh. EH11 3LN.
Tel: 031-444-3000 Fax: 031-455-7247

FRIARTON: The Governor, HM Prison,Friarton, Perth. PH2 8DW.
Tel: 0738-25885 Fax: 0738-30544

GLENOCHIL: The Governor, HM Prison, King O'Muir Road, Tullibody, Clackmannanshire FK10 3AD.
Tel: 0259-760471 Fax: 0259-762003

GREENOCK: The Governor, HM Prison, Gateside, Greenock. PA16 9AH.
Tel: 0475-87801 Fax: 475-83154

INVERNESS: The Governor, HM Prison, Porterfield, Inverness. IV2 3HH.
Tel: 0463-233320 Fax: 0463-236595

LONGRIGGEND: The Governor, HM Remand Institution, Longriggend, Airdrie.. ML6 7TL.
Tel: 0236-830392 Fax: 0236-83717

LOW MOSS: The Governor, HM Prison, Low Moss, Glasgow. G64 2QB.
Tel: 041-762-4848 Fax: 041-772-6903

NORANSIDE: The Governor, HM Prison, Fern, Angus. DD8 3QY.
Tel: 0356-650217

PENNINGHAME: The Governor, HM Prison, Penninghame, Newton Stewart. DG8 6RG.
Tel: 0671-2886 Fax: 0671-3470

PERTH: The Governor, HM Prison, Edinburgh Road, Perth. PH2 8AT.
Tel: 0738-22293/5 Fax: 0738-30545

PETERHEAD: The Governor, HM Prison, Peterhead, Aberdeen. AB4 6YY.
Tel: 0779-79101/4 Fax: 0779-70529

POLMONT: The Governor, HM Young Offender Institution, Polmont, Falkirk. FK2 OAB.
Tel: 0324-711558 Fax: 0324-714919

SHOTTS: The Governor, HM Prison, Scott Drive, Lanarkshire. ML7 4LF
Tel: 0501-20620 Fax: 0501-22545

iii NORTHERN IRELAND PRISON SERVICE

HEADQUARTERS: Northern ireland Office, Dundonald House, Newtownards Road, Belfast. BT4-3SU.
Tel: 0232-520700 Fax: 0232-658957

COLLEGE: NIPS College, Woburn House, Millisle, Co. Down. BT22 2HS.
Tel: 0247-861581 Fax: 0247-861062

BELFAST: The Governor, HM Prison, Crumlin Road, Belfast. BT14 6AE.
Tel: 0232-741100 Fax: 0232-352010

The Governor, HM Young Offender Institution, Hydebank Wood, Belfast. BT8 8NA.
Tel: 0232-693111 Fax: 0232-641429

MAGHABERRY: The Governor, HM Prison, Lisburn, Co. Antrim. BT28 2NF.
Tel: 0846-611888 Fax: 0846-619516

MAGILLIGAN: The Governor, Magilligan, Limavady, Co.Londonderry. BT49 OLR.
Tel: 0504-763311 Fax: 0504-765931

MAZE: The Governor, HM Prison, The Maze, Lisburn. BT27 5RF.
Tel: 0846-683111 Fax: 0846-689769

iv STATES OF JERSEY PRISON SERVICE

JERSEY: The Governor, HM Prison La Moye, St Belades, Jersey CI.
Tel: 0534-44181

v STATES OF GUERNSEY PRISON SERVICE

GUERNSEY: Guernsey Prison, Les Nicholls, Baubigny, Guernsey CI.
Tel: 0481-48376

vi ISLE OF MAN PRISON SERVICE

DOUGLAS: The Governor, HM Prison, Victoria Road, Douglas IoM.
Tel: 0624-621306

vii SPECIAL HOSPITALS (DEPT OF HEALTH)

BROADMOOR: The Director, Broadmoor Hospital, Crowthorne, Berks. RG11 7EG.
Tel: 0344-773111

MOSS SIDE: The Director, Moss Side Hospital, Maghull, Liverpool. L31 1HW.
Tel: 051-531-0022

PARK LANE: The Director, Park Lane Hospital, Liverpool L31 1HW.
Tel: 051-520-2244

RAMPTON: The Director, Rampton Hospital, Retford, Notts. DN22 0PD.
Tel: 0777-84321

CARSTAIRS: The Superintendent, State Hospital, Carstairs, Scotland. ML11 8RP
Tel: 0555-840293

SECTION TWO

ADVICE

(with thanks to THE PRISON REFORM TRUST)

1. Unconvicted & Civil Prisoners

Statement of principle: unconvicted prisoners

Unconvicted and Civil Prisoners have additional rights and facilities to those of convicted prisoners. The Prison Service has developed the following **Statement of Principle** on how unconvicted prisoners should be treated.

'Unconvicted Prisoners are presumed to be innocent. Subject to the duty to hold them and deliver them to court securely and the need to maintain order in establishments, they will be treated accordingly and, in particular, will be allowed all reasonable facilities to:-

i Seek release on bail
ii Preserve their accommodation and employment
iii Prepare for trial
iv Maintain contact with relatives and friends
v Pursue legitimate business and social interests
vi Obtain help with personal problems.

They will receive health care appropriate to their needs. They will have opportunities for education, religious observance, exercise and recreation and, where possible, for training and work.'

Additionally, HM Prison Service has committed itself to the **Citizen's Charter** and have publicly undertaken to:

- Give you an Information Pack on first admission
- Provide detailed information about facilities and services at your own establishment
- Your preferences will be taken into account wherever possible in deciding what work you will do and what education or training you will receive
- Regular Prisoner Surveys will be set up in all establishments to find out what you think about regimes, conditions and other aspects of prison life
- You will be treated fairly and given reasons for decisions: these will be given in writing if you make a formal complaint
- If you have a complaint you can take it up with a member of staff or ask to see the Governor, use written requests and complaints procedures or raise it with a member of the BoV, outside agency or prison Ombudsman: more information on Requests and Complaints is contained in Chapter 3.
- A Code of Standards is being prepared and Prisoners Compacts are also being used on a trial basis in a number of establishments. These Compacts tell you about the facilities,

opportunities and choices available to you in prison and what is expected of you in return.

Unconvicted Prisoners

An ***Unconvicted Prisoner*** is someone who has been remanded in custody while waiting for their trial or court appearance. They are classed as ***Unconvicted*** until they have been found guilty (or have pleaded guilty) to any charge in respect of which they are then either sentenced to a term of custody, or are remanded in custody awaiting sentence.

Civil Prisoners

A ***Civil Prisoner*** is the term used to describe a person who is in prison for contempt of court, for debt or for the failure to comply with an order of the court in relation, for example, to parental maintenance **AND FOR NO OTHER REASON.** If you are in custody for non-payment of fines or other monies due as a result of conviction, you will **NOT** be classed as a civil prisoner. Ask your Landing or Wing Officer if you are not sure whether you are a civil prisoner. Rules about the treatment of civil prisoners are set out in **STANDING ORDER 12**, a copy of which is available in the prison library; you may purchase your own copy of SO.12 for £1.00.

Association for Civil Prisoners

As a civil prisoner you will usually be in the company of other civil prisoners and will not be required to associate with any other class of prisoner unless you wish to and the Governor approves. In practice the shortage of accommodation in many establishments means that civil prisoners are placed where there is space, which normally means with convicted prisoners. You can object to this if you wish, but you should be aware that 'standing on the rules' in prison often results in a harsher regime being experienced than might otherwise be the case—it makes good sense to strike a sensible balance.

Clothes: 'suitable, tidy and clean'

As an unconvicted or civil prisoner in a male prison or remand centre you can wear your own clothes as long as they meet the prison standards of being: '*suitable, tidy and clean*' (Prison Rule 20(1)).

- '**Suitable**' means they cannot be confused with any part of a prison officers' uniform and are not otherwise objectionable on security grounds.
- '**Tidy**' means in reasonable condition, and
- '**Clean**' is self-explanatory

Visitors can bring clean clothes which can be exchanged for clothes that need washing. Washing facilities are usually limited in prison and you may not be able to wash more than your underwear and socks. If you do not get regular visits you may find it more difficult to wear your own clothes and keep them clean—but shortage of visits alone is not a ground on which own clothes can be denied, as long as you agree to keep them clean.

Security

In adult-male prisons you can be given a prison uniform if you want. The jacket and trousers are brown, while convicted prisoners wear grey/blue. At court appearances you will always wear your own clothes unless they are unsuitable or insufficient—in which case the prison must provide ordinary (discharge) clothing for you to wear. Own clothing can be denied on security or disciplinary grounds (Prison Rule 50(1)(h)), in which case you will be given a prison uniform to wear. If civilian clothing was denied because of an attempt to escape, you will probably be placed on the Escape List and have to wear clothing with bright yellow patches on the arms and legs—your cell light will also be left on 24 hours a day and you will have to place all clothing outside your cell each night. The Governor decides when you can come out of 'patches' though a review should be carried out regularly.

Females

No female prisoners wear prison uniform, but clothing must meet the prison standard of being 'suitable, tidy and clean'. If you do not have enough clothing of your own the prison should give you ordinary clothes, but not uniforms.

Facilities for food and drink

Before March 1988 unconvicted prisoners could have food brought in by relatives and friends. Food or sweets cannot now be handed in, however tobacco or cigarettes are still allowed to be handed-in on a visit, provided they are in SEALED packets. The same does not apply to convicted prisoners. A full list of the approved items which may be held in possession are set out in **Annexe G.** Phone cards and, in most establishments, batteries cannot be handed in on visits but can be purchased from the canteen. Cards which operate prison telephones will not operate outside of prison and *vice versa.*

Cash, cheques and postal orders

Generally the simplest and cheapest way is for relatives or friends to send money for you to spend at the canteen where you should be able to buy cigarettes, tobacco, toiletries, sweets etc. Money sent in, together with any you had on arrival, is referred to as '**Private Cash**'. If friends or relatives do send money in it is best to use postal orders by Recorded Delivery mail—they should *not* send cash, nor cheques if at all possible. Cash has often gone missing and on average it takes THREE WEEKS for the prison cashier to clear a cheque.

Letters which arrive at the prison by Recorded Delivery have to be opened in the presence of the prisoners to whom they are addressed, which obviates any dispute about what was or wasn't in the envelope. Postal orders should be made payable to The Governor, with the prisoner's name in brackets.

Books, newspapers and magazines

All prisoners, unconvicted and convicted, can receive newspapers and periodicals. Officially, other than in C & D establishments, reading material should be sent direct from the newsagent or publisher, though few prisons stand on this rule. All prisons have a contract with a local newsagent to deliver newspapers and periodicals. Prisoners can either purchase these through the library using earnings or private cash, or their relatives can send money direct to the newsagent and place an order: make sure that your visitors state your name and number in full. The number of books and newspapers which you may keep in your cell can be limited by the Governor, half a dozen books and at least the same number of newspapers is the usual limit, though very few prisons today enforce a limit at all unless the hoard becomes a fire risk.

Radio, sound system, games

A number of other items, including a radio, sound system, games and personal toiletries are allowed in cells. Further details are given in the next chapter: '**Starting Your Sentence**'.

Voting rights

Unconvicted prisoners who are at least 18 years old on the date of an election are entitled to vote under the **Representation of the People Act 1985**. Under this Act an Electoral Registration Officer (ERO) must grant an application to vote by post or proxy at a particular election. The ERO must be satisfied that the applicant's circumstances on polling day mean that he or she cannot reasonably be expected to vote in person at the allocated polling station.

Details have been recently sent to all prison governors concerning providing remand prisoners with more information about their voting rights. If you think you would like to vote you should approach your Personal Officer or Wing Governor.

Health

Under **Prison Rule 17(4)**, unconvicted prisoners can apply to be treated by the doctor or dentist of their choice. The Governor, in consultation with the Medical Officer, will decide if there are 'reasonable grounds'. You will be expected to pay the expenses of the doctor or dentist.

Work and pay

Unconvicted prisoners do not have to work inside prison but may do so if they wish (**Prison Rule 28(5)**). Work is not always available for unconvicted prisoners. If no work is available you will receive a small amount of money (average £2.50) each week to cover basics such as tobacco, toiletries, etc. If you are given the opportunity to work you may earn a little more money (£2–3), but if you are offered work and refuse, you will not receive any money at all, and the prison does not have to offer you further work.

Record, photographs and fingerprints

All prisoners may be photographed on reception and subsequently according to **Prison Rule 40(2)**. **Circular Instruction 2/90** and **Standing Order 17** provide that unconvicted prisoners, civil prisoners, fine defaulters and Immigration Act detainees should not be routinely photographed, and civil prisoners should only be fingerprinted in exceptional circumstances; e.g. Category A prisoners. All photographs, including negatives, and fingerprints, will normally be destroyed (in your presence if you wish) if you are discharged or acquitted AND have not been previously convicted of a crime.

Private affairs

You are strongly advised to make arrangements for your private and business affairs to be looked after in case you should be convicted and returned to custody. The Governor has descretion in respect of 'newly convicted' prisoners to grant extra letters and visits in order that you may put your affairs in order (SO.5A). In local prisons extra visits after sentence may be difficult to obtain because of the pressure of space, so it makes good sense to do whatever you can ***before*** sentence to sort out your affairs.

Witnesses who may be of help to you

If you are waiting trial and want witnesses to appear for your defence in court—but do not have a legal representative to act for you—then you should be given every help to write to your relatives and friends and get witnesses to attend the hearing. If you are conducting your own defence, you are still entitled to advice under the legal aid **Green Form Scheme** from a solicitor, who will be able to help with the details. You can write to the Crown Prosecution Service with the names of witnesses (CPs addresses are in Section Three) but, other than in the case of **expert evidence**, this is often inadvisable as it reveals the defence cards while still in the hand. A witness summons can be obtained and any solicitor will inform you how to obtain one in respect of a witness who is not willing to attend voluntarily.

Bail

This information should be of help if you are:-

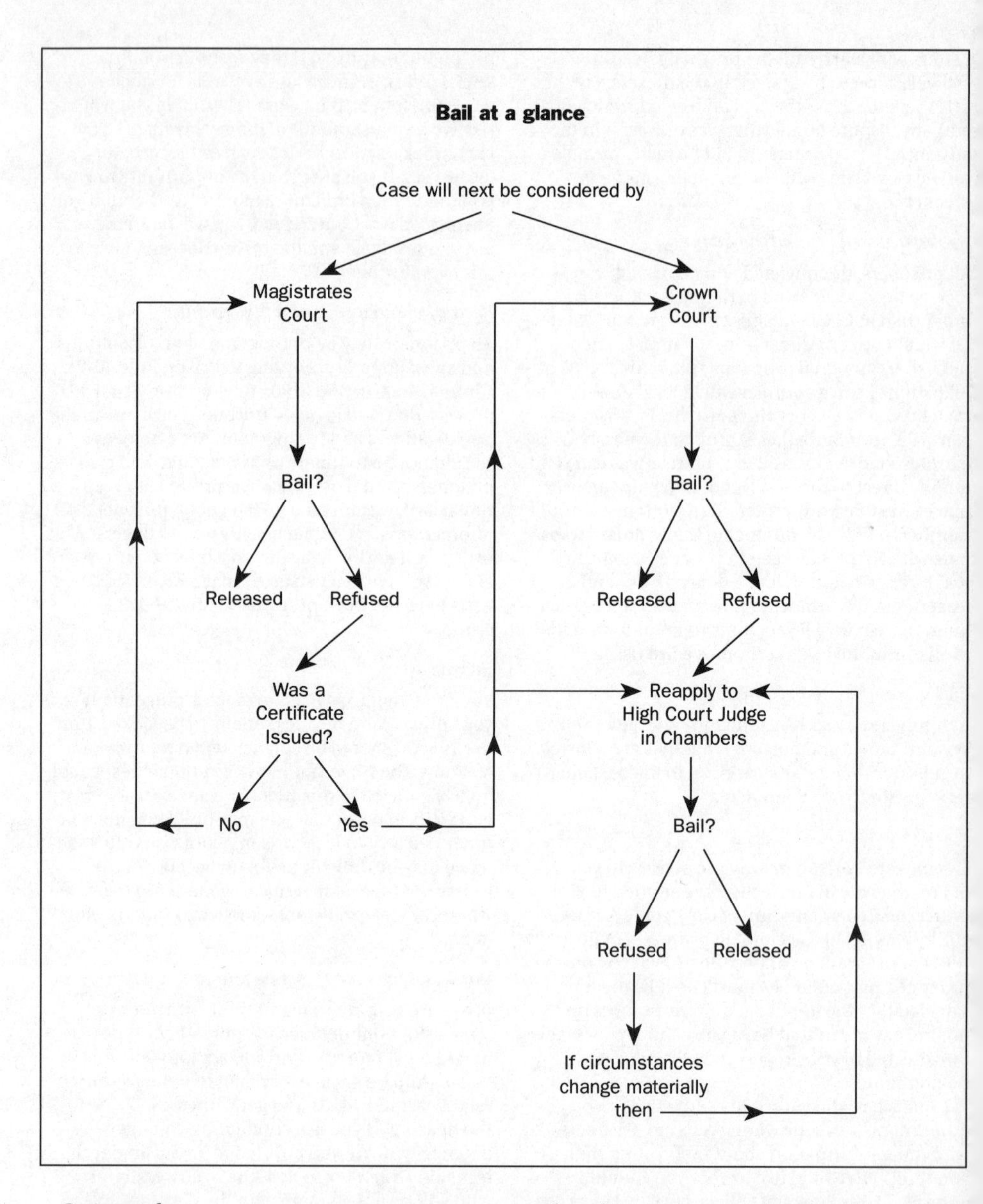

- **On remand**
- **Awaiting trial**
- **Awaiting sentence**. This includes being committed in respect of a suspended sentence, a breach of a probation order or an order of conditional discharge.

If there is anything in this section which you do not understand, you should ask to see one of the **Legal Aid Officers** in the prison; these are prison officers who have been trained to advise on bail matters. The magistrates have sent you to prison until you have to appear again before them or the Crown Court. This information will explain how you can ask for bail and, if bail is granted, what you and your relatives and friends must do in order to secure your release. If you want to apply for bail see the Legal Aid Officer.

How to ask for bail

You can ask for bail each time your case is considered by the **magistrates court**. You can also ask your solicitor—if you have one—to ask for you. If the court refuses bail you will be told why in writing. Do not lose this information as it may be helpful next time bail is considered. You can ask the **Crown Court** for bail. If, when your case was last considered by the magistrates, the court gave you a certificate saying they had heard full argument on your bail application, you can ask the Crown Court for bail. You will need to send the certificate to the Crown Court when you do so. **The Crown Court cannot consider a bail application if you have not been given a Certificate**. If the magistrates have refused you bail you can still ask a High Court Judge in Chambers to grant bail.

Sent for trial at the Crown Court

You can write to the Clerk of the magistrates court which committed you for trial, or ask your solicitor to go or write for you. You can ask your solicitor to apply to the Crown Court. If you do not have enough money for your own solicitor and you have not been granted legal aid, you may make an application for bail to the Crown Court through the Official Solicitor. If you have been refused bail by either the magistrates or by the Crown Court, you can make an application to a High Court **Judge in Chambers**: There are three ways of doing this:

1. If you are paying for your own solicitor, ask him to do it for you. Your solicitor can then go to the Judge or arrange for counsel to go. You will have to pay your solicitor to do this.
2. If you have legal aid for a solicitor he can help you write to the Official Solicitor but you will have to pay for this; the Official Solicitor will then approach the Judge. Legal aid will NOT pay for your solicitor to go to the Judge, or help you write to the Official Solicitor—your solicitor does not have to help you voluntarily, though many of course will do so.
3. You can complete the Judge in Chambers forms held by the prison Legal Aid Officer and these will be forwarded to the Official Solicitor for you.

Sent for sentence to the Crown Court

The magistrates court cannot grant you bail, but you can ask the Crown Court or a Judge in Chambers as if you were awaiting trial.

Points to remember

- The Governor will let you have a special letter to write to the court or your solicitor. The Governor can give you a special form if you are writing to the official Solicitor. If you need help with the letter or application form you should ask to see one of the prison Legal Aid Officers.
- **ALWAYS** give reasons why you think bail should be allowed.
- **Study the form that states why you were refused bail** last time and address each ground of refusal. Send a copy of the form with your application. If your last appearance was before the Crown Court, you will only have a copy of the Bail Refusal form if your lawyer asked the court to give you one.
- **You can apply more than once to the same court for bail**, but it is not much use doing so unless you can show a change of circumstances relative to at least one of the grounds of refusal last time you applied.

What to do when bail has been granted

If you are allowed bail, you must appear in court when told to do so. If you do not appear, without reasonable cause, you will have committed an offence and you may be arrested and charged with absconding; it will also be very difficult for you to obtain bail again in the future. You may also have to obey certain conditions, such as reporting daily to the police. If you break these conditions you may be arrested and kept in prison until your case is heard.

Sureties

You may also have to find one or more relatives or friends willing to promise in writing that they will be prepared to pay a sum of money if you do not appear in court. The relatives or friends who do this are called ***Sureties***. They can visit you during normal visiting hours to discuss the possibility of their acting as sureties. You cannot be released until the written undertaking of your sureties has been accepted. If you do not appear before the court when told to do so the relatives and friends who have acted as sureties may have to pay some or all of the money they agreed to pay—or go to prison themselves. A surety can also withdraw from their written undertaking at any time in writing, in which case you may be taken into custody until the court can reconsider the matter.

Attendance of sureties

If you think you may be granted bail when you appear at a magistrates court it is a good idea to make sure relatives and friends who would be willing to act as sureties are at the court. If bail is granted and the magistrates approve your sureties, you will not be sent back to prison.

Non-attendance

If bail is granted when you or your relatives who will act as sureties are not in court, you must tell them to go to the court or any police station if the court is too far away or it is too late in the day for the court still to be open. If the magistrates or police think your relatives or friends are suitable persons to be sureties they may either:

- ask them to sign an undertaking and then issue a certificate that tells the Governor that this has been done, or
- the court may give your relatives or friends a

certificate which says it is satisfied that they could pay the sum of money if ordered to do so.

Your relatives or friends must sign the certificate in the margin and take it to the prison before you can be released. They can visit the prison to do this at any time on a weekday. The Governor will ask them to sign an undertaking for the magistrates or police if they have not already done so.

Remember

Before going to the prison your relatives or friends MUST go to the magistrates or police first, to obtain a certificate that they have signed an undertaking or that they are suitable persons to be sureties for you. Your release will be delayed if they go to the prison first without a certificate.

Remission: civils sentenced before 1st October 1992

If you were committed to prison for contempt of court or similar offences **before October 1st 1992**, you may be granted remission of up to one-half of that terms if committed for 12 months or less, and up to one-third if committed to prison for a longer term. But the period in custody will not be reduced to less than five days. If you are in prison as a civil prisoner for any reason other than contempt of court—or similar offences—you will NOT be eligible for any remission of sentence.

Sentenced on or after 1st October 1992

If you are a civil prisoner sentenced ***on or after* October 1st 1992** and serving 12 months or less, you will be released at the half-way point of your sentence. Civil prisoners sentenced to longer than 12 months will serve two-thirds of their sentence before being unconditionally released.

Rights of appeal

You may have rights to appeal or take other action for release from orders which are being enforced against you.

Contempt of court

If you have been committed to prison for contempt of court you may appeal. If you were committed by a Magistrates Court you should appeal to the **Crown Court** either through your solicitor if you have one or, if you prefer, act on your own behalf. Your appeal **MUST** be lodged within 21 days of the date of committal. If you were committed by another court, for example a County Court or the Crown Court, you should consult your solicitor or, if you prefer, appeal yourself by contacting-

The Appeals Clerk
Royal Court of Justice
Strand
London WC2N 2LL

Remember

Depending on the type of court in which you were sentenced, you may have no more than **fourteen days** in which to lodge your appeal at the court office.

2. Starting Your Sentence

After being sentenced to prison you will usually be taken first to a local prison, or remand centre if you are under 21. However, if you are a male, under 18 serving a sentence up to 12 months, you should be taken straight to the nearest Young Offender Institution for your age.

Reception procedure

Once at the prison you will have to go through the reception process. This includes removal and storage of any private property that you cannot keep, issue of prison uniform for men, issue of bedclothes, a shower or bath and a (often cursory) health assessment. You will be allocated to a cell, be given a prison number which will remain with you throughout your sentence irrespective of what prison you transfer to, and you will also receive a **reception letter** so that you can contact your family/friends to tell them where you are. Make sure you stress in your letters the importance of clearly displaying your prison number on all mail sent to you.

Reception Board

You will be seen by a Reception Board or have reception interviews on the day following your admission—other than a Sunday. At these interviews you will be given a security category, allocated a job within the prison if there is work available and placed on the **Escape List** if this is judged necessary either by your behaviour or previous record. You will also be able to discuss any problems that you have with the prison probation officer. Though these Reception Boards are in theory extremely good, the practice often leaves much to be desired; the whole process can be over in less than five minutes with one prisoner after another being wheeled in conveyer belt style. Make a note of any questions you want to ask before you go in, and don't be afraid to speak up—you will not get another chance with so many officials around the one table.

Appeals: how does a prisoner appeal?

1. If you were convicted at the Crown Court you may apply for leave to appeal against sentence, conviction, or both, to the Court of Appeal (Criminal Division). You must lodge your appeal at the Royal Courts of Justice within 28 days of the date of sentence.
2. You cannot appeal to the Court of Appeal if you were convicted and sentenced at the magistrates court, though if you were convicted at the magistrates court, committed for sentence and sentenced at the Crown Court you may, in certain circumstances, appeal to the Court of Appeal.
3. The Court of Appeal can consider an appeal against conviction even if you pleaded guilty, but you will have to put forward very good grounds as to why the conviction should be set aside.

Advice and assistance

It is important to get advice **before** you seek leave to appeal against either sentence or conviction. If you apply without any real grounds the court, when it finally hears the appeal, can order that any time spent in custody 'as an appellant' shall ***not*** count towards sentence. In practice this is rarely done—though it is not by any means unheard of. If you were legally represented at the Crown Court, the solicitor and barrister who acted for you are best placed to advise on whether you have grounds for an appeal. They are both under a professional duty to give you advice on the merits of an appeal, in writing if you wish, and if they advise that you have grounds, they will complete the necessary paperwork for you and send it to the court. The legal aid granted at your trial cover the preliminary work for any appeal.

New lawyers

If you are dissatisfied with the legal team who acted for you at the Crown Court, you may apply to the **Registrar of Criminal Appeals** for legal aid for the purposes of advice and assistance from a different legal team; though you have to present good grounds for doing so. Faced with advice after conviction that there are *no grounds of appeal*, it is often tempting to change solicitors, though frequently their advice is destined to be the same. Think carefully before changing solicitors—don't blame the messenger because you don't like the message! If you are not happy with the advice that there are no grounds of appeal, ask your solicitor to set out in writing the legal reasons behind the advice—and in a form that you can understand. If you were not legally aided at the trial, you may still apply to the Registrar for legal aid for advice and assistance on appeal.

Appeal visits

You will be allowed reasonable facilities to write to and be visited by a solicitor for the purpose of your appeal. If you are acting for yourself the Governor can grant you special letters and visits for contact with any person in connection with your appeal.

Bail on appeal

If you want to be released on bail pending an appeal, you may make an application to a judge of the Court of Appeal on Form B. Time spent on bail does *not* count towards sentence.

Time limits

If you wish to lodge the appeal yourself, you should ask to see the Legal Aid Officer in the prison who will give you the necessary forms to complete; though you have 28 days to lodge the appeal from the date of sentence, you may make an application for an extension of that time limit and, again, the Legal Aid Officer will have the necessary form for this.

Security categories

Since publication of the **Mountbatten Report** in 1967 all *adult male* prisoners have been classified on reception and placed into one of four security categories—female prisoners and young offenders are not subject to formal security classification.

CATEGORY A: Prisoners for whom escape would be highly dangerous to the public or police, or to the security of the nation;

CATEGORY B: Prisoners for whom the very highest conditions of security are not necessary, but for whom escape must be made very difficult.

CATEGORY C: Prisoners who cannot be trusted in open conditions but who do not have the will or resources to make a determined escape attempt.

CATEGORY D: Prisoners who can be trusted to serve their sentence in open conditions.

Appeal

You will not be told the reasons for your security classification—though in some cases it will be obvious from the nature of the offence or the length of your sentence. Though there is no formal appeal procedure against a security classification, it can be challenged in the High Court by way of judicial review if the correct procedure has not been followed, or the decision is legally *unreasonable*: for example a prisoner serving three months for theft would not normally be placed in Category A. Your solicitor will be able to advise whether you have grounds for judicial review.

What are the effects

Categorisation effects the conditions in which you will be kept—only **Category D** prisoners, for example, can be located in an open prison. **Category A** prisoners (and there are sub-categories of Category A which range from **'High Risk'** to **'Exceptional Risk'**) are subject to extra restrictions being placed upon them. Visitors have to be vetted by the police, their photographs are kept at the prison gate, your clothes will have to be placed outside your cell each night—and the cell light will be kept on 24 hours a day to facilitate the frequent visual checks by staff. Additionally two officers and a dog-handler have to escort the Category A prisoner when moving around inside the prison, while movement outside the jail requires a major police escort.

Reviews

Categorisation of long-term prisoners is looked at on a regular basis—three or six-monthly reviews are normal—and you can submit a written request form to Headquarters if you believe you have been wrongly classified—only in the most obvious cases will they intervene.

Allocation

Unless you are serving a short sentence, say less than six months, you will usually be sent to a **'training prison'** or Young Offender Institution soon after sentence; though in many cases this can take weeks if not months to arrange. Allocation depends on the length of the sentence you are serving, your security classification and where spaces are available.

Special factors

Any special factors affecting your allocation from your point of view should be brought to the attention of the Allocation Unit staff or the Governor. These will be taken into account, but it is not always possible to meet your wishes. For example, it would obviously be helpful for your visitors if you were allocated to a prison which had good public transport links, but many prisons are difficult to get to in this way and, at the end of the day, it is available space which is often the decisive factor.

Grendon Underwood

Some prisons, such as Grendon Underwood near Aylesbury, have special therapeutic regimes for violent or sexual offenders, and for those who genuinely wish to understand why they offend and what they can do about it. If you are interested you should ask prison staff about the availability of such a placement, or write direct to the Governor of Grendon—address in the **Establishment Section** of the *Handbook*.

What is 'Sentence Planning'?

Sentence planning is being introduced gradually for different groups of prisoners. You will be informed if sentence planning arrangements apply to you at your establishment. The aim of sentence planning is to ensure that the best use is made of your time while in custody and to provide an opportunity to keep your progress under review throughout the sentence. A sentence plan will be drawn up which will assess your needs and set targets for you to try and achieve, in order to meet those needs. It is hoped that it will enable you to acknowledge and tackle your offending behaviour and give you planned experience of work, training and education, to help you prepare for release.

Open reporting

Your involvement in the preparation and review of such plans will be a crucial feature. Sentence planning will be an open process, which means that you will be able to see, discuss and comment on what has been written about you.

Parole effects

If you are eligible to be considered for early release on parole, sentence planning may inform the Parole Board of any progress towards release which you have made since the start of your sentence. Similarly, for the many prisoners who will be subject to a period of compulsory supervision by the Probation Service after release, sentence planning will inform the supervising officer of the activities undertaken while in custody and identify any matters which may need to be addressed during the period of supervision.

Benefits

There is often a feeling among prisoners that sentence planning has nothing to offer; as understandable as that approach may be, it is misconceived. **You** are the one who has to serve your sentence, it is **your** victim, **your** family and **you** who will suffer. **You, and you alone** decide whether you are coming back to prison once you are released. One way of making the best of your chances of going 'straight' on release, is to analyse the reasons why you ended up in prison in the first place. This way you are in a much stronger position in the future when similar circumstances arise, not only to recognise them as dangerous, but also you will be better equipped to deal with them in a constructive way before it's too late.

Segregation

Pursuant to **Rule 43 of the Prison Rules**, prisoners can be segregated from other prisoners either for their Own Protection **(OP)** or in the interests of the Good Order And Discipline of the prison **(GOAD)**. **Rule 46 of the Young Offender Rules** has similar provisions.

Own protection

If your offence is of a type generally disapproved of by other prisoners, such as sexual or violent offences against women, children or the elderly, and prisoners who have 'grassed' on fellow prisoners or who have belonged to the police or prison service in the past, you can ask to be placed on **Rule 43/46 (OP)**. The Governor does **not** have to agree to your request, it is a matter for him to decide and he may feel that you can safely be located in another part of the prison and arrange for you to be moved there on normal location—i.e. in association with other prisoners. In practice, however, a request for segregation is normally granted, but you should not make the request lightly for segregation is a very serious step to take and it may well have continuing ramifications not only during your current sentence, but any future ones you are unfortunate enough to serve.

Regime and effects

Prisoners who are segregated under Rule 43/46 (OP) can usually associate with other prisoners who are segregated for their own protection, but are kept apart from prisoners on normal location. This may mean, for example, that you will only receive the flat rate minimum wage because you are not allowed to work, and you may spend far more time locked in your cell because of the restricted regime. Once you have gone **'on the numbers'** (Rule 43/46), other prisoners will make assumptions about you which may bear no relation to the truth, and it will make a return to normal location for you in the future very difficult indeed, if not impossible.

Application

If having considered the matter carefully, you feel that you need to be segregated then you should talk the matter over very carefully with the Governor. If you feel that you need segregation when you first come to prison, then you should inform the Reception Officer when you are called forward to give your details. . . remember things are often not as bad as they may at first appear, and once you have chosen segregation you will rarely be able to escape completely from its effects in the future.

Good order and discipline

Segregation under Rule 43/46 (GOAD) is a management and control measure which takes out of general circulation prisoners who the Governor believes are a threat to the 'good order and discipline' of the prison. Prisoners segregated for this reason are not allowed to associate with other prisoners and are frequently housed in the punishment block—despite the claims that GOAD segregation is not a punishment, distinguishing the two regimes is often almost impossible.

Legal challenge

A decision to segregate under Rule 43/46 is susceptible to challenge in the High Court by way of judicial review (**R v Secretary of State ex.p Haigh (1990)**. Circular Instruction 37/90 requires that GOAD prisoner must be told of the reasons for the segregation 'as far as practicable'. **Reasons** should be given in writing if the prisoner requires them. The Governor must obtain the authority of the Board of Visitors (or the Secretary of State) if the segregation is to continue beyond the first three days. Such an authority if given lasts for one month (fourteen days in in Young Offender Institutions) but may be renewed for a like period *ad infinitum*.

Canteen

The prison canteen is a small shop which you can usually visit once per week. Prisoners in some prisons are paid in cash, but the vast majority of establishments employ a credit system. Prisoners' earnings can be spent there on tobacco, sweets, biscuits, toiletries, batteries, stationary etc.

Private cash

Your own money which you brought with you to the prison, or which has been sent in by relatives and friends (known as 'private cash') can also be used to buy certain items—the items which convicted prisoners can purchase from private cash are restricted, broadly speaking, to toiletries, batteries and greetings cards, and there is a (hopelessly inadequate) limit on the amount of private cash you may spend in one year.

Prices and profits

Prison canteens charge 'outside' prices and the profit is split between the **Central General Purpose Fund** held centrally (used to equip new prisons with recreational equipment) and a **Local General Purpose Fund** for your prison's recreational needs. Both funds are subject to audit by the National Audit Office. The range of stock held in prison canteens is generally very small and it is one area which has been in need of reform for many years. The provisions of the **Sale of Goods Act 1979** apply to purchases made from the prison canteen. This means that, for example, the goods you purchase must be of **'merchantable quality'**, they should be **'as described'** on the package and **'fit for the purpose'** for which they were sold. If any of these '*implied undertakings*' (which are set out in section 14 of the Act) are breached the prison Governor is obliged in law to replace the item or refund the money—the choice is yours. Phone cards are an area where the Prison Service has sought to pass requests for replacements to British Telecom. However, the legal fact remains that the 'consumer contract' entered into when you bought the phone card is between you and the Governor—under the Sale of Goods Act it is the Governor (not BT) who remains responsible in law for replacing defective items.

Personal possessions: general items

What you are allowed in the way of personal possessions varies from one prison to another: a full list of approved items that you MAY be allowed to keep in your possession are set out in **Annexe C**. Generally you are allowed a combined sound system or a radio and a choice of cassette or compact disc player. These may include an internal mains adapter but must not be run from any external power source. The radio can receive long wave, medium wave, short wave **(1–18MHz)** and **VHF/FM (88–108MHz)** but no other. It may have an external aerial, but not one with long, strong wires.

Books, jewellery and photographs etc

You may keep in your cell at least six newspapers and periodicals and at least the same number of books. You can normally have a **calendar**—though many prisoners aren't keen!—**a diary, an address book, phone cards bought internally, postage stamps, unpadded greetings cards, unglazed photographs, and pictures, hobbies materials, games, batteries, writing and drawing materials, a wrist watch, a manual typewriter, a battery operated shaver, personal toiletries, a wedding ring or plain ring, a medallion or locket, smoking requisites**—except in establishments where smoking is prohibited—up to a certain limit, and **religious articles** as approved by the Governor. **Batteries, phone cards and tobacco**—except for unconvicted prisoners—cannot be handed in or sent in and may only be purchased through the prisoners' canteen.

Local prisons

Many local prisons—those which service the main city-centre courts and are usually full of 'locals'—restrict the amount of personal possessions, though a radio, watch and toiletries are allowed in all prisons. In some cases it may be necessary for you to formally apply to have permission to have an item, even though it is on the approved list—typewriters and musical instruments are common examples.

Your 'stored' property

In prison there are only limited facilities for the storing of property. In relation to the property that is taken from you on reception and stored in the custody of the Governor, the prison service owes you a legal duty to take care of it and if, through negligence, they lose or damage it, then you may claim compensation for the loss from the prison authorities; requests for compensation are usually settled on an *ex gratia* (by favour) basis if the prison authorities feel they may be liable. If compensation is refused you may seek damages in the local County Court. Your stored property will be kept in sealed containers—usually plastic bags or boxes. On first reception as a convicted prisoner, you will be asked to sign a **'Property Card'** to certify that the details are correctly recorded—**in busy Receptions mistakes happen, read it before you sign**. The containers will then be sealed in your presence and *should* only be opened again in your presence. All property will be returned to you when you leave the prison on transfer or discharge and, again, you will be asked to sign the Property Card to confirm it is correct.

Property in possession (IP)

As a prisoner you are only allowed to have in your possession those items of property which the Governor authorises you to have—see **Annexe C**. When you are allowed to have an item of property in your possession you will have to sign a **Disclaimer**—either incorporated into the Property Card or separately—which states that you accept full responsibility for any loss or damage that may be caused to it. **Once this disclaimer is correctly signed it provides the Home Office with a complete defence to any action you may bring to recover compensation for loss or damage to your property caused other than by the negligence of the prison authorities or their employees.** Subject to the restrictions on what you are allowed, what possessions you **choose** to have in your possession is a matter you need to think carefully about. It will not come as any surprise to learn that some of your fellow prisoners often confuse the property of others for their own, and you should remember that your property will be not be under your control when you are out of your cell or dormitory as a result of work or recreation. Think carefully before you decide whether to have valuable items in your possession.

Transfer

On transfer to another establishment your private cash will not be sent with you, but will follow as a paper credit transfer to the receiving prison later—a delay of six weeks is common. If transfer to another prison necessitates a stay at another prison en route, what you will be allowed will be restricted to the following items:

- **a bar of soap**
- **flannel**

- **comb**
- **toothpaste and brush**
- **safety razor and shaving cream**
- **a bottle of shampoo**

—a radio (or similar item)

- **book, biro and writing paper.**

Items carried with you on the journey—e.g. a wrist watch—are held at your own risk.

Association

This is the name given to the time spent out of your cell and with other prisoners, either for meals, exercise, recreation, or educational classes. Association is considered as a **privilege** and may be withdrawn:

- as a punishment
- while you are waiting for a disciplinary adjudication
- for your own protection
- for the protection of others if you are considered violent, disruptive or subversive.

3. Requests & Complaints

Four ways to complain or make a request

You can use:

- the **internal** prison procedures, or
- contact the **Board of Visitors**, if it is a matter that can be dealt with inside the prison, or
- you can contact the Prison Service **Area Manager** at **Prison Service HQ (Cleland House, Page Street, London SW1P 4LN)** if it is something—such as a disciplinary adjudication which can only be dealt with at a higher level.
- On 19th April 1994 Home Secretary Michael Howard announced the appointment of Sir Peter Woodhead as **Prisons Ombudsman**. The office of Ombudsman, which should be operational by November 1994, will be able to investigate grievances from prisoners on all matters for which the Prison Service has responsibility with certain exceptions. See 'Prisons Ombudsman' below.

You can also take your complaint outside of the prison, by writing to your MP, solicitor, probation officer or penal reform groups—see chapter on **Useful Organisations'**. Who you write to first really depends upon what your request or complaint is about, but for the majority of cases it makes sense to use the internal complaints procedure as you will get a written reply quite quickly. Of course if your complaint raises matters of a legal nature, you may want to consult your solicitor first for advice as to whether the internal complaint may prejudice your claim.

Basic principles

The basic principle is that requests or complaints will usually be dealt with inside the prison by your landing, wing or personal officer on an informal basis. However, if the matter cannot be sorted out in that way you should make an oral (spoken) application to your landing or wing officer and you should be seen that day.

In writing

If your discussion with the wing manager does not resolve things, you can make a Governor's Application. Within two days, you should be seen by a senior member of staff—you have no absolute right to see the 'No.1' or governing Governor. If this proves fruitless the normal way forward at this stage will be for you to make a formal written request or complaint. There is an official form for this and you should note the case number written on the form when handed to you. Also keep a copy of what you wrote. Within **seven days** of returning the form you should receive a reply: in practice many weeks can pass before the form finds its way back to you.

Reasoned replies

The reply you receive may not contain an answer to your problem, but you should be told when you can expect a full reply. If your request or complaint is refused you should be given reasons for the refusal. If you are still unhappy you can appeal to the Prison Service Area Manager, contact the Board of Visitors, or write to someone outside of the system.

Who are the 'Board of Visitors'?

Boards of Visitors were created by the **Prison Act 1898**, when they were established for local prisons. Non-local prisons already had Visiting Committees elected by magistrates at the Quarter Sessions. When Quarter Sessions were abolished by the Courts Act 1971 Boards of Visitors were established for all prisons. The rationale for their creation was the desire to inject into the penal system some degree of independent scrutiny; whether that has been achieved or not depends on which side of the cell door you happen to be standing. Currently there are some 2000 members in post, representing every prison in the country. Members are drawn from the local community which surrounds the prison, but they are not selected by that community, nor are they answerable to it; selection is by—and answerability is to—the Home Secretary.

Powers

You can contact the Board of Visitors at any time, either by asking to speak to them personally, or by making a written request or complaint. They will not usually take up matters until you have been through the internal channels, and it is important to bear in mind that the Board of Visitors have no operational powers at all; they can make representations on your behalf to the Governor or draw the matter to the attention to the Secretary of State if they feel it necessary, but they cannot 'order' the Governor to do anything. Until recently the Boards of Visitors have been closely allied with the prison disciplinary system, though they lost their disciplinary powers in April 1992 and now have only a pastoral function to discharge.

Area Managers: 'reserved subjects'

All prisons in England and Wales fall into one of fifteen different areas, each headed by an Area Manager based at Prison Service Headquarters who are generally promoted from serving prison governors. The Area Manager can deal with appeals against replies to written requests or complaints and with direct applications about **reserved subjects**. Reserved Subjects are ones which cannot be dealt with at a local level, such as adjudications and early release. Requests and complaints to the Area Manager in Prison Service Headquarters should be made in writing, either using the appeal form (if you are appealing against the reply you have got from your own prison) or a Request/Complaint form if you are making a request or complaint about a reserved subject. You should get a reply within **six weeks** of your form reaching Headquarters; though it can take up to **two weeks** for the form to be processed at a local level and dispatched to Headquarters.

Confidential access

If you do not want to disclose the nature of your complaint or request to the officers on your wing or landing, you can write direct to the Governor, Area Manager or Chairman of the Board of Visitors using a sealed envelope. This is called **Confidential Access** and there is a special envelope provided for this purpose. It is particularly useful if you are making allegations against staff, though there are important limitations which you need to understand.

How confidential is 'confidential'?

Confidential Access is meant to be used only when prison staff cannot deal with the complaint or request. You should fill in the Request/Complaint form and seal it in the special envelope marked **'Prisoners' Confidential Access'**. You should address the envelope to whoever you want to deal with the matter. You should also say on the form why you want it dealt with confidentially. **It is up to the person whose name you have placed on the envelope to decide how to deal with matters you raise. This may mean that the confidentiality you requested is not respected in cases where the Governor adjudges it to be unnecessary.**

Prison Ombudsman

Until recently there was no formal appeal against a decision taken at Headquarters; the only way forward was to write to someone outside the prison system, but now that has finally changed—at least in most respects. Lord Justice Woolf, in his report into prison disturbances in 1990, recommended that a **Prisons Ombudsman** be established in order to inject an independent element into the complaints procedure. On 19th April 1994 Home Secretary Michael Howard announced the appointment of the Prisons Ombudsman in a written answer to a Parliamentary Question from Mr David Willets MP. The Home Secretary said:

> 'I am pleased to announce that I am appointing Sir Peter Woodhead KCB as the Prisons Ombudsman. Sir Peter plans to take up post in May [1994], and our intention is that his new office will be established and will start to receive and investigate prisoners' complaints in the autumn. I welcome this as a significant step in further safeguarding the fair and just treatment of prisoners.'

Sir Peter was Deputy Supreme Allied Commander in the Atlantic until the end of 1993 and he retired from the Royal Navy in April 1994. His appointment fulfils a commitment by the Government to implement a recommendation in the Woolf Report to appoint an independent complaints adjudicator for prisoners. It is in keeping with the Citizen's Charter principle that wherever possible those making complaints should be able to have access to someone independent of the service in question. Sir Peter will make recommendations to the Prison Service and, where necessary, the Home Secretary on individual cases and will publish an annual report. He will have unfettered access to prison service documents, establishments and individuals. There will be tight time limits for all major stages of dealing with complaints: the Prisons Ombudsman will have **an eight week target to investigate and respond to complaints—rising to 12 weeks where the subject is particularly complex.** Contracted out prisons and services will be eligible for investigation. The Prisons Ombudsman operates from an independent office in central London with a support staff of twelve. Sir Peter, who is married with two grown up children and lives at Woking in Surrey, will have three **Assistant Ombudsmen** to help with his investigations. They are:

- Adam Sampson (ex-Deputy Director of the Prison Reform Trust) 0171 389 1462.
- Sarah Down (ex-legal adviser to the Housing Association Ombudsman) 0171 389 1405, and
- Michael Loughlin (a Prison Service civil servant) 0171 389 1438.

The **Office Manager** is Barry Patton (0171 389 1303), and the Ombudsman's Investigators are:

- Jennifer Hall (0171 389 1509)
- Michael Griffiths (0171 389 1591)
- Stephen Ruddell (0171 389 1318)
- Mark May (0171 389 1446)

How to complain to the Ombudsman

There are four important points to note:

1. Only inmates can complain
2. Request/complaint procedure must have been exhausted
3. There are strict time limits
4. There are subjects the Ombudsman cannot deal with.

Those who have difficulty reading and writing can ask their family, friends or a solicitor for help, but no one can complain for you—the complaint must carry your signature. Letters to the Ombudsman should be sealed in a 'Prisoners' Confidential Access' envelope available in every establishment—but first you **MUST** have exhausted the internal request/complaint procedure, including appeal to the Area Manager. You may appeal to the Prisons Ombudsman, however, if you have submitted an appeal to the Area Manager and have not received a reply within six weeks. Delay in contacting the Ombudsman could be fatal to your complaint: You must contact the Ombudsman within **ONE MONTH** of receiving a reply from Prison Service HQ, or as soon as the time limit for the HQ reply has expired. **IF YOU DELAY, YOUR COMPLAINT MAY NOT BE LOOKED INTO.** Sir Peter will be able to investigate grievances from individual prisoners on all matters for which the Prison Service is responsible, **EXCEPT (i) complaints about the clinical judgement of prison medical staff, (ii) the Home Secretary's exercise of his responsibility for deciding release dates for life sentence prisoners, (iii) any matters where there are outstanding legal proceedings.**

What happens next?

When your complaint is received by the Ombudsman, a member of his staff will ensure: it is signed by the prisoner; has been made within the time limits; is after exhaustion of the request/complaint procedure; and is about a subject the Ombudsman can deal with. In most cases the Ombudsman will then request copies of relevant paperwork from the Prison Service and in some cases, though not all, those involved in the complaint may be interviewed by a member of the Ombudsman's staff or someone he has asked to act on his behalf. When the inquiry is completed, both the inmate and the Prison Service will receive a copy of the formal findings. If the complaint if upheld the Ombudsman will recommend that the Prison Service take some positive action. The Prison Service will reply to the Ombudsman within six weeks and the inmate will receive a copy of the reply setting out what is to be done. In some cases it may be impossible to put things completely right, because of changed circumstances. If the complaint is not upheld you may approach outside agencies or a solicitor for support. Complaints should be sent to the Ombudsman at the following address:

Prisons Ombudsman, St Vincent House, 30 Orange Street, London WC2 7HH
Tel: 0171-389-1527. Fax: 0171-389-1492

Outside Agencies

There are many different people and organisations outside prison who may be able to take up your complaint or request—**see Useful Organisations**. Not all will be effective in doing so and most will expect you to have gone through the internal request/complaint procedure before taking the matter up with them. Even though you may have the support of outside agencies, your request or complaint may still not be resolved to your satisfaction. However if you are dissatisfied with the answer you have got through the official channels, you can write to an outside agency to see if it can help.

Legal and general

Some organisations that may be able to help are included in the chapter on **Useful Organisations**. Do read the chapter carefully to ensure you are writing to the right organisation. In addition to those bodies listed you can also take up the matter with:

- ***Your Solicitor.***
  This is particularly important if it is a legal matter, such as an assault. In cases where a crime has been committed you could also consult the police, though it is wise to seek legal advice before doing so.
- ***Commission for Racial Equality.***
  You can write to the CRE if you feel that you have been the victim of racial discrimination. The address to write to is:

  C.R.E., Elliot House, 10/12 Allington Street, London SW1E 5EH

Also see the chapter on Race Relations.

- *The Queen or Parliament.*
  Everyone has the right to Petition either the Queen or Parliament; see **Standing Order 5** in the library. A Petition to the Queen can simply be in the form of a letter. Normally it will be passed to the Home Office or Prison Service for reply. A Parliamentary Petition has to be written according to a certain set format. The prison should have a copy of the Rules in relation to Parliamentary Petitions, or you can obtain a copy free from the Petitions Office at the House of Commons. **Parliamentary Petitions** have to be sent to a Member of Parliament and it is for the member to decide when (if at all) the Petition is read out on the floor of the House. Parliamentary Petitions can also be addressed to a member of the House of Lords and the format for this is different from that of a Petition addressed to the House of Commons and can be obtained from the Petitions Office.
- *The European Parliament.*
  All British subjects have the right to petition their Member of the European Parliament. The procedure for doing so is similar to that for writing to your MP and is set out in Standing Order 5.
- *European Commission for Human Rights.*
  Once you have exhausted all domestic remedies which are open to you, you may submit a petition to the ECHR alleging that your complaint discloses a violation of any of the Articles set out in the European Convention on Human Rights and Fundamental Freedoms; a copy of which is available in the prison library. You must apply to the Commission within SIX MONTHS of the date when you exhausted your last domestic remedy. More information can be obtained from:

  The Secretary, Council of Europe, Commission of Human Rights, BP 437 R6, 67006 Strasbourg Cedex, France.

Research request

Prisoners who have taken or are taking proceedings in the ECHR, may like to contact **CHARLES WILSON**, a Senior Lecturer in Criminology **(Portsmouth University, Winston Churchill Avenue, Portsmouth, Hants. PO1 3AS)** who is conducting research into cases brought before the ECHR by prisoners.

4. Visits, Letters & Phone Calls

HM Prison Service and the Citizen's Charter

HM Prison Service has publicly committed itself to the Citizen's Charter. In relation to Visits the Prison Service has said:

> Our aim is to ensure that visitors to prisons, including prisoners' families, friends and legal representatives, are treated courteously and professionally at all times: We will try to provide decent facilities for visitors, convenient visiting times, helpful information and a reasonable amount of privacy at all our establishments. Staff who come into contact with prisoners and the public will normally wear name badges.

VISITS

Keeping in contact with the outside world is obviously very important while you are in prison. **Prison Standing Order 5**, a copy of which will be available in the library, sets out the minimum number of letters and visits allowed, and also the minimum length of visits. The way in which the rules are applied varies quite a lot. In some prisons there is overcrowding, pressure for visiting space is heavy and you will only receive the minimum entitlement, but extra letters and more frequent and longer visits, in better conditions, are available at many prisons—particularly training prisons.

Unconvicted prisoners: 90 minutes minimum per week

If you are an unconvicted prisoner you are allowed visits totalling *at least* 90 minutes per week. This is a strict entitlement, which can be reduced only in the most exceptional circumstances—and then only with the Home Secretary's express consent.

Arrangements

It is up to the Governor to decide how visits are spread over the week, and then arrangements will vary. At most prisons you may continue (as in the past) to be allowed a visit of at least fifteen minutes every day excluding Sunday (and in some cases Christmas Day and Good Friday). But the Governor can now introduce different arrangements under which you would get fewer visits but lasting longer than fifteen minutes. Under this arrangement you should still always be entitled to

- visits on at least three days each week adding up to at least 90 minutes
- a visit either Saturday or Sunday, normally every weekend and at least once a fortnight.

One visit a day

Visitors to unconvicted prisoners generally do not need a visiting order to gain entry to the establishment—a ***visiting order*** is an official pass which visitors to **convicted** prisoners are issued with by the prison authorities. Up to three adults and your children are allowed on any one visit, but it is important that they all enter the prison gate *at the same time.* It is a good idea to work out who is going to visit you each day—if a second party of visitors arrive at the gate after you have already had one visit that day they will, other than in wholly exceptional circumstances, be turned away.

Special circumstances

Where daily visits are the rule, you may find that the 15 minute limit is strictly imposed—down almost to the second! Even in such establishments longer visits should be allowed whenever possible, and particularly where a close relative is unable to travel frequently, perhaps as a result of age, ill-health or the distance (more than 50 miles) they have to travel to the prison. If this applies to someone who visits you regularly you could arrange to have them visit less frequently, but stay for longer, by submitting a request form and explaining the circumstances.

Convicted prisoners: 60 minutes per month minimum

If you are a convicted prisoner—including those convicted but currently unsentenced—you are entitled to a minimum of two thirty minute visits every four weeks. This is a statutory entitlement and cannot be reduced. Visits while you are undergoing cellular confinement may be postponed, but you will not lose your entitlement and they should, in any event, only be postponed where there is clear evidence that allowing you the visit would pose an unacceptable risk to the good order and discipline of the prison.

Visiting Orders

Before a visit can take place you need to send out a *Visiting Order* with the names of your visitors on it. You do not have to specify a particular date for the visit and up to three adults and four children are normally allowed to visit at once. The first Visiting Order (VO) is handed out during the reception process when you first enter prison as a convicted prisoner. The first VO is known as a **'Reception VO'**—extra to your normal entitlement—and must be used within seven days of convicted-admission. Your first (proper) VO will be available fourteen days after the Reception VO was issued and will be valid for 28 days. If your visitors are unable to use the VO within that period, they should return it to the prison and a new one will be issued in lieu.

In possession of the VO

It is vital that your visitors bring the VO with them when they visit, otherwise the prison may turn them away. If your visitors report that a VO has not arrived, they should contact the prison probation officer and explain the situation. A copy of the VO is kept at the prison and it should be possible for the issue of the VO to be confirmed and the visit allowed; they should not simply turn up at the gate, but telephone beforehand and explain the situation.

Handing-in property on a visit

Visitors to convicted prisoners are not usually allowed to hand anything to *the prisoner* at a visit, but they can offer cigarettes to be smoked *during* the visit (except in Young Offender Institutions where there is a no smoking rule in force and in those adult prisons where smoking on visits has been banned). Many prisons have a small WRVS canteen in the visiting room, at which drinks and sweets may be purchased by your visitors, and only items or drinks purchased from it may be consumed on the visit. Convicted prisoners are not allowed to take *anything* away with them after the visit is over. All prisoners are subject to a search—often a strip search—after a visit. If your visitors wish to hand something in for you on a visit—such as a radio, sound system or other authorised article—they should hand it to the officer in charge of the visits on entry. Normally property will not be accepted unless you have previously obtained official approval by going on application.

Handing-out property on a visit

If you wish to hand out property on a visit you will need to make a formal application. If the article is something which you have made as a result of hobbies, you must usually submit the article to security at least seven days prior to the visit. If the article is something you have stored in reception—clothing for example—you normally need to give at least three days notice. You are not allowed to hand out any item to the visitors of another prisoner. At maximum security (dispersal) prisons, you may ask for permission to hand out letters or documents during your visit and to receive letters from your visitor. At lower security establishments, formal applications are not usually required and will be allowed without permission unless the staff have grounds to suspect that the rules in relation to correspondence (Standing Order 5B) are being breached.

Extra visits

Many prisons allow visits to last longer than thirty minutes (some allow up to two hours) and extra visits (**'privilege' visits**) are often allowed to supplement the statutory entitlement and so allow a visit each week. You may also be allowed one or more 'special' visits if you are seriously ill, if there is a family crisis, or if you need to sort out your business or legal affairs after conviction.

Searching visitors: take note

Your visitors may sometimes be asked to permit themselves and their property to be searched before a visit can take place. This is necessary to ensure that visitors do not bring in unauthorised articles. The search will normally be limited to a 'rubdown' search. In some cases, particularly where staff have reason to suspect that a visitor may have concealed unauthorised items or substances so that they cannot be detected by a 'rubdown' search, visitors can then be asked to submit to a 'strip-search'. No search by prison staff can be carried out without the visitor's consent. All searches must be carried out with courtesy and consideration and by an officer of the same sex as the visitor. If a visitor declines to be searched then they may be offered a 'closed visit'—where no physical contact is possible—or the visit may be refused completely. A growing number of prisons, aware of the possible litigation that could flow from an unauthorised search, are now contacting the local police who may arrest the visitor and take them to the police station.

Financial assistance for visits

Your visitor may be able to get financial help for some visits, including travel costs and, where necessary, overnight accommodation if:-

a. your visitor is your wife, daughter, husband, son, mother, sister, father, brother or someone with whom you have been living as man and wife at the same address for at least four months ***before*** imprisonment or who has a child from the relationship. It may also include adoptive step- and half brothers and sisters, parents and children; **AND**
b. your visitor is receiving **Income Support, Family Credit, Disability Working Allowance** or holds a **Department of Health Certificate for full (AG2) or limited (AG3) help**. Such certificates are available to people on low incomes who do not get any of the above benefits, and can be obtained on application to the **Dept of Health, Benefits Unit, Newcastle, NE2 1DB—using Form AG1**.

Disqualified

Visitors, even where they otherwise satisfy the above criteria, are **NOT** eligible to apply for assisted prison visits if they are:

- partners in a same-sex relationship, or
- parents- brothers- or sisters-in-law.

The Assisted Prison Visits Unit, PO Box 2152, Birmingham, B15 1SD.
Tel: 021.626.2797. APVU Director: *Tony Price*

The APVU pays for

- the return fare to the prison or place of custody
- something towards food and drink if the visit means being away from home for five hours or more
- something towards the cost of overnight stays if the APVU thinks this is necessary in the circumstances, and
- other *unavoidable* expenses.

Escorts

APVU will pay for someone to escort a prisoner's close relative who is too ill or young to travel alone, if the relative (or person who supports them) qualifies for assisted prison visits. The APVU Scheme covers all prisons, remand centres, YOI's, people detained under the Immigration Act 1971 and prisoners, sentenced or remanded by the courts, and held in police custody. The scheme **does not** cover hospitals of any sort, special schools, bail hostels, military corrective training centres nor any prison outside the UK.

Making the application

Assistance may be claimed for visits at **two weekly** intervals, starting from your reception into prison whether you are convicted or on remand. Each visitor is allowed a **maximum** of 26 assisted visits in 12 months. Visitors should obtain a claim form available from any DSS office, sending it, **every four weeks**, to the **APVU** at the address below. The claim form has been completely revised and is easier to complete. You now have the option of claiming for two visits at once, as long as you travel by the same means each time. You can still claim for two visits even if you do not have two VO's when you submit the form—as long as you have one VO and the date for the second visit, the claim will be processed.

10 days in advance

Payment is usually made in advance of the visit, so long as the claim is submitted to the Unit at least 10 days before the visit is due—10 days before the **first** visit if you are making a claim for two visits. However, since October 1994, the APVU has sought to deal with claims within eight working days—and from April 1995, they hope to reduce this to five working days. If you are visiting a convicted prisoner, you should send a photocopy of the Visiting Order but not the original. There is more information about assistance with visits in the claim form. If there is anything you do not understand or are not sure of, write or telephone the APVU at the address/number shown below.

Fraud Prevention

The APVU has a duty to ensure that public funds issued for the purpose of assisted prison visits are used for that purpose and no other. Visitors will receive a slip of paper which they should have stamped at the prison on the day of their visit, to prove their attendance, and return it to the APVU. If the APVU discover that money issued for assisted prison visits has been used for a purpose other than visiting, criminal prosecution could well be the result.

Appeals procedure

There is no independent body which can review a refusal of the APVU to provide funding for a visit. However the APVU have themselves set up a system whereby appeals against refusal are dealt with by a person inside the APVU one grade higher than the person who took the initial decision. All appeals should be dealt with within one calendar month.

APVU STATEMENT OF PURPOSE: 'Our purpose is to promote contact between prisoners and their families by helping with the costs of visits. We seek to serve the public by ensuring that assistance is given to relatives who are on low incomes and is used on visiting. We will deal with claims sympathetically and flexibly, as soon as possible.'

Informing your visitors of a transfer

All prisoners, other than those in Category A or on the Escape List, should be told if they are to be transferred to another prison, sufficiently far in advance to allow them to write to anyone who is intending to visit to save them a wasted journey. Convicted prisoners are entitled to as many extra free first class letters as they need to let anyone who has a valid visiting order (one issued in the last twenty-eight days) know when they are being transferred. You will have to make an application for these 'special' letters and it is a good idea to do so as soon as you are informed of your transfer. If there is not sufficient time to write, then you can ask staff at the prison you are being transferred *from* to telephone anyone who has an outstanding visiting order, or use your phone card, if available, if you prefer to do so.

Transfer letters

Unconvicted prisoners are entitled to only one extra free letter, but you can ask for more if there are several people who may turn up to visit you after your transfer. It is up to the Governor whether he allows more letters for this reason. If there is not enough time to write before your transfer then staff should make one telephone call to warn anyone likely to visit you of your transfer. If more than one call needs to be made then it is up to the Governor whether this is allowed. Alternatively you can contact your visitors using your phone card if you have one and telephone facilities are available.

Category A & E.List prisoners

For security reasons, **Category A or E.List** prisoners are never told in advance of any transfers. If you are such a prisoner, or if for any other reason you have been unable to contact potential visitors before your transfer, you should be given a copy of **Form F1994** as you leave the prison. During the journey fill in the names and details of anyone who needs to be told of your move and hand it to the senior officer in charge of the reception at your receiving establishment. Reception staff there should make sure that the people you have named are telephoned that day.

Accumulated visits

If you are a convicted prisoner held in a prison that is too far from your relatives or friends for them to visit easily, you can 'save' at least three (and up to 26) visits. Six months after your transfer from the local prison to which you were sent after conviction, you can apply to the Governor (or in the case of Category A, complete a Request/Complaint form) for temporary transfer to a prison near to where your visitors live. In some cases this may be possible before the six months eligibility period is up. All your accumulated visits are taken during the time you are at your temporary prison (usually 28 days) and you are then returned to your own prison. You become eligible for more accumulated visits six months later if sufficient visits have been saved.

Inter-prison visits

Visits between two close relatives who are in different prisons are allowed once every three months. Application has to be made and both have to surrender a visiting order for the visit.

Segregation

If you are segregated as a punishment, any visit may be put off until the end of the period of segregation if the Governor has reason to believe the visit would pose an unacceptable risk to the good order and discipline of the prison. This is not normal practice, but it can and does happen, and if your visitors have to travel a long distance you should inform them of this possibility so that they can phone the prison and confirm that the visit can go ahead.

Visits in advance

You can apply to have visits in advance of the date that they are normally due, in special circumstances—for instance if a visitor is going away on holiday. The date of your next visiting order will be calculated from the date on which the last one was officially due—not from the date on which it was issued.

Children in care

If your children are in care, either in a Children's Home or a foster home, application can be made for the children to visit in private conditions. If those responsible for the care of the children are unable or unwilling for this to happen, application can be made for you to visit the children at their home. If permission is given by those caring for the children, such visits can take place once every three months—subject to staff availability—and visiting orders need not be surrendered for this purpose.

Samaritans

If you are despairing and feel unable to cope it may be possible to have a visit from a 'Samaritan', or to telephone or write to the local branch. Chapter 6 on 'Welfare Services' tells you more about how the Samaritans may be able to help. It also explains about how to get visits from a Prison Visitor or a Voluntary-Associate if you are not getting many visits from family or friends. If you are writing to the Samaritans you should mark the envelope accordingly and the letter will not then be subject to censorship by prison staff.

In private

If you wish to phone the Samaritans using a phone card to talk to them in confidence, you should inform the monitoring officer via your wing manager; your call will not then be listened to. In many establishments it is possible to call the Samaritans in private conditions, without using a phone card. Your wing manager or prison probation officer should have details. You should bear in mind that though your letter (or phone call) to the Samaritans will not be subject to official vetting, the fact that you have contacted them may well be recorded on your prison record.

Legal visits: in sight but out of hearing

Your legal adviser has the right to visit you in sight but out of the hearing of prison staff. You do not need to use a visiting order for your legal adviser to visit, though in some establishments—notably the larger local prisons—your lawyer has to pre-book the visit with prison because of shortage of space. Visits from a legal adviser can take place at any reasonable time—including evenings if special arrangements are made—and there is no fixed duration or restriction on frequency for such visits.

Police visits: caution

You may discover that the police wish to visit you while you are in prison and you need to think very carefully beforehand how you will react if they wish to visit you; in certain cases you have no choice but to see them.

Compulsory visits

You have no choice but to see the police if they wish to either:

- charge you with an offence, or
- interview you in connection with an offence

Right of silence

You are not obliged to answer any of their questions and you may terminate the interview once you have been charged or, in the case where the police seek to put questions to you, after they have explained what it is they wish to question you about.

Witnesses

You may ask for a witness to remain in the room with you while you are being interviewed by the police and a prison officer will remain if you ask. If you decide to be interviewed you should, in any event, take handwritten notes of the questions and any answers that you may choose to give but it is often vital to take legal advice before allowing any questions to be put to you. There is nothing improper or prejudicial in asking the police to defer their interview until such a time as you have had an opportunity of speaking with a solicitor.

Non-compulsory visits

If the police wish to interview you about a matter in which you may have been a **witness** rather than a **culprit**, or about other matters in which there is no question of you being charged with an offence, you are NOT obliged to see them. If you wish to decline the visit you may do so. You may be required to tell the police yourself.

Visitors: three golden rules

- **If you say you are going to visit—then visit.** There is nothing more frustrating and soul-destroying for a prisoner locked in his cell, having spent the last week looking forward to the visit and a couple of hours carefully getting ready for it, to lay on his bed and watch the minutes of the visiting session tick away, locked on the wrong side of the door.
- Secondly, and equally important, **don't be late.**
- Finally **if you can't make the visit due to unforeseen circumstances, then telephone the prison probation officer** and say so; that way a message will be passed to the prisoner concerned.

Special transport and facilities

Some prisons—see ***Establishment section***—organise special transport for visitors, which usually amounts to the prison minibus collecting visitors at railway stations and returning them there after the visit. A small charge (£1.00 or so) is usually made. At some prisons and Young Offender Institutions there is a No Smoking policy in force and neither the prisoner nor visitor are allowed to smoke during the visit. Some prisons provide creche facilities for visitors and others provide nothing at all. Disabled access is usually very difficult at our prisons, although most officers will help lift wheelchairs up stairs if asked. There are usually toilet facilities available during the visit and in some establishments there are Visitors Centres where visitors can go for refreshments before or after a visit.

Reclaiming for wasted journeys

If you arrive at the prison to find that the person you intended to visit has been moved, you may be able to claim back **from the prison** the cost of the journey and any overnight stay that proved to be necessary. Arrangements are made for prisoners before transfer to inform their potential visitors, though sometimes transfers take place at very short notice and it is not possible to make contact. As long as the prisoner has tried to contact you, either by telephone or in writing (and neither were successful) you are entitled to claim back the cost of the visit from the prison. The prison will not give you any money if you travelled on a warrant or if the APVU paid your costs. But they will pay you if you paid your own costs and they should provide a note for the APVU, explaining what happened, so that the APVU can pay for you to visit at the new establishment.

Visiting unconvicted prisoners

If you are visiting an unconvicted remand prisoner you will find that the visiting arrangements differ from prison to prison. In some prisons there will be canteen facilities and a pleasant atmosphere while, in others, both will be absent. Always take **coins** with you in case a drinks machine is fitted, and if the prisoner you are visiting is a smoker, take some **cigarettes** with you for during the visit. Unconvicted prisoners are entitled to a minimum of 90 minutes visiting time a week, and each prison varies the time on which visits can take place: see Section One for details of individual establishments. Normally remand prisoners should be allowed at least three visits a week, normally including one at the weekend at least once a fortnight. Check with the prison if you are unsure of visiting arrangements and, for remand prisoners, you will not usually require a visiting pass for entry to the prison. Unconvicted prisoners can have clean clothes brought in (except at weekends in some London prisons and other overcrowded prisons), but usually they have to apply first for this to be allowed. Remember, remand prisoners are only allowed a certain number of visits per week, so you could contact others who may be visiting the same person to make sure you don't go on the same day; you could be turned away. Up to three adults are usually allowed in on the same visit, with children, although at Brixton Prison, for example, it is only two adults with children under five (children **over five** count as 'adults'!)

Visiting convicted prisoners

If you are visiting a convicted prisoner you will need to have a valid visiting order in your possession when you arrive at the prison gate. Prisoners are allowed a visit once every fourteen days and visits last at least thirty minutes. At some prisons prisoners only get this basic visits allowance but once transferred to a training or dispersal prison, visits are often longer and sometimes made more frequent by the use of 'privileged' visiting orders. At some prisons, privileged visiting orders have to be used during the week.

LETTERS

There are different rules for unconvicted and convicted prisoners.

Unconvicted prisoners: censorship and restrictions

You can send out as many letters as you like at your expense and you are allowed two second class 'ordinary' letters per week from the prison at public expense. All incoming letters—other than those from a legal adviser—are opened and examined for contraband. Outgoing letters will not be subject to routine reading unless you are provisionally in Category A, but the Governor may consider it necessary in exceptional circumstances to examine and read outgoing correspondence in order to prevent its use to plan escapes. Correspondence with a legal adviser will not normally be read (see below). There are no restrictions on the number or length of incoming letters unless in exceptional circumstances the Governor has ordered that all of your letters must be read.

Letters for your defence etc

If you are an unconvicted prisoner with no private cash, letters connected with the defence of your case, or to tell visitors you are to be transferred, will be sent first-class at public expense, in addition to the two second-class weekly 'ordinary' letters you are given. In urgent domestic or business situations, extra letters may also be allowed.

Convicted prisoners: censorship and restrictions

You can send out one letter a week on which the cost of second-class postage is paid at public expense and usually there is no limit on the number of extra letters which you can pay for from prison earnings or private cash (first or second class). However, if you are in a maximum security establishment or a prison where the Governor has ordered routine reading of mail for a short period, the Governor may set a limit on the number and length (subject to a minimum of four sides of A5 paper) of your letters. These letters are usually written on prison note paper with the name and address of the prison at the top. You are allowed to buy paper from the prison canteen, but the name and address of the prison still have to appear at the top of the first sheet unless a special application is made. In certain circumstances—for example where you are writing to your children who do not know you are in prison—you may be given permission to use the private address of the prison, which is usually the 'street address' of the establishment. Stamped addressed envelopes can be sent in by people who want you to write to them. At maximum security prisons all letters will normally be read as they enter or leave the prison, apart from legal correspondence.

At lower security establishments letters will not be read unless you are in Category A or on the escape list, or unless the Governor has reasonable grounds for believing that you are breaking the rules in relation to correspondence—though all letters are still opened to check for any illegal enclosures.

Reception and extra letters

The first letter should be given to you as part of the reception process (reception letter, first class). Extra 'free' letters can be provided at the discretion of the Governor, if you are newly convicted, to settle private or business affairs, or if you have domestic problems, are arranging accommodation or employment for your release, are writing to your probation officer or are taking legal action—including an appeal.

Restrictions on incoming mail

There is no limit placed on the number of letters which you can receive except at those prisons where routine reading of mail is in force, Governors may limit incoming mail to one letter received for every one which you send out. In these circumstances you will be told when excess mail is being sent to you (normally stamped on your incoming letter when you receive it) and you will be allowed to pick which of the letters you have been sent you particularly want to read; the rest will be returned to sender or stored in your property.

Letters in lieu of a visit

If you do not get a visit, an extra (free) letter can be allowed in lieu of a visit. At Christmas, you will be allowed to buy at least one extra letter from your earnings and up to twelve Christmas cards with stamps from the prison canteen out of earnings or private cash.

Correspondents and the stopping of letters

All prisoners can write to and receive letters from any person or organisation, as long as the contents of the letter do not breach any of the restrictions on correspondence set out in Standing Order 5B.34 (copy in the library). These restrictions relate to such things as an escape plan or anything which effects prison security, anything which helps anyone to commit a criminal or prison disciplinary offence, anything effecting national security (instructions for making weapons or coded messages etc), threats, blackmail, or anything racially offensive or obscene. In these circumstances the letter you write will be stopped, may be referred to the police or other appropriate authority and you will normally be given a fresh letter in order to 'rewrite' the one which has been stopped from leaving the prison. See 'Other Correspondence' below.

Legal correspondence

Until recently a prisoner could only enjoy uncensored and privileged correspondence with a legal adviser if the contents of the correspondence related to proceedings which had already been issued; all letters to and from your lawyer before the issue of proceedings could be read by the prison authorities. On 19th May 1993 the Court of Appeal handed down a unanimous judgement which held that any letter from a prisoner to a legal adviser, whether proceedings were pending or merely contemplated, was privileged and could not be read or stopped unless there were identifiable grounds for believing it was not to or from a lawyer, or that it contained illicit enclosures (**R. v Secretary of State for the Home Department, ex.p Leech**). The Court of Appeal also held that where the letter was read by the prison authorities they were under a common law duty to keep the contents of the letter confidential. The Home Secretary later abandoned his attempt to appeal the decision to the House of Lords.

Censorship of legal correspondence

Letters which you write to your legal adviser can be sealed before posting. Any letter sent to you from your lawyer should have been sealed inside an envelope which carries your name and prison number. This envelope should then be sealed inside a second outer envelope, addressed to the Governor, and enclosing a covering letter from your solicitor asking the Governor to pass the enclosed sealed envelope to you—unopened. Whether the letter is incoming or outgoing the prison authorities have the power to open the letter, but this can only be done:

- in your presence, and
- after reasons have been given.

Opening legal correspondence

If an envelope purporting to come from your solicitor is thought to contain illicit enclosures, the Correspondence Officer may open it to check for such enclosures—but only in your presence and after he has explained his reasons. If no illicit enclosures are discovered the contents of the envelope should be passed to you unread.

Reading legal correspondence

If the prison authorities wish to read the contents of legal correspondence, either because they have reason to believe a letter purporting to be bona fide legal correspondence is bogus—in that it is not from a genuine legal adviser—or the contents of the letter are believed not to relate to bona fide legal business, then the Correspondence Officer cannot read the correspondence of his own volition. Instead he must seal the letter (unread) in an envelope in your presence and send it to the Governor, stating in writing his grounds for believing that the contents of the letter should be read. **only the Governor** (or **'the person who for the time being is in charge of the establishment'**) can order that the contents of the letter be read. It will be a very rare event for the Governor to order the contents of the letter be read and, as stated above, in such circumstances there is a duty of confidentiality in relation to the contents of the letter. The decision by the Governor to order that the legal correspondence be read, is susceptible to challenge in the High Court by way of judicial review.

Probation letters

You can write to your probation officer by applying for a 'probation letter' and this will be sent second class at public expense.

Correspondence with the media

You can send a letter to the press for publication, or to radio or television, as long as it is not in return for payment—though unconvicted prisoners can be paid. Letters to the press or other media must not be about your own crime or past offences, or those of others, unless it is a serious comment about crime, justice, conviction, sentence or the penal system. You also cannot refer to individual prisoners or members of staff so that they can be identified and your letter or article must not break any of the other rules in SO.5B in relation to correspondence. This means that ordinary letters or articles to press or other media are now allowed, though once they were firmly forbidden. The above restrictions on both content and payment, interestingly, are not requirements of the Prison Act or the Prison Rules made under the Act, but a stipulation contained in Home Office Standing Orders which have no force of law. Accordingly it is susceptible to challenge in the courts by way of judicial review.

Inter-prison letters

Letters between convicted prisoners at different establishments are allowed if you are close relatives or co-defendants and the letters relate to trial and sentence. Otherwise, they normally require to have the approval of both governors who can disallow them (though rarely do) if they think it is in the interest of either prisoner or in the interests of security or the good order and discipline of either prison.

Stopping letters

Other letters can be stopped if they are to a person or organisation who the Governor believes to be 'planning or engaged in activities which present a genuine and serious threat to the security or the good order of the establishment, or other Prison Service establishments'. The Prison Service has no powers to stop you writing to your spouse, fiancé(e), parent, child, brother or sister unless any of these persons has made a request in writing to the prison authorities asking that further letters should not be sent to them. If that happens you will be asked to co-operate by not writing and given the opportunity to discuss the matter with staff. The Prison Service also cannot stop you writing to your lawyer or MP. You must however apply to the Governor if you wish to advertise for a pen friend, and convicted prisoners must also apply to the Governor if they want to write to the victim of their offence or a member of the victim's immediate family.

You should be told of any letter stopped by the prison for any reason; a replacement letter will then be issued and you will be allowed to re-write the letter so that it does not break any of the rules set out above.

Language

Letters can be written in any language, although letters written in languages other than English are sometimes held up because they have to be translated so that they can be read. If a letter is going abroad the 'free' letter will be sent by the cheapest post, i.e. surface mail. You can pay the difference to have it sent by air mail from private cash or prison earnings.

PHONE CALLS

Card phones for prisoners' use are being made available in all establishments. Prisoners are able to buy specially produced Prison Service cards from the prison canteen—public phone cards will not work on prison telephones. You can use both earnings and private cash and there is now no fixed limit in Standing Orders on the number of cards you can buy. In addition, money spent on phone cards will not count against your private cash allowance. The Governor can, however, set a monthly limit on the amount of private cash you can spend on phone cards and also restrict you to having a maximum of two valid cards in your possession at any one time; 'possession' means in your cell, or on your person, or any card over which you are exercising any degree of control.

Monitoring

Section 2 of the **Interception of Communications Act 1985** provides that it will not be an offence to intercept a telephone call if there are reasonable grounds for believing **'that the person to whom, or the person by whom, the communication is sent has consented to the interception'**. In all prisons where monitoring is in force a warning in regard to it should have been brought to your attention, either verbally or in writing. By then using the 'phone, runs the legal reasoning, you are consenting to the interception (monitoring) of your call within the meaning of section 2 of the Act. At open prisons phone calls are not monitored but, at others, prison officers are expected to monitor a random sample of telephone conversations some of the time. They can listen to **both** sides of the conversation. The restrictions on the content of phone calls are the same as the restrictions which apply to correspondence—if you can't write it, you can't say it! If you breach any of the restrictions on correspondence set out in SO.5B while making a phone call, you could be disconnected. It is also possible that your call could be tape-recorded; *interception of communications* includes tape-recording.

Telephone calls in lieu of visits

In some prisons, prisoners who are not receiving visits may use up a visiting order by making a supervised free telephone call instead of having a visit. If your relatives are overseas, you may be permitted call in this way, but if you want to make additional calls using the official phone then the Governor can, at his discretion, insist that your relatives pay some or (frequently) all of the costs. There is no 'right' to a phone call in lieu of a visit.

Telephone calls on reception and to lawyers

Unconvicted prisoners should be allowed access to official telephones to make urgent contact with their lawyers. This usually happens through the prison Legal Aid Officer or prison probation officer. Such conversations should be out of the hearing of prison staff. At some prisons unconvicted prisoners are also allowed to make a phone call home immediately after first reception from court.

FURTHER INFORMATION

More information about visits, letters and phone calls is contained in Standing Order 5. A copy (along with any amendments) should be available in the prison library (usually on 24 hour loan). Alternatively for £1.00 you can purchase on application to the Governor your own copy of the order, and any other published orders. If you have any problem about urgent matters which need a telephone call or an additional letter, see your landing officer or make application to the Governor—in really urgent cases it is helpful to remember that there is nothing to prevent you from using the prisoners' telephone to call the Governor (or anyone else) by dialling the number of the prison and asking to be connected.

5. Prison Discipline & Punishments

Over 100,000 offences against prison discipline are punished by the authorities each year. The number of prisoners appearing before a disciplinary hearing (known as an **adjudication**) tends to be higher in Young Offender Institutions and female prisons.

'Proper opportunity'

An important feature of disciplinary adjudications is that you must be given 'a proper opportunity' to put your side of the case. If you are charged with a disciplinary offence think about what you plan to say in your defence or in mitigation, and whether there are others who saw what happened who might appear as witnesses. This chapter tells you the basics of what to expect from an adjudication. If you want to know more, the Prison Service have published a manual (**the 'Yellow Book'**) on adjudications and there will be a copy available to you through the prisoners library; whether you have been charged with an offence or not, you may borrow the manual at any time and you can buy your own copy of the manual from the Home Office Library, Queen Anne's Gate, London SW1. Additionally, Oxford University Press have recently published an excellent book called **Prison Law:**

Text & Materials, your library should have a copy and you are advised to read it. You should also read Section Four (i) of the *Handbook*.

OFFENCES AGAINST DISCIPLINE

Consequentials

Prison Rule 47 sets out the 22 offences against prison discipline you may be charged with. These range from very serious charges (hostage taking, escape) to less serious charges (intentionally failing to work properly). If you are suspected of an offence against Prison Rule 47 which is also a offence against the criminal law (e.g., possession of drugs or assault), the prison authorities may refer the matter to the police. If evidence is subsequently led in court, irrespective of the verdict or whether the charges are withdrawn from the jury at some later point because there is 'no case to answer', this **bars** the prison authorities from taking any **Consequential** disciplinary proceedings against you in respect of the incident which led to the appearance in a criminal court. Only if *no evidence at all* (such as the Crown offering no evidence at the commencement of the trial) is led may the prison authorities bring consequential disciplinary against you, but in any event they must have charged you internally 'as soon as possible' after the offence—and in any event within 48 hours of the offence being discovered: see (*R. v Dartmoor Prison Board of Visitors ex.p Smith* **(TLR 1984)**.

Catch-all offences

Rule 47 of the Prison Rules contains two catch-all offences against discipline. Rule 47(19) says it is an offence to disobey any lawful order or fail to comply with any rule or regulation of the prison. Rule 47(21) says that anything which offends against good order and discipline may be punished, even if it is not expressly prohibited by the rules; though the basis of the offence must have some foundation in Standing Orders if not the Rules themselves. The High Court has previously quashed a decision to convict a prisoner of failing to carry out an order to place his bed outside his cell, on the grounds that such an instruction was not authorised by Standing Orders: *R v Swansea Prison BoV, ex.p McGrath*, (The Times, November 1984)

Judicial review

You should also bear in mind that in addition to the internal appeal procedures following a disciplinary adjudication, the House of Lords have held that the High Court can judicially review any disciplinary adjudication—and quash the sentence and conviction—if the procedure at the hearing was unfair, the finding of guilt was irrational, or the Governor misapplied the law: reported *sub nom*, *Leech v Deputy Governor Parkhurst Prison*. [1988] 1 All ER, 485(HL). Under Order 53 of the Rules of the Supreme Court (RSC) you have **three months** in which to lodge your application for leave to apply for judicial review at the High Court: the three month period begins on the date when grounds for the application first arose—delay in applying can be fatal.

RULE 47 OF THE PRISON RULES 1964

A prisoner is guilty of an offence against discipline if he:-

1. Commits any assault;
2. Detains any person against his/her will;
3. Denies access to any part of the prison to any officer;
4. Fights with any person;
5. Intentionally endangers the health or personal safety of others or, by conduct, is reckless whether such health or personal safety is endangered;
6. Intentionally obstructs an officer in the execution of his duty;
7. Escapes from prison or from lawful custody;
8. Fails to comply with any condition upon which he is temporarily released under Rule 6 of the Prison Rules;
9. Has in his possession—
   a. any unauthorised article, or
   b. a greater quantity of any article than he is authorised to have;
10. Sells or delivers to any person any unauthorised article;
11. Sells or, without permission, delivers to any person any article he is allowed to have only for his own use;
12. Takes improperly any article belonging to another person or to a prison;
13. Intentionally or recklessly sets fire to any part of a prison or any other property, whether or not his own;
14. Destroys or damages any part of a prison or any other property other than his own;
15. Absents himself from any place where he is required to be;
16. Is disrespectful to any officer or any person visiting a prison;
17. Uses threatening, abusive or insulting words or behaviour;
18. Intentionally fails to work properly or, being required to work, refuses to do so;
19. Disobeys any lawful order.
20. Disobeys or refuses to comply with any rule or regulation applying to him;
21. In any way offends against good order and discipline;
22. a. Attempts to commit,
    b. Incites another prisoner to commit, or
    c. Assists any other prisoner to commit or

attempt to commit any of the foregoing offences.

Being placed 'on report'

Disciplinary charges are usually brought as a result of prison officers seeing what they believe to be 'an offence against discipline' and placing you 'on report'. The prison officer will usually tell you at the time that a charge will be brought against you, but he is not under any statutory duty to do so. The Prison Rules require that any charge must be laid as soon as possible and the High Court have held this is a mandatory requirement where *as soon as possible* 'means what it says': (*R. v Dartmoor Prison Board of Visitors ex.p Trevor Smith* (**TLR 1984**). In any event the charge sheet must be given to you within a period of 48 hours of the discovery of the offence.

Charging and procedure

As soon as it has been decided that a charge will be laid against you, you should be given a **Form 1127 Notice of Report** (known to prisoners as 'The Telegram'). This notice must be given to you at least two hours before the case is heard by the Governor. At the same time as being given the F1127, you should also receive another form (**F1145**) which sets out briefly how the adjudication will take place. You can prepare a written statement on the back of the F1127 and ask for more paper if you need it. You can also name any witnesses you wish to call or any legal representation you wish to apply for. You do not have to write anything on the back of the form, but it can be useful to record matters which at a later date may be in dispute: witnesses, representation etc.

Reference books

You may find it useful to consult the legal sectionof the *Handbook*, **The Manual on Conduct of Adjudications** (**The Yellow Book**, Home Office) and **Prison Law: Text & Materials** (OUP) before the hearing. Copies should be available in the prisoners library, though in some prisons it may not be kept on open display and you will have to ask the librarian for it. If you have difficulties obtaining them submit a formal request form. If you are subject to **interim segregation** prior to the adjudication you will not be allowed to visit the library, in which case you should ask the staff to obtain a copy for you prior to the hearing. You can also consult **Standing Order 3D**, which contains a brief summary of the disciplinary system and guidance on punishment. You can purchase your own copy of **Prison Law** from **Oxford University Press**, (Walton St, Oxford OX2 6DP). The **Yellow Book** is available from the Home Office.

Medical examination

Before the hearing you will normally be examined—usually very briefly—by a medical officer; some doctors have however refused to become involved at all in the disciplinary process. The purpose of the medical 'examination'—often conducted from a distance of six feet in less than three seconds flat—is for the medical officer to determine whether you are fit to plead and undergo punishment of **Cellular Confinement** if you are found guilty.

Interim segregation

You may be segregated in the punishment block (**under Rule 48**) from the time the offence was discovered by an officer until seen by the Governor. Strictly this should not happen automatically, but it is 'par for the course' in most prisons. To quote from **Alice in Wonderland**: *'Sentence first, verdict last'*.

Legal representation and assistance

Prisoners do not have a right to legal representation at a disciplinary adjudication, though you do have a right to ask for it and a right to expect that the application will be considered fairly by the Governor. You can, alternatively, ask for the assistance of a friend at the hearing, known as a **'McKenzie Man'**; see below. The High Court, in the 1984 case of *R. v Board of Visitors Albany Prison, ex.p Tarrant et al*, confirmed the principle of legal representation or McKenzie assistance, and expressed a non-exhaustive list of factors which the Governor should consider when deciding whether to grant you representation or assistance. These are:

Important factors

1. The seriousness of the charge and, particularly where there is more than one charge, the potential penalty.
2. Whether any points of law are likely to arise. Some offences contain terms such as 'reckless' and 'intentionally', and defining these terms has occupied our courts for centuries. If you are charged with an offence you contest, which involves these or other similar terms, then you should apply for representation.
3. The capacity of the prisoner to conduct his own defence. If you have difficulty understanding the hearing, asking questions, do not speak and/or understand English well, these are all factors which could give rise to your asking for representation or assistance—an interpreter can also be applied for.
4. Procedural difficulties. If you are segregated prior to the hearing it may only be possible to interview witnesses who can help you if you have a solicitor who can do this for you.

Similarly if the defence depends on effective cross-examination, only a trained lawyer will be able to do it properly.
5. The need for reasonable speed in making the adjudication. Granting legal representation will cause a delay to the hearing and the Governor is entitled to consider what effect this may have in the prison.
6. The need for fairness between prisoners and prison officers. If the Governor grants legal representation to you, it would also be appropriate to grant it to the reporting officer and, again, the Governor can consider what effect legal representation may have on the prison.

The overriding obligation is to comply with the statutory duty of ensuring you have a proper opportunity of presenting your case; if that requires legal representation, then the Governor must grant it. If representation is granted, and it is by far the exception rather than the rule, it will be paid for by the authorities.

McKenzie man

In 1970 Mr McKenzie applied to the courts for a divorce and his wife contested it. Mr McKenzie was not legally aided and decided to conduct the case himself with the help of a friend—who was a solicitor's clerk, though not acting in that capacity. The judge objected to the presence of the friend and said that Mr McKenzie must either act for himself or retain a lawyer. Mr McKenzie appealed against the decision and the Court of Appeal held that the judge had been wrong. Everyone can have a friend beside them in court—which includes prison hearings—to sit quietly, take notes and make suggestions, but they cannot speak for you. In the prison setting a prisoner does not have the RIGHT to a McKenzie Man—prisons are not places where the public have an automatic right of entry as in a courtroom—but you do have a right to ask for one and a right also that your request will be considered fairly. (1984: *ex.p Tarrant*). Re-affirmed by the Court of Appeal in 1991: *R v Leicester City Justice, ex.p Barrow et al.* You may choose who you wish to be your McKenzie Man, though the Governor may veto a particular person where he has good grounds for doing so. You could call a fellow prisoner, the prison probation officer or prison chaplain.

Disciplinary hearings

Governor grades now conduct all disciplinary hearings. The Reporting Officer has the burden of proving your guilt, beyond reasonable doubt, to the Governor. The adjudication room is normally located within the punishment block. The reporting officer must not be in the room before the prisoner enters it: *R v Governor Pentonville prison, ex.p Watkins* [unreported 4.12.91]. The Governor will sit behind a table and you will be brought into the room with two escorts, one in front and one behind, who will take up a position on either side of you in front of the Governor. The room should have a chair for you to sit on, and the Governor will provide a desk and writing materials if you wish to make a note of the proceedings. The escorting officers, at those times when the Governor requires you to stand, should stand by your side—they are not be allowed to **'eyeball'** you (where they stand staring into your eyeballs) as was the practice at one time, and if they do so it can be reviewed in the High Court.

Procedure

At the start of the hearing the Governor will ask if you have been served with the Notice of Report **(F1127)** and the Notice of Procedure **(F1145)**. Both forms will be taken from you and held by the Governor. He will ask if you understand the procedure and the charge, and he will ask whether you have had enough time to prepare your defence and whether you wish to apply for representation or assistance. The charge is then read and you will be asked whether you plead guilty, or not guilty.

If you plead 'guilty'

The officer who placed you on report reads out a statement of his evidence, detailing what happened and why you were placed on report. You will then be allowed to ask the officer questions, though you may be required to put these questions through the Governor. You may also comment on his evidence. If you disagree with the officer's version of events, you should say so and you may call witnesses to support your evidence. If, when the Governor believes the facts are clear he or she accepts the plea of guilty, you will then be asked if you wish to make a plea in mitigation. This is your opportunity to explain why you did what you did. A member of staff will then read out a conduct report (which relates only to your current sentence, not your criminal record or previous sentences), which you may comment on. The Governor will then announce your punishment.

If you plead 'not guilty'

The reporting officer who placed you on report will be asked to read out a statement of his evidence, at the end of which you will be given an opportunity of asking the officer any questions—though you may be required to put your questions through the Governor. The reporting officer may call witnesses in support of his case, though if he does so it is usual for the Governor to ask questions of the witness rather than the officer. If you disagree with the evidence of the reporting officer or any witnesses he may call on his behalf, you should say so and explain why. You will be allowed to question every witness who is called to give evidence against you. You will then be asked to reply to the charge and comment on the evidence. You may call witnesses in your defence and the Governor can only deny hearing your witnesses where he has very good reasons to do so; Governors have been criticised in the past by the High Court for failing to hear material defence witnesses without valid cause. The witnesses you call will then be questioned by you and, in addition, the Governor is entitled to ask questions himself and so is the reporting officer.

Summing up

You will be allowed to sum-up your case and the Governor will announce the verdict in respect of each charge. If you have been found guilty of an offence you will be allowed to make a statement in mitigation, and call witnesses in support of it. The Governor will then announce the findings.

Punishments

The punishments which can be imposed and the maximum penalties are set out in **Rule 50.** With the exception of a caution and prospective awards of added days, any punishment may be suspended for up to six months. Prospective awards are given to remand prisoners who, at the time, have no sentence to which days can be added, but which take effect if convicted and sentenced to custody. The punishments available to adults are shown below—figures in [square brackets] relate to Young Offender Institutions:

1. **Caution**
2. **Loss of Facilities** (privileges) for up to 28 days [14 days]
3. **Stoppage of Earnings** 28 days [14 days]
4. **Cellular Confinement** for up to 14 days
5. Up to 28 **Additional Days** in custody
6. **Exclusion from Associated Work** for up to 14 days [n/a]. It is a common practice—though contrary to Prison Service Instructions—for a sentence of NAL to be served in the Segregation/Punishment Unit.
7. For unconvicted prisoners found guilty of escape or an attempt to escape, **forfeiture of the right to wear their own clothing** [n/a].

   Additionally, in **Young Offender Institutions only**, the following punishments are allowed:
   1. **Removal from Activities** for up to 14 days
   2. Two hours **Extra Work** per day for up to 14 days.
   3. **Removal from Wing** or unit for up to 14 days.

Disciplinary appeals

Prison **Rule 56(1)** gives the Secretary of State the power to quash any sentence or finding of guilt. Appeals against a disciplinary adjudication are a **reserved subject** and accordingly can only be dealt with by Headquarters on the appropriate form available on application. You should also remember that you may apply to the High Court for judicial review of the adjudication and your solicitor will tell you whether you have appropriate grounds for doing so.

Terminating punishments

A Governor can terminate or reduce most punishments where it appears they have served their purpose and the offences are unlikely to be repeated. If you received **Additional Days** you can apply to have them cancelled. Before doing so you must be sure that it is at least **SIX MONTHS** (four months for Young Offenders) since:

a. The last offence for which you received additional days or loss of remission, **and**
b. the last time, if any, you applied to have them cancelled.

If you think you are eligible you should apply first to staff on your wing. They will check your eligibility and then you will be asked to make a written statement to support your application. A member of staff on your wing will write a report on you and this, together with any record you have of offences in prison, will go to the Governor. It is unlikely that all your additional days will be cancelled, but it is worth applying to get more of it back later if you are still in custody and meet the conditions.

Prison mutiny

If there is a major disturbance in the prison, and if you take part in it, you may be prosecuted for prison mutiny. If you are convicted you may receive a prison sentence of up to ten years, or a fine, or both. Section 1 of the **Prison Security Act 1992** defines prison mutiny by saying:

> 'There is a prison mutiny where two or more prisoners, while on the premises of any prison, engage in conduct which is intended to further a common purpose of overthrowing lawful authority in that prison.'

If you find yourself caught up in a prison mutiny you should leave the scene at the earliest possible opportunity. If you remain when you had a reasonable opportunity to leave, then irrespective of whether you actually cause any damage or injury, you may be deemed to be involved and so liable to the same consequences as those prisoners who started it. In addition to the formal disciplinary system, the prison authorities can employ a range of other measures for maintaining control.

Control and restraint (C&R)

All prison officers receive basic and ongoing **Control and Restraint** training which is based on the martial art of Akido. By use of painful locks and holds a three-man **'C&R'** team can remove a prisoner from one place to another and subdue him completely by increasing the pressure—and so the pain. Theoretically you should be given the opportunity of walking to wherever it is intended you should go, and only if you refuse should the team be ordered in. One officer will take the right wrist and a second will take your left wrist. The third officer should hold your head in his hands and lead the way—some establishments have unlawfully extended the C&R repertoire by wrapping a towel around the prisoners' face and this unauthorised practice amounts to an assault. If you find yourself placed in locks applied by a C&R Team, do not resist. The pain level can be increased markedly by the simple appliance of pressure and you risk injury: one female prison officer in 1994 had her arm broken in three places and her elbow dislocated during what was termed *C&R training.* If the locks are professionally and properly applied, and you do not resist, you should feel no pain. The use of C&R techniques is only lawful if it entails use of the **minimum amount of force necessary in the circumstances.** If the minimum force necessary in the circumstances is exceeded, then the application of the C&R technique becomes an unlawful assault.

Transfer and segregation

Transfer may be made in the interests of good order and discipline. Prisoners should be told the reasons for the transfer, so far and as soon as is practicable. However prisoners have no **right** to be informed of the reasons before the transfer takes place. The House of Lords has held that disciplinary transfers and segregation are susceptible to challenge by way of judicial review: *ex.p Haigh 1992.* Rule 43 can be used to segregate you from other prisoners against your will. It tends to be used if you are felt to be acting in a violent, threatening or subversive way. Segregation beyond three days requires the written authority of the Secretary of State or a member of the Board of Visitors; only exceptionally is that authority refused.

Special accommodation

Non-Medical cases. Strip Cells and Body Belts The Governor may order that a prisoner who is violent or refractory should be:

a. **temporarily confined in a special cell (strip cell), and/or**
b. **placed in a mechanical restraint, i.e.**
   - **a body belt with iron cuffs for a male prisoner and leather cuffs for a female prisoner;**
   - **handcuffs (male prisoners only);**
   - **leather wrist straps (female prisoners only)**

Such measures may be taken only if it is necessary to prevent the prisoner injuring himself, another prisoner or member of staff, or to prevent a serious disturbance. Also, if a prisoner who needs to be moved from one part of the prison to another kicks out at staff, **ankle straps** may be used to prevent injury to the prisoner or other people. Special accommodation or **mechanical restraints** must never be used as a punishment and their use should be stopped as soon as the prisoner has ceased to become violent or refractory. **Mechanical restraints should not be used on persons under 17 years of age.** The use of special accommodation or mechanical restraints should be reported immediately to:

- the **Medical Officer** (restraint must be ended at once if the Medical Officer says that there are medical reasons why such a measure should not continue: though this is more a theoretical safeguard rather than a practical one;
- The **Board of Visitors**, who are required to give authority for the use of such measures beyond the first twenty four hours—refreshingly there is evidence of a few Boards refusing to grant authority, or restricting its duration.

Further information is contained in **Standing Order 3E** available for purchase or loan through the prisoners library.

Special accommodation

Medical Cases. The Medical Officer may order that a prisoner who poses a danger to himself or to staff or others should be temporarily held in a protective room—padded cell. Alternatively the prisoner may be placed in a **loose canvas restraint jacket** if physical restraint is needed. Such measures must never be used as a punishment and should be stopped as soon as they are no longer necessary. The use of protective rooms or canvas jackets should be reported immediately to the Governor and the Board of Visitors; and the Governor and Board of Visitors should also be told about prisoners who need to be held in an unfurnished room: in some establishments, this is very much a management afterthought.

Drug offences

Possession of a controlled drug offends against not only the Misuse of Drugs Act, but also against the Prison Rules as an unauthorised article. Moreover, if an officer suspects that you have a controlled drug in your mouth and you appear to swallow before opening your mouth for examination, this may be construed as obstructing an officer in the execution of his duty. The **Criminal Justice and Public Order Act 1994** contains measures which allow prison officers to require urine samples from prisoners for drug testing. Prisoners who test positive for illicit drugs, or who refuse to provide a urine sample for testing, will have committed an offence under the Prison Rules. It is unclear at the time of writing (October 1994) how the authorities intend to proceed, but the intention appears to be that HM Prison Service will conduct a pilot study of random testing in several prisons before random testing is launched on a national basis: the pilot study is expected to begin in Spring 1995. No prisoner will be forced to provide a specimen of urine: no inmate can be forceably catheterised for example. There are few support systems in place and inmates need to have sight of the system behind it: including the safeguards that must be built-in to ensure that samples provided remain free from interference. The desire to reduce the amount of drugs in our jails is a commendable one, but any method that seeks to achieve that by bringing prison officers into a face-to-face confrontational situation with the prisoner, is destined to create far more problems than it will ever solve.

6. Welfare & Religious Matters

WELFARE

Basic welfare needs are usually dealt with by prison staff. It may be best to discuss any problem first with either your personal officer, if you have one, or the officer in charge of the wing, block or accommodation.

Shared working in prison (SWIP)

The prison and probation services work together to meet social and welfare needs of all prisoners. Probation officers are seconded to the prison service, usually for an initial period of two years, and they should be able to offer you help during your sentence and as you prepare for release. Specially trained prison officers share the welfare work in many establishments, allowing them greater understanding of the inmate's problems and improving their input when it comes to writing reports.

Confidential

Normally whatever you discuss with a probation officer is confidential, but in the prison setting probation officers are accountable to the prison Governor and they have a clear duty to report to him anything which threatens the security, good order or discipline of the prison. SWIP officers should also respect the confidentiality of your discussions unless it impinges on the security or good order of the establishment.

All establishments

There are probation officers working in every prison and Young Offender Institution. In Young Offender establishments, where personal officers should help with most needs, their work is different from that in adult prisons; where probation officers work from an office somewhere in the prison.

How can they help?

The first contact you will have on reception is likely to be with a prison officer who should be able to help with any immediate and practical day to day problems. You should meet your probation officer soon after arrival. He or she may be able to help you with other and more serious and different problems, including those which may have resulted in your offending in the first place. The two main areas where prison probation officers can help you are, assisting your contact with your family outside, while helping you prepare for your release on the inside.

Family and personal matters

The division of work between probation officers and prison officers varies in different prisons. Your prison probation officer should be able to see that you get help and advice with personal-domestic problems, such as outstanding debts, relationships, or problems with visits. In some establishments SWIP officers will help with this kind of problem, though normally they tend to deal with routine matters like sending letters, making telephone calls and basic hygiene and health.

Preparation for release

Probation officers should also be available to help you prepare for release by:

- helping with arrangements for home leave
- putting you in touch with your 'home' probation officer (who may supervise your parole) and
- contacting outside bodies who may be able to help arrange accommodation, training, education or employment after your release.

Tackling your offending behaviour

During your sentence you may be asked to go to groups or courses. These will help you, with the probation officer, to look at the causes, behaviour or problems (such as alcohol or drug abuse, gambling, financial pressures) which resulted in your being sent to prison. These courses may take place in groups with other prisoners with the same problems so that you can work together to find ways to stop the offending pattern from being repeated.

The probation officer may also be able to help put you in touch with outside specialists who will help deal with your particular problem.

Sex Offender Treatment Programme

HM Prison Service has seven establishments which act as **Assessment Centres** for the Core Sex Offender Treatment Programme (SOTP):

- Albany, Dartmoor, Full Sutton, Maidstone, Wakefield, Wandsworth, Whitemoor.

Ten **Treatment Centres** currently operate the Core SOTP:

- Acklington, Channings Wood, Leyhill, Littlehey, Risley, Swinfen Hall, Usk, Wayland, Whatton, Wymott.

In addition there is one **Advanced Treatment Centre**, HMP Woodhill, which operates the Concentrated Core SOTP, for serious, persistent, offenders. Inmates who wish to apply for a place on the SOTP, should speak with their prison probation officer in the first instance.

Pre-release courses etc

During your sentence you may be offered the opportunity to attend a **Pre-Release and prisoner Development** course. These are available in many—but by no means all—establishments, and are usually lead by prison officers who have been trained for the task. The sessions involve prisoners a lot and cover a wide range of topics. These include **relationships, communication and social skills, gambling, drugs, alcohol, health, accommodation, employment, benefits and rights**. Outside groups such as NACRO, CAB and AA often take part in appropriate parts of the course. You cannot be forced to attend such a course, and some are notably better than others—but even if it does no more than get you out of the cell, you will have benefited by it.

Parole

As you come up to consideration for parole, both 'home' and prison probation officers write reports for the Parole Board. You can show your willingness to work with a probation officer and to cooperate with the conditions in a parole licence by keeping in regular touch with the home and prison probation officers.

Aftercare

The Probation Service may be able to help you after your release. You can ask for voluntary assistance if you are discharged as 'time served' (at your earliest date of release). If you are released on licence the Probation Service **supervises** you. The job of the supervising probation officer is to make sure that you stick to the conditions on the licence—in which respect they act as the disciplinary agent of the Parole Board. A parole licence lets you serve the rest of your sentence in the community. All young offenders and prisoners released on life licence are supervised by a probation officer.

Board of Visitors

Boards of Visitors should not be confused with prison visitors—see below. The Board of Visitor's main task is to act as a watchdog to ensure that the prison rules are complied with and that you are being treated fairly—see 'Requests and Complaints' chapter for more information. The Board is made up of local people, some of whom are magistrates—and all of whom have been selected by the Home Secretary. If you have a complaint, or something to do with prison life that you want the Board to look into, you can ask to see a Board member who is visiting the prison. You can ask to see the whole Board if you wish—they usually meet once a month—though in a large number of prisons the Board insists its work is done by a quorum of usually three members.

General reputation

The general reputation of the Board of Visitors' (BoV) among prisoners has never been good—though there are some notable exceptions (Wandsworth being one). Some of the more professional Boards put copies of their Annual Report in the prisoners' library and a few openly campaign to improve standards. Sadly however there still remain many Board members who are more interested in the social status Board membership is perceived as bringing, rather than discharging professionally the duties Parliament has entrusted to them. Now that Boards have been stripped of their disciplinary powers (as from April 1992), it remains to be seen whether they will enjoy the degree of independence which Parliament clearly envisaged they should represent when they were first created more than a century ago: whatever may be the result in the future it is already very clear, from a perusal of BoV annual reports, that many deeply resent the loss of such powers, and waste few words in arguing for its swift return. BoV's have their own association **AMBoV** (Association of Members of the BoV), though not all BoV members belong to it—sadly.

Samaritans

The Samaritans have strong links with many prisons, forged in the last ten years as a result of the increasing prison suicide rate. They are local volunteers who befriend people for whom life may be getting too much to bear. Sometimes when you are in prison you may be feeling very anxious or despairing and would like to talk things over with someone who is unconnected with the prison and who will not—no matter what the circumstances—

divulge any part of your conversation to the prison authorities. In far too many prisons the medical response when a prisoner seeks help for anxiety is still to replace his clothing with a humiliating nylon suit and toss him into a strip cell that is dimly lit, often claustrophobic, and far more certain of aggravating the situation than resolving it. If you wish to see a Samaritan, there are a number of ways of doing it.

- **Ask a member of staff to arrange a visit**
- **Phone the local branch from the prisoners' telephone**
- **Write either to your local branch or to**
  Chris
  PO Box 1250
  Slough SL1 1ST

You may be able to get a special letter (free) to write to the Samaritans. The organisation may also be able to provide emotional support to your family if they are having a tough time while you are inside. An increasing number of prisons are providing **Listener** Schemes, in which selected prisoners are trained by the Samaritans. They will listen (in confidence) to your problems, they may not always have the answer but they will understand what you are going through and provide a sympathetic ear and often helpful advice.

Prison visitors: fancy a chat?

Prison Visitors are usually organised by the prison chaplain. They are local people who are available to see any prisoner who asks for a visit. These visits may be very helpful for prisoners who might not otherwise get social visits. Prison visitors are 'independent' of the prison authorities and, while your conversations with them will not be routinely relayed to staff within the jail, prison visitors do have a duty to the Governor to inform him of anything which effects the security of the prison. Therefore prison visitors are able, within those limits, to talk with you on a more informal and open basis. If you would like a prison visitor you should contact the chaplain. The visits will normally take place in your cell or interview room and you are free to end the arrangement at any time. These visits do not count against your entitlement to ordinary social visits.

Voluntary Associates/Volunteers

Voluntary Associates/Volunteers are usually linked to the probation service. They are like prison visitors who can make friends with prisoners by visiting and letter writing. When it comes to the time for release your VA will usually be able to help you with practical problems as well as being a supportive friend. Visits from a VA take place in the visiting room like any other social visit and it will not count against your allowance of ordinary visits. Other prisoners need never know your visitor is a VA if you don't want them to know—some prisoners prefer to keep this quiet. If you are interested in having a VA then talk to the prison probation officer about it or write to:

The New Bridge, 27A Medway Street, London SW1

The New Bridge is an independent body, who also publish the national newspaper for prisoners, *INSIDE* TIME.

Other help

Most prisons are visited by a wide range of people and organisations for example Alcoholics, Gamblers and Narcotics Anonymous. Your landing officer or probation officer will be able to give you details of how to go about meeting with these people.

RELIGION

Every establishment has a Chaplaincy Team to help prisoners practise their religion; this is made up of the Church of England Chaplain and the Roman Catholic and Methodist Chaplains. Visiting ministers are also appointed to each prison to meet the needs of prisoners of the non-Christian religions and other Christian denominations. Freedom to practise religion is Prison Service policy and if you have any difficulties see the prison Chaplain.

What rights do I have?

The observance of religion in prisons is covered by in **Standing Order 7A**, which is available for reference in the prisoners library, or you can purchase your own copy for £1.00 on application. This states that 'The Prison Service respects the need for all prisoners to be free to practise their religion.' Once you have declared your religious affiliation you may attend main services of your declared religion. If you have registered as 'Nil Religion', you may still attend worship. The time kept for the main acts of Christian worship on a Sunday must be kept free from activities that might discourage attendance.

Who can't go to church?

You do not lose your right to attend the main service because you are undergoing punishment, segregated under the Rules, on the Escape List, in Category A, or in hospital. You may only be stopped from attending prison church services in the following circumstances:

- **If the Medical officer advises against attendance**
- **If the Governor judges that you have misbehaved, are likely to misbehave, or are likely to cause a disturbance by your presence. The Governor may ban you from the church service for a maximum of one month, but it may be renewed from month to month for ever more**

- **If you are located in a special unit.**

Non-Christian faiths

Prisoners of faiths other than Christianity share in the right to practise their religion. Such prisoners are entitled to the diet and dress which accord with the requirements of their religion, together with observance of any special days. The arrangements for members of the Buddhist, Hindu, Muslim, Jewish and Sikh religions are to be found in the **Directory and Guide on Religious Practices Manual in HM Prison Service.** This is available in the prison library or you can purchase your own copy. The Prison Service hope to produce similar guides for other religions shortly. In addition to the accommodation provided for Christian worship there should also be clean and appropriate accommodation provided for the meetings and prayers of non-Christian groups.

'Nil religion'?

Upon arrival in prison you should have been asked whether you belong to any religion. You may state your religion or ask to be registered as **'Nil Religion'**. The Chaplain should also visit you at some stage to ensure that you have been registered correctly and ask if you have religious needs. Generally you will only be allowed to attend services and meetings of the religion in which you have registered.

Changing your religious registration

If you wish to alter your religious registration, you will need to satisfy the Governor that you are genuine in your intention to join a different religion. He or she will also consult both the minister from the religion you wish to leave, and the one to which you have applied to join. Unless the application is obviously frivolous, change of religious registration is usually granted; though subsequent applications may be viewed with some suspicion.

Chaplains and Visiting Ministers

If you wish to see a Chaplain or Visiting Minister you may make application to do so. A written form should normally be available from a wing officer. Each day the Chaplain is required to visit those of his religion who are ill or undergoing cellular confinement.

Contacts with the outside

Chaplains and Visiting Ministers may help you to keep alive your contact with the outside world, perhaps by arranging for a priest or minister from your home area to visit you. Chaplains and Visiting Ministers may have contact with your family in various ways and, for those prisoners refused permission to go to an outside registry office, they are able to conduct wedding ceremonies inside the prison with approval of Headquarters.

Reports

Prison Chaplains are often asked to contribute to Parole and Life Licence Prisoner Reports. You can ask for a representative of your own religion to write your report.

7. Health & Hygiene

Health

While you are in prison your health care is the responsibility of the **Health Care Services for Prisoners**—formerly known as the (much criticised) Prison Medical Service. Although not a part of the mainstream NHS—despite constant calls for integration—much of the health care is provided by local family doctors who are contracted to come into the prison for morning sick parades and who are paid by the Prison Service. Larger prisons also have a number of prison medical officers who are full-time members of the Health Care Service for Prisoners. The Prison Service pays for all treatment provided or arranged by medical officers.

Treatment by own doctor?

If you are unconvicted, you can apply to the Governor to be examined and treated in prison by a doctor or dentist of your own choice. The Governor will decide in consultation with the medical officer whether there are reasonable grounds for this. You would be expected to pay any charges made by the visiting doctor or dentist. If you are involved in legal proceedings, in which medical examination is necessary by an independent doctor, then you have the right to be visited by an external doctor for that purpose.

Consent

Standing Order 13(25) states:

Circular Instruction 4/1988 further specifies that no radiographs [X-rays] may be taken without the consent of the patient, but neither the Prison Rules nor European Prison Rules deal directly with the issues of consent to treatment or the relationship between a prison medical officer and the prison administration.

The subject of 'consent' was raised in the Court of Appeal case of *Freeman v Home Office (1984)*. Freeman had alleged that he had been held down and forcibly injected and could not have been said to have consented to treatment because he was not told what was wrong with him nor the effect of the medication or its likely side-effects. The Court of Appeal held that a prison doctor acts as a doctor inside the prison and not as a senior member of the prison's management. The court held consent had been given by the prisoner and therefore it did not rule on the important point of whether the issue of consent to treatment should have been viewed as within the ambit of **s.58** *Mental Health Act 1983*—which would have required the prison doctor to record the prisoner's refusal of consent in writing, and then obtain a second psychiatric opinion agreeing to the administration of the proposed drugs. The boundaries of consent therefore remain blurred, but other than in exceptional circumstances you are free to accept or decline any medical treatment offered to you. If you do not wish to receive any treatment at all from the prison authorities, irrespective of the situation, then you should record that view in writing and lodge a copy with the Governor and the prison medical officer by way of recorded delivery post. You may rescind the refusal at any time by service of an appropriate counter-notice, lodged again with the Governor and prison medical officer. The British Medical Association's booklet on **Medical Ethics** makes the further point that a prisoner is entitled to exactly the same standard of care as if he were a person at liberty in the community.

Second opinions

If the prison medical officer cannot deal with your medical problem or needs a second opinion an outside specialist may be asked to see you either in prison or in an outside NHS hospital. If you go to the outside hospital, you will remain in the custody of the Prison Service.

Medically confidential

All prisoners undergo a medical examination on reception. The doctor will ask you questions about any health problems you have or have had in the past. These details will be recorded in your **Inmate Medical Record** (**IMR**) and is treated as being medically confidential. Your IMR will normally follow you from prison to prison, though your outside medical records will only be called for if the prison doctor thinks there are good grounds for requesting them—and you will have to sign to consent to it. Therefore the prison doctor may not know of any health problems you have unless you tell him/her and, as a result, you will not get any treatment for them.

HIV/AIDS: one prick is all it takes

Many prisoners are very concerned about the risk of AIDS at the moment. **Acquired Immune Deficiency Syndrome (AIDS)** is caused by a virus called HIV—although people who are HIV positive do not always develop AIDS, and people who are not HIV positive cannot contract the illness. While there is as yet no cure for AIDS, nor any vaccine against it, already it is well established that intravenous drug misuse or unsafe sexual activity represent the greatest risks.

Transmission of the HIV virus

You **CANNOT** catch HIV through normal social contact with someone who has it. **There is NO RISK at all from ANY of the following situations:**

- **shaking hands**
- **brushing past**
- **using the same toilet, plates and cutlery**
- **being spat on or bitten by someone with HIV**

There is NO RISK as long as you do not:

- **get involved in risky types of sexual activity**
- **share needles and syringes to inject drugs**
- **share needles to tattoo.**

The **only** way in which HIV can be passed on is when **blood or semen** from someone who has HIV, **enters the bloodstream** of someone else. Most people who have HIV have caught it through sharing needles ('works') with other people who inject drugs or as a result of unsafe sexual intercourse—vaginal or anal.

World Health Organisation

The risks of transmission can be significantly reduced—but not ruled out—by not sharing needles or using a condom, though unfortunately both clean needles and condoms are banned in prison—despite recent recommendations of the World Health Organisation that prisoners should be able to obtain exactly the same health care services in prison, as they would receive were they outside.

Intravenous drug injection

You cannot tell from looking at a person whether they have HIV or not and, because of the horrendous potential consequences, it is safer to assume that anyone you come into contact with ***could*** be HIV positive. Sharing needles to inject drugs is extremely risky and due to the few illegal syringes which will be found in any prison, the dangers of injecting while inside are particularly great. Some prisons provide bleach or sterilisation tablets and used properly these will effectively kill the virus.

Homosexuality in prisons

The view of the Prison Service is that homosexuality in prison is an offence against the criminal law and, therefore, the Prison Rules. The Prison Service do not consider that a prison cell is a 'private' place within the meaning of the Sexual Offences Act 1967—though this is an interpretation, somewhat convenient, which has not been tested in court and is the subject of much legal debate. As a consequence (even if both male prisoners are over the age of consent) any homosexual act amounts to a criminal offence. As as result, whatever may be the legal merit at the end of the day, the Prison Service for the moment steadfastly refuses to permit or provide condoms for prisoners, on the basis that there is no 'legitimate use' for such items in prison; again seemingly contrary to the recommendations of the World Health Organisation and in ignorance of the fact that, as a result, some prisoners will leave prison with a potentially terminal illness they did not possess when they arrived.

'In custody'

A special Home Office leaflet, 'AIDS Inside and Out', is available to all prisoners. The Terrence Higgins Trust (see **Useful Organisations** chapter) have a special section ('In Custody') for prisoners and they have also produced a leaflet on HIV/AIDS in prison which is available free on request.

Testing

The prison doctor will need to know if you have been receiving any medical or psychiatric treatment, and if you have any problems with alcohol or drugs. You will also be asked about whether you have HIV (the virus which can lead to AIDS), or have come into contact with the body fluids of anyone who may have been HIV positive. The prison medical officer can arrange for you to be tested for HIV, though it is a step you should think very carefully about. Despite the regulations which state that medical information shall be kept confidential, prison medical staff have been known to disclose such information to non-medical staff—particularly if there has been a violent or blood-spilling incident in which staff or other prisoners have been involved—and it is possible that your condition could become generally known.

Counselling

The level of counselling available for HIV/AIDS prisoners is generally derisory and even the **National AIDS Helpline**—free of charge 24 hours a day to the public—is denied to prisoners because '0800' *freephone* numbers are electronically rejected by prison telephones exchanges—why?

Medicines and specialist treatment

You will not be allowed to keep any medicines you have been taking outside—all medicines must be issued from the prison pharmacy. It is important to let the medical officer know if you are allergic to any form of medicine. If you suffer from asthma, inhalers may be issued from the prison pharmacy, but some prisons do not allow prisoners to keep asthmatic inhalers in their cells overnight. If this causes you problems you should see the medical officer.

Dental and optical treatment

Dental and optical services are available to you as a prisoner. You should apply to see the medical officer if you wish to have your teeth and eyes checked. In most establishments a waiting list will be in use for all but emergency treatments. You will not have to pay for a dental check-up or any other type of service provided by the prison dentist. Whether you have to pay for optical services or not will depend on how long you have been in prison if you are unsentenced, how long you still have to serve if you are sentenced and the cost of the spectacles or lenses which you choose. The optician will be able to give you further details if you are in doubt.

Informing the next-of-kin

If you become seriously ill while you are in prison, the Governor should make sure that your family or next of kin are told and they may be able to visit. Prisoners who have a chronic illness which is expected to result in death or who are likely to be bedridden until their release date may, in certain circumstances, be granted early release. There would need to be friends or relatives outside willing and able to provide or arrange the necessary care.

Access to Medical Records Act 1990

This Act provides for the right to inspect a medical record or part of a record, and the right to be provided with a copy of a record or part of a record—for which you may have to meet the photocopying costs. The Act entitles patients to see information put on their health records **after 1st November 1991**. There is no legal right to see information recorded on your medical record before this date, though medical officers may be able to provide it.

Restrictions

Access will not be given to records which, in the opinion of the medical officer or other health professional involved, would give information likely to cause serious harm to the physical or mental health of the patient or of any other individual. The medical officer will not give access to records if the information contained within them was provided by an individual other than the patient who could be identified from that information. Reports made as a result of a request from a court/Parole Board, are not regarded as being records made in connection with the care of the individual concerned and access to these records will not be allowed.

Corrections

If you believe that a part of the **IMR** is incorrect, misleading or incomplete, you can apply for it to be corrected. If the record holder—prison medical officer—accepts that the information is inaccurate, it must be corrected. If the medical officer disagrees, he must append a note to the record describing your views on why the information is inaccurate or misleading.

Applying for access

You may make an application to see your medical records, in writing or verbally during the course of a consultation—usually during the morning sick parade. Access should be given within forty days of the application for access. If your medical record is at another establishment your request will be passed on, though Standing Orders state that no prisoner should be accepted at an establishment unless his Inmate Medical Record has come with him or can be faxed to the receiving establishment that day.

Fees

There is **no fee** made for giving access to records. However, if the applicant is provided with a copy of a record, or part of a record (other than for legal purposes when the request should be made by your lawyer), a fee may be charged to cover the cost of the copy and postage when copies are sent by post.

Clothes

The Prison Service rules and standing orders say that prisons have to provide clothing that is clean, aired, in reasonable condition and adequate for warmth and health. Clean underclothing, socks and shirts should be provided. The number of items issued at any one time and/or the frequency of exchange may vary from prison to prison.

Bedding

Unlike Scottish prisons, English prisons generally do not allow you have your own duvet sent in and you will have to use the sheets and blankets provided by the prison. Bedding should be clean, aired and in reasonable condition and both mattress and bedding are to be aired for at least one hour per week, according to prisons standing orders. **Prison Rule 24** says that bedding should be adequate for warmth and health.

Personal hygiene

All prisoners have a bath or **shower** at reception and you should then be able to have a hot bath or shower at least 'once per week' according to **Prison Rule 26**. This phrase has been interpreted literally by the Prison Service and, in some prisons, a shower on a Monday can be followed by one a week the following Friday and still be within the 'week' in the rules.

Shampoo and shaving

You should be provided with necessary toilet articles, **soap, shampoo, razors and toothpowder are available on request**, though you can purchase civilian varieties from the canteen. Men will be expected to shave daily, unless you already have a beard. If you want to grow a beard or moustache—which changes your appearance from the last occasion when the prison authorities took your photograph—you have to make an application to do so. Generally it will be permitted.

Haircuts

Female prisoners cannot have their hair cut without their consent, unless the medical officer orders it—in practice the same applies to male prisoners, but men (and especially young offenders) can still be required to have their hair cut for the sake of 'neatness'; though the legal authority for this rule is considered to be somewhat dubious, especially as **Rastarfarians** are entitled to retain their dreadlocks.

Exercise

All prisoners not engaged in outdoor work, or detained in an open prison, shall be given exercise in the open air for not less than one hour in all each day, if weather permits. **(Rule 27)**. If the exercise consists of physical training, then it may be given indoors instead of the open air. It may also be reduced to half an hour per day if association is the general rule of the prison, or the working day is more than five hours or outside activities are available in the evenings. If you are segregated or on punishment, you retain the right to one hour of exercise, though you may be required to exercise alone.

Food

Prison food according to **Prison Rule 21**, should be 'wholesome, nutritious, well prepared and served, reasonably varied and sufficient in quantity'. Again according to the rules the food should be inspected regularly by the medical officer and by a member of the Board of Visitors. The Governor should taste the food every day at lunch time, but all of these inspections normally take place in the prison kitchen.

Diets

It is also Prison Service policy that food should, as far as practicable, take account of the religious requirements and cultural preferences of prisoners from different ethnic groups.

- **Vegetarian diets should be provided on request.**
- **Vegan diets should normally be provided to Buddhist prisoners upon request and to other**

prisoners who normally follow a vegan—no animal or dairy products—diet.

- **Halal meat should be issued to Muslims on request.**
- **Kosher meat should normally be available to prisoners who follow Jewish dietary laws.**
- **A rice-based diet should be available on request.**
- **It is normal practice for prisons to allow special food to be brought in for the celebration of religious festivals.**
- **Cocoa will be provided instead of tea/coffee for Mormons.**

Transfer and advice

Problems may arise on transfer to a new prison as the prison kitchen may not have the food you need. In this case you should apply to see the Governor, your religious minister or the Board of Visitors. Because some prisons allow cooking in the wings there are dangers of contamination if food hygiene practices are not followed. You can get advice on food hygiene either from the prison catering or medical officers, or the Environmental Health Officer (EHO) at the local Council. EHO's now have statutory powers under the **Food Safety Act 1990**, to inspect all prison kitchens, and any other place where food is eaten, cooked or stored. They can issue written advice to caterers about hygiene issues which give concern but which are not a breach of the **Food Hygiene (General) Regulations 1970**. If there is a contravention of the Regulations, EHO's may issue Enforcement Notices, requiring the offending place to be brought into line with the law—and if not, they can close it down completely. No prison kitchen has yet been closed down, but in June 1993 the kitchen at Pentonville prison, north London, came very close to it after no less than eight breaches of the Regulations were discovered and the Governor forced to put them right.

Smoking, or non-smoking?

If you are a non-smoker and do not want to share a cell with a smoker, ask the Governor for a cell change. The prison authorities are constantly being pressured by individuals and trade unions to create more *No Smoking* Areas. A growing number of prisons now operate a *No Smoking* policy during visits and more could follow.

8. Race Relations

Policy Statement

The Prison Service has a public **Policy Statement** about Race Relations and it should be clearly displayed in every prison. The full Statement is set out in **Annexe A** of the Handbook. It says that the Prison Service is committed absolutely to a policy of racial equality and to the elimination of discrimination in all aspects of its work. It also says that the Prison Service is opposed to any display of racial prejudice either by word or conduct by any member of staff. The Prison Service is also opposed to racial discrimination by one prisoner against another prisoner. In its report 'Racial Attacks and Harassment' published in June 1994 the Home Affairs Committee called on the Government to reconsider its opposition to an offence of racially-motivated violence for behaviour which it describes as 'evil and destructive'. The Committee, referring to modern-day life in the UK, concluded that 'racial attacks and harassment and the spread of literature which preaches racial hatred are increasing and must be stopped'.

Humanity, respect and equal access

The statement goes on to say that all prisoners should be treated with humanity and respect, regardless of their race, religion or culture. All prisoners should have equal access to the facilities provided in prison. These include jobs, education, library services, exercise and accommodation.

Race relations manual

The Prison Service policy is set out in greater detail in the 'Race Relations Manual'. The manual is for use by prison staff, but a copy should be available in the prisoners library. Alternatively, the **Race Relations Liaison Officer (RRLO)** may be able to lend you a copy.

Disciplinary offence

All prison staff should know the Prison Service's policy on race relations. They should also know that it is a disciplinary offence for staff to use racially abusive language.

Who can help?: Race Relations Liaison Officer (RRLO)

Every prison has a RRLO who must keep up to date with the law, departmental instructions and race relations policies. The RRLO should be known, and available, to prisoners. He or she should be able to help if you have a problem or query of a racial nature. If you think you have been discriminated against you may to talk first to the RRLO. Some larger prisons have an officer on each wing who you can talk to about race relations problems.

Can you help?

RRLO's should also know about different ethnic minority groups in the prison. You may feel that you can help the RRLO by telling him or her about your cultural background or about your community. For example if you come from a group which is only a very small minority population in the UK you may be able to help the RRLO with names and addresses of outside contacts. The names of bookshops, publishers and suppliers of videos would be helpful. You may also be able to help with such matters

Race Relations Management Team (RRMT)

Every prison also has a Race Relations Management Team (RRMT). It is made up of prison staff and includes the RRLO and a Governor. In some cases people from outside the prison may be at its meetings—though our Prison Service has yet to learn the benefits of having inmates involved with such meetings. The RRMT should meet regularly to make sure that the Service's policies on race relations are being carried out. They should check that ethnic minority prisoners are being treated fairly in such matters as work and education.

Reported racial incidents

The RRLO will inform the RRMT about any incident of a racial nature in the prison. If you complain to an RRLO—or via a formal Request/Complaints form—the complaint will be looked at in the normal way and the RRMT will be informed at its next meeting.

Different discriminations

Racial discrimination can take many forms. For example someone may be refused a job because of the colour of their skin—the Home Office have already been successfully sued by a prisoner in Parkhurst for this reason. This is called **'direct discrimination'**, because there is a positive act (job refusal) in practice. **'Indirect discrimination'** is when a rule or policy discriminates against a racial group. Some discrimination happens without our realising it, known as 'unconscious discrimination'. Sometimes a particular facility (a snooker table for example) may be taken over by one group to the exclusion of other racial groups, whose members may feel unable to use it. That too is a form of indirect discrimination.

Equally available to all

The Prison Service policy is to try to make sure that everything is equally available to all prisoners regardless of race. This does not prevent people from exercising genuine preferences for particular kinds of activities, or from wanting to be with other members of the same group, provided this does not exclude others. If you feel kept out of any part of prison life because of your race or colour, you may be a victim of racial discrimination.

Possible areas of discrimination

The following list sets out areas of prison life where discrimination may occur. It is meant to be able to help you ensure that you are not being discriminated against:

- Accommodation should be available on a fair basis. Usually a rota system works fairly. No areas should be taken over by one racial group.
- Work and Training should be available equally to all prisoners, on the basis of how well they can do the job, or how much they will benefit from a training course. Popular areas of work, or the best paid ones, should not be given to one particular group while keeping out others.
- Education classes should be equally available to all prisoners on the basis of their needs and suitability. Special classes can be provided to meet the needs of groups such as prisoners with difficulties speaking English.
- Religion and opportunities for its practise should be available equally to all prisoners
- Diet should reflect prisoners' religious beliefs and as far as possible take account of their culture.
- Libraries and information, such as prison leaflets, newspapers and books, should be available to all ethnic groups in the prison, and reflect their various cultures. Foreign language books should be available, as should translations of the Race Relations Policy Statement, the 'How To Make A Complaint' booklet, and the summary of the White Paper on the Government's plans for the Prison Service.
- Discipline should be applied to all prisoners equally and with no regard to their race or ethnic group. Prisoners from one ethnic group should not be unfairly treated or given harsher punishments than those from other ethnic groups. Proven racial discrimination in disciplinary decisions would be a forceful ground of appeal.

Complaints about racial discrimination: who to see

You may feel that you have been discriminated against (for example over work, or education) or that you have been racially abused. If so you can inform the RRLO. You may also complain to the Governor or Area Manager via a Request/Complaint form—submitted under 'Confidential Access' if you feel it appropriate. For more information see the *Handbook* chapter on Requests and Complaints.

If there is a simple case of misunderstanding, the RRLO may be able to settle the matter by talking to everyone. If you make a formal complaint however, this will be fully investigated.

You can also complain to the **Commission for Racial Equality**. The CRE are able to investigate complaints under the terms of the Race Relations Act 1976. You can write direct and in confidence to the CRE at:

Commission for Racial Equality, Elliott House, 10/12 Allington Street, London SW1E 5EH

Standing Order 7A

There is a **Standing Order (7A)** on Religion which should be available in the prison library

Equal opportunities

Members of other religious groups have the same right to practise their faith as Christian prisoners. Members of other religions should be given the same opportunity to do so in prison whenever this is possible. This means that a suitable place should be provided for meetings and services. The prison should also take account of various times of prayer, holidays and festivals. The prison should also help you if you have any needs relating to hygiene, dress or diet.

The **Prison Act 1952** says that the Prison Chaplain, though a practising minister of the Church of England, should ensure that every prisoner is able to practise his or her religion. Every prisoner is entitled to see a visiting minister of his or her religion.

If you are unhappy with the religious arrangements in prison, or of no-one has asked a representative of your religion to visit the prison, you should inform the Chaplain or the **RRLO** about it.

Religious registration

When you first arrive in prison you will be asked to state your religion. If you want to go to religious services you will be expected to go to those of the religion you have declared. It is not usually possible for you to attend meetings of faiths other than your own and visiting ministers are not permitted to see prisoners who do not belong to their religion and who have not asked to see them. Although Rastafarianism is not registered as a religion in prisons, those following the Rastafarian faith are entitled to have their needs met, for example a vegetarian diet, retaining their locks and suitable headgear etc.

Changing your religious registration

If you want to be recorded as belonging to a different religion you can ask the Governor. But some faiths are not keen to accept a new person unless they think he or she really wants them to change. You may have to talk to a representative of that religion.

Standing Order 7A states that prisoners who wish to change their religious registration should make an application to the Governor, who will then ensure that the appropriate chaplain's or visiting ministers are informed.

Prisoners who wish to consult a minister or representative of a religion other than one for which they are registered, may be permitted to do so without changing their religious registration, provided that:

- **the Governor is satisfied after consultation with the appropriate chaplains that the prisoner has a genuine interest in exploring the faith represented by the minister; and**
- **the Governor is satisfied that the prisoner is not seeking to cause undue disruption, for example by asking to see a succession of ministers of different religions.**

Directory and Guide

The **Directory and Guide to Religious Practices in HM Prison Service** gives guidance on provisions for all religions. A copy will be available in the prisoners library.

9. Social Security & Discharge Grants

Where to find help

One of the most immediate effects of being sent to prison is on your finances and those of your family. Very often this means that you or your family will have to claim social security to make ends meet. This chapter sets out the main social security regulations as they effect prisoners and their families.

While you are in prison, the only social security benefit that you can claim is to cover your housing costs. You cannot claim income support, unemployment benefit, or any of the other personal benefits and allowances. Nor can your family claim for you. But if you were claiming benefit before you went into prison, if you have a house or flat you want to keep for when you are released, or if your family are going to be claiming benefit while you are inside, you need to act quickly to sort out your finances. If you want more detailed information or advice you should contact either your local DSS office, Welfare Rights Centre, Law Centre, Citizen's Advice Bureau or Probation Officer.

When you first go into prison

When you first go into prison, you should contact the DSS quickly to sort out your benefit affairs; you can do this by applying for a special letter to write to the DSS, or ask your solicitor to write on your behalf.

If you were claiming benefit for yourself and your family

Your partner should go immediately to the DSS and make a fresh claim. Even if you are on remand and expect to be granted bail, it is important that this is done quickly so that your family does not lose any benefits, such as the lone parent premium. They should consult their CAB or Law Centre for advice about claiming welfare benefits.

If you were single and claiming benefit

You should inform the DSS as soon as possible after being received into custody. Sometimes this may be difficult, particularly if you are remanded to a police station for further inquiries or due to local prison overcrowding; your lawyer should write to the DSS on your behalf. It is important to make contact with the DSS so that you do not face difficulties when claiming benefit on your release from prison. It is also particularly important if you were living with your parents, and both you and they were claiming benefit. In that case, it is possible that they were having money deducted from their housing benefit because you were living with them. If so you must tell the **Housing Benefit Office** so that they can get their money increased—money may still be deducted however if you are on remand.

If you were working

Your family may have to claim benefit while you are in prison. They should seek advice from an advice agency about their entitlement. However, they should go to their DSS as soon as possible to make a claim for benefit; if they delay, they may lose money as a result.

Getting your rent paid

If you were living in rented accommodation before you were in prison, or if you own your own home, you will probably be anxious to keep your accommodation for when you are released. You or your family may be able to claim benefit in order to pay your housing costs.

If you were living with your family in rented accommodation

Your family may be able to claim **Housing Benefit** to cover the cost of the rent. If you were already claiming Housing Benefit, you should write to the **Housing Benefit Office** (and the DSS if you were claiming other benefits too) to inform then of the situation. Your family should also contact the Housing Benefit Office to take over your claim or make a fresh claim.

If you were living alone in rented accommodation

The situation is more complicated in these circumstances. You will only be able to claim Housing Benefit for the first 52 weeks that you are in custody, and Housing Benefit will only cover the ***essential rent***—not your water rates, standing charges for gas or electricity, nor your council tax. The council may also refuse to pay Housing Benefit if you are going to be in prison for more than **15 months**. This means that prisoners who are likely to be inside for longer may not be able to hold on to their accommodation unless they can afford to continue to pay the rent and bills from their own resources.

Can I claim Housing Benefit while in prison?

Housing Benefit helps pay the rent while you are in prison for up to 52 weeks if:

1. **You intend to go back to your property when released.**
2. **You do not rent out the property while in prison.**
3. **You are not likely to be away for a continuous period of much more than a year.**
4. **You do not have more than £16,000 in capital (i.e. savings etc).**

How do I make a claim

Claim from the local council which covers the area where your property is located (not the one nearest the prison). If you were claiming Housing Benefit before you were in prison, you should write to the Housing Benefit Office (and the DSS if you were claiming other benefits) to make a fresh claim based on the change in your personal circumstances—i.e. being sent to prison. If you were not claiming Housing Benefit you should write to your local council to ask for a claim form, if you need help filling it in you could ask your personal officer if you have one, or the prison probation officer. Housing Benefit is available to both remand and convicted prisoners if they meet the criteria.

Who needs to know?

Anyone who was living in rented accommodation—whether private, council or housing association—should write to the landlord or estate manager to let them know what is happening. You will need to tell them how long you expect to be away and whether anyone will be looking after the property while you are away.

What happens if I lose my accommodation?

If you will not be able to keep your accommodation, i.e. because you will be in prison too long and have no resources to meet the rent, you should consider giving up your accommodation in order to avoid debts such as rent arrears on release. You might be able to obtain assurances of accommodation on release (ideally in writing) if your landlord is a housing association or local council.

Paying your mortgage

If you are buying your own home, you or your family may be able to get help paying the mortgage while you are in prison.

If you were living with your family

If your family are going to be living in the flat or house while you are in prison, they may be able to get help in paying the *interest* on the mortgage. They need to make a claim from the DSS as soon as possible after you go into prison. A local welfare rights worker can help with advice.

If you were living alone

You can claim Income Support to help with the interest payments on the mortgage. However **this only applies while you are an unconvicted remand prisoner; as soon as you are convicted all help with your mortgage interest will cease.** Even if you are an unconvicted remand prisoner, for the first 16 weeks of your claim only HALF of the interest will be paid. After that you will be able to claim the full cost of the interest payments, including interest on any arrears that have built up over the first 16 weeks. It also helps pay interest on loans taken out to repair or improve your property. You need to write to the DSS to claim this as it is not done automatically.

Can I claim mortgage interest benefit?

To be able to claim you must:

1. **Intend to go back to the property when released**
2. **Not rent out the property in your absence**
3. **Not be likely to be away for a continuous period of much more than a year**
4. **Not have more than £8,000 in capital (i.e. savings etc)**

Who needs to know?

Whatever happens you ought to tell the mortgage company, bank or building society of the situation. If you are going to be switching to interest only payments, or if you are not going to be able to afford to make any payments at all, you need to tell them. They may be able to arrange for the repayments to be frozen or for the sale of the property.

Water rates and standing charges

You cannot get any help with these payments while you are in prison. You could write to the water authority and the gas and electricity boards to tell them of the situation and ask them whether you can pay them once you are released. Otherwise, if you are going to remain in prison for a long time, it may be worth having these services disconnected.

Council tax

Most prisoners will not have to pay council tax while they are in prison—although prisoners are not exempt for any time spent in police cells before their first court appearance. However you will have to claim exemption from the tax as soon as you arrive in prison. To claim exemption, you will have to write to the Council Tax Registration Officer (CTRO) at your local authority using a form that you can obtain from the prison. If you do not claim your exemption you will face a bill when you are released. You will have to pay the tax if you are imprisoned for fine default or council tax defaults.

Home leave

When you are released on home leave, you will be given a travel warrant or money for your journey, money to cover any essential extra travel (e.g. reporting to your probation officer etc) and a small amount of money for food.

Can I claim income support on home leave?

It is a requirement of the income support regulations that in order to be eligible for income support a person must show that he is not 'a prisoner' and is 'actively seeking work'. The issue was recently considered by the Court of Appeal in the case of *Chief Adjudication Officer v Carr: 1994.*

In November 1991 Mr Carr was serving a sentence of imprisonment and during a five day home leave he applied for income support. He established that during the period of his temporary release licence he was not 'a prisoner' in terms of the regulations and, in a novel attempt to get around the 'available for work' requirement, he sought to rely on the 1987 Income Support Regulations which provided that a prisoner 'discharged from prison' did not have to be actively seeking work during the first seven days of discharge. This approach was successful before the Social Security Commissioner who ruled that Mr Carr was eligible for income support during the period of his home leave. However, because of the importance of the case, the DSS Chief

Adjudications Officer appealed to the Court of Appeal.

Court of Appeal

On the 27th May 1994, the court held that a person on home leave WAS eligible for income support but ONLY if he could show that he was actively seeking work during the period of his leave. The court accepted that Mr Carr was not 'a prisoner' during the period of his home leave, but rejected his argument that he did not have to show he was actively seeking work on the basis that the exemption on which he sought to rely applied only to to those who were *discharged* from prison **at the end of their sentences**. As Mr Carr was unable to show he had been actively seeking work during the period of his home leave, his claim for income support failed. Unless the case is taken to the House of Lords—which seems unlikely given that this was a unanimous decision of the Court of Appeal—the position is unlikely to alter without changes in the Social Security Regulations. You may therefore make an application for income support on home leave if you can show that you are actively seeking work during this period—but the burden of establishing that you are actively seeking work rests with you: letters from potential employers and written evidence of arrangements for job interviews will all help to support your application.

Are there any other funds available?

If the people you are staying with are on DSS benefits they may be able to claim a grant for the duration of your leave. If they are not on DSS benefits and cannot afford to keep you while you are on home leave, you should apply to the prison probation officer as soon as you know that home leave has been granted. The Prison Service have a small fund of money from which payments like this can be made. If you are going to a hostel or staying in lodgings the prison will pay for your accommodation and meals.

DISCHARGE GRANTS

When you are released from prison you will receive a travel warrant to take you back to your home or wherever you intend to travel. Most prisoners will also receive a discharge grant.

Am I eligible for a discharge grant?

You will NOT receive a discharge grant if:

- you are under 16
- you are serving less than 15 days
- you were in prison for fine default or non-payment of council tax
- you were a civil prisoner
- you were on remand awaiting deportation
- you are going straight to hospital
- you are travelling to an address outside the UK, or
- you are not eligible to get income support.

This means that 16–17 year olds will not usually receive a discharge grant unless there is a real need to look for, get and pay for accommodation before being released. It also means that no-one with savings of over £8,000 or who is discharged to hospital will receive a discharge grant.

How much will I get?

The amount of money you will receive depends on your age and whether you have a home to return to, or will be homeless on release. If you are returning home, the level of grant depends on your age and will be the equivalent of one week's income support for a person of your age, plus any (one) premium for which you may qualify—see below.

DSS BENEFIT RATES WITH EFFECT FROM 1 APRIL 1995; FIGURES IN (BRACKETS) SHOW RATES EFFECTIVE UNTIL THEN.

Personal Allowances
Weekly Rate .
Income Support (IS), Housing & Council Tax benefits (HB & CTB)

Single:	16–17 (IS)	£28.00	(£27.50)
	16–17 (Higher IS & HB)	£36.85	(£36.15)
	18–24	£36.85	(£36.15)
	25 & over	£46.55	(£45.70)
Couple:	both aged 16–17	£55.65	(£54.55)
	one or both aged 18+ (both must be eligible for IS)	£73.05	(£71.70)
Lone parent	16–17 (IS)	£28.00	(£27.50)
	16–17 (Higher IS & HB)	£38.65	(£36.15)
Dependent children:			
	aged under 11	£15.95	(£15.65)
	aged 11–15	£23.45	(£23.00)
	aged 16–17	£28.00	(£27.50)
	aged 18	£36.85)	(£36.15)

Premiums:	**Single**	**Couple**
Family (Couple & Lone Parents)	£10.25	£10.25
*Lone Parent (IS)	£5.20	n/a
*Lone Parent (HB & CTB)	£11.35	n/a
*Pensioner (65–74)	£18.80	£28.30
*Enhanced Pensioner, 75–79 (not disabled)	£20.95	£31.15
*Higher Pensioner (60+ disabled, or 80+)	£25.35	£36.15
*Disability	£20.00	£28.55

**Only one of these can be paid. Highest paid if you qualify for more than one premium. Couples in receipt of Income Support will also receive £1.40 per week to help off-set the VAT now on fuel, single people receive £1.*

Unemployment Benefit
Statutory Sick Pay.
Over Pension Age: £59.15 (£57.60) Lower Rate: £47.80
Under Pension Age: £46.45 (£45.45) Standard Rate: £52.50

Will I get the higher level of payment?

If you can't return home but are going to a hostel or lodgings, or have tried and failed to find an address to be discharged to, you will be paid a higher level of discharge grant. All 16–17 year olds who qualify for a discharge grant will not get one at the higher level. Generally, you will not get the higher grant unless you have rented accommodation—such as a hostel or bed and breakfast—arranged before you are released. The only exception is where the probation officer has tried, with your co-operation, to fix something up but has been unsuccessful. If you decide not to return home you will not be able to get the higher grant unless there is good reason, like wanting to go into a rehabilitation hostel or having a firm offer of a job elsewhere.

Income Support

You only qualify for income support from the day that you sign on, and any delay in making a claim could cost you money. Your discharge grant does not count as part of your benefit, and you should not wait until it runs out before you claim.

When is it paid?

Income support is paid **fortnightly in arrears** (i.e. for the fortnight just passed), so if you are claiming income support you will not actually receive any money until two weeks after you leave prison. You may be owed some benefit for the period before you were sent to prison, i.e. if you were due to sign on the day you were sent to prison you may be owed two weeks benefit. If you run out of money before you receive your first payment, you can go to the Social Security and apply for a crisis loan from what is called the social fund. However you will have to pay this money back and the payments are deducted automatically from your giro every fortnight—i.e. you are paid your benefit minus the amount of the loan repayment.

Reclaiming benefits for remand periods

If you have been found not guilty after a period on remand, or released with a non-custodial sentence, you may be able to claim back benefit if you had been receiving any of the following before you went to prison:

- Sickness, Retirement or Invalidity Benefit
- Widow's Benefit, Disability or Child Special Allowance
- Maternity Allowance, any retirement pension, Age Addition
- Severe Disablement Allowance, Disablement Benefit
- Reduced Earnings Allowance and Industrial Death Benefit

Increases for dependents (i.e. wife and children) can also be paid on release.

National Insurance Contributions

National Insurance contributions determine whether you can apply for such things as unemployment benefit and the state pension. If you have not paid the appropriate number of contributions you will only be able to claim income support. While you are in prison, you are not making any National Insurance contributions towards unemployment benefit or your pension. When you are released you may decide that it is worth catching up with the payments you have missed; though for many prisoners, it may not be worth doing this.

Benefit advice

If you are in any doubt about how to claim and what you are entitled to, you should consult your probation officer or get advice from a Citizens Advice Bureau or other welfare rights adviser. The DSS have national **Freephone Benefit Advice Lines** on which you can obtain confidential advice in relation to any DSS benefit.

DSS BENEFITS: FREEPHONE ADVICE LINES
0800 666555 (English)
0800 289011 (Welsh)
0800 521360 (Punjabi)
0800 289188 (Urdu)
0800 252451 (Chinese)
0800 882200 (Disabilities)

This service is not linked to your local DSS office, so although individual advice is given, you will still have to go to your local office to make a claim when released. Also, because prison telephones do not accept 0800 numbers, you will have to arrange for the call via the prison probation/SWIP officer while in prison, or you can use the service while on leave prior to release.

Community Care Grants (CCG)

You can apply to the social fund for a CCG for things you will need when you are released; such as clothing and furniture. You can apply up to six weeks before you are due to be released. Some DSS offices refuse to accept these applications if they are unsure that you will be returning to the area. A decision on your application will therefore be delayed until you are released.

How do I apply?

To get a CCG you must be likely to be on income support when released. If you apply early to the DSS, they may be in a position to make a decision on your application before you are released. To apply ask for Form SF300 available from the DSS office which covers the area where you will live on release—*not* the office closest to the prison. You should include as much information as possible on your application—ie how long you have been in prison, details of illness, disabilities, alcohol and drug problems etc. The Social Fund does not have rules saying discharged prisoners *must* be paid grants. The Social Fund allows grants to be paid but does not order that they must. This is because there is only a limited amount of money in the Social Fund and the Social Fund Officer in charge of grants for your area, has a legal duty not to over spend his annual Social Fund budget. If your application is refused, you may ask for the decision to be reviewed and you should get advice from a welfare rights worker.

Housing advice

If you will be homeless on release, there are a number of associations and other organisations which provide accommodation specifically for ex-prisoners. Much of this housing is hostel-type accommodation, but some is in independent living units. To get details, you should contact your home or prison probation officer as soon as you know your release date. However you should be aware that such accommodation is not in plentiful supply and they may not be able to guarantee you a place.

Stop press

On 24th October 1994 the Government unveiled new plans to replace unemployment benefit with a new jobseekers allowance as from **April 1996**. The allowance will be paid for a maximum of six months, rather than 12 months like the current unemployment benefit, and jobseekers will have to enter into an agreement to actively look for work. Partners of unemployed will be allowed to work for up to 24 hours a week before any benefit is lost, instead of 16 hours at present, and jobseekers who continually refuse work or advice to make themselves more acceptable to employers (by taking training courses or even just smartening themselves up) can lose benefit and be required to undertake 'tasks of benefit to the community'. Full details next edition

10. Release

Sentenced before 1st October 1992

If you were sentenced on or **before 30th September 1992** the arrangements for working out your sentence have not changed at all. You will be entitled to release at the two-thirds point of your sentence—or at the half-way stage if you are serving 12 months or less. If you are serving over 12 months, you will be eligible for parole at the one-third point of your sentence—or six months after sentence, which ever is the longer.

Parole?

You will be reviewed for parole automatically. However, reviews after 1st October 1994 will be under the new procedures created by the Criminal Justice Act 1991, which are described below. The '**restricted policy**' on parole in relation to those prisoners serving more than five years for violence, sexual or drug offences, introduced by Leon Brittan in October 1983, which restricted parole to a few months at the end of the sentence, have now been rescinded.

If parole is granted

If you are released on parole licence you will be supervised by the Probation Service until the two-thirds point of your sentence. You will be liable to recall to prison during this period if you breach the conditions of the parole licence. If you do not gain parole you will be released at the two-thirds point of your sentence, but any previous loss of remission or **Additional Days Awarded (ADA's)** will set back your release date appropriately. All young offenders sentenced to detention in a YOI are supervised on release for at least three months—unless they turn 22 years of age, at which point the supervision ceases.

Sentenced on or after 1st October 1992

The **Criminal Justice Act 1991** introduced major changes concerning release from custody. Amongst the important new features are:

1. **All prisoners will spend at least half their sentence in custody, as opposed to the old minimum of one third.**
2. **Those prisoners serving sentences of less than four years will be automatically released at the half-way point of their sentence.**
3. **Prisoners serving four years or more become eligible for release on parole at the half-way point of their sentence. If granted parole they will be supervised until the three-quarter point of the sentence; some sex offenders will be supervised for 100% of their sentence if the trial judge so orders.**
4. **All Young Offenders and all those sentenced to**

12 months or over will be supervised in the community on release.

ADA's are added to sentences for breaking prison rules (replacing the old remission system). They will automatically set back your release date and eligibility for parole but not the date on which the full sentence ends—the Sentence Expiry Date (SED).

At Risk—all prisoners will be 'at risk' on release. This means that if you are convicted of a new imprisonable offence between release and the SED, a court can make you serve all or part of the remainder of your original sentence, from the date of the new offence to the SED.

'orking out your release date

orking out release dates can be complicated by riods on bail and in custody on remand—partic- arly if you are remanded for different offences by fferent courts on different dates. Any time spent manded in custody or in police cells will be garded as part of your sentence and will count wards your release and review dates. **Prison anding Order 3C** gives diagrams which explain w to calculate release dates and is available in e prison library.

ntences up to and including twelve months

u should be told your **Automatic Release Date** RD) within 24 hours of being sentenced, and d also of your **Sentence Expiry Date (SED)**. The RD will be the half-way point of your sentence. u will be released automatically at this point less you had any ADA's.

er twelve months and less than four years

u should be told your **Conditional Release Date** RD) and your SED. The CRD (the old **EDR**) will the half-way point of your sentence. You will be eased automatically at this point, subject to any)A's, under supervision to the three-quarters int of your sentence (known as the **Non-Parole ate or NPD**).

ntences of four years or more

u should be told your **Parole Eligibility Date** ED) within a few days of sentence—often this is ne at the Reception Board. This is the earliest te on which you can be released on parole and is e half-way point of your sentence, plus any)A's. If you do not get parole, you will automati- lly be released on your ARD at the two-thirds int of your sentence (the former EDR). You will subject to supervision until the three-quarters int of your sentence—the NPD. You should also informed of your SED (the former LDR).

ne defaulters

ou are sentenced to twelve months or less, your ease date will be at half of the term being served and you will be released unconditionally at this point. Over 12 months and you will be released at two-thirds unconditionally. In both cases you will not be eligible for consideration for release on parole licence.

Parole

The new 'parole' scheme applies **ONLY** to those prisoners serving **four years or more**, and is now called **Discretionary Conditional Release (DCR)**. Release is not automatic, but depends on the Parole Board, and in some cases the Home Secretary. assessing whether you are suitable for early release. If successful, you will be under supervision until the **three-quarters point of your sentence—or to the very end for some sexual offenders**.

How does it work?

Parole is granted on the basis of reports by probation, police and prison staff on your home circumstances, plans for release, conduct in prison, etc. About four months before your PED you will have the opportunity to see these reports and to make written representations stating why you believe you should get parole and what you will do on release.

Interviews and process

About three months before your PED you will be seen by a member of the Parole Board, who will write a report for the Board. You will be able to see and comment on this report. About two months before your PED a panel of Parole Board members will meet to consider your case. They will focus on the risk to the public, the prevention of further offending and the rehabilitation of the offender. If the panel decides against parole, or decides in favour of parole in the case of a prisoner serving less than seven years, the prison will be notified immediately. If the panel recommended parole in the case of a prisoner serving seven years or more, the case will be referred to the Home Secretary for a decision.

Further parole reviews if refused

If you are refused parole, you may be entitled to further reviews at yearly intervals. These will depend on the length of your sentence and on the time left between your PED and NPD—known as the **'parole window'**—a second review will only be available if you have a sentence of 6.5 years or more. You will receive a third parole review only if you are serving 12.5 years or more, a fourth if you are serving 18.5 years or more and so on.

The parole answer

When a decision has been made, a notification will be sent to the prison setting out the detailed reasons for the decision, and you will be given a copy.

There is no formal right of appeal against a parole decision but you can use the complaints procedure. Additionally, in certain circumstances, you may be able to challenge the decision in the High Court by way of judicial review proceedings. These circumstances can arise if the decision has not been made fairly—perhaps because you were not shown copies of appropriate reports—and the correct procedure has not been followed. Your solicitor will be able to advise you, though you should be aware that even if you win the judicial review, it does not mean that you will be granted parole; only that the Parole Board will have to meet to consider your case afresh and follow the appropriate procedure.

'Early' and 'special' parole reviews

Apart from a straight 'yes' or 'no' in response to your parole application, you may be granted an early review or a special review. An *early review* means that the date of the next review is being advanced. A *special review* may be granted where a prisoner would not normally be entitled to one. Special and early reviews will only be granted exceptionally, for example to monitor a prisoner's progress on a drugs rehabilitation course.

Young Offender Institution Supervision

On release you will be under supervision for at least three months, *even if this takes you past your SED.* Supervision will end earlier only if you reach your 22nd birthday within three months of release. On supervision you will have to report regularly to your probation officer or social worker. If you breach your conditions you may be taken to court and face a fine or up to 30 days in custody.

Adult sentences up to twelve months

Your release will be unconditional (Automatic Unconditional Release, AUR). This means that you will not be supervised by the Probation Service but you will still be 'at risk' until your SED. Before you are released you will be given a notice explaining what this means and you will have to sign it.

Sentences over twelve months but less than four years

Your release will be conditional (**Automatic Conditional Release, or ACR**). This means that you will be on licence and receive supervision on release. This will last until the three-quarters point of your sentence, plus any ADA's, this is called your **Licence Expiry Date (LED)**. You will be 'at risk' until your SED.

Conditions for release

Shortly before your release, you will be handed your ACR licence which sets out the conditions that apply to you and the name and address of your supervising officer. The conditions will be explained to you and you will have to sign the licence agreeing to abide by them. Conditions will normally involve reporting to your probation officer regularly, living at an approved address, receiving visits from your probation officer and keeping out of trouble. In some cases you will have to agree to not make contact with certain named individuals—often someone connected with your offence, be they co-accused or victim. You may also have to agree to work only at employment approved by your supervising officer. Breach of the ACR licence is a criminal offence in itself, for which you can be sentenced to six months, receive a fine—or both.

Sentences of four years or more

When you are released (either on parole or automatically at your NPD) you will be on licence and supervised by a probation officer, up to the three-quarters point of your sentence—or to the end of your sentence in the case of some sexual offenders.

> While you are on parole licence you may be 'dragged-back' to prison—even if you have not committed a criminal offence.

The Drag-Back Clause

If your behaviour gives '**cause for concern**' your supervising officer can apply to the Home Office to have you recalled, under the 'drag-back' clause of the parole licence. The final decision has to be made by the Parole Board, but you can be kept in prison in the meantime. It is difficult to define what may be considered as 'cause for concern', because it will be different in each case. If you committed your offences while 'high' on drink or drugs, your behaviour could be said to give cause for concern if you are involved in these activities while on licence. Similarly if you spend most of your days on the pavement outside the bank, having been released on licence from a sentence for bank robbery, it might just cross your supervising officer's mind to wonder what you're up to! That example may be taking it to an extreme, but it illustrates the point.

If you are dragged-back

If you are returned to prison you have the right to be informed of the reasons, and in sufficient detail to enable you to make realistic and cogent written representations to the Parole Board, who have the authority to order your re-release. If the Parole Board do not order your re-release, then you may be able to challenge the decision by way of judicial review in the High Court; your solicitor will advise whether you have a case. In any event you will be considered again for parole at 12 monthly intervals, in the normal way, if you have at least 16 months of your sentence still to serve.

Deportees serving less than four years

If you are liable to deportation or removal from the mainland as a result of an Exclusion Order, you will be released automatically (to be deported or excluded) at the half-way point of sentence (the ARD) for those serving under twelve months and at the CRD for those serving more than 12 months, but less than four years.

Deportees serving four years or more

You will become eligible for release on licence at the half-way point of sentence (your PED). You may be released at any point between half-way and two-thirds (NPD) at which point you will be released automatically to be deported or excluded. It will be a matter for the Home Secretary to decide at what point to release those serving long sentences. Cases of deportees will no longer be considered by the Parole Board.

What is 'home leave'?

Home leave is intended to help you re-adjust to the world outside prison and make arrangements for your release. It is important to understand there is no 'right' to home leave: you have to apply and the decision is made by the Governor after taking account of the the recommendation of the Home Leave Board (usually comprising a governor grade, a prison officer who knows the applicant, and a seconded probation officer)—**though a new system, which will be introduced in March 1995, may alter this: see below.** The Home Leave Board will consider your prison behaviour and a report into your home circumstances by your home probation officer who will have visited the accommodation address you have given. You cannot be released on home leave without 'suitable accommodation' and you will not usually be allowed to stay at the home of someone recently released from prison unless that person is a blood relative or a bona fide sexual partner.

Can I apply for home leave?

The rules on who can apply for home leave are complicated. You will not be able to apply for any type of leave if you are a Category A prisoner, subject to extradition proceedings, mentally ill or disordered. You are also unlikely to get home leave if you are appealing against conviction or sentence, or have been involved in serious incidents in prison—usually classified as those involving the loss of remission or imposition of ADA's. If your home is in Scotland, Northern Ireland, the Isle of Man or the Channel Islands you will not normally be prevented from visiting your home if leave is granted: though the current home leave system is uncertain.

Changes on the horizon

On November 1st 1994, following a number of high profile press reports on prisoners who had been granted leave in circumstances deemed subsequently to be inappropriate, the Home Secretary revealed to the Prison Service Annual Conference that he would '*shortly be announcing changes*' to the home leave system, which '*will introduce more rigorous risk assessment in every case*' by taking into account '*the views of the police and of victims and not rest solely on performance in prison*'. The new changes to the system of 'risk assessment', which all Governors were instructed to introduce with effect from 1st December 1994, include providing a route for victims and the police to object to the leave being granted, and the Home Office have made it clear such views will be taken into account—see end of chapter. **Failure to return from leave will become a specific criminal offence.** The new scheme will see a 40 per cent reduction in home leave and will consist of three new types of Licence.

Home leave system with effect from March 1995

1. **COMPASSIONATE LICENCE.**
   This will be confined to urgent personal matters such as funerals, visits to close relatives who are near to death, domestic crises and urgent hospital appointments. This type of leave will normally be restricted to those in category D, or analogous establishments.
2. **RESETTLEMENT LICENCE.**
   This will be available to prisoners nearing the end of their sentences. It is intended to help prisoners re-establish family ties and links with the local community, and to provide an opportunity to seek accommodation or work before release. Prisoners serving **12 months or less** will NOT be eligible for resettlement licence. Those serving **between one and four years** will have to serve at least ONE THIRD of their sentence, subject to a minimum of four months after sentence, before becoming eligible. Prisoners serving **over four years** will NOT be eligible until they have served at least HALF of their sentence, that is the date of their first parole application. If parole is granted, such prisoners will receive resettlement leave four weeks before release, if parole is refused they will have to wait for a set period beofre applying for resettlement leave.
3. **FACILITY LICENCE.**
   This will replace the current temporary release licence and is intended to enable suitable prisoners to undertake education, training, work experience and community service projects in the community. To be eligible for a facility

licence, inmates must have served a quarter of their sentence and be either Category C or D. Prisoners in Category A or B, are not eligible.

Temporary release for young offenders

There are a number of different kinds of temporary release for young offenders. These include attending colleges, outward bound courses and community service projects. Different Young Offender Institutions are able to offer different options. The eligibility for home leave is similar for Young Offender Institutions as for adult establishments.

Home leave for young offenders

If you are serving a fixed sentence of over 12 months, or if you are a lifer with a provisional release date, you can apply for resettlement licence (five days plus travelling time) to be taken shortly before your ARD, CRD or NPD. You will not be considered for resettlement licence leave until you have served at least four months from your date of sentence. Young offenders and female prisoners who are analogous to Category C or D adult male prisoners, will be eligible for facility licences and compassionate licences under the same arrangements as for adult males.

Section 53 detainees

Section 53 of the Children and Young Persons Act 1933 allows Crown Courts to impose sentences (of *detention*) longer than 12 months on young people under 18 years of age where otherwise they could not do so. If you have been sentenced to detention for life or during Her Majesty's Pleasure (HMP), you should consult the Governor. But if you have been given a fixed length sentence under section 53(2), your position will depend upon whether you were sentenced before, or after, 1st October 1992.

S.53s sentenced before 1st October1992

- You can be released on licence ***at any time*** during your sentence. In practice you will not be considered for release on licence until you have served one third of your sentence.
- You will be released before the end of your sentence only if your release is recommended by the Parole Board. There is no automatic right to be released at the half-way point, the two-thirds point, the three-quarters point or any other stage of your sentence except the very last day.
- Your date of release depends on what the Parole Board thinks of your progress.
- After release you will remain on licence, under supervision of a probation officer or a social worker, until the end of your sentence or for three months, whichever is the longer.

S.53s sentenced on or after 1st October 1992

Your eligibility for release will be exactly the same as if your sentence had been one of detention in a Young Offenders Institution for the same length of time. You should read the parts of this chapter in relation to automatic conditional release for those serving less than four years) or discretionary conditional release if you were sentenced to four years or more.

Release from prison

When you are released from prison all of your private property and clothing should be returned to you and you will receive a travel warrant and a discharge grant unless you fall into one of the excluded categories—see the chapter on *Social Security and Discharge Grants*. You will usually go before a discharge board just before your release and be asked about where you are going to live, whether you have sufficient clothing for your release etc.

Clothing

In many prisons you will get the chance to try on your clothes a few days before you are released. If your clothes no longer fit you, or if they are not warm enough for the time of year, the Prison Service has to provide 'liberty clothing' from a standard range of civilian clothes kept at the prison. It is particularly important if you have been arrested in midsummer, and are to be released in midwinter, to make sure you remember to ask about clothing a few days before you are released. If you leave it until the morning of your release, you may find you have left it too late.

Travel warrant

When you are released after serving a sentence you are entitled to the cost of your fare home, or to any other place in the British Isles where you intend to settle. Fares are usually paid through a travel warrant given to you at the time of release.

Private property and money

When you are released you have to sign for your stored private property and private cash and you should also receive any prison earnings due to you. It is important that you check everything, otherwise you may sign for something you have not received. If you have recently been transferred from another prison, your private cash may not have been transferred, so it is important that you point this out so that appropriate arrangements can be made. If you have difficulty obtaining money that has not been transferred, you should consult your home probation officer or solicitor.

Discharge grants

The discharge grant is explained more fully in the chapter on *Social Security and Discharge Grants*. The grant is supposed to cover your living expenses until you receive income support from the DSS a ***fortnight after your release***. It is roughly equivalent to one week's benefit. If you run out of money before you get your first income support payment, you can apply for a loan from the Social Fund at the DSS or apply for a Community Care Grant—see Social Security chapter. In the case of loans, you will have to repay the loan and this is taken automatically from your income support payments. If you are released after being on remand, or serving less than 15 days, awaiting deportation, going straight to a hospital or are in prison for fine default or as a civil prisoner, you will not get a discharge grant at all. You will receive a travel warrant, some subsistence money and a letter for the DSS. Whether you get a discharge grant or not, it is vital that you go to the DSS **as soon as possible** after your release to sort out your benefits; preferably on the day of release or, at the latest, the very next working day.

Health

You will be examined by the Medical Officer as soon as possible before discharge—in most cases this will be the previous day. If you are ill you can ask to stay in prison until you feel better(!), but it is up to the Medical Officer and the Governor. If you are unfit to travel alone, any family or friend will be asked to collect you or, if this is not possible, you will be taken to your destination by a prison officer in plain clothes.

Release time

You will normally be released before 0845 and quite often a lot earlier than that. If your release date falls on a weekend or public holiday, you will be released on the last working day before then. However, if you are getting out on parole, and your release date falls on a weekend or public holiday, you will normally have to wait until the first working day *after* your release date to be liberated. If your release is likely to give rise to publicity, with journalists and camera crews at the gate, you can ask the Governor to transfer you to another prison from which you can be released, though you will have to demonstrate your fears are genuine.

Gate arrest

Many prisoners are worried by the prospect of being arrested at the gate by waiting police officers, particularly if you have been visited in prison by the police during your sentence and refused to see them. Prison Standing Orders state that in any case where it is known that a prisoner will be arrested on his release, the prisoner will be informed by the Governor beforehand, so that he can contact family and a lawyer. There is, however, no obligation on the part of the police to inform the Governor that they intend to gate arrest, and they may simply turn up and do so quite legally.

The last breakfast!

You will be provided with your breakfast on the day of your release. If prison tradition is to be believed, it is important that you eat the last breakfast—otherwise you will return to eat it on another day!

Rehabilitation of Offenders Act 1974

The Rehabilitation of Offenders Act 1974 enables some criminal convictions to become 'spent', or forgotten, after a 'rehabilitation period'. A rehabilitation period is a set length of time from the date of conviction. After this period, with certain exceptions—see below—an ex-offender is not normally obliged to mention the conviction when applying for a job or obtaining insurance, or when involved in criminal or civil proceedings. A copy of the Act should be in the prisoners' library.

Rehabiliation periods

The length of the rehabilitation period depends on the **sentence** imposed—not the **offence** committed. For a custodial sentence, the length of time actually served is irrelevant for the purposes of the Act; the rehabilitation period is determined by the length of sentence imposed, not the amount of time actually served before release.

When does a conviction become 'spent'?

Sentences of more than 30 months can never become 'spent' and always have to be disclosed. Other convictions become spent after a fixed period of time, which runs from the date of conviction—not release or any other date. See table below.

SENTENCE	REHABILITATION PERIOD	
	Aged 17 or over on conviction	Aged Under 17 on conviction
Prison (immediate or suspended) or, Youth Custody, or Detention in a YOI FOR SIX MONTHS OR LESS:	7 Years	3.5 Years
Prison (immediate or suspended) or Detention in a YOI FOR MORE THAN 6 MONTHS BUT NOT EXCEEDING 30 MONTHS	10 Years	5 Years
Fine Or Community Service	5 Years	2.5 Years
Absolute Discharge	6 Months	6 Months

With some sentences the rehabilitation period varies

Probation, Supervision, Care-order, Conditional discharge or Bind-over: 1 YEAR or until the order expires— whichever is the longer.

Attendance Centre orders: 1 YEAR from expiry

Hospital Orders—with or without a restriction order attached: 5 YEARS or 2 YEARS after the order expires

Further convictions

Once a conviction becomes spent, it remains spent, even if a person is convicted of further offences in the future.

Criminal records

A person's offence will still remain on record even after it has become spent—the debt to society may have been paid, but the police keep all the receipts! Records held on the Police National Computer will be deleted only when the person has not come to police attention for twenty years. Records will NOT be deleted, however, if they include custodial sentences of more than 6 months, evidence of mental illness, evidence of indecency or homicide. To obtain a copy of your list of previous convictions held on the Police National Computer, you should apply by letter to your local Chief Constable, who may require that a fee be paid to cover the costs. You can only obtain a list of your OWN convictions. If there are errors in the list provided by the police, you can insist that they be removed, and you can also lodge a complaint with the **Data Protection Registrar, Data Protection Office, Wilmslow, Cheshire**, about the matter.

Can I keep quiet about my record?

Applicants with a criminal record who are asked on an application form—or at an interview—whether they have criminal convictions, can answer 'no' if the convictions are 'spent' and the job applied for is not exempt from the Act—such as a Health Service post, armed forces, police or other similar occupations. Under the Rehabilitation of Offenders Act it is not lawful to dismiss someone from employment because they did not disclose a spent conviction, unless the employment falls into a category exempt under the Act.

What if my convictions are not 'spent'?

One of the greatest problems faced by any released prisoner is what you do about the fact that you have been in prison. When you go for a job interview and an employer asks where you have been working for the past few years, at that moment in time you have to make a decision. You can either tell lies and cover up the fact that you have been in prison, or you can tell the truth and accept the great likelihood that you will remain unemployed and on the dole—the temptation is a profound one. Once you actually begin to build your future on a foundation of lies and deceit, however, you are at the top of a very slippery slope which leads, inevitably perhaps, once more to prison.

Do I have to disclose my convictions?

If you have convictions which are not spent, you do **NOT** have to disclose them **UNLESS** you are asked; either at an interview or on the application form. The dilemma has no easy answer: If you are asked and you do not disclose convictions that are not 'spent' then, if the convictions are subsequently discovered, you may—on the one hand—have had enough time with the firm to demonstrate your usefulness and you **may** survive or, as is perhaps more likely, you could be sacked without notice—and you may additionally have committed the offence of obtaining a pecuniary advantage by deception, contrary to the **Theft Acts 1968/1978**. If you are dismissed you will not be eligible for any accrued holiday pay or payment in lieu of notice: those are only afforded under a contract of employment and by telling lies you have cancelled any contract that may otherwise have existed. You must make the decision about whether to disclose your record, and you are the one who will have to live with consequences: by concealing them, you could already be on your way back to prison.

Can I move abroad?

The Act covers Great Britain. Other countries have their own rules about those they will give visas and work permits to. If you conceal convictions when required to disclose them, any visa or work permit issued as a result will have been obtained fraudulently and, as a result, will almost certainly be revoked if discovered. Embassies and overseas employment agencies may be able to provide further information on who they allow to enter their country—and, more to the point, who they don't!

What about the Foreign Legion?

Candidates for the Foreign Legion must be aged between 17 and 40, and those under 18 must bring their parents' permission in writing. Those who have decided to apply to join the Legion must present themselves at one of the recruiting offices in France with a passport: the main office is at Nogent-Sur-Marne in Paris—Express underground, line RER A4 in the direction of Boissy St.Leger. A British born Warrant Officer is based there to help English speaking applicants. At the recruiting office candidates are given a medical examination and aptitude test: fail either and you have to meet your own costs home. If successful in the medical/aptitude examinations candidates are sent to Legion Headquarters in Southern France where an intensive three week testing course takes place. Success at that stage results in full selection and transfer to a regiment for a 16 week training course. Basic contract is five years and the rules are basically the same as in any other Army. The Legion regulations ban recruitment of anyone who, at any time, has been convicted of murder or drug offences. Be warned: the Legion conducts very searching background tests which include checks with Interpol and police in the home country—you will NOT be able to conceal your convictions. Don't expect too much information or details about the Legion from the French Embassy in London: British law expressly prevents them from providing specific details on the Legion to anyone who enquires!

Victim Helpline

In November 1994 the Home Secretary announced changes to the system by which home leave and temporary release of prisoners are granted. One such change is the introduction of a **Victim Helpline (Tel: 0345 585112):**

Victim Helpline, PO.Box 4278, Birmingham B15 1SA.

The Head of the Helpline Unit, Tony Price, has explained the operation of the Unit as follows:

'The Helpline is open between 0900 and 1600 hours Monday to Friday. Details are taken of the caller (name, address, telephone number and connection with prisoner) to deter the non-genuine. The operators ask for details of the prisoner and the caller's areas of concern (eg, harassment, possible early or temporary release, etc). The Helpline staff then seek to identify and locate the prisoner. The caller will be contacted by letter asking for further details if it has not been possible to identify the prisoner. For prisoners in custody, the Helpline staff will write to the caller to confirm that his/her concerns have been passed on to the Governor and will be taken into consideration with all other available information in any future decisions. A record of the call is sent to the Governor of the establishment where the prisoner is being held. The information is considered along with all other available information in the following circumstances:

- where the prisoner is eligible to apply for, or has applied for, home leave or other temporary release
- where the prisoner is undergoing a parole review or may do so in the future
- where the prisoner is soon to be released on licence.

The representations made by the victim should be given due weight alongside other factors in considering temporary release, in accordance with Instruction to Governors 70/1994.'

It is important to note that there is no mechanism for informing the prisoner that these concerns have been expressed, and there is therefore no opportunity for the prisoner to comment, correct or contradict what has been said. No checks are made by the Victim Helpline Unit to ensure that the caller is genuinely the victim of the prisoner as they purport to be.

11. Women Prisoners

Introduction

Most of what has been said in the other chapters of the Advice Section applies to both women and men in prison, but there are some differences in the way prisons for women are run which will be covered in this chapter.

Male officers

As part of the Prison Service staff mobility scheme, there are now some male officers working in women's prisons; however females cannot at any time—or under any circumstances—be strip searched by or in the presence of a male officer.

Female prisons: few and far between

There are only 12 prisons in England and Wales which take women and girls. This means you may be kept far apart from your home area, family and friends.

Prison Life

Unconvicted women prisoners have exactly the same rights and privileges as men in the same situation as regards wearing your own clothes, writing and receiving letters, visits, etc. The main differences are for *convicted* female prisoners.

Clothes

Women and girls in prison do not wear prison uniform. You can wear your own clothes as long as the prison regards them as 'suitable' or, if you have not got enough clothes of your own, you can get clothes from the prison. The number of clothes you can have at any one time is limited and you should be able to use a washing machine to keep them clean. Clothes can also be exchanged on visits or swapped with clothes stored with your private property. There is also a clothing allowance—to help pay for your clothes while you

Female Establishments in England and Wales:

1. **RISLEY** (Cheshire). Remand/recently-sentenced only.
2. **PUCKLECHURCH** (Bristol). Remand/recently-sentenced only.
3. **LOW NEWTON** (near Durham). Remand/recently-sentenced only.
4. **HOLLOWAY** (London). Remand and convicted prison. Also national centre for the treatment of females with psychiatric problems.
5. **NEW HALL** (near Wakefield). Takes both remand and sentenced women, including life sentence prisoners following their initial induction stage.
6. **STYAL** (Cheshire). Closed, convicted-only prison.
7. **COOKHAM WOOD** (Kent). Closed, convicted-only prison.
8. **BULLWOOD HALL** (Essex). Closed, convicted-only prison.
9. **DURHAM** (H Wing). Forty females, high security conditions.
10. **ASKHAM GRANGE** (York). Open, convicted only.
11. **DRAKE HALL** (Staffs). Open, convicted only.
12. **EAST SUTTON PARK** (Kent). Open, convicted only.

are in prison. The amount differs according to the length of your sentence and you should apply to the Governor for details of your clothing allowance.

Hair

The prison cannot make you have your hair cut unless the medical officer orders it to be cut on medical grounds or in the interests of health or cleanliness; the medical officer has to state why, and it has to be approved by the Governor.

Toiletries

Certain toiletries will be supplied but if you wish to purchase additional items, these can be obtained from the prison canteen. Skin and hair care products for the particular use of black women are not always available and can be expensive, but you should be able to order anything you need. If this does not seem possible you should apply to see the Governor. If you have a skin condition which means you must use a particular cream etc, it can be prescribed by the medical officer.

Sanitary protection

A sufficient supply of sanitary towels or tampons should be provided at the appropriate time according to prison Standing Order 12. Paper to wrap used towels should also be provided and they should be incinerated without delay. Also according to Standing Order 14, prisoners can be provided with a supply of warm water in the evenings on request. You should also be allowed to approach a female prison officer rather than a male prison officer for sanitary protection should you so wish.

Visits

There is no difference in the level and the frequency of visits in male and female establishments. Convicted women and girls should be allowed a visit once every 14 days. Visits during weekdays should normally last at least one hour and at weekends thirty minutes. Establishments will, however, try to allow visits to last longer whenever possible. This will be subject to local circumstances, in particular staffing levels at weekends—which is a more popular time for visiting. Visitors can at present claim the cost of travel from the Assisted Prison Visits Unit once every 28 days—see chapter on **Visits, Letters and Phone Calls**.

Mother and Baby Units: Holloway, Styal and Askham Grange

If you are pregnant and likely to have the baby while you are in prison or have recently given birth to a baby, you may be able to go to one of the three Mother and Baby Units (M&BU) which exist at Holloway, Styal or Askham Grange prisons. The aims of the M&BU are:

'To create as many opportunities as possible for the mother to exercise and develop her parental responsibilities, duties and skills and to maximise the potential for the child's proper development.' (M&BU Regimes, HM Prison Service 1992, p.2).

Pregnant women are usually sent to one of these three prisons and receive their ante-natal care either in the prison or a nearby hospital. According to prison **Standing Order 13**, pregnant women prisoners should not be alone at night, but should share a room or have a bed in a hospital ward so that there are others around to call on for help if necessary. If you refuse to share a room you will be asked to sign a form saying that you have chosen to on your own and understand that this may mean help is not so easily available should you need it. There should be a call button in your cell if you are alone. Pregnant women should also not be left alone if they are in labour.

Disciplinary segregation when pregnant

If you commit an offence against prison discipline while you are pregnant you will probably not be punished by being segregated. If you are, then you will spend the days in the segregation unit and should be able to share a room at night.

Can my baby stay with me in prison?

If you are likely to give birth during your time in prison or have a small baby when you are sent to prison, you can apply to have your baby with you in prison. **The M&B Unit at Holloway takes babies up to 9 months old, but at Styal closed prison and Askham Grange Open prison, the age limit is 18 months.** In reply to a report by HMCIP on Askham Grange prison on 14th July 1993, Chief Executive of HM Prison Service, Derek Lewis, emphasised that the Prison Service was flexible in the way the age criterion was applied and he accepted that every case needed to be judged on its respective merits. The 18 month age limit was based on Department of Health advice on the age at which babies needed to begin experiencing everyday phenomena. A decision to allow a baby to remain an extra month or two would be taken if it was in the best interests of the child. A multi-disciplinary team, involving the local social services, a paediatrician, a Health Visitor, a doctor and prison staff will consider your application. They will consider many factors before deciding whether you should be allowed to keep your baby with you including:

- **Whether your baby will exceed the Unit age limit by the time you are due for release**
- **If your children were in care before you were sent to prison**
- **If you are suffering from a mental or physical illness which would effect your ability to look after your baby**
- **If you are considered to be a disruptive influence who may not co-operate with the running of the Unit.**

There are a limited number of mother and baby unit places. Space may not always be available, but more places are planned. If you are given a place in the Unit, you have to sign to say you will be responsible for your baby in accordance with the regime of the Unit. The way that Units are run varies, but it is usual for their to be rules about when you can bath your baby, not having your baby in your bed etc. Babies are usually left in a nursery for at least four hours a day while you are at either work or classes.

Can I be separated from my baby?

While you are in a Mother and Baby Unit you can still be disciplined for breaking prison rules like any other prisoner. As a very last resort you can be placed in segregation and kept away from your baby for up to 28 days, but you should not be prevented from seeing your baby regularly and even feeding the baby if practicable. Although disciplinary action itself should not damage your chances of keeping your baby in a mother and baby unit, the Prison Service can decide to move you to another prison because of your behaviour and this could mean that you are separated from your baby—for example if you are at Askham Grange, with a 12 months old baby, and you are moved to Holloway, your baby would be over the age limit for the Holloway Unit.

DoH inspection of M&BUs

The report of the second of three multi-disciplinary inspections of facilities for mothers and babies in prison, together with a study of social work arrangements for the children of imprisoned foreign women, was recently published by the Department of Health. The inspectors found that prisons had attempted to create a suitable environment for mothers and their babies and a regime to enable them to take up their roles as mothers on return to the community. But at no prison was the system well established and bedded in the culture of the mother and baby units said the inspectors. Further information about Mother and Baby Units can be obtained from HM Prison Service HQ: Sue McDougall (071-217-6682) or Jackie Jee (071-217-6444). Copies of the inspection reports can be obtained from the Department of Health, and should be available through the prison library.

Visiting expenses

If your child or children are not in prison with you, but are living with their father or friends or relatives, they can be brought on fortnightly visits if you are convicted (or more frequently if you are unconvicted) in the usual way. Travelling expenses, payable through the Assisted Prison Visits Unit (see chapter on Visits, Letters and Phone Calls for more information) to those on benefits or low income, are payable to people who would not normally qualify (i.e. friends rather than relatives, and same-sex partners) if they bring your children with them.

Extended and external visits

In some women's prisons you can get extended visits for your children, which are conducted in a more relaxed atmosphere than normal visiting sessions. If your children are in care the foster parents or children's home may be able to arrange for the children to visit you, in which case arrangements will be made for the visit to be in private. If this is not possible, you can make an application to visit the children where they are living. This depends on permission from the Prison Service, and the people caring for your children, but if there is agreement then the visits can take place every three months and you will not have to use a VO.

12. Young Offenders

Most of the other chapters in the Advice Section apply equally to young offenders and adult prisoners. But there are some differences in the way Young Offender Institutions (YOI's) are run. Some of these differences are set out in this chapter.

Headquarters allocation

If you have been sentenced to detention for life, or at Her Majesty's Pleasure, or if you have been sentenced to detention under Section 53 of the Children and Young Persons Act 1933, the decision about your allocation will be taken at Prison Service Headquarters. The decision will be based on reports sent by the local prison or remand centre you are in. If you are under 17 years old you could be sent to a children's home or Youth Treatment Centre instead of a YOI.

Local allocation

If you have been sentenced to detention in a YOI for a fixed length of time, the decision about which YOI you should go to will be taken at the local prison or remand centre unless you are a male aged under 18; in which case you should be taken immediately to the appropriate YOI from court. The staff will decide first whether you should go to an open or closed YOI, and then normally send you to the nearest YOI of that type to your home area. In a few cases they might send you to a YOI further from your home for a particular reason, such as need medical treatment or a special course which is not available in the nearest YOI to your home.

CLOSED YOIs

AYLESBURY. CASTINGTON. DEERBOLT. DOVER. FELTHAM. GLEN PARVA. GUYS MARSH. HINDLEY. HOLLESLEY BAY COLONY. HUNTERCOMBE/FINNAMORE WOOD. LANCASTER FARMS. LOW NEWTON. NORTHALLERTON. ONLEY. PORTLAND. READING. STOKE HEATH. SWINFEN HALL. WERRINGTON. WETHERBY.

OPEN YOIs

HATFIELD. THORN CROSS.

Reception

The **reception process** includes:

- **storing property if you are not allowed to keep it with you.**
- **If you are male, giving you your uniform.**
- **Giving you bedclothes.**
- **A short medical examination.**

You will be told where you are to live. You will be given a YOI number and a 'reception letter', so that you can write to a relative or friend to tell them where you are.

Induction

Induction is the name given to your first few days in a YOI. During this time you will be interviewed by staff. They will ask you a number of questions. Your answers will be used to try and make sure that you get the right opportunities for education or work, and to prepare your sentence plan.

Sentence plan

A sentence plan should be made as soon as possible after you first arrive and should start straightaway. It should set out the various stages of your sentence and the activities in which you will take part. Your supervising officer or social worker, if you have one, will give you information that will be used in making your plan. If your sentence is long enough, your progress during your sentence might change parts of the plan.

Personal

All YOI have Personal Officer Schemes. You will probably have a particular officer as your personal officer. In some YOI's you may find that a pair or group of officers share this task to make sure that there is someone available for you to see. You should ask these officers for help with any questions, problems or complaints. They will play an important part in making and changing your sentence plan.

Visits and family contact

The rules about visits and letters are explained in detail in the chapter '**Visits, Letters and Phone Calls**'. You should be able to get at least one visit every 14 days but, wherever possible, YOI's try to let you have more frequent visits. You will be told how often visitors can come and for how long. YOI's should also provide facilities for visitors, for example, places for children to play and for mothers to feed babies. *Families should be told that, as well as visiting you, they may also ask to see your personal officer or a senior member of staff.*

Letters

You can send out one letter a week on which the postage (normally second class) is paid for you by the authorities. You can also send at least two extra

Bullying

The amount of bullying that goes on in YOIs can be quite high, particularly in those which have dormitory rather than cellular accommodation. If you are the subject of bullying by those older or stronger than yourself, it is vital that you realise you do not have to suffer in silence and there are a number of things you can do to stop it. Those who prey on weaker or younger inmates get away with it because their victims are, perhaps understandably, afraid to speak out for fear of what will happen afterwards. Indeed the main reason we have such a problem with bullying is that the Prison Service, despite a number of well-resourced initiatives, has failed to convince a large number of victims that they can do something about it. If you are being bullied yourself, or see it happening to others, you MUST do something about it. Some young offenders suffer the anguish of daily physical assaults, weekly loss of canteen and constant humiliation. **NO-ONE HAS TO SUFFER SUCH MISERY IN SILENCE:** you are sent to prison AS punishment, not FOR punishment. There are courses designed to help those who bully others and, by speaking out, you are helping them to help themselves. If you are being bullied or see it happening to others you can discuss it with:

- **your Personal Officer**
- **Probation Officer**
- **Medical Officer**
- **Chaplain**
- **Governor**
- **Listener**
- **Older inmates**

Some young offenders have committed suicide as a result of being bullied: no-one has the right to frighten another person (and particularly a weaker one) to death.

letters a week for which the postage has been bought from your earnings or private cash.

The personal officer will also make sure that the supervising probation officer or social worker in your home area is told about your sentence plan. He or she should also tell the supervising officer what progress you make during your sentence.

Education

There should be educational classes at every YOI. The YOI rules say that these should as far as possible 'be such as will further your personal responsibility, your interests and skills and help you to prepare for your return to the community'.

Under school-leaving-age

If you are under school leaving age you must attend education or training classes for at least **15 hours per week**. If you are over school leaving age but in a juvenile establishment or unit this level of education or training should be available to you if you wish.

'Senior' young offenders

If you are in a YOI for prisoners aged 18–20, educational classes to meet your needs should be available in the evenings. Basic education classes for people who need help with reading or dealing with numbers should also be available during the working day.

Training

There should be training courses in all YOI's. The aims of YOI training are to develop personal responsibility, encourage your interests and skills and improve your chance of finding a job when you are released. Training course should also help you acquire qualifications.

Work

The YOI Rules say that, as with training courses, work should 'help you to develop personal responsibility, encourage your interests and skills and help you to prepare to return to the community'. In other words you should not be asked to do unnecessary jobs, although some routine work such as cleaning is needed in all establishments.

Physical Education

There should be physical education (PE) in all YOI's. This might be in working hours as well as in the evenings and at weekends. You should take part in PE for at least two hours every week. If you are in a YOI or a separate part of a YOI for juveniles (aged under 18) you will be expected to take PE for at least five hours per week. If you are below school leaving age, physical education classes do not count towards the 15 hours you must spend in education classes.

Remedial PE

Special facilities should be provided if you have an injury or need to have a special physical activity.

Open air

In some YOI's physical education classes will take place outdoors, but in others all classes may take place indoors. But in these YOI's you should be able to spend some time in the open air each day.

Community Service Volunteers

In closed establishments, some young offenders take part in the Young Offender Programme run by Community Service Volunteers (**CSV**). Towards the end of their sentence some offenders may take part in a four week residential community project. This may include, for example, working in a shelter for the homeless, or centres for the mentally handicapped or for alcoholics. This is a means of getting work experience as part of your preparation for release and to do something useful for the community.

Recreation and association

You should have at least one hour a day for recreation and association. This is a time when you can mix freely with other prisoners, play games such as pool or watch television.

Weekends

YOI's should provide more recreation and association at weekends. In some establishments Saturday mornings are set aside for cleaning of kit and inspection of bed spaces/cells.

Church services

All YOI's set aside time on a Sunday for church services which you can attend if you want to. Services should be available for different religions. More information on religion is in the chapter on Welfare and Religion and also in the chapter on Race Relations.

Voluntary work outside the YOI

At weekends you might be asked to do voluntary work outside the YOI. This is also a time when visits from outsiders, such as sports and youth clubs, may be possible. Weekend programmes might also include educational classes. This depends on whether local education officers and other staff are available. Where classes are available, they should concentrate on leisure time activities including arts and crafts.

Smoking

You will not be allowed to buy cigarettes or tobacco if you are aged under 16 or if you are in an establishment or unit for juveniles. In units and YOI's for juveniles no smoking is allowed. In YOI's for prisoners aged 18–20 smoking may be allowed only in designated places.

Grades

In some establishments for male and juvenile and short termers, there is a grade system. Your grade can be moved up and down by a review board. Prisoners in higher grades enjoy better facilities and privileges.

Pay

Pay is provided so that you can buy items from the canteen for your own use. You will be told how much your pay will be and how much of your private cash you may spend.

Voluntary Associates and Prison Visitors

Details of voluntary associates and prison visitors are in the chapter Welfare and Religion. These are members of the public who visit prisoners in their spare time. If you are interested in seeing a voluntary associate or prison visitor, you should speak to your personal officer.

Pre-Release Classes

Pre-Release Classes and Inmate Development courses are usually led by prison officers and are available at most YOI's. Many prisoners find the communication and relationships sections of the course can help in coming to terms with a custodial sentence. The problems are examined from the point of view of prisoners and also of their families. Other parts of the course deal with problems such as gambling, problem drinking, finding a job, accommodation, benefit entitlements, health etc. Outside groups such as NACRO, CAB and Alcoholics Anonymous often take part in the courses. Some probation services also run pre-discharge courses or workshops in the community for people who will be returning to that area after release.

Temporary release

Temporary release is available to some prisoners. You may be able to be released temporarily if you want to take part in the workshops or courses run by the probation service. These normally take place in your home area, but can sometimes take place in the area near your establishment.

Home leaves

You can also ask for a period of temporary release for other purposes connected with resettling in the community or for urgent compassionate reasons e.g. to visit a seriously ill close relative. All requests for temporary release will be considered on their merits but you do not have a right to have a period of temporary release. Some prisoners may be eligible for periods of home leave—see the 'Release' chapter.

Supervision: compulsory if under 22

All young offenders released from custody are subject to probation or social service supervision after release, unless they are 22 years old by the time they are released. This does not apply if your sentence was for the non payment of fines etc.

Requirements

The requirements of supervision will be set out in a notice from the Home Secretary, which you will be given on release. The supervision period begins on your release and lasts for at least three months. If you are released from a sentence of over 12 months, you will probably be under supervision on licence, for more than three months. You will find more information about this in the chapter on Release.

Supervision and the law

It is a criminal offence not to comply with the requirements of supervision. If you do not comply, you can be sentenced to up to 30 days or fined up to £400. Only people detained for fine default or contempt of court are not subject to supervision on release. You should make sure that you understand the conditions of supervision before your release. Your supervisor should discuss them with you when you meet him or her.

Parole

If you are released on parole, the parole licence will last until the date on which you would have been released on remission. This is called your Earliest Date of Release (EDR). When the parole licence expires, a period of supervision, as explained above, will begin. This lasts until your LDR or until two years after your release, whichever comes first.

Release

When you are released, you should receive the following:

- **Travel warrant** for a rail/bus ticket to your home.
- Return of your cash and private **property**—check carefully that it is correct *before* you sign.
- A written explanation of your **notice of supervision**, and your parole licence if applicable.
- Where appropriate, a **certificate** for 16 and 17 year olds who are unable to live at home.
- **Educational and training certificates** received in custody.
- A **discharge grant**—although most prisoners under 18 will not receive this. See the chapter on **Social Security and Discharge Grants.**

Benefits and training

To get benefit you must register for unemployment benefit and make a claim for income support straight away. You may be asked to apply for a place on a government-run Youth Training Scheme or **Employment Training** scheme. If you attend a Pre-release or Development course, you will probably receive advice on finding a job and about training opportunities. Prison officers in many establishments can also give advice about job finding. Other information will be available in the library. Your supervising officer or social worker should give you more advice on trying to find a job when you are released.

13. Foreign Prisoners

Introduction

If you are yourself a foreign national imprisoned in the UK, or you are otherwise connected with an imprisoned foreign national, this chapter is for you. It gives basic information to foreign nationals held in prisons in England and Wales. More detailed information is available from organisations listed later in the chapter, or from the Race Relations Liaison Officer (RRLO) at the prison. First, however, a few words for everyone.

What are the problems

The five main problems experienced by foreign prisoners are

- **The lack of information:** Many foreign offenders have a lack of knowledge about the British criminal justice system and how it operates, this includes a basic lack of understanding about the prison system. Many foreign prisoners are not kept abreast of developments in their cases, particularly in relation to immigration matters where lengthy delays are par for the proverbial course.
- **Communication:** Language in any country is a major method of communication and it creates serious problems when there is a difficulty with the written and spoken word. These barriers may mean that foreign prisoners are ignorant of the basic rights they possess, are unsure of how to obtain help, or complain about improper treatment.
- **Culture:** Foreign prisoners have different religious and dietary needs and they have a right to have those needs respected while they are in prison. Differences in cultural backgrounds, and ignorance of the details, can become sources for resentment and discrimination.
- **Isolation:** The visits that many British nationals take for granted are often impossible for those who come from overseas. Family and friends suffer in addition to the prisoner as both endure the fear and worry which comes from being isolated.

- **Fear & Mistrust:** Lack of knowledge of the system and difficulties in communicating are themselves responsible for increasing the feelings of fear and mistrust that imprisonment in such conditions frequently engenders. Many foreign prisoners find it difficult to establish trust in their lawyer, probation officer or medical staff to whom they turn for help. In many cases their fear comes from simply not knowing what these services are designed to do for them.

Remember these points next time you see such a prisoner attempting to make sense out of what is, even to UK nationals, this bewildering world we call 'prison'

Three words of warning

If you are a foreign national here are three words of warning:

1. Do not expect the British criminal Justice system to operate in the same way as your own—the chances are it is quite different.
2. Holding a non-British passport does NOT give you immunity from the laws applicable to the United Kingdom.
3. It is vital that you understand all your rights. If you have difficulty with English you have the right to the services of an interpreter.

Holding centres

On 15th June 1994 Derek Lewis, Director General of HM Prison Service said that the Prison Service is to reduce the number of prisons used to hold immigration detainees. These detainees were held there detainees are held at 41 different locations but, by September 1994, this will be reduced to five: **Birmingham, Holloway, Rochester, Doncaster and Haslar**. 'By focusing resources on five prisons' said Mr Lewis, 'the Prison Service and Immigration and Nationality Departments will be able to provide more language and support services for foreign nationals. . . . It will allow immigration staff the opportunity to visit each of the five prisons on a daily basis and staff in those prisons to develop an expertise in dealing with a consistent population. At a time of rising prison population the move will also help the Prison Service by removing immigration detainees from local prisons.'

Courts and counsel

There are two kinds of lawyer in England and Wales, a **Solicitor** and a **Barrister**. The solicitor will help you to prepare your case for court, while the barrister will present your case at the trial. Legal fees are normally paid by the Legal Aid Fund, though if you have sufficient money legal aid can be refused. There are also two sets of courts. The **Magistrates Court** in which your case will be initially heard, is presided over by non-lawyers (mainly), called **Magistrates**. For serious offences their duty is to forward to a more senior court those cases which are required to be tried there, or which are too serious to be tried by the Magistrates. The senior criminal court is called the **Crown Court**, presided over by a Circuit Judge, or High Court Judge, who have been promoted from the ranks of practising lawyers—usually Barristers.

Deportation

When you were sentenced to imprisonment the court may have recommended that you be deported on completion of your sentence. If the court made no such recommendation, it remains open to the Home Secretary to exercise his administrative powers to remove you from the UK if he believes your removal will be conducive to the public good. Before a deportation order can be made all relevant circumstances have to be taken into account and each case is considered on its individual merits. You can appeal against a deportation order, either to the Court of Appeal if the trial judge recommended your deportation, or to an independent appeals body if the Home Secretary has sought to deport you of his own motion. Your RRLO will have all the details and probably written in your own language.

Repatriation

If you are a foreign national you may be allowed to transfer to your own country to complete a sentence imposed by a court in the UK. You have no 'right' of repatriation: it is entirely a matter of discretion for the appropriate UK authorities, and those in your home country. If you require further details of repatriation, your prison probation officer will be able to tell you whether you qualify and, if so, inform you of the necessary steps to take in your establishment.

Customs and Excise

If you were arrested by Customs Officers in relation to drugs, the Officer will estimate the value of the drugs based on their weight and purity. The drugs are then sent for expert analysis to an chemist independent of the Customs & Excise. You will be served with a form that informs you that you have 28 days to appeal against the destruction of the large majority of the drugs, only a small sample of drugs and wrappings being kept as evidence for the trial. The Customs Officer will also give you a list of property taken from you, study the form carefully. There are three columns: Seized, Detained and Exhibited, and Custodial. Property that is listed as **Seized** will not be returned to you. Property listed as **Detained and Exhibited** may be returned to you if you are acquitted at the close of your trial. Property listed as **Custodial**, is that which you are allowed to retain.

Embassies

Most Embassies adopt a diplomatic low profile attitude when their nationals are imprisoned in the UK. Your Embassy cannot intervene to obtain your release from prison or from prosecution. Your Embassy will neither recommend nor provide you with legal representation, nor will they attend your trial with you. They are unlikely to offer any form of legal advice or interpretation of British laws. You are unlikely to receive any financial help from your Embassy towards paying for a lawyer, though they may help you transfer funds from your own country. Your Embassy will not give any financial help to any relatives visiting you from abroad. Details of some Embassies are given at the end of the chapter.

Information available

Some official information is already available in translation, and you should be able to obtain this from the prison library:

- Prisoners' Information Pack (Prison Reform Trust/HM Prison Service publication.
- Prison Rules 1964 as amended
- Immigration leaflets
- 'How To Make A Complaint' booklet
- Repatriation White Paper
- Custody, Care & Justice
- Race Relations Statement
- Life Sentence Information
- Parole Information
- F2042 Notice for the Information of Inmates.

Language Line

In addition to the above, HM Prison Service have also paid for all prisons to have access to Language Line—a telephone interpreting service offering over 140 languages, available 24 hours a day seven day a week. The costs of the calls are paid for by the Governor out of his annual budget. A Language Line Information Pack was sent to all prisons in April 1993.

Language Line, 18 Victoria Park Square, London E2 9PF.
Interpreters: 081-981-9911. Administration: 081-983-4042

Other translation services

The following bodies are able to assist with translation, though they may require a fee for their services:

- **Institute of Linguists**
  24a Higbury Grove
  London N5 2AE
  071-359-7445
  Language department with translators. Also operates the **Association of Community Interpreters**
- **The Ethnic Switchboard**
  081-682-0216
  Hourly fee payable. Many linguists, including medically trained.
- **British Red Cross Emergency Multi-lingual Phrasebook.**
  The Red Cross
  9 Grosvenor Crescent
  London SW1
  071-235-5454
- **Greater London Translation Unit**
  5–5A Westminster Bridge Road
  London SE1 7XW
  071-928-9889
  Translation, interpretation and printing services in: Arabic, Chinese, Farsi, Greek, Gujarati, Hindi, Italian, Malayalan, Punjabi, Portuguese, Somali, Spanish, Tamil, Urdu, and Vietnamese.

Immigration: contacts and addresses

The Home Office Immigration Department
Lunar House
Wellesley Road
Croydon CR9 2BY
081-760-1563/2473
Headquarters of the Immigration Department

The Home Office Nationality Department
3rd Floor, India Buildings
Water Street
Liverpool L2 OQN
051-227-3939
Deals with most cases of Nationality.

Asylum Department
Quest House
Wellesley Road
Croydon CR9 2BY
081-760-4838
Deals with most cases of asylum.

UK Immigration Advisory Service
190 Dover Street
London SE1 4YB
071-357-6917/7511
Offers a range of services including information about appeals.

Joint Council for the Welfare of Immigrants
115 Old Street
London EC1V 9JR
071-251-8706

Greater Manchester Immigration Aid Unit
400 Cheetham Hill Road
Manchester M8 7EL
061-740-7722

Independent Immigration Support Agency
3rd Floor, Spencer House
Digbeth
Birmingham. B5 6DD
021-622-7353

Embassies and Commissions

Belgian Embassy
103 Eaton Square
London SW1W 9AB

Bolivian Embassy
106 Eaton Square
London SW1W 9AD
071-235-4248
Contact: Mrs Gabriella Vargas

Brazilian Embassy
32 Green Street
London W1Y 4AT
071-499-0877
Contact: Mr Romvaldo/Mrs C Sinclair

Candian High Commission
Macdonald House
1 Grosvenor Square
London W1X OAB
071-629-9492
Contact: Mr A Charbonneau

Colombian Embassy
Flat 3a, Hans Crescent
London SW1X OLR
071-589-9177
Contact: Ms Liliana Bonila-Otoya

French Embassy
58 Knightsbridge
London SW1X 7JT
071-235-8080
Contact: Mrs Colette Muguet-Shukor

German Embassy
23 Belgrave Square
London SW1X 8PZ
071-235-5033
Contact: 1st Secretary

Guyana High Commission
3 Palace Court
Bayswater Road
London W2
071-229-7684

Indian High Commission
Aldwych
London WC2B 4NA
071-836-8484

Embassy of Israel
2 Palace Green
London W8 4QB
071-937-8050

Italian Embassy
14 Three Kings Yard
London W1Y 2EH
071-629-8200

Royal Netherlands Embassy
38 Hyde Park Gate
London SW7 5DP
071-584-5040

New Zealand High Commission
Haymarket
London SW1 4TQ
071-930-8422

Nigerian High Commission
9 Northumberland Avenue
London WC2 5BX
071-839-1244
Contact: Ms Iris Amoah

High Commission for Pakistan
35 Lowndes Square
London SW1X 9JN
071-235-2044

Embassy of the Philippines
9A Palace green
London W8 4QE
071-937-1600
Contact: Estrella Berenguel

High Commission for Singapore
9 Wilton Crescent
London SW1X 8SA
071-235-8315
Contact: Tan Wah Sern

South African Embassy
Trafalgar Square
London WC2N 5DP
071-930-4488

Spanish Embassy
16th Floor Portland House
London SW1E 5SE
071-235-5555
Contact: Araceli Garcia

Turkish Embassy
43 Belgrave Square
London SW1X 8PA
071-235-5252
Contact: Mrs Gulgun Taslica

American Embassy
Grosvenor Square
London W1A 1AE
071-839-5783

Useful independent contacts

Immigration law and procedures are extremely complex, and it is vital to obtain professional legal (and general) advice as soon as possible. Listed below are the names of independent advisors who have wide experience of immigration matters.

- **Wesley Gryk:** solicitor, BM Birnberg & Co, 103 Borough High Street, London SE1 1NN (071-403-3166) has both an expert knowledge and a sound track record in this complex area.
- **Nick Hammond/Rosemary Abernethy:** both probation officers with Middlesex Area Probation Service who together run the Foreign Nationals Illegal Drug Importers Project at

Heathrow Airport. Well informed on legal/welfare difficulties faced by foreign prisoners convicted of drug traffiking.

Ayesha Tarzi: ILPS Foreign Offenders Co-ordinator, Central Resources Dept, Lansdale House, 57 Buckingham Gate, London, SW1E 6AJ (071-931-8722). Co-author of 'Prison Within a Prison' on the experiences of foreign nationals imprisoned in the UK. Well informed on contacts, and wide-ranging linguist.

Prison Reform Trust . . . Publications 1994/5

59, Caledonian Road, London N1 9BU.
Tel: 071-279-9815. Fax: 071-833-5543

IISSION STATEMENT
he work of the Prison Reform Trust is aimed at reating a just, humane and effective penal system. /e do this by: inquiring into the workings of the ystem; informing prisoners, staff, and the wider ublic; and by influencing Parliament, overnment and officials towards Reform.

EYOND CONTAINMENT—the penal response to ex offending. £4.95, ISBN 0 946209 21 9. Seven napters, written by acknowledged experts in this eld, this book covers all aspects of the penal esponse.

LACK WORKERS IN THE PRISON SERVICE by obin Alfred. £2.95, ISBN 0 946209 22 7. The report scusses racism in the Prison Service and focuses particular on the personal experiences of black aff.

HE WOOLF REPORT—A SUMMARY. £3.45 ISBN 946209 19 7. This booklet summarises Lord istice Woolf's main recommendations in an easy--read format.

EFORM, RENEWAL AND REHABILITATION by r Robert Runcie. £1.95 ISBN 0 946209 16 2. In this amphlet the former Archbishop of Canterbury esents one of the most significant theological ontributions to penal debate for many years.

ACKLING FINE DEFAULT. £2.95 ISBN 0 946209 6. This report sets out an agenda for better prac-e and makes an important contribution the role monetary penalties and their enforcement

IV, AIDS & PRISONS. £2.95 ISBN 0946209 12 X. is report details the dilemmas HIV and AIDS use in prisons and recommends steps to reduce e risk.

RISON RULES: A WORKING GUIDE. Edited & vised by Nancy Loucks. Each Prison Rule and uivalent European Prison Rule is cited in full, Standing Orders and Circular Instructions with full commentary.

A LOOK INSIDE. £6.25 A pack designed for students aged 13 upwards, with factsheets on Prison Life, Women in prison, Remand, Young People in custody and the alternatives to it.

PRISON REPORT. Quarterly magazine of the Prison Reform Trust, packed with articles, news and features. Annual subscription of £15 includes 40% discount on other PRT publications.

REPORT OF THE COMMITTEE ON THE PENALTY OF HOMICIDE. £5.95 ISBN 0 945209 25 1. The report of an independent inquiry—chaired by ex-Lord Chief Justice, Lord Lane, into the mandatory life sentence for murder.

PRIVATISATION & MARKET TESTING IN THE PRISON SERVICE. £4.95 ISBN 0 946209 26 X. The Government's policy of private sector involvement in the penal system explored in five widely different contributions.

PRISON MAGAZINES: A SURVEY & GUIDE. £3.95 ISBN 0 946209 27 8. This PRT report reviews a selection of prison magazines and identifies some of the problems they have encountered.

THE CHANGING ROLE OF PRISON BOARDS OF VISITORS. £3.95 ISBN 0 946209 27 8. Based on interviews with current board members, this report presents a detailed account of how boards operate in practice.

FEAR IN PRISONS A DISCUSSION PAPER by Joanna Adler. £2. This PRT paper, based on research at three prisons, investigates the nature of both staff and prisoner fears.

Payment can be by cheque or postal order, made payable to the Prison Reform Trust, or (subject to a minimum order of £10) by credit card.

N.A.C.R.O. . . . Publications 1994/5

NACRO, The National Association for the Care and Resettlement of Offenders, is an independent voluntary organisation working to prevent crime and promote the resettlement of offenders in the community.

NACRO ADVICE LEAFLETS. Pack includes leaflets on: Planning for Release, Housing, Employment, Education & Training, DSS Benefits, Alcohol and Drugs. Single pack free, multiple copies £1 each.
KEEPING YOUR HOME. Gives information to prisoners on getting housing costs paid while inside.

Includes standard letters to the various officials. Single pack free, multiple copies 20p each.
OUTSIDE HELP. Gives practical information for the families and friends of people in prison to help them keep in touch and know how the system works. Single pack free, multiple copies 20p each.
INFORMATION ON CRIMINAL JUSTICE. NACRO also produces a wide range of publications giving factual information about crime and criminal justice and outlining policies and strategies for change. Two subscription mailings are available: a quarterly criminal justice mailing, providing up-to-date information on the latest developments in criminal justice and penal affairs, containing the NACRO Criminal Justice Digest, briefing papers and factsheets: and a quarterly Youth Crime section mailing containing essential information for practitioners and others interested in youth crime and young offenders.

To order publications or to receive a catalogue containing further details and an order form, please contact:
NACRO PUBLICATIONS, 169 CLAPHAM ROAD, LONDON SW9 OPU. Tel: 071 582 6500

;ECTION THREE

JSEFUL ORGANISATIONS

CONTENTS

If you operate a relevant organisation that you would like to have listed in this section, please send full details to the Handbook address shown in the introduction: mark your envelope 'Useful Organisations'.

he following pages list dozens of organisations ıat cater for prisoners and their families in a wide ariety of ways: from advice, counselling and sup- ort, to bus services and vetted escorts for children ·anting to visit their parents in prison. Details of ıl the approved Bail and Probation hostels in ngland and Wales are given, along with details of əlf-help groups.

'lease note

: you represent an organisation listed in this sec- on, please advise us of any changes so that mendments can be made for the next edition. If ou represent an organisation that is NOT cur- əntly listed in this section, and which you would ke carried in the next edition, then please write vith FULL DETAILS—and about 100 words xplaining what it is you do and how you do it. 'here is no charge for this service.

'RISON REFORM TRUST

.5 NORTHBURGH STREET
ONDON EC1V OAH
EL: 071 251 5070
AX: 071 251 5076
·irector: Stephen Shaw
:hair: Jon Snow

PRT is a national charity which campaigns for better conditions in prison and greater use of alternatives to custody. It is able to deal with enquiries about various aspects of imprisonment and complaints about treatment of individuals in prison, but not with cases of wrongful conviction. PRT also produces various publications and a quarterly journal. One of the best penal reform groups around.

JUSTICE

59 CARTER LANE
LONDON EC4V 5AQ
TEL: 071 329 5100
FAX: 071 329 5055

JUSTICE campaigns for law reform. It is sometimes able to help prisoners by investigating cases where there is a valid complaint about conviction or sentence. Emphasis is mainly on longer sentence prisoners. Heavily over-burdened with casework, but committed to those cases they do take on.

NATIONAL PRISONERS' MOVEMENT

BM-PROP
LONDON WC1N 3XX
TEL: 081 542 3744
Director: Geoff Coggan

Founded by Dick Pooley on the exercise yard of Dartmoor prison in 1972, the National Prisoners' Movement (formerly known as PROP) handles enquiries from prisoners and their families. NPM is able to provide legal and medical back-up in cases of complaints about prison treatment. An organisation which has built a solid reputation for getting things done.

P.A.I.N.
BM-PAIN
LONDON WC1N 3XX.
TEL: 081 542 3744
Co-ordinator: Geoff Coggan

Prisoners' Advice and Information Network is an umbrella organisation which incorporates the NATIONAL PRISONERS MOVEMENT, WOMEN IN PRISON, RADICAL ALTERNATIVES TO PRISON, INQUEST and the BLACK FEMALE PRISONERS' SCHEME. Your letter will be passed by PAIN to the right section. Created by Geoff Coggan of NPM.

INQUEST
ALEXANDER NATIONAL HOUSE
330 SEVEN SISTERS ROAD
LONDON N4 2JP
TEL: 081 802 7430
Contact: Deborah Coles

INQUEST is an advice, information and support group concerned with deaths in custody. Many of these deaths raise issues about treatment and care of people in prisons, psychiatric hospitals or police cells. INQUEST can help families with legal representation and preparation for the inquest; ensuring these deaths are properly investigated. A group who have brought deaths in cutody into the spotlight and achieved excellent results.

NATIONAL ASSOCIATION FOR THE CARE & RESETTLEMENT OF OFFENDERS (NACRO)
169, CLAPHAM ROAD
LONDON SW9 OPU
TEL: 071 582 6500.
Information Officer: Mervyn Barrett

NACRO provides various services for ex-prisoners, including housing, resettlement and education. They also administer a number of employment training schemes. There are offices in different parts of the country, so to get an idea of how NACRO may be able to help you, write to the London office. Often under-rated by prisoners, NACRO is an essential point of contact for those approaching release.

PRISONERS' ADVICE SERVICE
57 CHALTON STREET
LONDON NW1 1HU
TEL: 071 388 8586
Solicitor: Simon Creighton.
Caseworker: Vickie King

The PAS was launched in May 1991 and has become a bedrock of resolving disputes in prisons. PAS takes up complaints about prison treatment but has no facilities to deal with miscarriages of justice other than internal adjudications. A professional service well used by prisoners. Now a wholly independent charity.

PRISON CHARITY SHOPS TRUST
24, ST.ANN'S TERRACE,
LONDON NW8 6PJ

Prison Charity Shops scheme is a shared venture between the Prison Services throughout the United Kingdom and the Prison Charity Shops Trust. Quality merchandise produced in prisons is offered for sale in 'time...' shops with the profits donated to charity. The big drawback is that individual prisoners do not receive any money from the sale, unlike items sold in the HALOW (London) shop—see below.

SOCIETY OF VOLUNTARY ASSOCIATES
BRIXTON HILL PLACE
LONDON SW2 1HJ
TEL: 081 969 9133

SOVA promotes voluntary action in the penal field by recruiting, training and deploying volunteers to work alongside statutory agencies. SOVA volunteers work in IT schemes, family groups, day centres, hostels, prisons and Young Offender Institutions. SOVA represents an excellent way of getting involved in prison work on a voluntary basis.

THE NEW BRIDGE
27A MEDWAY STREET
LONDON SW1P 2BD
TEL: 071 976 0779
FAX: 071 976 0767
Director: Eric McGraw.

THE NEW BRIDGE provides a befriending service to prisoners during sentence and after release. There is a job-finding and advisory service for those seeking employment in Greater London. The New Bridge publish INSIDE TIME, the prisoners' national newspaper. The TV docu-drama 'Knock-Back' gave TNB a staid image. 'Inside Time' changed that, though many governors still refuse to allow the paper to be circulated.

NATIONAL ASSOCIATION OF PRISON VISITORS
49B HARTINGTON STREET
BEDFORD MK41 7RL
TEL:0234 359763

NAPV co-ordinates the activities of prison visitors and promotes prison visiting, especially in those prisons where there are no PV's or very few. PV's are not to be confused with Boards of Visitors. NAPV has close links with the Home Office which has stilted its image with prisoners; equally, this level of contact has enabled PV's to solve a problem when other avenues have failed.

THE ALDO TRUST (NACRO)
169 CLAPHAM ROAD
LONDON SW9 OPU
TEL: 071 582 6500

The ALDO TRUST provides financial assistance to individual prisoners. It concentrates on three broad areas: education, recreation and outside links. Requests have to come from prison probation staff—NOT PRISONERS DIRECT. Grants usually about £10 and applications on behalf of groups of prisoners accepted also. Decisions fairly fast.

TERRENCE HIGGINS TRUST
52–54 GRAYS INN ROAD
LONDON WC1X 8JU
TEL: 071 242 1010

THT provides information, counselling, advice and support on all matters relating to prisoners who are HIV+. THT also has a special division 'IN CUSTODY' specifically for prisoners. Also provides a 'Buddy' service which befriends prisoners who are HIV+ or have AIDS. By far the best organisation for prisoners who are HIV positive. Gives advice on special diets available to HIV+ prisoners.

WOMEN IN PRISON
(U3) ABERDEEN STUDIOS
22 HIGHBURY GROVE
LONDON N5
TEL: 071 226 5879

WIP is an ex-prisoner organisation campaigning on the issue of female imprisonment. Contact from any female prisoner, on any subject, is welcome. Founded by Chris Tchaikovsky. Conditions for female prisoners are often marginalised when set against the larger male population and Women in Prison provides an important voice which is often missing from penal debates.

BRIXTON CARES
13 LOUGHBOROUGH PARK
BRIXTON
LONDON SW9 8TP
TEL: 071 738 4818

BC is a local community group based in the Brixton 'frontline' area. It specialises in visiting prisoners in London prisons and helping them through the criminal justice process from arrest onwards. They can arrange for black prison visitors. Primarily for black prisoners, BC also runs a holiday scheme and supplementary school to cater for black children who may have one or both parents in prison.

BLACK FEMALE PRISONERS' SCHEME
444 BRIXTON ROAD
LONDON SW9 1BZ
TEL: 071 733 5520

BFPS provides advice and assistance for black women both while in prison and after release. Information about housing, deportation problems, discharge grants and benefits given. For 10 years BFPS has been a vital link between black female prisoners and the community—well worth making contact no matter where you are in your sentence.

PARTNERS OF PRISONERS & FAMILIES SUPPORT GROUP
ST MARKS CHEETHAM
TETLOW LANE
MANCHESTER. M8 7HF
TEL: 061 740 8600

POPS is a registered charity run by prisoners' families who offer moral support and friendship to prisoners' families and partners. Although based in Manchester members of POPS are willing to help anyone from the North of England or North Wales. Founded by Farida Anderson in 1989, POPS has earned a good reputation both inside and outside prison; a group which will grow rapidly in the years to come given the funding.

WOMEN PRISONERS' RESOURCE CENTRE
1 THORPE CLOSE
LADBROOK GROVE
LONDON W10 5XL
TEL: 081 968 3121

WRPC workers regularly visit all female prisons to give advice and information about housing and other facilities open to women returning to the London area. They also offer advice and support to female prisoners after release. Well organised and reliable.

CREATIVE AND SUPPORT TRUST (CAST)
37–39 KINGS TERRACE
LONDON NW1
TEL: 071 383 5228

CAST have workshops where women released from prison can train in various skills. Under-rated as a result of it not being well-known; an organisation which has much to offer female prisoners who need help on release.

GAY RIGHTS IN PRISON
82 BARNETT ROAD
HOLLINGDEAN
BRIGHTON BN1 7GH

GRIP assists gay, lesbian and bisexual prisoners. It offers correspondence, visiting, housing on release and general support. Said to have branches in London, Derby and short-term hostel available in Brighton. However, this much needed minority group appears to have faded into almost non-existence in recent years.

IRISH COMMISSION FOR PRISONERS OVERSEAS
BERRYMEAD GARDENS
LONDON W3 8AA

Fr Paddy Smith at the ICPO provides help and information for Irish born prisoners and their families. An organisation which has much work to do if it is to improve its disappointing reputation among Irish prisoners in the UK.

THE PEOPLE'S PLACE
338 OLD STREET
LONDON EC1V 9LT
TEL: 071 729 5050

TPP provides a range of services mainly for black offenders and ex-offenders aged 17–25, along with their families and dependents. Services include advice and counselling, support and befriending through correspondence and visits while in prison. Good reputation for reliability and consistancy in contact.

RASTAFARIAN ADVISORY CENTRE
17A NETHERWOOD ROAD
LONDON W14
TEL: 071 602 3767

RAC offers a befriending service to Rastafarian and other black prisoners. Visits to prisoners are arranged and they provide support to families as well as offering help and advice on release. Based in London and more of help to those in the SE Region.

JOINT COUNCIL FOR THE WELFARE OF IMMIGRANTS
115 OLD STREET
LONDON EC1V 9JR
TEL: 071 251 8706

JCWI offers help, information and advice to prisoners who have problems with immigration laws or who are threatened with deportation. Very heavy caseload often prevents delivery of a keep-you-informed service. Knowledgable and up to date.

NATIONAL ASSOCIATION OF CITIZENS ADVICE BUREAUX
115 PENTONVILLE ROAD
LONDON N1 9LZ
TEL: 071 833 2181

NACAB co-ordinates around 1000 CAB offices around the country. Some prisons already have CAB staff visiting once per month. Able to provide advice and information and advocacy on a huge range of issues. Excellent results reported from those prisons where CAB staff provide advice sessions—if your prison doesn't have this facility, organise it.

ANGULIMALA
THE FOREST HERMITAGE
LOWER FULBROOK
WARWICK CV35 8AS

The Buddhist Prison Chaplaincy Organisation. Makes available facilities for the teaching and practice of Buddhism in prison. If you are having difficulties practising your Buddhist religion, this is the place to take your complaint if internal avenues fail.

SOLO PROJECT
SUMNER ROAD
LONDON SE15
TEL: 071 252 8022

SOLO is an educational/training advice and counselling service for offenders and ex-offenders based in Southwark. Plenty of job contacts in the London area and a good success rate.

PRISON LINK PROJECT
CHI COMMUNITY CENTRE
48A SEVEN SISTERS ROAD
LONDON N7 6AA.
TEL: 071 607 7373

PLP provides a confidential advice, information and referral service for prisoners due to be released, ex-prisoners and the family and friends of prisoners and ex-prisoners. They can offer support and advice in housing, jobs and training, education, welfare benefits, health and legal problems. Excellent all-round help, support and advice service.

SERIOUS OFFENDERS FAMILIES ASSOCIATION (SOFA)
7 PEEL STREET
SPRING BANK
HULL HU3 1QR
TEL: 0482 28284

SOFA supports the other innocent victims of crime—the family of the offender. Support to those in the Humberside area is provided by those who are themselves the family members of serious offenders. A good idea which deserves to spread throughout the country.

NARCOTICS ANONYMOUS
PO BOX 417
LONDON SW10 ORN
TEL: 071 351 6794

NA is a non-profit making fellowship of men and women for whom drugs had become a major problem. They are recovering addicts who meet regularly to help each other remain drug-free. Often viewed cynically by the authorities, NA does much good work for those who genuinely want to be drug-free.

VISITORS TRAVELLING EXCHANGE
16 STUART MANTLE WAY
ERITH
KENT DA8 3LQ

VTE is run by Mrs Jay Leffew who provides a central exchange for people wishing to share the cost of travel/boarding when visiting prisoners. An excellent scheme.

THE BOURNE TRUST
189A OLD BROMPTON ROAD
LONDON SW5 OAR
TEL: 071 370 0883

BT—formerly known as Catholic Social Service for Prisoners—provides practical help, counselling and support to prisoners, ex-prisoners and their families regardless of religious belief. Volunteers operate in Preston, Durham and London—information desk set up at Wormwood Scrubs. A general support group which also offers small financial grants.

PRISONERS' FAMILIES & FRIENDS
106 WESTON STREET
LONDON SE1 3QG

PFF offers an advice and information service to any relative or friend of a prisoner who contacts them. They can also visit prisoners families in the Inner London area only. Small group based in South London, friendly and helpful to those who need support.

HALOW (LONDON)
193 BROOK DRIVE
LONDON SE11 4TG
TEL: 071 793 7484
FAX: 071 793 7230
Contact: Julie Robertson or Jill Swift

HALOW: Help & Advice Line for Prisoners, Ex-prisoners, Partners, Families & Friends. Founded by two prisoners' wives, HALOW (London) provides excellent services: welfare advice, advocacy, penpals, support groups, counselling, shop selling prisoner-made items (with profit going to the prisoner). Bus services to HMPs: Bullingdon, Bullwood, Coldingley, Dartmoor, Ford, Frankland, Gartree, Grendon, Littlehey, L/Lartin, Whitemoor. Child Escorting Service, with vetted escorts.

AFTERMATH
PO BOX 414
SHEFFIELD S1 UP
TEL: 0742 326166

Founded by the irrepressible Shirl Marshall, AFTERMATH is a help and advice service for serious offenders' (murder, rape, GBH) families. Taking care of those we have left behind but never forget, AFTERMATH helps them comes to terms with often many years of separation.

GRUPO AMIGA
WOMEN IN PRISON
ABERDEEN STUDIOS
22 HIGBURY GROVE
LONDON N5

GA is an organisation which gives support to Latin American women in British prisons. Grupo Amiga's are all women and they all either speak Spanish or Portuguese. A relative newcomer to the Advice/ Support scene, but one which was long overdue.

PRISON LINK
25 TRINITY ROAD
ASTON
BIRMINGHAM B6 6AJ
Tel 021 551 1207

PL provides a transport, counselling and advice service for families of prisoners from ethnic minority groups, where the family is based in the West Midlands area. Provides free legal advice and arranges legal representation. Reliable and well established in the West Midlands.

THE HOWARD LEAGUE FOR PENAL REFORM

708 HOLLOWAY ROAD
LONDON N19 3NL
TEL: 071 281 7722

The Howard League is an independent charity working for reform of the criminal justice and penal systems.

PENAL AFFAIRS CONSORTIUM

c/o NACRO
169 CLAPHAM ROAD
LONDON SW9 0PU
TEL: 071 582 6500
FAX: 071 735 1673
Chair: Paul Cavadino

The Penal Affairs Consortium comprises 24 penal organisations most of which exist to help the prisoner—others, like the Prison Officers Association, do not! The aim is to provide a mechanism whereby member organisations can work together for penal reform by presenting joint views to Government, Parliament and the public. Consortium members: APEX TRUST, ACPO, AmBOV, BOURNE TRUST, BRIDGE-BUILDERS, HOWARD LEAGUE, INQUEST, IPMS, JUSTICE, LIBERTY, NACRO, NAPO, NATIONAL FORUM OF CARE TRUSTS, THE NEW BRIDGE, PRISONERS' ABROAD, PRISONERS' ADVICE SERVICE, PRISONERS' FAMILY & FRIENDS SERVICE, PRISONERS' RESOURCE SERVICE, PRISON GOVERNORS ASSOCIATION, POA, PRISON REFORM TRUST, RPS, SVA, WOMEN IN PRISON.

JUSTICE FOR ALL

THE MANCHESTER MCKENZIE ORGANISATION
CRIMINAL APPEAL ADVISORS/INVESTIGATORS
1 ALLERFORD CLOSE
ALEXANDRA PARK
MANCHESTER M16 7AY
TEL: 0161 226 5626
Contact: James Stevenson / Dr Peter Wright.

JFA has been operating for six years as a private non-profit making criminal investigation agency based in Manchester. It aims to assist anyone wrongfully convicted in the UK, provided there is a serious prospect of achieving justice. Good track record and extensive list of useful contacts.

SELF-HELP GROUPS

STANDING CONFERENCE ON DRUG ABUSE
1–4 Hatton Place, Hatton Garden, London EC1N 8ND.
Tel: 0171 430 2341
The main co-ordinating body for organisations working in the field of drug abuse.

RELEASE
169 Commercial Street, London E1 3BW
Tel: 0171 603 8654—24 Hrs
Provides advice on legal issues relating to drug problems, office staffed Monday-Friday 10–6pm.

RE SOLV
30a High Street, Stone, Staffs ST15 8AW
Tel: 01785 817885
National charity dealing with all aspects of solvent abuse.

MAINLINERS
205 Stockwell Road, London SW9 9SL
Tel: 0171 738 4656
Organisation run by ex-drug users and catering mainly for those who are HIV positive or who have AIDS.

CADA
359 Old Kent Road, London SE1 5JH
Tel: 0171 237 8784
Non residential drug treatment centre, home methadone detox, counselling and needle exchange scheme.

MIND
22 Harley Street, London W1N 2ED
Tel: 0171 637 0741
MIND is the co-ordinating body for withdrawal self-help groups around the country.

TURNING POINT
New Loom House, 101 Back Church Lane, London E1 1LU
Tel: 0171 702 2300
Charity with 23 projects ranging from information, counselling, residential homes. Operates nationwide for both drugs and alcohol.

PHOENIX HOUSE
47–49 Borough High Street, London SE1 1NB
Tel: 0171 407 2789
Provides residential services in London, East Sussex, Merseyside, Tyneside, Sheffield and Glasgow. Prison Liaison Worker: 0191 454 5544.

NARCOTICS ANONYMOUS
PO Box 704. London SW10 0RN
Tel: 0171 351 6794—24 Hrs
Large number of self-help groups around the country.

DRINKLINE
7th Floor Weddel House, 13–14 West Smithfield, London EC1A 9DL
Tel: 0171 332 0202

Information, advice and support for those with a drink problem.

ALCOHOLICS ANONYMOUS
PO Box 1, Stonebow House, Stonebow, York YO1 2JN
Tel: 01904 644026
The main organisation for those wishing to help themselves come off alcohol, branches throughout the country and in many prisons.

GAMBLERS ANONYMOUS
PO Box 88, London SW10 OEU
Tel: 0171 384 3040
Main organisation for those who wish to help themselves stay free of gambling. Also Gam-Anon for partners and family of those who have a problem with gambling—same number.

ACOMB HOUSE
141–143 Dickenson Road, Rusholme, Manchester M14 5HZ
Tel: 0161 224 7272
Caters for male ex-offenders, 40+ with alcohol, drug or mental problems.

EFFRA TRUST
Eurolink Business Centre, Unit 7, 49 Effra Road, Brixton, London SW2 1BZ
Tel: 0171 326 1013
Specialist organisation offering accommodation and support to ex-offenders with mental health difficulties. Room for 33 clients.

IRIS HOUSE TRUST
68 Bath Road, Worcester WR5 3EW
Tel: 01905 35388
Specialist parole hostel for those difficult to place, 24 hour staff cover. Nationwide catchment area, and 100 per cent Home Office funded. A proven track record with long term offenders.

HENDERSON HOSPITAL
2 Homeland Drive, Brighton Road, Sutton, Surrey SM2 5LT
Tel: 0181 661 1611
The Henderson Hospital has long been a well respected therapeutic community for adults 17–45. Group work but no medication. residents encouraged to stay for one year, though they are free to leave at any time. Hard but worthwhile therapy for those who complete the course.

CROWN PROSECUTION SERVICE HQ

50 LUDGATE HILL
LONDON EC4M 7EX
TEL: 0171 273 8000

CPS AREA OFFICES

NORTH
Benton House, 136 Sandyford Road, Newcastle upon Tyne NE2 1QE.
Tel: 0191 201 2390.

YORKS.
Area HQ, Ryedale Building, 60 Piccadilly, York YO1 1NS.
Tel: 01904 610726.

LANCS.
Royal Liver Building, Pier Head, Liverpool L3 1HN.
Tel: 0151 236 7575.

HUMBER.
Belgrave House, 47 Bank Street, Sheffield. S1 2EH.
Tel: 0114 273 1261.

NORTH WEST
Sunlight House, Quay Street, Manchester M60 3LU.
0161 837 7402.

MIDLANDS
2 King Edward Court, Nottingham, NG1 1EL.
Tel: 0115 948 0480, and
2 Colmore Row, Birmingham B3 2QA.
Tel: 0121 629 7200.

WALES
16 Cathedral Road, Cardiff CF1 9LJ.
Tel: 01222 783000.

ANGLIA
58 Victoria Street, St.Albans. AL1 3HZ.
Tel: 01727 818100.

THAMES
Artillery House, Heritage Way, Worcester WR9 8YB.
Tel: 01905 795477.

S/WEST
Hawkins House, Paynes Hill, Exeter, EX2 5SS.
Tel: 01392 422555.

LONDON
Portland House, Stag Place, London SW1E 5BH.
Tel: 0171 915 5700.

APPROVED PROBATION AND BAIL HOSTELS

AVON
Bridge House, 74–78 Filton Road, Bristol BS7 0PD
Tel: 0117 942 5851. 17+yrs, 29 places.

BERKS
St. Leonards Hostel, 2 Southcote Road, Reading RG2 2AA
Tel: 01734 573 171. 17+yrs, 23 places.

Manor Lodge, 8 Straight Road, Slough SL4 2RL
Tel: 01753 868 807. 17+yrs, 22 places.

Wellesley House, Vansittart Road, Slough SL4 5DB
Tel: 01753 857 010. 17+ yrs, 18 places.

CAMBS
5 Wesleyan Road, Peterborough PE1 3RZ
Tel: 01733 51678/9. 17+yrs, 32 places.

CHES
Bunbury House, Alswick Drive, Ellesmere Port
L65 9HE
Tel: 0151 357 3551/4. 17+yrs, 22 places.

CLEVE
13 The Crescent, Middlesborough TS5 6SQ
Tel: 01662 826 606. 17+yrs, 26 places.

DEVON
Lawson House, 14 Paradise Place, Plymouth PL2
Tel: 01752 568 791. 17+yrs, 20 places.

DORSET
11 Cecil Road, Boscombe, Bournemouth BH5 1DU
Tel: 01202 391 756. 17+yrs, 18 places.

HERTS
294/298 St. Albans Road, Watford WD2 5PE
Tel: 01923 35983. 17+yrs, 26 places.

HUMBER
41 Queens Road, Hull HU5 2QW
Tel: 01482 446284/5. 17+yrs, 22 places.

LANCS
Highfield House, Lydia Street, Accrington BB5 0PX
TEL: 01254 395 997. 17+yrs, 18 places.

LEICS
Charnwood Lodge, 42 Fosse Road South, Leicester
LE3 0QD
Tel: 01254 395 997. 17+yrs, 18 places.

LINCS
Wordsworth House, 205 Yarborough Road, Lincoln
LN1 3NQ
Tel: 01522 28520.17+yrs, 26 places.

LONDON (Inner)
Ellison House, 370 Albany Road, London SE5 0AJ
Tel: 0181 769 8096. 17+yrs, 25 places.

St. Edmunds, 298 Leigham Court Road, Streatham
SW16 6RZ
Tel: 0181 769 8096. 17+yrs, 25 places.

St. Mungos, 9 Cologne Road, Battersea
SW11 2AH
Tel: 0171 223 3006. 17+yrs, 25 places.

Shenley Hostel, 204 Bedford Hill, SW12 9HJ
Tel: 0181 675 2693. 17+yrs, 30 places.

LONDON (NE)
Westbourne House, 199 Romford Road, Forest Gate
E7 9HL
Tel: 0181 534 2483/0673. 17+yrs, 40 places.

LONDON (SE)
4 Beckenham Road, Beckenham, Kent
Tel: 0181 658 3515. 17+yrs, 20 places.

LONDON (SW)
69 North Road, Kew, Richmond upon Thames TW9
4HQ
Tel: 0181 876 6303/4. 17+yrs, 17 places.

MANCHESTER
Bradshaw House, 147 Walmersley Road, Bury
B09 5DE
Tel: 0161 761 6419. 17+yrs, 29 places.

St. Joseph's, Miller Street, Eccles M30 8PF
Tel: 0161 789 5337. 17+yrs, 29 places.

Ascot House, 195 Wellington Road North, Stockport
SK4 2PB
Tel: 0161 443 3400. 17–25 yrs, 22 places.

MERSEYSIDE
Canning House, 55 Canning Street, Liverpool
L8 7NN
Tel: 0151 709 4959. 17+yrs, 27 places.

Southwood Hostel, 24 Southwood Road, Liverpool
L17 7BQ
Tel: 0151 727 2401. 17+yrs, 23 places.

MIDDLESEX
2 Corfton Road, Ealing, London W5 2HS
Tel: 0181 997 7127. 17+yrs, 20 places.

71–73 Shoot-up-Hill, London NW2 3PS
Tel: 0181 452 4209/4200. 17+yrs, 20 places.

NORFOLK
1 Drayton Street, Norwich NR3 2DF
Tel: 01603 429 488. 17+yrs, 29 places.

NORTHANTS
45–48 Lower Meadow Court, Northampton NN3 1YX
Tel: 01604 648704/645722. 17+yrs, 23 places.

NOTTS
5 Astral Grove, Hucknall, Nottingham N15 6PY
Tel: 0115 963 2835/962 3992. 17+yrs, 15 place.

SUFFOLK
The Cottage, 795 Old Norwich Road IP1 6LH
Tel: 01473 47139. 17+yrs, 18 places.

Lightfoot House, 37 Fuchia Lane, Ipswich IP1 5AA
Tel: 01473 728 198. 17+yrs, 22 places.

SURREY
St. Catherine's Priory, Portsmouth Road, Guildford
GU2 5EB
Tel: 01483 571 635. 18–26yrs, 19 places.

WARWICKS
33 Kenilworth Road, Leamington Spa CV32 6JG
Tel: 0192 636 331. 17+yrs, 19 places.

McIntyre House, 125 Edward Street, Nuneaton
CV11 5RD
Tel: 01203 382 889. 17+yrs, 21 places.

WEST MID
33 Portland Road, Edgbaston, Birmingham
B16 9HS
Tel: 0121 454 0394. 17+yrs, 21 places.

23 Wellington Road, Bilston, Wolverhampton
WV14 6AH
Tel: 01902 497688. 17+yrs, 15 places.

96 Edgbaston Road, Moseley, Birmingham B12 9QA
Tel: 0121 440 2657. 17+yrs, 20 places.

31 Trinity Road, Aston, Birmingham B6 6AJ
Tel: 0121 523 4401. 17+yrs, 26 places.

85 Stonnall Road, Aldridge, Walsall WS9 8JZ
Tel: 01922 59574. 17+yrs, 12 places.

Sycamore Lodge, Clay Lane, Oldbury B69 4TH
Tel: 0121 552 9930. 17+yrs, 32 places.

W. YORKS
84 Cardigan Road, Headingley, Leeds LS6 3BJ
Tel: 0113 275 2860. 19–25yrs, 23 places.

Elm Bank, Bradford Road, Cleckheaton BD19 3LW
Tel: 01274 878606. 17+yrs, 17 places.

263 Hyde Park Road, Leeds LS6 1AG
Tel: 0113 275 5702. 17+yrs, 28 places.

6 Walmer Villas, Manningham, Bradford BD8 7ET
Tel: 01274 494 846. 17+yrs, 18 places.

30 Albion Street, Dewsbury WF13 2AJ
Tel: 01924 242 748. 17+yrs, 24 places.

S. GLAM.
Mandeville House, 9 Lewis Street, Cardiff CF1 8JY
Tel: 01222 394 592. 17+yrs, 26 places.

N. WALES
Plas-y-Wern, Ruabon, Wrexham, Clwyd LL14 6RN
Tel: 01978 821 202. 17+yrs, 18places.

MISCELLANEOUS ADDRESSES

ADVISORY SERVICE FOR SQUATTERS
2 St. Pauls Road, London N1
Tel: 0171 359 8814.

ALONE IN LONDON SERVICE
188 Kings Cross Road, London WC1
Tel: 0171 278 4224.
Help for under 21s in London.

APEX TRUST
2 Fore Street, London EC2
Tel: 0171 638 5931.
Employment service for ex-offenders.

CHAR
5–15 Cromer Street, London WC1
Tel: 0171 833 2071.
Housing campaign for single homeless.

GEESE THEATRE COMPANY
220 Moseley Road, Birmingham. B12 ODG.
Tel: 0121 446 4370.
Theatre company for prisons.

GINGERBREAD
35 Wellington Street, London EC2.
Tel: 0171 240 0953.
Single parent association.

HOMES FOR HOMELESS PEOPLE

90–92 Bronham Road, Bedford MK40.
Tel: 01234 210549.
Accommodation placement service.

LIBERTY
21 Tabbard Street, London SE1 4LA.
Tel: 0171 403 3888.
National Council for Civil Liberties.

PRISONERS' ABROAD
82 Rosebery Avenue, London EC1R 4RR.
Tel: 0171 833 3467.
Helps UK nationals jailed abroad.

SHOP
67–71 Grove Crescent Road, London E15 1BH.
Tel: 0181 534 9111.
Housing organisation for ex-Prisoners.

SECTION FOUR

Part 1. PRISONERS AND THE LAW

By **Vicky King** (Caseworker) and **Simon Creighton** (Solicitor)
of the **Prisoners Advice Service**

The law as stated is correct to 30 September 1994 and refers only to England and Wales. Scotland and Northern Ireland have their own prison rules.

1. INTRODUCTION

The law relating to prisons and prisoners is straightforward in terms of legal theory: the primary legislation is contained in the Prison Act 1952 and the secondary legislation in the Prison Rules 1964 and Young Offender Institution Rules 1988—they are set out in Annexe B.

However, because the legal theory is so simple, the day-to-day practice in prisons around the country has become extremely complex and difficult. The primary and secondary legislation which does exist is so basic that it has to be supplemented by a constant stream of documents sent out to Governors from Headquarters, intended to guide them on interpretation of the Rules, and inform them about changes in the implementation of both penal policy and practice.

2. ORDERS, ADVICE & INSTRUCTIONS

Standing Orders (SO), and Advice and Instructions to Governors (AG/IG)—which have now replaced Circular Instructions (CI)—provide detailed guidance to prison staff on how to implement policy and exercise their discretion. SO, which cover all aspects of prison life, are being continually updated by AG/IG and, although they possess no force of law, a failure by prison staff to heed the advice or instructions they contain may provide evidence of negligence, or irrationality in the decision making process—both of which we will deal with later.

3. PRIMARY & SECONDARY LEGISLATION.

The primary legislation relating to the operation and management of prisons is the **Prison Act 1952**. This Act of Parliament gives the Secretary of State for the Home Department (the Home Secretary) legal powers 'to make Rules for the regulation and management of prisons. . . . and for the classification, treatment, employment, discipline and control of persons required to be detained therein' (Section 47(1)). Using this secondary legislative power the Home Secretary issued the Prison Rules in 1964 (as amended most recently in 1992), which provide the administrative framework for the treatment of prisoners in England and Wales.

The Prison Rules are well-known for the large

amount of discretion that they grant to the prison authorities, and for the provisions allowing the Home Secretary to give further directions at a later date. They make reference to a few specific areas, such as the amount of exercise time or the certification of accommodation, but by and large it has only been through the intervention of the courts that the precise nature of prisoners' legal rights and entitlements have been clarified. Consequently, this area of law is very fluid and it is constantly being updated as new court judgements are delivered.

4. CASELAW

The starting point for an examination of the current legal position in relation to prisoners' rights is the case of *Raymond v Honey* [1982] AC 1. This landmark case established that prisoners retain all civil rights which are not taken away expressly by Act of Parliament (such as the right to vote in an election), or impliedly by the fact of imprisonment (such as the right to free movement). The practical effect of the ruling in *Raymond*, however, is somewhat limited by the fact that prisoners' are not permitted to sue the prison authorities for a breach of the Prison Rules alone: (*R v Deputy Governor of Parkhurst prison, ex.p Hague* [1992] AC 58). The effect of *Hague* is that prisoners must prove they have suffered some form of injury or loss *in addition to and as a direct result of* the breach of the Rules. The House of Lords in *Hague* did, however, affirm that the High Court can review all decisions made by the Prison Service, by way of an application to the High Court for Judicial review. It is worthwhile to divide the most common matters on which prisoners take litigation into two areas.

5. PUBLIC AND PRIVATE LAW REMEDIES

Firstly, in what may be termed the field of 'public law', there are routine administrative decisions which will affect every aspect of a prisoner's sentence concerning such matters as categorisation, transfers and home leaves. All such decisions are discretionary and as such may only be challenged by way of **judicial review** in the High Court.

Secondly, prisoners commonly require advice regarding **negligence** by prison staff which will have resulted in some form of financial loss (usually with lost property), or physical injury. As prisoners have no right to simply bring an action for breach of statutory duty when the prison authorities breach the Prison Rules, they must rely instead on the civil (or private) law principles of negligence in order to obtain redress.

6. JUDICIAL REVIEW (Order 53 RSC)

Judicial review is perhaps the most important safeguard of prisoners' legal rights. The scope of this remedy, which is available only from the Queens Bench Division of the High Court, is widely misunderstood and must be explained to provide a context for the remainder of this chapter. There are three basic grounds which can give rise to an application for judicial review:

- **Illegality** is an error of law or an abuse of power—a Governor imposing a greater amount of disciplinary punishment than the Rules gave him authority to impose, would be acting *illegally* in law.
- **Irrationality** occurs when the person who makes the decision that is complained of, has acted so absurdly that no reasonable person would have made that decision—placing a prisoner serving seven days in Category A, all other things being equal, could be *irrational* in law.
- **Impropriety** is when a decision has been made in breach of natural justice—a Governor who wrongly prevents the calling of witnesses at an adjudication, for example, would have acted with procedural *impropriety*.

The High Court does not operate as an appeal court and will only **review** the administrative decision made. This means that there will not be a rehearing of the facts and the Court will only examine the decision to make sure it has been properly made, is within the law, and was subject to the correct procedure being followed. An application for judicial review can only be made once all other internal areas of appeal (such as the requests/complaints system) have been exhausted. The application must be lodged at the High Court (Crown Office) as soon as possible and, in any event, not later than **three months** from the date when the decision was made—though the Court has power in exceptional cases to extend this period. Judicial review is also a *discretionary remedy*. This means that the Court is not bound to find in the favour of a prisoner even if it believes the decision is wrong in law. Cases where the Court would still find against a prisoner would include occasions when it felt that the administrative difficulties in quashing the decision complained of would outweigh the benefits: an example of this approach occurred in the case of *R v Secretary of State for the Home Department, ex.p Davies* ([1994] Court of Appeal, unreported). This case involved a prisoner who challenged the lawfulness of Common Fund deductions from his pay and sought return of the money taken. The Common Fund was abolished in February 1990, prior to Mr Davies' application for judicial review, and the Court felt that in view of the relatively small amount of money involved for each prisoner and the administrative problems resulting from reimbursement, it was not practical to allow the application. It is also important to note that if the High

Court quashes a decision by way of judical review, that does not mean the matter is definately at an end. The effect of a decision being quashed is simply to place all parties back where they were before the decision was made. This means the prison authorities could quite lawfully recommence the process, avoiding the errors made on the first occasion. This has not been the case in England to date, though in a recent Scottish case where a disciplinary adjudication of a prison Governor was quashed by the Court of Session—for the first time in Scotland—the prison authorities drafted in a governor from a different establishment and re-heard the case: (*Leech v The Governor of HM.Prison Edinburgh* ([1994] Court of Session 13 May unreported at present). At that second hearing all charges against the prisoner were dismissed and the matter brought to an end, but it illustrates the point that success does not prevent a rehearing. The following is a brief look at the most common areas upon which prisoners seek advice in relation to judicial review.

(a) Adjudications & Prison Discipline.

There are 22 offences against discipline in Prison Rule 47. A list of them, together with an explanation of procedures for charging, internal adjudications and legal representation are contained in Chapter 5 of the Advice Section. Therefore, this explanation will cover external matters, where cases may be referred to the police for investigation: a complex disciplinary offence around which a body of caselaw has built up. CI.3/92 provides guidelines to Governors on when breaches of prison discipline should be referred to the police for investigation. These include the following:

- serious assaults, rape, non-consensual buggery and threats to kill where there appears to be intent;
- escapes and serious attempts at escape from closed establishments or secure escorts;
- possession of unauthorised articles such as firearms, knives, all Class A drugs, and Class B drugs where there is intent to supply;
- criminal damage where the damage exceeds £2,000 and arson (unless there was little or no risk of the fire taking hold);
- robbery involving the use of threats of serious violence or a weapon; and
- mass disobedience.

However, even in these cases referral to the police is not mandatory and a Governor retains a discretion whether to deal with the matter internally.

(b) Police Investigations

In cases where the police are to be asked to investigate, a disciplinary charge must still be laid in the usual way and the adjudication should be opened at the establishment. The Governor must satisfy himself that there is a charge to answer at this stage. Once so satisfied, the hearing will then be adjourned pending the outcome of the police investigation. If there is no prosecution as a result of the police investigation, the Governor must then decide whether to continue with the disciplinary charge. Governors are advised that they should dismiss a disciplinary charge if it is similar to the aborted criminal charge, and relies on the same evidence. Governors should also consider dismissal of the disciplinary charge, if to proceed would appear unfair. Otherwise internal proceedings may be resumed at the discretion of the Governor (Standing Order 3D, 7). In practice, it is rare for an adjudication to proceed in such circumstances. If the referral to the police results in prosecution, then the disciplinary charge should not be proceeded with.

The vast majority of offences against discipline (a total of 100,700 in 1993) are not referred to the police, but are dealt with internally. In the majority of cases charges are straightforward and rely on factual evidence submitted by the officer who laid the charge, which the prisoner may try to disprove.

(c) 'Unauthorised Possession'

One of the more complex charges which a prisoner can face is that laid pursuant to Prison Rule 47(9) which makes it an offence against discipline for a prisoner to have:

'in his possession or under his control:
a) any unauthorised article;, or
b) any article in greater quantity than he is authorised to have'.

This covers a variety of situations ranging from having too much tobacco in possession, through to being found in possession of a controlled drug. In order to reach a finding of guilt the Governor has to satisfy himself about five things:

a. the article (drugs, tobacco etc) actually exists;
b. the article is what it is alleged to be;
c. the article was found where it was said to be found
d. the prisoner:
   1. knew what the article was, and
   2. exercised some degree of control over it.

(*R v Deputy Governor of Camp Hill prison, ex.p King* ([1984] 3 All ER, 897 CA). See also: *R v Parkhurst Prison Deputy Governor & Another*, ex.p *Leech & Another* ([1988] 1 All ER, 485 HL).

Thus, if two prisoners are sharing a cell and one was found to be in possession of cocaine, the other prisoner could not be convicted if he believed the substance to be milk powder, or if he knew the substance was cocaine, but exercised no control over it.

(d) Appeals

Where a prisoner is found guilty of an offence against prison discipline, he may seek to have the verdict quashed under Prison Rule 56(1). In practice this involves appealing the finding of guilt to the Area Manager through the request/complaint procedure. There is no rehearing of the case and a review is conducted on the papers alone. The Area Manager may quash the finding of guilt, or remit or mitigate any punishment(s) imposed.

(e) Categorisation

Prison Rule 3(1) states that:

'Prisoners shall be classified, in accordance with any directions from the Secretary of State, having regard to their age, temperament and record, and with a view to maintaining good order and facilitating training and, in the case of convicted prisoners, of furthering the purpose of their training and treatment . . .'

The Home Secretary has used these provisions to divide prisoners into four categories (see Chapter 3 in the Advice Section). A prisoner's security category will determine the conditions in which their sentence is served. Most prisoners are categorised after their initial reception into prison by the Governor, who will have regard to CI.7/88 in making the decision. There is no formal process for reviewing categories thereafter, though it is intended to be reviewed at least annually and a prisoner may make such an application at any time. CI.7/88 states that every prisoner must be in the *lowest* security category which meets their security risk at each stage of their sentence; implying thereby that regular reviews should be carried out. In the case of prisoners perceived to be high risk, classification will be referred to the Category A Section at Prison Service Headquarters for a final decision to be taken. The Category A Section receives annual reports on each Category A prisoner, in order to review their security classification. There is no formal right of appeal against categorisation, although it is open to prisoners to request a review through the request/complaint procedure. This however has proved difficult because, other than in the limited case below, prisoners have no right to know the reasons why they have been placed in a particular security category.

The case of *R v Secretary of State for the Home Department ex.p Duggan* ([1993] TLR, 17 December) established that Category A prisoners have the right to know the reasons for their security classification. Lord Justice Rose commented in *Duggan*:

'A prisoner's right to make representations is largely valueless unless he knows the case against him and secret, unchallengable reports which may contain damaging inaccuracies are, or should be, anathema in a civilised democratic society.'

As a result of *Duggan* the gist of the annual reports submitted to the Category A Section must now be disclosed to the prisoner and, subject to any exemptions arising from public interest immunity, the prisoner has the right to be given reasons for any future decision to maintain him as a Category A prisoner. The legal reasoning in *Duggan* found its focus in the fact that as security categorisation has a direct affect on release prospects, a prisoner should have the right to sufficient information to allow proper representations to be made. Changes as a result of this case have only recently been introduced, and at present the Home Office are adhering very closely to the wording of the judgement by disclosing the bare minimum. It is important to note that disclosure in this way only applies to Category A *reviews*. The initial decision to classify a prisoner as Category A was specifically exempted in the judgement, on the grounds that the decision may need to be taken urgently 'in the public interest'. A prisoner who is allocated to Category A for the first time, will not be told the reasons for that decision.

(f) Compassionate Release

The Home Secretary has the power to order the release of a prisoner on compassionate grounds if he is satisfied that exceptional circumstances exist which justify such a decision (s.36 Criminal Justice Act 1991). The detailed guidelines for the exercise of this power are currently contained in CI.36/92, and there are two main cases where compassionate release will be considered:

- cases of terminal illness, and
- tragic family circumstances which were unforeseen at the time of sentencing.

The basic principles applied in such cases are that:

- the release of the prisoner will not put the safety of the public at risk; and,
- the Home Secretary will not normally intervene solely on the basis of the facts known to the sentencing/appeal court; and,
- there is some specific purpose to be served by early release.

The application must be made to HM Prison Service HQ, and can be commenced either by the prison Governor, or by a prisoner directly.

When decisions are made on medical grounds, the Home Secretary will need to be satisfied that the prisoner is suffering from a terminal illness and that death is likely to occur soon, or that the prisoner is bedridden or similarly incapacitated. The risk of further offending must be past and there must be some significant benefit from early release. In order to satisfy the criteria for tragic family circumstances, it must be shown that there is a real and urgent need for the prisoner to be *permanently* with his family, that release will bring some *significant* benefit and that the risk of further offending is past.

Successful applications are invariably made on

edical grounds and not tragic family circumances. Instances have included cases where prisners are very close to death and in a few ceptional cases, where further imprisonment ould be very likely to result in death: eg where a isoner has a history of heart disease and prison nditions are likely to result in a further, probably tal, attack. Attempts have been made to extend e principles and to more closely define the pows and obligations of the Home Secretary, both in ational courts and through the European ommission of Human Rights (eg: *R v Secretary of ate ex.p Grice* ([1993] unreported). However, as e Home Secretary retains a very wide discretion, has proved difficult to make such advances. The ly method of challenge is by way of judicial view.

) Lifers

andatory life sentences are divided into two elents. Firstly, the penal element which is set by e Home Secretary to reflect the minimum period at a lifer should serve in the interests of 'deternce and retribution'. This is known as the **'tariff riod'**.

All life sentence prisoners have to serve up to eir tariff date, and there is no prospect of release forehand—unless the criteria for compassionate lease is met.

In setting the tariff the Home Secretary seeks commendations from the trial judge and the rd Chief Justice as to an appropriate period to be rved. The Home Secretary sets the tariff taking to account both judicial views and other factors cluding public policy considerations. The Home cretary is under no obligation to set the tariff in e with the judicial view, and it is apparent that me Home Secretaries have set the tariff at a conerably higher number of years than the judiry had recommended.

Because mandatory lifers have not had the right know the basis upon which their tariffs were set, whether the Home Secretary had set it at a her level than recommended by the judiciary, it s increasingly considered that the procedure was fair. The case of *R v Secretary of State ex.p Doody* 993] 3 WLR 154) aimed to rectify this position. e House of Lords in *Doody* gave a comprehene judgement which examined the principles of ness in administrative decisions and overturned vious authorities on this area. The judgement es mandatory lifers the following rights:

- o **know the judicial view** of the minimum eriod that they should serve and the gist of the easons why the judiciary made that recommenlation; and,
- o **make representations** in respect of their tariff efore it is set; and,
- o be **informed of any reasons for departure** rom the judicial view when the tariff is set.

This means that mandatory lifers should now have the information necessary to ascertain whether they have been treated fairly, and the means with which to challenge any tariff decisions which appear to be unfair.

Lifers whose tariffs were set before the new arrangements came into effect also benefit and are told the gist of the judicial recommendation as to tariff, and the level at which the tariff was set. They are given an opportunity to make representations to the Home Secretary in order that their tariff periods can be reviewed. Though the *Doody* judgement had been eagerly awaited by lifers and their representatives, in practice the information being disclosed is often inadequate and the Home Secretary has so far refused to rescind any tariff decisions. Further cases on the nature and extent of disclosure in tariff setting are due to be heard in the High Court at the end of 1994, and will be covered in the next edition.

Lifers usually begin their sentences in one of three main lifer centres and remain there for approximately 18 months to three years for assessment. Following this the Lifer Management Unit will decide upon the next allocation and it is possible for the lifer to progress through to category C conditions before they reach their first **Local Review Committee** (LRC) date.

This LRC takes place three years before the tariff is due to expire and is the first stage at which a mandatory lifer's prospects for release upon completion of the tariff will be considered by the Parole Board. If the Parole Board recommend either a provisional release date upon completion of the tariff, or a move to Category D conditions, the recommendation will be considered by the Home Secretary who has a right of veto. Most mandatory lifers must complete a period in both open conditions and a Pre-Release Employment Scheme Hostel before they are released on licence.

The second part of the mandatory life sentence is the period at which a lifer may be held because release is deemed to pose too much of a *'risk'*. This begins when the tariff period has been served, and may last indefinitely. The decision to hold a lifer at risk will be made by the Parole Board and Home Secretary on the basis of reports from prison staff. Mandatory lifers are entitled to disclosure of such reports and are given an opportunity to make representations upon them. However, even in cases where mandatory lifers have served beyond the tariff period, and are not considered to pose any risk, the Home Secretary still has the power to detain on the basis that release may undermine the public confidence.

The recent case of *R v Secretary of State ex.p Pegg* ([1994] The Independent 9 September) emphasised the willingness of the High Court to intervene in this area. The Court decided that the Parole Board has a duty to give full reasons for its decisions. It stated that the courts must be vigilant in exercising powers of judicial review over the Board and the Home Secretary in the case of mandatory lifers as the fundamental rights of such prisoners are important, and the system created for dealing with them under the Criminal Justice Act 1991 is procedurally unfair—referring to the discrepancy in the treatment of discretionary and mandatory lifers.

The process of release for mandatory lifers is distinct from that for discretionary lifers. The case of *Thynne, Wilson & Gunnell v United Kingdom* ([1990] 13 EHRR, 666, Series A No.190), established that discretionary lifers have the right to have regular and independent reviews of their detention once they have passed their tariff period. The Criminal Justice Act 1991 established **Discretionary Lifer Panels** (DLP)—hearings at which discretionary lifers are entitled to have legal representation and disclosure of reports made about them by the Prison Service. DLP's have the power to direct the Home Secretary to release a discretionary lifer, but are only able to make recommendations to the Home Secretary as to the progression of such a life sentence prisoner through the system if it is considered that the lifer may be a 'risk'.

(h) Rule 43(GOAD)

Rule 43 of the Prison Rules provides that prisoners who are believed to be a threat to the Good Order and Discipline (GOAD) of a prison may be removed from normal location and segregated. A Governor may segregate a prisoner a for up to three days, but this period may be extended for up to a month with the authority of a member of the Board of Visitors or a representative of the Home Secretary. However, at the end of that month there is no requirement to return a prisoner to normal location and a decision to continue the period of segregation may be taken from month to month. CI.26/90 gives guidance to both Governors and Boards of Visitors on the use of segregation in the interests of good order and discipline. In particular it states the Rule is:

'. . . designed to assist Governors to prevent trouble . . . it is not necessary to wait until a prisoner has actually shown that it is his intention to do so; and it is right to take into account a history of disruptive behaviour . . .'

IG.28/93 outlines a 'management Strategy for Disruptive Prisoners' and replaces CI.37/90. The new Instruction provides a five stage programme to deal with sentenced prisoners in Category B conditions who are identified as posing serious control problems. The stages of the programme are as follows:

i. Internal Action at the Parent Establishment
If a prisoner becomes disruptive or subversive disciplinary action should be considered, the reasons should be identified and the prisoner should be counselled in an attempt to change their behaviour. Relocation within the prison should be considered as should the possibility of segregation under Rule 43 (GOAD). If these fail, or if the circumstances are exceptional, then a prisoner may be transferred to another establishment.

ii. Temporary Transfer from Parent Establishment
Initially the prisoner will be moved to the segregation block, and from there to another prison as identified by the Population Management Section at Prison Service Headquarters. The Governor of the parent establishment will inform the receiving Governor as to the background to the move. The transfer will then take place and will be for a maximum of one month with the expectation that the prisoner will be returned to the parent establishment when that time has lapsed. If, however, the parent establishment does not want that prisoner back, the Governor can make representations to this effect and the final decision rests with Prison Service Headquarters.

iii. Centrally Managed Transfers to other Prison
Those prisoners who do not return to their parent establishment will be reallocated to other Category B prisons by Headquarters. The Governors of the receiving establishments are required to accept such allocations, although they do have a right of appeal.

iv. Control Review Committee Special Unit
Special Units were set up to deal with persistently disruptive prisoners who have a history of disruptive and aggressive behaviour. This is likely to be characterised by one or more of the following:

a. violence to inmates or staff
b. frequent disciplinary reports
c. acts of serious damage to property in prison
d. dangerous behaviour such as hostage taking or roof-top protests
e. history of mental abnormality—for allocation to Parkhurst Special Unit (Not SSB)
f. failure to respond to stages 1 and 3 above.

If a Governor believes that a prisoner meets these criteria then he may refer the case to the Special Unit Selection Committee. Before allocation to a Special Unit is sanctioned a governor may apply have an inmate transferred to the Special Assessment Unit at HMP Woodhill.

v. Continuous Assessment Scheme
Persistently disruptive prisoners who are deemed not to be suitable for a Special Unit, or who are transferred out of Special Units because of their behaviour whilst there, are kept under constant assessment by Prison Service Headquarters. In practice this means that they are usually allocated to another Category B prison and held in the Segregation Block—although the Governor has authority to locate them elsewhere in the prison.

Ieadquarters review such cases every six weeks nd can order further transfers around the system or an indefinite period. Several important points hould be observed throughout this process:

prisoners should not be transferred as a punishment;
prisoners should be advised in writing of the reasons for their transfer or segregation within 24 hours;
request/complaints referring to transfers should be answered within seven days by the Governor who made the decision to transfer; and
visitors to the prisoner should be notified of the transfer.

;rievances surrounding decisions to segregate and ransfer prisoners are extremely common, particuarly where detailed reasons for the decision are ot given. In the case of *R v Secretary of State for he Home Dept ex.p Ross* ([1994] TLR, 9 June CA) he Court of Appeal held that Governors are bliged to make a statement giving general reasons or the transfer and so an extremely brief reason vould not be acceptable. However, Governors do ot have to give 'chapter and verse detailing the risoners' conduct'.

The cases of *R v Parkhurst Prison Deputy ;overnor and Another ex.p Hague and Weldon* [1992] 1 AC 58 HL) decided that prisoners subected to intolerable conditions such as segregaon and disciplinary transfer CANNOT bring an ction for false imprisonment. However, dependng on the facts of each case, there are potential ctions for negligence, assault, misfeasance in ublic office (see below) or termination of such onditions by judicial review. In practice an pplication to terminate the conditions will rarely e practical. It is usually the case that by the time n application can be heard by the Court, the risoner will have been moved by the Prison ervice.

. NEGLIGENCE

a) Lost Property Cases

;.38/94 gives Governors the authority to deal with laims for lost property up to £3,000 and thus any laim up to that value should be put to the ;overnor in the first instance through the equest/complaint procedure—or by instructing a olicitor under the Green Form Scheme. If the laim is turned down then an 'appeal' to the Area Manager can be lodged. Claims exceeding £3,000 re dealt with by the Area Manager but will be eferred to the Treasury for final authority to settle laims in excess of £20,000. In submitting a comensation claim for lost property full details of the ost items should be given: where/when purchased nd the circumstances of the loss. Receipts should e obtained if possible.

i. Stored Property
If Stored Property is either lost or damaged in reception or in transit then, so long as it is clear from the property cards that the prisoner is the owner of the property and it was held by the prison authorities, then the Prison Service will be liable.

ii. Property in Possession
The Prison Service does not normally accept liability for property held '*in possession*' (i.e. property held in the prisoner's cell) on the basis that the inmate may have given it to other prisoners or exchanged it for other items. Four exceptions to this general rule are shown below, and are based on the law of negligence:

a. **Where the prisoner has been removed from normal location (to the segregation block for example) without prior warning and has therefore been unable to secure his property.**
b. **Where the prisoner has been removed from normal location because of illness.**

In both of these situations, property 'in possession' at the time of removal from normal location is deemed to be no longer under the control of the inmate, and thus responsibility reverts back to the Prison Service. Therefore it is crucial to determine whether the cell was sealed immediately after removal from normal location. If the cell:

i. was not sealed immediately, or
ii. was unsealed at any point before cell clearance, or
iii. if property shown on the cell clearance sheet was never returned to the prisoner then the Prison Service is liable for the loss unless they establish otherwise (eg: *Winson v Home Office*, Central London County Court 1993, C/No: 83065).

c. **Where the prisoner has been on temporary release.**

The Prison Service will argue that the prisoner should have taken reasonable steps to secure his property before temporary release. It is therefore important to ascertain whether the prisoner was advised by staff to store property in reception during his absence from the prison, or if the prisoner asked to do so and this was refused. If prisoners are temporarily released on a daily basis they should be warned of the increased risk to their property by staff.

d. **Where the prisoner has absconded or escaped.**

The Prison Service will not accept liability for property lost between the time of the abscond/escape and the disappearance being confirmed. When the disappearance is confirmed prison staff should take immediate action to secure the 'in possession' property: the cell should be sealed and then cleared without delay. CI.48/92 states that the property should be stored until six months after the date of abscond/escape. At that time the next of kin should be contacted to ask if they wish to claim the property. If after three years the property still has not been claimed, CI.48/92 further states that it may be disposed of either by competitive tender, or if the items have no value they may be destroyed.

In all cases a failure to handle a prisoner's property in accordance with the instructions in the Inmate Personal Records System Manual will create a strong presumption in favour of paying compensation (Prisoners' Requests/Complaints Procedure Staff Manual, Annexe I, para 2), it is therefore important to check that the relevant signatures are on property cards, and that there is no evidence that the property has been mis-recorded at some stage.

If the claim is unsuccessful then consideration should be given to taking legal action to recover compensation for the loss. In most cases, the amount of the claim will fall below the level for which legal aid is normally granted and thus prisoners will experience difficulty in gaining legal representation to recover the value of their property. It is possible to argue that the value of a relatively small claim is substantially greater to a prisoner due to the low level of prison wages (eg a claim of £500 is equal to at least six months of prison earnings). However, in most cases legal aid will be refused—for which see 8[a] below.

(b) Personal Injury Cases

Whilst the risk of injury in prison at the hands of a fellow prisoner or staff is not as great as the public may perceive, heightened tension in the system caused by overcrowding, declining staffing levels and poor regime may give rise to claims for personal injury. Claims for personal injury need not be as a direct result of assault but simply on the basis of negligence by Prison Service staff in failing to protect a prisoner from foreseeable injury. These claims are particularly important in light of the fact that there is no right of action for breach of statutory duty.

Where a prisoner is assaulted by another prisoner, the Governor of the establishment should decide whether to deal with the matter as an internal disciplinary offence, or whether to report it to the police. In making this decision the Governor should have regard to the seriousness of the assault and the wishes of the victim (CI. 3/92 and IG.33.94). Prisoners are often unwilling to give evidence against fellow inmates because of the fear of repercussions, however it is important to realise that if no complaint is made to the police then there will be no prospect of success in applying for compensation from the Criminal Injuries Compensation Authority (CICA).

The CICA, formerly the CIC Board, is a Government agency empowered to pay compensation to the victims of violent crime who have suffered personal injury (including mental injury). Prisoners experience great difficulty in making successful claims as the CICA is able to refuse claims on the basis of the applicant's behaviour, character or way of life. The CICA may take into account the applicant's criminal record even where the convictions are entirely unrelated to the incident in which the injury occurred (*R v CICB ex.p Thompstone* ([1984] 1 WLR, 1234 CA). Despite this, it is still worth submitting a claim to the CICA where an assault has taken place. However, because of the obstacles involved, it is prudent to instruct a solicitor to handle the application. If compensation is refused the solicitor should advise as to the merits of an application for judicial review of that decision.

In terms of civil action where a prisoner has been assaulted by another prisoner, there are two possible avenues of redress:

- Investigation of a civil action against the assailant may be considered. However, as it is unlikely that a prisoner would have the financial means to pay compensation to his victim this is generally not worth pursuing.
- An action against the Home Office for negligence. The Prison Service owes a duty of care to prisoners to take reasonable care for their safety (*Palmer v Home Office* ([1988] The Guardian 31st March, CA).

Prisoners, therefore, can be awarded damages for injuries at the hands of other prisoners which may be attributed to a failure by the prison authorities to provide reasonable protection (e.g. *Porterfield v Home Office*). In order to take such an action, the prisoner must establish that the prison authorities knew of the danger to the prisoner and that they failed to take reasonable steps to prevent the assault. Therefore in order to enhance chances of success it is of primary importance that where a prisoner fears that he is to be attacked, this is reported to Prison Service staff and that a request for transfer or segregation is made.

Allegations of physical assault by Prison Service staff are very common throughout the system. These may take the form of injuries sustained as a result of a lawful activity such as during the application of Control and Restraint techniques, or officers acting entirely outside the scope of their duty. Similar remedies apply as outlined above—reporting the matter to the police, applying to the CICA, and suing the officer(s) concerned for assault.

There are three further types of action that may be taken in such cases:

i. for negligence
ii. assault and battery
iii. misfeasance in public office.

The case of *R v Secretary of State for the Home Department ex.p Hague & Weldon* (above) established that prisoners may bring actions for negligence by prison staff where they have suffered personal injury. In particular there is a right to bring an action for *Assault and Battery,* where there is negligence coupled with a lack of reasonable care on the part of the officer causing the injury. Such claims may arise where excessive force is used to carry out an otherwise lawful activity (eg where someone is removed from normal location under Control and Restraint techniques), or where a restraint has been imposed for too long (e.g. when a prisoner is no longer considered to be a danger to himself or to others).

Racz v Home Office ([1994] 2 WLR, 23) established that prisoners can bring an action for *Misfeasance in Public Office.* In order to bring a successful claim it must be shown that:

- an officer has caused damage to a prisoner,
- the officer's actions were motivated by malice, and
- the officer was aware he did not possess the authority to take that action.

3. CASES IN COURT

(a) D.I.Y. Litigation

Where legal aid is not available, prisoners may commence their own proceedings. Applications for judicial review (see Order 53 of the Rules of the Supreme Court for procedure) can be brought by litigants in person—though as judicial review is a very complex legal field it will be rare indeed for a prisoner to possess the necessary legal expertise. Negligence actions can be brought in the County Court local to the prison in which the inmate is located. A summons form and explanatory leaflet (Ex-50) can be obtained by written request to the Chief Clerk at local County Court—addresses and phone numbers are in the phone book under 'Courts'. Those prisoners who bring their own negligence proceedings, need to be aware of the following points:

i. The proper defendant is the Home Office (not the Governor of the prison in which the loss took place)
ii. The address where the summons can be served is that of the Treasury Solicitor (Queen Anne's Chambers, 28 Broadway, London SW1)
iii. The court fee payable on issuing the summons may be waived in cases of financial hardship by making an application to the Lord Chancellor's Department (Great Peter Street, London SW1)
iv. The claim is for 'negligence': not maladministration or breach of statutory duty.
v. If attendance at court is necessary, either for the final hearing or interim applications, the normal rules on production at court will apply—see below.
vi. Obtaining relevant and necessary documents by way of an application to the court for Discovery of documents, may help to establish exactly what happened. If the Governor conducted an inquiry into the loss, for example as the result of the prisoner using the Request/Complaint procedure, the Court can be asked to order the defendant Home Office to disclose to you the contents of that investigation, including copies of statements that may have been taken from staff, together with copies of the respective property cards (e.g. *Leech v Home Office,* (1986 Lewes County Court).

(b) Production at Court in Civil Matters

There will be many occasions where prisoners will wish to be produced at court, these will include matrimonial and child care cases, and where they are taking action against the prison authorities. The Criminal Justice Act 1962 (s.29(1)) empowers the Home Secretary to order production of a prisoner at any court where it is considered to be 'desirable in the interests of justice'. Caselaw has established that if so produced a Governor may recover the costs of production (including transport, escorts and staff subsistence).

Whilst this remains the law, the views of Lord Donaldson in *R v Secretary of State ex.p Wynne* ([1991] The Times 27 December) are extremely helpful to use in applications for productions at a civil court. Lord Donaldson stated that where a prisoner has applied for production at court, in exercising his discretion as to whether to grant the application the Home Secretary should have consideration as to the necessity of the presence of the prisoner. Particular regard should be had as to whether the proceedings are oral or could be conducted in writing, and whether the prisoner is legally represented. A decision not to produce a prisoner in a case where the proceedings are oral, and there is no legal representation, would be susceptible to judicial review. Lord Donaldson further considered that a prisoners' inability to pay the costs of production would not constitute sufficient grounds for refusal to produce, and in any case escort costs should be limited to those of transport from the nearest prison to the court. In those cases where the legal action is against the Prison Service, if the Home Secretary were to be seen to be exercising his discretion to the detriment of a prisoner, it could be seen as the improper advancement of his own case. This was a hypothetical argument in the case of *Wynne,* where the prisoner had not actually completed the formal part of the application for production. However, at the present time the Prison Service have been overturning refusals for production upon being reminded of Lord Donaldson's observations on this matter.

9. EUROPEAN CONVENTION ON HUMAN RIGHTS

The UK is a signatory to this Convention and has agreed to accept the decisions of the Court in individual cases since 1965. The Convention provides basic safeguards as to the rights and freedoms of individuals and deals with such areas as the right to a fair trial, the right to a private and family life, and the prevention of torture or inhuman or degrading treatment or punishment.

The method of making an application under the Convention is very straightforward. All that is necessary is for a letter to be sent to the Secretary of the European Commission, at the Council of Europe in Strasbourg, France, setting out the facts of the application and the Article(s) in the Convention which it is alleged have been violated. The Commission will then decide whether the application should be allowed to proceed, both legally and procedurally.

Procedurally, it is only possible to make an application to the Commission once all UK based avenues of redress have been exhausted. This will mean that all internal Prison Service appeals procedures have been tried and that all potential legal methods before the UK courts including appeals, have been attempted. If there is no remedy in English law for the complaint, then an opinion from a lawyer to that effect may be necessary. The complaint must be made to the Commission within a period of SIX MONTHS from the date of exhaustion of UK remedies.

The Commission has the power to determine whether the application is admissible. This may be done without communicating the application to the UK Government (e.g. if the application is outside the relevant time limits), or it may invite observations from both the Government and the applicant. In such cases it is common for an oral hearing to be fixed to decide upon admissibility.

If an application is declared admissible, the decision will be communicated to the parties to try and procure a friendly settlement. If this cannot be achieved, then the case will be referred to either the full court or the Committee of Ministers. If an application is declared inadmissible, there is no right of appeal.

Generally, very few cases put to the Commission are admissible. One of the major problems applicants face is in exhausting all domestic remedies and in making the application within the relevant time limits. The procedure once the application is before the Commission is relatively straightforward in legal terms, but has proved to be very slow and the time the Commission take to reach decisions may be measured in years rather than months. However, prisoners have won important rights through this procedure, such as the introduction of Discretionary Lifer Panels (*Thynne, Wilson & Gunnell v UK* (above)) and greater scope for privileged correspondence with legal advisers (*Campbell v UK* (1992)).

Vicky King and **Simon Creighton** (Solicitor), operate the **Prisoners' Advice Service [PAS]**, 57 Chalton Street, London NW1 1HU. (Tel: 071 388 8586). PAS is a well-respected independent charity, which has advised thousands of prisoners, their families and friends, since opening in May 1991.

STOP PRESS

MISCARRIAGES OF JUSTICE

On 28th November 1994 the Divisional Court of the Queens Bench handed down a judgement in four cases brought by prisoners against the Home Secretary: *R v Secretary of State for the Home Department, ex.p Hickey et al.* Each case challenged the procedure followed by the Home Secretary when determining a request by or on behalf of a prisoner to refer a case back to the Court of Appeal (Criminal Division), pursuant to section 17 Criminal Appeal Act 1968.

The s.17 power of the Home Secretary is the only method of reopening a case which has already failed on appeal: 'Following trial on indictment there can only be a single application for leave to appeal' said Lord Justice Simon Brown who delivered judgement in each of the four cases. 'If that application or the appeal fails, section 17 alone provides the mechanism for unlocking the door back into the criminal appeal system'.

The s.17 system which allows the Home Secretary to refer a case back to the Court of Appeal has been the subject of much criticism, not least by the Royal Commission on Criminal Justice who, in their Report on Correcting Miscarriages of Justice, said such powers should be entrusted to a new body independent of both the Government and the Courts. For the moment, however, it remains in place.

When a s.17 request is received by the Home Secretary it is considered and a decision is taken as to whether further inquiries are necessary as a result of it—in a recent 12 month period the Home Secretary received 725 such requests, of which 55% were refused without any inquiry being found necessary. In cases where an inquiry is ordered, the Home Secretary has refused to disclose the reports produced by those inquiries and the Court ruled that was unlawful.

For however long into the future the Home Secretary retains his powers of referral, he will now have to disclose the reports, or the substance of them, and allow the prisoner to make further representations as a result of them, before any final decision is taken in respect of the s.17 request.

How much information should be disclosed is a legal grey area: 'The guiding principle should always be that sufficient disclosure should be given to enable the [prisoner] properly to present his best case' said Lord Justice Simon Brown: 'That can only be done if he adequately appreciates the nature and extent of the evidence elicited by the Secretary of State's inquiries'.

SECTION FOUR

Part 2. **ADJUDICATIONS IN PRISON**

Custody, Care and a Little Less Justice

Peter M. Quinn. LL.B., BCL. Governor, HM Prison Service HQ, London. Visiting Fellow, Faculty of Law, U.W.E (Bristol)

HAVE YOU GOT SOMETHING TO SAY?

Peter Quinn's excellent paper on the pages that follow, brings a fresh approach to the vexed issue of disciplinary adjudications. His clear reasoning and cogent arguments make for a profound, compelling and, perhaps, controversial read: can you do the same for the 1996 edition?

Have you got something important to say about a serious aspect of our penal system? Can you present your case, radical or otherwise, with clarity and in a way that advances the penal debate using arguments that stand up to scrutiny? If so, then I'd like to hear from you. You choose the topic: I only require that it be relevant to prisoners and original.

All submissions MUST:

i. be no more than 6,500 words in length,
ii. be typed, double-spaced, on one side of A4 only,
iii. be properly referenced, and
iv. arrive at the Handbook address shown in the Introduction NO LATER than 1st JUNE 1995. Mark your envelope: 'Something To Say'.

The author of the published submission will receive a free copy of the 1996 Handbook, in addition to free hardback copies of the Concise Oxford English Dictionary and the Oxford Thesaurus. Submissions cannot be returned so please only send copies.

ABSTRACT

The writer considers the Home Office responses to Lord Justice Woolf's report on the 1990 prison disturbances in so far as they affect the disciplinary adjudication. He fears that, with the removal from Boards of Visitors of their adjudicatory function, elements of natural justice have been placed in jeopardy. It may not be possible for a prison Governor to come to a hearing without bias, or hints that he is a judge in his own cause: the adjudicating Governor may be in breach of Article 6 of the European Convention on Human Rights. The writer offers a way forward whereby discipline may be maintained in prisons through the application of a redrafted Prison Rule 47 and a revision of the present procedure.

BACKGROUND

One of the many consequences of Lord Justice Woolf's (1991) monumental inquiry into the 1990 prison riots was that the Home Secretary was required to address the question of justice in prison with greater urgency than hitherto. Whatever the causes of the riots, the Home Office had, according to the report, simply failed to convince a significant number of prisoners that they were being treated with fairness during their sentence. Dialogue took place during Woolf's public seminars which indicated a shift in thinking within the highest levels of Prison Service management about justice, internal discipline and the punative sanctions available to help maintain discipline. This thinking became crystallised in the 1991 white paper *Custody, Care and Justice* (Home Office 1991) which, whilst paying tribute to the dedicated work of boards of visitors in the past, proposed to remove from them the power to adjudicate and to punish prisoners. That should have come as no surprise.

Whilst influential voices had previously been raised against a splitting of their functions (Weiler Report, (Home Office 1975); May Report, (Home Office 1979)) others (Jellicoe Report, (Martin 1975); McKenna 1983; Prior Report, (Home Office 1985)) had argued for the removal of the adjudicatory role. The Home Office had vacillated. Douglas Hurd announced to the 1986 annual conference of boards of visitors that they were to lose their adjudicatory function, but the Minister of State for prisons, Lord Caithness, told the same conference the following year that they would not. Lord Justice Woolf's voice was simply too powerful to be ignored and his recommendation, adopted in the white paper, was that boards of visitors should drop out of the process completely. All future infractions of internal discipline should be disposed of by the governor within the existing powers of punishment or, if serious enough, should be referred to the police who would be invited to mount a criminal investigation. The changes were implemented by an amendment to the Prison Rules which came into force on 1 April 1992: what has been gained as a result of this change?

GAINS AND LOSSES

In the first place boards of visitors are no longer faced with the contradiction of being the body which both safeguards the rights and privileges of prisoners through their watchdog role, while at the same time taking them away through their adjudicatory role. Secondly, being freed from responsibility for adjudicating, boards have more time to develop and to devote to their statutory duties under Part IV of the Prison Rules. They may thus become more effective as the Secretary of State's eyes and ears inside establishments. Thirdly as was pointed out to the Woolf Inquiry team at one of their public seminars, boards of visitors had ordered 1,723 punishments of unsuspended forfeiture of remission of over 28 days. Now that the maximum number of days that can be added by a governor is 28 in respect of any one offence, there will be some inroad into the figure of 600–700 people remaining in prison beyond their originally calculated release date. This, Woolf described as: 'an astonishing extra burden on the Prison Service [which] needs to be controlled and relieved'. The more intriguing question, however, remains whether anything has been lost as a result of change.

The loss, it is contended, is that degree of independence vested in the adjudicator which ensures the application of the principles of natural justice. It has been long argued that boards of visitors were seldom truly independent. They were often seen by critics and certainly by a large number of prisoners as being in cahoots with management. Until recently they had a management role in that under Prison Rule 94(4) as formerly drafted, they could suspend members of staff from duty. However much boards might have been suspected of sacrificing their independence there remained the authority of the European Court of Human Rights which, in *Campbell & Fell v UK* (1982) declared them, as adjudicators, to be 'an independnent and impartial tribunal established by law'. They thus fulfilled one of the requirements of Article 6 of the European Convention for the Protection of Human Rights (Council of Europe 1950).

THE INDEPENDENT & IMPARTIAL GOVERNOR

Boards of visitors are appointed by the Secretary of State and not by the Director General of the Prison Service. Governors on the other hand, whilst ultimately working to the Home Secretary's command, do so through the management line of area manager, operational director and Director General. This has not been fundamentally affected by the Prison Service's change to agency status on 1st April 1993. Until the decision of the House of Lords in *ex.p Leech* (1988), the domestic courts, in accord with the apparent policy of 'hands off' in prison matters, firmly rejected the notion of an 'independent governor'. Analogies drawn were between the governor and the commanding officer or sea captain (*Fraser* v. *Mudge* (1975)), the schoolmaster (*ex.p St.Germain* (1979)) or the manager (*ex.p King* (1984)). Waller.LJ in the Court of Appeal perceived 'the importance of the Officer charged with maintaining discipline not being interfered with by the court'. Governors had readily agreed with the view of the adjudication as being part of the managerial role in keeping a smooth running prison. Their then trade union (Home Office Prison Department 1987) saw it as essential for the governor to be 'involved in day to day management e.g. adjudications' and Jenkins (1987), then a serving governor, wrote of adjudications being 'regulatory or managing rather than a simple persuit of justice'. Governors training to take adjudications remains fairly rudimentary and sits within management modules at the Prison Service College. In *ex.p Leech* (1988) however, the House of Lords decided that governors' adjudications are directly reviewable by the divisional court by way of *certiorari* in exactly the same way as those of boards of visitors. Governors are required to apply the rules of natural justice and to reason in a judicial manner when hearing charges against inmates. The managerial element of the adjudications was tossed aside. Adjudicating governors owed their *vires* not to any management line to higher authority but to the statutory instrument under which were performed their duties. Lord Bridge stated it thus:

A prison governor may, in general terms, be described as a servant of the Secretary of State but he is not acting as such when adjudicating on a charge of a disciplinary offence. He is then exercising the independent power conferred upon him by the Rules. The Secretary of State has no authority to direct the governor...as to how to adjudicate on a particular charge or what punishment should be awarded. If a Home Office official sought to stand behind the governor at a disciplinary hearing and tell him what to do the governor would properly send him packing. (at p.497)

NATURAL JUSTICE IN PRACTICE

During 1993, the last year for which figures are presently available, over 100,700 offences against discipline were punished (Home Office 1994). Despite the increased number of serious prison offences which now will be dealt with by the courts, it is clear that adjudicating will remain a substantial part of the governor's role. Speaking as Governor of Durham Prison in March 1992 Martin Mogg told a seminar of governors at Low Newton Remand Centre that he found it '*hard to give proper consideration to the rules of natural justice when you have 19 or 20 adjudications to get through in a morning*'. Mogg's expression of concern goes to the core of this paper. Just how possible is it for the governor to be independent and impartial in adjudicating and if it is not possible, what does that say for natural justice at such hearings?

Lord Bridge's view of the adjudicating governor acting outside the role of state servant may be to enunciate the domestic law correctly, but it is to misunderstand the realities of prison life and to pay little regard to the decisions of the European Court of Human Rights. Classically the governor has been seen as:

responsible to the Commissioners (broadly predecessors of the Prisons Board) for everything that goes on in his establishment. (Among) the principal aspects of his work are the maintenance of security and good order and discipline (Home Office and Scottish Home Department 1958, p.44)

Further, despite the governor's role as general manager of the prison, the casework-cum-counselling ethos implies that many still have an interest in, concern for or relationship with, their charges. Williams (1990) has it that:

It is untrue that helpful, caring approaches—even friendship and counselling in some cases—never occur between governors and prisoners. . . . With long term prisoners the governor of the institution can become similarly involved not least because of intractable discipline problems with some inmates. (p.59)

So management issues, personal relationships and discipline problems may become seamless parts of a whole often implying that, at adjudication, the *de novo* principle may be in jeopardy.

INSTITUTIONAL PRESSURES

The governor is the manager of the organisation within which the alleged offence has taken place and is the employer of the reporting officer. Certainly, in adjudicating, the governor's mind will be on maintaining the good order of the prison and the delicate balance that exists between the staff disciplinary function and the preservation of the tolerable life for inmates. The governor will attempt to come to a hearing with an open mind. Yet the experience of managing the prison day in and day out will make it hard to avoid bias. Morris (1975) noted the argument that a governor may well be seen as a judge in his own cause. The governor may well know the strengths and weaknesses of the principal characters at the hearing. If for example the charge is one of assault, the governor may already have seen papers indicating difficulties that a particular officer has had with a particular inmate. The governor, faced with a simple conflict of evidence, may be inclined to accept the staff version of events since, in the absence of other clarifying factors, there is a knowledge of what staff expect. Prison officers tend to classify governors as representing one or other extreme of a continuum. They may be 'the prisoners' friend' or a 'staff man'. Thus the inter-personal and inter-professional relationships between staff and staff, and staff and governor, may all have their influence on the hearing. Governors may find themselves subject to formal protest raised by the Prison Officers Association over the manner in which they have adjudicated. A governor may be swayed by the exigencies of the regime to order a particular punishment in the hope that it may have some general deterrent effect or because of some more mundane institutional reason such as that the segregation unit is full. Indeed the governor may have had to decide whether or not a particular prisoner who faces charges will have had to be segregated prior to the adjudication and thus, in performing a managerial function, will have had to weigh in the balance the prisoner's dangerousness, previous behaviour or chances of having done that which has been alleged. What have the courts made of this conundrum?

THE JUDICIAL APPROACH

For as long as adjudications could be seen as part of the management function prior knowledge was seen as a positive advantage serving to enhance adjudicatory skills. In *ex.p King* for example Griffiths LJ had it that:

With the governor's knowledge of the personalities with whom he is dealing, I suspect that he will usually be left in no doubt as to the truth of the matter . . . The board of visitors are entirely independent and in all probability they do not know the prisoner or if they do, not nearly as well as the Governor.

It was, of course, *ex.p King* that was overturned by the decision in *ex.p Leech* (supra). But that *ex.p King* has been overturned does not affect institutional dynamics. It does affect what is expected of a governor by subordinates and superiors. The requirement to adjudicate will be part of the governor's job description and the need to keep good order and discipline now forms a part of the Prison Service's (1993) new business and corporate plans to which every governor is committed. A novel twist to the argument is presented in that provision is made in the Criminal Justice Act 1991 for prisons to be contracted out to the private sector. It is enacted that custody officers, the equivilent of prison officers in the contracted out prisons, should assume a broad range of the duties of the latter group but the director of such a prison is statutorily excluded from adjudicating (s.85(3)a). Adjudications are conducted by a controller who is 'a crown servant appointed by the Secretary of State' (ss.85(1)b; 85(4)) partly for that purpose. Paradoxically then, the adjudicator is independent of the contracted out prison but not of the Secretary of State as Lord Bridge would have it. With the job specification of the Controller of Wolds remand prison (Prison Governors' Association 1992) we learn that she is a member of the prison governor grade who is tasked *inter alia* 'to deal with all prison disciplinary cases and authorise confinement and restraint'. The judicial and the managerial functions thus appear fused into one. The controller of the contracted out prison has a similar management line to that of a conventional governor though in place of an area manager she is accountable to the head of the Custodial Contract Unit with the Home Office and ultimately to the Permanent Under Secretary rather than to the Director General. Being independent of the management of Group Four, who run the establishment, she will come to her adjudications *de novo*, without bias and without being judge in her own cause. Her statutory position, reinforced by her job specification written by crown servants, implies that she adjudicates because that is required of her by the Secretary of State.

EUROPEAN ARTICLE 6

Neither the European Commission nor the Court of Human Rights has yet been required to address the question of the adjudicating governor's role. An indication as to how they might recommend or decide may be gleaned from *Engel and others v Netherlands* (1976) and *Sramek v Austria* (1984). *Engel* arose out of infractions of a military disciplinary code some of which were criminal in character and others purely disciplinary (cf Prison Rule 47 *infra*). As to whether or not the hearing of such charges attracted the protection of Article 6(1) of the Convention, that is, were disciplinary charges tantamount to criminal charges, the Court held *inter alia* that one of the factors to be taken into account must the severity of the punishments risked. Since the soldiers risked such penalties as 'strict arrest' or 'service in a disciplinary unit' the charges fell within 'the criminal sphere'. Thus the Article applied. The susceptibility of up to 28 extra days detention however it is styled would place governors' adjudications clearly within the *Engel* test. In *Sramek* a member of a tribunal was a civil servant under the authority of the state official bringing the action. The government agreed that the superior officer was precluded from giving instructions to the subordinate nor was there evidence that there had been any such attempt. The Court found a violation of the Article since 'the parties could maintain legitimate doubts about that person's independence'. The prisoner at adjudication might reasonably harbour legitimate doubts about the governor's independence, not because the Secretary of State had given instructions but that, given the heirarchial relationship, it appeared that he was in a position to do so. Similarly, the prisoner could question the governor's objective impartiality because of the kind of managerial concerns that have been examined.

AMERICAN PRACTICE

Robertson (1991) addressed the question of impartiality at internal hearings within prisons in the United States. Due process does not prohibit internal hearings as long as no adjudicator has been 'involved in the investigation or prosecution of a particular case or has had any personal involvement in the case'. Personal involvement may be direct (for example, the investigation of an incident or the decision to charge) or indirect (for example, personal knowledge of material facts or manifest command influence) (cf *Sramek*).

BIAS AND ITS AVOIDANCE

It is not impossible for the adjudicator in a conventional prison to avoid bias. The governor may genuinely come to a hearing with no prior knowledge of the inmate and no institutional pressures conspiring to affect judgment. Most infractions of internal discipline tend not to be particularly serious nor committed by notorious desperados.

Akester, in her evidence to Lord Justice Woolf (1990, paper E1,p.32) noted that they tended to be about little things—'scraps over the hot plate and goodness knows what'.

In other cases the governor may address the question of bias and apply the test in *ex.p Topping*. Here magistrates had seen court papers that revealed seven further pending charges against the accused yet they proceeded. The Divisional Court quashed the conviction since they had failed to exercise their discretion as to whether or not they should discontinue the hearing. The test to be applied is whether there would be an appearance of bias to a reasonable person observing the proceedings with a complete knowledge of the relevant facts. A governor would on many occasions be in a position akin to that of the justices in *ex.p Topping* yet custom and practice would generally be to continue with the adjudication. Governors would doubtless argue that operational necessities mean that they must adjudicate and must do so speedily, after all detailed instructions as to how they are to act are laid down by the Secretary of State (Home Office Prison Service 1992) despite Lord Bridge's view that they are not his servants when they do so.

There is, of course, a difference between hearings in the magistrates court and disciplinary proceedings in prison, yet the importance of preserving natural justice by the avoidance of bias is common to both. Clapham (1992) stated the position thus:

the law relating to bias seems to be reasonably clear. It is not what the adjudicator feels about possible bias, nor indeed what the accused feels, but what the man on the Clapham omnibus, sitting in court with full knowledge of the relevant facts, considers fair and reasonable. If he feels that the accused is unlikely to receive a fair trial, because of ostensible bias, then an appearance of bias will lead to his convictions being quashed and a new trial being ordered. (p.394)

The foregoing presupposes that governors know of the test in *ex.p Topping*. The writer has argued elsewhere (Quinn 1992) that whereas many governors are graduates, only a handful have read law or have much acquaintance with it and the case put forward by Evans and Le Jeune (1987) for an increase in legal awareness training for civil servants has gone unheeded in so far as governors are concerned.

THE RIGHTING OF WRONGS

A prisoner who is aggrieved at the outcome of an adjudication has one of two courses of action in seeking a remedy. One way, as has been seen since *ex.p Leech*, is to seek judicial review. The other way is to seek an internal remedy by way of the established requests and complaints procedure. In the latter case the record of a disputed hearing is lifted to area manager level. In practice the matter is reviewed by a member of that person's support staff who will pass comments on to one of a team of three senior executive officers who make a recommendation to the area manager concerned. One of the three present post-holders has a law degree but that is not seen as being a requirement of the job. The Directorate of Inmate Administration informed the writer that during 1992, 470 findings at adjudications were quashed or punishment mitigated by the Secretary of State under Prison Rule 56(1). Yet it will be appreciated that to whatever degree an adjudicating governor strives to be impartial or independent of the Secretary of State, the review process rests firmly with his servants.

A WAY FORWARD

It has been argued in this paper that whereas Lord Bridge would have a governor cast aside the hat of servant of the Secretary of State when adjudicating, it is well nigh impossible to do that.

Conversely the 'noise' surrounding an adjudication will be wrapped up so closely with the management of the prison that it will be similarly impossible for a governor to come to the hearing with an open mind. There is a solution, but it is one that is likely to be unpopular both within the Home Office and amongst governors themselves since it smacks of administrative inconvenience and a diminution of governors' powers.

Inconvenience is not a reason to deny something which is correct in principle as we know from the *dicta* of Lane.LJ in *ex.p St.Germain (no.2)*. 'Mere administrative difficulties *simpliciter*' he said 'are not in our view enough. Convenience and justice are often not on speaking terms'. A starting point might be to develop the notion put forward by Fitzgerald giving evidence to the Woolf public seminar on behalf of the National Council for Civil Liberties. He said, in part:

The government should have no power to take away liberty whatever form that liberty is cast in—be it the forfeiture of remission, the postponement of parole or as I see the white paper itself says that additional days in prison could be ordered. If additional days spent in prison are to be ordered for misconduct then it is absolutely fundamental that governors who are not independent and impartial should not have the power to make orders. In fact it would be a clear breach of Article 6(1) of the European Convention of Human Rights. (Evidence to Lord Justice Woolf 1990, paper E1, p.106)

Prison Rule 47 lays down offences against discipline. As presently drafted it includes some which are patently criminal in character for example fighting (Rule 47(4)) or fire-raising (Rule 47(16)), and those which are essentially disciplinary in character, for example non-compliance with the terms of a temporary release licence (Rule 47(16)) or being disrespectful (Rule 47(16)). Others form a hybrid, for example having in possession an unauthorised article (Rule 47(9)a) which may or not be criminal in character depending upon the nature of the article. A final catch-all, 'in any way offending against good order and discipline' (Rule 47(21)) is of dubious legality for want of legal certainty. It is possible to envisage a re-drafting of the Rule which might separate out those charges which have the colour of criminal acts from those which do not. Under a revised system a governor would have *vires* only in respect of those which do not and would lose the statutory authority given under s.42 of the 1991 Criminal Justice Act to add days within the term of the sentence following a finding of guilt. A model for this presently exists in the system of 'minor reports' prevailing in Young Offender Institutions. Here trivial offences are tried with the minimum of formality, usually by the governor or uniformed principal officer; the sanction being strictly limited. It would accord both with evidence given to the Woolf seminar (1990, paper E1, p.63) by Caffarey on behalf of the Prison Service and with the recommendation of Lord Justice Woolf himself that there should be a progressive move towards less reliance upon added days in prison and more reliance upon deprivation of privileges as a sanction.

THE NOTION OF THE PERIPATETIC ADJUDICATOR

Who should adjudicate in cases that are criminal in character but which, for whatever reason, do not reach the courts? Essentially it must be a person who stands aside from the day to day management of the prison. According to the Fitzgerald model it should not be a governor but according to Lord Bridge it can be. One solution might be to look to each area manager and that person's support team. Perhaps each of the Prison Service's 15 administrative areas should have assigned to it a peripatetic adjudicator who might visit each prison in the area as occasion demanded. Ideally such a person should be independent of the Home Office—maybe a retired lawyer or magistrate. This would satisfy not only Fitzgerald's concern that the adjudicator should not be a governor but also Lord Bridge's 'independence' requirement. Most important it would place prison practice in harmony with Article 6(1) of the Convention. Such ideas would need refining but may offer a way forward both in terms of the very necessary maintaining of internal discipline and of ensuring adherence to the rules of natural justice. Could discipline be maintained if governors' powers to adjudicate were to be reduced? That, of course, is untested yet Alpert (1978) found that the implanting of greater legal normality into a prison system (in that case the provision of legal services) was a step which reduced tension, anxiety, hostility and also infractions of discipline among inmates. Under the present model, a governor in awarding 28 added days can, in effect, order the equivilent of a two month prison sentence without any of the safeguards available to a defendant in open court. In light of the foregoing arguments it is posited that such a power should no longer be vested in the governor, and indeed the Prison Governors' Association (1993) in its recent discussion document (March 1993) urged that consideration should indeed be given to the use of (an) 'independent adjudicator for offences which attract additional days'.

Whilst it is clear that there is no short-term prospect of the review of disputed hearings being taken out of the hands of civil servants a new factor is about to enter the equation. The implementation of another of Lord Justice Woolf's proposals means that, at the time of writing, the appointment of an independent prison ombudsman is imminent. Whereas the locus for the review of disputed adjudications will remain with the area manager, once that process has been completed the prisoner will have access to the prison ombudsman. That office will have the power to recommend an alternative decision to the Secretary of State if it is seen that the area manager was at fault.

CONCLUSION

Palley warned the British Institue of Human Rights (1980) conference on judicial review of prison discipline that we should guard against an 'over judicialised procedure' at adjudication but saw manifest fairness as the overriding factor. During the time that has elapsed since that conference the climate has changed with the emergence of 'the active judiciary' (Gearty 1991). The need to be fair permeates all recent caselaw and it has become apparant that prison authorities can no longer depend upon judicial abstention to guard their activities from scutiny in the courts. That Mr Leech and Mr Prevot, with whom his case was joined, are the only prisoners ever successfully to have had governors' adjudications overturned at judicial review, cannot be seen as a reason for complacency. It can only be a matter of time before further litigation calls into question the fairness of governors' adjudications as presently constituted. The cost of litigation and the inevitable adverse publicity accruing to the Prison Service should prisoners once again be successful should not be the reason for change. That should come about partly since manifest fairness will itself help towards the maintenance of peaceful prisons. The kind of change outlined will also help place the adjudication room on all fours with Lord Justice Woolf's aspirations that the prison regime as a whole should be informed by considerations of justice.

NOTE

The views expressed are those of the writer and are not necessarily those of HM Prison Service or the Home Office. The writer is grateful to Colin Warbrick of the Department of Law, University of Durham, for his helpful comments on this paper. This is an updated version of an article first published in the Howard Journal of Criminal Justice Vol.32, 1993. It is reproduced here by kind permission of the publishers Basil Blackwell Ltd.

REFERENCES

Alpert, G.P (1978)
Legal Rights of the Prisoner: An analysis of Legal Aid, Lexington: Heath.

British Institute of Human Rights (1980):
'Judicial review of prison discipline' (report of a meeting held at Queen Mary College, University of London, 5 June), London: BIHR.

Clapham, B. (1992):
'Should judges and JP's always declare an interest', Justice of the Peace, 156, 376–7, 393–4

Council of Europe (1950):
Convention for the Protection of Human Rights and Fundamental Freedoms with subsequent Protocols, Strasbourg: Council of Europe.

Evans., S. & Le Juene, M. (1987):
Report on Training in Legal Awareness, London: Cabinet Office.

Evidence to Lord Justice Woolf's public seminar (1990):
'Justice in Prison', City University, 30,31, October 1990; public seminar papers E1/E2.

Gearty, C. (1991):
'The prisons and the courts', in J.Muncie and R. Sparks (Eds), Imprisonment: European Perspectives, London: Harvester Wheatsheaf with the Open University.

Home Office (1975):
The Report of the Working Party on Adjudication Procedures in Prison (The Weiler Report), London: HMSO.

Home Office (1979):
Report of the Committee of Inquiry into the United Kingdom Prison Services (The May Report), Cmnd. 7673.

Home Office (1985):
Report of the Committee of the Prison Disciplinary System (The Prior Report), Cmnd.9641–1, 9641–2.

Home Office (1991):
Custody, Care and Justice, Cm. 1647.

Home Office (1994):
Statistics of Offences Against Prison Discipline and Punishments: England and Wales,1993. Cm.2664

Home Office Prison Department (1987):
'Note of a meeting held on 12th February 1987 with the Society of Civil and Public Servants (Governors' Branch), London HOPD (P8 Division), (internal circulation).

Home Office Prison Service (1992):
Standing Order 3D: Offences, Adjudications and Punishments, London: Home Office Prison Service.

Home Office and Scottish Home Department (1958):
Report of the Committee on Renumeration and Conditions of Service of Certain Grades in the Prison Service (The Wynn-Parry Report), London: HMSO.

Jenkins, M.J. (1987):
'Control problems in dispersals', in A.E.Bottoms and R.Light (Eds.), Problems of Long-term Imprisonment, London: Gower.

McKenna, B. (1983):
Justice in Prison, London: Justice.

Martin J.P. (1975):
Boards of Visitors of Penal Institutions: Report of a Committee set up by Justice, the Howard League and NACRO (The Jellicoe Report), Chichester and London: Barry Rose.

Morris, T. (1975):
in BIHR, Detention: Minimum Standards, Chichester and London: Barry Rose.

Prison Governors Association (1992):
PGA Magazine, March, No.16.

Prison Governors Association (1993):
'Discussion document' considered at the PGA Annual Conference, Newbold Revel, March 10–11.

Prison Service (1993):
Business Plan 1993–94, 5; Corporate Plan 1993–96, 16–17, London: Prison Service.

Quinn, P.M. (1992):
'Prison discipline, justice and Woolf: the demise of the adjudicating board', Cambrian Law Review, 17, 7–25.

Robertson, J.E. (1991):
'Impartiality and prison disciplinary tribunals', New England Journal on Criminal and Civil Confinement, 17, 301–35.

Williams, B. (1990):
Working with Prisoners, Birmingham Venture.

Woolf, Sir H. (1991):
Prison Disturbances: April 1990. Report of an Inquiry by the Rt.Hon. Lord Justice Woolf (parts 1 and 2) and His Honour Judge Stephen Tumim (Part 2),Cm. 1456.

TABLE OF CASES

Campbell & Fell v UK
(1982) 5 EHRR, 207
Engel and others v Netherlands
(1976) ECHR. Series A, 22
Fraser v Mudge
(1975) 3 All ER, 78.
R v. Hull Prison Board of Visitors ex.p St.Germain et al
(1978) 2 All ER, 198 QBD;
(1979) 1 All ER, 545, CA;
(1979) 3 All ER 545.
R v. Deputy Governor of Camphill Prison ex.p King
(1984) 3 All ER, 897.
R v. Deputy Governor of Parkhurst Prison and another ex.p Leech and another,
The Times, 5 February 1988;
reported sub.nom **Leech v Parkhurst Prison Deputy Governor** (1988) 1 All ER, 485 HL.
R v. Liverpool Justices ex.p Topping
(1983) 1 WLR 119
Sramek v. Austria
(1984) Eur.Ct. H.R. Series A, No.84.

108 Cowley Road, Oxford OX4 1JF

;ECTION FIVE

UMMARIES OF INSPECTION REPORTS

'y His Honour **Judge Stephen Tumim** HM Chief Inspector of Prisons.

ıblished between October 1993 and September 1994.

cluding extracts from various BoV Annual Reports.

ESTABLISHMENTS

BLUNDESTON · CASTINGTON · CHELMSFORD · DORCHESTER · EAST SUTTON PARK · ERLESTOKE · EXETER · FELTHAM · FORD · FULL SUTTON · GRENDON · HAVERIGG · HOLLESLEY BAY COLONY · HULL · HUNTERCOMBE/FINNAMORE WOOD · KIRKLEVINGTON GRANGE · LINDHOLME · LITTLEHEY · LIVERPOOL · NORTHALLERTON · NORTH SEA CAMP · PENTONVILLE · PRESTON · ROCHESTER · STOCKEN · SWALESIDE · SWINFEN HALL · THORN CROSS · THE VERNE · WAKEFIELD · WANDSWORTH · WORMWOOD SCRUBS

troduction

s Honour Judge Stephen Tumim, who is now in
s second term as Her Majesty's Chief Inspector
Prisons (HMCIP) for England and Wales, has
n wide acclaim for his hard-hitting no-non-
nse prison Inspection Reports. Based at the
me Office, this jovial Judge with a fondness for
ckie-bows', has been a persistent campaigner
reform—and with a voice often too powerful to
ore. Since his appointment in 1987 Stephen
mim has radically rewritten the theory of prison
pection, and translated it into practice with
ee highly respected proactive Inspection Teams
o leave few prison stones unturned—if any.
ere are two types of inspection carried out by
ICIP.

e Full Inspection

is follows a well defined path, with the date it
l start made known to the prison in advance.
average of eight inspectors descend on the
son, including specialists in building and
alth care, and for five days they examine over
) specific matters; the inspection is often
ended to six days to encompass a weekend
it. All full inspections include early morning
and visits during the night, meetings with senior managers, staff, inmates, union officials and members of the BoV. A **Full Inspection Report** is subsequently published and usually runs to about 130 pages.

The Short Inspection

These normally last about two days, are usually unannounced and are used to see what progress has been made since the last full inspection was carried out. Short inspections allow the inspectors to see how the prison normally operates, without prior notice of the visit, and they follow a path that allows inspectors fairly wide discretion. The resulting **Short Inspection Report** runs to about 15 pages of text, but has proved especially useful: most media interest relates to comments made in Short, rather than Full, Inspection Reports.

Inspection to publication

Stephen Tumim and his staff inspect around 44 penal establishments in England and Wales each year, both types of inspection being conducted in roughly equal measure. The resulting reports are sent to the Home Office before publication, so that an official response from the prison authorities can be published at the same time as the Report. In the past this has commonly led to delays of a year or more before publication of the Report. Now, after a string of complaints from HMCIP, the period between submission to the Home Office and subsequent publication has been cut to as little as six weeks, though six months is still far more likely for the majority of Reports—at least twice as long as it generally could (and should) be.

Boards of Visitors Annual Reports

Regrettably, BoVs are not (yet?) required to publish their annual Reports. While a large number staunchly refuse to let others 'in' on what they whisper each year to the Home Secretary there are a growing number of others who, refreshingly, are freely choosing to speak up. What follows are summaries of Inspection Reports published by HMCIP between **1st October 1993 and 30th September 1994**, along with extracts of Board of Visitors' annual reports where copies have been provided or obtained. The purpose of this section is threefold: to show trends that are developing, to bring together in one section summaries of all the most recently published Inspection Reports, and to expand upon the short review given of each Report in the respective establishment entry. Unlike our Boards of Visitors, Judge Stephen Tumim makes available all of his Inspection Reports (some for a small fee) to anyone who writes to request a copy. Copies of past and present HMCIP Reports should be available in the library of the prison to which the Report refers, though copies are also available from the address below. Short Inspection Reports are normally free, but there is a small charge for Full Inspection Reports—£1.50 each at present.

Publications Unit, Room 1024, Home Office,
50 Queen Anne's Gate, London SWIH 9AT
Direct line: 071 273 3072/2302
DIRECTOR: **Nigel Owens**

HM PRISON BLUNDESTON

There are striking similarities between the Report (published 29th June 1994) of an inspection of Blundeston training prison in October 1993 and the one in 1987. Then there was an air of resignation and a need for the prison to be revitalised, high levels of adjudications but good staff/inmate relationships. It is clear said HMCIP that the prison has to some extent been revitalised and the morale of staff has improved since the 1987 inspection. In other respects however the conclusions of the earlier Report remain valid.

HMYOI CASTINGTON

Castington has built a solid reputation for containing young offenders with histories of violent offences said HMCIP in a Report, published 22nd March 1994, of an inspection carried out in July 1993. There was too much lock up. Young offenders were locked up on Wednesdays & weekends from tea time until the following morning. The offending behaviour programmes left much to be desired and HMCIP also criticised Castington for insufficient work training opportunities.

A 'listeners' scheme was being developed, however there were few opportunities for the inmates to earn trust and responsibility so that young men were subject to as much supervision after three years as they were after three days in the establishment, regardless of how they behaved. Adjudications had risen from around 250 in 1987 to 2,004 in 1994. Overall, however, there was much more to admire than criticise. Castington's Governor, Chris Harder, responding to the Report said that a working party had been set up to look at ways in which long-term prisoners could earn greater trust and responsibility. Other areas being looked at include: a review of officers' working patterns and the provision of staff to supervise evening associations; improved work opportunities for prisoners; improved courses to help prisoners tackle behavioural problems; and the updating of suicide and lifer risk-assessment training for all officers.

HM PRISON CHELMSFORD

The outstanding feature of Chelmsford was the quality of the relationships between staff and inmates which generated a relaxed atmosphere in which prisoners seemed content to be held said HMCIP in a Report (published 1st February 1994) of an inspection in September 1993.

Morale of the staff was adjudged to be good. Improvements since the last inspection in 1990 included the gradual installation of integral sanitation, a more flexible use of staff, the refurbishment of the Health Care Centre, and a new £2.5m kitchen that was far too large for its purpose, with extravagant fittings and facilities; a waste of public funds. There was promise for the future in the development of a programme on C.wing for remand prisoners and in the life skills and anger management courses which had been introduced. PE staff continued to make good use of the inadequate indoor facilities.

The shortage of constructive activity remained a concern which had consequences for prisoners and for society when they were released: inactivity does nothing to reduce offending. There were no

·aining opportunities and the education pro- ·ramme was not operating at the time of the ıspection: the prison came virtually to a halt at 600 and no progress had been made since our last ıspection in introducing PE and structured asso- iation in the evenings. HMCIP also expressed oncern about the lack of space for domestic visits.

The fact that the Governor and other members f senior management had been in post for several ears had helped to encourage good relationships, ut work and other training opportunities must be rovided if Chelmsford is to provide anything ıore than a warehousing function.

The Governor of Chelmsford, David Sinclair, aid: 'I believe the positive aspects of the report ill be welcomed by everybody as a recognition of ıe commitment shown by staff at all levels. urther progress is essential, and the steps taken llowing the 1990 Report show the will is there'.

IM PRISON DORCHESTER

enior management deserve credit for what has een achieved at Dorchester, said HMCIP in a eport (published 10th March 1994) of an inspec- on in September 1993. Dorchester is unusual mong local prisons in having an effective personal fficer scheme in operation in all wings and for all risoners including remands. The pre-release ourse has been replaced by inmate development ıodules which allow problems to be addressed at n earlier stage and which again are available to all risoners including remands. Sentence planning as been introduced for all prisoners serving one ear or more and effective systems are in place to ıonitor prisoners' progress. The prison is clean nd brightly decorated, with pictures on the walls ı the wings. Staff are proud of their prison and ncourage inmates to respect that environment.

However, evening association is limited to two r three days a week for the majority of prisoners. he regime for vulnerable prisoners is restricted nd that for young offenders is not sufficiently ctive. The education contract holders appeared ot to understand that the syllabus should be ased upon prisoners' needs as identified through entence planning. Living conditions had been nhanced by the installation of integral sanitation nd the conversion of some of the recesses to pro- ide extra showers.

IMP & YOI EAST SUTTON PARK

taff-prisoner relationships at this women's estab- shment were very good said HMCIP in a Report ublished 15th June 1994) of an inspection in ovember 1993. However, physical constraints nposed by buildings mean there is a lack of privacy for prisoners and an absence of any supervised activities in the evenings and at weekends. Education could be improved. There had been relatively little abuse of the system of town and overnight visits; the majority of prisoners valued the opportunity to spend time with their families and had responded in a positive manner. Generally HMCIP was encouraged by much of what they saw at the establishment but considered that it has not yet reached its full potential. HMCIP felt sure however however that the establishment was moving forward led by a committed senior management team.

HM PRISON ERLESTOKE

The treatment of prisoners in Erlestoke was impressive said HMCIP in a Report (published 5th October 1993) of a short inspection in April 1993.

Basic facilities were good. Cells were of a fair size with no shared occupancy. Men had ready access to showering facilities, sufficient clothing and space within the wings. Most had their own keys to privacy locks on their cells doors. Visiting facilities were welcoming, albeit the prison's isolated location made for difficult travelling for visitors. The programme of activities was equally impressive. Relationships are the strength of Erlestoke and with the implementation of sentence planning and an inmate development unit men have a good chance of tackling offending behaviour and preparing themselves for release. The programme of activities was equally impressive. Relationships are the strength of Erlestoke and with the implementation of sentence planning and an inmate development unit, men have a good chance of tackling offending behaviour and preparing themselves for release.

The food provided was satisfactory but unimaginatively presented. Breakfast was meagre. The heated trolleys used to transport the food to the wings were dirty and HMCIP were told a four-week menu cycle was operated, but perusal of the menu book indicated that meals were repeated more frequently than this.

HM PRISON EXETER

There was considerable overcrowding at this local prison and remand centre, said HMCIP in a Report (published 21st June 1994) of an inspection in September 1993. Nevertheless most inmates spent a good deal of time out of their cells. Initiatives to improve the regime were constantly under review, and there was a well established ethos of inmate/staff respect and co-operation. Evening association, however, was limited. Young prisoners were held in the remand centre, which offered the poorest accommodation. There was insufficient work or other out of cell activities for them and bullying was fairly common.

The segregation unit was gloomy and forbidding, cramped and dungeon-like because of the thick pillars supporting the ceiling in the middle of the landing. The regime for prisoners was very limited. There was insufficient work. Association was limited and education needed to be focused on their special needs. Young offenders were locked in a bare cell for most of the day and had few opportunities to make use of the facilities on offer.

There were still significant delays in getting patients accepted into NHS psychiatric facilities. One patient had been admitted at the time of the inspection in a grossly psychotic state. A consultant had been contacted but was unable to assess the patient until the end of the week. The senior medical officer was unwilling to treat the patient against his will and so the patient deteriorated until by mid-week he was lying all day on a mattress on the floor talking to no-one. At that point arrangements were made to try and get him into hospital. In the community a general practitioner could expect to have such a patient admitted on the day he was seen. This should be the same for the prison. There was a Listeners Suite for suicidal prisoners: there had been one suicide in 1989 and one in 1993.

The inspectors concluded that there was a tradition of providing a sensible, relaxed regime. The prison has struggled with recent changes, particularly the extensive building programme, and related inconveniences which have had adverse effects of morale. However HMCIP felt there was an underlying expectation that matters were improving.

Responding to the Report, the Prison Service said that since the inspection the Governor has moved young offenders requiring segregation to the main segregation unit where they have access to exercise and education. In addition a workshop offering employment for up to 15 segregated prisoners, including young offenders, is under development. Two extra psychiatric sessions have been added and full psychiatric ward rounds are now conducted by an outside specialist.

HMYOI & REMAND CENTRE FELTHAM

Measures taken to improve family ties, including family visits on the units and the flourishing visitors centre, were welcomed by HMCIP in a Report (published 10th December 1993) of a brief inspection in August 1993. The inspectors were encouraged to see the beginnings of a positive programme for sentenced juveniles. The arrangements in reception were more civilised. Relationships between many staff and prisoners had improved since the last inspection, but the treatment of young prisoners still gave cause for concern. The basic lifestyle was unsatisfactory. Many prisoners spent too much time in cells which were barren of furniture and devoid of stimulation. Sentence planning was at best mediocre and the involvement of personal officers patchy. The attitudes of some staff seemed to be offhand and uninterested. Some remand prisoners were issued with only one pair of underpants a week. During August 1993 no educational classes took place and there had been no evening classes for over 12 months. The shortage of suitable training opportunities was lamentable. The three training courses offered 32 places for a population approaching 800.

Medical interviews were conducted at speed. Some 60–70 inmates a day reported sick but only about 3 of them were subsequently seen by the doctor, these figures may indicate that the filtering process was excessively severe. There was no time to establish any understanding with the prisoner—contrary to the standards set by the Directorate of Health Care. Most of the 23 patients in the Health Care Centre suffered from psychiatric or personality disorders. Half had been admitted because of anxieties about suicide. One subnormal patient with a history of sexual assaults for whom there had been (despite several applications) no offer of treatment or care in the NHS, could not cope on ordinary location and had spent his first two years in health care centres. Plans which existed in 1991 to employ a trained psychiatric nurse had not been implemented.

Some positive steps had been taken to address the problem of bullying including the siting of closed-circuit television cameras and monitors for staff in reception, outside the prison shop, in some shower rooms and other areas. A small self-contained unit, the Lee Waite Unit holding up to 16 prisoners known or suspected of being involved in serious bullying, had been established. However the levels of threatening behaviour and taxing were clearly still high. The inspectors were disappointed, especially as the Prison Service's initiative in tackling bullying had been largely based on work undertaken at Feltham, but that establishment was unable to provide information on the number of incidents of bullying and the effectiveness of the Lee Waite Unit had not been evaluated.

Some prisoners came from as far away as Cornwall, Newport, Great Yarmouth and Liverpool—distances which cannot be conducive to the development of resettlement plans or the maintenance of family links. Cells in the YOI were badly in need of redecoration, graffiti was commonplace and much cell furniture was damaged. Rubbish abounded and very few cells had curtains. The inspectors found an obviously distressed juvenile in a cell, where he had been for many hours,

vith only cardboard furniture. There were no pic-
:ures, books or other distractions from his plight.
\ssociation for some remand prisoners was under
:wo hours a day, although those who had earned
nost privileges were out of cell for about 12 hours
)er day.

Feltham Board of Visitors Report

)espite deep cleaning in some units there was no
;eneral improvement in the conditions of many
;howers and lavatories, which were appalling.
ntegral sanitation was not installed in the Health
:are Centre when it was refurbished during the
'ear. There was concern about the level of associa-
ion. There was, for example, no evening associa-
ion at weekends and juveniles only had
ssociation on alternate weekday evenings.
\ssociation was frequently cancelled because of
lemands for escorts. There were still no evening
:lasses. A mosque and Radio Feltham, an in-house
etwork run by prisoners, were established during
he year.

The level of personal officer work continued to
'ary and, as a result, sentence planning was frag-
nentary. There was respect between officers and
risoners in the special unit for bullies but this was
ften lost when prisoners returned to normal loca-
ion because of the lack of personal officer work
nd different attitudes. There was a high level of
ncidents (109) involving the use of control and
estraint techniques and a sharp increase in the
umber of drug finds, although some of this may
ave been due to more effective search proce-
ures. By the end of the year only those juveniles
rom outside Feltham's catchment area who could
ot be managed elsewhere were being sent to
eltham.

IM PRISON FORD

ord did not have a clear purpose said HMCIP in a
eport (published 13th December 1993) of an
ispection in June 1993.

The Governor's idea that the regime prepared
r inmates for release was not shared in practice
y a large number of staff, many of whom had
een at Ford for far too much of their service. It
'as impossible to escape the feeling of inertia in
ie living units. Sentence planning and personal
fficer work had not really taken off, nor had staff
een given suitable incentives for close involve-
ient with inmates. There were pockets of good
ractice being pursued by individuals unsup-
orted, and in some cases they thought hindered,
y other staff.

There were aspects of the prison which were
dmirable—the visits and catering arrangements,
ie introduction of two town visits a month, the
splendid new education department. There had been an improvement in the quality of work offered to prisoners. Positive initiatives had been taken towards suicide prevention.

Responding to the the Report the Director General of HM Prison Service said the Chief Inspector's criticisms had already been taken to heart in an overhaul of the management structure by the new Governor and his management team. This, coupled with preparation of the establishment's Business Plan, will point towards a vigorous regime designed to stretch inmates and prepare them for release.

HM PRISON FULL SUTTON

Full Sutton's reputation for disorder was gradually receding said HMCIP in a Report (published 3rd June 1994) of a short inspection of this dispersal prison in November 1993. Staff were regaining control, conditions for prisoners were good and the atmosphere on the assessment/treatment unit was impressive because of its focus and the commitment of staff.

HM PRISON GRENDON UNDERWOOD

Although some of the 1960's fabric has a worn out look, the same cannot be said of the ethos of Grendon which continues to flourish said HMCIP in a Report (published 5th October 1993) of an inspection in May 1993. Men with backgrounds including very serious offending were taking the opportunity to confront underlying problems assisted by committed and skilful staff. The specialised training needs of staff involved in therapeutic activities, which have long been recognised, were still not being addressed suitably. As to how successful this therapeutic regime is in improving men's chances of not reoffending, a recent study of reconviction statistics gives cause for optimism: of 214 men covered by the study, 33.3% were reconvicted within two years if release, compared with a national reconviction rate for adult males of between 42% and 47%. There is a case for a wider study of the results based on larger samples.

The spontaneity and constructive approach of staff and inmates was impressive. The prison was clean and well-cared for. Time out of cell was 13 hours a day, although observation of the assessment unit indicated a lack of sufficient daytime activity. The quality of food was satisfactory but the kitchen should be replaced. Visiting arrangements had been improved since the last inspection and a bright new Visitors Centre was opened by the Minister of State. The atmosphere in the prison was very friendly, with common use of forenames.

Relationships between staff and inmates were based on an understanding of the purpose of Grendon and largely used to good effect.

HM PRISON HAVERIGG

If this training prison is to remain part of the penal estate for the foreseeable future, further investment is needed, said HMCIP in a Report (published 13th July 1994) of an inspection in January 1994. Most prisoners are housed in former RAF huts, each in a poor state of repair. The small communal toilet areas in a number of huts were dirty, smelly and unhygienic. Cleaning standards were generally poor and there is considerable vandalism. The huts were a haven for bullying and trafficking, primarily in drugs. The portable buildings housing Rule 43 prisoners were even more spartan than the worst of the old huts in the main prison. Conditions were cramped and association space and facilities were limited. The regime remained impoverished, most prisoners were lying on their beds or watching television in a claustrophobic room.

Nevertheless the atmosphere at the prison was relaxed. Employment opportunities more than matched the inmate population. Work with lifers was commendable. All prisoners serving six years or over were entitled to apply for family visits which took place once per month. There were opportunities for prisoners and relatives to prepare a meal or snack together, to watch television or walk around the prison farm. Due to the need in the north to move prisoners at short notice from local prisons to training establishments, receptions at Haverigg have been arriving in large numbers, stretching further the resources available to put them through a satisfactory induction programme.

HMP & YOI HOLLESLEY BAY COLONY

The routine in the YOI was not so impressive in 1990 said HMCIP in a Report (published 29th June 1994) of an inspection in December 1993. Staff were more optimistic, with younger officers keen to take on more fulfilling work. Fewer prisoners were held under Rule 43 for their own protection. The Governor had plans to increase time spent out of cell for all prisoners. NVQ's were being introduced into many areas of the regime and a job search facility would soon assist prisoners to find work on release. But young offenders still spent too much time idle and there was insufficient encouragement for them to make use of the facilities and bullying was still a significant problem.

HM PRISON HULL

BoV Report 1993/4: Staff at this local prison have had to cope with exceedingly high numbers of prisoners. There has been an increase in the number of hours prisoners on certain wings spend out of their cells, an increase in the visits allowance and the introduction of more realistic mealtimes. But it is a matter of regret that more structured work is not available. There is still no association area for C.wing, which has a large population of remand prisoners. There is overcrowding in C and D Wings, creating tension in the prison. The morale of the education staff has been undermined by the contracting out process but their professionalism has ensured that there has been minimum disruption to the service. The regime for vulnerable prisoners was reduced to one hour's exercise per day and occasional visits to the gymnasium. On occasions these prisoners have had to double up, with one prisoner having to sleep on the floor. The number of mentally disturbed prisoners continues to be high despite efforts to divert them from custody. Far too many prisoners are held, albeit for their own safety, in strip conditions. A prisoner committed suicide on C.wing during the year. A 'listeners' scheme is being set up.

HMYOIs FINNAMORE WOOD & HUNTERCOMBE

BoV Report 1993/94: Tendering for prison education has been a disaster which has radically lowered the morale of education staff. An enormous amount of time was spent by staff in dealing with the upheavals arising from it. The result is that an external college with no previous experience of handling prison education is struggling at both institutions. The Board is concerned about the long delays in getting replies to requests and complaints, from the Area Manager. It condemns the Prison Service for refusing to release its report of an investigation into an assault by prison staff on a prisoner being transferred to another prison. It is also concerned that the Crown Prosecution Service's failure to prosecute offences committed by prisoners is sending the wrong message. The Board is also concerned about the future of Boards of Visitors following the Home Secretary's decision not to appoint a President to Boards of Visitors. In order to take on the task of monitoring the performance of the establishment contracts in the future, the Board believes that there is a need to reorganise the structure and leadership of the Boards in order to prevent their demise. From April 1st 1994, Finnamore Wood became an open prison.

HM PRISON KIRKLEVINGTON GRANGE

Kirklevington was a clean, tidy and well maintained prison with which the inspectorate were favourably impressed said HMCIP in a Report (published 19th May 1994) of an inspection in November 1993. The excellent leadership provided by the governor had been instrumental in rebuilding staff morale after an earlier decision to close the prison. There were clearly defined objectives and an impressive contract between the Governor and Area Manager. The environment was calm and co-operative and a high emphasis was placed on helping prisoners to confront their offending behaviour. The prison had soon achieved a high degree of acceptance within the local community and a positive awareness existed which took account of the needs of all ethnic groupings. A recommendation to the Director General that the Grange should begin to hold lifers is currently being considered by the Home Office. If accepted the first lifers should arrive by January 1995. HMCIP also recommended to the Area Manager that an additional member should be appointed to the probation team.

Recommendations to the Governor: leaking flat roofs should be covered; Health and Safety policy should be rewritten promptly and audits carried out annually; BoV room should be fitted with a telephone and there should be more combined staff training with staff at Holme House. A study needs to be conducted to ensure racial factors do not play any part in the inmate selection process for the Grange and education cover should be provided for weekends. PE staff should be increased by one. Liaison with outside probation should be carried out by personal officers. The Health Care Contract should be amended to allow the Medical Officer to contribute to management meetings and the hospital should be resited so allowing the Health Care Centre to become a residential block. Consideration should be given to arranging more economical part time nursing cover, deficiencies in the kitchen should be corrected and plans to provide education in exercise, diet and cancer prevention should not be delayed. A multi-disciplinary HIV/AIDS group should be set up. Overall, HMCIP were most favourably impressed with their inspection of the Grange.

HM PRISON LINDHOLME

In their Report (published 21st July 1994) of an inspection in March 1994, the inspectors voiced their concern that Category D prisoners continue to be held in closed conditions. H.wing was dirty, smelly and badly in need of major refurbishment. In general, however, the inspectors were heartened by much of what they found at the prison. A sensible regime development plan and sound inmate/staff relationships supported by compacts provide a good basis for future progress.

HM PRISON LITTLEHEY

There was praise for Littlehey from HMCIP in a Report (published 4th May 1994) of an inspection in January 1994. Prisoners who in other establishments would be segregated for their own protection felt safe enough to take part in the full range of activities with other inmates. The personal officer scheme was working well, teamwork was impressive and staff at all levels were encouraged to develop initiatives. Inmates had association seven nights a week, the weekend education programme was excellent, prisoners were purposefully occupied. Staff moral was high said HMCIP. According to the 1993/4 Annual Report of the Littlehey BoV, however, a change in the type of prisoner being sent to Littlehey, and the tendency to send them much earlier in their sentence, has destabilised the prison. The system of adjudications was ineffective and did not provide sufficient disincentives for prisoners to commit offences. The reluctance to prosecute inmates for serious offences caused serious concern. There were five escapes in 1993, four absconds and 35 home leave failures—a rise which the BoV maintains is directly attributable to the changes in adjudications. The Board's relations with some members of staff had deteriorated due to its loss of disciplinary powers, with some staff taking the view that BoV members were acting merely as 'busybodies'. The BoV remains disturbed at the length of time it takes to transfer mentally ill inmates to the appropriate hospital facility.

HM PRISON LIVERPOOL

Liverpool was a severely overcrowded local prison said HMCIP in a Report (published 23rd November 1993) of an inspection carried out in May 1993. Following the Strangeways riot, Liverpool's catchment area had been extended to include some courts previously covered by that prison and it helped to alleviate the use of police cells. The effect of this had been to inhibit the development plans to improve the regime. Of particular concern was the limited time prisoners spent out of their cells, especially the unconvicted population, and the poor facilities and impoverished regime for the mentally ill in the Health Care Centre which is unfit for patient care because of its design deficiencies. The operating theatre was an expensive wasted resource and was structurally unsafe. The surgical unit (staffed by qualified civilian nurses) had good standards for patients and the nurses who staffed it; however the remainder of the Health Care Centre was poor and was a cause of low morale among the officers there. A simple refurbishment and redecoration would be insufficient and a waste of money. There have been five suicides at Liverpool in the last five years—three in the Health Care Centre.

As a result of the increased demand for places, Liverpool had essentially become a short stay prison where it was impossible to have a meaningful induction programme for new inmates; sentence planning and the proper assessment of inmates was severely inhibited and, because of the overcrowding, there was insufficient space to allow much association on the wings. At the same time, because of the external commitment, continuity of staff on the wings was diminished and this, in turn, led to fewer officers being involved in dealing with inmates personal problems. However the inspectors found Liverpool to be, in most respects, a well-managed and well-run establishment. Relations between management, staff and inmates appeared sound and relaxed.

HMRC NORTHALLERTON

This establishment was struggling to recover from the effects of a change of role from YOI to Remand Centre, said HMCIP in a Report (published 9th September 1994) of an inspection in March 1994. Throughcare at the Centre had been thrown into disarray by the change of role, and the Personal Officer scheme had all but died out. Association facilities were limited and there were no activities on offer during the evenings. Insufficient use was made of both education and PE facilities, the majority of inmates were offered only part-time work, although the inspectors concluded that control was being exercised firmly but fairly with good inmate/staff relationships. Inmates who become ill at Northallerton are transferred to Holme House prison or located in the segregation unit. transfers to Holme House were sometimes difficult to arrange and the segregation unit was not a satisfactory location for sick prisoners. It was particularly disturbing to find that prisoners who were considered suicidal were located there. Responding to the Report, the Prison Service said that a development plan had already been prepared to answer many of HMCIP's criticisms.

HM PRISON NORTH SEA CAMP

The quality of relationships between staff and prisoners at North Sea Camp in Lincolnshire and the prison's work aimed at helping prisoners not to re-offend were praised in by HMCIP in a Report (published 23rd November 1993) of an inspection in July 1993. Since the inspection the prison has opened a Job club and, with the probation service, has set up a scheme to allow prisoners (within six weeks of discharge) periods of supervised leave to help re-establish themselves in the community.

HM PRISON PENTONVILLE

Despite the bleak and spartan surroundings in which prison officers and prisoners at this local prison worked and lived, the inspectors were impressed by their general cheerfulness. The Report (published 22nd March 1994) of an inspection in July 1993 said that many of the prisoners were prepared to accept the limitations of the regime because of the prison's proximity to their homes. They also seemed to have a genuine appreciation of the efforts of the Governor and his staff to make improvements to their quality of life. The staff seemed to have been stimulated by the changes to the regime which had recently been introduced.

These changes had lead to prisoners spending almost 40 hours a week out of cell (compared with 13 hours in 1990), to more realistic mealtimes and to the introduction of evening visits. But there was little for them to do but watch television or play games in the workshops which had been converted for association purposes. Work opportunities for convicted prisoners were limited. The inspectors had grave reservations about holding immigration detainees in the prison and were very uneasy about holding detainees on the same wing and subjecting them to the same regime as unconvicted prisoners, as a group immigration detainees gave the impression of being distressed, despondent and, in some cases, desperate.

The inspectors were particularly concerned about the provision of health care services. New arrivals could wait in reception several hours before they saw a doctor. Staff feared that the imminent move of the Health Care Centre to unsuitable F.Wing might become permanent since the planned rebuilding of the old Health Care Centre had been stopped. Nursing staff complained about the lack of training, poor detailing, poor communication and poor regimes for patients. Although there had been some improvement in the preceding months, it was still commonplace for the transfer of mentally disordered prisoners to hospital to take several weeks. Occasionally even court diversion schemes were proving unsuccessful in securing hospital beds. A 'listeners' scheme had been set up. The inspectors concluded that after a long period of marking time Pentonville was beginning to move forward but there was much still to be done. They would like to see recent initiatives at the prison sustained and supported by the provision of extra resources which the establishment urgently needs.

Responding to the Report, the Governor, Bill Abbott, said that since July's inspection a range of improvements have been carried out, including: relocation of the Health Care Centre pending complete refurbishment of its old premises; the recruitment of new medical staff and improvements in management and training; on-going work to give all prisoners 24 hour access to sanitation by the end of the year; and an increase in the amount of time prisoners spend in employment and training.

HM PRISON PRESTON

With few exceptions, conditions for prisoners at Preston were unsatisfactory, said HMCIP in a Report (published 28th July 1994) of an in inspection of this local prison in January 1994. Some of the cells were dowdy and squalid, with flaking paintwork and many were barren of furniture. Convicted inmates are lodged in dirty cells with nothing more than a bed, mattress and bucket. Those inmates who did not use the gymnasium could only expect one shower per week unless they were living in B.wing. Few of the cells in B.wing had privacy curtains around the toilets and none were suitable for two prisoners as well as integral sanitation. There were no plans to give all prisoners access to in-cell sanitation by the target date of 31st December 1994. Instead all prisoners outside B.wing were likely to have to put up with the squalid indignity of slopping out in 1995.

However, in spite of these conditions, prisoners were generally content to be at Preston. This was primarily because it was convenient for their families to visit, but also because it represented a reasonably safe environment compared with some other establishments. Some improvements had been made to conditions on the landing which held prisoners under psychiatric observation, although the subterranean position of the unit is fundamentally unsuited for its purpose. There were often considerable difficulties and delays in transferring prisoners to psychiatric hospitals. Sentence planning was weak on setting targets for prisoners to tackle offending behaviour. The personal officer system was practically non-existent. The regime for most vulnerable prisoners was barren and there was enormous scope to improve the quantity and quality of work training together with educational and offence focused activity. As it was, there was too little of a constructive nature to occupy prisoners when they were out of their cells. While wrangling between the Prison Service and the Prison Officers Association (POA) has been going on, conditions for prisoners continue to be unsatisfactory. There is not enough to do: the standard of throughcare and challenging offending behaviour is abysmal. Cells are squalid and the POA has successfully prevented them being improved by self-help painting. There must be serious doubts about Preston's suitability to remain a local prison because of the very large sums of capital investment that would be required for rebuilding and refurbishment. In spite of the personal qualities of many staff and the good humour of prisoners, Preston presents a depressing picture. It fell a long way short of the Prison Service's declared statement of purpose and of the good practice recommended by the Woolf Committee. The inspectors were overwhelmingly reminded of prisons of many years ago. In Preston it was as if nothing had changed since the 1960s. The Prison Service is examining which establishments would be most suitable for market testing. The inspectors were not aware of all the factors involved in such decisions, but the treatment of and conditions for prisoners should be at the heart of them. Establishments with impoverished regimes and poor conditions which fail to gain the co-operation of the majority of staff to improvements may lend themselves to being taken over by private companies—conditions and the regime at Preston must be improved, one way or another.

HM PRISON ROCHESTER

Rochester lacked a unified sense of purpose said HMCIP in a Report (published 29th October 1993) of an inspection in April 1993. The Category C and D prisoners, who were housed in A.wing in poor quality dormitory accommodation, had a very restricted regime in comparison with other similar establishments. Their freedom of movement within the grounds, employment opportunities, and use of the extensive facilities of the prison were limited by the need to keep them apart from other prisoners. Many of the vulnerable prisoners in C.wing could not make use of the already limited availability of the education/activities centre because of essential work commitments. They were sometimes also prevented from attending offending behaviour groups for the same reason. The young prisoners on B and E Wings also suffered from the need to share facilities with the two other groups of prisoners. They resented the fact that they had minimal access to the facilities available. The establishment presented a picture of uncertainty; an unhappy series of compromises operating with an uneconomic use of resources.

Responding to the Report Derek Lewis, Director General of HM Prison Service, accepted that the differing needs of each group of prisoners posed problems but said that for the foreseeable future Rochester will continue to hold all three.

HM PRISON STOCKEN

What was being achieved at Stocken, and the direction it was taking, is the best way of securing Stocken's future said HMCIP in a Report (published 19th May 1994) of an inspection in October 1993. Facilities, inmate-staff relationships and opportunities for work, education and training were praised by the inspectorate. However Judge Tumim criticised the catering service and the design of the kitchen as well as the role of the Chaplaincy who were not well thought of by either prisoners or staff. There were five recommendations to the Director General concerning the Chaplaincy; sale of off-lying land; permission for lifers to work outside the prison; improvements in catering service and the fitting of power points in all cells. There were lengthy recommendations to the Governor (56 in all) covering the whole spectrum of the prison from improving fire precautions to the development of the 'Genesis' addiction project. There should be an end to receptions being located in the segregation unit, washing and drying facilities should be installed on all wings and all visitors should from time to time be searched. Cell searches should be conducted by staff unconnected with the respective living unit. Lunch should not be served before noon and not left in trolleys. Targets for replying to request/complaint forms should be met and the quality of replies should be improved. There should be access to the library at weekends, an increase in specialist PE staff and consideration should be given to prison transport being used to meet visitors at local railway stations. The quality of sentence planning should be improved, as should the induction programme. More training and support should be given to staff working in the inmate development unit. Dental surgery should be equipped to appropriate hygiene standards and priority on the waiting list should be given to those experiencing pain. Access to the medical officer should be improved with more time being devoted to morning surgery, and inmates should be able to have private interviews with the Medical officer. The aims and purposes of the Job Club should be explained to all staff, and staff who supervise family visits should be given more training in counselling. Overall the prison was heading in the right direction and its design should act as a model for the building of similar prisons in the future.

HM PRISON SWALESIDE

The Swaleside **Board of Visitors Annual Report 1993**, published April 1994, identified five 'Areas of Concern'. The £1m that was being spent refurbishing the prison kitchen, which had been built only five years previously, was an extraordinary waste of public money. The inordinate delays experienced by deportees granted parole subject to deportation, and those granted cross-border transfers within the UK, caused much frustration and waste of valuable staff time. The BoV also expressed concern about the destabilising effect caused by the large number of transfers in and out, the sharp increase in the number of cell fires at the prison, and a serious increase in the number of assaults on staff. The BoV said four further matters required immediate attention.

For the third year running the BoV raised the problem of mentally disturbed prisoners in Swaleside. At the time of writing 45 prisoners (nearly 10% of the population) are receiving psychiatric treatment. Inmates being confined in the segregation unit for 23 hours/day was inhumane and unacceptable. Transfers from Cat.C prisons without explanation may not be a punishment in theory, but to those at the sharp end it is most certainly seen and accepted as a punishment. An alleged assault by staff at Wandsworth had been promptly passed to that establishment for investigation: five months elapsed and in spite of numerous determined efforts no explanation or investigation report was forthcoming, a prevarication the Board found completely unacceptable.

Many constructive and positive things are happening at Swaleside, the building work is already under way for the Drugs Unit and for the new Visitors Centre, and looks close for the staff rest rooms. The reception area is being upgraded. The Board are greatly encouraged and impressed by the high quality and performance of the Swaleside staff. Their co-operation and support of the Board's role is much appreciated.

HMYOI SWINFEN HALL

The regime at Swinfen Hall was constructive and forward looking and the training programme was well-regarded by prisoners said HMCIP in a Report (published 7th December 1993) of an inspection carried out in June 1993. Staff were well motivated and committed to the principle of challenging prisoners' behaviour. It was refreshing to find such a united and positive staff staff culture in the prison. The establishment had a long tradition of looking after young offenders and had benefited in recent years from good management which had promoted a very caring approach to inmates. Personal officers were the inmates' first point of reference if they had problems and the regime was built around a personal officer system in which each wing officer was given the responsibility of preparing and managing the sentence plans of a small number of inmates. However there were inadequate facilities on the wings for personal officers to do their work. The contribution of the personal officers was reflected in the atmosphere between staff and inmates, which was relaxed and mutually helpful, and the apparent absence of bullying in the establishment. HMCIP was encouraged by the time spent out of cell each day by inmates at Swinfen Hall and the Governor's expressed wish to increase this time. However, more purposeful activities were needed and work training opportunities needed to be expanded. The regime would benefit from the provision of more practical training courses rather than having to depend so heavily on education for full-time occupation of inmates. The group work treatment programme which primarily addressed offending behaviour were run on a multi-disciplinary basis and were well received by inmates. The Chief Inspector stated that there was an impressively high level of co-operation amongst those who ran them and a high degree of interest was shown by all staff in what they were aiming to achieve. The overall impression was very favourable. The regime was constructive and the staff well-motivated and committed to the principle of challenging inmates' offending behaviour. It was refreshing to find such a united and positive staff culture in a penal establishment and credit must be given to the current and previous managements for achieving and maintaining this.

HMYOI THORN CROSS

Thorn Cross is clean with a cheerful prison population, said HMCIP in a Report (published 10 March 1994) of an inspection in August and September 1993. Staff showed enthusiasm and were clearly doing work they enjoyed and doing it well. Instructors on the catering course, for instance, not only trained prisoners but helped them secure employment on release. The vocational training and construction industry training courses and physical education were good features but formal education had suffered over the last year because of tension between the Home Office and teachers and the successors of local education authorities.

The anomaly whereby juveniles do not qualify for a discharge grant at the end of their sentence was a particular problem at Thorn Cross. The inspectors said there is a clear need for juveniles to be given financial assistance on discharge, particularly where the alternative is a return to circumstances in which the risk of re-offending is greater. Consideration should be given to introducing an ex-gratia payment of similar scale to the discharge grant.

Responding to the Report, the Governor, Iain Windebank, said that most of the educational difficulties are on their way to being resolved and that the introduction of a discharge grant for juveniles is being considered by the Prison Service.

HM PRISON THE VERNE

Some of the factors which contributed to the disturbance at Wymott in September 1993 were present at The Verne when the establishment was inspected in February 1994, said HMCIP in their Report published 15th July 1994. There were severe limits to the control staff could exercise to prevent bullying, racketeering and misuse of drugs, because of the large number of inmates and the open nature of the prison. Vandalism was increasing and disciplinary sanctions were ineffective in controlling the behaviour of some disruptive prisoners. Staff relationships with prisoners were generally good and certainly much stronger than those at Wymott. But there is a danger that staff will start to lose the confidence necessary to retain close links with prisoners. In the most recent protest over food, which occurred just before the inspection, it appeared that a small group of disruptive inmates exerted influence over others to force them to take part. This was also a feature of the Wymott disturbance. During the six months before the inspection 425 prisoners had been received at The Verne, stretching the prison's ability to cope and provide a proper training regime. Transferring unsuitable prisoners to other establishments was extremely difficult to organise and expensive to carry out. Similar features were seen at Wymott when there was a very quick turnover of prisoner population before the disturbance. HMCIP was not satisfied that all prisoners who were demonstrably unsuitable and unwilling or unable to conform could be reallocated before they produced serious control problems. HMCIP said the inspection lends further weight to the view that the categorisation system is flawed: inmates who do not present a threat to security can nonetheless pose serious control problems and the latter factor needs to be taken into account when their allocation is determined.

HM PRISON WAKEFIELD

While work to install integral sanitation was well advanced at Wakefield, said HMCIP in a Report (published 10th May 1994) of a short inspection in December 1993, the decision to place two toilets in each small dormitory without any privacy screen was insensitive. Considerable progress had however been made since the last inspection, with the Health Care Centre being completely refurbished, but not all matters had received attention.

Efforts to transfer mentally disordered prisoners to secure psychiatric facilities were still proving difficult, the Redgra pitch still needed replacement, cells still lacked picture boards, the request/complaints system remained confused, the much-needed Visitors Centre had not yet been provided and there was still no formal induction programme for inmates. HMCIP were nevertheless impressed by the calm, clean and safe environment that Wakefield offered both inmates and staff.

With two catering staff on long term sick leave, some 300 hours of TOIL were owed to kitchen staff, and the shortfall in supervision was reflected in the somewhat slipshod attitude of the inmate work party. Many prisoners complained about the food, though HMCIP, who found the general standard to be satisfactory, argued the timing of meals was unacceptable.

By 6 December 1993 there had been 909 disciplinary charges brought against prisoners in Wakefield during the year, a figure which HMCIP described as low and confirmed the quality of the relationships between staff and inmates. A total of 1,831 request/complaint forms had been issued in the year to the end of October 1993, 242 of which were subsequently declared out of date when they had not been returned within three months. Prisoners alleged that staff lost forms which complained about them, and officers claimed that prisoners destroyed the forms themselves. HMCIP was unable to determine where the truth lay because no attempt was made to account for forms issued and not handed in. This weakness should be remedied.

Wakefield allowed less items in possession than other dispersals and this created conflict. A radical and far-reaching review of regimes was being undertaken at the time of the inspection which would bring standards into line with other establishments. Workshop hours would rise from 19 per week to 27 and time out of cell would increase from 9.5 to 11.75 per day. Meal times were also set to change with dinner at 1215 rather than 1100, and tea at 1715 rather than 1600. Censorship of mail had moved into the wings since the last inspection and away from its former central office. Mail for Cat A's was fully censored both incoming and outgoing, though there was a reduced censorship for other categories of inmates.

HMCIP recommended that full use be made of the Health Care Centre, with waiting times to see the dentist and optician reduced. More female officers should be recruited and supervision in the kitchen should be reviewed. Card phones should be fitted with acoustic hoods, consideration should be given to inmate members on welfare and conditions committees, and a system should be found for tracking request and complaint forms after issue to inmates. The BoV should have a room and telephone of its own, all staff members should wear name badges, dormitory toilets should be screened and further action should be taken in respect of matters outstanding from the last inspection. Situated about half a mile from Wakefield city centre, the present prison dates from 1842 and is of radial design. Wakefield is the main centre for lifers and is strangely both the largest and cheapest-to-run dispersal prison in the system.

HM PRISON WANDSWORTH

BoV Annual Report 1993/4: The Board of Visitors called for the reinstatement of plans to renovate two wings before the end of 1994 where conditions are described as unacceptable. A and B wings were due to be improved as part of the Government's commitment to end slopping out but cuts in the refurbishment budget mean that this undertaking will not now be met. Physical conditions on A.wing, which accommodates 250 remand prisoners, are extremely poor: slopping out, flooding in recesses, lack of showers, continuing cockroach infestation, inadequate equipment for association. The rising population has put a strain on some units and has affected sentence planning. Plans to locate men nearer their families have also been a casualty. There has only been one fire drill this year, in the Admin Block, the alarm was let off early and the Fire Officer was with Security so he was unable to observe the evacuation; there was also some confusion about whether it was real or false. The Board deplored the failure of prison officers to wear name badges, contrary to Prisons Board policy. The Board were assured in a letter from the Home Office in May that staff will not be given a choice of whether to wear badges. By December 1993 there was no discernible change, and it is rare to see a prison officer wearing a name badge at Wandsworth.

A Visitors Centre opened in February 1994. The introduction of a new regime has lead to increased workshop hours and employment for 97 per cent of convicted prisoners. Association was introduced in January 1994 though there is evidence of increased bullying, intimidation and drug use because of insufficient supervision. There were an increasing number of attempted suicides during the year. Two men hanged themselves. A 'listeners' scheme operates in the VPU. The Board continues to be concerned about delays in investigating and prosecuting crimes committed in prison. In the year ending 31st December 1993, there had been a total of 202 drug finds at Wandsworth—an average of 17 per month.

HM PRISON WORMWOOD SCRUBS

Wormwood Scrubs was in many respects marking time, said HMCIP in a Report (published 1st

February 1994) of an inspection in August 1993. New buildings would shortly be ready for occupation and would provide some of the best facilities in the country. In use however were old, cramped, inadequate buildings which did little to promote civilised behaviour and a constructive approach to imprisonment. Some staff, in anticipation of refurbishment, had lost interest in the appearance and maintenance of the wings for which they were responsible and had let its standards of cleanliness and hygiene slip.

Time out of cell had increased to about 11 hours per day for lifers and eight hours per day for all other prisoners—six hours daily at weekends. But there was a lack of purposeful activity, particularly for unconvicted prisoners. Most on A and B wings were accommodated two to a cell and still slopped out. The regime for vulnerable prisoners on Rule 43 was often curtailed. Inmate/staff relationships appeared both relaxed and constructive. Psychologists and probation staff praised the uniformed staff's enthusiasm for shared working and the interest they show in dealing with prisoners' problems. The positive attitudes of staff have contributed significantly in making poor physical conditions more tolerable for prisoners. Efforts were being made by the Governor to bring about further improvements to the regime. The management team were discussing proposals to change staff attendance systems which would expand the prisoners' working day and mean more realistic mealtimes.

Responding to the Report the Director General, Derek Lewis, said that cleanliness and hygiene have been improved generally. Toilets will be installed in A and B wings this year. New buildings, including a new accommodation wing, Health Care Centre, kitchen, reception area and workshop complex are due to be occupied this year, and will mean extra space for activities.

SECTION SIX

ANNEXES

ANNEXE A **HM Prison Service**

People, policies, facts and figures

[A] PEOPLE & POLICIES

The senior management team of HM Prison Service is collectively known as The Prisons Board. Its role is to monitor performance, decide the Service's priorities—within the framework of policy and resources agreed by Ministers—and to set goals and performance targets to ensure this work is carried out. The Prisons Board consists of six directors and four non-executive directors from outside the Prison Service. The Board is chaired by the Director General.

THE PRISONS BOARD

DIRECTOR-GENERAL: **Derek Lewis**

NON-EXECUTIVE DIRECTORS: **Bill Bentley; Urmilla Banerjee; Sir Duncan Nichol; Geoffrey Keeys**

DIRECTOR OF SERVICES: **Richard Tilt**
Responsible for:
Prisoner Services (Head: Lynette Gill)
Parole; Sentence Planning; Throughcare; BoV Section; Assisted Prison Visits; Lifer Section.
Building Planning Services (Head: Tim Wilson)
Prison Building; Programmes at new and existing establishments.
Works Services (Head: Ron Haines)
Managing the development and maintenance of the existing estate.
Industries & Farms Services (Head: Robert Fulton)
Support to establishments in managing their industrial, agricultural and horticultural enterprises.
Activity Services (Head: Eddie Gray)
Education; Physical Education; Chaplaincy; NVQ; Programmes for Problem Behaviour; Suicide Awareness.
Supply & Transport Services (Head: David Kent)
Procurement; Stores; Supplies; Transport; Catering.
Management Services (Head: Robin Masefield)
Management Consultancy Service; Market Testing Support Unit; Office Services; HQ Reorganisation Implementation project.

DIRECTOR OF HEALTH CARE: **Rosemary Wool**
Responsible for:
Professional Development (Head: David Howells)
Professional Development for Health Care Services

Nursing Services (Head: Bob Lockett)
Professional Development of Nursing Staff
Strategic Development (Head: Libby Joyce)
Strategic Development and Research
Health Group (Head: Richard Weatherill)
Health and Safety policy; Planning for Health Gain.

DIRECTOR OF PROGRAMMES: **Tony Pearson**
Responsible for:
Programmes Group (Head: Kevin Head)
Women; Young Offenders; Unsentenced prisoners; Vulnerable Prisoners; Community Prisons; Prison Discipline; Prison Ombudsman; Prisoner Privileges; Incentives; International Work; Race Relations; Transfer/Repatriation; Home Leave/Family Ties.
Areas: Central; East Midlands; Mercia; North East; North West; Trans Pennine; Yorkshire.

DIRECTOR OF CUSTODY: **Philippa Drew**
Responsible for:
Custody Group (Head: Phil Wheatley)
Security; Control; Incident Management; Intelligence; Population Management; Strategic Estate Planning; Category A Prisoners; Lifer Policy.
Areas: The Chilterns; East Anglia; Kent; London North; London South; South Coast; Wales & West; Wessex.

DIRECTOR OF PERSONNEL: **Tony Butler**
Responsible for:
Training Services (Head: John Dring)
Prison Service Colleges; Training Units.
Pay & Industrial Relations Group (Head: Ian Boon)
Industrial Relations; Pay & Related Conditions of Service.
Personnel Services (Head: Liz Grimsby)
Personnel Management; Conduct & Performance; Staff Ideas; Superannuation; Pay Casework; Expenses; Staff Care & Welfare; Senior Grade Management; Equal Opportunities; Better Jobs; Accelerated Promotion Scheme.

DIRECTOR OF FINANCE: **Brian Landers**
Responsible for:
Internal Audit Services (Head: Steve Jenner)
Independent Review of the Agency's internal control system.
Finance Group (Head: Simon Hickson)
Financial Planning, Control, Accounts and Systems.
Planning Group (Head: Julian Le Vay)
Framework Document; Corporate & Business Planning; Performance Monitoring.
PSIT Services & Strategy (Head: Ray Corrigan)
Systems & Software; Specification & Development; IT Infrastructure; Contract & Services Management; Project Management; IT Security; Administration; Information Systems Strategy.

The Prisons Board formulated the document properly known as the ***Statement of Purpose***—though more colloquially referred to as the 'Mission Statement'. The Prisons Board also defined a statement of the Prison Service's ***Vision, Goals and Values*** to clarify the aims of the mission statement. The text of both are reproduced here by kind permission of HM Prison Service.

The Purpose

Her Majesty's prison service serves the public by keeping in custody those committed by the courts. Our duty is to look after them with humanity and help them lead law-abiding and useful lives in custody and after release.

The Vision

Our vision is to provide a service, through both directly managed and contract-out prisons, of which the public can be proud and which will be regarded as a standard of excellence around the world.

The Goals

Our principal goals are to:

- Keep prisoners in custody
- Maintain order, control, discipline and a safe environment
- Provide decent conditions for prisoners and meet their needs, including health care
- Provide positive regimes which help prisoners address their offending behaviour and allow them as full and responsible a life as possible
- Help prisoners prepare for their return to the community
- Deliver prison services using resources provided by Parliament with maximum efficiency.

In meeting these goals, we will co-operate closely with other criminal justice agencies and contribute to the effectiveness and development of the criminal justice system as a whole.

The Values

In seeking to realise our vision and meet our goals, we will adhere to the following values:

- **Integrity** is fundamental to everything we do. We will meet our legal obligations, act with honesty and openness, and exercise effective stewardship of public money and assets.
- **Commitment** by our staff and to our staff. Staff are the most important asset of the Prison Service. They will be empowered to develop and

use their skills and abilities to the full, while being held accountable for their performance. Teamwork will be encouraged. They will be treated with fairness, respect and openness. Their safety and well-being will be a primary concern.

Care for prisoners. Prisoners will be treated with fairness, justice and respect as individuals. Their punishment is deprivation of liberty and they are entitled to certain recognised standards while in prison. They will be given reasons for decisions and, where possible, involved in discussions about matters affecting them. In working with prisoners, we will involve their families and others in the community as much as possible.

Equality of Opportunity. We are committed to equality of opportunity and the elimination of discrimination on improper grounds.

- **Innovation and Improvement** are essential to the success of the Service, requiring the acceptance of change and the delivery of continuing improvements in quality and efficiency.

Goals, indicators & Targets

Eight key performance indicators have been agreed by Ministers for the Prison Service's principal **Goals**. There is at least one **Key Performance Indicator** (KPI) for every goal. A key **Target** is set by Ministers every year, in the Business Plan, for each KPI. The KPIs and targets do not cover every aspect of the Service's work. The Prisons Board monitor a wide range of indicators relating to other aspects of the service's work.

ioals	*Key Performance Indicators*	*Key Targets 1993/94*
.eep prisoners in custody.	The number of escapes from prison establishments and escorts.	To ensure that the number of escapes from prison establishments and from escorts, expressed as a percentage of the average prison population, is fewer than in 1992/93.
laintain order, control, iscipline and a safe nvironment.	The number of assaults on staff, prisoners and others.	To reverse, over the period of the corporate plan, the rising trend of assaults on staff, prisoners and others, expressed as a percentage of the average prison population.
rovide decent conditions for risoners and meet their needs, cluding health care.	The proportion of prisoners held in units of accommodation intended for fewer numbers.	To ensure that by 31st March 1994 no prisoner is held three to a cell in accommodation which is intended for one prisoner, subject to ensuring that no prisoners are held in police cells unless this is absolutely unavoidable.
	The number of prisoners with 24 hour access to sanitation.	To provide 24 hour access to sanitation in at least 4,700 more prison places (excluding new and renovated accommodation), as part of the programme to provide all prisoners with this facility by 31st December 1994.
ovide positive regimes which lp prisoners address their fending behaviour and allow em as full and responsible a e as possible.	The number of hours a week which, on average, prisoners spend in purposeful activity.	To ensure that prisoners spend, on average, at three per cent more hours a week in purposeful resulting in an average of 24.9 hours per week per prisoner.
	The proportion of prisoners held in establishments where prisoners are unlocked on weekdays for a total of at least 12 hours.	To ensure that by 31st March 1994 at least 34 per cent of prisoners are held in establishments where prisoners are unlocked for a total of at least 12 hours on weekdays.

cont./

Goals	*Key Performance Indicators*	*Key Targets 1993/94*
Help prisoners prepare for their return to the community.	The proportion of prisoners held in establishments where prisoners have the opportunity to exceed the minimum visiting entitlement.	To ensure that by 31st March 199 at least 90 per cent of prisoners are held in establishments where prisoners have the opportunity to exceed the minimum visiting entitlement.
Deliver prison services using the resources provided by Parliament with maximum efficiency.	The average cost per prisoner place.	To ensure that the average cost per prisoner place does not excee £23,561.

Area Managers

The prison estate in England and Wales is divided into 15 different areas, each under the control of an Area Manager who has control of between seven and eleven establishments and who is selected from experienced senior prison governors. Area Managers are the link between the Prisons Board and prison establishments. They are responsible for ensuring that the Service fulfils its stated purpose, lives up to its values and that individual establishments work to achieve their objectives efficiently and effectively, meeting goals and targets set by the Prisons Board. Area Managers are responsible to one of the two Operational Directors on the Prisons Board.

AREA 1. NORTH EAST
AREA MANAGER: **Al Papps**
Responsible for:
- Acklington
- Castington
- Durham
- Frankland
- Full Sutton
- Holme House
- Kirklevington Grange
- Low Newton

AREA 2. NORTH WEST
AREA MANAGER: **Ian Lockwood**
Responsible for:
- Garth
- Haverigg
- Hindley
- Kirkham
- Lancaster
- Lancaster Farms
- Preston
- Thorn Cross
- Wymott

AREA 3. YORKSHIRE
AREA MANAGER: **Maurice Codd**
Responsible for:
- Askham Grange
- Deerbolt
- Everthorpe
- Hatfield
- Hull
- Northallerton
- Rudgate
- Thorpe Arch
- Wetherby

AREA 4. TRANS PENNINE
AREA MANAGER: **Terry Bone**
Responsible for:
- Leeds
- Liverpool
- Manchester
- New Hall
- Risley
- Styal
- Wakefield

AREA 5. EAST MIDLANDS
AREA MANAGER: **Joe Mullens**
Responsible for:
- Lincoln
- Lindholme
- Moorland
- Morton Hall
- North Sea Camp
- Nottingham
- Ranby
- Stocken
- Whatton

AREA 6. MERCIA
AREA MANAGER: **Dai Curtis**
Responsible for:
- Brockhill
- Drake Hall
- Hewell Grange
- Shrewsbury
- Stoke Heath

Sudbury/Foston
Swinfen Hall
Werrington

REA 7. CENTRAL
REA MANAGER: **Jim Blakey**
esponsible for:
Ashwell
Birmingham
Brinsford
Featherstone
Gartree
Glen Parva
Leicester
Long Lartin
Stafford

REA 8. LONDON NORTH
REA MANAGER: **Amy Edwards**
esponsible for:
Bedford
Grendon/Spring Hill
Holloway
Littlehey
Oxford
Pentonville
Wellingborough
Whitemoor
Woodhill
Wormwood Scrubs

REA 9. EAST ANGLIA
EA MANAGER: **Tom Murtagh**
esponsible for:
Blundeston
Bullwood Hall
Chelmsford
Highpoint
Hollesley Bay Colony
Norwich
Wayland

REA 10. THE CHILTERNS
EA MANAGER: **Arthur de Frisching**
esponsible for:
Aylesbury
Bullingdon
Coldingly
Huntercombe/Finnamore Wood Camp
Mount
Onley
Reading

REA 11. WALES & WEST
EA MANAGER: **John Wilkinson**
esponsible for:
Bristol
Cardiff
Eastwood Park
Erlestoke

- Gloucester
- Leyhill
- Pucklechurch
- Swansea
- Usk/Prescoed

AREA 12. LONDON SOUTH
AREA MANAGER: **Peter Kitteridge**
Responsible for:
- Albany
- Belmarsh
- Brixton
- Camp Hill
- Feltham
- Latchmere House
- Parkhurst
- Wandsworth

AREA 13. KENT
AREA MANAGER: **John Hunter**
Responsible for:
- Aldington
- Blantyre House
- Canterbury
- Cookham Wood
- Dover
- East Sutton Park
- Elmley
- Maidstone
- Rochester
- Standford Hill
- Swaleside

AREA 14. SOUTH COAST
AREA MANAGER: **Alan Rayfield**
Responsible for:
- Downview
- Ford
- Haslar
- Highdown
- Kingston
- Lewes
- Send
- Winchester

AREA 15. WESSEX
AREA MANAGER: **John May**
Responsible for:
- Channings Wood
- Dartmoor
- Exeter
- Guys Marsh
- Portland
- Shepton Mallet
- The Verne

HM Prison Service: Race Relations Policy Statement

1. The Prison Department is committed absolutely to a policy of racial equality and to the elimination

of discrimination in all aspects of the work of the Prison Service. It is opposed also to any display of racial prejudice, either by word or conduct, by any member of this Service in his dealings with any other person.

2. All prisoners should be treated with humanity and respect. All prisoners should be treated impartially and without discrimination on the grounds of colour, race or religion. Insulting, abusive or derogatory language towards prisoners will not be tolerated.

3. Race relations concern every member of the Prison Service. It is the responsibility of every member of staff to ensure that the Department's policy is carried out in relation to other members of staff as well as prisoners.

4. Members of minority religious groups have the same right to practice their faith as those of the majority faith. Wherever feasible in prison circumstances arrangements are made to give them the same practical opportunity to do so.

5. All inmates should have equal access to the facilities provided in the establishment including jobs. The distribution of inmates throughout the establishment and its facilities should as far as practicable and sensible be broadly responsive to the ethnic mix of the establishment.

6. No particular racial group should be allowed to dominate any activity in the establishment to the unfair exclusion of others.

[B] FACTS & FIGURES

Agency Status: How it Works

In February 1988 the *Next Steps* initiative was launched in response to a report from the Prime Minister's efficiency unit. The aims were to improve management in government and deliver a better quality of service to the public. Agencies are each headed by a Chief Executive who works under a policy and resources framework agreed with the relevant Minister who remains answerable to Parliament. The three main documents which detail the agency status of HM Prison Service are the:-

Framework Document which outlines the Service's responsibilities and accountability and sets out the key performance indicators.

Corporate Plan 1993–1996 which sets out the strategy for achieving the six main goals over the next three years.

Business Plan which gives key targets and programmes of work for the financial year ahead.

All three documents are available, free of charge, from HM Prison Service HQ, Room 810, Abell House, John Islip Street, London SW1P 4LH.

Agency Status: What it Means

The theory of agency status borrows heavily from both best management practice and modern management theory: devolve authority and responsibility from headquarters to individual governors in the field, establish clear lines of accountability, give people budgets and let *them* work out the most efficient and effective means of delivery at establishment level. The benefits of agency status are often difficult to determine in advance because it represents the process of reform rather than the product. Agency status allows the Prison Service to operate at arms length from central Government: the benefits which flow from it therefore depend, to a large extent, on what the Prison Service chooses to make of the opportunities which this more distant operational relationship represents. Properly utilised it allows local management a flexibility of operation hitherto unknown, but there are dangers. Devolving increased authority to a local level, brings with it the reality that changes made in the name of 'reform' then necessarily travel a much more subjective path. The perceptions and practices of the Governor *in situ* rarely coincide with those of his peers elsewhere or his successor when he departs. As a result, the 'reforms' introduced in such an atmosphere are by neccessity piecemeal and all too frequently have been transient and fragmented. For that reason it is crucial that increased delegation does not slip into a 'hands off' approach by senior management who must lead the way with the right policies and firm leadership from above. It is early days yet, but given the right approach agency status could mean that the reforms sorely needed for donkey's years are now closer to reality than at any time in the past. Time alone will tell whether HM Prison Service embraces this opportunity—or squanders it.

Competition

There has recently been an increasing use of competition to spur progress in the penal system, and it is an initiative that stretches from top to bottom. The post of Director General of HM Prison Service (the pre-Agency status equivalent of Chief Executive) was openly advertised in an open competition for the first time and resulted, in January 1993, in Derek Lewis taking over from Joe Pilling. Three months before, in October 1992, the rebuilt Manchester prison was offered for tender—and awarded to the in-house team, amid fierce competition, in July 1993. In September 1993 the Home Secretary announced that ten per cent of prisons will be run by the private sector in due course, including **The Wolds, Blakenhurst, Doncaster, six new prisons and seven other establishments, new and old**. Buckley Hall is due to open in October 1995 under private sector management.

Population

The average population in custody—including those detained in police cells—in 1993 was **44,600**; this is 1200 lower than in 1992 and the lowest figure for any year since 1984. The average population in police cells was **14** in 1993, this compares with 1,080 in 1992 and is the lowest annual figure since 1979. The population increased during 1993 from 42,200 in January 1993 to **47,500** in December 1993. This rise in the prison population during 1993 reverses a steep fall during 1992. The remand population increased by an average of 200 a month from 9,200 at the end of December 1992, to **11,700** at 31st December 1993. The sentenced population increased from 32,800 at the end of December 1992, to **35,000** by 31st December 1993. The number of sentenced receptions in 1993 was **52,000**, 2% higher than in 1992. Receptions of untried prisoners was **53,700**, 7% higher than in 1992. The **Long Term Projection** envisages a prison population of **56,600** by the year 2001. The expensive use of police cells to hold remand prisoners (at £1,792 per prisoner per week) ended—albeit briefly—on 12th February 1993. Since then however the prison population has risen steeply: on 31st December 1993, the latest date for which prison figures are available, it stood at **47,500**. On 1st March 1994, **358** remand prisoners were again being held in police cells. There were **1,560** female prisoners on 31st December 1993 (3.3% of the prison population) and **5,131** young offenders (10.8%).

Vulnerable Prisoners

On 31st December 1993, a total of **1,180** prisoners were segregated for their own protection under Prison Rule 43 or Young Offender Rule 46: **1,087** adult males; **78** males under 21; **15** adult females; nil females under under 21. In addition, **1,605** prisoners in this category were in need of long-term protection and were held in national VPU's.

Accommodation

During 1992–94 well over **4,000** prison places were added to the prison estate with the seven establishments which opened between April 1992 and July 1994: Blakenhurst; Doncaster; Woodhill; Wolds; Holme House; Lancaster Farms and Highdown. All had integral sanitation and provided a mixture of extra local, remand and young offender accommodation. Additionally nearly **900** extra places were provided in existing establishments, a similar number were re-opened after refurbishment and integral sanitation has been completed during the year in **4,300** cells.

Key Changes in Establishments

Reading changed from a local prison to a remand centre.

Kirklevington Grange changed from a YOI to an adult trainer.

Northeye closed.

Oxford closed as a satellite of Wormwood Scrubs.

Security

HM Prison Service met its 1992–93 target on escapes [to reduce the number of escapes and absconds below the level of the year before] but not on absconds: there were **389** escapes and **1,951** absconds, compared with **473** and **1,731** respectively the year before. Prisoners **escape** if they do so from inside a closed establishment or get free while under escort. Prisoners **abscond** if they go missing from inside an open prison, work party or fail to return from a period of temporary release. The goal of the Prison Service is that no Category A prisoner escapes, and no Category B prisoner escapes from inside a Category B prison.

Intelligence Evaluation Unit

An Intelligence Evaluation Unit was set up in November 1993 as the result of the report by Hadfield and Lakes on security for Category A prisoners. Its aims are to:

- Gather security information
- Analyse trends and developments
- Disseminate learning swiftly
- Inform policy development.

Work to improve physical security at prisons included:

- Low cost perimeter alarm and CCTV systems
- Electronic overlocking
- Installing CCTV
- Improving cell security
- Improving dog units
- Providing new perimeter walls and security fences
- Reviewing security departments and intelligence procedures at establishments
- Establishing a standard system to gather and evaluate intelligence information in prisons

Assaults

There has been a rising trend of assaults in prison. In 1992–93 a total of **4,472** assaults was recorded (10.2% of the average prison popution): **2,411** on staff and **2,061** on prisoners. In the future incidents will be analysed to identify factors which lead to assaults, and smaller more manageable units will be created in wings of Victorian prisons.

Prison Building

Nearly **£310.7 million** was spent on prison building in 1992–93. Six new prisons were opened—

providing over **3,000** places, and 20 of the 21 prisons in the current building programme have now opened. Preliminary work is planned to start in 1995–96 on prisons, at Fazakerley on Merseyside and Bridgend in South Wales. These will provide a further **1,200** places. All new prisons are organised in living units of 50–70 prisoners. Twenty-three new capital schemes costing over **£5 million** each were under way or completed during the course of the year, including refurbishment of wings at **Brixton, Liverpool, Pentonville, Rochester, Stafford and Wandsworth**. Nearly 900 additional places were gained from changes at **Birmingham, Risley, Bedford and Guys Marsh**.

Overcrowding

The ten most overcrowded local prisons were:

- **Wormwood Scrubs (72% overcrowded)**
- **Leicester** (66%)
- **Shrewsbury** (60%)
- **Birmingham** (59%)
- **Leeds** (45%)
- **Lincoln** (42%)
- **Chelmsford** (39%)
- **Cardiff** (35%)
- **Gloucester** (32%)
- **Liverpool** (30%)

Security, Control & Justice

Maintaining the balance between security, control and justice in prison, as recommended by Lord Justice Woolf, has occupied the minds of staff at Headquarters since that report was published. The five inter-related concepts of **respect, fairness, individuality, care and openness** have been developed into the prison service's five basic values as set out in section [A] of this annexe.

Code of Standards: Update

The publication *Custody, Care and Justice* committed the prison authorities to producing a Code of Standards to spell out what was needed to provide decent conditions for prisoners, and establishing a benchmark for allocating resources and making improvements. Eleven task forces made up of governors, area managers, other headquarters staff and interested outsiders have now begun detailed drafting of the Code.

Life Sentence/Parole Reviews

Discretionary and mandatory lifers now have access to reports which are to be placed before the Parole Board when their case for release is being considered. This disclosure will be extended to all parole reviews from October 1994.

Women

Three guidance booklets have been produced for females in relation to Mother and Baby Units, dealing with admissions policy, guidance for staff and guidance for unit managers and governors.

Health Care

About half of all establishments now have multi-disciplinary HIV/AIDS teams. A report on the review of services for mentally disordered offenders, published in July 1992, made 276 recommendations and the prison authorities are developing strategies to deal with them. Improved co-operation between prison and medical authorities has resulted in the increased transfer of **611** prisoners to hospital—compared with **445** in 1991/92, and less than **100** in 1985. At Belmarsh three prison service Medical Officer posts have been replaced by three psychiatric registrars seconded from the NHS under the clinical supervision of a consultant psychiatrist. The aims are to reduce the amount of time taken for the completion of psychiatric reports for remand prisoners, and the transfer of mentally ill prisoners to hospital.

Positive Regimes

During the year the prison authorities achieved an average of 23.68 hours spent on structured activities per week, falling just short of their target for 1992/93 of 24.18 hours. The target to be achieved in 1993/94 has been set at 24.9 hours of structured activity per week. The second key performance tar get in this area for 1993/94 is to ensure that 34 per cent of prisoners are held in establishments where prisoners are unlocked for a total of 12 hours on weekdays.

Working Incentives & Information

A new incentive pay scheme, introduced in December 1992 increased the average basic wage to £6 per week. The aim is to reach an average of £[illegible] per week. Pilot schemes have been undertaken at Styal, Featherstone and Latchmere House where some prisoners are earning 'realistic wages' in excess of £100 per week. Prison Service Industries and Farms (PSIF) currently produce goods to a value of around £55 million. Employment places i[illegible] workshops fell from **6,830** places in 1991/92, to **6,435** in 1992/93. The average working week, however, increased for prisoners to 29 hours (gross) compared with 25 hours in 1991/92. Prisoners hel[illegible] to produce all the bacon, pork and preserves used in prison kitchens, around 80 per cent of the vegetables and 70 per cent of the milk

Education & PE

Student hours increased to 7.57 million in 1992/93, from 7.55 million in 1991/92. The net hourly cost per student was £3.57 and the average class size increased from 7.96 to 8.06 in 1992/93—the target is eight. Open University operated in 80 prisons and of the 332 prisoners who completed a year of study, two-thirds (224) passed. The **Further and Higher Education Act 1992** led to a decision by ministers in July 1992 that future educational services should be bought in from educational suppliers. In October 1992, 241 organisations were invited to tender, 155 did so and, by October 1993, 124 contracts had been awarded. **KOESTLER AWARD SCHEME**, which promotes artistic talent in prisons, YOI's and special hospitals, attracted a total of 1700 entries in 1994, of which 550 won awards or were highly commended. There was an increase of 76,000 inmate hours in PE in 1992/93: a total of 5.06 million compared with 4.99 million in 1991/92. There was a greater uptake in Category C prisons—recognising the generally young population—and a lower uptake in locals—recognising their shortage of facilities. Vocational and academic awards increased by 55 per cent, particularly good was the **Community Sports Leaders Award**.

Offending Behaviour

The prison authorites provide a range of treatment programmes for behavioural problems:

- **Sex Offender Programme.** Core programme which makes the offender face up to the consequences of their actions and teaches them how to stop themselves relapsing in the future. There is an extended programme for the most serious offenders.
- **Anger Management Programme.** Tackles and challenges disruptive behaviour.
- **Cognitive Skills Programme.** A course on 'How to think before you act'.
- **Drug & Alcohol Misue Programme.** Detoxification, counselling and life-style training.

Visits

Over 90 per cent of establishments now allow more than the statutory entitlement of two visits per month for convicted prisoners and 90 minutes per week for untried. Over 70 establishments now have creches or play areas for children and a grant of £325,000 in 1992/93 was paid to help run 31 Visitors Centres. In 1993/94 grants of £488,000 should support 36 Visitors Centres.

Bail Information Schemes

A total of 34 establishments now have Bail Information Schemes. This will be extended to all Local Prisons and Remand Centres by the end of 1994/95.

Pre-Release Hotels

There are now seven PRH providing a total of 107 places: **Birmingham, Bristol, Maidstone, Nottingham, Wakefield and Askham Grange**. Two 'Resettlelement Prisons' at **Latchmere House and Kirklevington Grange** have been opened, and **Blantyre House** provides a resettlement programme for 95 Category C prisoners.

Prisons Link Project

The PLU provides training and information for prison staff on offering advice and help to prisoners in housing and employment matters. The PLU is funded by the Prison Service and run by NACRO. By 1996 all prison establishments should have a pool of PLU-trained staff.

Drugs

The Home Secretary has laid before Parliament legislation to authorise the requesting of urine samples from prisoners, for drug testing, and to make it a disciplinary offence for a prisoner to refuse when so requested. In a report 'Drug Use in Prison', published 28th July 1994, AVERT, the AIDS education and research trust, and The Centre for Research on Drugs and Health behaviour say that 'proposals to introduce mandatory urine screening to detect drug use, if accompanied by disciplinary action, would not be conducive to creating a proper climate for provision of treatment and help. The use of such measures would also be counterproductive when used as a measure to control drug-free wings and expel those who have not been able to comply with the treatment regime.' The organisations argue that 'drug problems in prison may now be developing more rapidly than the current ability of prison authorities to respond effectively'. They call on all custodial institutions to provide, as a minimum, a wide range of treatment opportunities—notably long-term methadone programmes and materials to clean syringes.

'DRUG USE IN PRISON', available from AVERT, 11–13 Denne Parade, Horsham, West Sussex RH12 1JD. Price £9.95.

ANNEXE B. i. The Prison Act 1952
ii. Prison Rules 1964
iii. The Young Offender Institution Rules 1988

i. Prison Act 1952

(15 & 16 Geo 6 and 1 Eliz 2 c 52)

Central administration

Section
1 General control over prisons
3 Officers and servants of Prison Commissioners
4 General duties of Prison Commissioners
5 Annual report of Prison Commissioners
5A Appointment and functions of Her Majesty's Chief Inspector of Prisons

Visiting committees and boards of visitors
6 Visiting committees and boards of visitors

Prison officers
7 Prison officers
8 Powers of prison officers
9 Exercise of office of chaplain
10 Appointment of prison ministers
11 Ejectment of prison officers and their families refusing to quit

Confinement and treatment of prisoners
12 Place of confinement of prisoners
13 Legal custody of prisoner
14 Cells
16 Photographing and measuring of prisoners
17 Painful tests
19 Right of justice to visit prison
21 Expenses of conveyance to prison
22 Removal of prisoners for judicial and other purposes
23 Power of constable etc. to act outside his jurisdiction

Length of sentence, release on licence and temporary discharge
24 Calculation of term of sentence
25 Remission for good conduct and release on licence of persons sentenced to terms of imprisonment
28 Power of Secretary of State to discharge prisoners temporarily on account of ill health

Discharged prisoners
30 Payments for discharged prisoners

Provision, maintenance and closing of prisons
33 Power to provide prisons, etc
34 Jurisdiction of sheriff, etc
35 Prison property
36 Acquisition of land for prisons
37 Closing of prisons

Offences
39 Assisting prisoner to escape
40 Unlawful conveyance of spirits or tobacco into prison, etc
41 Unlawful introduction of other articles
42 Display of notice of penalties

Remand centres, detention centres and Borstal institutions
43 Remand centres, detention centres and youth custody centres

Rules for the management of prisons and other institutions
47 Rules for the management of prisons, remand centres, detention centres and Borstal institutions

Miscellaneous
49 Persons unlawfully at large

Supplemental
51 Payment of expenses out of moneys provided by Parliament
52 Exercise of power to make orders, rules and regulations
53 Interpretation
54 Consequential amendments, repeals and savings
55 Short title, commencement and extent

An Act to consolidate certain enactments relating to prisons and other institutions for offenders and related matters with corrections and improvements made under the Consolidation of Enactments (Procedure) Act 1949
[1 August 1952]

Central administration

1 General control over prisons
All powers and jurisdiction in relation to prisons and prisoners which before the commencement of the Prison Act 1877 were exercisable by any other authority shall, subject to the provisions of this Act, be exercisable by the Secretary of State.

2 *(Repealed by the Prison Commissioners Dissolution Order 1963, SI 1963/597.)*

3 Officers and servants of Prison Commissioners
(1) The Secretary of State [may, for the purposes of this Act, appoint such officers and servants as he] may, with the sanction of the Treasury as to number, determine.

(2) There shall be paid out of moneys provided by Parliament to [the officers and servants appointed under this section] such salaries as the Secretary of State may with the consent of the Treasury determine.

4 General duties of Prison Commissioners
(1) [The Secretary of State] shall have the general superintendence of prisons and shall make the contracts and do the other acts necessary for the maintenance of prisons and the maintenance of prisoners.

(2) [Officers of the Secretary of State duly authorised in that behalf] shall visit all prisons and examine the state of buildings, the conduct of officers, the treatment and conduct of prisoners and all other matters concerning the management of prisons and shall ensure that the provisions of this Act and of any rules made under this Act are duly complied with.

(3) [The Secretary of State and his officers] may exercise all powers and jurisdiction exercisable at common law, by Act of Parliament, or by charter by visiting justices of a prison.

5 Annual report of Prison Commissioners
[(1) The Secretary of State shall issue an annual report on every prison and shall lay every such report before Parliament.]

(2) The report shall contain—

(*a*) a statement of the accommodation of each prison and the daily average and highest number of prisoners confined therein;

(*b*) such particulars of the work done by prisoners in each prison, including the kind and quantities of articles produced and the number of prisoners employed, as may in the opinion of the Secretary of State give the best information to Parliament;

(*c*) a statement of the punishments inflicted in each prison and of the offences for which they were inflicted . . .

[5A Appointment and functions of Her Majesty's Chief Inspector of Prisons
(1) Her Majesty may appoint a person to be Chief Inspector of Prisons.

(2) It shall be the duty of the Chief Inspector to inspect or arrange for the inspection of prisons in England and Wales and to report to the Secretary of State on them.

(3) The Chief Inspector shall in particular report to the Secretary of State on the treatment of prisoners and conditions in prisons.

(4) The Secretary of State may refer specific matters connected with prisons in England and Wales and prisoners in them to the Chief Inspector and direct him to report on them.

(5) The Chief Inspector shall in each year submit to the Secretary of State a report in such form as the Secretary of State may direct, and the Secretary of State shall lay a copy of that report before Parliament.

(6) The Chief Inspector shall be paid such salary and allowances as the Secretary of State may with the consent of the Treasury determine.]

Visiting committees and boards of visitors

6 Visiting committees and boards of visitors
(1) . . .

(2) The Secretary of State shall appoint for every prison . . . a board of visitors of whom not less than two shall be justices of the peace.

(3) Rules made as aforesaid shall prescribe the functions of . . . boards of visitors and shall among other things require members to pay frequent visits to the prison and hear any complaints which may be made by the prisoners and report to the Secretary of State any matter which they consider it expedient to report; and any member of a . . . board of visitors may at any time enter the prison and shall have free access to every part of it and to every prisoner,

(4) . . .

Prison officers

7 Prison Officers
(1) Every prison shall have a governor, a chaplain and a medical officer and such other officers as may be necessary.

(2) Every prison in which women are received shall have a sufficient number of women officers; . . .

(3) A prison which in the opinion of the Secretary of State is large enough to require it may have a deputy governor or an assistant chaplain or both.

(4) The chaplain and any assistant chaplain

shall be a clergyman of the Church of England and the medical officer shall be duly registered under the Medical Acts.

(5) . . .

8 Powers of prison officers

Every prison officer while acting as such shall have all the powers, authority, protection and privileges of a constable.

9 Exercise of office of chaplain

(1) A person shall not officiate as chaplain of two prisons unless the prisons are within convenient distance of each other and are together designed to receive not more than one hundred prisoners.

(2) Notice of the nomination of a chaplain or assistant chaplain to a prison shall, within one month after it is made, be given to the bishop of the diocese in which the prison is situate; and the chaplain or assistant chaplain shall not officiate in the prison except under the authority of a licence from the bishop.

10 Appointment of prison ministers

(1) Where in any prison the number of prisoners who belong to a religious denomination other than the Church of England is such as in the opinion of the Secretary of State to require the appointment of a minister of that denomination, the Secretary of State may appoint such a minister to that prison.

(2) The Secretary of State may pay a minister appointed under the preceding subsection such remuneration as he thinks reasonable.

(3) [The Secretary of State] may allow a minister of any denomination other than the Church of England to visit prisoners of his denomination in a prison to which no minister of that denomination has ben appointed under this section.

(4) No prisoner shall be visited against his will by such a minister as is mentioned in the last preceding subsection; but every prisoner not belonging to the Church of England shall be allowed, in accordance with the arrangements in force in the prison in which he is confined, to attend chapel or to be visited by the chaplain.

(5) The governor of a prison shall on the reception of each prisoner record the religious denomination to which the prisoner declares himself to belong, and shall give to any minister who under this section is appointed to the prison or permitted to visit prisoners therein a list of the prisoners who have declared themselves to belong to his denomination; and the minister shall not be permitted to visit any other prisoners.

11 Ejectment of prison officers and their families refusing to quit

(1) Where any living accommodation is provided for a prison officer or his family by virtue of his office, then, if he ceased to be a prison officer or is suspended from office or dies, he, or, as the case may be, his family, shall quit the accommodation when required to do so by notice of [the Secretary of State].

(2) Where a prison officer or the family of a prison officer refuses or neglects to quit the accommodation forty-eight hours after the giving of such a notice as aforesaid, any two justices of the peace, on proof made to them of the facts authorising the giving of the notice and of the service of the notice and of the neglect or refusal to comply therewith, may, by warrant under their hands and seals, direct any constable, within a period specific in the warrant, to enter by force, if necessary, into the accommodation and deliver possession of it to [a person acting on behalf of the Secretary of State].

Confinement and treatment of prisoners

12 Place of confinement of prisoners

(1) A prisoner, whether sentenced to imprisonment or committed to prison on remand or pending trial or otherwise, may be lawfully confined in any prison.

(2) Prisoners shall be committed to such prisons as the Secretary of State may from time to time direct; and may by direction of the Secretary of State be removed during the term of their imprisonment from the prison in which they are confined to any other prison.

(3) A writ, warrant or other legal instrument addressed to the governor of a prison and identifying that prison by its situation or by any other sufficient description shall not be invalidated by reason only that the prison is usually known by a different description.

13 Legal custody of prisoner

(1) Every prisoner shall be deemed to be in the legal custody of the governor of the prison.

(2) A prisoner shall be deemed to be in legal custody while he is confined in, or is being taken to or from, any prison and while he is working, or is for any other reason, outside the prison in the custody or under the control of an officer of the prison [and while he is being taken to any place to which he is required or authorised by or under this Act [or the Criminal Justice Act 1982] to be taken or is kept in custody in pursuance of any such requirement or authorisation.]

14 Cells

(1) The Secretary of State shall satisfy himself from time to time that in every prison sufficient accommodation is provided for all prisoners,

(2) No cell shall be used for the confinement of a prisoner unless it is certified by an inspector that its size, lighting, heating, ventilation and fittings are adequate for health and that it allows the prisoner to communicate at any time with a prison officer.

(3) A certificate given under this section in respect of any cell may limit the period for which a prisoner may be separately confined in the cell and the number of hours a day during which a prisoner may be employed therein.

(4) The certificate shall identify the cell to which it relates by a number or mark and the cell shall be marked by that number or mark placed in a conspicuous position; and if the number or mark is changed without the consent of an inspector the certificate shall cease to have effect.

(5) An inspector may withdraw a certificate given under this section in respect of any cell if in his opinion the conditions of the cell are no longer as stated in the certificate.

(6) In every prison special cells shall be provided for the temporary confinement of refractory or violent prisoners.

15 *(Repealed by the Criminal Justice Act 1967, ss 66 (2), 103 (2), Sch 7, Pt I.)*

16 Photographing and measuring of prisoners
The Secretary of State may make regulations as to the measuring and photographing of prisoners and such regulations may prescribe the time or times at which and the manner and dress in which prisoners shall be measured and photographed and the number of copies of the measurements and photographs of each prisoner which shall be made and the persons to whom they shall be sent.

17 Painful tests
The medical officer of a prison shall not apply any painful tests to a prisoner for the purpose of detecting malingering or for any other purpose except with the permission of [the Secretary of State] or the visiting committee or, as the case may be, board of visitors.

18 *(Repealed by the Criminal Justice Act 1967, ss 65, 103 (2), Sch 7, Pt I.)*

19 Right of justice to visit prison
(1) A justice of the peace for any county . . . may at any time visit any prison in that county . . . and any prison in which a prisoner is confined in respect of an offence committed in that county . . . , and may examine the condition of the prison and of the prisoners and enter in the visitors' book, to be kept by the governor of the prison, any observations on the condition of the prison or any abuses.

(2) Nothing in the preceding subsection shall authorise a justice of the peace to communicate with any prisoner except on the subject of his treatment in the prison, or to visit any prisoner under sentence of death.

(3) The governor of every prison shall bring any entry in the visitors' book to the attention of the visiting committee or the board of visitors at their next visit.

20 *(Repealed by the Courts Act 1971, s 56, Sch 11, Pt IV.)*

21 Expenses of conveyance to prison
A prisoner shall not in any case be liable to pay the cost of his conveyance to prison.

22 Removal of prisoners for judicial and other purposes
(1) Rules made under section forty-seven of this Act may provide in what manner an appellant within the meaning of [Part I of the Criminal Appeal Act 1968], when in custody, is to be taken to, kept in custody at, or brought back from, any place at which he is entitled to be present for the purposes of that Act, or any place to which the Court of Criminal Appeal or any judge thereof may order him to be taken for the purpose of any proceedings of that court.

(2) The Secretary of State may—

(*a*) . . .

(*b*) if he is satisfied that a person so detained requires [medical investigation or observation or] medical or surgical treatment of any description, direct him to be taken to a hospital or other suitable place for the purpose of the [investigation, observation or] treatment;

and where any person is directed under this subsection to be taken to any place he shall, unless the Secretary of State otherwise directs, be kept in custody while being so taken, while at that place, and while being taken back to the prison in which he is required in accordance with the law to be detained.

23 Power of constable etc to act outside his jurisdiction
For the purpose of taking a person to or from any prison under the order of any authority competent to give the order a constable or other officer may act outside the area of his jurisdiction and shall notwithstanding that he is so acting have all the powers, authority, protection and privileges of his office.

Length of sentence, release on licence and temporary discharge

24 Calculation of term of sentence
(1) In any sentence of imprisonment the word 'month' shall, unless the contrary is expressed, be construed as meaning calendar month.

(2) . . .

25 Remission for good conduct and release on licence of persons sentenced to terms of imprisonment
(1) Rules made under section forty-seven of this Act may make provision whereby, in such circumstances as may be prescribed by the rules, a person serving a sentence of imprisonment for such a term as may be so prescribed may be granted

remission of such part of that sentence as may be so prescribed on the ground of his industry and good conduct, and on the discharge of a person from prison in pursuance of any such remission as aforesaid his sentence shall expire.

(2)–(6) . . .

[(7) A person who is committed to prison in default of payment of a sum adjudged to be paid by a conviction shall be treated for the purposes of subsection (1) of this section, . . . , as undergoing a sentence of imprisonment for the term for which he is committed, and consecutive terms of imprisonment shall be treated for all the purposes of this section as one term.]

26, 27 *(Repealed by the Criminal Justice Act 1967, s 103 (2), Sch 7, Pt I.)*

28 Power of Secretary of State to discharge prisoners temporarily on account of ill health

(1) If the Secretary of State is satisfied that by reason of the condition of a prisoner's health it is undesirable to detain him in prison, but that, such condition of health being due in whole or in part to the prisoner's own conduct in prison, it is desirable that his release should be temporary and conditional only, the Secretary of State may, if he thinks fit, having regard to all the circumstances of the case, by order authorise the temporary discharge of the prisoner for such period and subject to such conditions as may be stated in the order.

(2) Where an order of temporary discharge is made in the case of a prisoner not under sentence, the order shall contain conditions requiring the attendance of the prisoner at any further proceedings on his case at which his presence may be required.

(3) Any prisoner discharged under this section shall comply with any condition stated in the order of temporary discharge, and shall return to prison at the expiration of the period stated in the order, or of such extended period as may be fixed by any subsequent order of the Secretary of State, and if the prisoner fails so to comply or return, he may be arrested without warrant and taken back to prison.

(4) Where a prisoner under sentence is discharged in pursuance of an order of temporary discharge, the currency of the sentence shall be suspended from the day on which he is discharged from prison under the order of the day on which he is received back into prison, so that the former day shall be reckoned and the latter shall not be reckoned as part of the sentence.

(5) Nothing in this section shall affect the duties of the medical officer of a prison in respect of a prisoner whom the Secretary of State does not think fit to discharge under this section.

Discharged prisoners

29 *(Repealed by the Criminal Justice Act 1961, ss 21, 41 (2), Sch 5.)*

[30 Payments for discharged prisoners

The Secretary of State may make such payments to or in respect of persons released or about to be released from prison as he may with the consent of the Treasury determine.]

Provision, maintenance and closing of prisons

33 Power to provide prisons, etc

(1) The Secretary of State may with the approval of the Treasury alter, enlarge or rebuild any prison and build new prisons.

(2) The Secretary of State may provide new prisons by declaring to be a prison any building or part of a building built for the purpose or vested in him or under his control.

(3) A declaration under this section may with respect to the building or part of a building declared to be a prison make the same provisions as an order under the next following section may make with respect to an existing prison.

(4) A declaration under this section may at any time be revoked by the Secretary of State.

(5) A declaration under this section shall not be sufficient to vest the legal estate of any building in the [Secretary of State].

34 Jurisdiction of sheriff, etc

(1) The transfer under the Prison Act 1877 of prisons and of the powers and jurisdiction of prison authorities and of justices in sessions assembled and visiting justices shall not be deemed to have affected the jurisdiction of any sheriff or coroner or, except to the extent of that transfer, of any justice of the peace or other officer.

(2) The Secretary of State may by order direct that, for the purposes of any enactment, rule of law or custom dependent on a prison being the prison of any county or place, any prison situated in that county or in the county in which that place is situated, or any prison provided by him in pursuance of this Act, shall be deemed to be the prison of that county or place.

35 Prison property

(1) Every prison and all real and personal property belonging to a prison shall be vested in the Secretary of State and may be disposed of in such manner as the Secretary of State, with the consent of the Treasury, may determine.

(2) For the purposes of this section the Secretary of State shall be deemed to be a corporation sole.

(3) Any instrument in connection with the acquisition, management or disposal of any property to which this section applies may be executed on behalf of the Secretary of State by an Under-

Secretary of State or any other person authorised by the Secretary of State in that behalf; and any instrument purporting to have been so executed on behalf of the Secretary of State shall be deemed, until the contrary is proved, to have been so executed on his behalf.

(4) The last foregoing subsection shall be without prejudice to the execution of any such instrument as aforesaid, or of any other instrument, on behalf of the Secretary of State in any other manner authorised by law.]

36 Acquisition of land for prisons

(1) [The Secretary of State may purchase by agreement or] compulsorily, any land required for the alteration, enlargement or rebuilding of a prison or for establishing a new prison or for any other purpose connected with the management of a prison (including the provision of accommodation for officers or servants employed in a prison).

[(2) The [Acquisition of Land Act 1981] shall apply to the compulsory purchase of land by the Secretary of State under this section . . .]

(3) In relation to the purchase of land by agreement under this section, [the provisions of Part I of the Compulsory Purchase Act 1965 (so far as applicable) other than sections 4 to 8, section 10, and section 31, shall apply].

37 Closing of prisons

(1) Subject to the next following subsection, the Secretary of State may by order close any prison.

(2) Where a prison is the only prison in the county, the Secretary of State shall not make an order under this section in respect of it except for special reasons, which shall be stated in the order.

(3) In this section the expression 'county' means a county at large.

(4) For the purposes of this and the next following section a prison shall not be deemed to be closed by reason only of its appropriation for use as a remand centre, detention centre or [youth custody centre].

38 *(Repealed with a saving by the Criminal Justice Act 1972, ss 59, 64 (2), Sch 65, Pt II, in this title post and Vol 12, title* Criminal Law.*)*

Offences

39 Assisting a prisoner to escape

Any person who aids any prisoner in escaping or attempting to escape from a prison or who, with intent to facilitate the escape of any prisoner, conveys any thing into a prison or to a prisoner or places any thing anywhere outside a prison with a view to its coming into possession of a prisoner, shall be guilty of felony and liable to imprisonment for a term not exceeding [five years].

40 Unlawful conveyance of spirits or tobacco into prison, etc

Any person who contrary to the regulations of a prison brings or attempts to bring into the prison or to a prisoner any spirituous or fermented liquor or tobacco, or places any such liquor or any tobacco anywhere outside the prison with intent that it shall come into the possession of a prisoner, and any officer who contrary to those regulations allows any such liquor or any tobacco to be sold or used in the prison, shall be liable on summary conviction to imprisonment for a term not exceeding six months or a fine not exceeding [level 3 on the standard scale] or both.

41 Unlawful introduction of other articles

Any person who contrary to the regulations of a prison conveys or attempts to convey any letter or any other thing into or out of the prison or to a prisoner or places it anywhere outside the prison with intent that it shall come into the possession of a prisoner shall, where he is not thereby guilty of an offence under either of the two last preceding sections, be liable on summary conviction to a fine not exceeding [level 3 on the standard scale].

42 Display of notice of penalties

The Prison Commissioners shall cause to be affixed in a conspicuous place outside every prison a notice of the penalties to which persons committing offences under the three last preceding sections are liable.

Remand centres, detention centres and Borstal institutions

The reference in the heading above to borstal institutions should be construed as a reference to Young Offender Institutions which are now provided under s 43 post in place of borstals.

[43 Remand centres, detention centres and Young Offender Institutions

(1) The Secretary of State may provide—

(*a*) remand centres, that is to say places for the detention of persons not less than 14 but under 21 years of age who are remanded or committed in custody for trial or sentence;

(*b*) detention centres, that is to say places in which male offenders not less than 14 but under 21 years of age who are ordered to be detained in such centres under the Criminal Justice Act 1982 may be kept for short periods under discipline suitable to persons of their age and description; and

(*c*) Young Offender Institutions, that is to say places in which offenders not less than 15 but under 21 years of age may be detained and given training, instruction and work and prepared for their release.

(2) The Secretary of State may from time to time direct—

(*a*) that a woman aged 21 years or over who is serving a sentence of imprisonment or who has been committed to prison for default shall be detained in a remand centre or a youth custody centre instead of a prison;

(*b*) that a woman aged 21 years or over who is remanded in custody or committed in custody for trial or sentence shall be detained in a remand centre instead of a prison;

(*c*) that a person under 21 but not less than 17 years of age who is remanded in custody or committed in custody for trial or sentence shall be detained in a prison instead of a remand centre or a remand centre instead of a prison, notwithstanding anything in section 27 of the Criminal Justice Act 1948 or section 23 (3) of the Children and Young Persons Act 1969.

(3) Notwithstanding subsection (1) above, any person required to be detained in an institution to which this Act applies may be detained in a remand centre for any temporary purpose or for the purpose of providing maintenance and domestic services for that centre.

(4) Sections 5A, 6 (2) and (3), 16, 22, 25 and 36 of this Act shall apply to remand centres, detention centres and Young Offender Institutions and to persons detained in them as they apply to prisons and prisoners.

(5) The other provisions of this Act preceding this section, except sections 28 and 37 (2) above, shall apply to such centres and to persons detained in them as they apply to prisons and prisoners, but subject to such adaptations and modifications as may be specified in rules made by the Secretary of State.

(6) References in the preceding provisions of this Act to imprisonment shall, so far as those provisions apply to institutions provided under this section, be construed as including references to detention in those institutions.

(7) Nothing in this section shall be taken to prejudice the operation of section 12 of the Criminal Justice Act 1982.]

44–46 *(Repealed by the Criminal Justice Act 1982, s 78, Sch 16.)*

Rules for the management of prisons and other institutions

47 Rules for the management of prisons, remand centres, detention centres and Young Offender Institutions

(1) The Secretary of State may make rules for the regulation and management of prisons, remand centres, detention centres and [youth custody centres] respectively, and for the classification, treatment, employment, discipline and control of persons required to be detained therein.

(2) Rules made under this section shall make provision for ensuring that a person who is charged with any offence under the rules shall be given a proper opportunity of presenting his case.

(3) Rules made under this section may provide for the training of particular classes of persons and their allocation for that purpose to any prison or other institution in which they may lawfully be detained.

(4) Rules made under this section shall provide for the special treatment of the following persons whilst required to be detained in a prison, that is to say—

(*a*)–(*c*) . . .

(*d*) any . . . person detained in a prison, not being a person serving a sentence or a person imprisoned in default of payment of a sum adjudged to be paid by him on his conviction [or a person committed to custody on his conviction].

(5) Rules made under this section may provide for the temporary release of persons [detained in a prison, [remand centre, youth custody centre], or detention centre, not being persons committed in custody for trial [before the Crown Court] or committed to be sentenced or otherwise dealt with by [the Crown Court] or remanded in custody by any court].

Miscellaneous

48 *(Repealed by the Criminal Justice Act 1961, s 41 (2), (3), Sch 5.)*

49 Persons unlawfully at large

(1) Any person who, having been sentenced to imprisonment, . . . [custody for life or youth custody] or ordered to be detained in a detention centre [or a Young Offenders Institution], or having been committed to a prison or remand centre, is unlawfully at large, may be arrested by a constable without warrant and taken to the place in which he is required in accordance with law to be detained.

(2) Where any person sentenced to imprisonment, . . . or [youth custody], or ordered to be detained in a . . . detention centre, is unlawfully at large at any time during the period for which he is liable to be detained in pursuance of the sentence

or order, then, unless the Secretary of State otherwise directs, no account shall be taken, in calculating the period for which he is liable to be so detained, of any time during which he is absent from the [place in which he is required in accordance with law to be detained].

Provided that—

(*a*) this subsection shall not apply to any period during which any such person as aforesaid is detained in pursuance of the sentence or order or in pursuance of any other sentence of any court [in the United Kingdom] in a prison, [youth custody centre, remand centre or detention centre];

(*b*), (*c*) . . .

(3) The provisions of the last preceding subsection shall apply to a person who is detained in custody in default of payment of any sum of money as if he were sentenced to imprisonment.

(4) For the purposes of this section a person who, after being temporarily released in pursuance of rules made under subsection (5) of section forty-seven of this Act, is at large at any time during the period for which he is liable to be detained in pursuance of his sentence shall be deemed to be unlawfully at large if the period for which he was temporarily released has expired or if an order recalling him has been made by the [Secretary of State] in pursuance of the rules.

50 *(Repealed in part by the Children and Young Persons Act 1969, s 72 (4), Sch 6; remainder spent upon the repeal of s 18 of this Act by the Criminal Justice Act 1967, ss 65, 103 (2), Sch 7, Pt I.)*

Supplemental

51 Payment of expenses out of moneys provided by Parliament

All expenses incurred in the maintenance of prisons and in the maintenance of prisoners and all other expenses of the Secretary of State . . . incurred under this Act shall be defrayed out of moneys provided by Parliament.

52 Exercise of power to make orders, rules and regulations

(1) Any power of the Secretary of State to make rules or regulations under this Act and the power of the Secretary of State to make an order under section thirty-four or section thirty-seven of this Act shall be exercisable by statutory instrument.

(2) Any statutory instrument containing regulations made under section sixteen or an order made under section thirty-seven of this Act, . . . shall be laid before Parliament.

(3) The power of the Secretary of State to make an order under section six or section thirty-four of this Act shall include power to revoke or vary such an order.

53 Interpretation

(1) In this Act the following expressions have the following meanings:—

'Attendance centre' means a centre provided by the Secretary of State under [section 16 of the Criminal Justice Act 1982];

'Prison' does not include a naval, military or air force prison;

. . . . .

(2) For the purposes of this Act the maintenance of a prisoner shall include all necessary expenses incurred in respect of the prisoner for food, clothing, custody and removal from one place to another, from the period of his committal to prison until his death or discharge from prison.

(3) References in this Act to the Church of England shall be construed as including references to the Church in Wales.

(4) References in this Act to any enactment shall be construed as references to that enactment as amended by any other enactment.

54 Consequential amendments, repeals and savings

(1) The enactments mentioned in the Third Schedule to this Act shall have effect subject to the amendments specified therein, being amendments consequential on the provisions of this Act.

(2) . . .

(3) Nothing in this repeal shall affect any rule, order, regulation or declaration made, direction or certificate given or thing done under any enactment repealed by this Act and every such rule, order, regulation, direction, certificate or thing shall, if in force at the commencement of this Act, continue in force and be deemed to have been made, given or done under the corresponding provision of this Act.

(4) Any document referring to any Act or enactment repealed by this Act shall be construed as referring to this Act or to the corresponding enactment in this Act.

(5) The mention of particular matters in this section shall not be taken to affect the general application to this Act of section thirty-eight of the Interpretation Act 1889 (which relates to the effect of repeals).

55 Short title, commencement and extent

(1) This Act may be cited as the Prison Act 1952.

(2) This Act shall come into operation on the first day of October, nineteen hundred and fifty-two.

(3) . . . Part II of the Fourth Schedule to this Act shall extend to Scotland, . . .

(4) Except as provided in the last preceding subsection or [the Criminal Justice Act 1961], this Act shall not extend to Scotland.

(5) This Act shall not extend to Northern Ireland.

(Schs 1, 2 repealed by the Criminal Justice Act 1961, s 41 (2), (3), Sch 5; Sch 3 repealed in part by the Mental Health Act 1959, s 149 (2), Sch 7, Pt I, the Criminal Justice Act 1961, s 41 (2), (3), Sch 5, and the Firearms Act 1968, s 59, Sch 7; the residue is spent upon the repeal of the Courts-Martial (Appeals) Act 1951, s 17, by the Courts-Martial (Appeals) Act 1968, s 60, Sch 6; Sch 4 repealed by the SL(R) Act 1974.)

ii. Prison Rules 1964

ENGLAND AND WALES

The Prison Rules 1964
as amended by
The Prison (Amendment) Rules of
1968, 1971, 1972, 1974, 1976, 1981, 1982, 1983, 1987, 1988, 1989, 1990, 1992

PART I
PRISONERS

PART II
OFFICERS OF PRISONS

pursuance of section 47 of the Prison Act 1952, amended by sections 23 (2) and 41 (1) of, and chedule 4 to, the Criminal Justice Act 1961, I ereby make the following Rules:

PART I
PRISONERS

General

urpose of prison training and treatment

The purpose of the training and treatment of nvicted prisoners shall be to encourage and sist them to lead a good and useful life.

aintenance of order and discipline

. (1) Order and discipline shall be maintained with firmness, but with no more restriction than is required for safe custody and well ordered community life.

(2) In the control of prisoners, officers shall seek to influence them through their own example and leadership, and to enlist their willing co-operation.

(3) At all times the treatment of prisoners shall be such as to encourage their self-respect and a sense of personal responsibility, but a prisoner shall not be employed in any disciplinary capacity.

Classification of prisoners

3. (1) Prisoners shall be classified, in accordance with any directions of the Secretary of State, having regard to their age, temperament and record and with a view to maintaining good order and facilitating training and, in the case of convicted prisoners, of furthering the purpose of their training and treatment as provided by Rule 1 of these Rules.

(2) Unconvicted prisoners shall be kept out of contact with convicted prisoners as far as this can reasonably be done.

(3) Nothing in this Rule shall require a prisoner to be deprived unduly of the society of other persons.

Privileges

4. There shall be established at every prison systems of privileges approved by the Secretary of State and appropriate to the classes of prisoners there, which shall include arrangements under which money earned by prisoners in prison may be spent by them within the prison.

5. Not allocated

Temporary release

6. (1) A prisoner to whom this Rule applies may be temporarily released for any period or periods and subject to any conditions.

(2) A prisoner may be temporarily released under this Rule for any special purpose or to enable him to engage in employment, to receive instruction or training or to assist him in his transition from prison life to freedom.

(3) A prisoner released under this Rule may be recalled to prison at any time whether the conditions of his release have been broken or not.

(4) This Rule applies to prisoners other than persons committed in custody for trial or to be sentenced or otherwise dealt with before or by the Crown Court or remanded in custody by any court.

Information to prisoners

7. (1) Every prisoner shall be provided, as soon as possible after his reception into prison, and in any case within 24 hours, with information in writing about those provisions of these Rules and other matters which it is necessary that he should know,

including earnings and privileges, and the proper method of making requests and complaints.

(2) In the case of a prisoner aged less than 18, or a prisoner aged 18 or over who cannot read or appears to have difficulty in understanding the information so provided, the governor, or an officer deputed by him, shall so explain it to him that he can understand his rights and obligations.

(3) A copy of these Rules shall be made available to any prisoner who requests it.

Requests and complaints

8. (1) A request or complaint to the Governor or board of visitors relating to a prisoner's imprisonment shall be made orally or in writing by the prisoner.

(2) On every day the governor shall hear any requests or complaints that are made to him under paragraph (1) above.

(3) A written request or complaint under paragraph (1) above may be made in confidence.

Women prisoners

9. (1) Women prisoners shall be kept entirely separate from male prisoners.

(2) Not allocated.

(3) The Secretary of State may, subject to any conditions he thinks fit, permit a woman prisoner to have her baby with her in prison, and everything necessary for the baby's maintenance and care may be provided there.

Religion

Religious denomination

10. A prisoner shall be treated as being of the religious denomination stated in the record made in pursuance of section 10 (5) of the Prisons Act 1952 but the governor may, in a proper case and after due enquiry, direct that record to be amended.

Special duties of chaplains and prison ministers

11. (1) The chaplain or prison minister of a prison shall—

(*a*) interview every prisoner of his denomination individually soon after the prisoner's reception into that prison and shortly before his release; and

(*b*) if no other arrangements are made, read the burial service at the funeral of any prisoner of his denomination who dies in that prison.

(2) The chaplain shall visit daily all prisoners belonging to the Church of England who are sick, under restraint or undergoing cellular confinement; and a prison minister shall do the same, as far as he reasonably can, for prisoners of his own denomination.

(3) If the prisoner is willing, the chaplain shall visit any prisoner not of the Church of England who is sick, under restraint or undergoing cellular confinement, and is not regularly visited by a minister of his own denomination.

Regular visits by ministers of religion

12. (1) The chaplain shall visit the prisoners belonging to the Church of England.

(2) A prison minister shall visit the prisoners of his denomination as regularly as he reasonably can.

(3) Where a prisoner belongs to a denomination for which no prison minister has been appointed, the governor shall do what he reasonably can, if so requested b[y] the prisoner, to arrange for him to be visited regularly by a minister of that denomination.

Religious services

13. (1) The chaplain shall conduct Divine Servic[e] for prisoners belonging to the Church of England at least once every Sunday, Christmas Day and Good Friday, and suc[h] celebrations of Holy Communion and weekday services as may be arranged.

(2) Prison ministers shall conduct Divine Service for prisoners of their denominations at such times as may be arranged.

Substitute for chaplain or prison minister

14. (1) A person approved by the Secretary of State may act for the chaplain in his absence.

(2) A prison minister may, with the leave of the Secretary of State, appoint a substitu[te] to act for him in his absence.

Sunday work

15. Arrangements shall be made so as not to require prisoners of the Christian religion to do any unnecessary work on Sunday, Christmas Day or Good Friday, or prisoners of other religions on their recognised days of religious observance.

Religious books

16. There shall, so far as reasonably practicable, be available for the personal use of every prisoner such religious books recognized by his

enomination as are approved by the Secretary of tate for use in prisons.

Medical attention, &c

Iedical attendance

7. (1) The medical officer of a prison shall have the care of the health, mental and physical, of the prisoners in that prison.
(2) Every request by a prisoner to see the medical officer shall be recorded by the officer to whom it is made and promptly passed on to the medical officer.
(3) The medical officer may call another medical practitioner into consultation at his discretion, and shall do so if time permits before performing any serious operation.
(4) If an unconvicted prisoner desires the attendance of a registered medical practitioner or dentist, and will pay any expense incurred, the governor shall, if he is satisfied that there are reasonable grounds for the request and unless the Secretary of State otherwise directs, allow him to be visited and treated by that practitioner or dentist in consultation with the medical officer.

pecial illnesses and conditions

8. (1) The medical officer shall report to the governor on the case of any prisoner whose health is likely to be injuriously affected by continued imprisonment or any conditions of imprisonment. The governor shall send the report to the Secretary of State without delay, together with his own recommendations.
(2) The medical officer shall pay special attention to any prisoner whose mental condition appears to require it, and make any special arrangements which appear necessary for his supervision or care.
(3) The medical officer shall inform the governor if he suspects any prisoner of having suicidal intentions, and the prisoner shall be placed under special observation.

otification of illness or death

9. (1) If a prisoner dies, becomes seriously ill, sustains any severe injury or is removed to hospital on account of mental disorder, the governor shall, if he knows his or her address, at once inform the prisoner's spouse or next of kin, and also any person who the prisoner may reasonably have asked should be informed.
(2) If a prisoner dies, the governor shall give notice immediately to the coroner having jurisdiction, to the board of visitors and to the Secretary of State.

Physical welfare and work

Clothing

20. (1) An unconvicted prisoner may wear clothing of his own if and insofar as it is suitable, tidy and clean, but, subject to that, the provisions of this Rule shall apply to him as a convicted prisoner. An unconvicted prisoner shall be permitted to arrange for the supply to him from outside prison of sufficient clean clothing
(2) A convicted prisoner shall be provided with clothing adequate for warmth and health in accordance with a scale approved by the Secretary of State.
(3) The clothing provided under this Rule shall include suitable protective clothing for use at work, where this is needed.
(4) Subject to the provisions of Rule 38 (3) of these Rules, a convicted prisoner shall wear clothing provided under this Rule and no other, except on the directions of the Secretary of State.
(5) A prisoner may be provided, where necessary, with suitable and adequate clothing on his release.

Food

21. (1) Not allocated
(2) Subject to any directions of the Secretary of State, no prisoner shall be allowed, except as authorised by the medical officer, to have any food other than that ordinarily provided.
(3) No prisoners shall be given less food than is ordinarily provided, except upon the written recommendation of the medical officer.
(4) The food provided shall be wholesome, nutritious, well prepared and served, reasonably varied and sufficient in quantity.
(5) The medical officer shall regularly inspect the food both before and after it is cooked and shall report any deficiency or defect to the governor.
(6) In this Rule 'food' includes drink.

Alcohol and tobacco

22. (1) No prisoner shall be allowed to have any intoxicating liquor except under a written order of the medical officer specifying the quantity and the name of the prisoner.
(2) No prisoner shall be allowed to smoke or

to have any tobacco except as a privilege under Rule 4 of these Rules and in accordance with any orders of the governor.

Sleeping accommodation

23. (1) No room or cell shall be used as sleeping accommodation for a prisoner unless it has been certified in the manner required by section 14 of the Prison Act 1952 in the case of a cell used for the confinement of a prisoner.

(2) A certificate given under the section or this Rule shall specify the maximum number of prisoners who may sleep or be confined at one time in the room or cell to which it relates, and the number so specified shall not be exceeded without the leave of the Secretary of State.

Beds and bedding

24. Each prisoner shall be provided with a separate bed and with separate bedding adequate for warmth and health.

Special accommodation

25. The governor or board of visitors may, on application by an unconvicted prisoner, permit him on payment of a sum fixed by the Secretary of State—

(*a*) to occupy a room or cell specially fitted for such prisoners and provided with suitable bedding and other articles in addition to, or different from, those ordinarily provided, and to have at his own expense the use of private furniture and utensils approved by the governor; and

(*b*) to be relieved of the duty of cleaning his room or cell and similar duties.

Hygiene

26. (1) Every prisoner shall be provided with toilet articles necessary for his health and cleanliness, which shall be replaced as necessary.

(2) Every prisoner shall be required to wash at proper times, have a hot bath on reception and thereafter at least once a week and, in the case of a man not excused or excepted by the governor or medical officer, to shave or be shaved daily, and to have his hair cut as may be necessary for neatness:

Provided that an unconvicted prisoner or a convicted prisoner who has not yet been sentenced shall not be required to have his hair cut or any beard or moustache usually worn by him shaved off except where the medical officer directs this to be done for the sake of health or cleanliness.

(3) A woman prisoner's hair shall not be cut without her consent except where the medical officer certifies in writing that this is necessary for the sake of health or cleanliness.

Daily exercise

27. (1) A prisoner not engaged in outdoor work, or detained in an open prison, shall be given exercise in the open air for not less than one hour in all, each day, if weather permits:

Provided that exercise consisting of physical training may be given indoors instead of in the open air.

(2) The Secretary of State may in special circumstances authorise the reduction of th period aforesaid to half an hour a day.

(3) The medical officer shall decide upon the fitness of every prisoner for exercise and physical training, and may excuse a prisoner from, or modify, any activity on medical grounds.

Work

28. (1) A convicted prisoner shall be required to do useful work for not more than 10 hour a day, and arrangements shall be made to allow prisoners to work, where possible, outside the cells and in association with one another.

(2) The medical officer may excuse a prisone from work on medical grounds, and no prisoner shall be set to do work which is not of a class for which he has been passed by the medical officer as being fit.

(3) No prisoner shall be set to do work of a kind not authorised by the Secretary of State.

(4) No prisoner shall work in the service of another prisoner or an officer, or for the private benefit of any person, without the authority of the Secretary of State.

(5) An unconvicted prisoner shall be permitted, if he wishes, to work as if he were a convicted prisoner.

(6) Prisoners may be paid for their work at rates approved by the Secretary of State, either generally or in relation to particula cases.

Education and social welfare

Education

29. (1) Every prisoner able to profit from the edu cation facilities provided at a prison shall be encouraged to do so.

(2) Programmes of evening educational classes shall be arranged at every prison and, subject to any directions of the Secretary of State, reasonable facilities shall be afforded to prisoners who wish to do so to improve their education by correspondence courses or private study, or to practice handicrafts, in their spare time.

(3) Special attention shall be paid to the education of illiterate prisoners, and if necessary they shall be taught within the hours normally allotted to work.

Library books

30. A library shall be provided in every prison and, subject to any directions of the Secretary of State, every prisoner shall be allowed to have library books and to exchange them.

Outside contacts

31. (1) Special attention shall be paid to the maintenance of such relationships between a prisoner and his family as are desirable in the best interests of both.

(2) A prisoner shall be encouraged and assisted to establish and maintain such relations with persons and agencies outside prison as may, in the opinion of the governor, best promote the interests of his family and his own social rehabilitation.

After-care

32. From the beginning of a prisoner's sentence, consideration shall be given, in consultation with the appropriate after-care organisation, to the prisoner's future and the assistance to be given him on and after his release.

Letters and visits

Letters and visits generally

33. (1) The Secretary of State may, with a view to securing discipline and good order or the prevention of crime or in the interests of any persons, impose restrictions, either generally or in a particular case, upon the communications to be permitted between a prisoner and other persons.

(2) Except as provided by statute or these Rules, a prisoner shall not be permitted to communicate with any outside person, or that person with him, without the leave of the Secretary of State.

(3) Except as provided by these Rules, every letter or communication to or from a prisoner may be read or examined by the governor or an officer deputed by him, and the governor may, at his discretion, stop any letter or communication on the ground that its contents are objectionable or that it is of inordinate length.

(4) Every visit to a prisoner shall take place within the sight of an officer, unless the Secretary of State otherwise directs.

(5) Except as provided by these Rules, every visit to a prisoner shall take place within the hearing of an officer, unless the Secretary of State otherwise directs.

(6) The Secretary of State may give directions, generally or in relation to any visit or class of visits, concerning the days and time when prisoners may be visited.

Personal letters and visits

34. (1) An unconvicted prisoner may send and receive as many letters and may receive as many visits as he wishes within such limits and subject to such conditions as the Secretary of State may direct, either generally or in a particular case.

(2) A convicted prisoner shall be entitled—

(*a*) to send and to receive a letter on his reception into a prison and thereafter once a week; and

(*b*) to receive a visit twice in every period of four weeks, but only once in every such period if the Secretary of State so directs.

(3) The governor may allow a prisoner an additional letter or visit where necessary for his welfare or that of his family.

(4) The governor may allow a prisoner entitled to a visit to send and to receive a letter instead.

(5) The governor may defer the right of a prisoner to a visit until the expiration of any period of cellular confinement.

(6) The board of visitors may allow a prisoner an additional letter or visit in special circumstances, and may direct that a visit may extend beyond the normal duration.

(7) The Secretary of State may allow additional letters and visits in relation to any prisoner or class of prisoners.

(8) A prisoner shall not be entitled under this Rule to receive a visit from any person other than a relative or friend, except with the leave of the Secretary of State.

(9) Any letter or visit under the succeeding provisions of these Rules shall not be counted as a letter or visit for the purposes of this Rule.

Police interviews

35. A police officer may, on production of an order issued by or on behalf of a chief officer of police, interview any prisoner willing to see him.

Securing release

36. A person detained in prison in default of finding a surety, or of payment of a sum of money, may communicate with and be visited at any reasonable time on a weekday by, any relative or friend to arrange for a surety or payment in order to secure his release from prison.

Legal advisers

37. (1) The legal adviser of a prisoner in any legal proceedings, civil or criminal, to which the prisoner is a party shall be afforded reasonable facilities for interviewing him in connection with those proceedings, and may do so out of hearing but in the sight of an officer.

(2) A prisoner's legal adviser may, subject to any directions given by the Secretary of State, interview the prisoner in connection with any other legal business out of hearing but in the sight of an officer.

Further facilities in connection with legal proceedings

37A (1) A prisoner who is a party to any legal proceedings may correspond with his legal adviser in connection with the proceedings and unless the governor has reason to suppose that any such correspondence contains matter not relating to the proceedings it shall not be read or stopped under Rule 33 (3) of these Rules.

(2) A prisoner shall on request be provided with any writing materials necessary for the purposes of paragraph (1) of this Rule.

(3) Subject to any directions given in the particular case by the Secretary of State, a registered medical practitioner selected by or on behalf of such a prisoner as aforesaid shall be afforded reasonable facilities for examining him in connection with the proceedings, and may do so out of hearing but in the sight of an officer.

(4) Subject to any directions of the Secretary of State, a prisoner may correspond with a solicitor for the purpose of obtaining legal advice concerning any course of action in relation to which the prisoner may become a party to civil proceedings or for the purpose of instructing the solicitor to issue such proceedings.

Removal, record and property

Custody outside prison

38. (1) A person being taken to or from a prison in custody shall be exposed as little as possible to public observation, and proper care shall be taken to protect him from curiosity and insult.

(2) A prisoner required to be taken in custody anywhere outside the prison shall be kept in the custody of an officer appointed or a police officer.

(3) A prisoner requiring to be taken in custody to any court shall wear his own clothing or clothing different from the dress worn at any institution to which the Prison Act 1952 applies.

Search

39. (1) Every prisoner shall be searched when taken into custody by an officer, on his reception into a prison and subsequently as the governor thinks necessary.

(2) A prisoner shall be searched in as seemly a manner as is consistent with discovering anything concealed.

(3) No prisoner shall be stripped and searched in the sight of another prisoner, or in the sight or presence of an officer not of the same sex.

(4) Not allocated.

Record and photograph

40. (1) A personal record of each prisoner shall be prepared and maintained in such manner as the Secretary of State may direct.

(2) Every prisoner may be photographed on reception and subsequently, but no copy of the photograph shall be given to any person not authorised to receive it.

Prisoners' property

41. (1) Subject to any directions of the Secretary of State, an unconvicted prisoner may have supplied to him at his expense and retain for his own use books, newspapers writing materials and other means of occupation, except any that appears objectionable to the board of visitors or, pending consideration by them, to the governor.

(2) Anything, other than cash, which a prisoner has at a prison and which he is not allowed to retain for his own use shall be taken into the governor's custody. An inventory of a prisoner's property shall be kept, and he shall be required to sign it,

after having a proper opportunity to see that it is correct.

(3) Any cash which a prisoner has at a prison shall be paid into an account under the control of the governor and the prisoner shall be credited with the amount in the books of the prison.

(3A) Any article belonging to a prisoner which remains unclaimed for a period of more than three years after he leaves prison, or dies, may be sold or otherwise disposed of; and the net proceeds of any sale shall be paid to the National Association for the Care and Resettlement of Offenders, for its general purposes.

(4) The governor may confiscate any unauthorised article found in the possession of a prisoner after his reception into prison, or concealed or deposited anywhere within a prison.

Money and articles received by post

42. (1) Any money or other article (other than a letter or other communication) sent to a convicted prisoner through the post office shall be dealt with in accordance with the provisions of this Rule, and the prisoner shall be informed of the manner in which it is dealt with.

(2) Any cash shall, at the discretion of the governor be—

(*a*) dealt with in accordance with Rule 41 (3) of these Rules; or

(*b*) returned to the sender; or

(*c*) in a case where the sender's name and address are not known, paid to the National Association for the Care and Resettlement of Offenders, for its general purposes:

Provided that in relation to a prisoner committed to a prison in default of payment of any sum of money, the prisoner shall be informed of the receipt of the cash and, unless he objects to its being so applied, it shall be applied in or towards the satisfaction of the amount due from him.

(3) Any security for money shall, at the discretion of the governor, be—

(*a*) delivered to the prisoner or placed with his property at the prison; or

(*b*) returned to the sender; or

(*c*) encashed and the cash dealt with in accordance with paragraph (2) of this Rule.

(4) Any other article to which this Rule applies shall, at the discretion of the governor, be—

(*a*) delivered to the prisoner or placed with his property at the prison; or

(*b*) returned to the sender; or

(*c*) in the case where the sender's name and address are not known or the article is of such a nature that it would be unreasonable to return it, sold or otherwise disposed of, and the net proceeds of any sale applied in accordance with paragraph (2) of this Rule.

Special control and restraint

Removal from association

43. (1) Where it appears desirable, for the maintenance of good order or discipline or in his own interests, that a prisoner should not associate with other prisoners, either generally or for particular purposes, the governor may arrange for the prisoner's removal from association accordingly.

(2) A prisoner shall not be removed under this Rule for a period of more than 3 days without the authority of a member of the board of visitors or of the Secretary of State. An authority given under this paragraph shall be for a period not exceeding one month, but may be renewed from month to month except that, in the case of a person aged less than 21 years who is detained in prison such an authority shall be for a period not exceeding 14 days, but may be renewed from time to time for a like period.

(3) The governor may arrange at his discretion for such a prisoner as aforesaid to resume association with other prisoners, and shall do so if in any case the medical officer so advises on medical grounds.

Use of force

44. (1) An officer in dealing with a prisoner shall not use force unnecessarily and, when the application of force to a prisoner is necessary, no more force than is necessary shall be used.

(2) No officer shall act deliberately in a manner calculated to provoke a prisoner.

Temporary confinement

45. The governor may order a refractory or violent prisoner to be confined temporarily in a special cell, but a prisoner shall not be so confined as a punishment, or after he has ceased to be refractory or violent.

Restraints

46 (1) The governor may order a prisoner to be put under restraint where this is necessary to prevent the prisoner from injuring himself or others, damaging property or creating a disturbance.

(2) Notice of such an order shall be given without delay to a member of the board of visitors, and to the medical officer.

(3) On receipt of the notice the medical officer shall inform the governor whether he concurs in the order. The governor shall give effect to any recommendation which the medical officer may make.

(4) A prisoner shall not be kept under restraint longer than necessary, nor shall he be so kept for longer than 24 hours without a direction in writing given by a member of the board of visitors or by an officer of the Secretary of State (not being an officer of a prison). Such a direction shall state the grounds for the restraint and the time during which it may continue.

(5) Particulars of every case of restraint under the foregoing provisions of this Rule shall be forthwith recorded.

(6) Except as provided by this Rule no prisoner shall be put under restraint otherwise than for safe custody during removal, or on medical grounds by direction of the medical officer. No prisoner shall be put under restraint as a punishment.

(7) Any means of restraint shall be of a pattern authorised by the Secretary of State, and shall be used in such manner and under such conditions as the Secretary of State may direct.

Offences against discipline

47. A prisoner is guilty of an offence against discipline if he—

(1) commits any assault;

(2) detains any person against his will;

(3) denies access to any part of the prison to any officer;

(4) fights with any person;

(5) intentionally endangers the health or personal safety of others or, by his conduct, is reckless whether such health or personal safety is endangered;

(6) intentionally obstructs an officer in the execution of his duty;

(7) escapes or absconds from prison or from legal custody;

(8) fails to comply with any condition upon which he is temporarily released under Rule 6 of these Rules.

(9) has in his possession—

(*a*) any unauthorised article, or

(*b*) a greater quantity of any article than he is authorised to have;

(10) sells or delivers to any person any unauthorised article;

(11) sells or, without permission, delivers to any person any article which he is allowed to have only for his own use;

(12) takes improperly any article belonging to another person or to a prison;

(13) intentionally or recklessly sets fire to any part of a prison or any other property, whether or not his own;

(14) destroys or damages any part of a prison or any other property, other than his own;

(15) absents himself from any place where he is required to be or is present at any place where he is not authorised to be;

(16) is disrespectful to any officer or any person visiting a prison;

(17) uses threatening, abusive or insulting words or behaviour;

(18) intentionally fails to work properly or, being required to work, refuses to do so;

(19) disobeys any lawful order;

(20) disobeys or fails to comply with any rule or regulation applying to him;

(21) in any way offends against good order and discipline;

(22) (*a*) attempts to commit

(*b*) incites another prisoner to commit, or

(*c*) assists another prisoner to commit or to attempt to commit,

any of the foregoing offences.

Disciplinary charges

48. (1) Where a prisoner is to be charged with an offence against discipline, the charge shall be laid as soon as possible and, save in exceptional circumstances, within 48 hours of the discovery of the offence.

(2) Not allocated

(3) Every charge shall be inquired into, by the governor.

(4) Every charge shall be first inquired into not later, save in exceptional circumstances, than the next day, not being a Sunday or public holiday, after it is laid.

(5) A prisoner who is to be charged with an offence against discipline may be kept apart from other prisoners pending the governor's first inquiry.

Rights of prisoners charged

49. (1) Where a prisoner is charged with an offence against discipline, he shall be

informed of the charge as soon as possible and, in any case, before the time when it is inquired into by the governor.

(2) At an inquiry into a charge against a prisoner he shall be given a full opportunity of hearing what is alleged against him and of presenting his own case.

Governor's punishments

50. (1) If he find a prisoner guilty of an offence against discipline the governor may, subject to rule 52 of these Rules, impose one or more of the following punishments:

(*a*) caution;
(*b*) forfeiture for a period not exceeding 28 days of any of the privileges under Rule 4 of these Rules;
(*c*) exclusion from associated work for a period not exceeding 14 days;
(*d*) stoppage of or deduction from earnings for a period not exceeding 56 days and of an amount not exceeding 28 days earnings;
(*e*) cellular confinement for a period not exceeding 3 days;
(*f*) in the case of a short-term or long-term prisoner, an award of additional days not exceeding 28 days;
(*g*) in the case of a prisoner otherwise entitled to them, forfeiture for any period of the right, under rule 41 (1) of these Rules, to have the articles there mentioned;
(*h*) in the case of a prisoner guilty of escaping or attempting to escape and who is entitled to it, forfeiture of the right to wear his own clothing under rule 20 (1) of these Rules.

(2) If a prisoner is found guilty of more than one charge arising out of an incident, punishments under this rule may be ordered to run consecutively but, in the case of an award of additional days, the total period added shall not exceed 28 days.

Forfeiture of remission to be treated as an award of additional days

51. (1) In this rule, 'existing prisoner' and 'existing licensee' have the meanings assigned to them by paragraph 8 (1) of Schedule 12 to the Criminal Justice Act 1991 (*a*).

(2) In relation to any existing prisoner or existing licensee who has forfeited any remission of his sentence, the provisions of Part II of the Criminal Justice Act 1991 shall apply as if he had been awarded such number of additional days as equals the number of days of remission which he has forfeited.

Offences committed by young persons

52. (1) In the case of an offence against discipline committed by an inmate who was under the age of 21 when the offence was committed (other than an offender in relation to whom the Secretary of State has given a direction under section 13 (1) of the Criminal Justice Act 1982 that he shall be treated as if he had been sentenced to imprisonment)—

(*a*) rule 50 of these Rules shall have effect, but—
 (i) the maximum period of forfeiture of privileges under rule 4 of these Rules shall be 14 days; and
 (ii) the maximum period of stoppage of earnings shall be 14 days;

(2) In the case of an inmate who has been sentenced to a term of youth custody or detention in a Young Offender Institution, and by virtue of a direction of the Secretary of State under section 13 of the Criminal Justice Act 1982, is treated as if he had been sentenced to imprisonment for that term, any punishment imposed on him for an offence against discipline before the said direction was given shall, if it has not been exhausted or remitted, continue to have effect as if made pursuant to rule 50 of these Rules.

(3) In the case of an inmate detained in a prison who, by virtue of paragraph 12 of Schedule 8 to the Criminal Justice Act 1988, on 1st October 1988 fell to be treated for all purposes of detention, release and supervision as if his sentence had been a sentence of detention in a Young Offender Institution, any award for an offence against discipline made in respect of him before that date under rule 50, 51 or 52 of the Prison Rules 1964, which were then in force, or treated by virtue of rule 5 (4A) as having been imposed under those Rules, shall, if it has not been exhausted or remitted, continue to have effect as if it were a punishment imposed pursuant to rule 50 or 51 of these Rules.

Particular punishments

53. (1) Not allocated

(2) No punishment of cellular confinement shall be imposed unless the medical officer has certified that the prisoner is in a fit state of health to be so dealt with.

Prospective award of additional days

54\. (1) Subject to paragraph (2), where an offence against discipline is committed by a prisoner who is detained only on remand, additional days may be awarded notwithstanding that the prisoner has not (or had not at the time of the offence) been sentenced.

(2) An award of additional days under paragraph (1) shall have effect only if the prisoner in question subsequently becomes a short-term or long-term prisoner whose sentence is reduced, under section 67 of the Criminal Justice Act 1967 (*b*), by a period which includes the time when the offence against discipline was committed.

Suspended Punishments

55\. (1) Subject to any directions given by the Secretary of State, the power to impose a disciplinary punishment (other than a caution) shall include power to direct that the punishment is not to take effect unless, during a period specified in the direction (not being more than six months from the date of the direction) the prisoner commits another offence against discipline and a direction is given under paragraph (2) below.

(2) Where a prisoner commits an offence against discipline during the period specified in a direction given under paragraph (1) above the person dealing with that offence may—

(*a*) direct that the suspended punishment shall take effect,

(*b*) reduce the period or amount of the suspended punishment and direct that it shall take effect as so reduced,

(*c*) vary the original direction by substituting for the period specified a period expiring not later than six months from the date of variation, or

(*d*) give no direction with respect to the suspended punishment.

Remission and mitigation of punishments and quashing of findings of guilt

56\. (1) The Secretary of State may quash any finding of guilt and may remit any punishment or mitigate it either by reducing it or by substituting another award which is, in his opinion, less severe.

(2) Subject to any directions given by the Secretary of State, the Governor may remit or mitigate any punishment imposed by a governor or the board of visitors.

57–62. Not allocated.

Other particular classes

Prisoners committed for contempt, &c

63\. (1) A prisoner committed or attached for contempt of court, or for failing to do or abstain from doing anything required to be done or left undone, shall have the same privileges as an unconvicted prisoner under Rules 20 (1) and 34 (1) of these rules.

(2) Such prisoners shall be treated as a separate class for the purposes of Rule 3 of these Rules but, notwithstanding anything in that Rule, such prisoners may be permitted to associate with any other class of prisoners if they are willing to do so.

(3) Not allocated.

64–71. Not allocated

Prisoners under sentence of death

Application of foregoing Rules

72\. The foregoing provisions of these Rules shall apply in relation to a prisoner under sentence of death only in so far as they are compatible with that sentence and with Rules 73 to 76 of these Rules.

Search

73\. A prisoner under sentence of death shall be searched with special care and every article shall be taken from him which it might be dangerous or inexpedient to leave in his possession.

Confinement

74\. (1) A prisoner under sentence of death shall be confined in a separate cell and shall be kept apart from all other prisoners.

(2) He shall be kept by day and night in the constant charge of 2 officers.

(3) He shall not be required to work, but shall, if he wishes, be given work to do in his cell.

(4) Subject to the provisions of Rule 75 of these Rules, no person other than a member of the board of visitors or an officer shall have access to a prisoner under sentence of death without the leave of the Secretary of State.

Visits

75\. (1) Every visit to a prisoner under sentence of death, other than a visit by the chaplain or a prison minister, shall take place in the sight and hearing of an officer.

(2) Such a prisoner may be visited by any relation, friend or legal adviser whom he wishes to see, and who is authorised to visit him by an order in writing of a member of the board of visitors or the Secretary of State.

(3) The chaplain shall have free access to every such prisoner belonging to the Church of England, and to every other such prisoner who wishes to see him.

(4) Where such a prisoner belongs to a denomination other than the Church of England, a minister of that denomination shall have free access to him.

Correspondence

76. A prisoner under sentence of death shall be given all necessary facilities to enable him to correspond with his legal advisers, relatives and friends.

PART II
OFFICERS OF PRISONS

General duty of officers

77. (1) It shall be the duty of every officer to conform to these Rules and the rules and regulations of the prison, to assist and support the governor in their maintenance and to obey his lawful instructions.

(2) An officer shall inform the governor promptly of any abuse or impropriety which comes to his knowledge.

Gratuities forbidden

78. No officer shall receive any unauthorised fee, gratuity or other consideration in connection with his office.

Search of officers

79. An officer shall submit himself to be searched in the prison if the governor so directs.

Transactions with prisoners

80. (1) No officer shall take part in any business or pecuniary transaction with or on behalf of a prisoner without the leave of the Secretary of State.

(2) No officer shall without authority bring in or take out, or attempt to bring in or take out, or knowingly allow to be brought in or taken out, to or for a prisoner, or deposit in any place with intent that it shall come into the possession of a prisoner, any article whatsoever.

Contact with former prisoners, &c

81. No officer shall, without the knowledge of the governor, communicate with any person whom he knows to be a former prisoner or a relative or friend of a prisoner or former prisoner.

Communications to the press, &c

82. (1) No officer shall make, directly or indirectly, any unauthorised communication to a representative of the press or any other person concerning matters which have become known to him in the course of his duty.

(2) No officer shall, without authority, publish any matter or make any public pronouncement relating to the administration of any institution to which the Prison Act 1952 applies or to any of its inmates.

Quarters

83. An officer shall occupy any quarters which may be assigned to him.

Code of discipline

84. The Secretary of State may approve a code of discipline to have effect in relation to officers, or such classes of officers as it may specify, setting out the offences against discipline, the awards which may be made in respect of them and the procedure for dealing with charges.

PART III
PERSONS HAVING ACCESS TO A PRISON

Prohibited articles

85. No person shall, without authority, convey into or throw into or deposit in a prison, or convey or throw out of a prison, or convey to a prisoner, or deposit in any place with intent that it shall come into the possession of a prisoner, any money, clothing food, drink, tobacco, letter, paper, book, tool or other article whatever. Anything so conveyed, thrown or deposited may be confiscated by the governor.

Control of persons and vehicles

86. (1) Any person or vehicle entering or leaving a prison may be stopped, examined and searched.

(2) The governor may direct the removal from a prison of any person who does not leave on being required to do so.

Viewing of prisons

87. (1) No outside person shall be permitted to view a prison unless authorised by statute or the Secretary of State.

(2) No person viewing the prison shall be permitted to take a photograph, make a sketch or communicate with a prisoner unless authorised by statute or the Secretary of State.

PART IV
BOARDS OF VISITORS

Disqualification for membership

88. Any person interested in any contract for the supply of goods or services to a prison shall not be a member of the board of visitors for that prison.

89–91 Not allocated

Board of visitors

92. (1) A member of the board of visitors for a prison appointed by the Secretary of State under section 6 (2) of the Prison Act 1952 shall subject to paragraph (1A below) hold office for three years, or such less period as the Secretary of State may appoint.

(1A) The Secretary of State may terminate the appointment of a member if he is satisfied that—

(*a*) he has failed satisfactorily to perform his duties,

(*b*) he is by reason of physical or mental illness, or for any other reason, incapable of carrying out his duties, or

(*c*) he has been convicted of such a criminal offence, or his conduct has been such, that it is not in the Secretary of State's opinion fitting that he should remain a member.

(2) When a board is first constituted, the Secretary of State shall appoint one of its members to be chairman for a period not exceeding twelve months.

(3) Subject to paragraph (2) above, at their first meeting in any year of office the board shall appoint one of their number to be chairman and one to be vice-chairman for that year and thereafter shall fill any casual vacancy in either office promptly.

(4) The vice-chairman's term of office shall come to an end when, for whatever reason, that of the chairman comes to an end.

Proceedings of boards

93. (1) The board of visitors for a prison shall meet at the prison once a month or, if they resolve for reasons specified in the resolution that less frequent meetings are sufficient, not fewer than eight times in twelve months.

(2) The board may fix a quorum of not fewer than three members for proceedings.

(3) The board shall keep minutes of their proceedings.

(4) The proceedings of the board shall not be invalidated by any vacancy in the membership or any defect in the appointment of a member.

General duties of boards

94. (1) The board of visitors for a prison shall satisfy themselves as to the state of the prison premises, the administration of the prison and the treatment of the prisoners.

(2) The board shall inquire into and report upon any matter into which the Secretary of State asks them to inquire.

(3) The board shall direct the attention of the governor to any matter which calls for his attention, and shall report to the Secretary of State any matter which they feel it expedient to report.

(4) The board shall inform the Secretary of State immediately of any abuse which comes to their knowledge.

(5) Before exercising any power under these Rules the board and any member of the board shall consult the governor in relation to any matter which may affect discipline.

Particular duties

95. (1) The board of visitors for a prison and any member of the board shall hear any complaint or request which a prisoner wishes to make to them or him.

(2) The board shall arrange for the food of prisoners to be inspected by a member of the board at frequent intervals.

(3) The board shall inquire into any report made to them, whether or not by a member of the board, that a prisoner's health, mental or physical, is likely to be injuriously affected by any conditions of his imprisonment.

Members visiting prisons

96. (1) The members of the board of visitors for a prison shall visit the prison frequently, and the board shall arrange a rota whereby at least one of its members visits the prison between meetings of the board.

(2) A member of the board shall have access at any time to every part of the prison and to every prisoner, and he may interview any prisoner out of the sight and hearing of officers.

(3) A member of the board shall have access to the records of the prison.

Annual Report

97. The board of visitors for a prison shall make an annual report to the Secretary of State at the end of each year concerning the state of the prison and its administration, including in it any advice and suggestions they consider appropriate.

PART V
SUPPLEMENTAL

Delegation by governor

98. The governor of a prison may, with the leave of the Secretary of State, delegate any of his powers and duties under these Rules to another officer of that prison.

Contracted out prisons

98A. (1) Where the Secretary of State has entered into a contract for the running of a prison under section 84 of the Criminal Justice Act 1991 (*a*) ('the 1991 Act') these rules shall apply to that prison with the following modifications—

(*a*) references to an officer in the Rules shall include references to a prisoner custody officer certified as such under section 89 (1) of the 1991 Act and performing custodial duties;

(*b*) references to a governor in the Rules shall be construed as references to a director approved by the Secretary of State for the purposes of section 85 (1) (*a*) of the 1991 Act except—

(i) in rule 43, 45, 46, 48, 49, 50, 56 and 98 where references to a governor shall be construed as references to a controller appointed by the Secretary of State under section 85 (1) (*b*) of the 1991 Act, and

(ii) in rules 77 (1), 81 and 94 where references to a governor shall be construed as references to the director and the controller;

(*c*) Rule 84 shall not apply.

(2) Where a director exercises the powers set out in section 85 (3) (*b*) of the 1991 Act (removal from association, temporary confinement and restraints) in cases of urgency, he shall notify the controller of that fact forthwith.

Interpretation

99. (1) In these Rules, where the context so admits, the expression—

'convicted prisoner' means, subject to the provisions of Rule 63 of these Rules, a prisoner who has been convicted or found guilty of an offence or committed or attached for contempt of court or for failing to do or abstain from doing anything required to be done or left undone, and the expression 'unconvicted prisoner' shall be construed accordingly:
'governor' includes an officer for the time being in charge of a prison;
'legal adviser' means, in relation to a prisoner, his counsel or solicitor, and includes a clerk acting on behalf of his solicitor;
'officer' means an officer of a prison;
'prison minister' means, in relation to a prison, a minister appointed to that prison under section 10 of the Prison Act 1952;
'short-term prisoner' and 'long-term prisoner' have the meanings assigned to them by section 33 (5) of the Criminal Justice Act 1991, as extended by sections 43 (1) and 45 (1) of that Act.

(2) In these Rules a reference to (*a*) an award of additional days means additional days awarded under these Rules by virtue of section 42 of the Criminal Justice Act 1991; and (*b*) the Church of England includes a reference to the Church in Wales.

(3) The Interpretation Act 1889 shall apply for the interpretation of these Rules as it applies for the interpretation of an Act of Parliament.

Revocations and savings

100. (1) The Rules specified in the Schedule to these Rules are hereby revoked.

(2) For the purposes of these Rules any appointment, approval, authority, certificate, condition, direction or restriction made, given or imposed under any provision of any of the Rules revoked by this Rule shall be treated as having been made, given or imposed under the corresponding provision of these Rules.

Citation and commencement

101. These Rules may be cited as the Prison Rules 1964 and shall come into operation on the fourteenth day after the day on which they are made.

HENRY BROOKE
One of Her Majesty's Principal Secretaries of State

Home Office
WHITEHALL
11th March 1964

Consolidated November 1991
DIA1

SCHEDULE Rule 100

RULES REVOKED

Rules	References
The Prison Rules 1949	SI 1949/1073 (1949 I, p. 3470)
The Prison Rules 1951	SI 1951/1343 (1951 II, p. 289)
The Prison Rules 1952	SI 1952/1405 (1952 III, p. 2631)
The Prison Rules 1956	SI 1956/1986 (1956 II, p. 1897)
The Prison Rules 1962	SI 1962/1471 (1962 II, p. 1602)
The Prison Rules 1963	SI 1963/468 (1963 I, p. 530)

iii. Young Offender Institution Rules 1988

1988 No. 1422

YOUNG OFFENDER INSTITUTIONS, ENGLAND AND WALES

The Young Offender Institution Rules 1988

Made	5th August 1988
Laid before Parliament	18th August 1988
Coming into force	1st October 1988

ARRANGEMENT OF RULES

PART I

Preliminary

Rule

In pursuance of sections 25, 43 (5) and 47 of the Prison Act 1952[a], I hereby make the following Rules:—

[a] 1952 c. 52; section 43 was substituted by the Criminal Justice Act 1982 (c. 48), section 11; section 47 was extended by the Criminal Justice Act 1961 (c. 39), section 23 (2), the Criminal Justice Act 1982, section 13 (5), and Schedule 17, paragraph 9 and the Criminal Justice Act 1988 (c. 33), Schedule 8, paragraph 14; and amended by the Criminal Justice Act 1961, Schedule 4, the Criminal Justice Act 1967 (c. 80), section 66 (5), the Courts Act 1971 (c. 23), Schedule 8, paragraph 33 and the Criminal Justice Act 1982, Schedule 14, paragraph 7. Section 47 of the 1952 Act was also affected by an amendment to section 52 (2) of that Act by the Criminal Justice Act 1967, section 66 (4). The Criminal Justice Act 1988, Schedule 8, paragraph 1, contains amendments affecting these provisions.

PART I
PRELIMINARY

Citation and commencement

1. These Rules may be cited as the Young Offender Institution Rules 1988 and shall come into force on 1st October 1988.

Interpretation

2.—(1) In these Rules, where the context so admits, the expression:—
'compulsory school age' has the same meaning as in the Education Act 1944;
'governor' includes an officer for the time being in charge of a young offender institution;
'inmate' means a person detained in a young offender institution;
'legal adviser' means, in relation to an inmate, his counsel or solicitor, and includes a clerk acting on behalf of his solicitor;
'minister appointed to a young offender institution' means a minister so appointed under section 10 of the Prison Act 1952;
'officer' means an officer of a young offender institution.
' "short-term prisoner" and "long-term prisoner" have the meanings assigned to them by section 33 (5) of the Criminal Justice Act 1991, as extended by sections 43 (1) and 45 (1) of that Act'.

(2) In these Rules a reference to (*a*) an award of additional days means additional days awarded under these Rules by virtue of section 42 of the Criminal Justice Act 1991; and (*b*) the Church of England includes a reference to the Church in Wales.

(3) The Rules set out in the Schedule to this Order are hereby revoked.

PART II
INMATES

General

Aims and general principles of young offender institutions

3.—(1) The aim of a young offender institution shall be to help offenders to prepare for their return to the outside community.

(2) The aim mentioned in paragraph (1) above shall be achieved, in particular, by—

(*a*) providing a programme of activities, including education, training and work designed to assist offenders to acquire or develop personal responsibility, self-discipline, physical fitness, interests and skills and to obtain suitable employment after release;

(*b*) fostering links between the offender and the outside community;

(*c*) co-operating with the services responsible for the offender's supervision after release.

Classification of inmates

4, Inmates may be classified, in accordance with any directions of the Secretary of State, taking into account their ages, characters and circumstances.

Release

5.—Not allocated.

Temporary release

6.—(1) An inmate to whom this rule applies may be temporarily released for any period or periods and subject to any conditions.

(2) An inmate released under this rule may be recalled at any time whether any conditions of his release have been broken or not.

(3) This rule applies to inmates other than persons committed in custody for trial or to be sentenced or otherwise dealt with before or by the Crown Court or remanded in custody by any court.

Conditions

Privileges

7. There shall be established at every young offender institution systems of privileges approved by the Secretary of State and appropriate to the classes of inmates thereof and their ages, characters and circumstances, which shall include arrangements under which money earned by inmates may be spent by them within the young offender institution.

Information to inmates

8.—(1) Every inmate shall be provided, as soon as possible after his reception into the young offender institution, and in any case within 24 hours, with information in writing about those provisions of these Rules and other matters which it is necessary that he should know, including earnings and privileges, and the proper method of making requests and complaints.

(2) In the case of an inmate aged less than 18, or an inmate aged 18 or over who cannot read or appears to have difficulty in understanding the information so provided, the governor, or an officer deputed by him, shall so explain it to him that he can understand his rights and obligations.

(3) A copy of these Rules shall be made available to any inmate who requests it.

Requests and Complaints

9.—(1) A request or complaint to the governor or board of visitors relating to an inmate's detention shall be made orally or in writing by that inmate.

(2) On every day the governor shall hear any oral requests and complaints that are made to him under paragraph (1) above.

(3) A written request or complaint under paragraph (1) above may be made in confidence.

Letters and visits generally

10.—(1) The Secretary of State may, with a view to securing discipline and good order or the prevention of crime or in the interests of any persons, impose restrictions, either generally or in a particular case, upon the communications to be permitted between an inmate and other persons.

(2) Except as provided by statute or these Rules, an inmate shall not be permitted to communicate with any outside person, or that person with him, without the leave of the Secretary of State.

(3) Except as provided by these Rules, every letter or communication to or from an inmate may be read or examined by the governor or an officer deputed by him, and the governor may, at his discretion, stop any communication on the ground that its contents are objectionable or that it is of inordinate length.

(4) Subject to the provisions of these Rules, the governor may give such directions as he thinks fit for the supervision of visits to inmates, either generally or in a particular case.

Personal letters and visits

11.—(1) An inmate shall be entitled—

(*a*) to send and to receive a letter on his reception into a young offender institution and thereafter once a week; and

(*b*) to receive a visit twice in every period of four weeks but only once in every such period if the secretary of State so directs.

(2) The governor may allow an inmate an additional letter or visit when necessary for his welfare or that of his family.

(3) The governor may allow an inmate entitled to a visit to send and to receive a letter instead.

(4) The governor may defer the right of an inmate to a visit until the expiration of any period of confinement to a cell or room.

(5) The board of visitors may allow an inmate an additional letter or visit in special circumstances, and may direct that a visit may extend beyond the normal duration.

(6) The Secretary of State may allow additional letters and visits in relation to any inmate or class of inmates.

(7) An inmate shall not be entitled under this rule to receive a visit from any person other than a relative or friend, except with the leave of the Secretary of State.

(8) Any letter or visit under the succeeding provisions of these Rules shall not be counted as a letter or visit for the purposes of this rule.

Police interviews

12.—A police officer may, on production of an order issued by or on behalf of a chief officer of police, interview any inmate willing to see him.

Legal advisers

13.—(1) The legal adviser of an inmate in any legal proceedings, civil or criminal, to which the inmate is a party shall be afforded reasonable facilities for interviewing him in connection with those proceedings, and may do so out of hearing of an officer.

(2) An inmate's legal adviser may, with the leave of the Secretary of State, interview the inmate in connection with any other legal business.

Further facilities in connection with legal proceedings

14.—(1) An inmate who is a party to any legal proceedings may correspond with his legal adviser in connection with the proceedings and unless the governor has reason to suppose that any such correspondence contains matter not relating to the proceedings it shall not be read or stopped under rule 10 (3) of these Rules.

(2) An inmate shall on request be provided with any writing materials necessary for the purposes of paragraph (1) of this rule.

(3) Subject to any directions given in the particular case by the Secretary of State, a registered medical practitioner selected by or on behalf of an inmate who is a party to any legal proceedings shall be afforded reasonable facilities for examining him in connection with the proceedings, and may do so out of hearing but in the sight of an officer.

(4) Subject to any directions of the Secretary of State, an inmate may correspond with a solicitor for the purpose of obtaining legal advice concerning any cause of action in relation to which the inmate may become a party to legal proceedings or for the purpose of instructing the solicitor to issue such proceedings.

Securing release of defaulters

15. Any inmate detained in a young offender institution in default of payment of a fine or any other sum of money may communicate with, and be visited at any reasonable time on a weekday by, any relative or friend to arrange for payment in order to secure his release.

Clothing

16.—(1) An inmate shall be provided with clothing adequate for warmth and health in accordance with a scale approved by the Secretary of State.

(2) The clothing provided under this rule shall include suitable protective clothing for use at work, where this is needed.

(3) Subject to the provisions of rule 42 (3) of these Rules, an inmate shall wear clothing provided under this rule and no other, except on the directions of the Secretary of State.

(4) An inmate shall where necessary be provided with suitable and adequate clothing on his release.

Food

17.—(1) Subject to any directions of the Secretary of State, no inmate shall be allowed, except as authorised by the medical officer, to have any food other than that ordinarily provided.

(2) The food provided shall be wholesome, nutritious, well prepared and served, reasonably varied and sufficient in quantity.

(3) The medical officer shall regularly inspect the food both before and after it is cooked, and shall report any deficiency or defect to the governor.

(4) In this rule, 'food' includes drink.

Alcohol and tobacco

18.—(1) No inmate shall be allowed to have any intoxicating liquor except under a written order of the medical officer specifying the quantity and the name of the inmate.

(2) No inmate shall be allowed to smoke or to have any tobacco except in accordance with any directions of the Secretary of State.

Sleeping accommodation

19.—(1) No room or cell shall be used as sleeping accommodation for an inmate unless it has been certified by an officer of the Secretary of State (not being an officer of a young offender institution) that its size, lighting, heating, ventilation and fittings are adequate for health, and that it allows the inmate to communicate at any time with an officer.

(2) A certificate given under this rule shall specify the maximum number of inmates who may sleep in the room or cell at one time, and the number so specified shall not be exceeded without the leave of the Secretary of State.

Beds and bedding

20. Each inmate shall be provided with a separate bed and with separate bedding adequate for warmth and health.

Hygiene

21.—(1) Every inmate shall be provided with toilet articles necessary for his health and cleanliness, which shall be replaced as necessary.

(2) Every inmate shall be required to wash at proper times, have a hot bath or shower on reception and thereafter at least once a week.

(3) Subject to any directions of the Secretary of State, a male inmate may be required by the governor to shave or be shaved and to have his hair cut as may be necessary for neatness or, as directed by the medical officer, for health or cleanliness.

(4) A female inmate's hair shall not be cut without her consent except where the medical officer directs that it is necessary for health or cleanliness.

Female inmates

22. The Secretary of State may, subject to any conditions he thinks fit, permit a female inmate to have her baby with her in a young offender institution, and everything necessary for the baby's maintenance and care may be provided there.

Library books

23. A library shall be provided in every young offender institution and, subject to any directions of the Secretary of State, every inmate shall be allowed to have library books and to exchange them.

Medical attention

Medical attendance

24.—(1) The medical officer of a young offender institution shall have the care of the health, mental and physical, of the inmates of that institution.

(2) Every request by an inmate to see the medical officer shall be recorded by the officer to whom it is made and promptly passed on to the medical officer.

(3) The medical officer may call another medical practitioner in consultation at his discretion, and shall do so if time permits before performing any serious operation.

Special illnesses and conditions

25.—(1) The medical officer shall report to the governor on the case of any inmate whose health is likely to be injuriously affected by continued detention or any conditions of detention. The governor shall send the report to the Secretary of State without delay, together with his own recommendations.

(2) The medical officer shall pay special attention to any inmate whose mental condition appears to require it, and make any special arrangements which appear necessary for his supervision or care.

(3) The medical officer shall inform the governor if he suspects any inmate of having suicidal intentions, and the inmate shall be placed under special observation.

Notification of illness or death

26.—(1) If an inmate dies, becomes seriously ill, sustains any severe injury or is removed to hospital on account of mental disorder, the governor shall, if he knows his or her address, at once inform the inmate's spouse or next of kin, and also any person who the inmate may reasonably have asked should be informed.

(2) If an inmate dies, the governor shall give notice immediately to the coroner having jurisdiction, to the board of visitors and to the Secretary of State.

Religion

Religious denomination

27. An inmate shall be treated as being of the religious denomination stated in the record made in pursuance of section 10 (5) of the Prison Act 1952[a], but the governor may, in a proper case after due inquiry, direct that record to be amended.

[a] 1952 c. 52.

Special duties of chaplains and appointed ministers

28.—(1) The chaplain or a minister appointed to a young offender institution shall—

(*a*) interview every inmate of his denomination individually as soon as he reasonably can after the inmate's reception into that institution and shortly before his release; and

(*b*) if no other arrangements are made, read the burial service at the funeral of any inmate of his denomination who dies in that institution.

(2) The chaplain shall visit daily all inmates belonging to the Church of England who are sick, under restraint or confined to a room or cell; and a minister appointed to a young offender institution shall do the same, as far as he reasonably can, for inmates of his own denomination.

(3) If the inmate is willing, the chaplain shall visit any inmate not of the Church of England who is sick, under restraint or confined to a room or cell, and is not regularly visited by a minister of his own denomination.

Regular visits by ministers of religion, etc.

29.—(1) The chaplain shall visit regularly the inmates belonging to the Church of England.

(2) A minister appointed to a young offender institution shall visit the inmates of his denomination as regularly as he reasonably can.

(3) The governor shall, if so requested by an inmate belonging to a denomination for which no minister has been appointed to a young offender institution, do what he reasonably can to arrange for that inmate to be visited regularly by a minister of that denomination.

(4) Every request by an inmate to see the chaplain or a minister appointed to a young offender institution shall be promptly passed on to the chaplain or minister.

Religious services

30.—(1) The chaplain shall conduct Divine Service for inmates belonging to the Church of England at least once every Sunday, Christmas Day and Good Friday, and such celebrations of Holy Communion and weekday services as may be arranged.

(2) A minister appointed to a young offender institution shall conduct Divine Service for inmates of his denomination at such times as may be arranged.

Substitute for chaplain or appointed minister

31.—(1) A person approved by the Secretary of State may act for the chaplain in his absence.

(2) A minister appointed to a young offender institution may, with the leave of the Secretary of State, appoint a substitute to act for him in his absence.

Sunday work

32. Arrangements shall be made so as not to require inmates to do any unnecessary work on Sunday, Christmas Day or Good Friday nor inmates of religions other than the Christian religion to do any unnecessary work on their recognised days of religious observance (as an alternative, but not in addition, to those days).

Religious books

33. There shall, so far as reasonably practicable, be available for the personal use of every inmate such religious books recognised by his denomination as are approved by the Secretary of State for use in young offender institutions.

Occupation and links with the community

Regime activities

34.—(1) An inmate shall be occupied in education, training courses, work and physical education provided in accordance with rule 3 of these Rules.

(2) In all such activities regard shall be paid to individual assessment and personal development.

(3) The medical officer may excuse an inmate from work or any other activity on medical grounds; and no inmate shall be set to participate in work or any other activity of a kind for which he is considered by the medical officer to be unfit.

(4) An inmate may be required to participate in regime activities for no more than 8 hours a day.

(5) Inmates may be paid for their work or participation in other activities at rates approved by the Secretary of State, either generally or in relation to particular cases.

Education

35.—(1) Provision shall be made at a young offender institution for the education of inmates by means of programmes of class teaching or private study within the normal working week and, so far as practicable, programmes of evening and weekend educational classes or private study. The educational activities shall, so far as practicable, be such as will foster personal responsibility and an inmate's interests and skills and help him to prepare for his return to the community.

(2) In the case of an inmate aged less than 17, arrangements shall be made for his participation in education or training courses for at least 15 hours a week within the normal working week.

(3) In the case of an inmate aged 17 or over who is illiterate or backward, arrangements shall be made for education appropriate to his needs, if necessary within the normal working week.

(4) In the case of a female inmate aged 21 or over who is serving a sentence of imprisonment or who has been committed to prison for default and who is detained in a young offender institution instead of a prison, reasonable facilities shall be afforded if she wishes to improve her education, by class teaching or private study.

Training courses

36.—(1) Provision shall be made at a young offender institution for the training of inmates by means of training courses, in accordance with directions of the Secretary of State.

(2) Training courses shall be such as will foster personal responsibility and an inmate's interests and skills and improve his prospects of finding suitable employment after release.

(3) Training courses shall, so far as practicable, be such as to enable inmates to acquire suitable qualifications.

Work

37.—(1) Work shall, so far as practicable, be such as will foster personal responsibility and an inmate's interests and skills and help him to prepare for his return to the community.

(2) No inmate shall be set to do work of a kind not authorised by the Secretary of State.

Physical education

38.—(1) Provision shall be made at a young offender institution for the physical education of inmates within the normal working week, as well as evening and weekend physical recreation. The physical education activities shall be such as will foster personal responsibility and an inmate's interests and skills and encourage him to make good use of his leisure on release.

(2) Arrangements shall be made for each inmate, other than one to whom paragraph (4) of this rule applies, to participate in physical education for at least two hours a week on average or, in the case of inmates detained in such institutions or parts of institutions as the Secretary of State may direct, for at least 1 hour each weekday on average, but outside the hours allotted to education under rule 35 (2) in the case of an inmate of compulsory school age.

(3) In the case of an inmate with a need for remedial physical activity, appropriate facilities shall be provided.

(4) A female inmate aged 21 years or over who is serving a sentence of imprisonment or who has been committed to prison for default and who is detained in a young offender institution instead of a prison shall, if not engaged in outdoor work or detained in an open institution, be given the opportunity of exercise in the open air for not less than one hour in all, each day, if weather permits; but the Secretary of State may in special circumstances authorise the reduction of the period aforesaid to half an hour a day:

Provided that exercise consisting of physical education may be given indoors instead of in the open air.

Outside contacts

39.—(1) The governor shall encourage links between the young offender institution and the community by taking steps to establish and maintain relations with suitable persons and agencies outside the institution.

(2) The governor shall ensure that special attention is paid to the maintenance of such relations between an inmate and his family as seem desirable in the best interests of both.

(3) Subject to any directions of the Secretary of State, an inmate shall be encouraged, as far as practicable, to participate in activities outside the young offender institution which will be of benefit to the community or of benefit to the inmate in helping him to prepare for his return to the community.

After-care

40.—(1) From the beginning of his sentence, consideration shall be given, in consultation with the appropriate supervising service, to an inmate's future and the help to be given him in preparation for and after his return to the community.

(2) Every inmate who is liable to supervision after release shall be given a careful explanation of his liability and the requirements to which he will be subject while under supervision.

Discipline and control

Maintenance of order and discipline

41.—(1) Order and discipline shall be maintained, but with no more restriction than is required in the interests of security and well-ordered community life.

(2) In the control of inmates, officers shall seek to influence them through their own example and leadership, and to enlist their willing co-operation.

Custody outside a young offender institution

42.—(1) A person being taken to or from a young offender institution in custody shall be exposed as little as possible to public observation and proper care shall be taken to protect him from curiosity and insult.

(2) An inmate required to be taken in custody anywhere outside a young offender institution shall be kept in the custody of an officer appointed under section 3 of the Prison Act 1952[a] or of a police officer.

(3) An inmate required to be taken in custody to any court shall wear his own clothing or clothing different from the dress worn at any institution to which the Prison Act 1952[a] applies.

[a] 1952 c. 52.

Search

43.—(1) Every inmate shall be searched when taken into custody by an officer, on his reception into a young offender institution and subsequently as the governor thinks necessary.

(2) An inmate shall be searched in as seemly a manner as is consistent with discovering anything concealed.

(3) No inmate shall be stripped and searched in the sight of another inmate or in the sight or presence of an officer not of the same sex.

(4) Not allocated.

Record and photograph

44.—(1) A personal record of each inmate shall be prepared and maintained in such manner as the Secretary of State may direct, but no part of the record shall be disclosed to any person not authorised to receive it.

(2) Every inmate may be photographed on reception and subsequently, but no copy of the photograph shall be given to any person not authorised to receive it.

Inmates' property

45.—(1) Anything, other than cash, which an inmate has at a young offender institution and which he is not allowed to retain for his own use shall be taken into the governor's custody.

(2) Any cash which an inmate has at a young offender institution shall be paid into an account under the control of the governor and the inmate shall be credited with the amount in the books of the institution.

(3) Any article belonging to an inmate which remain unclaimed for a period of more than 3 years after he is released, or dies, may be sold or otherwise disposed of; and the net proceeds of any sale shall be paid to the National Association for the Care and Resettlement of Offenders, for its general purposes.

(4) The governor may confiscate any unauthorised article found in the possession of an inmate after his reception into a young offender institution, or concealed or deposited within a young offender institution.

Removal from association

46.—(1) Where it appears desirable, for the maintenance of good order or discipline or in his own interests, that an inmate should not associate with other inmates, either generally or for particular purposes, the governor may arrange for the inmate's removal from association accordingly.

(2) An inmate shall not be removed under this rule for a period of more than 3 days without the authority of a member of the board of visitors or of the Secretary of State. An authority given under this paragraph shall, in the case of a female inmate aged 21 years or over, be for a period not exceeding one month and, in the case of any other inmate, be for a period not exceeding 14 days, but may be renewed from time to time for a like period.

(3) The governor may arrange at his discretion for such an inmate as aforesaid to resume association with other inmates, and shall do so if in any case the medical officer so advises on medical grounds.

Use of force

47.—(1) An officer in dealing with an inmate shall not use force unnecessarily and, when the application of force to an inmate is necessary, no more force than is necessary shall be used.

(2) No officer shall act deliberately in a manner calculated to provoke an inmate.

Temporary confinement

48.—(1) The governor may order an inmate who is refractory or violent to be confined temporarily in a special cell or room, but an inmate shall not be so confined as a punishment, or after he has ceased to be refractory or violent.

(2) A cell or room shall not be used for the purpose of this rule unless it has been certified by an officer of the Secretary of State (not being an officer of a young offender institution) that it is suitable for the purpose, that its size, lighting, heating, ventilation and fittings are adequate for health, and that it allows the inmate to communicate at any time with an officer.

(3) In relation to any young offender institution, section 14 (6) of the Prison Act 1952 shall have effect so as to enable the provision of special rooms instead of special cells for the temporary confinement of refractory or violent inmates.

Restraints

49.—(1) The governor may order an inmate, other than an inmate aged less than 17, to be put under restraint where this is necessary to prevent the inmate from injuring himself or others, damaging property or creating a disturbance.

(2) Notice of such an order shall be given without delay to a member of the board of visitors and to the medical officer.

(3) On receipt of the notice the medical officer shall inform the governor whether he concurs in the order. The governor shall give effect to any recommendation which the medical officer may make.

(4) An inmate shall not be kept under restraint longer than necessary, nor shall he be so kept for longer than 24 hours without a direction in writing given by a member of the board of visitors or by an officer of the Secretary of State (not being an officer of a young offender institution). Such a direction shall state the grounds for the restraint and the time during which it may continue.

(5) Particulars of every case of restraint under the foregoing provisions of this rule shall be forthwith recorded.

(6) Except as provided by this rule no inmate shall be put under restraint otherwise than for safe custody during removal, or on medical grounds by direction of the medical officer. No inmate shall be put under restraint as a punishment.

(7) Any means of restraint shall be of a pattern authorised by the Secretary of State, and shall be used in such manner and under such conditions as the Secretary of State may direct.

Offences against discipline

50. An inmate is guilt of an offence against discipline if he—

(1) commits any assault;
(2) detains any person against his will;
(3) denies access to any part of the young offender institution to any officer;
(4) fights with any person;
(5) intentionally endangers the health or personal safety of others or, by his conduct, is reckless whether such health or personal safety is endangered;
(6) intentionally obstructs an officer in the execution of his duty;
(7) escapes or absconds from a young offender institution or from legal custody;
(8) fails
  (*a*) not allocated
  (*b*) to comply with any condition upon which he was temporarily released under Rule 6 of these rules.
(9) has in his possession—
  (*a*) any unauthorised article, or
  (*b*) a greater quantity of any article than he is authorised to have;
(10) sells or delivers to any person any unauthorised article;
(11) sells or, without permission, delivers to any person any article which he is allowed to have only for his own use;
(12) takes improperly any article belonging to another person or to a young offender institution;
(13) intentionally or recklessly sets fire to any part of a young offender institution or any other property, whether or not his own;
(14) destroys or damages any part of a young offender institution or any other property other than his own;
(15) absents himself from any place where he is required to be or is present at any place where he is not authorised to be;
(16) is disrespectful to any officer or any person visiting a young offender institution;
(17) uses threatening, abusive or insulting words or behaviour;
(18) intentionally fails to work properly or, being required to work, refuses to do so;
(19) disobeys any lawful order;
(20) disobeys or fails to comply with any rule or regulation applying to him;
(21) on any way offends against good order and discipline;
(22) (*a*) attempts to commit,
  (*b*) incites another inmate to commit, or
  (*c*) assists another inmate to commit or to attempt to commit any of the foregoing offences.

Disciplinary charges

51.—(1) Where an inmate is to be charged with an offence against discipline, the charge shall be laid as soon as possible and, save in exceptional circumstances, within 48 hours of the discovery of the offence.

(2) Not allocated

(3) Every charge shall be inquired into, by the governor.

(4) Every charge shall be first inquired into not later, save in exceptional circumstances, than the next day, not being a Sunday or public holiday, after it is laid.

(5) An inmate who is to be charged with an offence against discipline may be kept apart from other inmates pending the governor's first inquiry.

Rights of inmates charged

52.—(1) Where an inmate is charged with an offence against discipline, he shall be informed of the charge as soon as possible and, in any case, before the time when it is inquired into by the governor.

(2) At an inquiry into a charge against an inmate he shall be given a full opportunity of hearing what is alleged against him and of presenting his own case.

Governor's punishments

53.—(1) If he finds an inmate guilty of an offence against discipline the governor may, subject to rule 60 of these Rules, impose one or more of the following punishments:

(*a*) caution;
(*b*) forfeiture for a period not exceeding 14 days of any of the privileges under rule 7 of these Rules;
(*c*) removal for a period not exceeding 14 days from any particular activity or activities of the young offender institution, other than education, training courses, work and physical education in accordance with rules 34, 35, 36, 37 and 38 of these Rules;
(*d*) extra work outside the normal working week for a period not exceeding 14 days and for not more than 2 hours on any day;
(*e*) stoppage of or deduction from earnings for a period not exceeding 28 days and of an amount not exceeding 14 days earnings.
(*f*) confinement to a cell or room for a period not exceeding 14 days;
(*g*) removal from his wing or living unit for a period not exceeding 14 days;

(*h*) in the case of an inmate who is a short-term or long-term prisoner, an award of additional days not exceeding 28 days.

(2) If an inmate is found guilty of more than one charge arising out of an incident punishments under this rule may be ordered to run consecutively, but, in the case of an award of additional days, the total period added shall not exceed 28 days.

54.—Not allocated

55.—Not allocated

Confinement to a cell or room

56.—(1) No punishment of confinement to a cell or room shall be imposed unless the medical officer has certified that the inmate is in a fit state of health to be so dealt with.

(2) No cell or room shall be used as a detention cell or room for the purpose of a punishment of confinement to a cell or room unless it has been certified by an officer of the Secretary of State (not being an officer of a young offender institution) that it is suitable for the purpose; that its size, lighting, heating, ventilation and fittings are adequate for health; and that it allows the inmate to communicate at any time with an officer.

Removal from wing or living unit

57. Following the imposition of a punishment of removal from his wing or living unit, an inmate shall be accommodated in a separate part of the young offender institution under such restrictions of earnings and activities as the Secretary of State may direct.

Suspended punishments

58.—(1) Subject to any directions of the Secretary of State, the power to impose a disciplinary punishment (other than a caution) shall include the power to direct that the punishment is not to take effect unless, during a period specified in the direction (not being more than 6 months from the date of the direction), the inmate commits another offence against discipline and a direction is given under paragraph (2) below).

(2) Where an inmate commits an offence against discipline during the period specified in a direction given under paragraph (1) above, the person dealing with that offence may—

(*a*) direct that the suspended punishment shall take effect; or

(*b*) reduce the period or amount of the suspended punishment and direct that it shall take effect as so reduced; or

(*c*) vary the original direction by substituting for the period specified therein a period expiring not later than six months from the date of variation; or

(*d*) give no direction with respect to the suspended punishment.

Remission and mitigation of punishments and quashing of findings of guilt

59.—(1) The Secretary of State may quash any finding of guilt and may remit a disciplinary punishment or mitigate it either by reducing it or by substituting a punishment which is, in his opinion, less severe.

(2) Subject to any directions of the Secretary of State, the governor may remit or mitigate any punishment imposed by a governor or the board of visitors.

Adult female inmates: disciplinary punishments

60.—(1) In the case of a female inmate aged 21 years or over who is serving a sentence of imprisonment or who has been committed to prison for default—

(i) rule 53 of these Rules shall not apply, but the governor may, if he finds the inmate guilt of an offence against discipline, impose one or more of the following punishments:

(*a*) caution;

(*b*) forfeiture for a period not exceeding 28 days of any of the privileges under rule 7 of these Rules;

(*c*) removal for a period not exceeding 14 days from any particular activity or activities of the young offender institution, other than education, training courses, work and physical education in accordance with rules 34, 35, 36, 37 and 38 of thése Rules;

(*d*) extra work outside the normal working week for a period not exceeding 14 days and for not more than 2 hours on any day;

(*e*) stoppage of or deduction from earnings for a period not exceeding 56 days and of an amount not exceeding 28 days earnings.

(*f*) confinement to a cell or room for a period not exceeding 3 days;

(*g*) in the case of an inmate who is a short-term or long-term prisoner, an award of additional days not exceeding 28 days;

(2) Not allocated

(3) If an inmate is found guilty of more than one charge arising out of an incident, punishments under this rule may be ordered to run consecutively, but in the case of an award of additional days, the total period added shall not exceed 28 days.

Forfeiture of remission to be treated as an award of additional days

60A.—(1) In this rule, 'existing prisoner' and 'existing licensee' have the meanings assigned to them by paragraph 8 (1) of Schedule 12 to the Criminal Justice Act 1991.

(2) In relation to any existing prisoner or existing licensee who has forfeited any remission of his sentence, the provisions of Part II of the Criminal Justice Act 1991 shall apply as if he had been awarded such number of additional days as equals the number of days of remission which he has forfeited.

PART III
OFFICERS OF YOUNG OFFENDER INSTITUTIONS

General duty of officers

61.—(1) It shall be the duty of every officer to conform to these Rules and the rules and regulations of the young offender institution, to assist and support the governor in their maintenance and to obey his lawful instructions.

(2) An officer shall inform the governor promptly of any abuse or impropriety which comes to his knowledge.

Gratuities forbidden

62. No officer shall receive any unauthorised fee, gratuity or other consideration in connection with his office.

Search of officers

63. An officer shall submit himself to be searched in a young offender institution if the governor so directs.

Transactions with inmates

64.—(1) No officer shall take part in any business or pecuniary transaction with or on behalf of an inmate without the leave of the Secretary of State.

(2) No officer shall, without authority, bring in or take out, or attempt to bring in or take out, or knowingly allow to be brought in or taken out, to or for an inmate, or deposit in any place with intent that it shall come into the possession of an inmate, any article whatsoever.

Contact with former inmates, etc.

65. No officer shall, without the knowledge of the governor, communicate with any person who he knows to be a former inmate or a relative or friend of an inmate or former inmate.

Communications to the press, etc.

66.—(1) No officer shall make, directly or indirectly, any unauthorised communication to a representative of the press or any other person concerning matters which have become known to him in the course of his duty.

(2) No officer shall, without authority, publish any matter or make any public pronouncement relating to the administration of any institution to which the Prison Act 1952 applies or to any of its inmates.

Quarters

67. An officer shall occupy any quarters which may be assigned to him.

Code of discipline

68. The Secretary of State may approve a code of discipline to have effect in relation to officers, or such classes of officers as it may specify, setting out the offences against discipline, the awards which may be made in respect of them and the procedure for dealing with charges.

PART IV
PERSONS HAVING ACCESS TO A YOUNG OFFENDER INSTITUTION

Prohibited articles

69. No person shall, without authority, convey into or throw into or deposit in a young offender institution, or convey to an inmate, or deposit in any place with intent that it shall come into the possession of an inmate, any article whatsoever. Anything so conveyed, thrown or deposited may be confiscated by the governor.

Control of persons and vehicles

70.—(1) Any person or vehicle entering or leaving a young offender institution may be stopped, examined and searched.

(2) The Governor may direct the removal from a young offender institution of any person who does not leave on being required to do so.

Viewing of young offender institutions

71.—(1) No outside person shall be permitted to view a young person institution unless authorised by statute or the Secretary of State.

(2) No person viewing a young offender institution shall be permitted to take a photograph, make a sketch or communicate with an inmate unless authorised by statute or the Secretary of State.

PART V
BOARDS OF VISITORS

Disqualification for membership

72. Any person interested in any contract for the supply of goods or services to a young offender institution shall not be a member of the board of visitors for that institution.

Appointment

73.—(1) A member of the board of visitors for a young offender institution appointed by the Secretary of State under section 6 (2) of the Prison Act 1952 shall subject to paragraph (1A) below hold office for 3 years or such less period as the Secretary of State may appoint.

(1A) The Secretary of State may terminate the appointment of a member if satisfied that—

(*a*) he has failed satisfactorily to perform his duties,

(*b*) he is by reason of physical or mental illness, or for any other reason, incapable of carrying out his duties, or

(*c*) he has been convicted of such a criminal offence, or his conduct has been such, that it is not in the Secretary of State's opinion fitting that he should remain a member.

(2) When a board is first constituted, the Secretary of State shall appoint one of its members to be chairman for a period not exceeding twelve months.

(3) Subject to paragraph (2) of this rule, at their first meeting in any year of office the board shall appoint one of their members to be chairman and one to be vice-chairman for that year and thereafter shall fill any casual vacancy in either office promptly.

(4) The vice-chairman's term of office shall come to an end when, for whatever reason, that of the chairman comes to an end.

Proceedings of boards

74.—(1) The board of visitors of a young offender institution shall meet at the institution at least once a month.

(2) The board may fix a quorum of not fewer than 3 members for proceedings.

(3) The board shall keep minutes of their proceedings.

(4) The proceedings of the board shall not be invalidated by any vacancy in the membership or any defect in the appointment of a member.

General duties of boards

75.—(1) The board of visitors for a young offender institution shall satisfy themselves as to the state of the premises, the administration of the institution and the treatment of the inmates.

(2) The board shall inquire into any report on any matter into which the Secretary of State asks them to inquire.

(3) The board shall direct the attention of the governor to any matter which calls for his attention, and shall report to the Secretary of State any matters which they consider it expedient to report.

(4) The board shall inform the Secretary of State immediately of any abuse which comes to their knowledge.

(5) Before exercising any power under these Rules, the board and any member of the board shall consult the governor in relation to any matter which may affect discipline.

Particular duties

76.—(1) The board of visitors for a young offender institution and any member of the board shall hear any complaint or request which an inmate wishes to make to them or him.

(2) The board shall arrange for the food of the inmates to be inspected by a member of the board at frequent intervals.

(3) The board shall inquire into any report made to them, whether or not by a member of the board, that an inmate's health, mental or physical, is likely to be injuriously affected by any conditions of his detention.

Members visiting young offender institutions

77.—(1) The members of the board of visitors for a young offender institution shall visit the institution frequently, and the board shall arrange a rota for the purpose.

(2) A member of the board shall have access at any time to every part of the institution and to every inmate, and he may interview any inmate out of sight and hearing of officers.

(3) A member of the board shall have access to the records of the young offender institution.

Annual report

78. The board of visitors for a young offender institution shall make an annual report to the Secretary of State at the end of each year concerning the state of the institution and its administration, including in it any advice and suggestions they consider appropriate.

PART VI
SUPPLEMENTAL

Delegation by governor

79. The governor of a young offender institution may, with the leave of the Secretary of State, delegate any of his powers and duties under these Rules to another officer of that institution.

Transitional

80. In the case of an inmate who, by virtue of paragraph 12 of Schedule 8 to the Criminal Justice Act 1988[a], falls to be treated for all purposes of detention, release and supervision as if he had been sentenced to detention in a young offender institution or who, under paragraph 13 of the said Schedule 8, is detained in such an institution, any award of an offence against discipline made in respect of him under rule 53 or 54 of the Detention Centre Rules 1983[b] or rule 53 or 54 of the Youth Custody Centre Rules 1983[c] shall, if it has not been exhausted or remitted, continue to have effect as if it had been made under rule 53 or 54, respectively, of those Rules.

One of Her Majesty's Principal
Secretaries of State

Consolidated Rules
DIA1 Division

November 1992

SCHEDULE
INSTRUMENTS REVOKED

The Detention Centre Rules 1983 (S.I. 1983/569)
The Youth Custody Centre Rules 19483 (S.I. 1983/570)
The Detention Centre (Amendment) Rules 1987 (S.I. 1987/1255)
The Youth Custody Centre (Amendment) Rules 1987 (S.I. 1987/1257)

---

[a] 1988 c. 33.
[b] S.I. 1983/569.
[c] S.I. 1983/570.

EXPLANATORY NOTE

(These notes are not part of the Rules)

These Rules make provision for the management of young offender institutions provided by section 43 of the Prison Act 1952 as amended by section 11 of the Criminal Justice Act 1982 and Schedules 8 and 15 of the Criminal Justice Act 1988 which comes into force on 1st October 1988 (S.I. 1988/1408). They replace the Detention Centre Rules 1983 (S.I. 1983/569) and the Youth Custody Centre Rules 1983 (S.I. 1983/570), as amended. They include provision for the treatment, occupation, discipline and control of inmates who may be detained therein, the conduct of officers of young offender institutions and the constitution, powers and duties of boards of visitors.

Rule 3 contains the aims and general principles of young offender institutions and rules 34 to 40 contain more detailed provisions regulating the regime. The provisions of the Rules are generally similar in substance to those of the Youth Custody Rules 1983, with some modifications to take account of the fact that the new sentence replaces both the detention centre order and the youth custody sentence. Rule 43 provides that an inmate may not be stripped and searched either in the sight of another inmate or in the sight or presence of an officer not of the same sex.

These Rules remove the disciplinary functions of boards of visitors. Transitional provision is made so that boards of visitors have continuing jurisdiction to deal with cases referred to them before the coming into force of these Rules.

The Rules increase the entitlement of a young offender to receive visits from once every four weeks to twice every four weeks.

The Rules abolish the separate disciplinary offence of failing to return to a young offender institution after a period of temporary release, which duplicates, in part, the offence of failing to comply with a condition of release.

These Rules make provision for the award of additional days which replaces forfeiture of remission as a punishment available to the governor of a young offender institution in respect of an inmate who is a short-term or long-term prisoner and who is guilty of a disciplinary offence.

The Rules also provide that the provisions of Part II of the Criminal Justice Act 1991 shall apply to an inmate who is an existing prisoner or licensee and who has forfeited any remission of his sentence as if he had been awarded the same number of additional days as the number of days of remission which he has forfeited.

In addition, the Rules prohibit smoking except in accordance with any directions of the Secretary of State and remove the requirement that inmates be searched only by an officer of the same sex.

ANNEXE C **Standard List of Articles Allowed *In-Possession* of Prisoners**

Warning

THE ITEMS SHOWN ARE ON THE APPROVED LIST OF ARTICLES ALLOWED 'IN POSSESSION' OF PRISONERS—BUT THE INCLUSION OF ANY ITEM IN THE LIST IS NOT TO BE TAKEN AS AN INDICATION THAT IT EITHER WILL OR MUST BE ALLOWED IN POSSESSION IN ANY PARTICULAR ESTABLISHMENT. MOREOVER, IF ONE ESTABLISHMENT ALLOWS A PARTICULAR ITEM IN POSSESSION, IT DOES NOT FOLLOW THAT OTHER ESTABLISHMENTS WILL SUBSEQUENTLY DO SO: THEY MAY NOT. TREAT THIS LIST AS AN INDICATION OF WHAT MAY BE PERMITTED IN POSSESSION AND CHECK BEFORE PURCHASE.

Six Lists

Annexe C contains six separate lists:-

1. General Items;
2. Clothing & Toiletries;
3. Cooking Items;
4. Recreation, Hobbies & Education;
5. Religious items;
6. Sports & Games.

Each list shows whether or not the item may be sent in by post, handed in on a visit (Y/N), or has to be purchased through the canteen by way of private cash (PC), earnings (E), or either (Y). The standard restrictions in respect of each item are also given.

Governor's Discretion

Details of precisely which articles are allowed in possession of prisoners are entirely at the discretion of the relevant Governor. For reasons of security, the good order and discipline of the prison or in the interests of anyone within it, the Governor may choose not to allow an article in possession, even though it is on the approved list.

Restrictions

Where an article is allowed, it will normally have to comply with the restrictions which are shown in the list; failure to observe them could lead to the article being refused by the prison authorities at the gate, or stored in reception where the item arrives by post. Governors have a discretion, however, to amend methods of obtaining articles, or relax particular restrictions, dependent on the security or status of their establishment. Treat this list therefore more as an indication of the various articles which are approved and the restrictions you can normally expect to be imposed if a particular item is allowed in possession.

Disclaimer

All items held in possession are held at the prisoner's own risk. The Property Card (F377M) contains a disclaimer, which all prisoners sign, to the effect that the prison authorities cannot be held liable for any loss or damage caused—other than through the negligence of prison staff. Moreover, articles held in possession are considered to be a'privilege' by the prison authorities and may be withdrawn as the result of a disciplinary punishment.

Finally

You must also bear in mind that alterations of items on the approved list take place at least once a year and you should, therefore, make sure that you are consulting the latest edition of the *Handbook* and have made a final check with the authorities before any purchases are made.

ITEM	SENT IN	HANDED IN ON VISIT	PRIVATE CASH EARNINGS	RESTRICTIONS
GENERAL ITEMS				
Air mail letter	Y	Y	Y	
Address Book	Y	Y	Y	
Bird Cage & Accessories	Y	Y	Y	Cage Must be i/p Before Bird
Bird Food	N	N	Y	Canteen Only
Bed Spread or Duvet	Y	Y	Y	Fire Retardent
Caged Bird	N	Y	Y	Budgerigar OR Canary—1 Only
Calendars	Y	Y	Y	
Curtains	Y	Y	Y	
Chain	Y	Y	Y	Max Length 24"
Diary	Y	Y	Y	
Ear Rings	Y	Y	Y	
Floormat	Y	Y	Y	6' × 4' Maxmimum
Flowers	N	N	Y	Direct from Florist or Canteen Only
Gas lighters	N	N	Y	Disposable Only
Greeting Card	Y	Y	Y	Not Padded
Medallion	Y	Y	Y	1.5" Circumference
Newspapers & Periodicals	Y	Y	Y	From Registered Newsagent Only
Personal Organiser	Y	Y	Y	
Photographs & Pictures Only	Y	Y	Y	Unglazed Posters 4'×3' max
Postage stamps	Y	Y	Y	
Phonecards	N	N	Y	Canteen only
Smoking Req'	Y	Y	Y	Lighter, flints, pipe cleaner
Pipe-pouch	Y	Y	Y	
Tablecloth	Y	Y	Y	
Tobacco	Y/Rem	Y/Rem	Y	125g wkly Remands, Sealed pkts Only
	N/Con	N/Con	E	62.5g wkly Cons
Wristwatch	Y	Y	Y	
Wedding Ring or Plain Ring	Y	Y	Y	
Writing Paper & Envelopes	N	N	Y	
Washing Powder	N	N	Y	Canteen Only.
Personal Tapes Family Messages	Y	Y	N/A	Subject to SO.5B Censorship
CLOTHING & TOILETRIES				
Bathrobes	Y	Y	Y	
Aftershave	N	N	Y	Non-Alcohol Stick

ITEM	SENT IN	HANDED IN ON VISIT	PRIVATE CASH EARNINGS	RESTRICTIONS
Comb	Y	Y	Y	
Razor	N	N	Y	Canteen Only
Flannel	Y	Y	Y	Not RED in colour (No DIY Red Bands!)
Flip-flops	Y	Y	Y	
Gloves	Y	Y	Y	
Hair Brush	Y	Y	Y	
Nail Brush	Y	Y	Y	
Nail Clippers	Y	Y	Y	
Shampoo	N	N	Y	Canteen only
Shaver	Y	Y	Y	Battery Only
Shorts	Y	Y	Y	4 Pairs Max
Sweatshirts	Y	Y	Y	4 Max. No Obscene Logos
T.Shirts				
Scarf	Y	Y	Y	
Socks	Y	Y	Y	4 Pairs Max
Sunglasses	Y	Y	Y	
Sweaters	Y	Y	Y	4 Max,
Talcum Powder	N	N	Y	Canteen Only
Television	Y	Y	Y	Battery Only with Current Licence
Toilet Tissues	Y	Y	Y	
Toilet Bag	Y	Y	Y	
Toothbrush	Y	Y	Y	
Toothpaste	N	N	Y	Canteen only
Towels	Y	Y	Y	
Track Suit	Y	Y	Y	No Hoods
Training Shoes	Y	Y	Y	2 Pairs Max
Underpants	Y	Y	Y	4 Pairs Max
Vests	Y	Y	Y	4 Max
COOKING ITEMS...				
Butterdish	Y	Y	Y	No glass
Can-Openers	Y	Y	Y	
Food Containers	Y	Y	Y	Plastic Only
Food and confectionary	N	N	Y	Canteen Only
Frying Pan/Wok	Y	Y	Y	1 Only
Mugs	Y	Y	Y	No Glass, 2 Only
Plates/Bowls	Y	Y	Y	No Glass
Spatula	Y	Y	Y	
Saucepan	Y	Y	Y	Not Pressure Type
Teapot	Y	Y	Y	No Glass
Tea Strainer	Y	Y	Y	

ITEM	SENT IN	HANDED IN ON VISIT	PRIVATE CASH EARNINGS	RESTRICTIONS
Vacuum Flask	Y	Y	Y	1.Ltr Max, No Pump
Whisk(hand)	Y	Y	Y	
RECREATION, HOBBIES & EDUCATION				
Adhesives	N	N	Y	Water-based only
Batteries			Y	1 Set in use and 1 Spare Set Only
Books	Y	Y	Y	Max of 12
Calulator	Y	Y	Y	Not Programmable or with Printout
Cassette Player, Combined radio cassette, CD, record player	Y	Y	Y	Battery Only. Radio MW/LW/FM (88–108MHz) SW(1–18GHz) Only
Canvas, cardboard & paper	Y	Y	Y	3' × 2' Max
Cassette tapes	Y	Y	Y	Transparent Cases and Max of 25
CD Player	Y	Y	Y	Battery Only
Computer	Y	Y	Y	Must be PC compatible, 2 disk drives may be fitted, monitor max and dedicated. No modems or printers in cell.
Headphones	Y	Y	Y	
Hobby Knife	Y	Y	Y	Contolled by Staff
Jigsaw puzzles	Y	Y	Y	3 i/p Only
Matchsticks	Y	Y	Y	1 Cheese
Musical Instruments	Y	Y	Y	On Application
Nails, Screws, Pins & Hinges	Y	Y	Y	
Model Kits	Y	Y	Y	
Paint/Brushes	Y	Y	Y	
Palette Knife	Y	Y	Y	Plastic Only
Pens & Pencils	Y	Y	Y	
Plywood/veneers	Y	Y	Y	3' × 2' Max
Record Player Batery Only	Y	Y	Y	
Records	Y	Y	Y	25 Max
Speakers	Y	Y	Y	2 Max
Typewriter	Y	Y	Y	Manual Only
Ring-Binders	Y	Y	Y	Not Padded
Rug Kits	Y	Y	Y	Tools with staff
Sandpaper	Y	Y	Y	No Emery Cloth
Soft-toy material	Y	Y	Y	

ITEM	SENT IN	HANDED IN ON VISIT	PRIVATE CASH EARNINGS	RESTRICTIONS
Soft leather	Y	Y	Y	Tools with staff
Varnish	Y	Y	Y	Controlled by staff
Video tapes	Y	Y	Y	12 Max
RELIGIOUS ITEMS				
Comb (Sikh)	Y	Y	Y	
Steel Bangle	Y	Y	Y	Sikh
Turban	Y	Y	Y	Sikh
Skull cap	Y	Y	Y	
Rosary	Y	Y	Y	
Prayer Mat	Y	Y	Y	
Prayer Hat	Y	Y	Y	
Prayer Suit	Y	Y	Y	Muslim
Crucifix	Y	Y	Y	
Passover dishes	Y	Y	Y	
SPORTS & GAMES				
Badminton Racquet	Y	Y	Y	
Chess/Crib	Y	Y	Y	
Darts	Y	Y	Y	
Flights	Y	Y	Y	
Football Boots	Y	Y	Y	1 Pr Only
Jockstraps	Y	Y	Y	
Playing Cards	Y	Y	Y	
Snooker Cue	Y	Y	Y	No Metal Cases
Shin Pads	Y	Y	Y	
Sweat Bands	Y	Y	Y	
Swimming Trunks	Y	Y	Y	
T/Tennis bats	Y	Y	Y	
W/Lifting Boots, Gloves/Straps	Y	Y	Y	Gym Use Only

ANNEXE D Answers to Parliamentary Questions October 1993–September 1994

Introduction

Members of either the House of Commons or the Lords can obtain information about the Prison Service by tabling a Parliamentary Question (PQ). Prior to April 1993 these PQ's were generally answered by the Minister with responsibility for prisons. Since HM.Prison Service acquired agency status, however, the majority of PQ's are now answered by the Chief Executive of HM.Prison Service, currently Derek Lewis, though the Home Secretary still remains ultimately accountable to Parliament for the penal system in England and Wales.

Fine Defaulters

According to a Parliamentary answer on 18th January 1994, in a letter to William Ross, Derek Lewis said that in 1992 the average length of sentence imposed for fine defaulters was 22 days; the average period served was 7.5 days.
In a letter to Martin Redmond , on 9th March 1994, Derek Lewis said that of a total of 74,920 receptions into Prison Service establishments in 1993 (provisional figures), 22,583 or 30% were fine defaulters. In a further letter the same day, to Lynne Jones, Derek Lewis said that the number of women received into custody for non-payment of a fine imposed for not possessing a television licence was 136 in 1991, 163 in 1992 and 292 in 1993.

According to a Parliamentary answer on 21st April 1994, in a letter to Lynne Jones, Derek Lewis provided provisional figures showing that during 1993, 845 of the 22,583 receptions into Prison Service establishments for fine default were people fined for using a TV without a licence.

According to a Parliamentary answer on 20th July 1994, in a letter to Joan Ruddock, A.J.Butler said that provisional information for 1993 shows that 21,280 males and 1,340 females were received into Prison Service establishments for fine default, accounting for 30% of all persons received under sentence.

In a written answer to a question from Jean Corston (22nd June 1994), David Maclean gave the following information (figures for 1993 are provisional) on receptions into Prison Service establishments for non-payment of a fine imposed for using a television without a licence, and non-payment of poll tax (community charge):

OFFENCE	1991	1992	1993
Non-payment of fine no TV licence	394	568	845
Non-payment of poll tax	113	504	1,157

Prison Rules Amendments

In a written answer to a question from Sir Ivan Lawrence (10th December 1993), Michael Howard said that he had laid the following Prison and Young Offender Institution Amendment Rules before Parliament to come into effect on 1st January 1994: to extend the scope of confidentiality for prisoners' legal correspondence to all correspondence between prisoners and their legal advisers or a court, whether or not legal proceedings have been commenced: and to increase the maximum period of cellular confinement a governor may impose as a disciplinary punishment from three to 14 days for adult prisoners and from three to seven days for young offenders.

Judges

In a written answer to a question from John Gunnell (12th July 1994), John Taylor gave the following information on the ethnic origin of judges in office on 31st March 1994:

JUDGES	TOTAL	WOMEN	BLACK	ASIAN
High Court	95	6	–	–
Circuit[1]	510	29	–	3
District[2]	290	25	–	1
Masters & Registrars[3]	49	6	–	–
Stipendary Magistrates[4]	46	6	–	–
Stipendary Magistrates[5]	34	2	–	1
Recorders	866	38	4	5
Assistant Recorders	385	58	6	2

1 Includes Official Referees.
2 Excludes District Judges of the Principal Registry of the Family Division.
3 Of the Supreme Court and District Judges of the Family Division.
4 Metropolitan area.
5 Provincial areas.

Rule 43 & 46 Prisoners

According to a Parliamentary answer on 17th March 1994, in a letter to Tom Cox, Derek Lewis gave the following information on the number of prisoners held on Prison Rule 43 and Young Offender Institution Rule 46 on 1st March 1994:

	Own Protection	Good Order and Discipline
Men	1,284	248
Women	11	3
Total	1,295	251

Prisoners in Local Prisons

According to a Parliamentary answer on 14th March 1994, in a letter to Lord Hutchinson, Derek Lewis said that the number of prisoners held in local prisons on 4th March 1994 was 16,653. This represented 35% of the prison population on that date and 34% of the total number of prisoners, including those held in police cells. The certified normal accommodation (CNA) of local prisons on 4th March 1994 was 13,902.

Cells

Additional prison In a letter to Lord Harris of Greenwich on 10th January 1994, Derek Lewis said that the Prison Service intends to create some 2,000 new places at existing establishments by building house blocks, at an estimated cost of £117m. There will be a staff increase of 1,050.

Prisoners in police According to a Parliamentary answer on 30th November 1993, in a letter to Jeremy Corbyn, Derek Lewis said that in 1992–93, the average daily cost of holding a prisoner was £254 in police cells and £75 in local prisons and remand centres.

In a letter to Joan Ruddock on 14th February 1994, Mr A Butler of the Prison Service said that the total cost of keeping prisoners, both sentenced and on remand, in police cells for the financial year 1992/93 was £9,974,035; further accounts relating to 1992/93 of £1,217,763 are under consideration.

In a letter to Lord Harris of Greenwich on 15th March 1994, Derek Lewis said that 358 prisoners were held in police cells on 1st March 1994: 196 by Greater Manchester; 63 by Merseyside; 40 by Lancashire; 23 by Northumbria; 20 by Humberside and 16 by South Yorkshire Police forces respectively.

Prisoners sharing On 28th January 1994, the latest date for which information was available, there were 39 prisoners sharing three to a cell intended for one, and 7,898 sharing two to a cell intended for one.

In a written answer to a question, from Lord Gray of Contin on 2nd February 1994, relating to progress towards providing prisoners with 24 hour access to sanitation, Earl Ferrers said that the percentage of prisoners sharing cells designed for one has been reduced from 38% in 1987/88 to 16% at the end of 1993.

According to a Parliamentary answer on 20th July 1994, in a letter to Joan Ruddock, A.J.Butler of the Prison Service said that since 1st April 1994, no prisoners had been sharing three to a cell designed for one.

Prison Building

According to a Parliamentary answer on 1st December 1993, in a letter to Mildred Gordon, Derek Lewis said that £620.3m will be assigned to the prison building programme over the next three years, including £43m for completion of the current prison building programme and the purchase of sites and infrastructure work for six new prisons. The remaining £577m will be spent on providing additional accommodation, repairs and modernising facilities in existing prisons.

Slopping Out

According to a Parliamentary answer on 4th March 1994, in a letter to Joan Ruddock, Mr A Butler of the Prison Service said that the number of prisoners with 24 hour access to sanitation has now risen to 90% compared with 60% in 1991. The target for the Prison Service for 1993/94 is to provide through the accelerated sanitation programme 24 hour access to sanitation in at least 4,700 existing prison places. In addition, a further 2,400 new and renovated places are scheduled for completion this year, all of which will have integral sanitation.

Time Out of Cell

According to a Parliamentary answer of 4th March 1994, in a letter to Joan Ruddock, Derek Lewis said that on 31st January 1994, 27.1% of prisoners were held in establishments where prisoners are unlocked for at least 12 hours on weekdays.

According to a Parliamentary answer on 21st June 1994, in a letter to Joan Ruddock, Derek Lewis gave the following information (which has been collated only since June 1993) on the percentage of prisoners held in establishments where prisoners were unlocked for 12 hours or more on weekdays:

	1993							1994				
MONTH:	Jun	Jul	Aug	Sep	Oct	Nov	Dec	Jan	Feb	Mar	Apr	May
	22	22	23	23	23	24	24	26	27	29	31	32

Hours in Purposeful Activity

According to a Parliamentary answer on 21st June 1994, in a letter to Joan Ruddock, Derek Lewis said that in May 1994 prisoners spent an average of 26.06 hours per week in purposeful activity.

Drug Misuse

According to a Parliamentary answer on 26th May 1994, in a letter to Joan Ruddock, A.J.Butler said that 30% of sentenced male foreign nationals (excluding fine defaulters) in Prison Service establishments on 31st March 1994, were under sentence for drug offences. The equivalent figure for females was 69%.

In a further letter to Joan Ruddock on 26th May 1994, A J Butler said that 74 of the 75 prisons surveyed so far provided some form of treatment or education programme for prisoners with drug misuse problems—and 72 provided treatment or education for prisoners with alcohol problems.

Drugs in Prisons

In a Parliamentary answer on 18th January 1994, in a letter to David Hinchliffe, Mr A Butler of the Prison Service said that the number of known drug addicts in prisons (i.e. the number of prisoners reported by prison medical officers to the Addicts Index at the Home Office) was 1,420 in 1990, 1,747 in 1991 and 2,586 in 1992.

In a written answer to a question from Joan Ruddock (4th March 1994), Peter Lloyd said that the proposals for drug testing in prisons brought forward in the Criminal Justice and Public Order Bill would be backed up by new prison rules making the use of drugs in prison and refusal to undertake a test a disciplinary offence—although prisoners may not be compelled to undertake a test. Mr Lloyd said there are no plans to link participation in tests more generally to the granting of privileges, but this will be considered as detailed plans are developed. Drug testing was expected to be used in a number of different circumstances, including where there is 'reasonable suspicion' that prisoners have misused drugs; on a random basis as a deterrent; and as part of compacts with prisoners relating, for example, to entry into drug rehabilitation units or privileges such as home leave.

In a written answer to Joan Ruddock (dated 6th July 1994), Derek Lewis on behalf of the Home Secretary said that the Prison Service's intelligence evaluation unit recently conducted a survey of nine establishments to gain better information on the extent of the drugs problem in prisons. The results indicate that: most of the establishments surveyed regarded themselves as having a significant drugs problem; most experienced significant problems with drugs other than cannabis; drug abuse created problems and could lead to bullying and inter-group rivalry; all establishments had found drugs following searches; most establishments had found visitors trying to smuggle in drugs. All the problems existed despite a range of active measures being taken by the establishments concerned to try and limit the entry of drugs and prevent the problem of drug use.

Assisted Prison Visits

According to a Parliamentary answer on 3rd December 1993, in a letter to Joan Ruddock, Derek Lewis said that the Prisons Board Executive Committee decided on 26th July 1993 to include the Assisted Prison Visits Unit as a candidate for market testing. Work on the first stage of the process will start in 1994. This will examine in detail the suitability or otherwise of the Unit for competitive tendering against the private sector.

According to a Parliamentary answer on 16th December 1993, in a letter to Baroness David, Derek Lewis said that although the Prison Service business plan indicates that the extension of the Assisted Prison Visits scheme to cover the second statutory monthly visit should take place this financial year, no final decision has been taken. Any decision must be in light of resources available to the Prison Service and 'it is not yet possible to say when it will be possible to finance the second visit per month'.

In a Parliamentary answer on 22nd February 1994 Derek Lewis, in a letter to Bridget Prentice, said that the assisted prison visits scheme for people on a low income would be extended from 5th April 1994 to cover the second statutory monthly visit.

In a written answer to a question from David Hanson (21st January 1994), Peter Lloyd said that homosexual partners of prisoners currently did not qualify for assisted visits because partner is defined as a person of the opposite sex. He added that consideration was being given to whether the scheme should be extended. Four days later, in a written answer to a subsequent question from Edwina Currie, Michael Howard said: 'I do not believe that taxpayers' money should be used for this purpose'.

According to a Parliamentary answer on 24th June 1994, in a letter to Tom Cox, Derek Lewis said that in the financial year 1993/94 the total number of successful applications to the assisted prison visits scheme was 74,280 and the total funds disbursed were £2,236,816.

Prison Privatisation

According to a Parliamentary answer on 1st November 1993, in a letter to Tom Cox, the Director General of the Prison Service, Derek Lewis, said that on 2nd September 1993 the Home Secretary announced that 10% of prisons—'about 12'—are to be managed by the private sector. This total includes the two already operated by the private sector (Blakenhurst and Wolds), the new prison at Doncaster, and six new prisons. 'About three' prisons currently managed directly by the Prison Service will therefore need to be brought under private sector management, but no decision has yet been taken on what prisons will be market tested.

Doncaster Prison Contract

In a written answer to a question from Sir Ivan Lawrence (12th January 1994), Michael Howard said that the Prisons Board has awarded the contract for the management of Doncaster Prison (a Category B local prison scheduled to open in July 1994) to Premier Prisons Ltd, a joint venture company owned by Serco Ltd and the Wackenhut Corrections Corporation. Mr Howard said that Wackenhut Corrections Corporation has experience in running penal establishments in the USA and Australia.

Prisoner Escorts in London

In a written answer to a question from Joan Ruddock (13th January 1994), Peter Lloyd said that approximately 335 full time equivalent prison officer posts are engaged on court escort and custody duties in the Metropolitan police district. Following the contracting out of the service to Securicor Custodial Services Ltd, the phased loss of a total of 250 prison officer posts is planned during the first year; the remaining 85 posts will be retained at local prisons where they should enable regime improvements to take place.

Penal Costs

According to a Parliamentary answer on 10th December 1993, in a letter to Alun Michael, Derek Lewis said the average monthly cost of custody was £2,142 per prisoner for 1992–93. In a written answer to a question from Alun Michael on the same date, the Home Office Minister, David Maclean, said that the average monthly cost of a probation order is estimated at £98, and the average monthly cost of a community service order is estimated at £95 (information taken from 'Probation Statistics England and Wales 1992').

In a written answer to Gerry Bermingham (20th January 1994), David Maclean said that weekly costs for 1991/92—the last year for which figures were available—were: probation order, £23; community service order, £22; bail hostel place, £179; average prison place, £442.

According to a Parliamentary answer on 20th July 1994, in a letter to Joan Ruddock, A.J.Butler said that the net operating cost per prisoner per month for 1993/94 is £2,326.

Cost of Prison Food

In a Parliamentary answer on 16th February 1994, in a letter to Martin Redmond, Mr A Butler of the

Prison Service gave information on the cost of food per prisoner per week in prisons in England and Wales whose management had not been contracted out. The average was £9.52 per prisoner per week.

Prison Education Expenditure

In a Parliamentary answer on 10th February 1994, in a letter to Sir Ivan Lawrence, Derek Lewis gave the following information on the total expenditure on education services in prisons: 1988/89, £19.5m; 1989/90, £22.9m; 1990/91 £25.5m; 1991/92, £29.5m; 1992/93, £31.5m

15 & 16 Year Old Prisoners

In written answers to questions from Joan Ruddock (28th February 1994), David Maclean said that in 1992 (provisional figures) 377 males aged 15 were received as untried or convicted unsentenced into Prison Service custody, of whom 141 subsequently received a custodial sentence. No female aged 15 was received as a remand prisoner in 1992. In 1993, a total of 553 males aged 15 were received into Prison Service custody under sentence; and a total of 25 females aged 15 were received into Prison Service custody under sentence.

Section 53 Prisoners

In a written answer to a question from Alex Carlile (30th June 1994), David Maclean said that on 30th April 1994 there were 250 persons sentenced to be detained in England and Wales at Her Majesty's Pleasure under section 53 Children & Young Persons Act 1933. Of these 61 were aged under 21 and 189 were adults.

Parole

In a written answer to a letter from Bernard Jenkins (7th March 1994), Michael Howard said he would provide openness in the parole process to prisoners sentenced before October 1st 1992 whose parole eligibility date (PED), or its anniversary, is October 1st 1994 or beyond. He said that under the openness arrangements the parole timetable takes about 26 weeks from start to finish. Prisoners should receive their parole dossiers about four months before their PED, be interviewed about their parole case by a parole board member about three months before their PED, and receive reasons for the parole decision about three weeks before their PED.

Life Sentence

Numbers According to a Parliamentary answer on 17th March 1994, in a letter to Tom Cox, Derek Lewis said that on 31st January 1994 there were 3,148 prisoners serving life sentences, of whom 3,040 were men and 108 were women.

Tariff disclosure In a written answer to a question from Viscount Mersey (4th November 1993), Earl Ferrers said that following the House of Lords judgement of 24th June 1993 [in *ex parte Doody*], the Home Office will commence a process of disclosure to all mandatory life sentence prisoners of the gist of the judicial advice which the Secretary of State received when setting the minimum period of custody the prisoner must serve; the Secretary of State's decision; and the reasons for any departure from the judicial view. It is estimated that it will probably be some 12 months before this process is completed for every mandatory life sentence prisoner (some 2,600) whose tariffs had already been set by Ministers prior to the House of Lords judgement.

Minimum sentence period In a written answer to a question from Don Dixon (3rd March 1994), Peter Lloyd said that of 806 mandatory life sentences considered by the Home Secretary from August 1990 to July 1993 inclusive, ministers set a minimum sentence period the same length as that recommended by the trial judge in 409 (50.7%) cases—in 325 (40.3%) of which the Lord Chief Justice agreed with the period recommended by the trial judge). In a further 244 (30.3%) cases, ministers set a period in accordance with the recommendation by the Lord Chief Justice. A period higher than either of the periods recommended by the judiciary was set in 112 (13.9%) cases. A period lower than either of the periods recommended by the judiciary was set in 3 (0.4%) cases. In the remaining 38 (4.7%) cases, ministers set a period between that recommended by the trial judge and that recommended by the Lord Chief Justice.

In a written answer to a question from Alex Carlile (30th June 1994), Peter Lloyd said that the number of mandatory life sentence prisoners for whom the Home Secretary increased the tariff period recommended by either the trial judge or the Lord Chief Justice was 57 in 1990 (August to December only), 32 in 1991, 19 in 1992 and four in 1993.

Deaths In a written answer to a question from Frank Field (13th December 1993), David Maclean said that seven individuals convicted of murder since the abolition of the death penalty have been convicted again of murder following release.

In a written answer to a question from Lord Longford (12th April 1994), Earl Ferrers said that during the past five years, 59 life sentence prisoners have died in custody.

In a written answer to a question from Lord Tebbit (11th May 1994), Earl Ferrers said that 72 people in England and Wales have been killed by people previously convicted of homicide in England and Wales between 1963–92. Of these, 18 had been killed by those who had been released from life sentences.

Prisoner Deaths

According to a Parliamentary answer on 25th May 1994, in a letter to Baroness Gould, Derek Lewis gave the following information about deaths in prison between 1989/93. The details relating to 1994 come from a Parliamentary answer on 20th July 1994, in a letter to Joan Ruddock, from A.J.Butler.

YEAR	SUICIDE	NATURAL CAUSES	KILLED BY INMATES
1989	48	31	0
1990	50	41	4
1991	42	27	4
1992	41	34	3
1993	46	37	4
1994	24 (to 18th July)		

Bail Hostels

In a written answer to a question from Lord Hutchinson (28th February 1994), Earl Ferrers said that current plans (taking into account previously announced closures and the opening of two more hostels) will mean a total of 107 hostels providing 2,680 places by April 1996.

In a written answer to a question from Joan Ruddock (13th April 1994), David Maclean said that on 1st April 1994 there were 2,597 places in approved bail and probation hostels, and that it is currently projected that there will be 2,560 places on 1st April 1995.

Remand Prisoners & Foreign Nationals

According to a Parliamentary answer on 13th April 1994, in a letter to Joan Ruddock, A J Butler of the Prison Service provided figures for the ethnic breakdown of the remand prison population on 31st December 1993:

	MALE	FEMALE	TOTAL
White:	8,685	293	8,947
Black African, Caribbean, other:	1,245	74	1,319
South Asian, Bangladeshi, Indian, Pakistani:	275	7	282
Chinese and other Asian, other Chinese, not recorded	201	14	215
ALL PERSONS	**10,375**	**388**	**10,763**

According to a Parliamentary answer on 20th June 1994, in a letter to Sir Russell Johnson, A.J.Butler said that on 30th April 1994, 303 prisoners had been remanded in custody for over one year but less than two years, and 38 for over two years—these provisional figures are for European Union nationals; the time since first remand to Prison Service custody includes any intervening time on bail.)

According to a Parliamentary answer on 24th June 1994, in a letter to Joan Ruddock, A.J.Butler gave the following information on remand prisoners in Prison Service establishments on 30th June 1994:

Time since first remand to Prison Service custody	NUMBER OF PERSONS MALES	FEMALES
All lengths	10,250	400
Up to and including one week	1,000	50
More than one week up to and including two weeks	800	50
More than two weeks up to and including four weeks	1,300	50
More than four weeks up to and including eight weeks	1,750	70
More than eight weeks up to and including three months	1,500	70
More than three months up to and including six months	2,300	80
More than six months up to and including 12 months	1,300	40
Over 12 months	400	10

According to a Parliamentary answer on 20th July 1994, in a letter to Joan Ruddock, A.J.Butler gave the following information on the ethnic origin of prisoners on 31st may 1994—provisional figures.

	MALE	FEMALE	TOTAL
White:	39,028	1,346	40,374
Black African, Caribbean, other:	5,283	363	5,646
South Asian, Bangladeshi, Indian, Pakistani:	1,372	28	1,400
Chinese and other Asian, other Chinese, not recorded	1,061	51	1,112
ALL PERSONS	**46,744**	**1,788**	**48,532**

According to a Parliamentary answer on 20th July 1994, in a letter to Joan Ruddock, A.J.Butler said that on 31st may (provisional figures) there were 3,780 non-British citizens (3,470 males and 310 females) in Prison Service establishments in England and Wales. This includes 600 male and 20 female nationals from the Irish Republic. A further 470 persons had no nationality recorded.

Racial Incidents

In a written answer to a question from Joan Ruddock (24th June 1994), Peter Lloyd said there were 9,762 racial incidents recorded by the police in England and Wales in the financial year 1993/94.

Termination of Community Sentences

In a written answer to a question from Gerry Bermingham (21st January 1994), David Maclean said that in 1992, 81% of probation orders terminated successfully (65% ran their full course, 3% were replaced by a conditional discharge, and 13% were terminated early by the courts for good progress); and 72% of community service orders terminated successfully (i.e. the specified number of hours was completed without termination of the order for failure to comply with its requirements, for conviction of another offence, or for other reasons).

Bind-Over Orders

In a written answer to a question from Baroness Faithful (21st February 1994), Earl Ferrers said that from 1st October 1992 to 31st December 1992—the latest date for which figures are available—97 bind-over orders were ordered on parents or guardians of offenders aged 10 to under 18 years who were found guilty of a criminal offence. This represents less than 1% of the total young offenders sentenced.

Unduly Lenient Sentences

In a written answer to questions from Phillip Oppenheim and Marion Roe (13th January 1994), Michael Howard announced that an order would be laid which will extend the Attorney General's powers to refer back to court cases involving the imposition of unduly lenient sentences. The order will bring within his powers offences of indecent assault, cruelty to children and making threats to kill. The Order takes effect as from 1st March 1994. Currently the Attorney General's power to refer back is restricted to Crown Court sentences for indictable-only offences. The new offences can also be dealt with in magistrates' courts, but may only be referred if the defendant is sentenced in the Crown Court. The Attorney General's powers of referral will also apply to attempts, conspiracy and incitement to commit any of those offences and will include convictions for aiding and abetting these offences.

In a written answer to Spencer Batiste (21st April 1994), Michael Howard said that 166 cases had been considered by the Court of Appeal following referral from the Attorney General, of which 95 references had resulted in an increased sentence.

In a written answer to a question from Jonathan Evans (7th July 1994), David Maclean said that on 1st March 1994 the Attorney General's power to refer unduly lenient sentences to the Court of Appeal was extended to cover the offences of indecent assault, making threats to kill and child cruelty. he said that all the most serious violent and sexual offences are now within the scope of the power.

Categorisation

According to a Parliamentary answer on 24th March 1994, in a letter to Tom Cox, Derek Lewis provided figures showing that on 1st March 1994 there were 641 Category A prisoners, of whom 638 were male and 3 were female.

According to a Parliamentary answer on 21st July 1994, in a letter to Joan Ruddock, Derek Lewis said that on 18th July 1994 there were 690 Category A prisoners, 6,050 Category B prisoners, 15,880 Category C prisoners and 6,150 Category D prisoners.

Secure Places

In a written answer to Anthony Coombs (22nd April 1994), John Bowis said that it is currently anticipated that, subject to planning procedures, construction of 110 of the proposed 170 additional secure places could be completed by the end of 1995 and the balance by mid-1995.

In a written answer to a question from Lynne Jones (7th July 1994), David Maclean said that the total costs of secure training orders are estimated to be in excess of £30 million a year. This estimate includes running, building and financing costs, the cost of post-release supervision, and Home Office administration costs.

Attendance Centre Orders

In a written answer to Baroness David (18th May 1994), Earl Ferrers said that the average cost of the 7,151 orders which were made in 1992 is estimated at £169.

After-care Hostel Grants

In a written answer to Baroness David (18th May 1994), Earl Ferrers said that in 1993/4 the average Home Office grant towards the cost of a bed in a voluntary after-care hostel for offenders was £1,662.

Income from Fines

In a written answer to Baroness David (19th May 1994), Lord Mackay said that in 1993/4 the total income from fines etc was £269,980,000. The total income from fines and fixed penalties only in the UK was £251,176,000.

Prisoners' Mental Health

According to a Parliamentary answer on 26th May 1994, in a letter to Joan Ruddock, A.J. Butler gave figures for the number of prisoners receiving some form of mental health care as at February 1994 and for the previous two years:

	FEB 94	FEB 93	FEB 92
Mentally disordered prisoners awaiting transfer to hospital:	136	123	92
Mentally disordered prisoners being treated in prison HCCs:	802	415	671
Other prisoners requiring mental health care:	1,766	2,343	1,515

Prisoners with HIV

According to a parliamentary answer on 21st July 1994, in a letter to Roland Boyes, Derek Lewis said that on 30th June 1994 there were 45 prisoners confirmed to have HIV; and that there were 207 centrally trained HIV counsellors throughout prison establishments in England and Wales.

Prison 'Listener' Schemes

According to a Parliamentary answer on 26th May 1994, in a letter to Joan Ruddock, A.J. Butler said Listener Schemes are now operating in 50 prisons and a further 14 prisons are scheduled to introduce them by the end of 1994.

Prisoners' Compacts

According to a Parliamentary answer on 26th May 1994 , in a letter to Joan Ruddock, A.J.Butler provided information showing that 20 establishments were operating prisoners' compacts and 14 establishments were operating on an experimental basis.

According to a Parliamentary answer on 20th July 1994, in a letter to Joan Ruddock, Derek Lewis said that 61 Prison Service establishments were operating prisoners' compacts on 30th June 1994.

Prisons' Cognitive Skills Programmes

According to a Parliamentary answer on 26th May 1994, in a letter to Joan Ruddock, A.J.Butler said that cognitive skills pilot programmes have been introduced in 11 establishments. 109 prisoners completed a cognitive skills programme during 1993/4.

ANNEXE E. **VTC/CIT Courses**

Who Provides What and Where?

The following pages contain a list of all Vocational and Constuction Industry Training Courses, and shows which establishments in England and Wales offer which courses.

Across the top of the following pages are the course numbers shown below. Down the left hand side of each page is a list of penal establishments. If a specific course is available in a particular establishment, an '✓' is shown where the two points meet.

No.	Course Name
1.	Beauty Therapy
2.	Braille
3.	Bricklaying
4.	Business Studies
5.	Computer-aided Design
6.	Carpentry
7.	Catering
8.	Computing
9.	Craft
10.	Drawing Office Skills
11.	Electrical Installation
12.	Electronic Wiring
13.	Fashion & Design
14.	Furniture Craft
15.	General Construction
16.	Hairdressing
17.	Home Economics
18.	Home Management
19.	Horticulture
20.	Industrial Cleaning
21.	Information Technology
22.	Light Vehicle Repairs
23.	Machine Setting
24.	Mechanical Engineering
25.	Micro Engineering
26.	Model Making
27.	Motor Mechanics
28.	Multi-skills
29.	Occupational Therapy
30.	Office Skills
31.	Painting & Decorating
32.	Parent Craft
33.	Plastering
34.	Plumbing
35.	Precision Engineering
36.	Radio/TV Servicing
37.	Skills Training
38.	Tailoring
39.	Technical Storekeeping
40.	Tiling
41.	Welding

Course No / Prison	1	2	3	4	5	6	7	8	9	10	11	12	13	14	15	16	17	18	19	20	21	22	23	24	25	26	27	28	29	30	31	32	33	34	35	36	37	38	39	40
Acklington						✓						✓		✓	✓										✓						✓			✓						
Albany				✓																					✓						✓									
Aldington																											7													
Ashwell												✓																												
Askham, Gr.							✓										✓																							
Aylesbury		✓					✓					✓								✓										✓	✓					✓				
Belmarsh			✓								✓									✓	✓						✓				✓									
Birmingham																															✓									
Blantyre				✓																																				
Blundeston																					✓										✓							✓		
Brinsford								✓																				✓									✓			
Bristol																															✓									
Bullingdon							✓													✓	✓																			
Bullwood												✓				✓																								
Camp Hill			✓									✓			✓						✓										✓									
Cardiff																															✓									
Castington			✓				✓															✓					✓				✓			✓						
Channings							✓	✓							✓					✓											✓									
Cookham Wood																														✓										
Dartmoor															✓										✓						✓			✓						
Deerbolt			✓			✓	✓				✓			✓						✓									✓		✓	✓		✓						
Dover			✓			✓					✓				✓						✓			✓	✓			✓				✓		✓						
Downview																✓		✓																						
Drake Hall	✓															✓														✓	✓									
East S-Pk														✓				✓																						
Elmley				✓																	✓						✓													
Erlestoke			✓							✓														✓							✓									
Everthorpe			✓			✓														✓									✓		✓									
Feather'st													✓							✓			✓													✓				
Feltham			✓																	✓											✓									
Finnamore																															✓									
Ford						✓	✓								✓						✓										✓									
Frankland														✓																	✓									
F-Sutton			✓																							✓	✓				✓				✓					
Garth			✓																								✓		✓		✓			✓						
Gartee									✓					✓																										
Glen Parva			✓			✓														✓			✓				✓				✓									
Grendon							✓																								✓									
Guys Marsh			✓			✓									✓												✓				✓									
Hatfield			✓												✓					✓							✓				✓									
Hewell Gr.															✓																✓									
Highdown																✓		✓		✓	✓						✓													
Highpoint																					✓			✓			✓													
Hindley						✓																									✓									

Holme Hse			✓																								✓			✓									
Hull											✓																												
Hunt'combe		✓												✓					✓											✓									
Kingston									✓																														
Kirkham											✓																												
Lancs Farm																			✓	✓							✓			✓	✓	✓							
Lancaster											✓									✓										✓									
Lewes		✓						✓																						✓						✓			
Leyhill							✓											✓	✓																				
Lindholme		✓			✓	✓	✓						✓					✓												✓			✓						
Littlehey		✓																	✓		✓					✓	✓			✓									
Liverpool		✓																												✓									
L-Lartin								✓	✓														✓																
Maidstone		✓	✓																										✓	✓									
Moorland						✓														✓							✓			✓									
Morton H																✓								✓															
Mount		✓																✓		✓						✓				✓									
Norwich		✓			✓									✓																									
Nottingham		✓																												✓		✓			✓				
North Sc																														✓									
Onley		✓			✓		✓												✓			✓								✓									
Parkhurst																				✓								✓		✓									
Preston																											✓												
Portland		✓			✓									✓					✓			✓				✓				✓									
Ranby		✓												✓																									
Risley										✓					✓				✓	✓										✓								✓	✓
Rudgate		✓												✓																									
Shepton M																														✓									
Stafford											✓				✓					✓							✓												
Standfd H		✓			✓									✓																✓									
Stocken						✓	✓											✓	✓		✓									✓									
Stoke Heath		✓																												✓									
Styal													✓			✓																				✓			
Swaleside		✓													✓				✓	✓				✓						✓									
Swinfen Hall		✓					✓																							✓									
Sudbury		✓																✓								✓				✓								✓	
Thorpe A						✓																					✓			✓									
Thorn C						✓								✓												✓				✓		✓							
Usk														✓																✓		✓							
Verne		✓			✓						✓			✓										✓		✓				✓		✓							
Wakefield	✓																						✓							✓		✓					✓		
Wayland		✓					✓			✓									✓		✓		✓			✓				✓									✓
Well'boro		✓			✓															✓						✓	✓			✓		✓							
Werrington		✓															✓									✓													
Wetherby		✓				✓																					✓					✓							
Whatton		✓																												✓		✓							
Whitemoor				✓								✓	✓							✓																			
Woodhill		✓																												✓									

ANNEXE F. **(Self-Inflicted) Deaths in Custody**

October 1993-September 1994

With thanks to Deborah Coles of INQUEST

Legend

R = Remand Inmate. S = Sentenced Inmate. JR = Judge's Remand (Convicted but Unsentenced).

No	Name	R/S	Cause	Date	Place
1	John Pringle	R	Hanging	14.10.93	HMP Exeter
2	Jeremy Parker	R	Hanging	17.10.93	HMP Woodhill
3	Pete Oliver	S	O/dose	17.10.93	HMP Nottingham
4	Lee Taylor	S	Hanging	05.11.93	HMP Long Lartin
5	Neil Kennedy	S	Hanging	08.11.93	HMP Holme House
6	Darrell Darson	R	Hanging	12.11.93	HMP Wolds
7	Michael Taylor	R	Hanging	18.11.93	HMP Exeter
8	Gary Symond	R	Hanging	26.11.93	HMP Norwich
9	Peter Hind	R	Hanging	28.11.93	HMP Bristol
10	William Stadman	R	Hanging	04.12.93	HMP Norwich
11	Keith Gilzene	R	Hanging	05.12.93	HMP Wandsworth
12	Ian Thomas	S	Hanging	08.12.93	HMP Wandsworth
13	Garfield Phinn	S	Hanging	17.12.93	HMP Dartmoor
14	Wayne Moorland	R	Hanging	17.12.93	HMP Liverpool
15	Philip Pryor	R	Hanging	24.12.93	HMP Lewes
16	Steven Cotterill	S	Hanging	31.12.93	HMP Holme House
17	Carl Trout	R	Hanging	08.01.94	HMYOI Moorlands
18	Brendan Tremble	R	Hanging	12.01.94	HMYOI Moorlands
19	Mr. Chadwick	R	Hanging	25.01.94	HMP Liverpool
20	Simon Quayle	R	Hanging	29.01.94	HMP Birmingham
21	Stephen Slavin	S	Hanging	09.02.94	HMP Liverpool
22	Mohammed Rahman	S	Hanging	11.03.94	HMP W.Scrubs
23	Ian Brook	S	Hanging	15.03.94	HMP Wakefield
24	Paul Tapon	S	Hanging	11.03.94	HMP Albany
25	Andrew Cook	S	Hanging	20.03.94	HMYOI Portland
26	Glyn Williams	S	Hanging	26.03.94	HMP Exeter
27	Ian Mountfield	R	Hanging	30.03.94	HMP Shrewsbury
28	John Clay	R	Hanging	31.03.94	HMP Leicester
29	Gordon Brown	S	Hanging	18.04.94	HMP Grendon
30	Joseph Stanley	JR	Hanging	10.05.94	HMP Cardiff
31	David Lewis	R	Hanging	12.05.94	HMP Manchester
32	Martin Howells	S	Hanging	21.05.94	HMP Usk
33	Paul Dobby	R	Hanging	02.06.94	HMP Leicester
34	Stephen Astbury	S	Hanging	06.06.94	HMP Grendon
35	Andrew Topliss	S	Hanging	15.06.94	HMP Lincoln
36	O. Akinbobola	R	Hanging	26.06.94	HMP Woodhill
37	Jamie Clydesdale	R	Hanging	26.06.94	HMP Bedford
38	Kirk Chean	JR	Hanging	28.06.94	HMP Brixton
39	Michelle Pearson	S	Hanging	05.07.94	HMP New Hall
40	Majid Farman		Hanging	17.07.94	HMP Wandsworth
41	M. Cunningham	R	Hanging	22.07.94	HMP Liverpool
42	Alan Boland	R	Hanging	26.07.94	HMP Wandsworth
43	William Cox	R	Hanging	28.07.94	HMYOI Moorlands

No	Name	R/S	Cause	Date	Plate
44	David Michael	R	Hanging	30.07.94	HMP Winchester
45	Christian Byrne	R	Hanging	01.08.94	HMP Swansea
46	Issac Gibb-Kirk	S	Hanging	02.08.94	HMP Hull
47	Andrew Bataty	R	Hanging	08.08.94	HMRC Low Newton
48	Jody Turner	S	Hanging	14.08.94	HMP Brinsford
49	Alvin Bay	S	Hanging	14.08.94	HMP Parkhurst
50	Shaun Webster	S	Hanging	16.08.94	HMP Doncaster
51	Anthony Watson	R	Hanging	20.08.94	HMP Brixton
52	Charles Anderson	S	Hanging	24.08.94	HMP Highdown
53	Gine Cellini	S	Hanging	25.08.94	HMP Garth.

R.I.P.

Breakdown by establishment

HMP Albany	1
HMP Bedford	1
HMP Birmingham	1
HMP Brinsford	1
HMP Bristol	1
HMP Brixton	2
HMP Cardiff	1
HMP Dartmoor	1
HMP Doncaster	1
HMP Exeter	3
HMP Garth	1
HMP Grendon	2
HMP Highdown	1
HMP Holme House	2
HMP Hull	1
HMP Leicester	2
HMP Lewes	1
HMP Lincoln	1
HMP Liverpool	4
HMP Long Lartin	1
HMRC Low Newton	1
HMP Manchester	1
HMYOI Moorlands	3
HMP New Hall	1
HMP Norwich	2
HMP Nottingham	1
HMP Parkhurst	1
HMYOI Portland	1
HMP Shrewsbury	1
HMP Swansea	1
HMP Usk	1
HMP Wakefield	1
HMP Wandsworth	4
HMP Winchester	1
HMP Wolds	1
HMP Woodhill	2
HMP W.Scrubs	1
TOTAL:	53

Establishments with more than one suicide

Liverpool	4
Wandsworth	4
Exeter	3
Moorlands	3
Brixton	2
Grendon	2
Holme House	2
Leicester	2
Norwich	2

In 1993/94, just nine establishments accounted for more than 45% of all suicides.

ANNEXE G. **Prisoner Respondents**

Background & methodology

In April 1994 questionnaires for completion by inmates were sent to the Governors of all 136 establishments in England and Wales by recorded delivery post: along with a questionnaire for completion by the Governor, and a letter to the Chairman of the BoV requesting a copy of their latest annual report. In July 1994 the national newspaper for prisoners, *Inside Time*, also carried the inmate questionnaire: in all **386** replies were received from a total of **65** establishments. Details of whether a particular Governor or BoV responded is shown in the respective establishment entry.

Please note

This section gives details of only those prisoners from whom we received a completed questionnaire, and who stated expressely within it that they did not object to being identified. If a particular prison is not shown below, it should not be taken as an indication that no inmate replied from that establishment: 289 of those who replied requested anonymity, while 25 requested that only their prison number appear. Similarly, the list of inmates named against a particular establishment below is not to be taken as a full list of all those who replied from that establishment, nor are any of the 'Prisoners' Comments' in the respective establishment entry necessarily attributable to all or any of those who are named.

Thanks

My thanks are due to all of those who replied, be they named or anonymous. I am grateful for the time you put into completion of the questionnaire, and the obvious effort (not to mention the humour!) that went into many of your comments.

MARK LEECH
EDITOR

HMP Albany	HF1140.
HMP Ashwell	JK1827. JM1648 Patrick Hamnett.
HMP Blundeston	NG0004. WA0643 Roger Ashford.
HMP Brixton	MX3886 Nicholas Usher.
HMP Bullingdon	PT2755 Blatchford. HL1600 Steve Dennis. BD0606.
HMP Camp Hill	VK2412 Paul Gibbon.
HMP Canterbury	LV3050. LV2515 Bowden. ND2340 Holbrook.
HMYOI Castington	DF1772 Andrew Jones.
HMP Channings Wood	WM2320 Chris Thomas. WS4617 P. Broome. CJ1623 G. Cook.
HMP Chelmsford	LX2454 Rhodes.
HMP Dartmoor	VJ2080 Wayne Collins. VM0847 Lewis. JT0291.
HMYOI Deerbolt	AG1851 John Thomas O'Neil. EW1623 Michael McCreath. EM1747 Anthony Bennett
HMP Drake Hall	RG2407.
HMP Durham	CM2238 M. Wilson
HMP Elmley	B79754. ND0889 Ian Cupid.
HMP Erlestoke	WE3387 Parvaz.
HMP Everthorpe	AF0935 D. Marsh. WA2041 L. Haddesley.
HMP Featherstone	A94037 Steve Dixon. RD0979 Andrew Williams. HT1164. JV3199 S. Priest.
HMP Frankland	CL2318.
HMP Full Suton	DH2017 G. Gabbard.
HMP Gartree	H10111. CV2583 I. Kentzer.
HMP Grendon	J98526 Haywood. NV0716. H27835 John Burke.
HMP Haverigg	EF2561 S. Thomas.
HMP Hewell Grange	JV0983 E. Chadwick.
HMP Hollesley Bay	WH2647 Rice. LX1249 Robbie Darby.
HMP Hull	CX2289 John Hastings. AA3520 I. Everett. CX3315. CX3988.
HMYOI Huntercombe	FC2581. FC2221 Jamie Purkiss.
HMP Kirklevington Gr:	EE3546 David Wilmott.
HMP Lancaster Farms	EW2244 Mark Kelly.
HMP Latchmere House	XC1798 Ken Stuart.
HMP Leicester	JD3835 A.C. Reid.
HMP Lewes	NV3844.
HMP Littlehey	H26454 Harrison. 802452 Baz Lewis. HE2875.

HMP Liverpool	FN1882 M. Creevy. FG1584 Francis McHugh. FN0328 K. McDonell. FG3661. FD3580. FD3810.
HMP Long Lartin	BP1076 Roy Fullerd. J29459.
HMP Manchester	EF2982 Jonathan Ashworth. EF0721 Carl Bolan. EF2754 Martin Clark. EF1421 Daly. EF2751 Martin Finnerty. EF1953 Shane. EF0520 Peter Smith. EF3222 Wall.
HMP Moorland	CE0280 K.D. Jones.
HMP Morton Hall	DA3154 A. Ogden.
HMP Norwich	LR2679.
HMP Nottingham	JK2074. N46456 Bradbury. T67099 Graham Galloway.
HMP Oxford	BT1768 Mark Tomlinson.
HMP Pentonville	PA1073.
HMYOI Portland	XE0609 Ian Hawkins.. WW2167.
HMP Reading	FC2159 Scott Oster-Ritter.
HMP Risley	NH3531.
HMP Send	PP1447 Smallwood.
HMP Stafford	BK1412 Dimpman. HT3138.
HMP Thorp Arch	HN3398 Robert Taswell.
HMP Usk	WG3562 Sid Court.
HMP Wakefield	H50278 Paul Blackburn.
HMP Wandsworth	PP0376 David Moore.. FJ0791 Richard O'Hara.
HMP Wayland	FJ1460 M. Brooks. HB1026 John Russell.
HMYOI Wetherby	CE3281 Stuart Hodson.
HMP Whitemoor	RD0659. B62006 Denis Nilsen.
HMP Winchester	VT3057.